ALEXANDER THE GREAT

ARRIAN (Lucius Flavius Arrianus, *c*. AD 86–161) was born into a wealthy and well-connected Greek family in Nicomedia (modern Izmit) in Bithynia, north-west Asia Minor. The family had long enjoyed Roman citizenship, and Arrian, helped by his friendship with the emperor Hadrian, made rapid progress to high military and political office at Rome and in the Roman imperial administration. He was consul in 129 or 130, and governor of the province of Cappadocia from 131 to 137. He retired to live in Athens, where he was elected archon (chief magistrate) for the year 145/6.

Arrian combined this distinguished record of public service with a literary career of a range and stylistic quality which established him as one of the foremost writers of the 'Greek renaissance' in the second century AD. From an early age until well into his retirement he published works in a wide variety of genres—history, biography, military theory, shorter essays, and philosophy: it is thanks to the young Arrian that we have a record of the *Discourses* of the Stoic philosopher Epictetus. Arrian is best known for his work on Alexander the Great. Based on the most reliable contemporary accounts, those of Ptolemy and Aristobulus, his *Anabasis*, together with its companion-piece the *Indica*, is our prime extant source for the history of Alexander and his campaigns. It is a fundamental text, and a dramatic story brilliantly told.

MARTIN HAMMOND was born in 1944 and educated at Winchester College and Balliol College, Oxford. He has taught at St Paul's School, Harrow School, and Eton College, where he was Head of Classics from 1974 to 1980, and Master in College from 1980 to 1984. He was Headmaster of the City of London School from 1984 to 1990, and of Tonbridge School from 1990 to his retirement in 2005. He has translated the *Iliad* (Penguin, 1987), the *Odyssey* (Duckworth, 2000), the *Meditations* of Marcus Aurelius (Penguin, 2006), and Thucydides' *Peloponnesian War* for Oxford World's Classics (2009). He is married, with two children.

JOHN ATKINSON is Emeritus Professor of Classics at the University of Cape Town. He has published commentaries on several books of Quintus Curtius Rufus' *Histories of Alexander the Great* in English, and on the whole of Curtius in two volumes for Mondadori (Fondazione Lorenzo Valla, in Italian).

OXFORD WORLD'S CLASSICS

*For over 100 years Oxford World's Classics have brought
readers closer to the world's great literature. Now with over 700
titles—from the 4,000-year-old myths of Mesopotamia to the
twentieth century's greatest novels—the series makes available
lesser-known as well as celebrated writing.*

*The pocket-sized hardbacks of the early years contained
introductions by Virginia Woolf, T. S. Eliot, Graham Greene,
and other literary figures which enriched the experience of reading.
Today the series is recognized for its fine scholarship and
reliability in texts that span world literature, drama and poetry,
religion, philosophy, and politics. Each edition includes perceptive
commentary and essential background information to meet the
changing needs of readers.*

OXFORD WORLD'S CLASSICS

ARRIAN

Alexander the Great
The Anabasis *and the* Indica

Translated by
MARTIN HAMMOND

With an Introduction and Notes by
JOHN ATKINSON

OXFORD
UNIVERSITY PRESS

OXFORD
UNIVERSITY PRESS

Great Clarendon Street, Oxford OX2 6DP
United Kingdom

Oxford University Press is a department of the University of Oxford.
It furthers the University's objective of excellence in research, scholarship,
and education by publishing worldwide. Oxford is a registered trade mark of
Oxford University Press in the UK and in certain other countries

First published as an Oxford World's Classics paperback 2013

Impression:15

British Library Cataloguing in Publication Data

Data available

Library of Congress Cataloging in Publication Data

Data available

ISBN 978-0-19-958724-7

Printed in Great Britain by
Clays Ltd, Elcograf S.p.A.

PREFACE

ARRIAN was one of the most distinguished and versatile Greek writers of the second century AD. What is not always the same thing, he is also an attractive author and good company, with a lively and lucid style of unobtrusive sophistication and subtle dramatic control. 'His work is the most complete and the most sober account of Alexander's reign' (Bosworth, *From Arrian to Alexander*, 13), but it is also a very good read, composed with considerable literary skill. In public life Arrian achieved the highest positions both in Rome and the Roman imperial service (senator, consul, provincial governor, successful military commander) and also subsequently in Athens (archon, or chief magistrate): and he combined this political, administrative, and military career with an equally successful role as what John Atkinson aptly terms a 'public intellectual'—philosopher, historian, essayist, man of letters. He started young (his record of the *Discourses* of the important Stoic philosopher Epictetus was compiled in his twenties, from notes taken at the great man's lectures), and continued writing well into his retirement at Athens. He is not without vanity (the very beginning and the very end of the *Anabasis* testify to that), and implicitly or explicitly he presents himself as the heir to Herodotus, Thucydides, and Xenophon, but he had good cause for satisfaction: he was celebrated in his own lifetime, and his work on Alexander became an immediate classic, outliving the sources on which it was based. And we have good cause to be grateful to Arrian: without him we would know much less about Alexander, and virtually nothing about Epictetus.

Arrian set out to write the definitive history of Alexander, and so it has proved. The bulk of this history is contained in the work conventionally known as the *Anabasis* [*Alexandrou*], which includes the most detailed account we possess of the four major battles in which Alexander defeated first the armies of Darius and then the formidable Indian king Porus. But Arrian had always planned (*Anab.* 5.4–6, 6.16, 6.28) and subsequently wrote and published a shorter companion-piece, the *Indica*, which after an introductory essay (*Ind.* 1–17) on the geography and sociology of India, full of lively details, gives an almost day-by-day account (*Ind.* 18–42) of Nearchus' coastal voyage with

Alexander's fleet from the mouths of the Indus to the head of the
Persian Gulf in 325–324 BC. Arrian himself regarded the *Indica* as an
integral part of his history of Alexander (*Ind.* 43.14), and we are
grateful to the editors of Oxford World's Classics for their ready
agreement to the inclusion of the *Indica* in this edition.

Names, Places, Distances

The representation in English of Greek names (or names written in
Greek) poses a familiar problem, to which there is no obvious or universally accepted solution. Given that at least some readers of Arrian
will want to make use of what is now the standard prosopography
of Alexander's empire, Waldemar Heckel's indispensable *Who's Who
in the Age of Alexander the Great* (Blackwell, 2006; Wiley–Blackwell,
2009), we have gratefully adopted Heckel's spelling of names, and
endorse the common-sense and user-friendly principles on which it
is based (p. vii of his Introduction): for the same reason our index follows the numbers used by Heckel to distinguish people of the same
name. Arrian's text names a multitude of places and geographical features, some of which can be identified, more or less securely, with
their modern equivalents: in those cases the modern name is given in
square brackets at the first occurrence (usually) of the ancient name
in the text of the translation, and also in the index. More generally,
we hope that readers will find useful the information of Map 1, which
plots Alexander's route on a map marking modern national boundaries, and so may help to answer questions of the type: 'Are we still in
Afghanistan?' Almost all distances, whether on land or by sea, are
given by Arrian in the usual Greek measurement by *stades*. The length
of the stade could vary quite widely, but the Athenian stade was just
under 200 yards, and that seems to fit with those distances given by
Arrian which can be securely confirmed. Since most of us cannot
think in stades, or form an immediate impression of what distance
is represented by, say, 85 stades (it sounds a lot, but isn't), Arrian's
stade measurements have been converted to miles. For land distances
we have assumed 9 stades to the mile, and for sea distances (almost
entirely in the *Indica*, where almost all distances are given in mul-
tiples of ten or a hundred stades) 10 stades to the mile.

I am grateful to Brian Bosworth and Waldemar Heckel for help and advice in the early stages; to Judith Luna of Oxford World's Classics for her unstinting support, encouragement, and guidance at every stage; and to Andrew and Aidan Crawshaw, for the loan every summer of their delightful house on the island of Andros, where this translation was both started and finished.

Above all, I am grateful to my collaborator, John Atkinson, the most congenial of colleagues with whom it has been a constant pleasure to work. I am responsible for the translation, the notes on the Greek text, and the index; John for all the rest of the book. John scrutinized each successive section of the translation in draft, and only he and I know how much, and how often, he improved what was first written. I have learnt much from him.

MARTIN HAMMOND

It has been a great privilege and a pleasure to work with Martin Hammond, who has such a wealth of experience as a translator. For me this project has been an enriching experience and I am very grateful to Martin for that, and at the mundane level for his attention to detail that has saved me from many unforced errors, and materially improved the presentation of the Introduction and Notes. I am also grateful to Judith Luna for defining what was required and reviewing the original draft material.

JOHN ATKINSON

Note

In the translation an asterisk indicates an Explanatory Note. An asterisk at the start of a paragraph indicates a Note which has reference to the whole of that paragraph or to a longer section of narrative beginning at that point.

CONTENTS

Introduction   xi

Select Bibliography   xl

Chronology   xliv

THE ANABASIS   1

    Book One   3

    Book Two   39

    Book Three   69

    Book Four   102

    Book Five   137

    Book Six   166

    Book Seven   195

THE INDICA   227

Appendix I: The Macedonian Army: Structures
and Terminology   266

Appendix II: The Macedonian and Persian
Courts and Imperial Administration   273

Appendix III: Finance and Linear Measures   275

Explanatory Notes   277

Notes on the Greek Text   335

Index   339

Maps   373

INTRODUCTION

ALEXANDER III, the Great, became the king of Macedon in 336 BC on the assassination of his father, Philip II. He was then 20 years of age, and began his reign in aggressive mode, campaigning north as far as the Danube and then into southern Romania to affirm Macedonian control of the area. In 335 he disabused the Greeks of the idea that the murder of Philip had freed them from Macedonian suzerainty, and the idea that he was too young and inexperienced to be taken seriously by the Macedonian senior officers. He took the leadership of the panhellenic military alliance set up by Philip, and in 334 launched his invasion of 'Asia', for the Persian Empire then stretched as far west as the Aegean shore of Asia Minor. The declared aim was to punish the Persians, in particular for Xerxes' invasion of Greece in 480. It is possible that Alexander really did think that he could conquer the Persian Empire from western Turkey and Egypt to the Punjab, and from the Makran in the south to Afghanistan in the north. But the record suggests that beyond the initial realistic aim of driving the Persians back out of Anatolia, the invasion was more an existential experience, for Alexander was ever the opportunist and pragmatic, and each mission accomplished created new challenges. So often he changed direction from what might have been predicted, and his victories over King Darius (Darius III Codomannus) and the Persian army in the major battles at Issus and Gaugamela were against the odds. As a commander he was exceptional not just because of personal courage and tenacity, but also because of his strength as a strategist and tactician. All this Arrian, as a military man himself, could appreciate, but he also saw the dark side.

The relatively short reign of Alexander (336 to 323 BC) marked one of the major turning-points in world history. The Greek city states continued to function after his death, but the world order had changed and a new era began, which came to be labelled the Hellenistic period. For Alexander, like many an autocrat, departed without leaving a viable succession plan. The senior officers who had survived the normal hazards of war and Alexander's paranoid suspicions were not united in purpose. Known as the Successors (*Diadochoi*), they acknowledged as king for a while Alexander's intellectually challenged half-brother Philip Arrhidaeus and then too Alexander's son by his Bactrian (Afghan) wife, born after his death. In 305 the leading Successors each took the title of king and demarcated his kingdom. Thus Alexander's empire was divided into the Hellenistic kingdoms, each with its ruling dynasty, the one that lasted the longest being Egypt under the Ptolemies, which survived till the suicide of Cleopatra in 30 BC.

Such is the ambiguity of dependency that while Alexander's campaigns furthered the spread of Greek culture, the Hellenistic kingdoms revealed the two-way effects of accommodation and assimilation. This pattern is well illustrated in Egypt by the Rosetta Stone and depictions of the Ptolemy of the day as a Pharaoh. And then there was the power of Roman imperialism, for by 30 BC what remained of the Hellenistic kingdoms was all under Roman control. These developments had some impact on the shaping of the Alexander legend. For example, in Egypt in the third century BC a revisionist account claimed Alexander as one of its own, as the bastard son of the Pharaoh Nectanebo. This developed into what is styled the *Alexander Romance*, later falsely attributed to Callisthenes (and thus conventionally referred to, as in this volume, as the Pseudo-Callisthenes), an account which over time generated derivatives in a broad sweep of cultures from Iceland to Indonesia. But in patriarchal, imperialistic Rome Alexander became the hero to be emulated or imitated, from Pompey the Great to Alexander Severus (emperor AD 222–35), and we have the image of the lanky Caligula once parading in the breastplate of the rather short Alexander. That last case readily explains why emulation of Alexander by unpopular autocrats was countered by hostile reworking of the legend.

The pattern has continued into modern times, each generation producing new variants to satisfy whatever passion or agenda it might nurse. Thus we have had Alexander welcoming into partnership the Aryan Persians as the Macedonians' kindred Herrenvolk, or promoting the unity of mankind and campaigning with rather Victorian values. The Cold War produced a more chilling image of Alexander, more in the mould of a Stalin. But interest in the 'real' as well as the imagined Alexander the Great continues strong. The last few decades have seen a stream of biographies and historical novels based on

the life of Alexander.¹ In the visual media there have been documen-
taries, feature films, and even a recent stage play.²

All this activity depends on a fairly limited amount of ancient
source material. Textual archival material is virtually limited to a
scatter of Greek inscriptions and Babylonian records. Contemporary
memoirs are known only from fragmentary quotations and more
substantial summaries or reworkings written some three centuries
or more after Alexander's death. To this group belongs Arrian,
though it may seem strange to label a text of the second century AD a
primary source for a chapter of history of the period 336 to 323 BC.
However, Arrian's concern to revive and justify the accounts of the
most authoritative and true primary sources³ gives his work special
value. Comparison with accounts written in the century or so before
Arrian's *Anabasis* shows that Arrian broke with the fashion of fiction-
alizing history and was not loading his material with a secondary level
of meaning.⁴ The title *Anabasis Alexandrou* (*Alexander's Expedition*)
indicates that this was primarily a military history, covering
Alexander's advance 'upcountry' or into the interior of Asia. The
Indica, based largely on Nearchus' account of his mission to take
Alexander's fleet from the Indus to the Tigris and Euphrates in late
325, is even closer to an archival record. Thus Arrian's *Anabasis*, with
its companion-piece the *Indica*, represents something of a time-
capsule, and is generally regarded as the most authoritative ancient
source on Alexander's campaigns.

At the same time Arrian clearly had ambition as a writer and a
belief in his own literary standing, and the *Anabasis* ranks as a 'classic'
not only as the major source on Alexander, but also as a work of literature, and it should be read as such.

---

¹ For example, Lane Fox, Cartledge, and Worthington (details in the Bibliography).
Novels include Mary Renault's trilogy: *Fire from Heaven* (New York, 1969), *The Persian
Boy* (London, 1972), and *Funeral Games* (London, 1981), Steven Pressfield's *Alexander:
the Virtues of War* (London, 2004), and A. Manfredi's trilogy: *Child of a Dream*, *The
Sands of Ammon*, and *The Ends of the Earth* (translated by I. Halliday, London, 2001).
² Notably Michael Wood's *In the Footsteps of Alexander* produced for the BBC, 1997;
Oliver Stone's movie *Alexander* (2000); and Juliet Jenkin's play *Mary and the Conqueror*
(Cape Town, 2011), which features Alexander and Mary Renault on stage with their
respective partners, Hephaestion and Julie Mullard.
³ Ptolemy and Aristobulus: see below the section on Arrian's sources.
⁴ As a representative of the Second Sophistic movement he had an agenda, but as is
explained below this was more supportive of the line of narrative he was following. We
also have to allow for the element of creative writing in battle scenes and speeches.

Arrian

ARRIAN'S CAREER

Lucius Flavius Arrianus was born about AD 86 in Nicomedia (mod. Izmit), the capital of the Roman province of Pontus and Bithynia in north-west Asia Minor. The family was Greek, but had acquired Roman citizenship, perhaps as early as 33 BC, and thus had been obliged to take the family name of their Roman benefactor, Lucius Flavius (consul 33 BC). As a member of a wealthy family which had a record of service to the community (for example, as municipal officers or priests) and perhaps some military service, our Arrian may have had from birth the legal status which would qualify him for admission to the career path of an *eques* (knight). This in turn presented the prospect of advancement to senatorial status and appointment to military and civil posts reserved for senators.

But first he is recorded as having studied under the Stoic philosopher Epictetus (*c.* AD 50–130) at Nicopolis, near Preveza in north-west Greece, in the period 107–9, or a little later. Sometime after that period of study Arrian produced the eight books of *The Diatribes of Epictetus*,[5] which he said represented the notes he had taken when listening to Epictetus. Hadrian, who went on to become the Roman emperor in 117, cultivated Epictetus' friendship, and it is possible that Arrian met Hadrian in Nicopolis.

Arrian is next attested, sometime in the period 111–14, as a member of the advisory council (or perhaps one should call him a staff-officer) of the governor of the province of Achaea, covering most of Greece. The governor, Avidius Nigrinus, was then a close friend of Hadrian, and Hadrian visited Athens. With this powerful Roman presence in a charm offensive in Athens, it was not surprising that the Athenians elected Hadrian to their top magistracy, the archonship, in 112. Arrian too had much to gain by courting the patronage of Roman Hellenophiles, which encourages the view that he began writing early in his career in the imperial service. Presumably he had the self-confidence to be sure that he could remain his own man, despite Epictetus' warnings against the dangers of becoming beholden to a ruler and of being shackled by official, familial, and social obligations (*Diatribes* 4.1.6–12).

[5] Otherwise translated as *Discourses*.

Just as the *Diatribes* is taken as evidence of a period of study in
Nicopolis, so the scattered references to the Parthian War in the surviving fragments of his *Parthica* have been taken as evidence that
Arrian went on to serve as an officer in Trajan's army during the war
in the Middle East against the Parthians in the period 114–17.[6] A
puzzle is that a citation of the *Parthica* refers to Arrian as commanding an operation in the area of the Caspian Gates [the Darial Pass] in
Georgia. But this was far to the north of Armenia where Trajan was
engaged in 114, after which the emperor pushed deep into southern
Iraq. Despite this puzzle, it seems quite possible that Arrian did serve
with Trajan in this war, and with equestrian, as opposed to senatorial,
rank. But the war was ill-conceived, and after capturing the Parthian
capital of Ctesiphon (*c*.40 km. south of Baghdad), and following the
Tigris down to the Persian Gulf, Trajan had to pull back and effectively abandon most of the territory he had won. He died in Cilicia,
southern Turkey, in 117 on his way back to Rome, and his cousin's
son, Hadrian, claimed to be the designated heir and assumed command of the army. He was to rule from 117 to 138.

Hadrian's route back to Italy took him through Nicomedia, and it
is generally assumed that Arrian, as a local dignitary, played a key
role in the city's reception of the new emperor. It was, then, probably
Hadrian who promoted Arrian to senatorial rank. This would have
been by the process of adlection, which meant the candidate's admission into the Senate without having first served in the successive
positions as prescribed for men born into senatorial families. He may
have been given the rank of one who had held the praetorship, for
which magistracy one had to be at least 30 years of age. With this
concessionary promotion, Arrian would have expected to wait some
ten to twelve years before he could be eligible for the consulship, and
indeed Hadrian had him appointed to that top position in 129 or 130.
His career in the period between adlection and the consulship is not
directly attested, but the pattern is established by the number of
known cases: Arrian would have held the command of a Roman
legion, followed by a term as the governor of a Roman province. An
Arrian is mentioned as the governor of Baetica, the most southerly
and Romanized province of Spain, and it is tempting to assume that

---

[6] The Parthians, from northern Iran, had won control of Iran by the mid-second century BC, and their empire lasted to about AD 227.

this was our historian, thus holding office there in the 120s.[7] It would also be significant as Baetica was the homeland of Hadrian's family.

After his consulship, in 129 or 130, he was assigned to the governorship of Cappadocia, that wild province in eastern Anatolia, west of the Upper Euphrates. This commission may have lasted from 131 to 137, and the reference to a campaign in Georgia could well belong to that context, rather than to Trajan's Parthian war. For in 135 the Alans, a nomadic tribe then living west of the Sea of Azov, raided south through Georgia and Azerbaijan and headed towards Cappadocia, but Arrian drove them back. Appointment to that difficult province is a mark in itself of Arrian's recognized military competence, even more so as his tenure of the post was twice as long as the norm. It was probably in 138, the year of Hadrian's death, that he was allowed to withdraw from the senatorial career track. Pulling out of the imperial service meant that he did not have to take his chances with the new emperor, nor have to wait around for five or more years in the hope of being awarded the prestigious governorship of Africa or Asia.

Released from the service, Arrian chose to settle in Athens (*Cynegeticus* [*Treatise on Hunting*] 1.4). There is no compelling evidence to support the opposing theories that he fell out of favour with the emperor Antoninus Pius (138–61) or returned to service to hold a further governorship.[8] But in Athens he presently gained the highest office, with his election to the archonship for the year 145/6.[9] At the end of his term as archon, he would have become automatically a member of the Athenian Areopagus council for life. He died sometime after the accession of Marcus Aurelius in 161.

LITERARY WORKS

The honorific inscription from Corinth which attests Arrian's governorship of Cappadocia hails him also as a 'philosopher', which we might translate as a public intellectual, and philosophy meant writing. Through his persona as the author of the treatise on hunting, Arrian gives his interests as hunting, military command, and philosophy (*On Hunting* 1.4), and in a dedication in Cordoba Arrian

---

[7] But it is also possible that he held this governorship only after his consulship.

[8] The governorship of Syria in the period *c.*138–41 has been suggested.

[9] The Athenian year began in July.

offered to Artemis, the goddess of hunting, poetry, as the gifts of the Muses, far better than gold and silver.[10] And indeed Arrian began writing as a young man, for, as noted above, the *Diatribes* may well have been completed not long after his period of study in Nicopolis, thus perhaps not long after AD 109. It was supposedly a record of sessions with Epictetus which Arrian attended, hence the lack of overall structure and the use of conversational, *koinē* Greek, as opposed to the literary, Attic dialect which Arrian used for other works. But elements in the work suggest that it was rather more a creative exercise, as Arrian worked his material up in the style of Xenophon's *Memorabilia* (*Recollections of Socrates*). This characterizes the double agenda which runs through the rest of his literary output: beside the material content was the challenge of switching between genres and linguistic registers. This gave him the scope to demonstrate the spread of his interests and familiarity with the work of diverse writers. But the key influence on him throughout was clearly Xenophon, not least because of the range of the genres which he covered.

Two relatively early works were the biographies of the 'philosopher king' Dion and the reformist liberator of Syracuse, Timoleon, but we know nothing of these works beyond their titles. Xenophon was again the model for the essay *On Hunting* (*Cynegeticus*). He makes much of his debt to Xenophon in that very different work, the *Periplus of the Euxine Sea* (*Circumnavigation of the Black Sea*), although it is cast as a report from himself to the emperor Hadrian, clearly while he was the governor of Cappadocia. The *Periplus* was dedicated to Hadrian, thus before the emperor's death in May 138, and probably while Arrian was still governor. The literary influence was by no means limited to Xenophon, for there are definite echoes of Herodotus and allusions to other literary works.

While he was in Cappadocia Arrian also wrote the *Order of Battle against the Alans*, which is taken to be a literary reworking in Greek of a report he would have made in Latin to Hadrian on his campaign of 135 to drive back the Alans and re-establish Roman control to the north-east of the province as far as Azerbaijan. This work was followed by a more general study, *The Science of Tactics*, which is dated to 136. Then his history of Trajan's Parthian War, the *Parthica*, may

---

[10] The dedication was apparently linked with a scheme to fund an annual festival in honour of Artemis.

also have been written after 135, if, as noted above, his reference in it to the Caspian Gates reflects his own action there.

Arrian is best known for his history of the campaigns of Alexander the Great, the *Anabasis*, but there is no agreement about when it was composed. Absolute dates are not ascertainable, and relative dating is tricky. For a start, when he wrote the *Anabasis* Arrian clearly considered himself an established writer: one of the masters of Greek, and well known because of the offices he had held (Preface 3; 1.12.4–5), there being no false modesty about Arrian. A complication is that he qualifies the reference to magistracies held with the expression 'in my own country', which might refer to Nicomedia and Bithynia, or Rome, or even Athens. Despite this uncertainty, the general view has been that Arrian wrote the *Anabasis* after about 140, when he had left Cappadocia and retired to Athens, though Bosworth has powerfully argued the case for treating it as an early work, perhaps written before 125.[11]

With the *Anabasis* he began a new string of books. In the latter part of the *Anabasis* he explicitly stated (5.5.1, 5.6.8, and 6.16.5) that he was planning a treatise on India, that is the *Indica*, which would cover Nearchus' account of his voyage from the Indus to the mouth of the Tigris,[12] if he could find the will and the inspiration (6.28.6). Another sequel to the *Anabasis* appears to be his *Events after the Death of Alexander*, which was presumably intended to take the story down to the foundation of the Hellenistic kingdoms, and thus at least to 304. But surviving fragments of this work indicate that Arrian did not get much beyond the death of Perdiccas in 321/0, covering in great detail events of about three and a half years in ten books, so either he abandoned the project for something else, or he died before he could complete it. This work would have been based on the magisterial memoirs of Hieronymus, who was perhaps the nephew of Alexander's secretary, Eumenes.

The Byzantine scholar Photius refers to another work, Arrian's history of his homeland, the *Bithyniaca*, running to eight books (of which only fragments survive). Photius implies that he took from the

---

[11] A. B. Bosworth, *A Historical Commentary on Arrian's History of Alexander*, 2 vols. (Oxford: Oxford University Press, 1980; 1995), i. 11. His case includes the point that elements in the *Order of Battle against the Alans* presuppose the *Anabasis*, which must therefore have been written before 135.

[12] Or the mouths of the Tigris and Euphrates (*Anab.* 6.19.5).

preface to this work that it was his fourth historical work, after the *Anabasis* and studies of Timoleon and Dion. As the biographies were early works, the *Anabasis* might then more appropriately also be seen as an early work, but scholars are generally more inclined to consider Photius' reference misleading and to treat the *Bithyniaca* as a late work, a labour of love for his motherland towards the end of his life.

Alexander's Life and Campaigns in the Framework of *the* Anabasis

Alexander was born on 20 July 356 BC. His father, Philip II, had assumed the kingship of Macedon in 359, and his mother was Olympias, a princess from Epirus. She was just one of the women Philip married to gain a hold on other dynasties in the region. The infant Alexander had a nurse, Lanice (4.9.3), whose brother later fell victim to Alexander, and his mentors included Aristotle. Anecdotes about the young prince attest his sharp mind, physical prowess, and bravery. Philip groomed him as heir to the throne, for instance by leaving him to act for a short period as regent in Macedon, and by allowing him an apprenticeship in the command of troops, notably at the battle of Chaeronea in 338. Arrian does not cover this early period, nor indeed the murder of Philip in October 336, which Arrian reports as simply the death of the king (1.1.1, though he later refers to the men involved in the conspiracy: 1.25.1–2). The narrative begins with Alexander's intimidatory mission to the Peloponnese and Athens and his campaigns to establish without any delay his control over Macedon's Balkan neighbours (1.1–6). Then Alexander returned to mainland Greece, with Thebes as the main target, as the Thebans had blockaded the Macedonian garrison. Thebes was retaken and destroyed (1.7–10). Arrian was well aware that the massacre and destruction did Alexander no credit, and so he was careful to spell out the mitigating circumstances (1.9.6–10).

At the time of his death, Philip was already committed to an invasion of the Persian Empire, but had achieved little more than establishing a bridgehead on the Asian coast of the Dardanelles. However, he had created in the so-called Corinthian League the framework of a panhellenic military alliance under Macedonian leadership ready for a war against the Persians in revenge for Xerxes' invasion of Greece and desecration of Greek temples in 480 BC. In 334 Alexander mobilized this multinational expeditionary force and invaded Asia Minor (1.11). He invoked memories of the Trojan War with ceremonies at the Hellespont and at the city of Troy (1.11.5–12.1). This was of little relevance to the proclaimed intent of a retaliatory invasion of the Persian Empire, but had much to do with countering a long-standing Greek perception that the Macedonians were not truly Greek. It also served to promote Alexander's model of charismatic leadership.

The first major battle was fought at the river Granicus, where Alexander routed the combined forces of Persians and Greek mercenaries from Persia's satrapies (territories under Persian control) in western Anatolia (1.12.8–16.7). He then headed south and received the capital of Lydia, Sardis, of strategic significance because of its position at the western end of the Persian Royal Road. Next, in the name of liberating Greek cities from Persian rule, he removed pro-Persian oligarchies from Ephesus and other Ionian cities, meeting the fiercest resistance at Miletus (1.17.9–19.11), and before the end of 334 he captured the Carian capital, Halicarnassus (1.20–3). The capture of these two cities was proof enough of Alexander's tactical genius and sheer determination.

In the context of his advance into Lycia and Pamphylia, Alexander received reports that Alexander of Lyncestis, then in command of the cavalry from Thessaly, was conspiring against him, and that Darius was trying to contact the Lyncestian with the promise of a large amount of gold if he could assassinate the Macedonian king (1.25). Meanwhile, Memnon, a Greek but serving Darius as his commander-in-chief in the Aegean, began a naval campaign in preparation for a counter-invasion of Macedonia and Greece (2.1–2). But in the spring of 333 Alexander headed north into central Turkey and entered the city of Gordium, where by cutting through the famous knot on Gordius' wagon he sought oracular support for his bid to become the king of 'Asia' (2.3). From Gordium Alexander headed east into Cappadocia and made a statement by crossing the river Halys (2.4.1–2), for in Cyrus' day this was the boundary between the West and the Persian Empire. Alexander dashed to Tarsus in Cilicia, and there was high drama when, after an ill-advised plunge into the Cydnus, he fell desperately ill (2.4.4–11; perhaps malaria). By now Darius had mobilized his army and was heading for Syria, while Alexander, after his recovery, advanced along the coast through the Cilician/Assyrian Gates [the Merkes Su Pass] towards Myriandrus [near Iskenderun], as he was planning to engage Darius in the plain beyond the Belen Pass (2.6.1–2). There was something of a comedy of errors, as Darius, unaware of Alexander's position, was persuaded to turn north and descend towards Cilicia via the Amanic Gates [the Toprakkale Pass] (2.7.1). Alexander was then surprised to learn that Darius was behind him, and turned back to confront Darius' large army in the narrow coastal plain near Issus (2.7–12), November 333. The Persians were routed and Darius fled, leaving his family to be captured by the Macedonians. Alexander rejected his offer of a truce on generous terms (2.13–14).

The next major action was the prolonged siege of Tyre, which ended in July/August 332 with a massacre (2.16–24). Alexander continued south, and met with similar determined resistance before Gaza fell to him (2.26–7). By November 332 Alexander was able to invade Egypt, encouraged by the readiness of the Persian satrap to surrender his satrapy without a fight (3.1.1–2). Arrian now covers Alexander's plans for the foundation of Alexandria, receipt of information on the political and military situation in the Aegean, Alexander's visit to the oracle of Ammon at Siwah, and the settlement of Egypt (3.2–5).

In the spring of 331 Alexander returned to Tyre, crossed the Euphrates (July/August), and then the Tigris. The eclipse of the moon on 20/21 September 331 was taken as a favourable omen before the imminent battle, which was fought on about 1 October at Gaugamela and ended with the complete defeat of Darius' vast army, which included scythe-chariots and armoured cavalry (3.7–15). The scale of the losses virtually sealed the fate of the Persian Empire.

Darius fled north from the battle site to Ecbatana [Hamadan] in Media, but Alexander turned south to take the key cities of Babylon, the administrative capital Susa, and the royal capital Persepolis (3.16–18). The first serious challenge to Alexander was from the Uxians, as he left Susa, with the decisive action at the Persian Gates in the Zagros mountain range. Arrian's brief reference to the occupation of Persepolis (3.18.10–12) conceals the fact that the army was there from January to May 330, and Arrian tries to rationalize the final torching of the capital, which he thought was a miscalculation on Alexander's part (3.18.12). It is at this point that Arrian introduces the first overt criticism of Alexander.

When the conditions allowed Alexander's army to continue north towards Ecbatana, Darius moved out, heading to Rhagae, near

Tehran, and Bactria, an area of Afghanistan, where he intended to regroup and build up a fresh army. But a group of Darius' officers, led by Nabarzanes and Bessus, arrested him, and when Alexander was close to overtaking them, they wounded Darius and left him to die (3.19–21). Alexander came upon the corpse and sent it back to Persepolis for burial (3.22.1–2, putting this in July 330). Greek troops who had served as mercenaries with Darius had fled into the Elburz mountains, and the peoples bordering on the southern part of the Caspian had sent troops to fight in Darius' army. Thus Alexander turned north, and invaded the territory of the Hyrcanians, Tapurians, and Mardians (3.23–4). Now he learnt that Bessus had assumed the title of King of Asia, and as head of the Persian Empire was assembling an army in Bactria (3.25.3). Alexander set off to invade Bactria, but was deflected south by the news of the defection of Satibarzanes, the Persian whom Alexander had reinstated as satrap of Areia. Satibarzanes had decided to switch to Bessus' side and had massacred the small guard force which Alexander had sent into Areia (3.25.4–8; at 25.2 they are described as more like military police). The campaign ended with the death in action of Satibarzanes, and the submission of peoples to the south of Bactria, the Drangians, Gedrosians, and Arachosians, and by now it was the winter of 330/29 (3.25.4–28.3). Arrian slips into the narrative of this campaign a brief mention of the conviction of the cavalry commander Philotas for misprision of treason, and the judicial murder of his father Parmenion (3.26–7).

On the approach to the pass in the Caucasus [Hindu Kush] Alexander founded a new city, Alexandria in the Caucasus (3.28.4), probably near Begram. Into Bactria Alexander made for Balkh, and Bessus retreated across the Oxus [Amu-Darya] and Alexander pursued him. Spitamenes and Dataphernes decided to save their skins by handing Bessus over, and Ptolemy was sent to effect the arrest. Alexander pushed on to Samarcand and then to the Tanaïs/Jaxartes [Syr-Darya], not least for the symbolic significance of crossing into Scythian territory and, as some saw it, passing from Asia back into Europe (3.28.5–30.11).

The rest of the campaigning season of 329 was spent in dealing with foci of resistance in Sogdiana, and with Scythian invaders (4.1–6). Alexander then crossed back into Bactria to winter at Zariaspa (Bactra [Balkh]; 4.7).

Now, at the midpoint of the *Anabasis*, Arrian introduces what

Bosworth labels 'the Great Digression' (4.7.4–14.4), following on the reference to the sadistic punishment of Bessus (4.7.3) and covering manifestations of resistance to the way Alexander began to cast himself in the role of emperor, adopting elements of the Persian dress-code and court rituals, most notoriously *proskynesis*, the ceremonial greeting performed when one approached the king. This exacerbated tensions within Alexander's court, first of all between the old guard of veterans of Philip's campaigns and those of Alexander's generation, between Macedonian chauvinists and those more prepared to tolerate his policy of assimilation. The generational divide led to the brawl in autumn 328, when Cleitus gave vent to the grievances of the veterans, and Alexander in a drunken rage stabbed him to death (4.8–9). Sometime later the official historian, Callisthenes, a relative of Aristotle, came into conflict with Alexander over the issue of *proskynesis*, and more generally Alexander's orientalizing (4.10–12). Then, in spring 327 (4.22.2), Callisthenes was accused of implication in a conspiracy of the Pages[13] to assassinate Alexander. Statements extracted under torture were believed and Callisthenes was put to death (4.12.7–14.4, where Arrian notes that Aristobulus attributed his death to natural causes).

But back in the winter of 329/8 Alexander was approached by envoys from the European Scythians seeking an alliance (4.15), and in the spring of 328 he crossed the Oxus back into Sogdiana, directing a five-pronged invasion (4.16.1–3). But Spitamenes organized a counter-offensive and with the support of Massagetan cavalry attacked the main Macedonian base in Bactria. Spitamenes was finally betrayed and killed while Alexander was wintering at Nautaca [Shakhrisyabz] in Sogdiana, 328/7 (4.16.4–17.7).

The spring offensive of 327 began with a battle for the Rock of Sogdiana. Oxyartes of Bactria had taken refuge there, and his daughter Rhoxane was among those captured, which introduces a romantic note, as Alexander went on to marry her (4.18.4–20.4). There was then a battle for the Rock of Chorienes, possibly at a gorge on the Vakhs (4.21). The action ended in wintry conditions, but still in the spring of 327, and Alexander waited in Bactria till the weather improved and he could recross the Hindu Kush to Alexandria in the Caucasus (4.22). The campaigning season was occupied by a series of

---

[13] Macedonian cadets training for enrolment in the regular army units.

actions north of the river Cophen [Kabul] in the Swat district and the old Persian satrapy of Gandhara between the Swat and the Indus (4.22.6–30.9). The climactic action was the battle at Mount Aornus, which, tradition had it, Heracles had been unable to capture. When the Indians holding this vantage-point were finally cowed into submission, Alexander met little further resistance before he reached the Indus (4.28–30).

Book 5 opens with two digressions: the first backtracks to cover the story of the celebrations in honour of Dionysus when Alexander visited the city of Nysa, to the west of the Indus, which according to the myth Dionysus founded when he campaigned into India. Arrian indicates that he included stories about Alexander's rivalry with Dionysus and Heracles as well-established traditions that he could not dismiss as totally incredible (5.1–3.4). The second digression deals mainly with the geography of India, and serves as a programmatic note on his plan for the *Indica* (5.4–6). He digresses again in speculating on how Alexander managed to bridge the Indus (5.7).

When Alexander reached the Hydaspes [Jhelum] the major challenge came from the Indian king, Porus, and a full-scale battle was fought on the river in April/May 326, ending in an overwhelming victory for the Macedonians (5.8.4–18.3). Porus was persuaded to surrender and Alexander paid him exceptional honour as a very worthy opponent and restored him to his royal position (5.18.4–19.3). Alexander also founded two cities to mark the battle site (5.19.4–6). The campaign continued to the Acesines [Chenab] and on to the Hydraotes [Ravi], beyond which the most dramatic action was the siege of Sangala (5.20–4).

When Alexander reached the river Hyphasis [Beas] in 326 he was minded to press on to the Ganges, but his troops refused to go further, and staged what is loosely called a mutiny, using the senior Coenus as their spokesman. The presentation of unfavourable omens allowed Alexander to be persuaded to turn back (5.25–9). Everything was done to avoid loss of face, but the relationship between Alexander and his Macedonian and Greek troops had been damaged. This was a real turning-point in the history of Alexander.

Back at the Hydaspes in early October 326 Alexander put his mind to sailing down the Indus to the sea (6.1). At this point Coenus died—officially, it was said, from some disease (6.2.1). The army set off downstream in early November, with Nearchus, the central character in, and principal source for, Arrian's *Indica*, as commander of the fleet (6.2.3), and Craterus and Hephaestion in command of the troops marching along the west and east banks respectively (6.2.2). The larger vessels took a pounding in the rough waters ahead of the junction of the Hydaspes and Acesines [Chenab] (6.4.4–5.4). The invasion of the territory of the Mallians (6.6.1–14.3) saw some high drama, as Alexander was very nearly killed in the assault on their main city when he jumped down from the walls ahead of his men and was briefly on his own, surrounded by Indians desperate to see him dead. He was rescued, but there was panic among the troops, who feared that he would not survive. Arrian exploits this episode for its dramatic value, but also uses it as an example of the contamination of the historical record by wilful or careless errors (6.11), and he uses this and other cases to demonstrate why he chose to favour Ptolemy and Aristobulus as the most trustworthy sources.

Alexander recovered and continued down to the junction of the Acesines and the Hydraotes [Ravi] (6.14.5), invading the territory of a succession of Indian peoples, including Musicanus' kingdom. This prince first surrendered without a fight, but then revolted. Betrayed to Alexander, he was hanged (6.17.2), as were the Brahmans who incited him to revolt. Alexander then reached Patala at the apex of the Indus delta (6.18.5). This would have been in July 325. From there he explored both streams of the Indus down to the sea, before returning to Patala (6.18–20). Here Nearchus with the fleet had to wait till the monsoon winds subsided before he could begin the voyage along the coast of the Arabian Sea (6.21.1–2), but Alexander was able to lead off with the army, probably in September 325, towards Baluchistan and the Persian satrapy of Gedrosia. This campaign (6.21.3–27.2) was dominated by the disaster of the march through the Gedrosian desert, where the shortage of food and water caused heavy casualties and the loss by death or slaughter of the baggage animals. The disaster was ennobled by some heroic actions, and when Alexander emerged from the desert there began what we might call a search for scapegoats (6.27.1).

The advance through Carmania (6.27.3–28.7) was marked by a purge of those charged with the abuse of power and dereliction of duty. The Alexander legend made much of a celebratory Bacchic carnival to mark the triumph of Alexander's deliverance of the army from the hell of Gedrosia (6.28). Arrian could not ignore this episode, but uses it to show that his principal sources, Ptolemy and Aristobulus (see below on Arrian's sources), lent no support to the extravagant (and anachronistic) elements in the myth.

From Carmania, not before the end of 325, Alexander headed back to Pasargadae, and was horrified to find that the tomb of Cyrus the Great had been desecrated. Under torture the Magi still refused to identify the culprits (6.29). Alexander returned to the ruins of Persepolis, and acted on a series of charges against the satrap, Orxines, whose execution added to the list of those purged after the march through Gedrosia (6.30.1–2; cf. 27.3–5 and 29.3, and 7.4.1).

At the beginning of Book 7 Arrian introduces another digression, with critical comment on the tradition of Alexander's last plans (7.1), which he caps with anecdotes about Alexander's humbling encounters with Diogenes the Cynic, Indian gymnosophists, and especially the guru Calanus (7.2–3). As Calanus died by suicide in Susiana, his story takes the reader back into the narrative, as Alexander was back in Susa (7.4.1). Here he took two members of the Persian royal family as wives, obliged his Companions, an elite of about ninety men in Alexander's court, to take noble Persian women as brides, and regularized as marriages the liaisons which some ten thousand of his Macedonian troops had formed with Asian women; he also settled the debts which his soldiers had accumulated (7.4.4–5.6). But the tensions were running deep as a force of thirty thousand young Asian conscripts joined the army; Asian cavalry units from various satrapies were incorporated; and the weddings at Susa signalled a policy of assimilation that offended and alarmed Macedonian chauvinists (7.6). This came to a head with a full-scale 'mutiny' at Opis (7.8–12.4). A reconciliation was effected but essentially on Alexander's terms, and those who had lost the will to fight or were unfit for service were discharged and sent back to Macedon with Craterus, who was given the additional mandate of replacing Antipater as Alexander's viceroy in Macedonia (7.12.3–7).

A reference to the apocryphal tale of an offer to Alexander of one hundred Amazons, with marital more than military intent (7.13.2–6), brings the story to Alexander's march to Ecbatana [Hamadan], and his personal tragedy with the death of his homosexual partner Hephaestion. His manifestations of grief were taken as further evidence of mental or moral decline: Arrian seeks to mitigate the charges (7.14). Towards the end of 324 Alexander was again operating against tribes in the Zagros mountains (7.15.1–2).

When he crossed the Tigris en route for Babylon Alexander received several warnings of unfavourable omens (7.16.5–18.6). But his focus was on building up a large fleet at Babylon, with the intention of launching an attack on the Arabs, who had refused to recognize his temporal power and, according to one tradition, his claim to be acknowledged as their third god (7.19.3–20.2). Alexander himself explored the Euphrates down to the sea, and received reports from Nearchus and others who had sailed in the Arabian Gulf (7.20.3–22.5), and again there was an omen of doom as he approached Babylon (7.22.2–5), and another ill omen as some nonentity unthinkingly rested his weary frame on Alexander's throne (7.24.1–3). This leads into the account of Alexander's last days (7.24.4–26.3), dominated by what purports to be the entry Arrian read in the 'Royal Journals' (*Ephemerides*) (7.25). He follows this with a summary of various tales claiming that Alexander was murdered, but for Arrian they lack credibility (7.27).

He concludes with a final assessment of Alexander, marking his achievements, addressing the vulnerable elements in his record, and calling for recognition of his superhuman stature (7.28–30). Alexander clearly had divine help, as Arrian could appreciate, since he too could not have written this work without God's help (7.30.3).

The Anabasis

SCOPE AND STYLE

Arrian certainly had pretensions, presenting himself as worthy to write the first adequate history of Alexander, like a Homer for Achilles (Alexander's ancestor), and a Xenophon for the Ten Thousand (1.12.1–5), and, like Alexander, Arrian could acknowledge divine assistance (7.30.3). But he would not be like Alexander's chosen chronicler, Callisthenes, who, with an inflated sense of his own importance, supposedly claimed to have been the creator of Alexander's fame (4.10.1–2; or as media specialists would say, the creator of the Alexander brand). In humbler terms in the Preface, Arrian gives his aim as to produce a more trustworthy account of Alexander's campaigns by giving precedence to Ptolemy (the Macedonian officer who after Alexander's death took Egypt as his kingdom, and assumed the royal title in 305) and Aristobulus (who apparently served Alexander as an engineer) as the most reliable of the primary sources, and to add in material from other sources where relevant, worth mentioning, and reasonably credible.

In the *Diatribes* Arrian had followed Xenophon's *Memorabilia* (*Memoirs of Socrates*); now he advertised the link with Xenophon by calling his work the *Anabasis Alexandrou* (*Alexander's Expedition*). The title was actually more appropriate for Arrian's work than it was for Xenophon's, as *ana*basis would mean an expedition upcountry or into the interior, and Alexander penetrated into the very heart of the Persian Empire. But Xenophon tells the story of the mercenaries who with himself joined Cyrus and were drawn into Cyrus' bid to seize the Persian throne from his brother Artaxerxes. The attempted coup failed with the death of Cyrus at the battle of Cunaxa in 401, and Xenophon and the ten thousand mercenaries headed north to escape from Persian territory (Xenophon, *Anabasis* Bks. 2–7): their heroic march was more down to the coast than into the interior. Thus Arrian signalled his identification with Xenophon, but clearly identified the contrast between Xenophon's wretched flight down to the sea (*kata*basis) and Alexander's glorious penetration into every part of the Persian Empire (Arrian 1.12.3–4).

But this is a work on a grander scale by virtue of the stature of the central character, the time-span of the action, the extraordinary extent of the geography covered, and the number of peoples whom Alexander conquered or encountered. Alexander changed the course of Greek history and built up a new empire. Thus Arrian sets the story in a much wider historical context, starting with the heroes of Homeric legend, Agamemnon, Achilles, and Priam; featuring the Persian kings Cyrus the Great, Darius I, and Xerxes; and working in the Athenian tyrant-slayers Harmodius and Aristogeiton, as well as more obviously the key figures in the Athenian democracy in Alexander's reign. Then there are episodes where Alexander is said to have rivalled Dionysus, Heracles, and the lesser likes of Perseus (3.3.2) and Semiramis (6.24.2–3). At the more mundane level Arrian goes beyond the military narrative to give, for example, some details of the instruments of incorporation, army appointments, provincial (satrapal) administration, and diplomatic exchanges.

Arrian's admiration for Alexander and somewhat naive political philosophy (evidenced at Pref. 2 and 7.5.2) did not mean that he was casual about the business of establishing historical truth. He was careful in his choice of sources and used them critically. He demythologizes the history, but does not suppress traditions that he considers dubious, for example on the supposed visit of Roman envoys to Alexander, which Arrian uses to demonstrate his critical ability and sense of history (7.15.5–6). Similarly Arrian retains the story of the Amazons who came to Alexander, but again takes the opportunity to display his erudition and to rationalize away the anachronistic elements in the story (7.13.2–6).

Arrian attributes numerous speeches to Alexander and other characters, and comparison with other sources shows that for some at least there was a common core to draw on, but he cannot have expected the reader to accept Alexander's lengthy speech to the troops at Opis (7.9–10), for example, as a verbatim record of what was actually said. Indeed, in this case Curtius Rufus' very different rendering of the speech in his *Histories of Alexander the Great* (Curtius 10.2.15–29) points to the creative element in this aspect of historiography and shows how speeches could be recast to assist in the characterization of the key figures in the drama.

If rhetorical exercises had some influence on the historian's approach to re-creating speeches and verbal exchanges, then perhaps Roman drama might also have had an influence.[14] Certainly there are elements of melodrama in Arrian's presentation of the troops' reaction to the speech at Opis (7.11), as in some scenes in the *Indica* (notably *Ind.* 34.6–12 and 35.8).

Digressions include relevant geographical matter (as in 5.4–6, 7.7.3–5, and 7.16.1–4), mythistorical notes in the style of Herodotus (as on the Cymaeans of Phrygia: 1.26.4), and details introduced out of their chronological context (as on Alexander's treatment of Darius' wife, taken prisoner after the battle of Issus: 4.20.1–3; and on Alexander's horse Bucephalas: 5.19.4–6). Authorial additions also include detail on Roman bridge-building techniques, where Arrian speculates on how Alexander might have bridged the Indus (5.7.3–5). And then there is the introduction of his plan for the *Indica* (5.4.3–5.2).

The narrative is also interrupted by passages where Arrian identifies errors in the tradition (as at 6.11.3–6) or comments on his historiographical principles (as at 2.12.8, 2.24.6, 6.11.2, and 7.3.6). Of course there are points where he passes judgement, and not just on

---

[14] The tragedies of Seneca illustrate the cross-pollination of drama and rhetorical exercises.

Alexander: he includes, for example, a critical but not unsympathetic obituary on Darius III (3.22.2–6).

In patches we have potted history, and errors crept in (as at 3.15.7), and some confusion when Arrian had difficulty in reconciling different sources (as at 4.7.1 and 4.18.1–3, where he appears to put the same event in successive winters). But the *Anabasis* should not be judged just by the criteria of historical accuracy and insight. Arrian was writing nearly five centuries after the events, and was revivifying undervalued sources rather than claiming to have new evidence. It is rather more to be appreciated as a work of literature. He knew where to make the narrative expansive and dramatic (as in 6.24.4–26.3), and where to increase the pace, as in his account of the battle of Issus (especially 1.15.6 ff.), and where to interrupt a staccato-style battle account with a little padding (as at 6.9.5) to delay the climax. Literary intent is also signalled in the intertextual references: in the notes we identify echoes of Homer, Herodotus, Thucydides, and of course Xenophon. Arrian was not only reviving a chapter in 'ancient' history but also out to make his contribution to 'classical' literature.

ARRIAN'S SOURCES

Genre was a factor in an historian's choice of sources. Arrian was writing history, and not 'universal' history, in the style of Herodotus, but rather a monograph, as he announced by adopting the title used by Xenophon, the *Anabasis*. But Plutarch wrote a biography of Alexander, and for this he needed anecdotal material and chance remarks as being more revealing of character than accounts of major battles and sieges of cities. Ideally Plutarch wanted autobiographical material, and for his life of Alexander he was at least able to read letters attributed to Alexander; and next in importance were the memoirs of those closest to him. Thus Plutarch cited Chares, the chamberlain or head of protocol, and Callisthenes, appointed by Alexander as his 'embedded' historian. He also referred to artistic representations of Alexander, and to the *Education of Alexander*, written by Onesicritus, whom we meet as the chief navigator in the *Indica*. By contrast, Arrian, writing a monograph on Alexander's campaigns, turned to the memoirs of those he judged the most authoritative on the military record: Ptolemy, a front-line commander, and Aristobulus, characterized as an army engineer, and of some value because of his overtly sympathetic attitude to Alexander. As both wrote after Alexander's death, when they had nothing to gain or risk by the way they wrote (Preface 2), they could also be taken as reliable guides to the political issues. It should be noted, however, that Aristobulus wrote very long after Alexander's death, and with a patently apologetic intent, and Ptolemy, who went on to establish a dynasty in Egypt, clearly had his own political motives. To his credit, Arrian used these sources critically, as at 5.14.4–6 where he rejects Aristobulus' version of Porus' son's action before the battle of the Hydaspes and explains why Ptolemy's account is more probable. In other cases he checked his main sources against others, and supplemented them where other sources had more to offer—hence the extension of his summary of Nearchus' record of the voyage from Patala to Susa into a separate book, the *Indica*, and his use of the 'Royal Journals', which he took to be an authentic archival record, at least for the days leading up to the death of Alexander (7.26). But it remains a criticism that Arrian did not signal that the protracted struggle for power after Alexander's death might have contaminated memoirs written in that context. An immediate case is Ptolemy's handling of Perdiccas' record, for in 321/0 Perdiccas, as regent for the mentally ill Philip Arrhidaeus and the toddler Alexander IV, invaded Egypt to bring the satrap Ptolemy into line: Perdiccas died in the attempt, and Ptolemy went on to claim the royal title. We can assume that when Ptolemy wrote his memoirs he would have been tempted to be less than dispassionate about Perdiccas. As it happens, in Book 1 we meet Perdiccas berserking at Thebes (1.8.1) and two drunken, undisciplined Macedonian soldiers from Perdiccas' brigade recklessly initiating an action at Halicarnassus without orders (1.21.1–3).

But Arrian was not blind to some questionable elements in Ptolemy's history. It suited his purposes to accept Ptolemy's account of the trial and conviction of Philotas and the judicial murder of his father Parmenion (3.26), but the very brevity of Arrian's summary suggests that his faith in Ptolemy was limited to acceptance of his record of the official version.

Still, one gains an impression of Ptolemy's style and value from passages where he features as a major participant in an action and can be presumed to have been Arrian's source, as in the battle for Sangala (5.22.4–24.5; cf. 4.24–5 and 29). On military matters he was Arrian's preferred source (6.2.4; cf. 7.15.1–3). Then there is the classic case of the story promoted by Cleitarchus (*c*.310 BC) and Timagenes (late first century BC) and others that Ptolemy acted heroically in the assault on the Mallian city, when he jumped down from the rampart to protect Alexander from his attackers: Arrian could cite his rejection of the myth, as Ptolemy recorded that he was on an independent mission at the time (6.11.8).[15]

From Aristobulus Arrian was able to access detailed documentary detail, as evidenced by Darius' battle-order at Gaugamela (3.11.3–7; cf. 7.19.3–6 on the fleet assembled at Babylon), and the recurring pattern in the accounts of sieges in Asia Minor suggests that these may have come from Aristobulus as a specialist in military engineering, though he was silent on how Alexander bridged the Indus (5.7.1). Aristobulus had a more general value because of his extraordinarily positive attitude towards Alexander, as the apologetic passages provided a navigational aid for Arrian, who clearly had to keep a line to the less adulatory, leeward side of Aristobulus.

In claiming credit for having identified the special value of Ptolemy and Aristobulus as sources for the history of Alexander's reign Arrian was distancing himself in particular from the work of Cleitarchus,[16] who in Hellenistic and Roman times, at least before the appearance of Arrian's *Anabasis*, enjoyed the status of being the most popular historian of Alexander's reign. And, as ever, celebrity status was a drawcard for detractors, and Cicero, Strabo, and Quintilian dismissed him as far from dedicated to the pursuit of historical truth. But Cleitarchus, who apparently completed his work by about 310 BC, was one of the first to produce a history of the Alexander era, and as his father Dinon was a historian, author of the *Persica*, it would be surprising if Cleitarchus did not aim to make his mark as a serious historian. Certainly Diodorus Siculus, who completed his universal history before about 30 BC, used Cleitarchus as his main source for Book 17, on Alexander. Then Curtius Rufus identified Cleitarchus as one of his sources for his *Histories of Alexander the Great* (a work in Latin, on the same scale as Arrian's *Anabasis*, and completed in or soon after AD 41). Trogus' *Philippica* (completed sometime before AD 6) covered Alexander in Books 11 and 12, known to us from the much later epitome by Justin;[17] and he too drew on Cleitarchus. These authors

---

[15] A point anticipated by Curtius Rufus 9.5.21.

[16] As indicated above he must have written before Ptolemy did.

[17] Justin probably wrote in the late second century AD, but some favour a much later date. The appropriateness of the label 'epitome' is also a matter of debate. On these

who followed the Cleitarchean tradition are rather dismissively referred to as the vulgate sources. Plutarch was more comprehensive in his review of the primary sources, and more eclectic in using them for individual episodes in his *Life of Alexander the Great* (best dated to between AD 110 and 115[18]). But he too recognized Cleitarchus as a major source.[19]

Thus, in distancing himself from Cleitarchus, Arrian was also setting himself above preceding Alexander historians from Diodorus to Plutarch. There are one or two cases where it is suggested that Arrian echoed Curtius Rufus, but the tradition of treating Arrian as apart from the 'vulgate' sources seems well justified; and genre as well as choice of sources separated Arrian from Plutarch.

The historical tradition on Alexander was contaminated (at least from an historian's point of view) by the way rhetoricians and philosophers appropriated elements of the story and developed them as improving *exempla* or rhetorical exercises. One such topic, popular in Hellenistic and pseudepigraphical texts, was the meeting between ruler and philosopher. Arrian could not resist this material and drew on it for his brief coverage of Alexander's encounters with the Brahmans of Nysa (5.1.3–2.4 with note on 6.16.5 and *Indica* 11.1–7, drawing on Megasthenes) and Diogenes the Cynic (7.2.1), and his bid to dissuade the Indian philosopher, or gymnosophist, Calanus from committing suicide (7.1.5–3.6). Such apocryphal material may also have influenced Arrian's re-creation of speeches attributed to Alexander, as in the exchange between Alexander and Coenus on the Hyphasis (5.25–7) and in his address to the mutineers at Opis (7.9–10). Pre-battle speeches (as in 2.17) were no doubt more free composition than authentic transcripts.

ARRIAN'S VIEW OF ALEXANDER

Over his career as a writer Arrian chose a variety of authors, genres, and even linguistic styles as his models, but the authorial comments

issues see *Justin, Epitome of the Philippic History of Pompeius Trogus, Books 11–12*; translated by J. C. Yardley, with commentary by W. Heckel (Oxford: Oxford University Press, 1997).

[18] Thus J. R. Hamilton, *Plutarch, Alexander: A Commentary* (Oxford: Oxford University Press, 1969), p. xxxvii.

[19] As, for example, on the role of Thaïs in urging Alexander to destroy Persepolis by fire, Thaïs later becoming Ptolemy's mistress (Plutarch, *Alexander* 38).

are not those of some adopted persona. His admiration of Alexander was clearly genuine. This might seem to be at odds with the values which Arrian said he learnt from Epictetus, who gave as a first principle the notion of god-given freedom and the free person, and enthused about the liberating effect of resistance to the tyrant or authority figure (*Diatribes* 4.1.6–12), and indeed Arrian slips in the point that it is unlikely that the Romans sent envoys to Alexander in 323, since they were second to none in their hatred of 'the whole tribe of kings' (7.15.6). But his history of Alexander is certainly not 'A Study in Tyranny': rather a celebration of the greatest leader in the Greek world, who 'made himself unambiguously king of two continents' (7.30.1). The simple truth may be that Arrian became more pragmatic with age, or found the philhellene Hadrian, or Antoninus, if he wrote later than 138, that much more worthy of respect than the bellicose Trajan.[20]

Despite many criticisms of Alexander in the body of his work—though the first direct criticism only occurs at 3.18.12—when he came to the final assessment (7.28–9) Arrian chose to stress the positive, and in this he could follow the lead of Aristobulus. Thus he explains Alexander's claim to divine parentage as a distancing strategy, and he could appreciate that Alexander must have had a divine mover (7.30.2–3). Arrian rationalizes that Alexander's adoption of Persian trappings and assimilation of Persians into his court and army were a pragmatic way of integrating the two empires and providing some protection against Macedonian chauvinists. He accepts Aristobulus' explanation that the episodes of excessive drinking arose from the demand of social interaction with his officers (7.29.4). But he gives greater prominence to Alexander's remorse for his misdeeds, which was a capacity that set him apart from the rulers of antiquity (7.29.1–2), and here Arrian has in mind Alexander's admission that the sack of Persepolis was an error of judgement, and his highly emotional expression of guilt after his killing of Cleitus (4.9).

Arrian's positive attitude to Alexander is shown not only in the openly eulogistic references, but also by other devices, including the omission of items that might tell against him, starting with the circumstances of the murder of his father, Philip II, the brutal killing of

---

[20] And panegyric had a programmatic function: thus, for example, Arrian expected a true king to be above lies and dissimulation (Preface 2; cf. 7.5.2–3).

Batis at Gaza (2.27), and the massacre of the Branchidae (covered by Curtius 7.5.28–35).[21] He could also cover with extreme brevity an episode that he could not omit. This can be seen in particular in 'The Great Digression' (4.7.4–14.4), in which Arrian compacts criticisms voiced of Alexander's orientalizing ways after the death of Darius and a series of quasi-judicial murders of those who were seen as a threat to Alexander. Some items could be brushed aside by discrediting the sources (as in 6.28, 7.12.5–7) or rationalized into a more acceptable form (7.14.4–7). Blame could be shifted onto others, as for the massacre of the Thebans in 335 (1.8.8 and 9.6); and for Alexander's excesses and outbursts of rage the guilty could range from sycophantic poets and sophists in his court (as at 4.9.9) to close associates in wantonly confrontational mood (like Cleitus, 4.9.1 and Callisthenes, 4.10.1). The narrative is dotted with references to massacres (quite a number between 5.21.6 and 6.11.1), generally without any comment but sometimes justified (4.6.5) or blamed on troops who could not control their anger (2.24.3, 4.23.5), though Arrian makes a criticism indirectly at 1.9.5 where he notes that Athenian atrocities at Melos and Scione brought more shame on Athens than shock to the Greek world. The number of criticisms, evasions, rationalizations, and lines of defence mean that the *Anabasis* is by no means a panegyric: Arrian's admiration had its limits.

ARRIAN'S OTHER AGENDA

Arrian is considered a representative of the Second Sophistic Movement, which is particularly associated with the second century AD. Both the Athenian and the later groups were associated in particular with the teaching of rhetoric, though the terms sophist and rhetorician could be used antithetically. In classical Athens the connotations tended to be derogatory,[22] the sophists seen as making money out of training the gullible to be glib and persuasive, however dubious the case. But the Greek sophists in the Roman Empire were more

[21] The Branchidae had been a priestly clan which controlled the oracle of Apollo at Didyma, near Miletus in Asia Minor. They may have been transplanted to Sogdiana by Darius I when he had the centre destroyed in 494/3. But the charge against the Branchidae in 329 appears from Callisthenes' official account to have been that the Branchidae had plundered the temple (sometime before 479). If the latter version is true, the Branchidae may have been moved to Sogdiana as refugees.

[22] As indeed in Arrian at 4.9.7–9.

generally and generously recognized as public intellectuals in a positive sense.²³ Their skills were also formally recognized as they were
called on to serve their mother-cities as speechmakers in courts,
political arenas, and commemorative events. They might speak as
diplomats for their cities and have a legally defined status.

The characteristic concerns of this intellectual elite included the
assertion of pride in Greek language, culture and history, a return to
classical Attic Greek in reaction to the *koinē* Greek that was the patois
in the globalized Roman Empire, and the promotion of a Greek renaissance that could resist the power of Rome at least in cultural terms.
In their different ways Plutarch and Arrian writing about Alexander
the Great were making their contribution to Greek public history.
Plutarch, probably writing the life of Alexander in the period AD
110–15, had reason to be warily positive about the emperor Trajan
who had set Rome on a new path after the murder of the 'tyrant'
Domitian in 96, for it was Domitian who in 89 had banished the philosophers, including Epictetus, from the city of Rome. Plutarch
paired off Alexander and Caesar in the *Parallel Lives*, giving due recognition to the Roman, and the issue was topical, and perhaps a little
sensitive, because Julius Caesar had plans to invade the Parthian
Empire, which came to nothing, and Trajan was at least planning to
do the same as some latter-day Alexander.²⁴ But when Arrian wrote it
was safer to write openly about Alexander, and his text was not
charged with coded references as were some earlier texts, such as
Curtius Rufus' *Histories of Alexander*, when memories of Alexander-
imitators like Pompey the Great, Julius Caesar, and the emperor
Caligula were fresher. Admittedly Trajan had embarked on his war
against the Parthians; but the mission was futile and ended in disaster, and Hadrian promptly abandoned that strategy. Trajan's failure
strengthened the image of Alexander's success.

For a public intellectual in the Greek world of his day to have such
an agenda was to be conformist, and carried little risk from a
Hellenophile emperor. Arrian thrived. His career path was most
impressive: starting as a Greek from Asia Minor with Roman citizenship, he served in the Roman army and provincial administration and
gained the consulship; he was recognized in Athens by election to the

²³ And Arrian uses the term sophist positively of the Indian Brahmans in 7.1.5–2.4.
²⁴ While Alexander was 'the Great' (*Magnus*), Trajan in 114 took the title *Optimus*
('the Best').

archonship. He was no less a philosopher and author of a series of substantial publications in a scatter of genres and in a succession of styles of Greek—*koinē*, Attic, and Ionic—with different proclaimed literary models. He was, then, driven by great personal ambition, and in the Greek context he was indeed a renaissance man.

The Indica[25]

Arrian's purpose was in part to rescue from oblivion Nearchus' record of his exploration of the coast as he led Alexander's fleet from the Indus to the Tigris, in the same way as the *Anabasis* was intended to reassert the importance of Ptolemy and Aristobulus as primary sources on Alexander's campaigns. Arrian labels the first seventeen chapters, on the geography and ethnography of India, a digression, drawing on Nearchus and Megasthenes (*Indica* 17.6–7), but clearly mainly on Megasthenes. In this section he refers to other writers, including Ctesias, Onesicritus, and Eratosthenes (*Indica* 3.1 and 6). But the main section, covering the next twenty-five chapters, is presented as a digest of Nearchus' account of his command of the fleet from the Indus to the mouth of the Tigris (6.28.6). Arrian might thus be styled Nearchus' epitomator, and in classical literature the epitome tended to be a mix of verbatim quotation, summary, and material taken from other sources or created by the epitomator.

Nearchus no doubt had some practical intent in logging names, topographical details, navigational pointers, and meteorological conditions, but by Arrian's day that information was largely redundant, and Arrian made no effort to update the material. Though his programmatic references to this book (5.6.8 and 6.16.5) may justify the translation of its title as *Treatise on India*, it was no handbook, but more a historical work to complement his *Anabasis*. Thus, in the same vein he offers some authorial comment on the source material, as at *Indica* 25.7–8, where he finds support from Eratosthenes[26] for

---

[25] It is conventional to refer to the work as the *Indica*, in line with his *Parthica* and *Bithyniaca*, but Arrian actually chose to call it his *Indikē xyngraphē*, which might imply a tighter focus, since it might mean 'An Indian Narrative', whereas *Indica* would suggest rather 'Indian Topics'. In any case Arrian marks the end of Indian territory at roughly the halfway mark in his book. Cf. P. A. Stadter, *Arrian of Nicomedia* (Chapel Hill, NC: University of North Carolina Press, 1980), 116–17.

[26] Eratosthenes is not mentioned at this point, but is at *Indica* 3.1, and more can be gleaned of his ideas from Strabo's *Geography*.

Nearchus' observations on noonday shadows in the Indian Ocean; at 31.9, where he takes Nearchus to task for wasting space in refuting palpably unscientific travellers' tales; and at 32.13, where he commends Nearchus for rejecting Onesicritus' proposal to cut across from the Carmanian coast to Ras Musandam in Oman.

But it was no less a work with serious literary pretensions. First of all Arrian chose to write the book in the Ionic dialect, and not Attic, which he had used for the *Anabasis* (*Ind.* 19.8), though the switch was not required by Nearchus' style, and Arrian effectively had to re-create the dialect for this purpose. He did not limit the use of Ionic for special effect to just one of the two main sections of the book, but in language and content he was consciously invoking more the memory of Herodotus (whose dialect was Ionic), particularly in the first section, where, for a start, the organization of the material into three parts, on physical geography, history, and human geography (plus the wild life), matches the scheme of Herodotus' treatment of Egypt in Book 2 of his *Histories*. Even if Arrian was here following the lead of Megasthenes, his effort in creating a text in a revived form of Ionic shows his personal interest in keeping alive the Herodotean tradition. The use of Ionic was a tour de force.

Literary intent is also reflected in his choice of sources, each of some literary merit and not too remote in time from Alexander's campaigns. Thus, beyond the primary sources he refers directly to no one later than Megasthenes and Eratosthenes, and ignores practical texts such as the contemporary *Periplus of the Erythraean Sea* ('The Circumnavigation of the Red Sea'). As noted above, this was no maritime handbook.

The book has a strange final chapter that is not really a conclusion, nor a coda. Chapter 43 refers to Hannon's exploratory expedition along the north-western coast of Africa and then to the geography of Cyrene. Unless the text is badly defective, this may be a muddled reference to Alexander's 'last plans', which seemed to include a campaign along the North African coast with an action against Carthage, and possibly the circumnavigation of Africa. But there is no explicit reference to the plans revealed just after Alexander's death. Furthermore this chapter does not appear to be a programmatic notice of some further publication. It is rather like the way a hypnotist clicks his fingers at the end of his show to bring his subject out of a trance and back to reality; in this case a device to bring the reader's attention firmly back from Nearchus to Arrian himself. The pattern is not uncommon in ancient texts and looks like a literary pretension, to wander off at the end of the book into some peripheral detail and then to abruptly stop.

Perhaps this odd ending to the *Indica* is a sign that with this work Arrian got as close to playfulness as he ever dared. For in the narrative section he also included some fanciful elements (34.7–10 and 35.8), whether or not they were faithfully copied from Nearchus, and the element of bathos in the allusion to performing elephants (14.5–6). Such oddities and the dialect might be intended to amuse the reader.

Arrian's work on Alexander and his *Events after the Death of Alexander* did indeed endure through late antiquity and the Byzantine period, as evidenced by writers who copied or quoted him, such as Dexippus (third century), Photius (ninth century), and Eustathius (twelfth century). In the West the *Anabasis* and *Indica* were translated into Latin in the fifteenth century, when Curtius Rufus' Latin *Histories of Alexander* was more entrenched, much as Cleitarchus' history of Alexander was the fashion before Arrian set a new standard by the way he turned to sources he considered more reliable. Thus in modern times it became axiomatic that Arrian was the principal source on Alexander. But now historians are more free in their criticisms of Alexander's failings, and Brunt in 1976 could conclude his section on Arrian in the Loeb edition with the line: 'He was a simple, honest soul, but no historian.' In this edition we do not avoid pointing out where a modern historian must be critical, but it is hoped that the reader will be guided to an appreciation of what Arrian achieved as a historian with literary ambition.

SELECT BIBLIOGRAPHY

Arrian

Bosworth, A. B., *A Historical Commentary on Arrian's History of Alexander.* Vol. 1: *Commentary on Books I–III* (Oxford: Oxford University Press, 1980); Vol. 2: *Commentary on Books IV–V* (Oxford: Oxford University Press, 1995). Vol. 3 is in preparation.

——*From Arrian to Alexander* (Oxford: Oxford University Press, 1988).

Brunt, P. A., *Arrian: History of Alexander and Indica*, Loeb Classical Library, 2 vols. (Cambridge, Mass., Harvard University Press, 1976 and 1983): text, translation, and notes.

——'From Epictetus to Arrian', *Athenaeum*, 55 (1977), 19–48.

Long, A. A., *Epictetus: A Stoic and Socratic Guide to Life* (Oxford: Oxford University Press, 2002), esp. 38–43.

Oldfather, W. A., *Epictetus: The Discourses as reported by Arrian, the Manual and Fragments*, Loeb Classical Library, 2 vols. (London and New York: Heinemann, 1926 and 1928).

Roisman, J., 'Ptolemy and his Rivals in his History of Alexander', *Classical Quarterly*, 34 (1984), 373–84.

Romm, James (ed.), *The Landmark Arrian: The Campaigns of Alexander* (New York, Pantheon, 2010).

Sisti, F., *Arriano, Anabasi di Alessandro*, 2 vols. (Turin: Fondazione Lorenzo Valla/Arnoldo Mondadori, 2001 and 2004).

Stadter, P. A., *Arrian of Nicomedia* (Chapel Hill, NC: University of North Carolina Press, 1980).

Swain, S., *Hellenism and Empire* (Oxford: Oxford University Press, 1996).

Whitmarsh, T., *The Second Sophistic* (Oxford: Oxford University Press, 2005).

Wirth, G., and von Hinüber, O., *Arrian, Der Alexanderzug, Indische Geschichte* (Munich: Artemis, 1985).

Other Ancient Sources

DIODORUS SICULUS

Welles, C. B., *Diodorus of Sicily, Vol. 8, Books XVI.66–95 and XVII*, Loeb Classical Library (Cambridge, Mass.: Harvard University Press, 1963): text, translation, and notes.

TROGUS AND JUSTIN

Yardley, J., and Heckel, W., *Justin, Epitome of the Philippic History of Pompeius Trogus, Books 11–12*; translated by J. C. Yardley, with commentary by W. Heckel (Oxford: Oxford University Press, 1997).

CURTIUS RUFUS

Heckel, W., and Yardley, J., *Quintus Curtius Rufus: The History of Alexander*, translated by J. Yardley, with an introduction and notes by W. Heckel (Harmondsworth: Penguin Books, revised edn. 2004).
Yardley, J., and Atkinson, J. E., *Curtius Rufus: Histories of Alexander the Great, Book 10* (Oxford: Oxford University Press, 2009): translation with commentary.

PLUTARCH

Hamilton, J. R., *Plutarch, Alexander: A Commentary* (Oxford: Oxford University Press, 1969).

THE ALEXANDER ROMANCE (OR PSEUDO-CALLISTHENES)

Stoneman, R., *The Greek Alexander Romance* (Harmondsworth: Penguin Books, 1991): translation.

GENERAL

Atkinson, J. E., 'Originality and its Limits in the Alexander Sources of the Early Empire', in A. B. Bosworth and E. J. Baynham (eds.), *Alexander the Great in Fact and Fiction* (Oxford: Oxford University Press, 2000), 307–25.
Heckel, W., and Yardley, J. (eds.), *Alexander the Great: Historical Texts in Translation* (Oxford: Blackwell, 2004).
Pearson, L., *The Lost Histories of Alexander the Great* (Oxford: Blackwell, 1960).
Stewart, A., 'Alexander in Greek and Roman art', in J. Roisman, *Brill's Companion to Alexander the Great* (Leiden and Boston: Brill, 2003), 31–66.
Stoneman, R., *Alexander the Great: A Life in Legend* (New Haven and London: Yale University Press, 2008).

Alexander the Great

Atkinson, J. E., 'Honour in the Ranks of Alexander the Great's Army', *Acta Classica*, 53 (2010), 1–20.
Badian, E., 'Harpalus', *Journal of Hellenic Studies*, 81 (1961), 16–43.
—— 'Nearchus the Cretan', *Yale Classical Studies*, 24 (1975), 147–70.

Badian, E., 'Alexander the Great Between Two Thrones', in A. Small (ed.), *Subject and Power: The Cult of the Ruling Power in Classical Antiquity* (Ann Arbor, Mich.: University of Michigan Press, 1996), 11–26.

Bosworth, A. B., *Conquest and Empire: The Reign of Alexander the Great* (Cambridge: Cambridge University Press, 1988).

——*Alexander and the East* (Cambridge: Cambridge University Press, 1996).

——and Baynham, E. J. (eds.), *Alexander the Great in Fact and Fiction* (Oxford: Oxford University Press, 2000).

Carney, E., and Ogden, D., *Philip II and Alexander the Great* (Oxford: Oxford University Press, 2010).

Cartledge, P. A., *Alexander the Great: The Hunt for a New Past* (London: Macmillan, 2004).

Eggermont, P. H. L., *Alexander's Campaigns in Sind and Baluchistan* (Leuven: Leuven University Press, 1975).

Engels, D., *Alexander the Great and the Logistics of the Macedonian Army* (Berkeley: University of California Press, 1978).

Hamilton, J. R., *Alexander the Great* (Pittsburgh: University of Pittsburgh Press, 1974).

Hammond, N. G. L., *Alexander the Great, King, Commander and Statesman* (London: Bristol Classical Press, repr. with corrections 1994).

Heckel, W., *Who's Who in the Age of Alexander the Great* (Oxford: Blackwell, 2006; New York and Oxford: Wiley–Blackwell, 2009).

——and Tritle, L. (eds.), *Crossroads of History: The Age of Alexander* (Claremont, Calif.: Regina Books, 2003).

—— ——and Wheatley, P. (eds.), *Alexander's Empire: Formulation to Decay* (Claremont, Calif.: Regina Books, 2007).

Holt, F. L., *Into the Land of Bones: Alexander the Great in Afghanistan* (Berkeley: University of California Press, 2005).

Lambrick, H. T., *Sind: A General Introduction* (Hyderabad, 1964).

Lane Fox, R., *Alexander the Great* (London: Allen Lane, 1973).

O'Brien, M., *Alexander the Great: The Invisible Enemy. A Biography* (London: Routledge, 1992).

Roisman, J. (ed.), *Brill's Companion to Alexander the Great* (Leiden and Boston: Brill, 2003).

Spencer, D., *The Roman Alexander: Reading a Cultural Myth* (Exeter: University of Exeter Press, 2002).

Tarn, W. W., *Alexander the Great*, 2 vols. (Cambridge: Cambridge University Press, 1948).

Thompson, M., *Granicus* (Oxford: Osprey, 2007).

Wood, M., *In the Footsteps of Alexander the Great* (London: BBC, 1997).

Worthington, I., *Alexander the Great, Man and God* (Harlow: Pearson, 2004).

——(ed.), *Alexander the Great: A Reader* (London: Routledge, 2003).

Further Reading in Oxford World's Classics

Herodotus, *The Histories*, trans. Robin Waterfield, introduction and notes by Carolyn Dewald.

Thucydides, *The Peloponnesian War*, trans. Martin Hammond, introduction and notes by P. J. Rhodes.

Xenophon, *The Expedition of Cyrus* (*Anabasis*), trans. Robin Waterfield, introduction and notes by Tim Rood.

CHRONOLOGY

356 Oct.: birth of Alexander the Great (date indicated by Arrian 7.28.1; but Plutarch, *Alexander* 3.5 gives July)

336 Philip's troops under Parmenion invade Asia Minor
Darius III made king of Persia
Oct.: assassination of Philip; Alexander becomes king

335 Alexander's campaigns in the Balkans; destruction of Thebes

334 Alexander crosses the Hellespont into Asia Minor, visits Troy
Victory over the Persians and their Greek mercenaries at the battle of the Granicus
Removal of Persians from the area with the capture of Sardis, Miletus, and Halicarnassus
Greek fleet sent home

333 Alexander cuts the Gordian knot, and crosses the river Halys
Darius mobilizes his army and heads for Syria
Sept.: Alexander falls sick at Tarsus in Cilicia
Nov.: rout of Darius' army at the battle of Issus

332 Jan.–Aug.: siege of Tyre
Siege of Gaza
Alexander invades Egypt; visits oracle of Ammon at Siwah

331 7 Apr.: foundation of Alexandria celebrated
Advance north to the Euphrates and east to the Tigris
Sept.: Darius' army routed at the battle of Gaugamela
Alexander takes Babylon, then Susa
Battle with the Uxians for control of the Persian Gates pass; Alexander enters Persepolis

330 Jan.–May: winter in Persepolis, which is then destroyed by fire
Agis' bid to liberate Greece defeated by Antipater
Alexander heads north in pursuit of Darius
c. July: Darius en route via Tehran to Bactria (Afghanistan) murdered by Bessus and associates; found by Alexander; the body is sent to Persepolis for burial
Alexander campaigns in the Elburz mountains
Allied Greek units demobilized and re-enlisted as mercenaries
Satibarzanes, satrap of Areia, defects; Alexander heads south via Herat and Farah
Macedonian commanders Philotas and Parmenion put to death
Winter: Alexander reaches the Hindu Kush, crosses into Bactria near Begram

329   Campaigns in Bactria, and across the Amu-Darya in pursuit of
          Bessus; advance to Samarcand and across the Syr-Darya into
          Scythia
       Spitamenes besieges the garrison in Samarcand and ambushes
          Macedonian troops at the Polytimetus (Zeravshan)
329/8 Alexander winters at Bactra (Balkh, Afghanistan)
328   Campaigns north of the Amu-Darya, in Sogdiana
       Nov.: Alexander kills Cleitus in Samarcand
328/7 Alexander winters at Nautaca (Shakhrisyabz, Uzbekistan)
327   Actions to capture the Rock of Sogdiana and the Rock of Chorienes;
          Alexander meets and marries the Bactrian girl Rhoxane
       Conspiracy of the Pages and execution of Callisthenes
       Alexander re-crosses the Hindu Kush, campaigns through the Swat
          district and Gandhara to the Indus
326   Advance from the Indus to the Hydaspes (Jhelum)
       May: defeat of Porus at the battle of the Hydaspes; at the Hyphasis
          (Beas) the troops refuse to go further
       Oct.: back at the Hydaspes, fleet assembled for descent of the
          Indus
325   The Mallian campaign: Alexander nearly killed in action
       July: the combined force reaches Patala; exploration of the Indus
          delta
       Sept.: Alexander leaves Patala for Gedrosia (Baluchistan)
       Oct.: Nearchus and the fleet set sail as the monsoon winds subside
       Alexander gets through Gedrosian desert with heavy casualties;
          begins a purge of the satraps
       Nearchus makes contact with Alexander in Carmania
324   Alexander reaches Pasargadae and Persepolis
       Nearchus and the fleet reach Susa
       In Susa a mass wedding ceremony: Alexander marries Darius'
          daughter
       30,000 Asian cadets join Alexander's army
       Mutiny of the Macedonian troops at Opis
       March to Ecbatana (Hamadan)
       Oct.: death of Hephaestion
       Further campaigns in the Zagros mountains
323   Alexander returns to Babylon
       10/11 June: death of Alexander
       Sept.: birth of Alexander's son by Rhoxane

THE ANABASIS

BOOK ONE

PREFACE

WHERE Ptolemy the son of Lagus and Aristobulus the son of Aris- *1*
tobulus agree with each other in the accounts they have written of
Alexander the son of Philip, I record what they say as unquestionably
true:* where they differ, I have chosen the version which seems to me
the more reliable, and also more worth relating. There have indeed *2*
been various other accounts of Alexander, and no one else has been the
subject of so many writers with such discrepancy between them, but
I have taken the view that Ptolemy and Aristobulus are more reliable
in their narrative. Aristobulus was with Alexander on his campaigns;
Ptolemy not only campaigned with Alexander but, as a king himself,
would have been particularly honour-bound to avoid untruth;* and
both composed their accounts when Alexander was dead and there
was no compulsion or profit* in writing anything other than what actually happened. I have included also some material from other writ- *3*
ers when I judged it worth relating* and not wholly implausible, but
this material I record simply as stories told about Alexander. And if
anyone is inclined to wonder why, with so many histories already written, I should have conceived the notion of writing this history of my
own, he should save the question until he has read through all those
other works and then taken up mine.

---

*History relates that Philip died in the year when Pythodelus was *1*
archon at Athens* [336 BC]; that on succeeding to the throne, as
Philip's son, Alexander marched to the Peloponnese; and that
Alexander was about twenty years old at the time. Once there he *2*
called a meeting of the Peloponnesian Greeks* and asked them to
give him the leadership of the campaign against Persia which they
had already granted to Philip. His request was agreed by all the various states except the Spartans:* they replied that it was not in their
tradition to follow others but to take the lead themselves. There had *3*
also been some stirrings in Athens, but the Athenians were thrown
into consternation by this early arrival of Alexander and offered him

yet more honours than had been given to Philip. Alexander returned to Macedonia and began preparations for the expedition into Asia.

4   *With the coming of spring he marched to Thrace against the Triballians and Illyrians, having heard that these tribes were restless. As they bordered his own territory, he had further reason for wanting them completely crushed: he could not leave them behind in any

5 other state while he set off on an expedition so far from home. Starting from Amphipolis he struck into the region of Thrace inhabited by the so-called independent Thracians,* keeping the city of Philippi and Mount Orbelus on his left. He crossed the river Nestus, and is said to

6 have reached Mount Haemus on the tenth day after that. There he was met in the narrows of the approach to the mountain by a large number of armed locals and the independent Thracians: they had occupied the high point of the Haemus pass along the army's route,

7 and were equipped to block its advance. They had collected wagons and positioned them in front of their troops as a stockade for a defensive action if they came under attack: but they also had the plan of letting the wagons roll down on the Macedonian phalanx* as it came up through the most precipitous stretch of the mountain. Their thought was that the more closely packed the phalanx met by the wagons in their downward path, the more explosive would be the force of their impact.

8   Alexander debated how best to cross the mountain in safety. He decided that the risk must be taken, as there was no other way through, and gave his orders to the hoplites.* When the wagons came down the slope, those with room to move on level ground should break ranks, stand apart, and let the wagons roll through the gap:

9 those who were trapped were to crouch in close formation, some actually face-down on the ground, linking their shields tightly together so that, with luck, the wagons bearing down on them would have the momentum to shoot over them and pass harmlessly on their way. In the event the supposition in Alexander's orders proved cor-

10 rect. One part of the phalanx divided, and the wagons rolled over the shields of the rest with little damage done—nobody died under them. Now that the main object of their dread had turned out to be harmless, the Macedonians took heart, raised a shout, and charged at the

11 Thracians. Alexander ordered the archers on the right wing (the easier side for this purpose) to advance in front of the phalanx and shoot at the Thracians wherever they attacked. He himself took the royal

guard, the foot guards, and the Agrianians and led them on the left.
So then with their constant shooting the archers kept back any *12*
Thracian attempts at a sally, and when the phalanx came to close
quarters it had little difficulty in dislodging from their position an
enemy consisting of light-armed troops and poorly equipped barbarians. The result was that the enemy did not wait to face Alexander's
attack from the left, but threw away their arms and, each man for
himself, fled down the mountain-side. Their dead numbered some *13*
fifteen hundred. Few of the men were taken alive (they were fast run-
ners and knew the local terrain), but all the women who had come
with them were captured, together with the children and all their
valuables.

Alexander sent the spoils back to the cities on the coast, putting *2*
Lysanias and Philotas in charge of the arrangements. He himself
crossed the ridge and marched on over Haemus towards the
Triballians,* reaching the river Lyginus, which is three days' march
from the Danube in the direction of Haemus. Syrmus, the king of the *2*
Triballians, had learnt some time before of Alexander's expedition
and had sent the Triballian women and children on to the Danube,
with instructions to cross over to one of the islands in the river called
Peuce. The Thracians who border the Triballians had also some time *3*
ago taken refuge on this island as Alexander was approaching, and
Syrmus himself had joined that refuge with his entourage: but the
main body of the Triballians fled back to the river which Alexander
had left on the previous day.

When he learnt of the Triballians' move, Alexander turned back *4*
himself and marched against them, catching them in the process of
making their camp. Thus caught, they drew up in battle-order close to
the wood which borders the river. In response, Alexander advanced
his phalanx in deep formation and ordered the archers and slingers to
run out ahead and start shooting volleys of arrows and sling-shots at
the barbarians, as a means of provoking them to move into open ground
away from the wood. When the range had shortened and the barbar- *5*
ians came under fire, they rushed forward to get hand-to-hand with the
archers, who were otherwise unarmed. Having drawn them out from
the wood, Alexander ordered Philotas* to take the Upper Macedonian
cavalry and charge their right wing, where the surge had made most
ground: Heracleides and Sopolis were ordered to lead the cavalry from
Bottiaea and Amphipolis against the left wing. He himself led the *6*

infantry phalanx, with the rest of the cavalry ranged in front of it, against the centre. At the skirmishing stage the Triballians did not have the worse of the encounter: but once the phalanx attacked with full force in close order, and the cavalry, no need for their javelins now, were simply riding them down with their horses in charge after charge,

7 they turned and fled through the wood towards the river. Three thousand of them were killed in the rout, but only a few of the fugitives were captured alive, as the wood in front of the river was very thick and the onset of night denied the Macedonians a thorough search. Of the Macedonians themselves Ptolemy reports that eleven cavalry were killed, and about forty infantry.

3 On the third day after the battle Alexander reached the river Danube.* This is the greatest river in Europe with the longest course across the continent, and forms a natural barrier to some very warlike tribes. Most of these are Celts—indeed the source of the river rises in Celtic territory—the furthest of whom are the Quadi and the

2 Marcomanni: the river then passes the Iazyges, a branch of the Sauromatae; on to the Getae, who think themselves immortal; on to the main body of the Sauromatae; and on past the Scythians all the way to its outlets, where it disgorges through five mouths into the Black

3 Sea. At the Danube Alexander found the warships which had come to meet him from Byzantium after passage through the Black Sea and up the river. He filled them with archers and hoplites and sailed against the island where the Triballians and Thracians had taken refuge, trying

4 to force a landing. But the barbarians offered opposition on the bank wherever the ships came in towards land; the ships were few in number with only a small force on board; most parts of the island were too steep for landing; and the current running past the island, as happens in a narrow channel, was swift and hard to negotiate.

5 At this point Alexander withdrew his ships and decided to cross the Danube against the Getae who lived on the far side of the river. One reason was that he could see large numbers of them gathered on the bank ready to oppose a crossing (there were some four thousand cavalry and more than ten thousand on foot): but also he was taken

6 with a yen* to go beyond the Danube. He himself joined those on the ships, but he had the men stuff their leather tent-covers with hay, and collected from the locality as many as possible of the dug-out canoes which were in plentiful use among the river-dwellers for fishing in the Danube and occasional visits along the river to their neighbours

(mostly for purposes of plunder). In this way he ferried across as many of his troops as the means available would accommodate. Those crossing with him amounted to some fifteen hundred cavalry and about four thousand infantry.

They crossed at night to a place where there was a deep cornfield, 4 which helped to conceal their approach to the bank. At dawn Alexander led them on through the field, ordering the infantry to use their pikes crosswise to flatten the corn* until they reached uncultivated ground. As long as the phalanx was advancing through the cornfield the cavalry followed behind: but as soon as they emerged 2 from the ground under cultivation Alexander in person took the cavalry off to the right wing and ordered Nicanor* to lead the phalanx forward in rectangular formation. The Getae did not even withstand 3 the first charge of the cavalry. Alexander's bold move had come as a shock to them: they were amazed that in one night he had so easily crossed the Danube, the greatest of rivers, without building a bridge for the crossing; the close-packed phalanx was terrifying, and the cavalry charge brutal. At first they fled to their city, about three and 4 a half miles from the Danube: but when they saw Alexander bringing on his phalanx at speed along the river, with the cavalry at the front, to avoid any ambush and encirclement of his foot-soldiers by the Getae, they now abandoned their city (it was poorly fortified), took up on horseback as many of the children and women as their horses could carry, and set out into empty country as far away from the river 5 as possible. Alexander captured the city and all the goods the Getae had left behind. He gave the spoils to Meleager and Philip to take back, while he himself razed the city and made sacrifice on the bank of the Danube to Zeus the Saviour and Heracles, and to the river itself for not denying him passage. Within that same day he brought all his men safe back to their camp.

Ambassadors now arrived to see Alexander from the independent 6 tribes bordering the Danube, including envoys from Syrmus the king of the Triballians: and envoys came also from the Celts who lived by the Ionian Gulf. These Celts were big in body and had a big opinion of themselves. All the envoys professed to have come in a desire for friendship with Alexander, and with all he exchanged reciprocal 7 assurances. He did ask the Celts what they feared most in the world, hoping that his own great name had reached as far as the Celts and yet further, and that they would say that they feared him more than

8 anything else. Their answer came as a disappointment. Living as they did in inaccessible country far away from Alexander, and seeing that his ambition lay elsewhere, they replied that their greatest fear was of the sky falling on them; their embassy to Alexander was prompted by admiration for him, but with no element of fear or self-interest. Even so he declared friendship with the Celts too, simply remarking that Celts were a pretentious lot.*

5   *He then advanced towards the territory of the Agrianians and Paeonians. Here messengers came with the news that Cleitus, the son of Bardylis,* had revolted and that Glaucias, king of the Taulantians, had joined him: they also reported that the Autariates intended to attack him on his march. In view of all this, Alexander determined to

2 move at speed. Langarus, the king of the Agrianians, had been openly in favour of Alexander even during Philip's lifetime, had visited him on a personal embassy, and was in attendance at this time with his foot

3 guards, the finest and best-armed troops he had under him. When he heard that Alexander wanted to know who the Autariates were and how strong in numbers, he told him not to give them a thought; they were the least warlike of the tribes in the area; he himself would invade their land, so they would have something of their own to worry about. With Alexander's sanction he did invade and set about ravaging their

4 territory. So the Autariates were kept occupied with troubles at home, and Langarus received high honour from Alexander, including the gifts regarded as the most prestigious at the Macedonian court. Alexander even promised to marry his sister Cyna* to Langarus when

5 he came to Pella: but on his return home Langarus fell ill and died.

   Alexander now marched along the river Erigon [Crna], making for the city of Pellium, which Cleitus had taken and occupied as the most strongly fortified in the region. On his arrival he made camp by the river Eordaïcus, and planned to assault the wall on the following day.

6 The forces with Cleitus occupied the ring of thickly wooded heights which commanded the city, so they could attack the Macedonians from all sides if an assault was made: but as yet Cleitus lacked the

7 support of Glaucias, the king of the Taulantians. Alexander advanced on the city. The enemy sacrificed three boys, three girls, and three black rams, then charged down to meet the Macedonians at close quarters: but once the engagement began they abandoned the positions they had occupied, strong though these were, and the bodies of their sacrificial victims were found still lying there.

On this day, then, Alexander confined them inside the city, camped *8* close by the wall, and proposed to blockade them with a circumvallation: but on the next day Glaucias, the king of the Taulantians, arrived with a large force. Alexander now recognized that he could not take the city with his present forces: large numbers of fighting men had taken refuge inside, and there were large numbers with Glaucias ready to attack him if he assaulted the wall. He sent Philotas out to *9* find food, telling him to take the baggage-animals from the camp and as many cavalry as he needed for protection. Glaucias learnt of this foraging expedition and set out to attack Philotas and his party, occupying the high ground which ringed the plain where they would be gathering the foodstuff. When it was reported to Alexander that there *10* was danger for the cavalry and baggage-animals if they were overtaken by night, he marched out at speed to their rescue, taking with him the foot guards, the archers, the Agrianians, and some four hundred cavalry. He left the rest of his troops where they were close by the city, as the risk of withdrawing the whole army was that the enemy in the city could break out and join forces with Glaucias. In *11* fact, when Glaucias became aware of Alexander's approach he abandoned the heights he had occupied, and Philotas' party was brought safely back to the camp.

It still seemed that the troops with Cleitus and Glaucias had Alexander caught in a difficult position. They occupied the com- *12* manding heights with large numbers of cavalry, javelin-men, and slingers, and a good force of hoplites; the men in the city were ready to attack Alexander's army as it withdrew; and it could be seen that the ground through which Alexander had to pass was narrow and wooded, bounded on one side by the river and on the other by a high mountain with a precipitous face, so that the army would not have been able to get through even just four abreast.

In this situation Alexander arranged his forces with the phalanx a *6* hundred and twenty files deep, and two hundred cavalry posted on either wing. He ordered complete silence and an instant response to commands. He first signalled 'spears upright' to the hoplites, then at *2* another sign he had them lower their spears to the ready and swing the massed points in coordination right and left. He now moved the entire phalanx forward at a smart pace, executing wheels on each wing alternately. After putting it through this rapid series of different *3* manoeuvres, he formed the phalanx in wedge-shape on the left and led it to the attack. All this while the enemy had been watching the speed and precision of the drill with amazement, and now they did not stay to meet the advance of Alexander's troops, but fell back from

4 the first line of hills. Alexander now ordered the Macedonians to raise their battle-shout and beat their spears on their shields: the Taulantians were yet more terrified by this din and hastily withdrew their forces to the city.

5 Seeing that a small group of the enemy had taken position on a hill along his intended route, Alexander ordered his Bodyguards and the Companions* with him to take up shields, mount their horses, and ride to the hill. If when they got there they encountered resistance from the enemy occupying the place, half of them should dismount

6 and fight on foot in between their mounted colleagues. In fact when they saw this move by Alexander the enemy abandoned the hill and took themselves off to the mountains on either side. At this Alexander seized the hill with his Companions and sent for the Agrianians and the archers, to a total of two thousand. He ordered the foot guards to ford the river, followed by the rest of the Macedonians in their detachments: once across each detachment should dress left, so that when all had crossed the phalanx would immediately present a solid line. He himself kept a covering watch from the hill for any enemy

7 movement. Seeing the force crossing, the enemy did charge down the mountains to attack the men with Alexander who would be the last to withdraw. Alexander let them get close, then rushed them with his own company while the main phalanx raised the battle-shout and prepared to attack them through the river. Faced by this concerted onslaught the enemy broke away and fell back. In this interval Alexander brought the Agrianians and the archers down to the river

8 at the double. He himself got across ahead of them, and when he saw the enemy closing in on the hindmost he had the catapults set up on the far bank and ordered fire at maximum range of all the missiles they could discharge: the archers had begun to cross, and he ordered them too to shoot from mid-stream. Glaucias' troops would not venture within range, and meanwhile the Macedonians crossed the river safely, and not one of them died in the withdrawal.

9 On the third day after this Alexander learnt that the troops with Cleitus and Glaucias were camped in disorderly fashion—no sentry-posts regularly manned, no palisade or ditch to protect them (presumably on the assumption that Alexander had taken fright and

disappeared), and the line of encampment dangerously extended. Taking with him the foot guards, the Agrianians, the archers, and the brigades of Perdiccas and Coenus, he crossed the river under cover of night, undetected so far. He had left instructions for the rest of the *10* army to follow, but seeing the immediate opportunity for an attack he did not wait for all his forces to gather, but sent in the archers and the Agrianians. Catching the enemy by surprise, and attacking in deep column formation designed to cause maximum impact at their weakest point, Alexander's men killed some of them still in their beds and easily rounded up those who attempted to escape: the result was that large numbers were caught and killed on the spot, and many more in the chaotic and panic-stricken flight; quite a few also were taken alive. Alexander's troops kept up the pursuit of the Taulantians as far as the *11* mountains: any who escaped only survived by throwing away their arms. Cleitus first took refuge in the city, but then set fire to it and left to find asylum with Glaucias and the Taulantians.

Meanwhile some of the Theban exiles who had been expelled from *7* the city made a covert return to Thebes at night, invited back by a group in the city with revolutionary intent. These exiles captured and killed Amyntas and Timolaus, two officers of the garrison occupying the Cadmea* who were outside their base quite unsuspecting of any enemy action. They then came before the assembly and incited *2* the Thebans to revolt from Alexander, making play with the fine old slogans of 'freedom' and 'independence', and urging that now at last was the time to be rid of the heavy hand of Macedonian rule. What told more with the general people was their assertion that Alexander had died in Illyria. There was indeed a strong and widespread rumour *3* to this effect, since he had been away long and no word had come from him, so that, as tends to happen at such times, in ignorance of the facts people assumed what they wanted to believe.

When Alexander heard of the situation at Thebes he realized that *4* he could not possibly ignore it. He had long been suspicious of Athens, and regarded this Theban insurgency as a serious affair, with the possibility that the revolutionary movement started at Thebes might be joined by the Spartans, whose disaffection was long-standing, by some others in the Peloponnese, and by the Aetolians, no firm friends. So he led his army down through Eordaea and Elimiotis and *5* past the heights of Stymphaea and Paravaea, and on the seventh day reached Pelinna in Thessaly. Starting afresh from there he was in

Boeotia six days later, so the Thebans had no idea that he had passed through Thermopylae until he was there with his entire army at
6 Onchestus. Even then the instigators of the rebellion claimed that the force which had arrived was an army sent from Macedonia by Antipater, and they maintained their insistence that Alexander himself was dead. They had no patience with anyone who reported that Alexander was at the head of his troops in person: it was, they said, another Alexander who had come, the son of Aëropus.*

7 On the next day Alexander left Onchestus and marched to Thebes, halting by the precinct of Iolaus. Here he made camp, to give the Thebans a period of grace, should they wish to reconsider their dis-
8 astrous decision and send out envoys to talk with him. So far from offering any prelude to an agreement, the Thebans had their cavalry and a good number of light troops sally out from the city towards the camp, and in shots fired at the outposts they actually killed a few
9 Macedonians. Alexander sent out some of his light troops and archers to repulse this assault, which they did easily enough, even though the Thebans were now coming on close to the main camp. On the next day Alexander moved his whole force round to the gates which lead to Eleutherae and Attica, but still refrained from a direct attack on the walls: he simply pitched camp not far from the Cadmea, to pro-
10 vide close support for its Macedonian garrison. The Thebans had built a double line of palisades to isolate the Cadmea, so that outside help could not reach the men blockaded there and they could not break out and disrupt Theban operations against the external enemy. Alexander still waited, camped where he was close to the Cadmea: he still hoped for reconciliation with the Thebans rather than the risk of
11 action against them. At this stage the Thebans who had the community's best interests at heart were anxious to go out to Alexander and obtain for the whole people of Thebes his pardon for the revolt: but the exiles and those who had brought them in had no reason to expect generous treatment from Alexander, especially as some of them were Boeotarchs,* and did everything in their power to press the people into war. Even so, Alexander still did not attack the city.

8 However, Ptolemy the son of Lagus says that Perdiccas,* who as officer in command of the camp guard had his own brigade in a forward position not far from the enemy palisade, did not wait for Alexander to give the signal for battle but started operations on his own initiative: he attacked the palisade, tore it apart, and charged in

on the Theban advance guard. After him Amyntas the son of 2
Andromenes, as a fellow officer in the same posting, led his own brigade into action when he saw that Perdiccas had broken inside the
palisade. Seeing this, Alexander brought up the rest of his army to
prevent the danger of these troops being caught isolated at the mercy
of the Thebans. He ordered the archers and the Agrianians to spread 3
out at the double inside the palisade, but still kept the royal guard and
the rest of the foot guards outside. Perdiccas was now forcing his way
through the second palisade, but he was wounded in the attempt and
fell on the spot: he was carried back to the camp in poor condition,
and only just survived the wound. But the troops he had led in the
breakthrough, joined now by the archers from Alexander, corralled
the Thebans into the sunken path leading down past the temple of
Heracles. The Thebans retreated as far as the temple with the 4
Macedonians in pursuit: but there they turned on their pursuers with
a shout, and it was now the Macedonians who were in flight. About
seventy of the archers were killed, together with their commander,
Eurybotas the Cretan: the rest ran for protection towards the
Macedonian royal guard and the king's foot guards. At this point, 5
seeing that his own men were in headlong retreat and that the Thebans
had lost formation in their pursuit, Alexander hit them with his phalanx in full battle-order. The Thebans were driven back inside the
gates, and their rout became such a panic that as they crowded into
the city through the gates they failed to shut them in time, and the
Macedonians closest behind them poured inside the wall after them
(the need to man so many outposts had left the walls undefended).
Some of Alexander's troops made their way round and up into the 6
Cadmea, then, joined by the Cadmea garrison, proceeded along the
Ampheum to enter the lower city: others climbed over the stretch of
wall already held by the party which had followed the rout inside, and
made for the market-place at the run. For a short while the Thebans 7
offered organized resistance by the Ampheum, but as the Macedonians
pressed in on them from all sides, with Alexander showing himself
here, there, and everywhere, the Theban cavalry rode out through
the city and scattered into the plain, leaving the infantry to save themselves as best they could. There followed a furious slaughter. It was 8
not so much the Macedonians as the Phocians, Plataeans, and other
Boeotians who began the indiscriminate killing of the now defence-
less Thebans. They broke into houses and killed the occupants; they

killed any who attempted to fight back; they killed even the suppliants at the altars; they spared neither women nor children.

9 For the size of the captured city, the sudden violence of the action, and not least the surprise of it for both victims and perpetrators, this Greek catastrophe shocked the rest of Greece as much as it did the

2 actual participants. The Athenian debacle in Sicily,* as measured by the number of dead, brought no less a disaster on the city of Athens: but their army was destroyed far from home; it consisted largely of allied rather than citizen troops; and their city still survived, to hold out for some considerable time thereafter in war against the Spartans, their allies, and the Great King. For these reasons the effects of this disaster were not of the same order: even for those afflicted there was a less immediate sense of loss, and for the Greeks at large no comparable horror at what had befallen them. Again, the Athenian defeat at

3 able horror at what had befallen them. Again, the Athenian defeat at Aegospotami* involved only the fleet, and the humiliation of the city was limited to the demolition of the Long Walls, the surrender of most of their ships, and the loss of empire. Otherwise Athens retained its established political system, and did not take long to recover its former strength, rebuilding the Long Walls, regaining supremacy at sea, and ultimately rescuing from extreme danger those very Spartans who had been fearsome enemies at the time and had come close to

4 annihilating the city. The Spartan defeats in turn at Leuctra and Mantinea shocked Sparta more by the unexpectedness of the reversal than for the number killed: and likewise the Boeotian and Arcadian attack on Sparta* under Epaminondas caused panic among the Spartans and their supporting allies at the time more as an unex-

5 pected sight than by the actual scale of the threat. And again the capture of Plataea* was no great calamity, given the small size of the city and the small number caught inside it (as the bulk of the population had long before taken refuge in Athens). As for the capture of Melos and Scione,* these were island towns and their fate was more a source of shame to the perpetrators than any great surprise to the Greek world in general.

6 In the case of Thebes, though, the impetuous irrationality of the revolt, the quick and easy capture, the widespread massacre (as happens within a tribe when old feuds are worked off), the total enslavement of a city pre-eminent among the Greeks of that time in power and military prestige—all this was understandably attributed to

7 divine anger. The Thebans, it was said, had in the end paid the price

for their betrayal of the Greeks in the Persian War, for their seizure of Plataea at a time of truce and the total enslavement of the city, for their agency in the un-Greek slaughter of the Plataeans who surrendered themselves to the Spartans, and for the desolation of a place where the Greeks had stood side by side against the Persians* and beaten off the threat to Greece; and also for adding their vote in favour of the destruction of Athens, when a motion for its enslavement was put to the Spartan allies. Indeed it was said that the disaster 8 had been preceded by many divine warnings: these had been ignored at the time, but later the memory of them caused people to reckon that the events had long been foretold.

Alexander delegated the arrangements for Thebes to the allies who 9 had taken part in the action. They decided to garrison the Cadmea and raze the rest of the city to the ground, sharing out the land (other than consecrated areas) among themselves: the children and women, and any surviving Theban men, were to be sold into slavery, with the exception of priests and priestesses, any guest-friends of Philip or Alexander, and any consular representatives* of the Macedonians. They say that out of reverence for the poet Pindar* Alexander spared 10 Pindar's house and his descendants. The allies also determined to rebuild and fortify Orchomenus and Plataea.

When news of the Thebans' fate reached the rest of the Greeks, the 10 Arcadians who had set out from their country to bring help to the Thebans condemned to death those who had incited them to offer the help, and the Eleans brought back their own exiles, as these were men favourable to Alexander. The Aetolians sent embassies from 2 each tribe to beg forgiveness for their own hint of revolution on news of the Theban revolt. The Athenians were celebrating the Great Mysteries* when some of the Thebans arrived straight from the action. They abandoned the Mysteries in panic, and began bringing their effects from the countryside into the city. The people met in 3 assembly, and on the motion of Demades chose from the whole citizen body ten ambassadors known to be particularly acceptable to Alexander, and sent this embassy to offer him on behalf of the people of Athens their formal (if belated) congratulations on his safe return from the Triballians and Illyrians and on his punishment of the Theban insurrection. Alexander's response to the embassy was generally good-natured, but he wrote a letter to the Athenian people demanding the surrender of Demosthenes and Lycurgus* and their

associates: he named Hypereides, Polyeuctus, Chares, Charidemus,*
5 Ephialtes, Diotimus, and Moerocles. These, he wrote, he held
responsible for the disaster which befell the city at Chaeronea and for
the subsequent wrongs committed on Philip's death against both
himself and Philip: he also declared that they were just as responsible
6 for the Theban revolt as the actual revolutionaries in Thebes. The
Athenians did not hand over the men, but sent another embassy to
Alexander asking him to forgo his anger* against those he had
demanded. Alexander did relent, it may be out of respect for the city
of Athens, or it may be because he was keen to start his Asian expedition and did not want to leave behind any suspect situation in Greece.
He did, though, order the exile of Charidemus alone of the men
whose surrender he had demanded but not received: Charidemus
went into exile in Asia at the court of King Darius.

11   After attending to these matters Alexander returned to Macedonia.
There he made the traditional sacrifice to Olympian Zeus which
had been established by Archelaus, and celebrated the Olympian
games at Aegae:* some say that he also held games in honour of the
2 Muses. At this time it was reported that the statue of Orpheus, the
son of Oeagrus the Thracian, in Pieria had sweated continuously.
The seers made various prophecies from this phenomenon, but one
of them, Aristander of Telmissus, told Alexander that it was an
encouraging sign: it meant that for all the composers of epic and lyric
and choral odes there would be much work ahead on poetry and
hymns celebrating Alexander and his achievements.

3   At the beginning of spring he marched to the Hellespont, leaving
Antipater in charge of affairs in Macedonia and Greece. He was leading an army of a little more than thirty thousand infantry (including
light-armed troops and archers) and over five thousand cavalry. His
route was past Lake Cercinitis towards Amphipolis and the Strymon
4 delta. He crossed the Strymon [Struma] and passed by Mount
Pangaeum on the road to Abdera and Maronea, Greek cities established on the coast. From there he reached the river Hebrus [Maritza]
5 and crossed it with ease. Then on through Paetice to the Black
River: he crossed that too and arrived at Sestos in a total of twenty
days after starting out from home. Coming then to Elaeus he sacrificed to Protesilaus* at his tomb, as Protesilaus was thought to
have been the first to set foot on Asia of the Greeks who went
with Agamemnon on the expedition to Troy. The intention of this

sacrifice was that his own landing in Asia should meet with better fortune than that of Protesilaus.

Parmenion was charged with ferrying across the cavalry and most 6 of the infantry from Sestos to Abydos: they made the crossing in a hundred and sixty triremes and a good number of freighters. The prevailing consensus is that Alexander sailed from Elaeus to put in at the Achaean Harbour, that he personally took the helm of his flagship for the crossing, and that at the mid-point of the Hellespont strait he sacrificed a bull to Poseidon and the Nereids and poured a drink offering into the sea from a golden bowl. They also say that he was the 7 first to disembark on the continent of Asia, and did so in full armour; that he set up altars both where he left Europe and where he landed in Asia to Zeus the Protector of Landings, to Athena, and to Heracles; that he then went up to Troy, sacrificed to the Trojan Athena, and dedicated his full set of armour in her temple, taking in its place some of the consecrated arms still preserved there from the Trojan War (which, it is said, his shield-bearers then used to carry before him into 8 his battles). The prevalent account also has him sacrificing to Priam at the altar of Zeus of the Forecourt, to avert Priam's anger at the race of Neoptolemus, of which he himself was a descendant.

When Alexander had gone up to Troy Menoetius, his ship's helms- 12 man, crowned him with a golden crown, followed by Chares the Athenian who arrived from Sigeum with some others, both Greeks and natives. Some say that Alexander placed a wreath on the tomb of Achilles, while Hephaestion, it is said, did likewise at the tomb of Patroclus. The story goes that Alexander called Achilles fortunate to have Homer as the herald of his lasting fame. And indeed Alexander 2 had good reason to envy Achilles' fortune in this respect. For all his other successes, this one field was left vacant and his achievements were not published to the world as they deserved,* either in prose or in any verse composition. There were not even any choral odes writ-ten for Alexander, as there were for Hieron, Gelon, Theron,* and a host of others who bear no comparison to him: the result is that Alexander's achievements are far less well known than even the most trivial of other deeds in the past. *For example the march of the Ten 3 Thousand with Cyrus into central Asia against King Artaxerxes, the fate of Clearchus and those captured with him, and the return march of these Ten Thousand led by Xenophon are, thanks to Xenophon, far more famous in the world than Alexander and Alexander's

4 achievements. Yet Alexander did not campaign in another man's army,* he did not retreat from the Great King, his victories were not confined to the defeat of those opposing a march back to the sea. On the contrary, there is no other single man, among either Greeks or barbarians, who has given evidence of achievements so many in number or so great in magnitude. That, I can affirm, was my own motive in embarking on this history: I did not think myself unsuited

5 to the task of making Alexander's achievements clear to the world. As for who I am to make this claim about myself, I have no need to record my name (it is by no means unknown in the world), nor to state my country or my family or any public office I may have held in my own land.* What I do set on record is that these works of mine are to me, and always have been from my youth, my country, my family, my public office. And that is why I would not disclaim for myself a supremacy in the Greek language, just as I regard Alexander as supreme in war.

6 From Troy Alexander came to Arisbe, where his entire force had encamped after crossing the Hellespont. On the next day he reached Percote, and on the day after that he passed by Lampsacus and camped by the river Prosactius, which flows from the Mount Ida range and discharges into the sea between the Hellespont and the Black Sea. From there he came to Hermotus, passing the city of Colonae on the way. He always had scouts sent ahead of the main

7 army: these were led by Amyntas the son of Arrhabaeus, who had under his command the squadron of Companions from Apollonia (their squadron leader was Socrates the son of Sathon) and four squadrons of the so-called 'advance guards'. Along the route of his march the city of Priapus was surrendered to him by its inhabitants, and he sent a detachment to take it over under Panegorus the son of Lycagoras, one of the Companions.

8 The Persian commanders were Arsames, Rheomithres, Petenes, and Niphates, and with them Spithridates the satrap of Lydia and Ionia and Arsites the governor of Hellespontine Phrygia. They were already encamped by the city of Zeleia with the barbarian cavalry and

9 the Greek mercenaries. When they received reports of Alexander's crossing into Asia they met to discuss the situation. At this debate Memnon* of Rhodes advised that they should not risk taking on the Macedonians, who far outnumbered them in infantry and had Alexander in person with them, whereas Darius was not there on

their own side: they should rather march on, destroy the fodder by trampling it with the cavalry, burn the crops in the ground, and not even spare the very cities in their path; Alexander would not stay in the country if denied provisions. It is said that in this Persian council 10 Arsites declared that he would not stand for the burning of even one house belonging to the people in his charge: and that the other Persians sided with Arsites out of a suspicion that Memnon was deliberately delaying hostilities to preserve his position with the King.

Meanwhile Alexander was advancing towards the river Granicus* 13 with his army in battle-order: he had formed the hoplites in a double phalanx, posted the cavalry on the wings, and ordered the baggage-train to follow behind. The forward party sent to reconnoitre the enemy position was led by Hegelochus with the lancer cavalry and some five hundred light troops. Alexander was not far from the 2 Granicus when riders came at speed from the forward posts to report that the Persians were ranged ready for battle on the far bank of the Granicus. Alexander then began to form his entire army for battle. But Parmenion came up to him and spoke as follows: *

'It seems to me, sir, that our best plan is for the time being to 3 make camp on the river bank, just as we are. The enemy are greatly outnumbered in infantry, and I doubt they will dare to camp for the night anywhere near us. That will make it easy for the army to cross the river at dawn: we shall have the initiative and be across before they can form for battle. As things are now, I think 4 there is risk in making an immediate attempt, because it is impossible to take the army across the river on a wide front. Much of it looks deep, and, as you can see, the banks here are very high, in places more like cliffs. We would straggle out of the water in column, the 5 weakest possible formation, to meet a concerted charge by the massed ranks of the enemy cavalry. A failure at the very beginning would cause immediate difficulties and threaten the outcome of the entire campaign.'

Alexander replied: 'I am well aware of that, Parmenion. But I 6 would be ashamed if, after crossing the Hellespont with ease, this lit-tle stream' (this was his term to disparage the Granicus) 'is to prevent us getting across just as we are. I would take that as false to Macedonian 7 prestige and false to my own short way with dangers: and I imagine that it would encourage the Persians to begin thinking themselves a

match for Macedonians, if they have met with no immediate justification for their fears.'

14   So speaking he sent Parmenion to take command on the left wing,
and moved across to the right wing himself. On the far right he had
posted Philotas the son of Parmenion with the Companion cavalry,
the archers, and the Agrianian javelin-men; posted beside Philotas
was Amyntas the son of Arrhabaeus with the lancer cavalry, the
2 Paeonians, and Socrates' squadron; next to these were positioned the
Companion foot guards, led by Nicanor the son of Parmenion; beside
them the brigade of Perdiccas the son of Orontes; then that of Coenus
the son of Polemocrates; then that of Amyntas the son of Andromenes;
3 then the troops under Philip the son of Amyntas. On the left wing the
far left was taken by the Thessalian cavalry, commanded by Calas the
son of Harpalus; next to them, the allied cavalry under Philip the son
of Menelaus; next, the Thracians under Agathon; to the right of them
the infantry, the brigades of Craterus, Meleager, and Philip, extending to the centre of the whole line.

4   The Persians' cavalry numbered some twenty thousand, and their
foreign mercenary infantry a little less than that number. They were
drawn up with the cavalry ranged in an extended phalanx along the
river bank and the infantry behind the cavalry (there was high ground
beyond the bank). They posted a particular concentration of cavalry
squadrons on the bank opposite where they could see Alexander himself ready to attack their left front—he was easy enough to pick out
for the magnificence of his armour and the awed attention of his
entourage.

5   For some time the two armies took no action, just standing there at
the river's edge in dread of what was to come, and there was deep
silence on both sides. The Persians were waiting for the Macedonians
to start their crossing, so they could fall on them as they came up out
6 of the water. But then Alexander leapt on his horse, calling on his
entourage to follow and prove their worth, and ordered Amyntas the
son of Arrhabaeus to charge into the river with the advance horse
guards, the Paeonians, and one brigade of the infantry, preceded by
Socrates' squadron led by Ptolemy the son of Philip (this squadron
7 happened to have the command of the whole cavalry for that day). He
himself led the right wing into the river, to the sound of trumpets and
the raising of the battle-cry. He kept his line extending across at an
oblique angle, in the direction of the pull of the current, to avoid

exposing his troops in column to the Persian attack as they emerged, but rather to give himself the best chance of taking on the enemy in frontal formation.

Where the advance party with Amyntas and Socrates were coming 15 close to the bank, the Persians kept up a volley of missiles from above, some shooting into the river from the height of the bank, others going down right to the water where there was lower ground. There was 2 shoving by the cavalry, one side trying to get out of the river and the other side trying to stop them, and great showers of javelins from the Persians, while the Macedonians fought with thrusting-spears. But the Macedonians suffered badly in this first onslaught. They were greatly outnumbered, and had to defend themselves from the river where the ground was not solid and they were below the enemy, whereas the Persians had the advantage of the high bank: moreover the best of the Persian cavalry had been positioned at this spot, and Memnon's sons and Memnon himself were fighting in their number. For all their 3 bravery, then, the first Macedonians to take on the Persians were cut to pieces by them, other than those who broke off to join Alexander as he approached. He was already close by, bringing with him the right wing, and he charged into the Persians at the head of his troops just where the whole bulk of their cavalry and the commanders themselves were positioned. A fierce fight developed round him, and in 4 this time brigade after brigade of the Macedonians made the crossing with little difficulty now. The fighting was from horseback, but in some respects it was more like an infantry battle, a tangled mass of horse against horse and man against man, as each side struggled to achieve its aim—the Macedonians to drive the Persians once and for all away from the bank and force them onto open ground, and the Persians to block their exit and push them back into the river. From 5 this point on the advantage lay with Alexander and his troops—it was not only their strength and experience, but also the fact that they were fighting with cornel-wood lances against light javelins.

At this stage of the battle Alexander's lance was broken. He called 6 for another from Aretis, a groom in the royal service: he too was in trouble with his lance snapped, but putting up a decent fight with the broken half he had left. He showed this to Alexander and told him to ask someone else. Demaratus, a man from Corinth and one of Alexander's entourage of Companions, offered him his own lance. Alexander took it up, then, seeing Mithridates the son-in-law of 7

Darius riding out far in front of the others and bringing a wedge of cavalry with him, charged out too in front of his own men and threw Mithridates to the ground with a thrust in the face. Then Rhoesaces

8 rode at Alexander and struck him on the head with his scimitar. He sheared off part of the helmet, but the helmet had absorbed the blow. Alexander threw him to the ground also, thrusting with his lance through the breastplate and into his chest. Spithridates had already raised his scimitar against Alexander from behind, but Cleitus the son of Dropidas* got him first with a slash at his shoulder which sliced off Spithridates' arm, scimitar and all. Meanwhile troop after troop of cavalry who had successfully negotiated the river kept coming up out of the water to join Alexander and his company.

16   The Persians were now harried on all fronts, with lances stabbing at their own and their horses' faces, constant pressure from the Macedonian cavalry, and great damage done by the light troops intermingled with the cavalry, and they began to give way—first at the point where Alexander was at the forefront of the action. When their centre had collapsed the cavalry wings on either side were also

2 broken, and there ensued a massive rout. About a thousand of the Persian cavalry were killed. There was not a long pursuit, as Alexander turned aside to deal with the foreign mercenaries. The mass of them were still where they had originally been posted—this was no principled resolution on their part, but rather a stunned reaction to the unexpected. Alexander brought his phalanx against them, ordered his cavalry to attack on all sides, and, surrounded as they were, took little time to massacre them: not one escaped, except by lying unnoticed among the dead, and about two thousand were taken prisoner.

3   The Persian commanders killed were Niphates, Petenes, Spithridates the satrap of Lydia, Mithrobuzanes the governor of Cappadocia, Mithridates the son-in-law of Darius, Arbupales son of the Darius who was son of Artaxerxes, Pharnaces the brother of Darius' wife, and Omares, the commander of the mercenaries. Arsites fled from the battle to Phrygia, where it is said that he committed suicide, aware that the Persians blamed him for their disastrous strategy at the time.

4   On the Macedonian side about twenty-five of the Companion cavalry died in the first attack. There are bronze statues of them set up in Dium: Alexander gave this commission to Lysippus, the only sculptor he chose for his own portrayal. More than sixty died from

the rest of the cavalry, and about thirty infantry. Alexander buried 5
them on the next day with their arms and other equipment: to their
parents and children he granted exemption from land taxes and all
other forms of personal state service or property levies. He showed
great care for the wounded, personally visiting every one of them,
inspecting their wounds, asking how they came by them, and giving
them the opportunity to brag about their exploits. He also buried the 6
Persian commanders and the Greek mercenaries who died in enemy
service. Those who had been taken prisoner he sent in chains to hard
labour in Macedonia, as they were Greeks who had fought for the
barbarian against Greece and in defiance of the concordat agreed by
all Greeks. He sent three hundred Persian panoplies to Athens to be 7
dedicated to Athena on the Acropolis, and ordered the inscription of
these words: 'Alexander the son of Philip and the Greeks except the
Spartans* dedicated these spoils from the barbarians occupying
Asia.'

Alexander appointed Calas satrap of the territory that had been 17
ruled by Arsites, and imposed on it the same taxes as had been paid
to Darius. When locals came down from the hills to surrender themselves, he told them all to return to their various homes. He absolved 2
the people of Zeleia from blame, as he recognized that they had been
forced to fight on the barbarian side: and he sent Parmenion to take
over Dascylium (which he did—the garrison had left).

He himself marched on towards Sardis. When he was about eight 3
miles away from the city he was met by Mithrenes, the commander
of the citadel garrison, and the leading men of Sardis: they surrendered the city to him, and Mithrenes surrendered the citadel and
treasury. Alexander himself camped by the river Hermus [Gediz], 4
which is a little more than two miles from the city, and sent Amyntas
the son of Andromenes into Sardis to take over the citadel. He kept
Mithrenes with him in a position of honour, and granted the Sardians
and the rest of the Lydians the right to their ancient Lydian institutions and autonomous status. He made a personal visit to the citadel, 5
where the Persian garrison had been stationed, and was impressed by
the strength of the place: it was very high, sheer on all sides, and
fortified with a triple wall. He had it in mind to build a temple to
Olympian Zeus on the citadel and set up an altar there, but as he was 6
surveying the citadel for the most suitable location a sudden storm
blew up (though it was summer-time) with heavy thunder and a

downpour of rain exactly where the Lydian royal palace stood. Alexander took this as divine confirmation of where he should build
7 his temple to Zeus, and gave orders accordingly. He left Pausanias, one of the Companions, in charge of the citadel of Sardis, Nicias in charge of the assessment and payment of tribute, and Asander the son of Philotas in charge of Lydia and the rest of Spithridates' satrapy, giving him as many cavalry and light troops as seemed sufficient
8 for present purposes. He sent Calas and Alexander the son of Aëropus to Memnon's territory with the Peloponnesians and the majority of the allied troops apart from the Argives: these were left in Sardis to garrison the citadel.

9 Meanwhile, when news of the cavalry battle reached them, the mercenary troops garrisoning Ephesus seized two Ephesian triremes and made their escape. With them went Amyntas* the son of Antiochus. He had left Macedonia to get away from Alexander: not that he had in fact met any harm at his hands, but he had taken against Alexander and thought it would be an indignity to meet with any unpleasant reprisal from him.

10 Alexander reached Ephesus after three days. He restored the exiles who had been banished from the city for supporting him, broke up the oligarchy, and installed a democracy: he also ordered that the taxes previously paid to the barbarians should now be contributed to
11 the temple of Artemis. With fear of the oligarchs removed, the people of Ephesus were quick to kill those who had called in Memnon, those who had plundered the sanctuary of Artemis, and those who had pulled down the statue of Philip* in the sanctuary and dug up the grave of Heropythus, the liberator of the city, in the market-place.
12 Syrphax, his son Pelagon, and the sons of Syrphax's brothers were dragged out of the sanctuary and stoned. But Alexander prevented any further inquisitions and vengeance, knowing that, if given licence to do so, along with the guilty the people would kill innocent men out of personal enmity or designs on their property. No other action won Alexander as much credit as his handling of Ephesus at this time.

18 About now envoys from Magnesia and Tralles came to Alexander offering to hand over their cities. He sent out Parmenion for this purpose, giving him two thousand five hundred mercenary infantry and about the same number of Macedonians, with some two hundred Companion cavalry. He also sent Alcimachus* the son of Agathocles with no smaller force to the Aeolian cities and those in Ionia still

under barbarian control. His instructions were to overthrow the oli- 2
garchies and install democracies throughout, to restore their own
local legislation in each city, and to remit the tribute they had been
paying to the barbarians. He himself remained in Ephesus, where he
made sacrifice to Artemis and held a pageant with his whole army
parading in full armour and battle-order.

On the next day he took the rest of the infantry, the archers, the 3
Agrianians, the Thracian cavalry, the royal squadron of the
Companions, and three further squadrons, and set out for Miletus.
What they call the outer city had been abandoned by its garrison, and
Alexander took it on first assault: he camped there with the intention
of walling off the inner city. Earlier Hegesistratus, the King's 4
appointee as commander of the Milesian garrison, had sent a letter to
Alexander surrendering the city: but with the Persian forces not far
away he had now changed his mind and was ambitious to save Miletus
for the Persians. But Nicanor brought up the Greek fleet and sailed
in with it three days before the Persians could reach Miletus: he
anchored with a hundred and sixty ships at the island of Lade, which
lies off Miletus. The Persian ships arrived too late, and when their 5
admirals discovered that Nicanor had already put in with his fleet at
Lade, they anchored under Mount Mycale. Alexander had won prior
control of Lade, not only by anchoring his fleet there, but also by
transporting the Thracians and about four thousand of the other
mercenaries to the island.

*The barbarian ships numbered about four hundred. Even so, 6
Parmenion urged a sea-battle on Alexander. He advanced various
reasons for encouraging hope of a Greek naval victory, relying particularly on a divine sign, as an eagle had been seen perching on the
beach astern of Alexander's ships. A victory, he argued, would be a
tremendous boost to the whole campaign, whereas a defeat would not
constitute a serious setback—the Persians would simply retain their
present domination of the sea. He said that he would gladly join the
fleet himself and run the risk with them. Alexander declared that 7
Parmenion's analysis was faulty and his interpretation of the omen
wide of the mark. It made no sense to engage a much larger force with
a small number of ships, or to set their own unpractised fleet against
the trained Cypriot and Phoenician navies; he was not prepared to 8
expose Macedonian expertise and daring to the barbarians on an
element where there could be no guarantee of success; if they were

defeated in the engagement it would do serious damage to their initial reputation in the war, not least because news of a naval defeat would
9 encourage revolt in Greece. These were the practical arguments he adduced to demonstrate that this was not the time to offer battle at sea. As for the omen, his own interpretation was different: the eagle was indeed a sign in his favour, but the fact that it was seen perching on land suggested to him that it meant he would defeat the Persian fleet from the land.

19   Meanwhile Glaucippus, one of the leading men in Miletus, was sent to Alexander by the people and the foreign mercenaries who had effective control of the city, offering equal access to their walls and harbours for both Alexander and the Persians, and requesting that on
2 those terms the siege should be lifted. Alexander told Glaucippus to get back inside the city without delay and warn the Milesians to be ready for battle the following morning. He personally supervised the application of siege-engines to the walls, and after quickly demolishing a section of wall and weakening a longer stretch he brought up his army ready to go over where the wall had been broken down or shaken loose. All this was shadowed by the Persians from Mycale, who could be little more than spectators of the siege of their friends and allies.
3   By now Nicanor and his fleet at Lade, seeing that Alexander's assault had begun, had rowed along the coast into the harbour of Miletus and anchored their triremes packed close together with prows facing outwards at the narrowest part of the harbour entrance, thus blocking the harbour to the Persian fleet and denying Persian aid
4 to the Milesians. The Milesians and the mercenaries were now threatened by the Macedonians on all sides. Some of them threw themselves into the sea and paddled on their upturned shields to an unnamed islet facing the city; others boarded small boats and desperately tried to outrun the Macedonian triremes, but were caught by the triremes at the harbour mouth; most of them were killed in the city itself.
5   With the city now in his power, Alexander sailed in person against those who had escaped to the island. He had ordered ladders to be carried in the bows of the triremes, so that the sheer cliffs of the island
6 could be scaled like a wall from the ships. When he saw that the men on the island were prepared to fight to the death, he was moved to pity for these evidently courageous and loyal soldiers, and offered them terms on condition that they now served in his army:* they

were Greek mercenaries, about three hundred in number. The Milesians themselves, those not killed in the capture of the city, were released and allowed their freedom.

The barbarians based at Mycale would sail up to the Greek fleet in 7 the daytime, hoping to provoke them into battle. Their anchorage overnight in Mycale was not comfortable, as they had to go some considerable distance to get their water supplies from the mouths of the river Maeander. While still blockading the harbour of Miletus 8 with his ships, so the barbarians could not force an entrance, Alexander sent Philotas to Mycale with the cavalry and three brigades of infantry, with instructions to prevent the Persians leaving their ships. Thus, denied water and the other necessities, the Persians were effectively under siege in their ships, and they sailed off to Samos: after provisioning there they sailed back to Miletus. They 9 ranged the bulk of their fleet out at sea in front of the harbour, in the hope of provoking the Macedonians to come out into open water, but five of their ships sailed into the harbour between Lade and the Macedonian camp, hoping to catch Alexander's ships unmanned, as they had discovered that most of the crews were away from their ships, out and about on details to collect firewood, provisions, or fodder. A number of sailors were absent, but Alexander had crewed ten 10 ships from the available hands as soon as he saw the five Persian ships approaching, and sent them out at speed to intercept, with orders to ram head-on. When the crews of the five Persian ships saw the Macedonians putting out against them (they had not expected this), they turned back while still at some distance and made for their main fleet. One of their ships (from Iassus, and not a fast sailer) was cap- 11 tured crew and all in the retreat, but the other four were quick enough to reach the safety of their own triremes. So the Persians then sailed away from Miletus with nothing achieved.

Alexander now took the decision to disband his navy. His reasons 20 were lack of funds at the time, and the realization that his fleet was no match for the Persians in a battle: he was not prepared to put even part of his force at risk. He also reckoned that with his land forces already in control of Asia he had no further need of a fleet,* and could break the Persian navy by capturing the cities on the coast, thus depriving them of recruitment sources for their crews and of land bases in Asia. This was how he interpreted the significance of the eagle: he would conquer the ships from dry land.

2   This decision implemented, Alexander set out for Caria, on reports
that a substantial force of barbarians and foreign mercenaries was
concentrated in Halicarnassus* [Bodrum]. He captured the cities
between Miletus and Halicarnassus at first assault, and made camp
against Halicarnassus about half a mile from the city, prepared for a
3   long siege. The site was naturally strong, and any apparent deficien-
cies in its security had long been completely seen to by Memnon,*
who was there in person and had now been appointed by Darius commander of Lower Asia and of the entire navy; a large number of foreign mercenary troops had been left in the city, together with many
of the Persians themselves; and triremes had the harbour blocked,
giving significant naval assistance to the defence.

4   On the first day, as Alexander approached the wall near the gates
leading to Mylasa,* there was a sally by the troops in the city and
some long-range shooting. Alexander's men had no difficulty in
repelling this assault with a counter-charge and shutting them back
in the city.

5   A few days later Alexander took the foot guards, the Companion
cavalry, and the infantry brigades of Amyntas, Perdiccas, and
Meleager together with the archers and the Agrianians, and went
round the city to the side facing Myndus,* to see if the wall was more
open to assault on that side, and also to explore the possibility of a
sudden quick raid to capture Myndus. He saw that possession of
Myndus would be a great benefit in the siege of Halicarnassus, and
there had in fact been some proposal of surrender from the Myndians,
6   if he could approach undetected at night. So he went in person up to
the Myndus wall around midnight, as agreed. There was no sign of
surrender from the men inside, and he had not brought with him his
siege-engines or ladders—he had not set out for a siege, but in expectation of the city's betrayal and surrender. Even so, he brought up the
Macedonian phalanx and ordered them to undermine the wall. The
Macedonians did bring down one tower, but its collapse did not lay
7   the wall open. The people inside put up a vigorous resistance, which,
combined with the arrival now of considerable reinforcements from
Halicarnassus by sea, made it impossible for Alexander to succeed in
this improvised and hasty attempt to take Myndus. So he returned
with nothing of his purpose achieved, and applied himself once more
to the siege of Halicarnassus.

8   First he began to fill in the moat which they had dug in front of the

city about forty-five feet wide and twenty-three feet deep. This was to facilitate the positioning of the siege-towers* for the bombardment of the defenders of the wall, and of the other engines for battering the wall. The moat was filled without difficulty and he began now to 9 bring up the towers. A night sally from Halicarnassus to set fire to the towers and the other engines which had been moved up or were nearly in position was countered and easily beaten back within the walls by the Macedonian guards, supported by other troops roused by the alarm. About a hundred and seventy of the men from 10 Halicarnassus were killed, including Neoptolemus* the son of Arrhabaeus and brother of Amyntas, one of those who had deserted to Darius. The losses among Alexander's troops amounted to sixteen, but some three hundred were wounded, as this was a sudden action at night and they were not wearing proper protective armour.

*Not many days later two Macedonian hoplites from Perdiccas' 21 brigade, tent-mates and drinking companions, were boasting to each other and talking up their own prowess and exploits. Rivalry ensued, heated by the wine. The result was that they armed themselves and set out on their own to attack the wall at the high point which faces in the direction of Mylasa: their idea was to prove their own virility rather than to provoke a dangerous clash with the enemy. Some of 2 the troops in the city saw them—just two men approaching the wall for no apparent reason—and ran out to confront them. The two men killed any who came close and hurled missiles at those who kept their distance, despite being outnumbered and handicapped by the lie of the land (their opponents could charge or fire at them downhill). At 3 this point more of Perdiccas' men ran out to join the fray, and others from the city too, and a fierce fight developed by the wall. The sally-ing party was again driven back inside the gates by the Macedonians, and indeed the city came close to being captured. At that time the 4 walls were not strictly guarded, and a stretch of two towers and the curtain wall between them had collapsed to the ground, which would have offered a relatively easy way in if the whole army had applied itself to the business. The next tower, too, had been weakened, and undermining could have brought it down without difficulty. But the enemy foreclosed this opportunity by building a crescent-shaped brick wall on the inner side as a replacement for the collapsed length of wall: with many hands available for the work this was easily accomplished.

5   On the next day Alexander brought up his engines against this new
wall, and once more there was a sortie from the city to set fire to the
machines. Part of the line of wickerwork shelters close to the wall,
and part of one of the wooden towers, were destroyed by fire, but the
rest were saved by the troops under Philotas and Hellanicus who had
been detailed to protect them. When Alexander also appeared at the
point of assault, the men who had sallied out ran back inside the wall,
dropping the torches they had brought with them, and most throw-
6   ing away their arms as well. And yet at first the besieged had the best
of it, given the natural advantage of their elevated position and the
fact that they could shoot at the troops up with the siege-engines not
only from in front but also from the towers left standing on either
side of the collapsed wall, which allowed them fire from the flanks
and almost at the rear of those attacking the replacement wall.

22   Not many days later Alexander again brought up his engines
against the inner brick wall and supervised the operation himself.
There was now a sally from the city in full force. Some attacked by
the collapsed stretch of wall where Alexander himself was positioned,
and others at the Tripylon gate, where the Macedonians were least
2   expecting it. The first party threw torches on the siege-engines, and
anything else which could start a fire and feed it into a blaze, but there
was a vigorous counter-attack by the men with Alexander, large
stones were hurled and missiles fired from catapults* on the wooden
towers, and this party was easily repulsed and sent running back into
3   the city. There was considerable slaughter in this area, proportionate
to the greater numbers and the greater daring of the sally. Some died
in hand-to-hand battle with the Macedonians, others in the rubble of
the collapsed wall, where the only open way through was too narrow
for their number and it was difficult to climb over the fallen
masonry.
4   The party making the sortie by the Tripylon gate were met by
Ptolemy the royal Bodyguard, bringing up the battalions of Adaeus
and Timander,* and some of the light troops. They too had no diffi-
5   culty in turning back this party from the city. In the retreat they had
to run back over a narrow bridge built over the moat, which collapsed
under their numbers and threw many of them into the moat, where
some were trampled to death by their fellows and others shot down
6   by the Macedonians from above. The greatest carnage took place
around the gates themselves. In the panic of the moment the gates

were shut too soon (the fear was that the Macedonians would burst in hard behind the fugitives), so many of their own side were denied entrance and were destroyed by the Macedonians right under the walls. The city would have been close to capture, if Alexander had 7 not decided to call off his army: he still hoped to save Halicarnassus if the inhabitants would make some positive move to surrender. The dead numbered about a thousand on the city side, and about forty of Alexander's men, including Ptolemy the Bodyguard, Clearchus, the commander of the archers, Adaeus (he was a battalion commander),* and some other Macedonians of note.

The Persian leaders, Orontobates and Memnon, now conferred 23 and decided that as things stood they could not hold out long under siege: they could see that part of the wall had already fallen and other parts were weakened by battering; many of their men had been killed in the sorties, and many others incapacitated by wounds. In view of 2 all this, round about the second watch of the night they burned the wooden tower which they in turn had constructed to counter the enemy engines, and the arsenals too in which their missiles were stored. They also set fire to the houses near the wall: other houses 3 caught alight from the huge blaze created by the arsenals and the tower, assisted by a wind in that direction. They themselves made a retreat either to the fortress on the island or to the citadel called Salmacis.* When this was reported to Alexander by some men who 4 took the opportunity to desert—and he could see the spread of the fire for himself—even though this was happening at about midnight he nevertheless led out his Macedonians and killed those who were still setting fires in the city: his orders were that any Halicarnassians found in their houses should be spared.

Dawn was now breaking and he could survey the strongholds which 5 the Persians and the mercenaries had occupied. He decided against besieging them,* thinking that he would waste much time on them because of the nature of the ground, and that there was no great point now that he had taken the whole city. He buried those who had been 6 killed during the night and ordered the officers in charge of the siege-train to take it back to Tralles. He then razed the city to the ground and set out himself for Phrygia, leaving behind as a garrison for Halicarnassus and the rest of Caria a force of three thousand mercenary infantry and some two hundred cavalry under the command of Ptolemy.

7   As satrap of all Caria he appointed Ada, the daughter of Hecatomnos
and wife of Hidrieus (he was both her brother and her consort, as is
the Carian custom). On his death Hidrieus had handed over power to
Ada (ever since Semiramis* female rule over men had been an
accepted institution in Asia). Pixodarus* had then driven her out of
8 her position and taken power himself. On his death his son-in-law
Orontobates was sent by the King to assume the Carian satrapy. Ada
was left with only Alinda as her domain, the strongest fortress in
Caria. When Alexander invaded Caria she went to meet him, offering
to surrender Alinda and adopting Alexander as her son. Alexander
handed back Alinda to her, and did not refuse to be called her son:
then when he had destroyed Halicarnassus and taken control of the
rest of Caria he gave her rule over the whole country.

24   Some of the Macedonians in Alexander's expedition had been
recently married before the campaign. Alexander thought he should
take care of these men, and sent them back from Caria to spend the
winter with their wives in Macedonia, putting them in the charge of
Ptolemy the son of Seleucus, one of the royal Bodyguards, and two
of his generals, Coenus the son of Polemocrates and Meleager the son
2 of Neoptolemus, as they too were among the newly married: a further
instruction was that, when they returned and brought back the group
they had escorted, they should have recruited as many cavalry and
foot soldiers as they could from Macedonia. This one act ensured
Alexander's popularity among the Macedonians as much as any
other. He also sent Cleander the son of Polemocrates to recruit troops
in the Peloponnese.

3   He dispatched Parmenion to Sardis with a squadron of Companion
cavalry, the Thessalian cavalry, the other allies, and the wagons: his
orders were then to proceed from Sardis to Phrygia. He himself
moved towards Lycia and Pamphylia, to gain control of the coast and
4 so deny the enemy any use of their navy. On his route he first came to
the fortress of Hyparna, where there was a mercenary garrison, and
took it in one assault, allowing the mercenaries to leave the citadel
under safe conduct. Then as he entered Lycia he won over the people
of Telmissus by agreement, and having crossed the river Xanthus he
received the submission of Pinara, the city of Xanthus, Patara, and
about thirty smaller towns.

5   By this stage it was already the depth of winter, but Alexander
pressed on into the region known as Milyas, which belongs to Greater

Phrygia but at the time was counted as part of Lycia by decree of the Great King. Here envoys from Phaselis came to offer friendship and to crown Alexander with a golden crown: envoys making similar overtures were also sent by most of the Lower Lycians. Alexander 6 told the Phaselites and the Lycians to hand over their cities to the officers he would dispatch for that purpose, and all were handed over. A little later he came in person to Phaselis and helped the inhabitants to destroy a strong fort which had been built by Pisidians to threaten the district, and was used as a base from which the barbarians caused much damage to the Phaselite farmers.

While Alexander was still in the area of Phaselis it was reported to 25 him that Alexander the son of Aëropus* was conspiring against him (he was not only one of the Companions but also at the time the commander of the Thessalian cavalry). This Alexander was the brother of Heromenes and Arrhabaeus, who had been party to the murder of Philip. He himself was implicated at the time, but Alexander had 2 absolved him, as he was one of the first of his friends to rally round him after Philip's death and had gone armed at his side when Alexander entered the palace. Later Alexander held him in an honoured position in his entourage, sent him to be his general in Thrace, and appointed him to the command of the Thessalian cavalry when Calas, the previous commander, was posted to a satrapy.

This is how the plot came to be reported. When Amyntas deserted 3 to Darius bringing proposals and a letter from this Alexander, Darius sent Sisines, a Persian in his intimate circle, down to the coast on the pretext of visiting Atizyes, the satrap of Phrygia, but his real mission was to meet this Alexander and offer him assurances that, if he were to kill Alexander the king, Darius would install him as king of Macedonia and present him with a thousand talents of gold as well as the kingdom. Sisines was captured by Parmenion and told 4 him the purpose of his mission. Parmenion sent him under guard to Alexander, and Alexander heard the same story from him. Alexander convened his council of friends and put the question of what should be done about his namesake Alexander. His Companions gave it 5 as their view that it had been a mistake in the first place for him to assign the best of the cavalry to a man of dubious loyalty, and that now it was imperative to get rid of him as soon as possible, before he could form yet closer relations with the Thessalians and use them for some revolutionary purpose. And they were also alarmed by an omen. 6

*Apparently, when Alexander was still besieging Halicarnassus and was taking a midday rest, a swallow had flitted about over his head chirping loudly and settled here and there on his bed giving

7 voice in a more than usually insistent way. Alexander was too exhausted to wake up, but the sound bothered him in his sleep and he brushed the swallow away with a light sweep of his hand. Far from flying off at this touch, the bird perched right on Alexander's head

8 and kept going until he was completely awake. Alexander took this business of the swallow seriously and recounted it to Aristander of Telmissus, a seer. Aristander told him that it signified a plot by one of his friends, and meant also that the plot would come to light, as the swallow is a domestic bird, friendly to man, and the most talkative of all birds.

9 So, putting this together with the story from the Persian, he sent Amphoterus (the son of Alexander and brother of Craterus) to Parmenion, with some men from Perge to accompany him as guides. Amphoterus wore local dress to avoid recognition along the way, and

10 reached Parmenion undetected. He did not bring any letter from Alexander (it was not thought sensible to commit anything to open writing in a matter such as this), but delivered the message he had been charged with orally. And so the other Alexander was arrested and kept under guard.*

26 Alexander now set out from Phaselis, sending part of his army through the mountains towards Perge on the road built for him by the Thracians (the route would otherwise have been long and difficult). He himself led his own section along the coastal path by the sea-shore, which is only open to passage when the winds are blowing from the north: if south winds prevail this shore route is impassable.

2 The winds had been from the south, but now he had strong northerlies setting in (not without divine intervention,* as Alexander and his men saw it) which gave him a quick and easy passage. As he marched on from Perge, envoys from Aspendus met him on the way with full authority to surrender their city to him, but they asked him not to

3 introduce a garrison. They left with their request about the garrison conceded: but Alexander required them to pay a fifty-talent contribution to his army's wages and to hand over the horses which they bred as their tribute in kind to the King of Persia. They agreed about the money and the surrender of the horses before they left.

4 Alexander proceeded towards Side. The inhabitants there are

Cymaeans from Cyme in Aeolis. The story they tell of themselves* is
that when the first colonists sent out from Cyme put into land here
and disembarked to make their settlement they immediately lost all
memory of the Greek tongue and spoke a foreign language from the
start—but not that of the neighbouring barbarians, rather a new and
hitherto unknown dialect of their own: and from that time the people
of Side have continued to speak a barbarian language unique in the
area. Leaving a garrison in Side Alexander advanced against Syllium, 5
a strong position with a garrison of foreign mercenaries as well as the
local barbarians themselves. He was unable to take Syllium at one
straightforward assault, and news had reached him on his march that
the Aspendians were reneging on all the terms of their agreement:
they had refused to hand over the horses to those sent to collect them
or to pay the money; they had brought their effects from the countryside into the city, had shut their gates against Alexander's emissaries,
and were repairing the dilapidated parts of their walls. On this intelligence Alexander marched for Aspendus.

   Most of Aspendus is built on a strong acropolis which rises sheer, 27
with the river Eurymedon running right past it. They also had a good
number of houses on the level round the acropolis, surrounded by a
low wall. As soon as they learnt of Alexander's approach, the inhabit- 2
ants abandoned this wall and the houses on the lower ground (thinking them impossible to defend), and all took refuge together on the
acropolis. When Alexander arrived with his force, he crossed the
deserted wall and camped in the houses which the Aspendians had
abandoned. When the Aspendians saw Alexander there in person 3
(they had not expected this) and his army surrounding them on all
sides, they sent envoys to request an accommodation on the previous
terms. Alexander could see the defensive strength of the place, and
had not come equipped for a long siege, but even so he refused to
settle with them on the same terms. He demanded their leading men 4
as hostages, the horses as previously agreed, and a hundred talents in
place of the original fifty; they were to be subject to the satrap
appointed by Alexander and to pay taxes every year to the
Macedonians; there would be a judgement made on the territory they
were accused of forcibly annexing from their neighbours.

   With all this conceded to his satisfaction, Alexander moved on to 5
Perge, and from there set out for Phrygia. His route lay past the city
of Telmissus. The people here are barbarians of the Pisidian race,

and the place they inhabit is on high ground with cliffs on all sides
6 and a difficult way past it. A mountain slopes down from the city to
this road and ends there, but opposite another mountain rises no less
sheer. These two mountains form effective gates to the road, so that
a small guard force holding the mountains can block any passage. On
this occasion the Telmissians had brought out their entire force and
7 were occupying both mountains. Seeing this, Alexander ordered the
Macedonians to camp where they were; he reckoned that when they
saw them making camp the Telmissians would not stay there in full
force, but most would return to the city (it was not far away), leaving
just a guard on the mountains. His supposition proved correct: most
8 of them left, and the guard detachments remained. He immediately
led an attack on them, taking with him the archers, the javelin battalions, and the lighter-armed hoplites. The guards did not hold out
under fire, and abandoned their position. Alexander then passed
through the narrows and camped close by the city.

28   Envoys now came to him from the people of Selge. They too are
warlike barbarians of the Pisidian race, and theirs is a large city. They
had long been enemies of the Telmissians, and so this embassy had
come to offer Alexander friendship: he made a treaty with them, and
2 from then on found them completely loyal. Alexander recognized the
impossibility of any quick capture of Telmissus, and set off for
Sagalassus. This too was no small city, populated likewise by
Pisidians, who were reputed to be the most warlike of this generally
warlike race. They were waiting for him now, having occupied the
hill in front of the city which offered as strong a defensive position as
3 the wall itself. Alexander drew up the Macedonian phalanx as follows. On the right wing, where he took up his own position, he had
the foot guards, and next to them he ranged the Companion infantry
all the way to the left wing, each brigade taking its position from that
4 day's sequence set for the commanding officers. On the left he gave
the overall command to Amyntas the son of Arrhabaeus. Posted in
front of the right wing were the archers and the Agrianians, and the
Thracian javelin-men, commanded by Sitalces, in front of the left
(the cavalry could serve no purpose in this rough terrain). The
Pisidian defence was joined by reinforcements from Telmissus.
5   Alexander's troops had begun their assault on the hill held by the
Pisidians, and were at the steepest part of the ascent when the barbarians launched group after group in attack on each wing, where the

ground favoured their line of attack and made it hardest for their enemies to advance uphill. They turned back the archers, less than fully armed as they were and the first to engage, but the Agrianians stood firm, as the Macedonian phalanx was already coming up close 6 behind, with Alexander in plain sight at its head. When the fighting turned hand-to-hand, it was unarmoured barbarians against hoplites: the barbarians were everywhere falling wounded, and finally gave way. Some five hundred of them were killed, but few were taken 7 alive: lightly armed and with knowledge of the area they could get away easily, whereas the Macedonians, weighed down by their armour and ignorant of the paths, had little enthusiasm for pursuit. Alexander, however, followed up hard behind the fugitives 8 and stormed their city: of his own men he had lost Cleander, the commander of the archers, and about twenty others. He then went on to attack the rest of the Pisidians, taking some of their fortresses and winning the surrender of others.

From Pisidia he passed into Phrygia by the lake called Ascania, 29 where salt crystallizes naturally and the locals make use of it without any need for salt from the sea. Four days later he reached Celaenae, where the acropolis, rising steep on all sides, was held under the satrap of Phrygia by a garrison of a thousand Carians and a hundred Greek mercenaries. These sent envoys to Alexander assuring him 2 that they would surrender the position if reinforcements did not reach them by the date which had been agreed (and they specified the day). Alexander thought this a better proposition than a siege of the completely unassailable acropolis. So he left fifteen hundred troops 3 as a guard on Celaenae, stayed there ten days himself, appointing Antigonus the son of Philip satrap of Phrygia and replacing him as general in command of the allies by Balacrus the son of Amyntas, and then set out for Gordium. He sent orders to Parmenion to bring his force and meet him there, and so he did. The newly married men who 4 had been sent back to Macedonia also came to Gordium, and with them a fresh levy of troops under the command of Ptolemy the son of Seleucus, Coenus the son of Polemocrates, and Meleager the son of Neoptolemus: there were three thousand Macedonian infantry, three hundred cavalry, two hundred Thessalian cavalry, and a hundred and fifty Eleans led by Alcias of Elis.

Gordium is in Hellespontine Phrygia, located on the river 5 Sangarius. The source of the Sangarius is in Phrygia, and the river

flows through the territory of the Bithynian Thracians to issue into
the Black Sea. Here there also arrived an embassy from Athens to
meet Alexander. Their request was for the release of the Athenian
prisoners who were captured at the river Granicus fighting on the
Persian side and were now among the two thousand captives impris-
6 oned in Macedonia. They left with no success for the time being in
their appeal for the prisoners: in the middle of the war against Persia
Alexander thought it dangerous to make any relaxation in the threat
to the Greeks who were prepared to fight against Greece for the barbarians. But his answer was that they should come again with the
same request when conditions were favourable.

BOOK TWO

AT this stage Memnon, who had been appointed by Darius com- 1
mander of the entire navy and in charge of the whole Asiatic coast,
was looking to shift the war into Macedonia and Greece.* Chios was
betrayed to him and he captured the island. From there he sailed
against Lesbos, where he met resistance from the Mytilenaeans but
won the submission of the other cities in Lesbos. With these secured 2
he landed at Mytilene, blocked off the city with a double stockade
from sea to sea on either side, and built five garrisoned forts which
gave him easy control of the inland territory. While part of his fleet
kept guard on the harbour of Mytilene he sent other ships to Sigrium,
the promontory of the island which was the usual landing-place for
merchant vessels from Chios, Geraestus, and Malea, to guard the sea
approach and so prevent any help coming to the Mytilenaeans by sea.
In the course of this operation Memnon fell sick and died, and this 3
was the most damaging setback to the King's cause at that time. As he
was dying Memnon had handed over his command (pending a decision
by Darius) to his nephew Pharnabazus, the son of Artabazus, and he and
Autophradates kept up a vigorous prosecution of the siege. Cut off from 4
their land and blockaded at sea by a large fleet, the Mytilenaeans sent
to Pharnabazus and reached an agreement to surrender on these
terms: the mercenaries sent by Alexander under the alliance should
leave the city; the Mytilenaeans should destroy the pillars recording
their alliance with Alexander, and become allies of Darius under the
Peace of Antalcidas* as agreed with the former King Darius; and
their exiles were to return with entitlement to half the property they
had at the time of their banishment. These were the terms the 5
Mytilenaeans agreed with the Persians, but as soon as Pharnabazus
and Autophradates had entry to the city they brought in a garrison
and Lycomedes of Rhodes to command it, and installed Diogenes,
one of the exiles, as tyrant over the city: they also exacted money
from the Mytilenaeans, using force to fleece the rich and otherwise
imposing a communal levy.

With these arrangements made Pharnabazus took the foreign mer- 2
cenaries on board ship and sailed for Lycia, while Autophradates went on to the other islands. At this point Darius sent down

Thymondas the son of Mentor to take over the mercenaries from Pharnabazus and bring them up to him in the interior, and also to instruct Pharnabazus to assume the whole of Memnon's command.
2 Pharnabazus handed over the mercenaries to him and sailed to join Autophradates and the rest of the fleet. Once their forces were joined they sent Datames, a Persian, with ten ships to the Cyclades, while they themselves sailed for Tenedos with a hundred ships. Putting in to what is called the 'North Harbour' of Tenedos, they sent word to the people of the island requiring them to destroy the pillars recording their treaty with Alexander and the Greeks, and to observe with the present King the Peace of Antalcidas as agreed with the former
3 Darius. The general feeling of the Tenedians was more in favour of Alexander and the Greeks, but in the present situation they could see no means of preserving themselves other than submission to the Persians. Although Alexander had instructed Hegelochus to assemble another naval force, he had not yet gathered a sufficient fleet for them to expect any timely help from that quarter. So in the end it was fear rather than any willing consent which brought the Tenedians over to Pharnabazus and his side.
4 Meanwhile Proteas* the son of Andronicus, acting on orders from Antipater, had collected a fleet of warships from Euboea and the Peloponnese to offer some protection to the islands and mainland Greece itself against the reported likelihood of a Persian naval attack. On receiving intelligence that Datames was anchored off Siphnos with ten ships, he set sail by night with fifteen ships from Chalcis on
5 the Euripus. He put in to the island of Cythnos at dawn and spent the day camped there, in order to gather more precise information about the ten enemy ships and to hold his attack on the Phoenicians manning them until night would add to their terror. When confirmation came that Datames and his ships were indeed anchored at Siphnos, he set out against them while it was still night and attacked at first dawn. They were caught unawares, and he took eight of their ships, crew and all. In the initial engagement with Proteas' ships Datames himself and two triremes managed to escape and get back safely to the main fleet.
3 When Alexander arrived at Gordium he was taken with a keen desire to go up the acropolis, where there was the palace of Gordius and his son Midas, and to see for himself Gordius' wagon and the
2 knot on its yoke. Local tradition had an elaborate story about this

wagon. Gordius, so the story went, was one of the Phrygians of old, a poor man with just a little land to farm and two yoke of oxen, one for his plough and one to pull his wagon. As he was ploughing one day an 3 eagle settled on the yoke and stayed perched there right through to the unyoking at the end of the day. Astonished at this sight, Gordius went to consult the seers of Telmissus about the prodigy (the people of Telmissus are skilled in the interpretation of omens, and the prophetic gift runs in families, inherited by the women and children also). As he approached a Telmissian village Gordius met a girl draw- 4 ing water and told her his experience with the eagle. She too came from one of the prophetic families, and she told him to return to the scene of the omen and make sacrifice there to Zeus the King. Gordius begged her to go with him and supervise the procedure in person. He then made the sacrifice under her direction, and came to marry the girl: they had a son called Midas. Midas had grown into a fine and 5 handsome young man when the Phrygians suffered the affliction of civil war. They had received an oracle saying that a wagon would bring them a king, and this king would put an end to their fighting. They were still discussing this very issue when Midas drove up with his father and mother, they and their wagon in full view of the assembly. The Phrygians deduced from the oracle that this must be 6 the man who the god told them would be brought to them in the wagon. They made Midas their king, and he did put an end to their civil war: and he dedicated his father's wagon on the acropolis as a thank-offering to Zeus the King for his sending of the eagle.

There was a further legend about the wagon, that whoever could undo the knot on its yoke was destined to rule Asia.* This knot was 7 tied with cornel bark, and no end or beginning could be seen. Alexander could find no means of untying the knot, but did not want to leave it intact, in case this failure provoked popular unrest. What he did next is variously reported. According to some he cut through the knot with a blow of his sword and observed that it was now undone: but Aristobulus says that he took out the pole-pin*—a knobbed bolt running through the pole which anchors the whole fastening—and so was able to pull the yoke over the end of the pole. I cannot say for 8 certain what actually happened with the knot, but there is no doubt that Alexander and his entourage left the scene thinking that the oracle about the wagon and the undoing of the knot had now been fulfilled, and in fact that night there was thunder and lightning from heaven in confirmation. Alexander responded by making sacrifice on the following day to the gods who had revealed these signs and shown him the way to undo the knot.

4 On the day after that Alexander set out for Ancyra in Galatia. There he was met by an embassy from the Paphlagonians, offering the submission of their people and ready to agree terms, with the
2 request that he should not invade their country in force: he imposed the condition that they must be subject to the authority of Calas, the satrap of Phrygia. He himself then marched on to Cappadocia and won the surrender of all the country on the near side of the river Halys [Kizilirmak] and much too beyond it.* Installing Sabictas as
3 satrap of Cappadocia he pressed on to the Cilician Gates. When he reached the site where Cyrus had camped* in his expedition with Xenophon, and saw that the Gates were strongly guarded, he left Parmenion there with the heavier-armed infantry brigades while he himself, at around the first watch, took the foot guards, the archers, and the Agrianians and advanced towards the Gates under cover of night, intending to fall on the guards when they were not expecting
4 an attack. His approach did not go undetected, but the very boldness of it brought him compensating advantage: when the guards realized that Alexander was leading the attack in person, they left their position and ran away. At dawn on the next day he took his whole force through the Gates and moved on down into Cilicia.

5 There he received reports about the likely intentions of Arsames. At first Arsames had planned to save Tarsus for the Persians, but when he learnt that Alexander had now passed through the Gates he was minded to abandon the city, and the Tarsians were consequently afraid
6 that he would turn to plunder as a prelude to this desertion. Hearing this, Alexander took the cavalry and the lightest-armed of his troops at full speed towards Tarsus, and knowledge of this impending attack sent Arsames hurrying out of Tarsus and back to King Darius without doing any harm to the city.*

7 *It was here that Alexander fell ill. Aristobulus' account attributes it to exhaustion,* but others say that Alexander, sweaty and overcome by the heat, had wanted a bathe and had dived into the river Cydnus for a swim (the Cydnus runs right through the city of Tarsus, and with its springs in the Taurus mountains and a course through
8 open country its water is cold and clear). The result was an attack of cramp, violent fever, and persistent inability to sleep. The doctors

thought he would not live, all except Philip, a doctor from Acarnania who was a close associate of Alexander, completely trusted as a physician and generally well regarded in the army: he wanted to administer a purgative, and Alexander told him to go ahead. He was engaged in *9* preparing the draught when Alexander was handed a note from Parmenion warning him to beware of Philip, as he had heard that Darius had bribed him to poison Alexander. Alexander read the letter and still had it in his hand when he took the cup containing the medicine. He passed the letter to Philip to read, and drank down the *10* dose as Philip was reading Parmenion's note. Philip's reaction made it immediately clear that there was nothing sinister in the potion: he showed no alarm at the letter, but simply reassured Alexander and told him to follow any further prescriptions he might make—if he did as he was told he would recover. The purge did its work and the *11* illness abated. Alexander had shown Philip that he trusted him as a friend, and demonstrated to the rest of his entourage that he was proof against suspicion of his friends and resolute in the face of death.

After this he sent Parmenion to the other Gates* (the pass, that is, *5* which divides Cilician from Assyrian territory) to forestall the enemy by seizing this pass and keeping it under guard: for this purpose he gave Parmenion the allied infantry, the Greek mercenaries, the Thracians commanded by Sitalces, and the Thessalian cavalry. Somewhat later *2* he himself set out from Tarsus, and on the first day reached the city of Anchialus, which legend tells was founded by Sardanapalus* the Assyrian. The circuit and groundwork of the walls speak of a city founded on a large scale and developed to great strength. Sardanapalus' *3* tomb was close by the walls of Anchialus, topped by the figure of Sardanapalus himself with his hands held together as if about to clap them, and inscribed with an epitaph in Assyrian script, which the *4* Assyrians said was in verse. However that may be, the meaning expressed by the words of the inscription was this: 'Sardanapalus the son of Anacyndaraxes built Anchialus and Tarsus in one day: but you, stranger, should eat, drink, and be merry, as all other human concerns are not worth—this' ('this' being a riddling reference to the noise of a hand-clap). They also said that 'be merry' was a euphemism for a cruder Assyrian word in the inscription.

From Anchialus Alexander came to Soli. He installed a garrison *5* there, and imposed a fine of two hundred talents of silver in punishment for the city's pro-Persian tendency.* From there he took with *6*

him three brigades of the Macedonian infantry, all the archers, and the Agrianians and marched against the Cilicians based in the mountains. In no more than seven days he returned to Soli with some of these
7 Cilicians forcibly dislodged and others brought to submission. Here he learnt that Ptolemy and Asander had been victorious over the Persian Orontobates, who was defending the citadel of Halicarnassus and had won control of Myndus, Caunus, Thera, and Callipolis: Cos and Triopium had also come over to his side. Their letter said that Orontobates had been defeated in a great battle, in which he had lost about seven hundred infantry and fifty cavalry, with at least one thou-
8 sand taken prisoner. At Soli Alexander made sacrifice to Asclepius,* personally led a parade of the whole army, held a torch-race, and organized festival games with competitions in athletics and the per- forming arts: he also gave the people of Soli a democratic govern- ment. He then set off in the direction of Tarsus, letting Philotas take
9 the cavalry through the Aleian plain to the river Pyramus, while he himself went to Magarsus with the infantry and the royal squadron of cavalry: there he sacrificed to the Athena of Magarsus. Next he came to Mallus and made the customary offerings for a hero to Amphilochus. He found the Mallians in a state of civil strife, and brought that to an end, also remitting the tribute which they had been paying to Darius, on the grounds that Mallus was a colony of Argos and he himself claimed descent from the Heracleidae of Argos.*

6   While he was still at Mallus Alexander received reports that Darius was encamped with his entire force at Sochi, a place in Assyria about two days' march from the Assyrian Gates. On this he called a meeting of his Companions and told them what was reported about Darius and his army: they recommended an immediate advance without
2 further preparation. Alexander thanked them for their advice and closed the meeting. Next day he led his army out on the march against Darius and the Persians. On the second day he passed through the Gates and camped by the city of Myriandrus:* during the night a fierce storm blew up, with rain and a violent wind, which kept him confined to camp.

3   Darius meanwhile had his army waiting idle. He had chosen a plain in Assyrian territory which was open on all sides, well suited to the sheer size of his army and ideal ground for the deployment of his cavalry. He was advised not to leave this spot by Amyntas* the son of Antiochus, the deserter from Alexander: the open space, Amyntas

urged, favoured the Persian numbers and all their gear for the fight. So Darius stayed on. But Alexander had spent a long time at Tarsus 4 because of his illness, quite some time over the sacrifice and parade in Soli, and further time in his expedition against the Cilicians in the mountains, and this delay caused Darius to deviate from his original plan. He was in any case readily susceptible to suggestions which particularly appealed to his fancy, and under the influence of the ingratiating advisers who surround and always will surround any king to no good end he was encouraged to conclude that Alexander was reluctant to advance any further, intimidated by the intelligence of Darius' own 5 approach. One after the other they fed his hopes, telling him that his cavalry would simply ride down and trample the Macedonian army. And yet Amyntas still insisted that Alexander would come 6 wherever he found Darius, and urged him to stay where he was. But the worse advice prevailed, as it was what Darius most wanted to hear at the time: and there must have been some supernatural influence also drawing Darius into the very position which gave him little benefit from his cavalry or from the huge number of his troops and their arsenal of javelins and arrows, and even denied him any spectacular display of his forces—instead he handed an easy victory to Alexander and his men. By now it was destined that the Persians should lose 7 control of Asia to the Macedonians, just as the Medes had lost it to the Persians, and before that the Assyrians to the Medes.

So Darius crossed the mountain range by the pass known as the 7 Amanic Gates and made for Issus, which brought him undetected to the rear of Alexander. Taking possession of Issus, he cruelly maimed and then killed all those he caught of the Macedonian sick who had been left there. On the next day he advanced to the river Pinarus.* When Alexander heard that Darius was at his rear he did not imme- 2 diately trust the report, but put some of his Companions aboard a thirty-oared ship and sent them back to Issus to see if this news was true. They sailed up in this vessel, their reconnaissance made easier by the bay which the sea forms in that area, and established that the Persians were indeed camped there. They reported back to Alexander that Darius was close at hand.

*He called together his generals and squadron commanders and 3 the commanding officers of the allies and told them that there was every reason for confidence: they had faced dangers before and emerged successful; they had already beaten the Persians, so this would be a contest between the victorious and the defeated; God was directing the battle more in their favour, having put it into Darius' head to move his forces from open country and constrict them in the narrows, an area of exactly the right size for the deployment of the Macedonian phalanx but too small for the Persians to make any tactical use of their numbers. And, he said, the Persians were no match

4 for them in physique or morale: these Persians and Medes, heirs to generations of soft living, would be facing Macedonians, who were long trained in the dangers and exertions of war; what was more, it would be a battle of free men against slaves. Where it was Greek against Greek, there was no comparison of motive: the Greeks with Darius were risking their lives for pay, and poor pay at that, but those fighting on their own side had volunteered to serve the cause of

5 Greece. Then again with the barbarians on either side: it would be the hardiest and most warlike in Europe—Thracians, Paeonians, Illyrians, Agrianians—against the laziest and most effeminate races of Asia. And finally they had Alexander to command them, as against Darius.

6 After listing all these factors which made for Macedonian superiority in the coming contest, Alexander went on to emphasize the great value of the prizes which they stood to win. The victory this time would not be over Darius' satraps, not over the cavalry ranged at the Granicus or the twenty thousand foreign mercenaries, but over all that was of any worth among the Persians and Medes and all the other nations in Asia subject to the Persians and Medes, and over the Great King himself, who was there in person. Nothing would remain for them to do after this contest—except to assume rule of the whole of Asia and put an end

7 to all their long hardship. And there was more. He reminded them of what they had already achieved for the common cause so brilliantly, citing individual acts of conspicuously noble bravery and naming the man as well as describing the deed: and in the most tactful way he touched on his own record of dangers faced in their battles.

8 It is said that in this speech he also referred to Xenophon and his Ten Thousand, saying that although that expedition did not compare to their own in numbers or in quality either, although Xenophon had none of the cavalry which supported their own army from Thessaly, Boeotia, the Peloponnese, Macedonia, Thrace, and elsewhere, although he had no archers or slingers except the few Cretans and Rhodians

9 he managed to raise from scratch for emergency service, even so the

Ten Thousand routed the Great King and all his force near Babylon itself, and successfully beat off the tribes opposing them on their return route down to the Black Sea.

He added all the usual encouragement which a brave commander gives to brave troops at a time like that, to firm their resolve in the dangers to come. They crowded round their king to take his hand and voice their approval, urging him to lead them on there and then.

For the time being, though, Alexander told his troops to take their 8 evening meal, while he sent a few cavalry and archers on to the Gates to reconnoitre the route back. Then at nightfall he took his whole army and marched to secure the Gates once more. By about midnight 2 he had re-established control of the pass, and for what remained of the night he rested his army on the rocky outcrop above it, with guard-posts set at the critical points. Towards dawn he moved on along the road leading down from the Gates. As long as the going was through a narrow defile enclosed on both sides he led the army in column: but as the terrain broadened he gradually opened out the formation from column to phalanx, bringing forward file after file of hoplites to right or left, to keep filling the space between the ridge on the right and the sea on the left. At first the cavalry had been ranged 3 behind the infantry, but as they moved on into more open ground Alexander began to deploy the army in battle-order. His infantry dispositions were as follows. On the far right wing, close up against the mountain, he placed first the royal guard and the foot guards under Nicanor the son of Parmenion, then next to them Coenus' brigade, and Perdiccas' brigade alongside that. These formed his hoplite line from the right to the centre. First on the left wing was Amyntas' bri- 4 gade, then Ptolemy's, and next Meleager's. Craterus had been given command of the infantry on the left, and Parmenion was the overall commander of the entire left wing, with instructions to leave no gap by the sea, to avoid encirclement by the barbarians whose numbers would otherwise outflank them on both sides.

When it was reported to Darius that Alexander was approaching in 5 battle-order, he sent about thirty thousand of his cavalry across the river Pinarus and some twenty thousand light troops with them, to give him time for the deployment of the rest of his army. At the front 6 of his hoplite forces, facing the Macedonian phalanx, he placed the Greek mercenaries, numbering some thirty thousand, and on either side of them about sixty thousand of the so-called Cardaces, who were

also hoplites: this was the number which could be accommodated on
7 a single front in the space where they were being deployed. In addition he posted about twenty thousand troops along the mountain
skirts to his left, threatening Alexander's right. Some of these succeeded in getting behind Alexander's line, as the contour of the foothills along which they were posted followed a deep indentation at one
point (rather like a bay in the sea) then crooked back again, so bring-
8 ing the troops on these hills to the rear of Alexander's right wing. The
main bulk of Darius' light and heavy troops, grouped in their national
regiments, extended to a quite useless depth behind the Greek mercenaries and the front-line barbarian phalanx. Darius' whole army
was said to number some six hundred thousand fighting men.*
9   The ground broadened out a little as Alexander moved forward,
enabling him to bring up his cavalry into the line: he posted the
so-called Companion cavalry and the Thessalians to join himself on
the right wing, and sent the Peloponnesians and the rest of the allied
cavalry to Parmenion on the left.
10   With his phalanx now organized, Darius recalled by prearranged
signal the cavalry he had posted in front of the river to cover the
deployment of his troops, and sent most of them to take up position
on the right wing by the sea, opposite Parmenion, as this was more
favourable ground for cavalry action. He also sent a section to the left
11 wing close up against the hills, but it became clear that they had little
use where the space was so confined, and he ordered most of these too
to ride round and join the right wing. He himself took position at the
centre of the whole line,* the traditional placing for the Kings of
Persia (Xenophon the son of Gryllus has written about the reason for
this order of battle).
9   At this point, seeing that almost all of the Persian cavalry had
transferred to face his own left wing by the sea, while he only had the
Peloponnesian and the other allied cavalry posted on that side,
Alexander sent the Thessalian cavalry urgently over to the left: to
prevent enemy sight of this manoeuvre he told them not to ride
across in front of the line, but to go round unobserved behind the
2 phalanx. In front of the cavalry on the right he now posted the 'scouts'
under Protomachus and the Paeonians under Ariston, and the archers under Antiochus in front of the infantry. At an angle to face the
hills behind him he deployed the Agrianians under Attalus and a
number of cavalry and archers, so that on the right wing his line was

forked, one part facing Darius and the main Persian army across the
river, the other facing the troops deployed in the hills to his rear. On *3*
the left wing the Cretan archers and the Thracians under Sitalces
were posted in front of the infantry, with the cavalry of that wing
further to their left. The foreign mercenaries formed a complete second line. Alexander thought his phalanx was not sufficiently solid on
the right, and expected that the Persians would far outflank him on
that side, so he ordered two squadrons of Companion cavalry to move
across inconspicuously from the centre to the right wing (these were
the squadron from Anthemus, whose commander was Peroedas the
son of Menestheus, and the so-called Leugaean squadron, commanded by Pantordanus the son of Cleander). At the same time he *4*
brought up the archers, a section of the Agrianians, and some of the
Greek mercenaries to the front line on the right and so extended his
phalanx to stretch beyond the Persian wing. The enemy posted on
the high ground had not come down to the attack, and a sally made
against them on Alexander's orders by the Agrianians and a few of
the archers had easily dislodged them from the foothills and sent
them retreating to the summit, so Alexander reckoned that he could
use the troops he had deployed opposite them to fill out his phalanx.
A detail of three hundred cavalry was sufficient guard against these
men on the hills.

   This, then, was the formation in which Alexander led his army on *10*
for a while, with frequent halts which gave the impression of an
advance with plenty of time to spare. The reason was that Darius
made no further corresponding movement: he kept the barbarians
where they had been at their initial deployment, and stayed by the
bank on his side of the river. In many places the banks were precipitous, but he had built a stockade along the more obviously accessible
stretches. From all this Alexander and his staff drew the immediate
conclusion that Darius was a broken man, a slave to his fate. With little *2*
distance now between the two armies, Alexander rode the length of
his line and encouraged his men to show their true quality, calling out
by name and proper title not only to his generals but also to squadron
and company commanders and those of the foreign mercenaries distinguished by rank or conspicuous service. He was answered by a universal clamour to be at the enemy with no more delay. Alexander *3*
continued the advance in line, keeping to a walking pace at first, even
though he now had Darius' force in sight: this was to prevent any

bulging and consequent split in the phalanx which could be caused by an accelerated approach. But as soon as they were within missile range, Alexander and his company stationed on the right wing led a charge into the river, to surprise the Persians with the speed of their attack and by this rapid move to close quarters to minimize the damage

4 done by the Persian archers. The result was as he had guessed. Once the fighting became hand-to-hand the Persian forces on the left wing gave way, and here Alexander and his company were achieving a brilliant victory. But Darius' Greek mercenaries took their opportunity where the Macedonian phalanx had broken and a gap opened up on

5 the right. While Alexander had charged at speed into the river, come hand-to-hand with the Persians stationed there, and was now pushing them back, the Macedonians in the centre were not so quick to engage, and finding the river banks sheer in several places could not keep the front of their phalanx to its original line. The Greeks concentrated their attack where they saw the greatest rift in the Macedonian

6 phalanx, and here the action was fierce: the Greeks were trying to push the Macedonians back into the river and reverse the defeat where their own side were being driven into flight, while the Macedonians fought to emulate the success now manifestly achieved by Alexander and to save the reputation of the phalanx, which up till then had been

7 famous for its invincibility. There was also an element of racial pride in the antagonism of Greeks and Macedonians. It was here that Ptolemy the son of Seleucus fell after distinguishing himself in the action, and about a hundred and twenty other notable Macedonians were killed.

11   At this point the brigades on the right wing, in view of their successful rout of the immediate Persian opposition, turned inwards against Darius' foreign mercenaries where their own centre was in trouble. They first drove them back from the river, then, outflanking the now broken section of the Persian army, charged into the mercen-

2 aries from the side and began cutting them down. At the start of the main engagement the Persian cavalry facing the Thessalians had not stayed on their side of the river, but charged across and made a forceful attack on the Thessalian squadrons. A fierce cavalry battle ensued on this wing, and the Persians did not give way until they realized that Darius had fled and the carnage inflicted on the mercenaries by

3 the Macedonian phalanx had left them isolated. There was now a complete and decisive rout. The Persian horses, carrying riders in

heavy armour,* suffered badly in the retreat, and the horsemen too came to grief as their great numbers crowded down narrow paths in disorderly and panic-stricken flight: they sustained as many casualties from trampling by their own side as from the enemy pursuit. The Thessalians went after them in earnest, with the result that the slaughter of cavalry in the rout was no less than that of the infantry.

As for Darius, as soon as his left wing was panicked by Alexander 4 and he saw it being broken away like that from the rest of the army, there and then, just as he was, still in his chariot, he set off in flight, one of the first to flee.* As long as he had level ground for his escape 5 he could stay safe in the chariot: but when he hit rough terrain with gullies and other obstacles he abandoned the chariot at that point, discarded his shield and king's robe, left robe, shield, and even his bow in the chariot, and continued his flight on horseback. Only the onset of night shortly afterwards saved him from capture by Alexander.

As long as there was daylight Alexander kept up his pursuit at full 6 stretch, but as it was now growing dark and hard to see the way ahead he turned back towards the camp: he did, though, take possession of Darius' chariot, and with it his shield, robe, and bow. He had in fact 7 been that much slower to start the pursuit because at the initial break in the phalanx he had doubled back himself and not turned to pursue until he had seen the foreign mercenaries and the Persian cavalry driven away from the river.

The Persian dead included Arsames, Rheomithres, and Atizyes, 8 who had all been cavalry commanders at the Granicus; of the Persian nobility there also died Sauaces, the satrap of Egypt, and Bubaces; in the general body of troops about one hundred thousand were killed (including more than ten thousand cavalry), such large numbers that Ptolemy the son of Lagus, who was with Alexander at the time, says that when the party in pursuit of Darius met a ravine in their path they could cross it over the bodies of the dead. Darius' camp was 9 captured at the first assault, and with it his mother and his wife, who was also his sister,* and his infant son: two of his daughters were captured as well, together with a few Persian ladies-in-waiting from the aristocracy. The other Persians had dispatched their women and general equipage to Damascus, and Darius too had sent to Damascus 10 the bulk of his money and all the other requirements of a luxurious lifestyle which go with a great king even on campaign, so no more than three thousand talents was found in the camp (but the money in

Damascus was also captured shortly afterwards by Parmenion on a special mission for that purpose). This, then, is how that battle ended: it was fought in the month Maemacterion* of the year when Nicocrates was archon at Athens [November 333 BC].

12   On the following day Alexander first visited the wounded, despite a sword-wound* of his own in the thigh. He then collected the dead and gave them a magnificent funeral with his whole army on parade in their most spectacular battle array. In his speech he made honourable mention of all who had performed some outstanding action in the battle, whether he had seen it himself or heard confirmed reports from others: and in recognition of this service he made grants

2   of money to each according to his deserts. As satrap of Cilicia he appointed Balacrus the son of Nicanor, one of the royal Bodyguards, and to fill his place in the corps of Bodyguards he chose Menes the son of Dionysius; as replacement commander of the brigade of Ptolemy the son of Seleucus, who had died in the battle, he appointed Polyperchon the son of Simmias; and to the people of Soli he remitted the fifty talents still outstanding from the fine he had imposed, and returned their hostages.

3   He did not fail to take care also of Darius' mother, wife, and children. Some of the Alexander historians say that on the very night of his return from the pursuit of Darius he entered Darius' tent, which had now been sequestered for his own use, and heard wailing and

4   other sounds of women in distress not far from the tent. He asked who these women were, and why they were billeted so close to him. He was told, 'Sir, they are Darius' mother and wife and children. They have heard that you have Darius' bow and royal robe and that his shield has been recovered. They think Darius is dead and they are

5   mourning him.' On hearing this Alexander sent Leonnatus,* one of his Companions, to them, telling him to explain that Darius was alive, that he had left his arms and robe in the chariot as he made his escape, and that these were all that Alexander had. Leonnatus entered their tent and gave them the message about Darius: he also told them that Alexander was allowing them to keep the status and trappings of royalty, and the title of queens, as there was no personal animosity in his war with Darius, but it had been a legitimate contest for the control of Asia.*

6   This is the account of Ptolemy and Aristobulus. There is also a story that on the next day Alexander himself visited the tent, with

Hephaestion* the only one of his Companions to go with him. Darius' mother, not knowing which of them was the king, as they were both dressed alike, approached Hephaestion as the taller of the two and made obeisance to him.* Hephaestion stepped back, and one of her 7 attendants pointed to Alexander and told her who he was. She retired in embarrassment at her mistake, but Alexander assured her that she was not wrong—Hephaestion was just as much Alexander as he was.

I record these stories without either vouching for their truth or 8 regarding them as wholly unlikely. If this is how it really happened, I applaud Alexander both for his compassion shown to the women and for the trust in his friend and the honour he paid him: and if his historians think it probable that Alexander would have acted and spoken in this way, I applaud him none the less for that too.

Darius fled throughout the night with a small retinue, but in the 13 daytime he took on a constant accretion of Persians and foreign mercenaries who had escaped from the battle, to a total of about four thousand: with these he made at speed for the city of Thapsacus* and the river Euphrates, to put the Euphrates between himself and Alexander as soon as possible. Amyntas* the son of Antiochus, Thymondas the 2 son of Mentor, Aristomedes of Pherae, and Bianor the Acarnanian—all commanders who had deserted to Darius—took some eight thousand of their troops just as they were straight from the battlefield and fled with them over the mountains, ultimately reaching Tripolis [Tripoli] in Phoenicia. Here they found hauled up on shore the ships which 3 had previously carried them from Lesbos. They launched as many as they thought sufficient for their transport, burnt the rest where they were in the dockyards, to delay any pursuit, and set off in flight first to Cyprus and then to Egypt, where not much later Amyntas met his death in some meddlesome venture, killed by the local people.

Meanwhile Pharnabazus and Autophradates, after spending some 4 time in Chios, installed a garrison there and sent part of their fleet to Cos and Halicarnassus, while they themselves put out with the hundred fastest ships and sailed to Siphnos. There Agis, the king of Sparta, came to meet them in a single trireme: his purpose was to seek money for the war and to ask them for the largest possible force of ships and troops to take back with him to the Peloponnese. At this 5 point reports came in of the battle at Issus, and they were shattered by the news. Pharnabazus set out for Chios with twelve triremes and

fifteen hundred of the foreign mercenaries, fearful that news of the
6 defeat would spark a Chian revolt. Agis got thirty talents of silver and
ten triremes from Autophradates, and put Hippias in charge of conveying them to his brother Agesilaus at Taenarum: he was to tell
Agesilaus to pay the crews in full and sail as fast as possible to Crete
and organize matters there. He himself remained for the time being
in the islands, but later went to join Autophradates at Halicarnassus.
7   Alexander appointed Menon the son of Cerdimmas as satrap of
Hollow Syria,* leaving him the allied cavalry for the defence of
the area, while he himself went on to Phoenicia. On his way there he
was visited by Straton, who was the son of Gerostratus the king of
Aradus and the surrounding district (Gerostratus himself, like the
other Phoenician and Cypriot kings, was serving in the fleet with
8 Autophradates). When he met Alexander, Straton crowned him with
a golden crown and ceded to him the island of Aradus and the large
and prosperous city of Marathus situated on the mainland opposite,
together with Sigon and the city of Mariamme and all the other places
within their kingdom.
14   *While Alexander was still at Marathus envoys arrived from
Darius, bringing a letter from him which they were to supplement
with their own oral plea for the return of Darius' mother, wife, and
2 children. The gist of the letter was as follows:

There had been friendship and alliance between Philip and Artaxerxes;
then when Artaxerxes' son Arses succeeded to the throne Philip had
started an aggressive move against King Arses without the provocation
of any unpleasantness from the Persians. In Darius' own reign Alexander
had not sent anyone to him to confirm the old friendship and alliance,
but had crossed into Asia with an army and done considerable harm to
3 the Persians. That was why Darius had come down to defend his country and preserve his ancestral kingdom. The outcome of the battle
was as some god had willed it: but now as king to king he was asking for
the release of his captive wife and mother and children, and wished to
establish friendly relations with Alexander and become his ally; and to
this end he proposed that Alexander should send back to him with
Meniscus and Arsimas (these were the envoys who had come from
Persia) officers empowered to give and receive pledges in his name.

4   Alexander wrote a letter in reply and sent Thersippus back with

Darius' emissaries, telling him to deliver the letter to Darius and take no part in any discussion. Alexander's letter read as follows:

'Your ancestors invaded Macedonia and the rest of Greece* without provocation and did us harm. I have been appointed leader of the Greeks and crossed into Asia on a mission to punish Persia for what you had started. You gave help to the Perinthians when my father had 5 a legitimate grievance against them, and Ochus sent a force into Thrace, which was part of our kingdom. My father was killed by conspirators suborned by you, as you yourselves boasted in your letters to everyone; together with Bagoas* you murdered Arses, then seized the throne illegitimately, flouting Persian law and doing an injustice to the Persian people; you sent letters about me to the Greeks, to alienate them and provoke them to war against me; you 6 offered money to the Spartans and some other Greeks, which other cities refused and only Sparta accepted; people sent by you corrupted my friends and tried to subvert the peace which I had established in Greece. In view of all this I marched against you, but it is you who are responsible for this enmity. I have been victorious in battle first 7 against your generals and satraps, and now against you and your own forces: by the gods' gift I am master of your country, and those of your men who survived the battle and took refuge with me are now glad to be in my care and willingly serve in my army.

'It is for you, then, to come to me as lord over all Asia. If you fear 8 harm at my hands when you come, send some of your friends to bring you back my guarantees. And when you have come you can ask me for your mother and wife and children and anything else you wish, and you shall have them: whatever you persuade me to give shall be yours. And in future address any communications to me as the king of Asia, 9 and do not write as an equal, but tell me as the master of all your possessions what it is that you need. Failing this, I shall plan to treat you as a criminal. But if you wish to dispute the kingship, stand your ground and fight for it: do not run away, as I shall come after you wherever you are.'

This was Alexander's reply to Darius. When he heard of the suc- 15 cessful capture of the money which Darius had sent to Damascus with Cophen the son of Artabazus, and that the Persians left there to guard it had also been captured together with all the rest of the royal

apparatus, he told Parmenion to take it all back to Damascus and keep
2 it safe there. Hearing that the Greek envoys who had come to Darius
before the battle were also seized, he ordered them to be sent to him.
They were the Spartiate Euthycles, from Thebes Thessaliscus the
son of Ismenias and the Olympic victor Dionysodorus, and from
3 Athens Iphicrates the son of the general Iphicrates.* When they presented themselves to Alexander he immediately released Thessaliscus
and Dionysodorus, even though they were Thebans. Part of the reason
was that he felt some compassion for the fate of Thebes, and he also
took the view that their actions were understandable when their country had been enslaved by the Macedonians and they were looking for
any help they could find from Darius and the Persians both for them-
4 selves and, if possible, for their country too. These thoughts inclined
him to be generous to both of them, but privately he said that he was
releasing Thessaliscus out of regard for the distinction of his family
in Thebes, and Dionysodorus because of his victory in the Olympic
games. In warmth of feeling for Athens and remembrance of his
father's fame he kept Iphicrates in his retinue and showed him particular favour for as long as he lived, and when he died of disease
5 Alexander sent his bones back to his relatives in Athens. As for
Euthycles, considering that he was from Sparta, a city blatantly hostile to Alexander at the time, and could come up with no convincing
claim to personal indemnity, Alexander at first kept him under guard
(though not in chains), but subsequently released him too as his successes began to multiply.
6   Setting out from Marathus, Alexander took Byblus and Sidon:
Byblus agreed terms of surrender, and at Sidon he was actually
invited in by the inhabitants, who had reason to hate the Persians and
Darius. From there he proceeded towards Tyre, and on his way he
was met by envoys sent on behalf of the community of Tyre with the
city's decision that they would follow whatever orders Alexander
7 gave them. Alexander expressed his thanks to the city and its envoys
(among other Tyrian notables the embassy included the son of the
king of Tyre, Azemilcus—he himself was serving in the fleet with
Autophradates), and told the envoys to inform the Tyrians on their
return that he intended to visit their city and sacrifice to Heracles.
16   At Tyre there is the most ancient temple of Heracles known to
human memory. This is not the Argive Heracles,* the son of Alcmene.
A Heracles was worshipped in Tyre many generations before Cadmus

left Phoenicia and occupied Thebes, where his daughter Semele was
born, the mother of Dionysus by Zeus. So Dionysus would be the 2
third generation from Cadmus, the same as Labdacus, the son of
Cadmus' son Polydorus, and the Argive Heracles would most likely
belong to the era of Oedipus the son of Laïus.* The Egyptians worship yet another Heracles, distinct from the Heracles of Tyre or
Greece (Herodotus says that the Egyptians count Heracles among 3
the Twelve Gods), just as the Athenians worship a different Dionysus,
the son of Zeus and Kore. It is to this Dionysus, rather than the
Theban Dionysus, that the mystic Iacchus hymn is sung. The 4
Heracles worshipped by the Iberians at Tartessus (where there are
Pillars named after him) must, I think, be the Tyrian Heracles, as
Tartessus is a Phoenician foundation and both the style of the temple
to Heracles built there and the nature of the sacrifices offered are in
the Phoenician mode. And the historian Hecataeus says that there is 5
no connection between Iberia and the Geryones against whom the
Argive Heracles was sent by Eurystheus to drive off his cattle and
bring them to Mycenae: according to Hecataeus, Heracles was not
sent to some island called Erytheia in the Great Sea outside, but
Geryones was king of the mainland area around Ambracia and
Amphilochia, and this was the region from which Heracles drove off
the cattle—of itself no mean labour to undertake. I know for a fact 6
that to this day this part of the mainland affords excellent pasture and
rears very fine cattle, and I think it perfectly possible that the fame of
these Epirus cattle had reached Eurystheus, and with it Geryones'
name as king of Epirus: whereas with the Iberians right at the edge of
Europe it is hardly likely that Eurystheus would have known either
the name of their king or the quality of the cattle thereabouts (unless
you want to bring in Hera at this point and have her brief Heracles
through Eurystheus, which would be using myth to cloak implaus-
ibility).

This, then, was the Tyrian Heracles to whom Alexander said he 7
wanted to make sacrifice. When the envoys reported back to the city,
the Tyrians decided to follow any other orders Alexander might give
them, but not to allow any Persian or Macedonian into their city: they
thought that this put the most plausible gloss on their policy for the
present, and would be their safest course in view of the still uncertain
outcome of the war. When he received this response from Tyre, 8
Alexander angrily dismissed the envoys who brought it, then summoned

a meeting of his Companions and the army leaders, including the brigade and squadron commanders, and spoke to them as follows:

17   'Friends and allies, I see two threats to our security. An advance on Egypt is not safe as long as the Persians control the sea. And the pursuit of Darius is not safe either if we leave behind us ambiguity in Tyre itself with Egypt and Cyprus still held by the Persians. This has

2 particular relevance to the situation in Greece. The Persians could regain control of the seaboard if we have taken our full force on an offensive against Babylon and Darius: they could then augment their fleet and carry the war to Greece, where the Spartans are in open conflict with us and our hold on Athens is secured at present more by fear than sympathy. But with Tyre destroyed the whole of Phoenicia

3 would be in our hands, and the Phoenician navy, which forms the largest and the strongest part of the Persian fleet, would in all likelihood come over to us—when their cities are in our control the Phoenician rowers and marines will not want to put themselves at risk in the service of others. After this Cyprus will need little persua-

4 sion to side with us, or else will fall easy victim to a naval attack. With the Macedonian and Phoenician fleets in combined operation, and with Cyprus too brought on side, we would be assured of supremacy at sea, and that of itself clears the way for our expedition to Egypt. When we have subdued Egypt, we shall have no further worries for Greece or our own country, and we can then make our move on Babylon with security ensured at home, our reputation enhanced, and the Persians cut off from the entire sea and all the land this side of the Euphrates.'

18   This argument readily convinced his officers of the need to attack Tyre. Further strengthening of Alexander's purpose came in the form of an omen: in a dream* that very night he saw himself approaching the walls of Tyre, and Heracles greeting him and escorting him into the city. Aristander's interpretation of this dream was that Tyre would be captured, but there would be labour in it, just as Heracles' achievements involved him in labour. And in fact the siege of Tyre

2 was clearly a substantial undertaking. The city was an island, fortified by high walls on all sides: and at the time the Tyrians had some clear advantage by sea, as the Persians still dominated the sea and they themselves still had a good number of ships at their disposal.

3   Nevertheless Alexander's argument had prevailed, and he proposed to build a mole from the mainland to the city. The gap is a

narrow stretch of shoaly water, all shallow pools and mud flats at the edge of the mainland, but the crossing deepens to a maximum of about three fathoms close to the city itself. However, there was a plentiful supply of stone and wood: they laid the wood on top of the stones, and it was easy to drive stakes into the mud, which of itself bound the stones together and kept them stable. The Macedonians 4 set to the task with great enthusiasm, and so did Alexander: he was in the midst of it, personally directing every operation, inspiring the men with his encouragement, and offering financial rewards for exceptionally meritorious work. In the early stages close to the mainland the construction proceeded without difficulty—no great depth to fill, and no interference. But as they advanced into deeper water 5 and at the same time nearer the city, they came under punishing fire from the high walls, dressed as they were specifically for building-work rather than battle, and the Tyrians, still in command of the sea, kept sailing up to the mole at various points in their triremes, which in many places made further construction impossible. In response 6 the Macedonians set up two towers equipped with catapults at the end of the mole, which had now pushed out far into the sea. The towers were hung with screens of skins and hides to prevent hits by fire-arrows shot from the wall, and also to protect the workforce against regular arrows: any Tyrians sailing up to harass the men building the mole would easily be turned back by missiles fired from the towers.

The Tyrians devised their own counter-stratagem. They filled a 19 horse-transport with dry brushwood and other flammable timber, fixed two masts in the foreship, and fenced the deck round them as far and wide as they could, to hold as much wood-litter and as many firebrands as possible: they then added pitch, sulphur, and anything else which would create an enormous blaze. Across the two masts 2 they rigged a double yardarm and suspended from it cauldrons of material which, poured or scattered on the fuel below, would feed the flames to a great height: and they piled ballast into the stern to weigh down the back of the ship and lift its prow. They then waited for a 3 wind blowing towards the mole, and used triremes with ropes attached to the stern of the ship to tow it out by the rear. When they were getting close to the mole and the towers, they set fire to the wood and the triremes gave a violent tug which sent the ship crashing onto the end of the mole: it was now alight, but the men on it swam away without difficulty. Soon the blaze was huge and beginning to 4

engulf the towers: and as the yardarms broke they poured on the fire the material which had been prepared to feed the flames. The men in the triremes hove to close by the mole and kept up a barrage of bowshots at the towers, making it too dangerous for fire-fighting parties
5 to get their equipment anywhere near. At this stage, with the towers now burning out of control, large numbers of men ran out of the city, boarded light boats, and landed at various points along the mole, where they easily broke through the protecting palisade and burnt all the engines which the fire from the ship had not reached.

6 Alexander ordered the mole to be built wider all the way out from the mainland, to accommodate more towers, and told his engineers to construct new engines. While this work was in train, he himself took the foot guards and the Agrianians and set off for Sidon to assemble there all the triremes now at his disposal, as there seemed little prospect of a successful siege as long as the Tyrians controlled the sea.

20 It was now that Gerostratus the king of Aradus, and Enylus the king of Byblus, on receiving the news that their cities were in Alexander's hands, had deserted Autophradates and his fleet and brought their own navies to join Alexander, together with the triremes from Sidon:
2 so about eighty Phoenician ships had come over to his side. In these same days there arrived nine triremes from Rhodes together with the state trireme they called the Guardship, three from Soli and Mallus and ten from Lycia, and a penteconter* from Macedonia commanded
3 by Proteas the son of Andronicus. Not long afterwards the kings of Cyprus also came in to Sidon with some one hundred and twenty ships: they had heard of Darius' defeat at Issus, and it alarmed them that the whole of Phoenicia was now in Alexander's control. Alexander absolved all these kings of any blame for their past actions, taking the view that they had joined the Persian fleet out of necessity rather than by their own deliberate choice.

4 In the interval while his new engines were being constructed and his ships fitted out as a task force for a naval offensive, Alexander took some of the cavalry squadrons together with the foot guards, the Agrianians, and the archers and marched inland towards Arabia, to the
5 mountain called Antilibanus. In ten days he reduced the whole area by conquest or capitulation and returned to Sidon, where he found that Cleander* the son of Polemocrates had arrived from the Peloponnese bringing with him some four thousand Greek mercenaries.

When he had his fleet organized, he put aboard on the decks as 6
many of the foot guards as he thought he would need for the action,
if the battle became a matter of hand-to-hand fighting rather than
purely naval manoeuvres to break through the enemy's line. He then
put out from Sidon and sailed against Tyre with his ships in battle
formation. He himself was on the right wing (that is, the wing which
extended out to sea) together with the Cypriot and Phoenician kings
except Pnytagoras, who jointly with Craterus commanded the left
wing of the entire line.

The Tyrians had previously intended to offer battle if Alexander 7
attacked them by sea, but now the sight of Alexander's fleet changed
their minds. It was much larger than they had expected (not knowing
at the time that Alexander had with him all the Cypriot and Phoenician
ships), and it was approaching in full formation for attack. Shortly 8
before reaching the city, and still in the open sea, Alexander's ships
had hove to in the hope of drawing the Tyrians out to battle, but
when there was no response to their challenge they surged forward
in that same formation with a great crash of oars. Seeing all this,
the Tyrians declined battle at sea, but, to prevent the enemy fleet
finding anchorage in any of their harbours, they blocked the entrances
with as many triremes crammed side by side as the mouths would
hold.

So when the Tyrians refused battle Alexander sailed against the 9
city. He abandoned any thought of forcing the harbour which faced
Sidon when he saw the approach blocked by rows of triremes moored
with their prows outward, and in any case the mouth of the harbour
was too narrow. Even so, the three triremes anchored furthest out
from the harbour mouth were attacked and rammed head on by the
Phoenicians: the ships were sunk, but the crews could easily swim to
safety on a friendly shore. So for the time being Alexander's ships 10
moored along the shore not far from the artificial mole, where there
seemed some shelter from the winds. On the next day he ordered the
Cypriots to take their contingent of ships under Andromachus as
admiral and set up a blockade of the city at the harbour facing Sidon,
and the Phoenicians to do the same at the harbour facing Egypt on
the other side of the mole (which was where Alexander's own tent
was pitched).

Alexander had recruited teams of engineers from Cyprus and all 21
over Phoenicia, and by now a large number of siege-engines had been

constructed: some were standing on the mole, others mounted on the horse-transports he had brought with him from Sidon or on those of

2 the triremes which were not fully fit for service. With all now ready they moved the engines into position both down the artificial mole and on the ships, which anchored at intervals alongside the wall and began a trial bombardment.

3 As a platform for defensive action the Tyrians set up wooden towers on the battlements facing the mole, and elsewhere countered with missiles and flaming arrows shot directly at the ships wherever the siege-engines were brought up, to deter the Macedonians from com-

4 ing close to the wall. The walls opposite the mole were about a hundred and fifty feet high* and correspondingly thick, made out of large blocks of stone cemented together. A further problem making it difficult for the horse-transports and triremes bringing up the siege-engines to get close to the city was that the sea in front of the walls had been piled with boulders, which prohibited an assault at close range.

5 Alexander determined to drag these boulders out of the sea. This was difficult work, carried out as it was from ships rather than solid ground, and progress was yet slower because of the Tyrian counter-measures: they sent ships with protective coverings across the anchor-lines of the triremes and cut their ropes, so making it impossible for the enemy

6 ships to moor close to. Alexander equipped several thirty-oared boats with similar protection and placed them at an oblique angle in front of the triremes' anchors, to block the approach of the Tyrian ships. Even so, the ropes were still cut by divers swimming under water. The Macedonians now replaced the ropes with chains running down to the

7 anchors, which put an end to the activity of the divers. So now they could set about the mound of boulders, fastening loops of rope round them and winching them out of the sea: they were then lifted on the catapults and thrown into deep water, where they could be piled without causing further obstruction. Where the wall had been cleared of these obstacles, the ships now came up alongside with relative ease.

8 With all other strategies now failing, the Tyrians decided to make an attack on the Cypriot ships blockading the harbour facing Sidon. For some time in advance they kept a screen of sails rigged across the harbour mouth to conceal the manning of their triremes, and then made their move about midday, when the enemy sailors were dispersed for their usual requirements at that time and Alexander was most likely

9 to retire to his tent from the fleet on the other side of the city. They had

manned three quinqueremes, three quadriremes, and seven triremes with their most skilful crews and, to fight from the decks, a force of their best-equipped and bravest marines who had already proved their courage in battle at sea. At first they slid out in line ahead, rowing very quietly with feathered oars and no one calling the stroke: but when they began to turn towards the Cypriots and were nearly within sight, they suddenly came on in full cry, cheering one another on and rowing flat out.

On that day it so happened that although Alexander retired to his 22 tent he did not spend his usual time there, and shortly returned to the fleet. The unexpected Tyrian attack on the blockading ships had 2 caught some of them completely empty, while amid all the noise of the onslaught desperate attempts were made to crew the others with any available sailors. The Tyrians went straight in to ram, and in this one strike sank the quinqueremes of King Pnytagoras, Androcles of Amathus, and Pasicrates of Curium, drove the rest of the ships ashore, and set about disabling them.

When Alexander learnt of the attack by the Tyrian triremes he 3 ordered most of the ships in his own fleet to take up position at the harbour mouth as soon as each was manned, to prevent any Tyrian ships breaking out on that side too, while he himself took his complement of quinqueremes and the first five or so triremes to be quickly crewed, and sailed round the city to engage the Tyrian sally. The 4 Tyrians on the walls could see the impending attack, and Alexander himself on board the enemy squadron. They shouted to the men on their own ships to turn back, but their shouts were inaudible through the din of the engagement, and they then tried to recall them with a succession of other signals. When the Tyrian ships finally became aware of Alexander's onset they turned around and fled for the harbour. A few of them made it safely in time, but most were rammed by 5 Alexander's ships and some put out of action: a quinquereme and a quadrireme were captured right at the mouth of the harbour. Not many of the marines were killed, as it was easy enough for them to swim away into the harbour when they could see that their ships were caught.

Now that the Tyrians could make no further use of their ships, the 6 Macedonians began to deploy their siege-engines against the wall. The strength of the wall was such that the engines brought up along the mole achieved nothing of note, and there was no greater success

when they applied some of the ship-borne engines to the wall on the
7 Sidon side of the city. So Alexander turned to the south side and
made exploratory attacks along the whole length of the wall facing
Egypt. It was here that a large expanse of wall was first shaken loose,
and a part of it broke off and collapsed to the ground. At the time
Alexander pressed the attack only to the limited extent of placing
ramps over the broken part of the wall, and the Tyrians easily beat
back this Macedonian assault.

23   Two days later, after waiting for the wind to drop and briefing his
brigade commanders for the operation, Alexander brought up the ship-
mounted artillery against the city. First he bombarded a long stretch of
the wall, and when what seemed a sufficiently wide breach had been
2 made he ordered the ships with the siege-engines to withdraw and sent
in two others carrying the ramps which he intended to lower across
the breach in the wall. One of these ships was taken over by the foot
guards, with Admetus in command, and the other by Coenus' brigade of the so-called 'Close Companions':* Alexander himself was
with the foot guards and ready to mount the wall wherever it proved
3 practicable. He ordered some of his triremes to patrol each of the two
harbours, looking for the chance to force an entry while the Tyrians'
attention was focused on the scaling-party. Those equipped with
missile-firing catapults or carrying archers on deck were instructed to
circle round the wall and run ashore where possible, or, failing that,
to take up a position within missile range. Under fire from all directions the Tyrians would thus face danger wherever they turned.
4   As soon as those two ships with Alexander were close up against
the city and the ramps had been lowered from them across the wall,
the foot guards swarmed up the ramps and onto the wall, their enthusiasm fired by the courageous leadership of Admetus in this operation
and the fact that Alexander was there with them, taking a vigorous
part in the midst of the action and able to observe any conspicuous
5 bravery shown by others in the face of danger. And in fact the first
part of the wall to be captured was that where Alexander had placed
himself: it was not difficult for the Macedonians to drive the Tyrians
off the wall once they had a means of access which was firm and not
completely vertical. Admetus was the first up on the wall and was
calling on his men to climb up after him when a spear hit him and he
6 died where he was. Alexander then followed with his Companions and
took the wall. When he had established possession of several towers

and the curtain wall between them, he moved on through the battlements towards the king's palace, an area which offered an easier way down into the city.

As for the naval forces, the Phoenicians blockading the harbour 24 facing Egypt forced their way in, broke the booms, and set about mauling the ships in the harbour, ramming some in the open water and driving the others ashore. The other harbour, facing Sidon, did not even have a boom: here the Cypriots sailed straight in and immediately took that part of the city. The main body of the Tyrians aban- 2 doned the wall when they saw it in enemy hands, and massed at what is called the Shrine of Agenor,* where they turned to face the Macedonians. Alexander made for them with his foot guards, killed some of them in the immediate fighting, and went after the others as they fled. There was large-scale slaughter, now that the force invad- 3 ing the harbour had gained control of the city and Coenus' brigade had also made entry. The Macedonians stopped at nothing in their fury. They were angered by the wearisome length of the siege, and by the action of the Tyrians when they had captured some of their men sailing in from Sidon: they had paraded them on the wall in full view of the camp, then cut their throats and thrown them into the sea. The 4 Tyrian dead numbered some eight thousand. Macedonian losses in the final assault were Admetus, who distinguished himself as the first to gain the wall, and twenty foot guards with him: over the whole siege they lost about four hundred.

A number had taken refuge in the sanctuary of Heracles. These 5 were, from Tyre itself, the leading authorities of the city and their king Azemilcus, and also a delegation of Carthaginians* who had come in observance of a long-standing custom to pay honour to Heracles in their mother-city. All these were granted an amnesty by Alexander, but he enslaved the rest, and a total of about thirty thousand Tyrians and foreigners caught inside the city were sold into slavery. Alexander 6 made sacrifice to Heracles and in his honour staged a parade of his entire force under arms, with a naval review as well: and he held athletic competitions and a torch-race in the temple precincts. He dedicated to the temple the siege-engine which had broken through the wall, and also the Tyrian ship consecrated to Heracles which he had captured in the attack by sea. To this he added an inscription—either of his own composition or by some other hand—of no great merit (which is why I have not seen fit to record it).

Such was the capture of Tyre, in the month Hecatombaeon* of the year when Nicetes was archon at Athens [July/August 332 BC].

25 *While Alexander was still engaged in the siege of Tyre, envoys came to him from Darius proposing a settlement: Darius was prepared to give Alexander ten thousand talents in exchange for his mother, wife, and children; to cede to Alexander all the country between the river Euphrates and the Aegean Sea; and to establish friendship and

2 alliance by giving his daughter in marriage to Alexander. Alexander reported this proposal to the council of Companions, where it is said that Parmenion told him that if he were Alexander he would have been glad to stop the war on these terms and run no further risks: to which Alexander replied that so would he if he were Parmenion, but since he was Alexander his response to Darius would be that which

3 he proceeded to send. He told Darius that there was no point in offering him money, or just a part of the country, as all the money and all the country already belonged to him; if he chose to marry Darius' daughter he would marry her with or without his consent; and Darius must come to him in person if he wished to meet with any sympathetic treatment. When Darius received this reply, he abandoned all thoughts of any settlement with Alexander and prepared again for war.

4 *Alexander now turned his mind to the expedition to Egypt. Most of what is called Palestinian Syria had already come over to him, but there was resistance from a eunuch called Batis* who governed the city of Gaza. He had brought in a force of Arab mercenaries and for some time had been stockpiling enough food to withstand a long siege: confident that the place was impregnable, he determined not to admit Alexander into the city.

26 Gaza stands a little over two miles from the sea. The approach to it is over deep sand, and the sea fronting it offers nothing but shallows. Gaza was a large city, built on a high mound with a strong surrounding wall, and it was the last centre of population at the edge of the desert on the route from Phoenicia to Egypt.

2 When Alexander came up to the city, he made camp that first day on the side where he judged the wall most vulnerable, and ordered the construction of siege-engines. His engineers gave it as their opinion that the height of the base mound made a mechanical assault on

3 the wall impracticable. Alexander took the view that this very impracticality made it all the more important to capture the place: success

against the odds would have huge deterrent impact on his enemies, and his reputation would suffer if reports of failure reached the Greeks and Darius. So he decided to build a mound all round the city, piling it to a height which would enable the engines to be brought up level with the wall. Construction was concentrated at the south wall of the city, where there seemed the best prospect of a successful assault. When they judged that the mound had reached the appropri- 4 ate height, the Macedonians positioned siege-engines on it and brought them to bear against the wall of Gaza.

As this began, Alexander made sacrifice. He had put on a garland and was just about to perform the ritual dedication of the first victim when a carrion bird flew over the altar holding a stone in its talons and dropped the stone on Alexander's head. He asked Aristander the seer what this omen signified. Aristander answered: 'Sir, you will take the city: but today you must look out for yourself.'

Thus warned, for a while Alexander kept back by the engines, out 27 of range. But then there was a sally in force by the Arabs in the city, who were attempting to set light to the engines and, with constant fire from their superior position, while the Macedonians had to fight back from below, began driving them down the artificial mound. At this point Alexander either deliberately ignored the seer or forgot his warning in the heat of the emergency: at any rate he brought up the foot guards and went to the support of his men where they were under the greatest pressure. He did succeed in preventing the igno- 2 miny of a forced retreat down the mound, but was hit by a catapult-shot which went straight through his shield and breastplate into his shoulder. The realization that Aristander had been right about the wound encouraged him to think that, by the same token, he would go on to take the city.

In fact Alexander's wound did not heal easily. But meanwhile the 3 siege-engines used in the capture of Tyre arrived by sea (he had sent for them). He now ordered the construction of a ramp all the way round the city, four hundred yards deep and two hundred and fifty feet high.* When the engines had been reassembled and brought up 4 the ramp into action they demolished a large section of wall; at various other points tunnels were dug and the subsoil removed without detection, and this excavation caused subsidence and the collapse of the wall in several places; and the Macedonians kept up an overwhelming barrage of missiles over a wide front, driving back the

defenders on the towers. Through all this, despite losing large numbers killed or wounded, the forces in the city held out against three
5 successive attacks. But in the fourth assault Alexander brought up the Macedonian phalanx to ring the city on all sides, and broke down long stretches of the wall, some collapsed by undermining and others battered to pieces by his siege-engines: the result was to open a relatively easy route of attack by means of ladders placed over the rubble.
6 So the ladders were brought up to the wall, and there was intense rivalry for first claim to its capture among the Macedonians who prided themselves on their courage. The first to scale the wall was Neoptolemus, one of the Companions and a member of the Aeacid family: following his lead brigade after brigade climbed up with their
7 officers. Once some of the Macedonians had got inside the wall they split into groups and forced open every gate they came to, so giving access to the whole army. As for the Gazaeans, even though their city was now overrun by the enemy, they closed ranks and fought on: and they all died where they were, each man fighting at his post. Alexander sold their children and women into slavery, and repopulated the city from the surrounding area: it then served as a garrison town in his prosecution of the war.*

BOOK THREE

ALEXANDER now set out for Egypt, as had been his original inten- 1
tion, and reached Pelusium in Egypt after six days' march from
Gaza. His naval arm sailed along the coast from Phoenicia to Egypt,
and he found the ships waiting at anchor in Pelusium. As satrap of 2
Egypt Darius had appointed the Persian Mazaces. He had been informed of the outcome of the battle of Issus and Darius' ignominious
flight, and knew also that Alexander now controlled Phoenicia, Syria,
and most of Arabia: furthermore, he had no Persian troops under his
command. He therefore gave a friendly reception to Alexander, and
welcomed him* to the country and its cities.

Alexander installed a garrison in Pelusium, and instructed his 3
naval officers to sail up the river as far as the city of Memphis, while
he himself made for Heliopolis. This was a march through the desert
with the Nile on his right, in the course of which all the local inhabitants surrendered their territory to his control. Having reached 4
Heliopolis, he then crossed the river and came to Memphis, where he
made sacrifice to the gods, specifically including Apis,* and held
games with competitions in both athletics and the performing arts, in
which he secured the participation of the most celebrated practition-
ers from Greece.

From Memphis he sailed downriver towards the sea, taking with
him the foot guards, the archers, the Agrianians, and the royal squadron of the Companion cavalry. After reaching Canopus and making a 5
circuit of Lake Mareotis he went ashore where the city of Alexandria
now stands and is named after him. He thought the site ideal for the
founding of a city there with the potential to prosper. So he was
seized with a passion for this project, and took personal charge of
mapping his city on the ground—where its central square was to be
built, how many temples there should be and to which gods (some
Greek, but also the Egyptian Isis), where the surrounding wall should
run. He made sacrifice in hope of sanction for these plans, and the
omens proved favourable.

There is also told a story which goes like this, and I would not 2
discount it. Alexander, it is said, wanted to leave the builders an
outline of the fortification, but they had no means to hand of marking

the ground. One of the builders came up with the answer: he collected all the barley-meal the soldiers had with them in their mess-
tins and dribbled it on the ground along the line* indicated by the
king. This was how the circuit of the walls Alexander intended for his
2 city was marked out. The seers pondered the significance of this, chief
among them Aristander of Telmissus, who was credited with having
given Alexander accurate predictions on many other occasions: they
declared that the city would prosper, and there would be particular
prosperity from the produce of the earth.

3   *It was at this time too that Hegelochus arrived in Egypt by ship with
news for Alexander. His report was as follows. The people of Tenedos,
reluctant collaborators from the start, had revolted from the Persians
and come over to their side; the democratic party in Chios had invited
his forces into the city despite the ruling junta installed by Autophradates
4 and Pharnabazus; Pharnabazus had been caught there and held captive,
together with Aristonicus, the tyrant of Methymna, who had sailed into
the harbour of Chios with five pirate sloops, unaware that the harbour
was now in Macedonian control (the men in charge of the harbour
boom had duped him into thinking that it was Pharnabazus' fleet
5 anchored inside); his troops had cut down all the pirates there and then,
but he was bringing Aristonicus to Alexander, as well as Apollonides of
Chios, Phesinus, Megareus, and all the others who had been party to the
defection of Chios and were at the time enforcing their control over the
6 island. He reported also that he had taken possession of Mytilene from
Chares,* and brought over the other cities of Lesbos by agreement as
well; he had sent Amphoterus to Cos with sixty ships in response to a
direct appeal from the people of the island, and when he himself sailed
to Cos he found it already taken over by Amphoterus.

7   Hegelochus brought all the other captives with him, but Pharnabazus
had managed to escape his guards in Cos and disappeared. Alexander
sent the tyrants back to their own cities, for whatever treatment the
people might decide:* Apollonides and the Chians with him were
consigned under strict guard to the city of Elephantine in Egypt.

3   After this Alexander was taken with a yen to visit the shrine of
Ammon* in Libya. One reason was to consult the god, as the oracle
of Ammon was regarded as infallible, and was said to have been con-
sulted by Perseus and Heracles—Perseus when he was sent against
the Gorgon by Polydectes, and Heracles on his missions to confront
2 Antaeus in Libya and Busiris in Egypt. Alexander was keen to emulate

Perseus and Heracles,* as he was descended from both of them: but a further reason was that he himself was beginning to attribute part of his paternity to Ammon,* just as the legends have Zeus as a father of both Heracles and Perseus. However that may be, in setting out to visit Ammon Alexander's intention was to acquire more precise knowledge about himself—or at least to say that he had acquired it.

He took the coastal route as far as Paraetonium,* a distance of about 3 a hundred and eighty miles, according to Aristobulus, through country which was desert but not waterless. From there he turned into the interior, where the oracle of Ammon was situated: this leg of the journey is across a desert largely of sand, and with no water. Alexander, 4 though, met with a good deal of rain, and this was attributed to divine intervention. So were the events which I now recount. Whenever a south wind blows in that region it piles great drifts of sand over the track, obliterating the markers, so there is just a virtual sea of sand and no means of knowing which direction to take—nothing to mark the route, and no hill, tree, or solid outcrop anywhere which travellers could use to plot their course in the way that sailors navigate by the stars. The result was that Alexander's expedition lost its way, and the guides were uncertain of the route. Now Ptolemy the son of Lagus says 5 that two snakes went hissing in front of the army, and Alexander told his commanders to trust this divine sign and follow them: the snakes, Ptolemy says, led the way to the oracle* and back again also. But 6 Aristobulus (and this is the main and prevalent version) has two crows flying ahead of the army as Alexander's guides. I am confident enough that Alexander did have some form of divine assistance, as all probability inclines that way, but the precise truth of the matter is obscured by the conflicting accounts given by his historians.

The site of the temple of Ammon is surrounded by desert, nothing 4 but waterless sand. The central site is a small oasis (about four and a half miles across at its widest), full of cultivated trees, olives, and date-palms, and is the only part of that region which catches dew. And a spring rises there which is quite unlike the normal springs 2 issuing from the ground. At midday its water is cold to the taste and yet colder to the touch, in fact as cold as can be; as the sun declines towards evening it grows warmer, warmer still from evening to midnight, and reaches its warmest at midnight; from midnight on it cools correspondingly, is cold by dawn, and at its coldest at midday.

3 This sequence occurs regularly every day. Natural salt deposits are mined in the area, and some of this salt is taken by priests of Ammon to Egypt. On these missions to Egypt they pack the salt in baskets woven from palm leaves and take it as a gift for the king or some other

4 figure. The grain of the salt is large (sometimes more than three fingers wide), and transparent as crystal. This salt is preferred, as purer than sea salt, for sacrificial purposes by the Egyptians and others who take their religious observance seriously.

5 Once there, Alexander toured the site with keen interest, and put his questions to the god.* Having heard all the answers he had hoped for, he set out back to Egypt. Aristobulus says that he took the same route on his return journey, but Ptolemy the son of Lagus has him taking another route, direct to Memphis.*

5 At Memphis several embassies reached him from Greece, and none was sent away with their request disappointed. There also arrived a force of four hundred Greek mercenaries sent by Antipater, under the command of Menoetas the son of Hegesander, and some five hundred cavalry from Thrace, commanded by Asclepiodorus the

2 son of Eunicus. Then Alexander sacrificed to Zeus the King, put on a parade of his whole force under arms, and held games with competitions in both athletics and the performing arts.

*He now turned to the organization of Egypt. He appointed two Egyptians, Doloaspis and Petisis, as provincial governors of the country, dividing the whole of Egypt between them: when Petisis declined

3 the office, Doloaspis took over the entire responsibility. As garrison commanders he installed Companions: at Memphis Pantaleon of Pydna, and at Pelusium Polemon the son of Megacles, from Pella. In command of the mercenaries he placed Lycidas, an Aetolian, with Eugnostus the son of Xenophantes, one of the Companions, as the administrative officer for that department and Aeschylus and Ephippus

4 the son of Chalcideus as superintendents. He gave the governorship of the adjacent territory of Libya to Apollonius the son of Charinus, and that of Arabia round Heroönpolis to Cleomenes of Naucratis. Cleomenes was instructed to allow the district officers to administer their districts under the long-established system, but to take personal control of the tax levy: and they were ordered to pay it over to him.

5 As generals of the army which he was leaving in Egypt he appointed Peucestas* the son of Macartatus and Balacrus the son of Amyntas, and as admiral of the fleet Polemon the son of Theramenes. To replace

Arybbas as a Bodyguard (he had died of disease) he appointed
Leonnatus* the son of Anteas; the captain of the archers, Antiochus, 6
had also died, and to take his place in command of the archers
Alexander appointed Ombrion, a Cretan. He put the allied infantry
under the command of Calanus, as their previous commander,
Balacrus, was to stay behind in Egypt. It is said that his division of 7
authority in Egypt between several officers was in response to what
he recognized as the formidable natural defences of the country, so he
did not think it safe to entrust control of the whole of Egypt to one
man. I would say that the Romans learnt from Alexander the need to
keep a close watch on Egypt, and so to exclude any senator from the
post of Prefect of Egypt, confining it to the equestrian rank.

At the first sign of spring Alexander set out from Memphis for 6
Phoenicia (he had bridges made over the Nile at Memphis and over all
its canals). When he reached Tyre his fleet was already there waiting
for him. At Tyre he sacrificed once more to Heracles, and held games
with competitions in both athletics and the performing arts.*
He was visited there by the Athenian state ship *Paralus*, which arrived 2
from Athens bringing Diophantus and Achilles as envoys—
but the entire crew of the *Paralus* also played a part in this embassy.
They succeeded in all the aims of their mission, in particular securing
from Alexander the release of all the Athenians who had been captured at the Granicus. Alexander had received reports of a resistance 3
movement in the Peloponnese, and now sent Amphoterus to support
the Peloponnesians* who were still committed to the war against
Persia and had no truck with the Spartans. Instructions were also
given to the Phoenicians and Cypriots to dispatch a further hundred
ships to the Peloponnese in addition to those he was sending with
Amphoterus.

Alexander himself was now setting out towards Thapsacus and the 4
Euphrates. As financial officers to administer tax collection he had
appointed Coeranus of Beroea in charge of Phoenicia, and Philoxenus
in charge of Asia west of the Taurus mountains. In their place as
keeper of his own travelling exchequer he appointed Harpalus the son
of Machatas, who had recently returned from exile. Harpalus had first 5
been exiled when Philip was still king, because of his loyalty to
Alexander. This had also, and for the same reason, been the fate of
Ptolemy the son of Lagus, Nearchus the son of Androtimus, Erigyius
the son of Larichus, and his brother Laomedon: they all went into

exile* when suspicion developed between Alexander and Philip after Philip married Eurydice and rejected Alexander's mother Olympias.

6 On Philip's death Alexander restored those who had been exiled on his account and gave them positions: he appointed Ptolemy as a Bodyguard, Harpalus to the treasury (as his physical disability made him unfit for service in war), Erigyius as commander of the allied cavalry, his brother Laomedon (who was bilingual, and could speak their language) as administrator in charge of the barbarian captives, and Nearchus as satrap of Lycia and the adjoining territory as far as

7 the Taurus mountains. Shortly before the battle of Issus Harpalus came under the malign influence of a man called Tauriscus and was induced to desert with him. Tauriscus made his way to join Alexander of Epirus* in Italy, and died there: Harpalus* took his refuge in the Megarid. However, Alexander persuaded him to return, with assurances that he would not be penalized for his desertion: nor indeed was

8 he when he did return—he was reappointed to the treasury. Alexander sent out Menander, one of the Companions, to Lydia as satrap, and appointed Cleander in his place to command the mercenaries. In place of Arimmas he made Asclepiodorus the son of Eunicus satrap of Syria, as he thought that Arimmas had been slack in the preparations required of him for the army's march into the interior.

7   *Alexander reached Thapsacus in the month Hecatombaeon of the year when Aristophanes was archon at Athens [July/August 331 BC]. There he found two bridges already spanning the river. What had happened was that Mazaeus, charged by Darius with the defence of the Euphrates, had for some time kept guard right by the river's edge with his force of three thousand cavalry and the same number of

2 infantry (of which two thousand were Greek mercenaries), and this had prevented the Macedonians from continuing the span of their bridge all the way to the opposite bank, for fear that Mazaeus' troops would attack that end of the bridge: but when Mazaeus heard of Alexander's imminent approach, he withdrew his entire force and was quickly gone. As soon as Mazaeus had decamped, the two bridges were carried over to the far bank and Alexander crossed over them with his army.

3   From there he marched on inland through the region called Mesopotamia, keeping the Euphrates and the mountains of Armenia on his left. He did not take a straight line from the Euphrates towards Babylon, as this alternative route was altogether easier on

the army—green fodder for the horses, food supplies from the country traversed, and not the same burning heat. Along the way some of *4*
the scouts sent out from Darius' army in various directions were captured: they reported that Darius was encamped by the river Tigris,
determined to prevent any attempted crossing by Alexander, and
that he had with him a much larger army than that with which he had
fought in Cilicia. Hearing this, Alexander made for the Tigris at full *5*
speed. Once there, he found no trace of Darius himself nor of the
guard he had left there. So he crossed the river. The speed of the current created difficulties, but there was no opposition.

He then rested his army. There was an almost total eclipse of the *6*
moon, and Alexander made sacrifice to the Moon, the Sun, and the
Earth, who are generally thought to cause eclipses. Aristander gave it
as his opinion that the change in the moon was favourable to the
Macedonians and Alexander, that the battle would take place during
that month, and that the sacrifices indicated a victory for Alexander.
Setting out from the Tigris, Alexander moved on through the coun- *7*
try of Assyria, with the Gordyenian mountains on his left and the
Tigris on his right. On the fourth day out from where he crossed the
river his scouts brought him reports that some enemy cavalry could
be seen in the plain, but they could not estimate their numbers. So
Alexander formed up his army and advanced as for battle: then other
scouts who had taken a closer view rode in and told him that as far as
they could tell the cavalry numbered no more than a thousand.

At this Alexander took with him the royal squadron, one squadron *8*
of the Companions, and the Paeonian contingent of the light cavalry,
and rode on at speed, telling the rest of the army to follow at the
march. When the Persian cavalry caught sight of Alexander's troop
closing rapidly on them, they set off in urgent flight. Alexander
pressed his pursuit, and though most of them got away some whose *2*
horses tired in the flight were killed, and others were taken alive together
with their mounts. From these it was learnt that Darius was not far off
with a large army.

*Darius' forces had been augmented by the support of the Indians *3*
who bordered the Bactrians, as well as the Bactrians themselves and
the Sogdians: all these were under the command of Bessus,* the satrap
of Bactria. Together with them came the Sacae, who are a Scythian
people, one of the tribes of Scythian race inhabiting Asia. They were
not subjects of Bessus, but came under the terms of their military

alliance with Darius: they were mounted archers, and their leader was
4 Mauaces. Barsaentes the satrap of Arachosia led both the Arachosians
and the so-called Mountain Indians; the Areians were led by the
satrap of Areia, Satibarzanes; Phrataphernes led the Parthyaeans,
Hyrcanians, and Topeirians, all of these cavalry; the Medes were
under the command of Atropates, and brigaded with the Medes were
5 the Cadusians, Albanians, and Sacesinians; the tribes bordering the
Red Sea were commanded by Orontobates, Ariobarzanes, and
Orxines; the Uxians and Susians had Oxathres the son of Abulites as
their leader; Bupares commanded the Babylonians, and the transplanted Carians and the Sittacenians were brigaded with the
Babylonians; the Armenians were led by Orontes and Mithraustes,
6 and the Cappadocians by Ariaces; the Syrians of both Hollow and
Mesopotamian Syria were commanded by Mazaeus. Darius' total
force was said to number up to forty thousand cavalry and one mil-
lion infantry. He also had two hundred scythe-chariots, and a few
elephants (about fifteen were brought by the Indians living this side
of the Indus).

7   With this force Darius had encamped at Gaugamela* by the river
Bumelus, about sixty-five miles from the city of Arbela. His position
was in an extensive stretch of flat ground: the Persians had in fact for
some time been busy levelling any areas too uneven for horses, to create freedom throughout for the deployment of chariots and cavalry.
Some had been suggesting to Darius that in the battle of Issus his real
disadvantage had been simply the confines of the theatre of operations, and Darius needed little persuasion to go along with this.

9   On receipt of this information from the captured Persian scouts,
Alexander halted where he was when the reports reached him and
stayed there for four days, resting his army after their march, and
fortifying the camp with a ditch and palisade: he had decided to leave
the baggage-train and the invalid soldiers in the camp, and to lead the
advance to battle with his combatant troops taking nothing with them
2 except their arms. So he gathered his force at night and led them out
at about the second watch, to engage the barbarians at dawn. On
hearing reports that Alexander's advance had started, Darius drew
up his army for battle: and Alexander was also bringing on his troops
in battle-order. The armies were now about six and a half miles apart,
but not yet in visual contact, as there were hills intervening between
them.

Alexander sighted the barbarians when he was about three and *3*
a quarter miles away and his army was now descending these hills.
He stopped his phalanx there, and called another conference of the
Companions, his generals and squadron commanders, and the leaders of the allied and mercenary troops, to discuss with them whether
he should lead the phalanx straight into battle there and then (as most
of them recommended) or follow Parmenion's advice: this was to *4*
camp where they were for the time being, and make a thorough survey of the whole terrain, to identify any questionable or impassable
areas and discover if there were trenches anywhere or hidden spikes
fixed in the ground, and also to gain a more precise view of the disposition of the enemy forces. Parmenion's opinion prevailed, and they
camped there with the site arranged in the intended order of battle.

Alexander took his light-armed troops and the Companion cavalry *5*
and made a tour of inspection round the whole area where the action
he planned would take place. On his return he reconvened the same
officers and told them that they had no need from him of encouragement for the fight: they had long been sufficiently encouraged by their
own bravery and the many successes they had already achieved. But *6*
he asked them all to fire up their own men—every company commander his own company, every cavalry leader his own squadron, the
brigade commanders their brigades, and the infantry leaders the
phalanx under their own command. They should tell their men that
in this battle they would not be fighting simply for Hollow Syria, for
Phoenicia, or for Egypt, as before, but at issue this time was who
should rule the whole of Asia. There was no need for them to spend *7*
many words inspiring the men to their honourable duty, when that
was already inherent in their nature: they should rather emphasize
the importance of individual discipline in the action, of strict silence
when that was the order of advance, and then again of giving voice to
a resounding shout at the appropriate moments, and, when the time
came for it, an utterly terrifying war-cry. The officers themselves *8*
should make sure they were quick to respond to the orders given, and
pass them on quickly to their units. They should all remember that
the whole outcome depended on individual performance—duty
neglected meant danger for all: constant attention to duty was a share
in success.*

In response to this address and a few more words of similar encour- *10*
agement his officers assured Alexander that he could rely on them.

So he gave orders for the army to take their dinner and rest. It is said that Parmenion came to his tent and advised him to attack the Persians at night: a night attack, he argued, would catch them unprepared and

2 disorganized, and also more likely to panic. Alexander's reply (others were listening to the conversation) was that a stolen victory was demeaning: Alexander's victories must be won in open fight without trickery.* This example of his grand manner probably reflected confidence in the face of danger rather than arrogance: and I am inclined to think that he had also made a careful assessment on something

3 like the following basis. Irrespective of an army's state of preparation—primed for battle or not—night actions have often confounded logic and foiled the stronger side, handing victory to the weaker, quite contrary to the expectations of both. Alexander was used to taking risks in his battles, but he could see that night was treacherous. Moreover, if Darius were again defeated, their stealthy attack by night would excuse him from conceding that he was an inferior leader

4 of inferior troops: whereas if the Macedonians suffered some unforeseeable reverse, they were deep into country friendly to the enemy and familiar to them, while they themselves had no local knowledge and were surrounded by enemies, not least their prisoners of war, who would join a night attack on them if they did not secure a clear and overwhelming victory—let alone if they lost. For these strategic considerations, as much as his apparent display of arrogance, I can only applaud Alexander.

11 Darius and his army remained throughout the night in their original formation and full battle-order, as they had no proper camp

2 perimeter and were also afraid of a night attack by the enemy. If there was one factor which particularly weakened the Persian position at this stage, it was this—that they were stood for so long under arms, and the fear naturally generated by the prospect of danger did not come in one immediate and automatic rush, but occupied their thoughts over a long period until it dominated their minds.

3 Darius' army was arranged as follows (Aristobulus reports that a document detailing Darius' order of battle was subsequently captured). His left wing was held by the Bactrian cavalry together with the Dahae and Arachosians; next to them were Persian contingents, mixed cavalry and infantry; then the Susians next to the Persians,

4 and the Cadusians next to the Susians. This was the line of the left wing as far as the centre of the entire phalanx. Placed on the right

wing were the troops from Hollow Syria and Mesopotamia, and further to the right the Medes; then in sequence the Parthyaeans and Sacae, the Topeirians and Hyrcanians, and the Albanians and Sacesinians, all these filling the line up to the centre of the entire phalanx. In the centre with King Darius were stationed the King's 5 Kinsmen, the Persian palace guard (who had golden apples for their spear-butts), the Indians, the transplanted Carians (as they are called), and the Mardian archers. The Uxians, Babylonians, Red Sea peoples, and Sittacenians were drawn up behind in depth. In advance 6 of the left wing, facing Alexander's right, were posted the Scythian cavalry, about a thousand Bactrians, and a hundred scythe-chariots. The elephants were positioned, together with fifty chariots, in front of Darius' royal squadron. In advance of the right wing were posted 7 the Armenian and Cappadocian cavalry with fifty scythe-chariots. The Greek mercenaries were drawn up either side of Darius and his attendant Persians directly opposite the Macedonian phalanx, as the only troops capable of matching it.

The disposition of Alexander's army was as follows. His right wing 8 was held by the Companion cavalry, with the royal squadron, led by Cleitus the son of Dropidas, in front: next to that was Glaucias' squadron, and then, in this order, the squadrons of Ariston, Sopolis the son of Hermodorus, Heracleides the son of Antiochus, Demetrius the son of Althaemenes, Meleager, and finally the squadron led by Hegelochus the son of Hippostratus. In overall command of the Companion cavalry was Philotas the son of Parmenion. The first unit of the Macedonian infan- 9 try phalanx, stationed next to the cavalry, was the royal guard of the foot guards, and then the rest of the foot guards, commanded by Nicanor the son of Parmenion; next to them, in successive order, came the brigades of Coenus the son of Polemocrates, Perdiccas the son of Orontes, Meleager the son of Neoptolemus, Polyperchon the son of Simmias, and Amyntas the son of Philip (this brigade was led by Simmias, as Amyntas had been sent to Macedonia to levy troops). The far left of the 10 Macedonian phalanx was held by the brigade of Craterus the son of Alexander, who was also the overall commander of the left wing of the infantry. Next to them were the allied cavalry, commanded by Erigyius the son of Larichus; then the Thessalian cavalry on the far left wing, led by Philip the son of Menelaus. In command of the whole of the left was Parmenion the son of Philotas, stationed with the Pharsalians, who formed the best and largest contingent of cavalry from Thessaly.

12 Such was Alexander's arrangement of his front line: but he also set a second line, so that his phalanx could face both ways. The commanders of this rearguard had orders to about-turn and engage the barbarians if they saw the Persian army encircling their own front
2 line. At an oblique angle, to cover any need to extend or close up the phalanx, were placed on the right wing, next to the royal squadron, half of the Agrianians, led by Attalus, together with the Macedonian archers under the command of Brison, and next to the archers the
3 so-called 'old' mercenaries with their commander Cleander. In front of the Agrianians and the archers there were contingents of cavalry—the light cavalry and the Paeonians—commanded by Aretes and Ariston, and in front of all these were stationed the mercenary cavalry under Menidas. Positioned in front of the royal squadron and the rest of the Companions, and opposite the scythe-chariots, were half of the
4 Agrianians and the archers, together with Balacrus' javelin-men. If the enemy cavalry tried to encircle the Macedonian wing, Menidas and his men had instructions to charge them in the flank once they had wheeled for the encircling manoeuvre.

Such were Alexander's dispositions on the right wing. At an angle on the left he had posted the Thracians under Sitalces, and next to them the allied cavalry commanded by Coeranus, and then the Odrysian
5 cavalry under the command of Agathon* the son of Tyrimmas. At the front of the whole oblique array on this side were placed the foreign mercenary cavalry commanded by Andromachus the son of Hieron. The Thracian infantry were detailed to guard the baggage-train.

The total strength of Alexander's army amounted to some seven thousand cavalry and about forty thousand infantry.

13 As the armies neared each other, it could be seen that Darius and the troops in his immediate area (the 'Golden Apple' Persians, the Indians, Albanians, and transplanted Carians, and the Mardian archers) were positioned to be directly opposite Alexander himself and the royal squadron. Alexander kept his own unit moving more to the right, and the Persians shifted correspondingly, far outflanking
2 Alexander with their left. The Scythian cavalry were by now riding across Alexander's line and engaging his advance units, but Alexander still continued his move to the right, and was close to getting clear of the ground which the Persians had levelled. At this point Darius, fearing that his chariots would be useless if the Macedonians went on to reach uneven ground, ordered the units posted ahead of his left

wing to ride round the Macedonian right, where Alexander was making this move, to prevent any further extension of that wing to the
right. In response to this Alexander ordered the mercenary cavalry 3
under Menidas to charge them. The Scythian cavalry and the
Bactrian squadrons posted with them launched a counter-charge
which, with far superior numbers, forced back Menidas' small contingent. Alexander now ordered the light cavalry under Aretes and
the Paeonians to join the mercenaries in a concerted charge on the
Scythians, and the barbarians began to give way. But the rest of the 4
Bactrians came up to confront the Paeonians and the mercenaries,
turned back into the fight those of their own men who were now trying to escape it, and brought about an intense cavalry battle. There
were more casualties on Alexander's side, because of the sheer pressure of the barbarian numbers and the fact that the Scythians and
their horses had more complete protective armour. Yet even so the
Macedonians stood up to their attacks, and, with squadron after
squadron laying into the enemy, gradually broke their formation.

Meanwhile the barbarians had launched their scythe-chariots 5
directly at Alexander, hoping to disrupt his phalanx. In this they
failed utterly. As soon as they were on their way they came under fire
from the Agrianians and the javelin-men under Balacrus who had
been posted in front of the Companion cavalry: the Agrianians
and Balacrus' men then grabbed the reins, pulled out the drivers, and
crowded round to slaughter the horses. Some chariots did pass 6
straight through the Macedonian lines, where the ranks moved apart,
as they had been ordered, to create a gap at the point of impact: the
result was that for the most part the chariots drove through unmo-
lested but also inflicting no harm on the objects of their attack. And
in fact these chariots too came to grief, captured by Alexander's army
grooms and the royal shield-bearers.

Darius was already advancing his entire phalanx when Alexander 14
ordered Aretes to charge the Persian cavalry attempting to ride round
his right wing and encircle it. For a while he himself continued the 2
oblique advance in column, but when the cavalry sent out to engage
the Persians encircling the right wing had forced a break in the
front line of the barbarian phalanx he wheeled for the gap, formed a
wedge of the Companion cavalry and the immediately adjacent infantry section, and led them on at full speed and in full cry straight for
Darius. For a short time it was hand-to-hand fighting: but when the 3

cavalry with Alexander and Alexander himself brought concerted pressure to bear, shoving with their horses and stabbing their lances at the Persians' faces, followed soon by the onslaught of a solid Macedonian phalanx bristling with pikes, the already fearful Darius could only see danger multiplied all round, and he was the first to turn and run. The Persian cavalry attempting to outflank the Macedonian wing were also thrown into panic by the vigorous counter-attack of the squadron under Aretes.

4   So in this part of the field there was a comprehensive rout of the Persians, and the Macedonians began following up and slaughtering the troops in flight. But Simmias and his brigade had to abandon any move to join Alexander in the pursuit, and were obliged to halt their phalanx and fight on where they were, as reports were coming in that

5   the Macedonian left was in difficulties. The line on this side had been broken, and some Indian and Persian cavalry punched through the gap and carried on all the way to the Macedonians' baggage-train, where a serious action developed. The Persians pressed their attack with confidence, as most of the men there were unarmed and had never imagined that an enemy force could cut through the double phalanx lines and get that far to threaten them: and what is more, when the Persians broke in, the barbarian prisoners of war joined the

6   action with their own attack on the Macedonians. However, the commanders of the reserve line behind the front phalanx quickly gathered what was happening, turned their division about face, as were their standing orders, and came up at the Persians' rear. Many of the Persians were killed where they were caught crowded among the baggage-animals, but some broke away and escaped.

The Persians on the right wing had not yet learnt that Darius had fled. They rode round Alexander's left wing and began a flanking attack on the troops under Parmenion.

15   At this point, with the Macedonians now under pressure from two sides, Parmenion sent a dispatch-rider at speed to Alexander, to report that his men were struggling and needed help.* On receipt of this message Alexander abandoned further pursuit and turned back with the Companion cavalry, making for the barbarians' right wing at the gallop. He first had to engage the fleeing enemy cavalry: these were the Parthyaeans, some of the Indians, and the largest and best

2   section of the Persian cavalry. What ensued was the fiercest cavalry battle of the whole action. The barbarians rallied, resuming the deep

formation of individual squadrons, and hurled themselves head on at
Alexander's troops. They had no use now for the usual cavalry tactics—no throwing of javelins, no manoeuvring of horses—but it was
each man for himself, trying to force his own way through as the only
means of survival: they were not fighting now for someone else's
victory, but for their very own lives, trading blows with reckless abandon. In this engagement about sixty of Alexander's Companion cavalry were killed, and Hephaestion himself, Coenus, and Menidas were
wounded. Nevertheless, here too Alexander came out victorious.

Such Persians as had managed to force through Alexander's troops *3*
set off in headlong flight, and Alexander was now in a position to
engage the enemy right wing. In the meantime the Thessalian cavalry
had put up a brilliant fight which matched Alexander's own success
in the action, and in fact the barbarians on this wing were already in
flight when Alexander came up to engage them. So Alexander turned
back and set out once more in pursuit of Darius, keeping it up for as
long as there was light: and Parmenion's troops followed, pursuing *4*
the enemy on their wing. When Alexander had crossed the river
Lycus [Great Zab] he camped there, to give his men and horses a
short rest, while Parmenion captured the barbarians' base camp,
together with the baggage-train, the elephants, and the camels.

Alexander rested his cavalry till midnight, then pressed on again at *5*
speed for Arbela, where he hoped to capture Darius as well as his
treasure and the rest of the royal apparatus. He arrived at Arbela on
the following day, having covered in his pursuit a total of about sixty-
five miles from the battlefield. He did not find Darius in Arbela (he
was continuing his flight without any pause), but Darius' treasure
and all his other apparatus were captured there, together with his
chariot and shield (both for the second time) and his bow.

On Alexander's side the losses were about a hundred men, and *6*
over a thousand horses dead of wounds or exhaustion in the pursuit
(almost half of which belonged to the Companion cavalry). The
barbarian dead were said to number some three hundred thousand,
but many more were captured than killed: captured too were the
elephants and all the chariots which survived the battle intact.

So ended this battle, in the month Pyanepsion* of the year when *7*
Aristophanes was archon at Athens. And Aristander was proved right
in his prophecy that Alexander would fight and win his battle in the
same month which saw the eclipse of the moon.

16   Immediately after the battle Darius set out to skirt the Armenian
mountains and make for Media. He had with him the Bactrian cavalry (as they had been posted close by him in that day's battle-order),
and was also accompanied by a retinue of Persians, the King's
2 Kinsmen, and a few of the 'Golden Apple' guards. In the course of
his flight he was joined by some two thousand of the foreign mercenaries, led by Patron of Phocis and Glaucus of Aetolia. His reason for
making his escape towards Media was the expectation that after the
battle Alexander would take the road to Susa and Babylon, as the
whole of this route was through inhabited country, and easy going for
the baggage-trains: and in any case Babylon and Susa stood as the
clear prizes of the war. The route to Media, on the other hand, was
not easy for a large army.
3   Darius was not wrong. On leaving Arbela Alexander immediately
advanced along the road to Babylon. He was not far from Babylon,
and now leading on his force in full battle-order, when the Babylonians
came out to meet him en masse, with their priests and magistrates,
bringing gifts from every section of the community and offering
4 to surrender their city, the citadel, and the treasury. Alexander
entered Babylon. There he directed the Babylonians to rebuild the
temples destroyed by Xerxes,* and in particular the temple of Bel, the
god whom the Babylonians worship above all others. He appointed
Mazaeus satrap* of Babylon, Apollodorus from Amphipolis general
in command of the troops to be left behind with Mazaeus, and
5 Asclepiodorus the son of Philon in charge of tax collection. He also
sent Mithrenes as satrap to Armenia (it was Mithrenes who had surrendered the acropolis of Sardis to Alexander). While at Babylon he
also met the Chaldaeans* and followed their advice in the matter of
the Babylonian temples, including a sacrifice to Bel according to their
prescription.
6   He himself now set out for Susa. On his way there he was met by
the son of the satrap of Susa together with a dispatch-rider from
Philoxenus.* Alexander had sent Philoxenus to Susa immediately
after the battle, and the contents of his written dispatch were that the
Susians had handed over their city, and that all the treasure was being
7 held in safe keeping for Alexander. Alexander reached Susa from
Babylon in twenty days.* On entering the city he took possession of
the treasure (some fifty thousand talents of silver) and all the rest of
the royal apparatus. Much else was found there and appropriated—all

that Xerxes had brought back with him from Greece, including bronze
statues of Harmodius and Aristogeiton.* These statues Alexander 8
sent back to Athens, and they stand there now in the Cerameicus, on
the route we take up to the Acropolis, roughly opposite the Metroön
and not far from the altar of the Eudanemoi (initiates of the two goddesses at Eleusis will know that the Eudanemos altar stands on the
Pavement).

At Susa Alexander made sacrifice in the way prescribed by ances- 9
tral custom, and held a torch-race and athletic competition. With
appointments made before he left—Abulites, a Persian, as satrap of
Susiana; Mazarus, one of the Companions, as garrison commander in
the citadel of Susa; Archelaus the son of Theodorus as general—he
then moved on towards Persis. *He sent Menes down to the coast as
governor of Syria, Phoenicia, and Cilicia, with some three thousand 10
talents of silver to take with him to the sea, from which he was to send
over to Antipater whatever he needed for the Spartan war. At Susa
too he was joined by Amyntas the son of Andromenes with the reinforcements he was bringing from Macedonia. The cavalrymen in this 11
new contingent were assigned by Alexander to the Companion cavalry, and the infantry were attached to the other brigades according
to their regional affiliation. Alexander also formed two companies in
each cavalry squadron (there had not previously been this subdivi-
sion in the cavalry), and appointed the company commanders from
the Companions who had given distinguished service in the field.

*Alexander set out from Susa and, after crossing the river Pasitigris 17
[Karun], invaded the country of the Uxians. The Uxians living in the
plains had been subject to the Persian satrap, and now surrendered to
Alexander: but the highland Uxians (as they are called) were not
Persian subjects, and they now sent envoys to Alexander saying that
they would only allow him to take his army through on the route to
Persis if they received from him the same toll which the King of
Persia used to pay them for his transit. Alexander sent them away, 2
telling them to meet him at the pass which they thought gave them
control over access to Persis, where he too would give them their
dues. He then took the royal bodyguard corps, the foot guards, and
eight thousand from the rest of the army, and marched by night, following, with Susian guides, a different way from the obvious route.
Having completed the whole of a rough and difficult journey in one 3
day, he fell on the Uxian villages, taking a great deal of booty and killing

many of them still in their beds: the survivors fled to the hills. He
pressed on at all speed to the pass, where it was expected that the
4 Uxians would gather in force to meet him and receive their dues. He
sent Craterus yet further forward, to seize the heights to which he
thought the Uxians would retreat when they came under pressure.
His own advance was so rapid that he reached and occupied the pass
before the Uxians could get there, and then from a superior position
5 he led his men in full battle-order against the barbarians. Astonished
by the speed of Alexander's operation, and disadvantaged now by the
very terrain which had been the key to their confidence, they turned
to flight without even attempting an engagement. Some of them were
killed by Alexander's troops as they fled, and many fell to their death
from the precipitous path. The majority made their escape into the
mountains, only to come up against Craterus' forces and die at their
6 hands. These then were the 'rightful dues' they received from
Alexander, and they had a hard time of it persuading him to accept
their plea to retain possession of their own country in return for the
annual payment of tribute. Ptolemy the son of Lagus says that Darius'
mother interceded on their behalf and begged Alexander to let them
live on in their country. The tribute imposed was a hundred horses
each year, five hundred draught animals, and thirty thousand sheep
or goats: this was because the Uxians were mainly herdsmen, and had
no coined money or arable land.

18   After this, Alexander gave Parmenion charge of the baggage-train, the
Thessalian cavalry, the allies, the foreign mercenaries, and all the heavier-armed units in the army, and sent them under his command to make
2 their way to Persepolis by the carriage road* which led there. He himself
took the Macedonian infantry, the Companion cavalry, the light cavalry,
the Agrianians, and the archers, and went by the mountain route at
speed. When he reached the Persian Gates,* he found them occupied
by Ariobarzanes, the satrap of Persis, with a force of some forty thousand
infantry and seven hundred cavalry: he had walled off the Gates, and
was camped there close behind the wall to deny Alexander passage.
3   For the moment Alexander stayed where he was and made camp:
but on the next day he formed up his army and led them in an assault
on the wall. When it became clear that the adverse terrain made it
impossible to take the wall, and his men were coming under constant
lethal fire from an enemy positioned high above them and equipped
with artillery, Alexander fell back on his camp for the time being.

Some of his prisoners of war now volunteered to show him another 4
route which would take him round behind the Gates. Enquiry
revealed that this was a rough and narrow path, so he left Craterus
there in charge of the camp with his own brigade and Meleager's, a few
of the archers, and some five hundred cavalry, and gave him instruc- 5
tions to attack the wall as soon as he learnt that Alexander had got all
the way round and was coming up close to the Persian camp (he would
know this easily enough from the signal given by the trumpets).

Alexander himself set out along this path at night. After covering
about eleven miles he divided his forces. For his own section he took
the foot guards, together with Perdiccas' brigade, the lightest-armed
of the archers, the Agrianians, the royal squadron of the Companion
cavalry, and one of the four-company cavalry units as well: with these
he turned to take the path leading back to the Gates, where the prisoners showed him the way. He told Amyntas, Philotas, and Coenus 6
to lead the rest of the army down into the plain, and to bridge the
river which he needed to cross on the route to Persepolis. He himself
struck out along what was a rough and difficult track, taking most of
it at speed. He fell on the first of the barbarians' outposts before light,
and annihilated it; most in the second outpost were also killed; in the 7
third the majority of the guards escaped, but even they did not run
for Ariobarzanes' camp, but fled in panic straight into the mountains
just as they were. So there had been no warning when Alexander
attacked the enemy camp towards dawn. At the very moment of his
assault on the perimeter ditch the trumpets sounded their message to
Craterus and his troops, and Craterus led them against the wall.
Caught between fire on all sides, the enemy never even came to blows, 8
and ran for escape. But they were corralled from both directions—Alexander threatening on one side, Craterus' troops rapidly
closing for attack on the other—and most of them were forced to
turn back to seek refuge in the walls: by this time, though, the walls
too were already in Macedonian hands. Alexander had accurately 9
guessed what did in fact happen, and had left Ptolemy* behind with
some three thousand of the infantry: the result was that most of the
barbarians attempting to flee were cut down at close quarters by the
Macedonians, while others, as flight turned to panic, threw themselves
to their death over the precipices. Ariobarzanes himself escaped with
a few cavalrymen into the mountains.

*Alexander marched on again at speed to the river, where he found 10

its bridge already constructed and took his army across without difficulty. He made full speed again from there to Persepolis, which enabled
him to arrive before the garrison had plundered the treasury. He also
captured the treasure held in the vaults at Pasargadae* from the time
11 of Cyrus the First. As satrap of Persis he appointed Phrasaortes the
son of Rheomithras. And he set fire to the Persian royal palace.
Parmenion had been urging him to preserve it: points included in his
advice were that there was no virtue in destroying what was now his
own property, and that the people of Asia would be less inclined to
accept him if they thought that even he had no plan to take the government of their country under his control, but was simply there for
12 a tour of conquest. Alexander said that he wanted to punish the
Persians for their destruction of Athens and burning of the temples
when they invaded Greece, and to exact retribution for all the other
harm they had inflicted on the Greeks. I myself share the view that
there was no sense in this action of Alexander's, and it could hardly
constitute punishment of the Persians in a distant past.

19   That done, Alexander marched on towards Media, as he was
receiving intelligence that Darius was there. Darius' plan had been to
remain where he was in Media, if Alexander were to stay put in Susa
or Babylon, in the hope that something close to rebellion might break
out* in Alexander's camp: if Alexander were to march against him, he
would go deeper into the interior through Parthyaea and Hyrcania
as far as Bactra [Balkh], ravaging all the country on his way and so
2 making it impossible for Alexander to advance any further. He sent
the women, the rest of the equipage he still had with him, and the
covered wagons to the pass known as the Caspian Gates, while he
stayed on in Ecbatana* [Hamadan] with the force he had gathered
from the available sources. It was this information which kept
Alexander on his march to Media, in the course of which he invaded
the country of the Paraetacae and subdued them, imposing as satrap
3 over them Oxathres, the son of Abulites the satrap of Susa. Along the
way reports came in that Darius had resolved to meet him in battle and
fight it out once more, as Scythian and Cadusian forces had come to
support him. Alexander gave orders for the baggage-animals, the rest
of the train, and the attendant detail of guards to follow at their own
pace, while he took the rest of the army and led it on in full readiness
4 for battle. He reached Media on the twelfth day. There he learnt that
Darius did not have the resources to fight: the Cadusians and

Scythians had not arrived in his support, and Darius had decided to make his escape. Alexander pressed on at yet greater speed. When he was about three days' march from Ecbatana, he was met by Bisthanes, the son of Ochus who had been King of Persia before Darius. He 5 reported that Darius had fled four days before, taking with him about seven thousand talents from the Median treasury and an army of some three thousand cavalry and six thousand infantry.

*When he reached Ecbatana Alexander sent the Thessalian cavalry and the rest of the allies back to the sea, after paying them the agreed wages in full and adding a personal gift of two thousand talents. He 6 gave out that it was open to any individual who so wished to sign up for continued service in his army as a mercenary, and a good number did enrol. He put Epocillus the son of Polyeides in charge of their conduct to the sea, with other cavalry as an escort (the Thessalians had sold their horses there and then). He also sent instructions to Menes to arrange triremes for their transport as soon as they reached the coast. He ordered Parmenion to deposit the bullion which was in 7 transit from Persepolis in the acropolis at Ecbatana and hand it into the care of Harpalus, whom he left in charge of the treasure with about six thousand Macedonians, some cavalry, and a few light troops to guard it. Parmenion was then to take the foreign mercenaries, the Thracians, and all other cavalry except the Companions and march them through Cadusian territory into Hyrcania. Cleitus, the com- 8 mander of the royal squadron, had been left behind ill in Susa: Alexander sent him instructions that when he reached Ecbatana from Susa he should take the Macedonians who had been left there for the time being to guard the treasure and proceed with them towards Parthyaea, which was also his own destination.

For his pursuit of Darius Alexander took with him the cavalry—the 20 Companions, the light cavalry, and the mercenaries under Erigyius— the Macedonian phalanx other than those detailed to guard the treasure, the archers, and the Agrianians. He marched at speed, with men falling behind from exhaustion and horses dying. Even so, he 2 pressed on and reached Rhagae on the eleventh day: this is a place one day's journey away from the Caspian Gates for someone moving as fast as Alexander. But Darius had got there before him, and was by now through the Caspian Gates. Many of those who joined Darius in his flight had deserted him in the course of it and were now dispersing to their own home regions, and quite a number had voluntarily

3 surrendered to Alexander. Realizing that he could not overhaul Darius with an infantry march, Alexander stayed where he was for five days and rested his army. At this time he appointed Oxydates to be satrap of Media: he was a Persian who had been arrested by Darius and imprisoned at Susa, which inclined Alexander to trust him.

4 Alexander then marched on towards Parthyaea. On the first day he camped close by the Caspian Gates, and on the second passed through the Gates and continued as far as there was cultivated country. Where that stopped he needed to lay in provisions for the onward journey through what he heard was desert, so he sent Coenus on a foraging expedition with some cavalry and a few of the infantry.

21 This was when a Babylonian noble called Bagistanes, together with Antibelus, one of Mazaeus' sons, came to him from Darius' camp. They reported that Darius had been arrested by Nabarzanes,* Darius' Grand Vizier, who was commanding the escort of cavalry accompanying his flight, Bessus the satrap of Bactria, and Barsaentes the satrap of

2 Arachosia and Drangiana. On hearing this Alexander pressed on even faster than before, taking with him only the Companions, the light cavalry, and a select corps of infantry chosen for their strength and speed on the march: he did not even wait for Coenus and his men to return from their foraging. He put Craterus in command of the remaining troops, with orders to follow on behind him without for-

3 cing the pace. His own group had nothing with them other than their arms and two days' rations. He travelled all through the night and until noon on the following day: having rested his troops for a short while, he went on all through the next night, and at the first glimmer of dawn reached the camp from which Bagistanes had set out back to

4 meet him. He found none of the enemy there, but he did learn that Darius was being carried under arrest in a covered wagon and that the supreme command now lay with Bessus in place of Darius. Bessus had been hailed as their leader by the Bactrian cavalry and all the other barbarians who had been with Darius in his flight, except for Artabazus and his sons and the Greek mercenaries: these were loyal to Darius, but, unable to prevent what was happening, they had turned off the main road and were making their own way into the mountains, having no part in the coup carried out by Bessus and his

5 supporters. The intention of those who had arrested Darius was to hand him over to Alexander, if they learnt that Alexander was coming after them, and so to win some credit for themselves: but if they

heard that he had turned back, their plan was to raise the largest army they could and preserve Persian power between them in unity. Bessus was to be their leader for the time being because he was a relative of Darius* and the arrest had been made in his satrapy.

When he heard all this, it was clear to Alexander that he must force 6 the pursuit. By now his men and their horses were becoming exhausted by the unremitting stress: but even so he drove on and covered a great distance throughout that night and the following morning, arriving at noon at a village* where Darius' abductors had camped the day before. He learnt there that the barbarians had 7 decided to travel by night, and asked the locals if they knew of any short-cut to reach the fugitives. They said they did, but it was a desert route without water. He told them to guide him along that path. He realized, though, that the infantry would not be able to keep up on foot with the fast pace he would set, so he dismounted some five hundred of the cavalry and ordered the infantry commanders and a group of their men chosen for their stamina to mount the horses with full infantry arms and armour. He instructed Nicanor the commander of 8 the foot guards and Attalus the commander of the Agrianians to lead the remainder of their contingents, as lightly equipped as possible, along the route taken by Bessus and his company, and the rest of the infantry were to follow in regular order. Alexander himself set off at 9 evening and led his party on at full speed. In the course of the night he covered about forty-five miles, and towards dawn he came on the barbarians. They were proceeding without formation and largely without arms, so only a few of them offered resistance: as soon as they saw Alexander there in person, the majority did not even attempt an engagement but took immediate flight, and those who did turn to face battle also fled when some of their number were killed. For a while 10 Bessus and his group continued on their way with the wagon carrying Darius, but when Alexander was now close on them Satibarzanes and Barsaentes stabbed Darius and left him where he was, then made their own escape together with six hundred cavalry. Darius died of his wounds shortly afterwards, before Alexander could see him alive.

Alexander sent Darius' body to Persepolis, with orders that it 22 should be buried in the royal tombs,* like the other Kings before him. As satrap of Parthyaea and Hyrcania he appointed Amminapes, a Parthyaean who had been with Mazaces in the surrender of Egypt to Alexander. Tlepolemus the son of Pythophanes, one of the Companions, was jointly appointed as superintendent of those provinces.

2   Such was the end of Darius, in the month Hecatombaeon of the year when Aristophon was archon at Athens [July 330 BC]. In warfare he was a consummate coward and incompetent, but in other matters did nothing to his discredit, if only for lack of opportunity, as his accession to the throne coincided with the start of hostilities by the Macedonians and the Greeks. So even if he had wanted to, he could not continue to oppress his subjects, as his situation was more dan-

3   gerous than theirs. His life was a series of disasters, with no let-up from the moment of his accession. First and immediate was the cavalry defeat of his satraps at the Granicus, then directly afterwards the enemy capture and possession of Ionia, Aeolis, both Phrygias, Lydia,

4   and all Caria except Halicarnassus: not much later Halicarnassus fell, and with it the whole seaboard from there to Cilicia. Next came his own defeat at Issus, where he saw his mother, wife, and children made captive. Then Phoenicia and all of Egypt were lost. Then at Arbela he brought disgrace on himself by being the first to flee, and lost there the greatest army ever gathered from the entire barbarian

5   race. A fugitive now from his own kingdom, and forced to keep on the move, he was finally betrayed by his own retinue to the depth of ignominy—all honour gone, a king led off in chains: in the end his

6   closest friends conspired to kill him. His was a disastrous life: but after death he received a royal burial, Alexander saw that his children were brought up and educated as they would have been if he were still king, and his daughter was married to Alexander.* When he died Darius was about fifty years old.

23   Alexander now joined up with the army units he had left behind in his pursuit of Darius and advanced into Hyrcania, a country which lies to the north of the road leading to Bactria: on one side it is enclosed by high wooded mountains, but it also has an area of plain which stretches to the Great Sea in that region [Caspian Sea]. He took this direction because he had learnt that the mercenaries with Darius had made their escape this way into the Tapurian mountains [Elburz mountains], and he also wanted to subdue the Tapurians

2   themselves. He divided his army into three parts. He himself took the largest part of his force, which was also the fastest-moving, by the shortest and most difficult route; he sent Craterus against the Tapurians with his own and Amyntas' brigades, some of the archers,

and a few cavalry; and Erigyius was ordered to take the mercenaries and the rest of the cavalry and convoy the wagons, the baggage-train, and all other personnel by the longer route following the main road.

Alexander crossed the first range of mountains and made camp. He 3 then took the foot guards, the fastest of the Macedonian phalanx, and some of the archers and went on by a rough and difficult path, leaving troops behind to mount guard on the roads at what seemed the dangerous points, where the barbarians living in the mountains might otherwise try to attack the rest of his forces as they followed after him. Taking just the archers with him he crossed over the pass to camp in 4 the plain beside a small river. While he was there Nabarzanes, Darius' Grand Vizier, Phrataphernes the satrap of Hyrcania and Parthyaea, and other Persian notables highly placed under Darius came and surrendered themselves. Alexander stayed four days in the camp to col- 5 lect the troops he had left behind on his own forward march. Most of them got through safely, though the mountain barbarians had attacked the Agrianian rearguard, but had the worst of the skirmish and went away.

Setting off from there Alexander moved on into Hyrcania and 6 reached the Hyrcanian city of Zadracarta.* He was now joined by Craterus and his section, who had found no sign of Darius' mercenaries but had annexed all the territory along their route either by force or through the surrender of the inhabitants. Erigyius also arrived at Zadracarta with the baggage-train and the wagons. Soon 7 afterwards Artabazus* came there to join Alexander with three of his sons, Cophen, Ariobarzanes, and Arsames: in the same party were Autophradates, the satrap of Tapuria, and envoys from the foreign mercenaries who had fought for Darius. Alexander allowed Autophradates to keep his satrapy, and gave Artabazus and his sons honoured places in his retinue, in recognition of their high Persian rank and especially their loyalty to Darius. The Greek envoys asked 8 him to give them an amnesty for the whole mercenary force. His reply was that he would never make any sort of terms with them: men who flouted the formal Greek consensus and fought for the barbarians against Greece were guilty of a serious crime. He required them to come in a body and surrender, leaving their subsequent treatment to his absolute discretion: if not, they must look out for their lives as best they could. Their response was to place themselves and the 9 others in Alexander's hands, and they asked him to assign them an officer to supervise the mercenaries' safe conduct to his camp. They were said to number about fifteen hundred. Alexander sent Andronicus the son of Agerrus for that purpose, and Artabazus with him.

24   He himself now moved against the Mardians, taking the foot guards, the archers, the Agrianians, the brigades of Coenus and Amyntas, half of the Companion cavalry, and the mounted javelin-men (by now he 2 had formed them into a separate division). With this force he overran most of the Mardians' territory, killing many of them whether they fled or (as some did) offered resistance, and capturing a good number alive. The fact was that for years no one had invaded their country with hostile intent, as the terrain was rough, the Mardians were poor, and not only poor but also fierce in a fight. So they had not feared an invasion by Alexander either, especially as he had already moved on some way past their land, and for this reason they were caught rather 3 off their guard. But many of them also took refuge in their highlands, where the mountains rise high and sheer, thinking that Alexander would surely not penetrate that far. When he did press on even to this final refuge, they sent envoys to surrender both themselves and their country. Alexander let the people go unharmed, and appointed Autophradates as their satrap, adding to the satrapy he had already been given over the Tapurians.

4   Alexander now returned to the camp which he had left on his expedition into Mardian country. There he found that the Greek mercenaries had come in, and there had arrived also the Spartan envoys sent on an embassy to King Darius—Callistratidas, Pausippus, Monimus, and Onomas—and an Athenian envoy, Dropides. He arrested these men and kept them under guard, but released the envoys from Sinope, on the grounds that the Sinopeans were not members of the Greek League, but as Persian subjects had what 5 seemed reasonable cause to send an embassy to their King. He released also those of the Greeks who had been in mercenary service with the Persians before the peace and alliance* made between Greece and the Macedonians, as well as an envoy from Carthage, one Heracleides. He made the other Greeks serve in his army for the same pay as they had received before, and appointed Andronicus as their commanding officer: it was he who had brought them in, and he had openly expressed his concern that the men's lives should be saved.

25   That done, Alexander made back for Zadracarta, which is the largest city in Hyrcania and its royal capital. He spent fifteen days there,

made the customary sacrifices to the gods and held an athletic competition, then marched into Parthyaea and on to the borders of Areia and the Areian city of Susia,* where again the regional satrap, Satibarzanes, came to present himself. Alexander allowed Satibarzanes 2 to keep the satrapy of Areia, and assigned Anaxippus, one of the Companions, to accompany him with about forty of the mounted javelin-men to act as police at various points along the army's march and prevent abuse of the inhabitants.

At this point some Persians came to meet Alexander with reports 3 that Bessus was now assuming the upright tiara and Persian royal dress, was calling himself Artaxerxes rather than Bessus, and was claiming to be King of Asia; he had with him the Persians who had escaped to Bactra and a good number of the Bactrians themselves, and was expecting the arrival of Scythian support as well.

Alexander was already on his way to Bactra with his entire force 4 now reunited, when Philip the son of Menelaus arrived from Media to join him, bringing with him the mercenary cavalry under his own command, the Thessalians who had volunteered to re-enrol, and Andromachus' foreign contingent. By now Parmenion's son Nicanor, the commander of the foot guards, had died of disease. As Alexander 5 continued on the road to Bactra news came in that Satibarzanes, the satrap of Areia, had massacred Anaxippus and his mounted javelin-men, was arming the Areians and mustering them at the city of Artacoana* (the royal capital of Areia), and had decided, on learning of Alexander's advance, to take his force from there to join Bessus in attacking the Macedonians wherever there was opportunity. When 6 he received this report Alexander halted the march to Bactra and moved at full speed against Satibarzanes and the Areians, taking with him the Companion cavalry, the mounted javelin-men, the archers, the Agrianians, and the brigades of Amyntas and Coenus, and leaving the rest of his force behind under the command of Craterus. He reached Artacoana after covering about sixty-five miles in two days.*

When Satibarzanes realized that Alexander was closing on him, he 7 was dumbfounded by the speed of the attack and took to flight, accompanied only by a handful of Areian cavalry, as when he fled most of his troops had deserted him once they too heard of Alexander's approach. Alexander went after all those known to be complicit in the revolt or to have left their villages at the time, and ruthlessly hunted them down wherever they were, killing some and enslaving the rest. As satrap of Areia he appointed Arsaces, a Persian.

8   Rejoining the force he had left under Craterus, Alexander now marched for Drangiana, and reached the Drangian royal capital.* The ruler of the province at this time was Barsaentes, who had been one of the conspirators involved in the attack on Darius as he continued his flight. On hearing of Alexander's approach he fled for refuge with the Indians living on this side of the Indus: but they arrested him and sent him to Alexander, who had him put to death for his betrayal of Darius.

26   *It was here that Alexander heard of the plot against him by Philotas the son of Parmenion. Ptolemy and Aristobulus say that he had received earlier reports of a plot when he was still in Egypt, but found it hard to believe given their long friendship, the honoured position in which he held Philotas' father Parmenion, and his trust in Philotas'
2   own loyalty. Ptolemy the son of Lagus gives the following account. Philotas was brought before the Macedonian army, Alexander pressed the charges vigorously, and Philotas spoke in his defence. Then those who had laid information about the plot came forward and offered clear proof that Philotas and his associates were guilty: the most telling evidence of guilt was that while Philotas himself admitted to having heard that some sort of plot was afoot against Alexander, he had said not a word of this to Alexander, even though he went to see him in
3   his tent twice every day. Philotas and all his fellow conspirators were executed with javelins by the Macedonians: and to deal with Parmenion Alexander sent Polydamas, one of the Companions, with letters to the generals in Media who were attached to the army under
4   Parmenion's command—Cleander, Sitalces, and Menidas—and they saw to Parmenion's murder. It may be that Alexander thought it inconceivable that while Philotas was laying his plot Parmenion had no part in his son's designs: or it may be that, even if he did have no part, it was now too dangerous to let him survive after his son's execution, given his high standing with Alexander himself and in the estimation of the rest of the army—not only the Macedonians, but also the foreign troops often assigned to him by Alexander, to whom he was a popular commander both in and beyond the call of duty.

27   They also say that Amyntas* the son of Andromenes was brought to trial at the same time, together with his brothers Polemon, Attalus, and Simmias: the charge was that, as close friends of Philotas, they

too had been complicit in his plot against Alexander. To the rank and 2
file what made their conspiracy more credible was the fact that as
soon as Philotas was arrested one of Amyntas' brothers, Polemon,
had deserted to the enemy. Amyntas, though, stayed to face trial with
his other brothers: he made a vigorous defence in front of the assembled Macedonians, and was acquitted of the charge. Immediately on
his acquittal he asked permission to go to his brother and bring him
back to Alexander, and the Macedonians agreed. He left that very day 3
and brought Polemon back. This was seen as yet stronger proof of his
innocence: but not long afterwards he was hit by an arrow while
besieging a village and died of his wound, so the only benefit Amyntas
gained from his acquittal was to die with his good name intact.

Alexander now put the Companion cavalry under the command of 4
two Captains of Horse, Hephaestion the son of Amyntor and Cleitus*
the son of Dropidas, with a corresponding division of the Companion
brigade into two sections: he was not prepared to have one man,
however close to him, commanding such a large body of cavalry,
especially as it was the most highly regarded and operationally effective of all his cavalry units. He came next to the territory of the people
formerly known as the Ariaspians, but later dubbed the Euergetae
('Benefactors') for the help they gave Cyrus the son of Cambyses in
his Scythian expedition. Alexander respected these people for the 5
service their forebears had rendered to Cyrus, and he discovered that
their system of government distinguished them from the other barbarians of that area, and had as good a claim to fairness as the best
examples in Greece. For these reasons he allowed them their freedom, and in addition offered them as much of the adjoining territory
as they wanted for themselves: in fact, despite the offer, they only
asked for a small portion. While there he sacrificed to Apollo, and
also arrested Demetrius, one of the Bodyguards, on suspicion of
complicity in Philotas' plot: to take Demetrius' place as Bodyguard
he appointed Ptolemy the son of Lagus.

That done, Alexander resumed his march to Bactra* against 28
Bessus, and on the way he received the submission of the Drangians
and Gedrosians: the Arachosians submitted also, and he appointed
Menon as satrap over them. He pressed on as far as the Indian tribes
on the borders of Arachosia, but at every stage of the journey through
these nations he had to face deep snow, with provisions in short supply and his men suffering. When news reached him that the Areians 2

had again revolted after Satibarzanes re-entered the country with two thousand cavalry provided by Bessus, Alexander sent Artabazus the Persian and two of the Companions, Erigyius and Caranus, to deal with them, and also ordered Phrataphernes, the satrap of Parthyaea,

3 to invade Areia in support. A fierce battle ensued between Satibarzanes and the troops under Erigyius and Caranus, and the barbarians gave no ground until in single combat with Erigyius Satibarzanes was killed by a spear-thrust in the face. Then the barbarians turned in headlong flight.

4 Meanwhile Alexander marched on to Mount Caucasus, where he founded a city and called it Alexandria* [Begram]. He sacrificed there to his customary gods, then crossed the mountain, appointing a Persian, Proexes, as satrap of the area and leaving Neiloxenus, one of the Companions, in the role of superintendent, with troops under his command.

5 Mount Caucasus is as high as any mountain in Asia, according to Aristobulus, and is largely bare, at least on this side. Caucasus is in fact a long mountain range, and it is said that even the Taurus mountains, which separate Cilicia from Pamphylia, are part of the Caucasus range,* as are several other great mountains with various different

6 names traditional in each location. Be that as it may, on this particular mountain in the Caucasus range Aristobulus says that nothing grows except pistachios and silphium.* Even so the area was well populated, and grazed by numerous flocks and herds. Sheep like silphium, and even a distant scent of the plant has them running to find it, nibble

7 the flower, and grub up and eat the root. For that reason the people of Cyrene keep their flocks as far away as possible from the places where their silphium grows, and some even fence off the silphium fields to prevent any sheep who do come near getting inside: silphium is a valuable crop for the Cyrenaeans.

8 Bessus had with him the Persians who had joined him in the arrest of Darius, some seven thousand men from Bactria itself, and the Dahae living on this side of the river Tanaïs [Syr-Darya]. With this force he was devastating the land leading down from Mount Caucasus, to create a dead area between himself and Alexander and prevent

9 Alexander's further advance by denying him a supply of food. But Alexander advanced none the less: it was a gruelling march through thick snow with provisions short, but still he came on. When Bessus received reports that Alexander was now not far off, he crossed the

river Oxus [Amu-Darya], burned the ships he had used for the crossing, and retreated to Nautaca* [Shakhrisyabz] in Sogdiana. He was
accompanied by the troops under Spitamenes and Oxyartes, including the cavalry from Sogdiana, and by the Dahae from the Tanaïs:
but the Bactrian cavalry dispersed to their various homes when they
learnt that Bessus had decided to avoid battle.

Alexander reached Drapsaca [Kunduz], and after resting his 29
army went on to Aornus and Bactra [Balkh], the largest cities in
Bactria, both of which he took at the first attack. He left a garrison
in the citadel of Aornus with Archelaus the son of Androcles, one of
the Companions, in command of it: the rest of Bactria had readily
submitted, and he appointed the Persian Artabazus* as satrap of the
country.

He himself made for the river Oxus. Flowing from Mount Caucasus 2
and discharging into the Great Sea* in its Hyrcanian reaches [Caspian
Sea], the Oxus is the greatest of all the rivers in Asia encountered by
Alexander and his men (only surpassed by the rivers of India, which
are the greatest rivers of all). Crossing the river seemed an impos- 3
sibility wherever Alexander made the attempt. It was some two-thirds
of a mile wide, and surprisingly deep for that width, in fact quite
some way deeper than might have been expected, sandy at the bottom
and fast-flowing as well, so piles driven into the bed could not take
firm hold in the sand and were easily wrenched from their footing by
the mere force of the current. A further difficulty was the lack of 4
timber, and it was clear that there would be a long delay if they had to
go far to bring back sufficient material for a bridge. So Alexander collected the men's leather tent-covers and had them stuffed with the
driest loose rubbish that could be found, then tied up and closely
stitched to make them watertight. Stuffed and stitched together,
there were enough to take the whole army across in five days.

Before the crossing Alexander picked out the oldest of the 5
Macedonians who by now were unfit for military duty and sent them
home, together with the Thessalians who had volunteered to remain
in service. He also sent Stasanor, one of the Companions, to Areia
with orders to arrest Arsaces, the satrap of Areia, whom he thought
guilty of deliberate failure of duty: Stasanor was to replace him in the
satrapy.

After crossing the river Oxus Alexander marched on at speed 6
towards what he was informed was the location of Bessus and his

force. In the course of this march men came to him from Spitamenes and Dataphernes with the message that if they were sent even a small contingent of troops and an officer to command them these two would arrest Bessus and hand him over to Alexander—they already had
7 him confined under guard, though not in chains. On hearing this Alexander relaxed the pace of his own advance, to give his army some respite, but sent Ptolemy the son of Lagus on ahead with orders to reach Spitamenes and Dataphernes at full speed: he was to take with him three units of the Companion cavalry, all the mounted javelin-men, infantry consisting of Philotas' brigade and one battalion of the foot guards, all the Agrianians, and half of the archers. Ptolemy set out as ordered with this force, and after covering in four days a dis-tance which would have taken ten days of a regular march he reached the site where the barbarians with Spitamenes had camped on the previous day.

30   There Ptolemy learnt that Spitamenes and Dataphernes were wavering about the surrender of Bessus. So he left the infantry behind, with instructions to follow on in full formation, while he himself rode out with the cavalry and came to a village where Bessus
2 had been left with a few soldiers. Spitamenes and his associates had already withdrawn from the village, reluctant to take a direct part in the handing over of Bessus. Ptolemy set his cavalry in a cordon round the village—it had a perimeter wall of sorts, with gates in it—and made a proclamation to the barbarians in the village that they would be left unharmed if they handed over Bessus. They admitted Ptolemy and his
3 troops into the village, and he arrested Bessus and set out on his way back. He sent a messenger ahead to ask Alexander how he should bring Bessus into his presence. Alexander told him to bring Bessus naked, bound, and collared, and to stand him on the right of the road along which Alexander and his army would process. Ptolemy did as instructed.

4   When he saw Bessus Alexander stopped his chariot and asked him why he had first seized Darius and taken him along in chains, then killed him, when Darius was his king, his kinsman, and his benefac-tor. Bessus said that this was not just his own idea, but a joint plan with the others accompanying Darius at the time, to win themselves
5 leniency from Alexander. At this Alexander ordered him to be flogged while the herald recited the specific crimes implied in his own ques-tion to Bessus. After this humiliation Bessus was sent to Bactra to be

executed there. This is Ptolemy's account of the capture of Bessus:
Aristobulus, though, says that it was the associates of Spitamenes and
Dataphernes* who brought Bessus to Ptolemy and handed him over
to Alexander naked, bound, and collared.

Alexander brought his cavalry back to strength with horses from 6
the locality, having lost a good number of horses in the crossing of
Mount Caucasus and the travel to and from the Oxus, and led on to
Maracanda [Samarcand], the royal capital of Sogdiana. From there 7
he advanced to the river Tanaïs [Syr-Darya]. This Tanaïs (which
Aristobulus says the local barbarians call by the different name of
Orxantes) is a river which, like the Oxus, has its source in Mount
Caucasus and also discharges into the Hyrcanian Sea [Caspian]. The 8
historian Herodotus speaks of a Tanaïs* as the eighth river in Scythia,
with its flow rising from a great lake and debouching into the yet
greater lake called Maeotis [Sea of Azov], but this will be a different
Tanaïs [Don]. Some make this other Tanaïs the boundary between
Asia and Europe. They take the view that, from the corner of the 9
Black Sea, Lake Maeotis and this Tanaïs which flows into it separate
Asia from Europe in the same way that the sea between Gadeira
[Cadiz] and the nomad Libyans opposite separates Europe in turn
from Libya:* doubtless they would also regard the river Nile as the
division between Libya and the rest of Asia.

Here a party of Macedonians who had spread out to forage was 10
massacred by the barbarians. The forces responsible, numbering
about thirty thousand, then retreated to a craggy mountain which
was precipitously steep on all sides. Alexander took his most mobile
troops to attack them. Several assaults on the mountain were 11
attempted by the Macedonians, and at first they were driven back by
volleys of fire from the barbarians: many of them were wounded,
including Alexander himself, who took an arrow right through his leg
which broke part of the fibula. But even so he captured the position:
some of the barbarians were cut down on the spot by the Macedonians,
and many others threw themselves to their death over the precipices.
Out of thirty thousand no more than eight thousand survived.*

BOOK FOUR

1 NOT many days later Alexander was visited by envoys from the Scythians known as the Abii,* an independent people living in Asia. In his epic Homer gives them the accolade 'most civilized of all men',* and their independence is largely due to their poverty and their civilized institutions. Envoys came too from the European Scythians,* who
2 are the most populous race in Europe. Alexander sent some of the Companions back with these envoys, ostensibly as an embassy to agree terms of friendship, but the main purpose of the mission was rather to afford the opportunity for a reconnaissance of the geography of Scythia, the numbers of the inhabitants and their way of life, and the weaponry they employed for battle.
3 He meanwhile was planning the foundation of a city on the river Tanaïs* to bear his name. The site seemed to him well suited for the growth of a city, and a foundation there would serve strategically for any future invasion of Scythia and as an outpost to defend the area against the incursions of the barbarians living on the other side of the
4 river. He thought that the large number of settlers attracted to it and the prestige of its name would see it develop into a great city. At this point the barbarians bordering the river seized and killed the Macedonian troops on garrison duty in their cities* and began to for-
5 tify them for greater defensive strength. Most of the rest of Sogdiana joined their revolt at the instigation of the men who had arrested Bessus, who thereby managed to bring about the defection of some of the Bactrians also. The Sogdians may have had a genuine fear of Alexander, or it may be that they were using as a pretext for revolt the fact that Alexander had summoned the barons of the whole region to gather for a joint conference* at Zariaspa [Balkh], the largest city in the area, which they suspected could only be to their detriment.

2 When Alexander was told of this revolt he ordered the infantry companies to build ladders, a set number for each company, and then he himself left camp and advanced to the nearest of the seven cities* in which the barbarians of the region were said to have taken refuge:
2 its name was Gaza. He sent Craterus to the city called Cyropolis,* the largest of them all, where the greatest number of the barbarians had concentrated. Craterus' instructions were to camp close by the city,

surround it with a ditch and stockade, and construct as many siege-engines as he needed: the purpose was to prevent the people in Cyropolis from bringing any help to the other cities by focusing all their attention on Craterus and his troops. As soon as he reached *3* Gaza, without pause or further preparation Alexander signalled an immediate attack on the wall (which was an earth-wall of no great height). He told his troops to bring their ladders up against it on every side of the circuit, and this assault by the infantry was accompanied by a barrage of fire at the defenders on the wall by his slingers, archers, and javelin-men, as well as volleys of missiles from the catapults: this intensity of fire quickly cleared the wall of defenders, and it was short work for the Macedonians to place their ladders and scale the wall. On Alexander's orders they killed all the men and took the *4* women and children as booty, with all else they could plunder. Alexander led straight on to the second city,* next placed after this one, took it in the same day by the same means, and inflicted the same treatment on the captured inhabitants. He then led on to the third city, and took it on the following day at one assault.

While he himself was engaged in this work with the infantry, he *5* sent the cavalry to the next two nearest cities, with instructions to keep a close guard on the men inside, in case they heard of the capture of their neighbouring cities and Alexander's own imminent approach and took to flight: if that happened, pursuit would be impracticable. It turned out exactly as he had foreseen, and his dispatch of the cavalry was just in time. When the barbarians occupying the two as yet uncap- *6* tured cities saw the smoke from the burning of the next city before theirs, and some survivors who escaped the full force of the disaster came in with first-hand accounts of the capture, they fled in a mass as fast as they could from each of the cities, but ran straight into the close-packed arrays of cavalry, and most of them were cut down.

After this capture and enslavement of these five cities in two days, *3* Alexander marched against the largest of all, Cyropolis. As founded by Cyrus, this was fortified with a higher wall than the others, and the greatest number of barbarians in the region, forming also their best fighting force, had taken refuge in it: capture in one quick assault was not therefore so easy for the Macedonians. However, Alexander brought siege-engines up to the wall, intending to use this means of attack to batter the wall down and send in his troops wherever a breach was made. But then he himself noticed the channels giving *2* outlet to the river which runs through the city full of water in the winter: they were dry at the time, and left a gap below the walls large enough for his men to creep through them into the city. So he took with him the bodyguards, the foot guards, the archers, and the Agrianians, and while the barbarians had their attention focused on the siege-engines and the troops pressing the attack there he used these channels to slip unnoticed into the city with just a few men at

3 first. Once inside he broke open the gates in that quarter and so readily admitted the rest of his troops. The barbarians could now see that the city had fallen to the enemy, but even so they turned to face Alexander and his men. They made a vigorous counter-attack, in which Alexander himself suffered a heavy blow to his head and neck* from a stone, Craterus was shot by an arrow, and many other officers were wounded also. Nevertheless the Macedonians drove the barbar-

4 ians out of the market-place, and meanwhile the wall, denuded now of defenders, was taken under their control by the contingents involved in the assault. In this first phase of the city's capture about eight thousand of the enemy were killed. The rest, out of a total number of some fifteen thousand fighting men gathered there, took refuge in the citadel. Alexander surrounded the place and blockaded it: after one day the lack of water brought their surrender.

5   The seventh city was taken in one assault. Ptolemy says that the people surrendered, but Aristobulus says that Alexander took this city too by storm, and killed all* he found inside it. Ptolemy adds that Alexander distributed the surrendered men among his army units, to be kept bound and guarded until he left the area: he did not want any of those involved in the revolt to remain behind in their own country.

6   Meanwhile an army of the Asian Scythians arrived at the banks of the Tanaïs. Most of them had heard that some of the barbarians on the other side of the river were in revolt from Alexander, and they intended to join in a general attack on the Macedonians if this did indeed develop into a substantial insurrection. News also came in that Spitamenes and his men had the garrison left behind in Maracanda

7 under siege in the citadel. At this Alexander sent Andromachus, Menedemus, and Caranus against Spitamenes' forces, with some sixty of the Companion cavalry and eight hundred mercenary cavalry (commanded by Caranus), and about fifteen hundred mercenary infantry. In overall command he placed Pharnuches,* his interpreter,

a man of Lycian origin who had expert knowledge of the language spoken by the barbarians of this area and was proving in other ways too a skilful intermediary.

He himself now completed the wall of his planned city in twenty 4 days, and settled there some of the Greek mercenaries, any of the neighbouring barbarians who volunteered to be part of the settlement,* and also some Macedonians who were no longer fit for active service in the army: he made his customary sacrifices to the gods, and held athletic and equestrian competitions. As for the Scythians, he could see for himself that they were not leaving the river bank: indeed 2 they were seen shooting arrows into the river (which was not very wide at that point), and, as is the way of barbarians, they hurled some insults at Alexander, boasting that he would never dare to come to grips with Scythians, or else he would learn the difference between Scythians and the barbarians of Asia. Provoked by this, he determined to cross and attack them, and began to prepare the leather floats for the way over. But when he sacrificed for sanction of the 3 crossing the omens were not favourable. Though impatient of the outcome, he restrained himself and stayed put. The Scythians kept up their taunts, and Alexander sacrificed again for the crossing: and again Aristander the seer declared that the omens indicated danger to his own person. Alexander replied that it was better to face any extreme of danger rather than, as conqueror of virtually the whole of Asia, to be ridiculed by the Scythians, as Darius the father of Xerxes had been* long ago. But Aristander refused to reinterpret the divinely vouchsafed signs to suit Alexander's wish to hear something else.*

But Alexander persisted. As soon as he had the leather floats ready 4 for the crossing, and his army lined up fully armed on the bank, at a signal the catapults began firing their missiles at the Scythian cavalry patrolling the other bank. Several were wounded by direct hits, and one was dropped from his horse by a bolt which struck right through his shield and breastplate. The Scythians were astounded at such long-range salvoes and the death of one of their braves, and retreated some way from the bank. Seeing the disruptive effect of the catapults, 5 Alexander had the trumpets sound the attack and began the crossing of the river, himself in the lead and the rest of the army following him. He put ashore the archers and slingers* first, with orders to start shooting at the Scythians to keep them away from the infantry phalanx as it came out from the river, until all the cavalry had crossed.

6 When the whole army was gathered on the far bank, he first launched against the Scythians one unit of the mercenary cavalry and four squadrons of the lancers. The Scythians took this attack: with much superior numbers they could ride circles round the Macedonians and shoot at will, easily avoiding any counter-action. Alexander then intermingled among the cavalry the archers, the Agrianians, and the rest of the light troops under Balacrus, and led this force against the

7 Scythians. When they were coming close, he ordered into attack three units of the Companion cavalry and all the mounted javelin-men: and he himself brought up the rest of the cavalry at the gallop and charged in with his squadrons in column. The result was that the Scythians could no longer employ the circling movements they had used so far. The Macedonian cavalry was now hard on them, and at the same time the light troops mixed in among the cavalry denied them the ability to wheel and turn without danger. There followed

8 now a spectacular rout of the Scythians: about a thousand of them fell, including one of their commanders, Satraces, and some one hundred and fifty were captured.* The pursuit was fast and tiring in the great heat, so the whole army was afflicted by thirst and Alexander

9 himself drank whatever water was available in that terrain. The water was in fact polluted, and his intestines suffered an attack of continuous diarrhoea. For this reason the pursuit of the Scythians was not pressed to the full: otherwise, if Alexander had not been taken ill, I think they would all have been killed as they fled. Alexander was carried back to the camp in a critical state, thus fulfilling Aristander's prophecy.

5   Not much later envoys came to Alexander from the Scythian king. Their mission was to present the defence that the recent incident was not a concerted act by the Scythian people, but the work of privateers out for plunder: and to assure Alexander that the king himself was willing to do whatever was required of him. Alexander sent him a courteous response, as he saw the dilemma: to disbelieve him yet fail to take punitive action would damage his own reputation, but also this was not the right moment for that action.

2   The Macedonians blockaded in the citadel at Maracanda responded to a direct attack on the citadel by Spitamenes and his troops with a sally of their own, which killed some of the enemy and drove off the whole of the rest: they themselves made a safe return to the citadel

3 with no casualties. And when Spitamenes heard reports of the

imminent approach of the relief force sent by Alexander to Maracanda, he abandoned the siege of the citadel and took himself off to the northern reaches of Sogdiana. Pharnuches and the generals with him were keen to drive Spitamenes completely out of the region, and pursued him as he retreated to the borders of Sogdiana. They had not calculated on meeting the opposition of the nomad Scythians as well. Spitamenes was able to add some six hundred Scythian cavalry to his 4 armament, and this reinforcement of Scythian allies stiffened his determination to meet the Macedonian advance. He drew up his forces in an area of level ground near the Scythian desert, but would neither invite nor initiate a direct engagement with the enemy: instead, he kept his cavalry circling in and out to fire their arrows at the infantry phalanx. Whenever Pharnuches' troops launched a 5 counter-charge, he had no difficulty in keeping clear of it, given that his men were mounted on faster and so far fresher horses, while Andromachus' cavalry had horses weakened by incessant travel and lack of fodder: and if the Macedonians remained where they stood or retreated, the Scythians would come back at them hard. With many 6 now being wounded by the arrows and some killed, the Macedonians formed their troops into a square and withdrew towards the river Polytimetus* [Zeravshan] and the wooded area close by it, to frustrate the barbarian archery and give a more effective role to their own infantry.

Without consulting Andromachus, the cavalry commander 7 Caranus attempted to cross the river in the hope that this would get his cavalry to safety. The infantry followed him: no such order had been given, and it was a panic-stricken and chaotic descent into the river down precipitous banks. Seeing this error on the part of the 8 Macedonians, the barbarians rode their horses straight into the river at several points along the bank. Some went in close pursuit of those who had already got across and were making away; others ranged themselves squarely in front of the men still crossing and penned them back in the river, while others shot at them from the flanks or 9 fell on the troops still entering the water. Caught in a hopeless situation on all sides, the Macedonians flocked for refuge on one of the small islands in the river. The Scythians and Spitamenes' cavalry surrounded the island and shot them all down: a few were taken prisoner, but these too were all killed.

Aristobulus, though, says that most of this force was destroyed in 6 an ambush—the Scythians had hidden in private parkland, and emerged from hiding to attack the Macedonians in the course of the main engagement. This was at the very time when Pharnuches was offering to resign his command in favour of his Macedonian colleagues in the expedition, on the grounds that he had no military experience, and had been sent by Alexander more to liaise with the barbarians than to take command in battles, whereas they were not 2 only Macedonians but also Companions of the king. Andromachus, Caranus, and Menedemus would not accept the command, partly to avoid any appearance of taking their own initiative in contravention of Alexander's orders, and partly because at this critical moment they had no wish to be involved in a possible disaster as more than individuals—certainly not as personally responsible for the mismanagement of the whole business. It was in this confusion and chaos, says Aristobulus, that the barbarians made the attack which cut them all down, with no more than forty cavalry and three hundred infantry left to survive and escape.

3   When this was reported to Alexander he was mortified by the fate of his soldiers and determined to march at full speed against Spitamenes and his barbarians. Taking with him half of the Companion cavalry, all the foot guards, the archers, the Agrianians, and the fastest of the phalanx infantry, he marched for Maracanda, hearing that Spitamenes had returned there and was once more 4 besieging the garrison in the citadel. He covered a hundred and seventy miles in three days,* and came up to the city just before dawn on the fourth. On the news of Alexander's approach Spitamenes and his 5 men stayed no longer, but left the city and fled. Alexander went after them in close pursuit: when he reached the site of the battle, he gave his soldiers an improvised burial, then continued to pursue the fugitives all the way to the edge of the desert. There he turned back and set about devastating the countryside and massacring the barbarians who had taken refuge in the various strongholds, as they too were alleged to have joined the attack on the Macedonians. In this he traversed the whole of the country watered by the river Polytimetus 6 along its course. From the point where the river water disappears there is only desert thereafter: and though full of water the river does indeed disappear into the sand.* Other large and perennial rivers also disappear in the same way in that region—the Epardus, which flows through the land of the Mardians; the Areius [Hari Rud], after which

the country of Areia is named; and the Etymandrus [Helmand], flowing through the territory of the Euergetae. In size all these rivers are 7
at least as large as the Peneius, the Thessalian river which runs
through Tempe on its course to debouch in the sea: but in comparison with the Peneius the Polytimetus is by far the larger river.

   After these operations Alexander came to Zariaspa, and stayed 7
there waiting for the worst of the winter to be over.* In this time he
was joined by Phratapherness, the satrap of Parthyaea, and Stasanor,
who had been sent to Areia to arrest Arsaces:* they brought Arsaces
with them in chains, together with Brazanes, Bessus' appointee as
satrap of Parthyaea, and some others who had been involved in
Bessus' revolt at the time. In this same interval Epocillus, Menidas, 2
and Ptolemy arrived from the coast (Ptolemy was the commander of
the Thracians who had escorted down to the sea the bullion sent with
Menes* and the allies who were discharged home). At the same time
Asander and Nearchus arrived bringing a Greek mercenary force,
and so did the two provincial governors of Syria, Menon and
Asclepiodorus,* these also bringing troops from the coast.

   Alexander now called the people of Zariaspa to a meeting and 3
brought Bessus before them. He charged him with treason to Darius,*
and ordered that Bessus should have his nose and ear-rims sliced
off, and then be taken to Ecbatana to be put to death in front of the
assembled Medes and Persians.

   *For my part, I cannot approve of this excessively severe punish- 4
ment of Bessus, but regard the mutilation of extremities as a barbaric
practice. And I agree that Alexander had been seduced into emulat-
ing the luxurious habits of the Medes and Persians and the way barbarian kings could live a life quite divorced from any equality with
their subjects. I wholly disapprove of the fact that he, a descendant of
Heracles,* adopted Median dress in place of traditional Macedonian
clothes, and saw no anomaly in changing to the Persian mitre* from
the headgear he had always worn before, when he was the victor and
they the vanquished. As I say, there is none of this that I can approve. 5
In fact I take Alexander's great achievements as the clearest proof
that nothing—not physical strength, not distinction of birth, not a
succession of military victories yet more extensive than Alexander's,
even if a man were to sail round the whole of Libya* and add that to
his conquest of Asia (as Alexander did indeed contemplate), even if
he won all three continents, Europe as well as Asia and Libya—none

of these things has any bearing on a man's happiness, unless the man of such apparently great success is also successful in self-control.

8   In this context I shall now relate the tragic end of Cleitus the son of Dropidas, and its consequences for Alexander, even though these events took place somewhat later.* The story is as follows. The Macedonians had a special day consecrated in honour of Dionysus,

2 and Alexander used to sacrifice to Dionysus on this day every year. On this particular anniversary, though, they say that Alexander neglected Dionysus and made his sacrifice, for whatever reason was in his mind, to the Dioscuri.* The subsequent drinking went on long—and indeed Alexander had already developed a new drinking habit on a more barbarian scale.* Anyway, in this particular drinking-bout talk turned to the Dioscuri and the way that their paternity had been removed

3 from Tyndareus and attributed to Zeus. Some of the company, attempting to ingratiate themselves with Alexander—the sort of flatterers who always have and always will corrupt and ruin the best interests of any king—claimed that Polydeuces and Castor bore no comparison to Alexander and his achievements. Others in their cups did not even stop short of Heracles: it was only jealousy, they said, which prevented living men from receiving the honours they deserved from their contemporaries.

4   For some time past Cleitus had not concealed his distaste for Alexander's shift to a more barbarian lifestyle and for the effusions of his toadies: and now, fired by the wine, he would not have them cheapen divinity or belittle the achievements of the heroes of old, simply to give

5 Alexander this gratification which actually did him no favours. In any case, he said, what Alexander had achieved was not as great and remarkable as they puffed it: he had not done it all by himself, but the main part had been taken by the Macedonians at large. Alexander was exasperated by this outburst, and I cannot condone it myself: I think that in such drunken company a man should be content to keep his own views to himself, while still not joining the others in their excess of flattery.

6 But when some of them turned the talk to Philip and, in a similar attempt to gratify Alexander, made the quite outrageous claim that Philip had achieved nothing great or remarkable, Cleitus lost all control and spoke out to champion Philip's achievements and denigrate Alexander and his. Violently drunk by now, he went on to pile contempt on Alexander; he himself, he said, had saved Alexander's life in

7 the cavalry battle against the Persians at the Granicus;* he even raised

his right arm in a dramatic gesture and declared, 'This is the very hand, Alexander, which saved you then!'

Alexander could no longer tolerate these drunken insults from Cleitus, and leapt up to get at him, but was restrained by his fellow drinkers. Still Cleitus kept up his abuse, and Alexander actually 8 shouted for his guards. When none of them responded to his call, he exclaimed that he had been reduced to the same state as Darius in the hands of Bessus and his colleagues—a king in nothing but name. The Companions could no longer hold him back, but he burst free and (according to some) snatched a lance from one of the Bodyguards and used it to strike Cleitus dead: others say that the weapon was a pike 9 taken from one of the foot guards. Although Aristobulus does not describe the cause of the drunken quarrel, he holds Cleitus solely responsible for his fate,* in that, according to him, when Alexander had become enraged and leapt up with murderous intent Cleitus was hurried out of the doors by Ptolemy the son of Lagus, one of the Bodyguards, and led away beyond the wall and the ditch surrounding the citadel (which was where all this happened), but could not control himself and went back again. Alexander was shouting 'Cleitus, Cleitus' when Cleitus came on him: he called out, 'Here I am, Alexander—here is your Cleitus', and it was then that he was killed with a thrust of the pike.

I myself think Cleitus greatly at fault for insulting his king, and I 9 pity Alexander for the circumstance which showed him up at the time as prone to two faults, neither of which should be indulged by a man of self-control—anger and drunkenness. But on the other hand 2 I commend Alexander for his subsequent behaviour, and his immediate recognition that he had done something terrible. Some say that Alexander fixed the pike in the wall and was ready to throw himself on it, thinking that he could not live on without shame when he had killed a friend in his cups. Most historians, though, do not have that 3 story, but say that Alexander took to his bed and lay there grieving, time after time calling out Cleitus' name and the name of his sister, Lanice, the daughter of Dropidas, who had been his nurse—and a fine return he had given her as an adult for all that care of his childhood! She had seen her sons die fighting for him,* and now he had 4 killed her brother with his own hand. He would not stop calling himself the murderer of his friends, and went without food or drink for three days, neglecting all other personal needs as well.

5   In response to these events some of the seers 'sang of the wrath' of
      Dionysus,* because Alexander had omitted his sacrifice. His friends
      ultimately managed to persuade him to eat, and to take some minimal
      care of his person: and he made good the sacrifice to Dionysus, as he
      was not unhappy to have the events attributed to divine wrath rather
6   than his own inherent faults. I find much to commend in Alexander's
      behaviour here: he did not brazen through any justification of a wrong
      done; he did not put himself yet further in the wrong by making a
      virtue of his crime or defending it; but he admitted that he had made
      an error,* as humans do.
7   Some say that Anaxarchus the sophist* was called to come and
      counsel Alexander, and that, finding him groaning on his bed, he
      chuckled and said that Alexander was forgetting why it was that the
      wise poets of old had Justice enthroned beside Zeus: they meant that
      justice was inherent in any action that Zeus determined. So too with
      any great king: whatever he causes to happen must be taken as just,
8   first by the king himself and then by the rest of the world. Though
      this argument consoled Alexander at the time, in my view Anaxarchus
      did Alexander a great disservice, something much more serious than
      this temporary indisposition, if indeed he did present as received wis-
      dom the notion that the obligation does not in fact lie on the king to
      think carefully about the justice of his actions, but on everyone else to
9   accept as just whatever the king does and however he does it. For
      example, the prevailing account has Alexander keen to introduce for-
      mal obeisance:* behind this was his conviction that his true father
      was Ammon rather than Philip, but he was already showing a taste
      for the culture of the Persians and Medes in his change of dress and
      other innovations in court procedure. Even on this issue there was no
      lack of flatterers to indulge his wish, including in particular two of the
      sophists he kept in his retinue, Anaxarchus* and Agis,* an epic poet
      from Argos.
10   It is said that this met with the disapproval of Callisthenes* of
      Olynthus, who had been a pupil of Aristotle. Callisthenes was some-
      what boorish in manner, but so far as this case is concerned I go
      along with him. On the other hand I think that Callisthenes was
      quite out of order in his claim (if it is accurately reported) that
      Alexander and all his exploits were dependent on him and the history
2   he would write: he had not come, so he declared, to borrow fame
      from Alexander, but to make him renowned in the world. And again,

for example, he said that Alexander's semi-divine status did not depend on the lies Olympias told about his birth, but on the account which he himself would compose in promotion of Alexander and publish to the world. Some also relate that Philotas once asked 3 Callisthenes who he thought was held in the greatest honour by the city of Athens, and his answer was Harmodius and Aristogeiton,* because they had killed one of the two tyrants and brought the tyranny to an end. Philotas followed his question by asking if a tyran- 4 nicide could find safe refuge wherever he wanted in Greece, and Callisthenes followed his answer with the response that Athens at least, if nowhere else, would provide a safe haven: the Athenians, after all, had done battle in support of the children of Heracles against Eurystheus,* who held a tyranny over Greece at that time.

Callisthenes' opposition to Alexander on the question of obeisance 5 is generally reported as follows. It had been agreed between Alexander and his sophists, and with the most distinguished Persians and Medes at his court, that mention of this subject should be introduced at a symposium. Anaxarchus began the discussion. He argued that there 6 was far greater justification for regarding Alexander as a god than Dionysus or Heracles, not only for the extent and scale of Alexander's achievements, but also because Dionysus was a Theban, with no connection to the Macedonians, and Heracles was an Argive, also unconnected, except with the family of Alexander through his Heraclid ancestry. So there was a stronger case for the Macedonians to award 7 these divine honours to their own king.* It could anyway not be doubted that when Alexander had left his mortal state they would honour him as a god: all the greater reason, then, to dignify him in life with the honour which would lose all value for him if conferred after death.

After this and more along the same lines from Anaxarchus, his fel- 11 low supporters of the proposal applauded his speech and were actually ready to begin offering obeisance, but most of the Macedonians were offended by the idea and received it in silence. The response 2 came from Callisthenes. 'Anaxarchus,' he said, 'I should state immediately that Alexander is deserving of every honour commensurate with human status. But men have made various distinctions between human and divine honours: examples are the building of temples, the dedication of statues, the consecration of precincts to the gods and sacrifice and libation made to them, the difference between a hymn

composed for worship of the gods and a speech made in praise of
3 men. Now a particular distinction is in the practice of obeisance. Men
greet each other with a kiss, but divinities, I imagine because they
have their seat far above us and we are not allowed to touch them, are
for that reason honoured with our obeisance, just as we stage dances
and sing paeans in honour of the gods. There is no great mystery in
this distinction, since even among the gods themselves there is variety in the honours paid, and indeed another layer of worship distin-
4 guishing the heroes from the gods. It cannot be right to blur all this
by raising mortals to an inflated status with extravagant honours, and
in so doing to demean the gods—as far as men can—by the indignity
of reducing the honour paid them to parity with men. Alexander
would not tolerate it either, if some unauthorized voting process,
show of hands or secret ballot, propelled a commoner into the hon-
5 ours of royalty. Much greater cause, then, for the gods to resent any
men who propel themselves, or allow others to propel them, into the
honours of divinity.

'In both reality and reputation Alexander is of all men far and away
the bravest of the brave, the most kingly of kings, the commander
6 most pre-eminently worthy of command. Yes, and you of all people,
Anaxarchus, attached to Alexander to guide him in the ways of wisdom, should have been the one to present the arguments I have
adduced and discourage any thoughts to the contrary. So for you actually to initiate this present proposal was quite improper. You should
have remembered that you are not attached as adviser to a Cambyses
or a Xerxes, but to a son of Philip, born to a line descended from
Heracles and Aeacus, whose forefathers came to Macedonia from
Argos, and who have ever since continued to rule the Macedonians
7 with a government based not on coercion but on law. Even Heracles
himself was not paid divine honours by the Greeks in his lifetime, nor
yet after his death until the god at Delphi sanctioned his worship as a
god.

'If raising this issue in a barbarian country implies that we should
adopt a barbarian way of thinking, then I for one, Alexander, would
urge you to remember Greece: it was for Greece that you undertook
8 this whole expedition, to add Asia to Greece.* So think now what you
will do on your return. Will you enforce obeisance on Greeks too, the
freest people on earth? Or will you exempt the Greeks but impose
this indignity on the Macedonians? Or will you personally make a

clean distinction in the matter of etiquette—human-scale and Greek-style honours from Greeks and Macedonians, barbaric honours only from barbarians? If Cyrus the son of Cambyses was, as it is said, the 9 first man to receive obeisance,* thereby establishing a tradition of this humiliation for the Persians and Medes, you should remember that this very Cyrus was taught a lesson by the Scythians, a poor but independent people, Darius also by another branch of the Scythians, Xerxes by the Athenians and Spartans, Artaxerxes* by Clearchus and Xenophon with their Ten Thousand, and now this Darius by Alexander—without any obeisance done.'

This speech by Callisthenes (and there was more in the same vein) 12 greatly displeased Alexander, but caught the mood of the Macedonians.* Realizing this, Alexander sent word telling the Macedonians to drop the subject of obeisance. But when the discussion then fell silent, the 2 senior Persians stood up one by one and made obeisance. One of the Companions, Leonnatus,* thought that a particular Persian had made an inelegant job of his obeisance, and laughed at what he saw as a cringing posture. Alexander was angry with him at the time, but was reconciled later. There is also recorded a story which goes like this. 3 Alexander sent round a golden loving-cup which came first to those who had agreed his proposal of obeisance: the first to drink from the cup then stood up, did obeisance, and received a kiss* from Alexander, and so it went on through all in turn. When the pledge came to 4 Callisthenes, he stood, drank from the cup, and without doing obeisance came up to give Alexander a kiss. It happened that at that moment Alexander was talking to Hephaestion, so did not notice whether Callisthenes had in fact performed the procedure of obeisance. But as Callisthenes approached for the kiss, one of the Companions, 5 Demetrius the son of Pythonax, told Alexander that he was coming without having done obeisance. Alexander refused to accept the offered kiss, and Callisthenes responded by saying, 'I shall go back, then, the poorer by one kiss'.

In this whole business I cannot in any way condone either 6 Alexander's arrogance at the time or Callisthenes' clumsy protest. I think that a man who has not disclaimed a place at court should be content to observe decorum in his own behaviour, and support his king as far as he can. So I would say that there was good reason for 7 Callisthenes to earn Alexander's hatred by his gross stupidity in making such an inappropriately frank outburst. I infer that this is why credence was readily given to those who denounced Callisthenes as a participant in the plot which was laid against Alexander by his Pages: some even alleged that he was the instigator of the conspiracy. The facts of the plot were as follows.

13   Since the time of Philip it had been an established custom that the sons of leading Macedonians* were enlisted into the king's service while they were in the adolescent years between puberty and manhood. Their general duties as valets to the king included the responsibility of keeping guard on him while he was sleeping. They would also take the horses from the grooms and lead them up whenever the king was to go riding, then, Persian-style, assist him to mount, and
2   join him in the competitive business of the hunt. One of these was Hermolaus the son of Sopolis, who was said to be a student of philosophy and for that reason an adherent of Callisthenes. The generally accepted account is that in one particular hunt, when a boar was charging at Alexander, Hermolaus let fly at the animal before Alexander, and brought it down with his cast. Having missed his own chance, Alexander was furious with Hermolaus and in his passion ordered him to be flogged in the sight of his fellow Pages, and confiscated his horse.
3   Embittered by this humiliating treatment, the young man Hermolaus told Sostratus the son of Amyntas, his contemporary and lover, that his life was not worth living without revenge taken on Alexander* for this insult. He had no difficulty in persuading
4 Sostratus, as his lover, to join him in the proposed action. These two then won over Antipater, the son of Asclepiodorus the ex-satrap of Syria, Epimenes the son of Arsaeus, Anticles the son of Theocritus, and Philotas the son of the Thracian Carsis. So when the night-watch roster came round to Antipater, it was agreed to attack Alexander that night in his sleep and assassinate him.
5   In fact, according to some, it just so happened that Alexander spent the whole of that night drinking until dawn. But Aristobulus has this account.* There was a Syrian woman subject to fits of divine possession who followed Alexander everywhere. At first she was a figure of fun to Alexander and his entourage: but as it became clear that she was accurate in all her utterances when possessed, Alexander ceased to ignore her, and the woman was given access to the king at any time of day or night, and by now would often watch over him while he slept.
6 And so on this occasion: with the divinity possessing her the woman

met Alexander as he was returning from the carousal and begged him to go back and continue drinking all night. Alexander took this as a sign from the gods and went back to his drinking, and so the action planned by the Pages fell through.

On the next day one of the conspirators, Epimenes the son of 7 Arsaeus, revealed the affair to Charicles the son of Menander, who had become his lover. Charicles passed this on to Epimenes' brother Eurylochus, and Eurylochus went to Alexander's tent and told the whole story to the Bodyguard Ptolemy the son of Lagus. He told Alexander, and Alexander ordered the arrest of all those named by Eurylochus. These were put on the rack, and under torture confessed their own involvement in the plot and gave the names of others as well.

Aristobulus says that they did in fact implicate Callisthenes as the 14 inspiration of their attempted coup, and Ptolemy says likewise. But most historians take a different view, that what made Alexander so ready to believe the worst of Callisthenes was his preconceived hatred of the man and the particularly close association between Callisthenes and Hermolaus. Some of my predecessors have also given the follow- 2 ing account. When Hermolaus was brought before the Macedonians he pleaded guilty to the conspiracy, saying that no free man could tolerate Alexander's presumptuous behaviour any longer: and he went through the whole list—the injustice of Philotas' death, the yet more illegitimate death of his father Parmenion and the others killed at that time, the drunken murder of Cleitus, the Median dress, the obeisance issue (a proposal not yet abandoned), Alexander's nights of drinking and days of sleeping. He could bear this no longer, he said, and had wanted to set himself and the rest of the Macedonians free of it. He and those arrested with him were then stoned to death by the 3 assembled company.

As for Callisthenes, Aristobulus says that he was shackled and taken with them as part of the army's baggage, until he died of disease: but Ptolemy the son of Lagus has him tortured on the rack and then crucified. So it is that even entirely trustworthy reporters who were there at the time with Alexander do not agree in their accounts of what actually happened, when the events were public knowledge and open to their own scrutiny. There are many other different ver- 4 sions of these same events related by various other writers, but I shall limit myself to the record I have given here. These events took place

a little later, but I have recorded them in the context of the affair of
Alexander and Cleitus, thinking this the more relevant place in my
narrative.

15   For the second time an embassy came to Alexander from the
European Scythians,* accompanied by the envoys which he himself
had sent to Scythia. The king of Scythia at the time of their mission
2 had subsequently died, and his brother was now on the throne. The
purpose of this embassy was to assure Alexander that the Scythians
were willing to do whatever he required of them, and the envoys
brought him gifts from their king which in Scythia are regarded as
the most honorific. They said that the king was willing to give his
daughter to Alexander in marriage, to confirm the friendship and alli-
3 ance with him. If Alexander should not see fit to marry the Scythian
princess, as an alternative the king would offer the daughters of the
regional barons and other dynasts throughout the land of Scythia to
Alexander's closest associates. He would also come in person, if summoned, to hear Alexander's requirements from Alexander himself.
4 At the same time Pharasmanes, the king of the Chorasmians, arrived
with fifteen hundred horsemen. He explained that his country bordered on Colchis and the territory of the Amazons, and, if Alexander
was minded to march against the Colchians and Amazons* and then
go on to subdue all the tribes extending from there to the Black Sea,
he undertook to act as his guide and to provision his army.
5   Alexander gave a courteous response to the Scythian emissaries, as
suited his interest at the time, but declined the offer of a Scythian
marriage. He thanked Pharasmanes and agreed a friendship and
alliance with him, but said that for his own purposes this was not the
time to march to the Black Sea.* He did, though, recommend
Pharasmanes to the Persian Artabazus, whom he had left in charge of
Bactria,* and to the other satraps with territory adjoining his, and
sent him back to his own area with these commendations set in train.
6 He told Pharasmanes that his immediate concern was India.* With
India subdued he would then be in possession of the whole of Asia;
with Asia in his control he would return to Greece and launch from
there a full-scale naval and land campaign against the Black Sea regions
through the Hellespont and the Propontis; and he asked Pharasmanes
to save his present offers for redemption when that time came.
7   Alexander himself returned to the river Oxus* with the intention
of advancing into Sogdiana, where it was reported that many of the

Sogdians had holed up in their forts and were refusing to obey the regional satrap imposed on them by Alexander. While he was camped at the Oxus a spring of water broke out of the ground not far from his own tent, and close by that another spring of oil.* This prodigy was 8 reported to Ptolemy the son of Lagus, one of the royal Bodyguards, and Ptolemy told Alexander. Alexander made the sacrifices which the seers specified for this phenomenon, and Aristander declared that the spring of oil was a sign of hardship to come, but also portended victory after the hardships.

So Alexander crossed with part of his force into Sogdiana, leaving 16 Polyperchon, Attalus, Gorgias, and Meleager* where they were in Bactria, with instructions to keep a tight hold on the country to prevent any further insurgency by the barbarians of the area, and also to take out those still in revolt. He himself divided the force he had 2 with him into five parts. He gave one to the command of Hephaestion, and another to the Bodyguard Ptolemy the son of Lagus; he put the third under Perdiccas, and the fourth brigade was commanded by Coenus and Artabazus. He himself took the fifth division and struck out with it into Sogdiana towards Maracanda. Each of the other divisions pursued their own line of invasion as and where opportunity presented, sometimes using force to annihilate groups congregated in the strongholds, sometimes winning them over in voluntary surrender. Between them these divisions covered most of Sogdiana, and when his entire armament had reconvened at Maracanda Alexander sent out Hephaestion with a commission to repopulate the cities already founded in Sogdiana, and dispatched Coenus and Artabazus into Scythia,* as news was coming in that Spitamenes had taken refuge there. He himself took the rest of the troops and swept through the areas of Sogdiana still held by the rebels, easily destroying these pockets of resistance.

While Alexander was engaged in this activity, Spitamenes and a 4 number of Sogdian fugitives who had joined him in retreating to the territory of the Scythian tribe called the Massagetae gathered a force of six hundred Massagetae cavalry and came up to one of the forts in Bactria. The fort commandant had not been expecting any 5 enemy action, and their attack took him and his garrison troops by surprise: they killed the soldiers, arrested the commandant, and kept him under guard. Encouraged by the capture of this fort, a few days later they approached Zariaspa. They had no intention of a frontal assault on the city, but they surrounded it and drove off a great deal of booty.

6   In Zariaspa there were a few of the Companion cavalry, left behind there as they were sick, together with Peithon the son of Sosicles, who had been put in charge of the royal entourage at Zariaspa, and Aristonicus the musician.* When they saw this raid by the Scythians (and they were by now sufficiently recovered to bear arms and ride their horses), they gathered the eighty or so mercenary cavalry left to garrison Zariaspa, and some of the Royal Pages,* and sallied out to

7 confront the Massagetae. Their first charge took the Scythians completely unawares, and they recovered all of the plunder, killing a good number of those who were driving the booty off. But their own return was disorderly, as no one was in charge, and they were caught in an ambush by Spitamenes and the Scythians in which they lost seven of the Companions and sixty of the mercenary cavalry. Aristonicus was killed there, having shown bravery beyond that expected in a musician. Peithon was wounded and captured alive by the Scythians.

17   When the report of this reached Craterus, he marched at full speed against the Massagetae: and when they heard of his imminent approach they set off in urgent flight towards the desert. Craterus kept close after them and overtook them (now joined by more than a

2 thousand other Massagetae horsemen) not far from the desert. A fierce battle ensued between the Macedonians and the Scythians, in which the Macedonians were victorious. A hundred and fifty Scythian cavalry were killed, but the rest made an easy escape into the desert, as the Macedonians were in no state to continue the pursuit.

3   Meanwhile Alexander relieved Artabazus of the satrapy of Bactria at his own request on grounds of age,* and appointed as satrap in his place Amyntas the son of Nicolaus. He left Coenus at Maracanda with his own brigade and Meleager's, about four hundred of the Companion cavalry, all the mounted javelin-men, some of the Bactrian and Sogdian troops, and the other contingents assigned to Amyntas. His instructions to this whole force were that they should take their orders from Coenus and spend the winter there in Sogdiana, to keep a guard on the region and look for the chance to trap and capture Spitamenes in his movements over the winter.

4   When Spitamenes and his men found that the Macedonians had installed garrisons all over the country, which denied them a safe retreat anywhere, they turned their attention to an attack on Coenus

and the troops under him, thinking they would have a better chance of success in this part of the country. They arrived at Gabae,* a Sogdian stronghold lying on the border between Sogdiana and the territory of the Massagetae Scythians, and had little difficulty in inducing some three thousand Scythian horsemen to join them in the invasion of Sogdiana. These Scythians are easily recruited into one 5 war after another: they live in conditions of extreme poverty, and theirs is a nomadic way of life without the permanent settlements which would make them fear consequences for their families.* When Coenus and his fellow officers learnt that Spitamenes was approaching with this cavalry force, they moved to confront them with their own troops. A fierce battle ensued, resulting in a Macedonian victory 6 such that more than eight hundred of the barbarian horsemen were killed in the fighting, while the losses on Coenus' side were about twenty-five cavalry and twelve infantry. In the consequent flight Spitamenes was deserted by the remaining Sogdians in his force and most of the Bactrians, who came in and surrendered themselves to Coenus. After this defeat inflicted on them the Massagetae Scythians 7 plundered the baggage-trains of the Bactrians and Sogdians who had been their fellows in the battle-line, and joined Spitamenes in the retreat to the desert. But when they heard reports that Alexander was on the move and making for the desert, they decapitated Spitamenes and sent his head to Alexander,* hoping that this gesture would protect them from his attention.

Meanwhile Coenus had returned to join Alexander at Nautaca 18 [Shakhrisyabz], and so had Craterus and Phrataphernes the satrap of Parthyaea with their troops, and Stasanor* the satrap of Areia, having carried out all of Alexander's instructions. While resting his 2 army at Nautaca (it was the depth of winter), Alexander dispatched Phrataphernes* to the Mardian and Tapurian region, to arrest and bring back the satrap Autophradates, who had ignored successive orders from Alexander for his recall. He sent Stasanor to the 3 Drangians as their satrap, and Atropates likewise to the Medes to take over the satrapy of Media from Oxydates, who seemed to him guilty of deliberate failure of duty. He dispatched Stamenes to govern Babylon, as news had reached him that Mazaeus, the satrap of Babylon, had died. And he sent Sopolis, Epocillus, and Menidas to Macedonia, to bring up the home army* to join him.

*At the first sign of spring Alexander advanced towards the Rock 4

of Sogdiana,* where he was told that many of the Sogdians had taken
refuge. The refugees on this rock were said to include the wife and
daughters of Oxyartes the Bactrian, who had put them there for safe
keeping (as he himself had revolted from Alexander)* in what he
assumed was an impregnable position. Alexander thought that once
this rock was taken the Sogdians still intent on revolt would have
5 no other recourse left to them. But when he and his army came
close to the rock, he found that on all sides it presented a sheer face
against attack, and the barbarians had laid in provisions for a long
siege. A heavy fall of snow made the approach more difficult for the
Macedonians, and at the same time kept the barbarians well supplied
6 with water. Even so, Alexander determined to attack the place, not
least because a sneering quip by the barbarians had angered him and
piqued his pride. He had invited them to agree terms, and was offering them the guarantee of a safe return to their homes if they handed
over the rock. They laughed and, speaking in their native language,
told Alexander that he must look for soldiers with wings to take the
7 rock for him, as ordinary humans gave them no concern. In response
Alexander immediately announced a reward of twelve talents for the
first man to scale the rock, with other prizes specified for the second,
the third, and so on down to the last man to reach the top, whose
reward would be three hundred darics.* The Macedonians were
already keen to make the attempt and this announcement whetted
their appetite yet further.

19   A unit numbering about three hundred was formed of all those
who had gained experience of rock-climbing in previous sieges. They
gathered a supply of the small iron pegs used to secure their tents, to
serve as pitons for fixing into the snow wherever it seemed frozen
solid or into any patches of bare rock grinning through the snow, and
they tied these pegs to stout linen ropes. Thus equipped, they set out
at night for the most precipitous face of the rock, which was for that
2 reason least well guarded. Fixing their pegs where they could, sometimes into solid ground wherever it showed through, sometimes into
the snow where it seemed least likely to crumble, they hauled themselves up the rock by various routes. About thirty of them fell to their
death in the climb, and their bodies, lost in the snow where they hap-
3 pened to fall, could not be found for burial. The rest completed the
ascent towards dawn, established possession of the summit of the
rock, and, as prearranged by Alexander, waved linen flags to signal

success to the Macedonian camp below. Alexander sent forward a herald to shout up to the barbarian defenders that they should surrender without further delay: he had found the men with wings, and the summit was now in their hands (with this he pointed to the soldiers up on the top).

The barbarians were aghast at a sight they had never thought possible, and supposed that the force occupying the summit was more numerous than they could see, and fully armed. So they surrendered themselves—such was the panic induced by the sight of these few Macedonians. In consequence many men's wives and children were captured, and most notably the wife and daughters of Oxyartes. One of Oxyartes' daughters was a virgin girl of marriageable age called Rhoxane.* Those who served with Alexander say that she was the most beautiful woman they had seen in Asia, second only to the wife of Darius, and that Alexander fell in love with her at first sight. For all his desire he was not prepared to violate her as a captive, but saw no reason not to marry her. And in this Alexander to my mind deserves more praise than censure.*

In the case of Darius' wife, who was said to be the greatest beauty in Asia, either he did not fall for her or, if he did, he kept his desire under control, though he was a young man at the height of success, which is when people tend to take what they want regardless. But he respected her and left her alone, showing great restraint as well as a prudent concern to establish a good name. Indeed there is a prevalent story that shortly after the battle fought between Darius and Alexander at Issus the eunuch attendant on Darius' wife as her guard managed to escape and rejoin Darius. As soon as he saw him, Darius' first question was whether his daughters, his wife, and his mother were still alive. Learning that they were, and retained their royal titles and the same entourage of servants as they had enjoyed at Darius' court, his next question was whether his wife was remaining faithful to him. Learning that she was, he then asked whether she had been forced to submit to violation by Alexander. The eunuch answered on his oath, 'Your wife, sir, is as she was when you left her, and Alexander is the model of nobility and restraint.' At this Darius stretched out his arms to the heaven and made this prayer: 'Hear me, Zeus, King of all. Yours is the power to ordain the fortunes of kings on earth. Grant now my best wish, and keep me sovereign over the Persians and Medes: you gave, and you can preserve. But if it is your will that I am no longer to be king of Asia, then give my empire, I pray, to none but Alexander.' This shows that even enemies will recognize an act of decency.

When Oxyartes heard that his children were held captive, the further news that Alexander had a care for his daughter Rhoxane gave him the confidence to present himself to Alexander, and he was received with the honour appropriate on this happy occasion.

21   With his work in Sogdiana completed and the rock now in his possession, Alexander advanced into the territory of the Pareitacae, as here too there was a stronghold said to be occupied by a good number of the barbarians: this was another rock, called the Rock of Chorienes.* Chorienes himself and several other local dynasts had taken defensive
2 refuge there. This rock extended over two miles from base to peak, and the circuit of its base was about six and a half miles. It was sheer on all sides, and there was only one way up, which furthermore was a narrow and difficult path, constructed as it was against the natural contours of the place. So it was hard to get up, even in single file and even without opposition. There was also a deep ravine enclosing the rock all round, so that anyone proposing to bring up an army to assault the rock would need before anything else to fill up the ravine, so as to have level ground from which to launch his army's attack.

3   Even so, Alexander set himself to the task, by now determined that there should be nowhere beyond his reach or immune to capture— such was the height of confidence to which high success had brought him. So he began felling the tall pines which grew in profusion all round the rock, and making ladders from them as the only means by
4 which his troops could get down into the ravine. During the daytime Alexander had half of the army at work under his own supervision: at night three of the Bodyguards, Perdiccas, Leonnatus, and Ptolemy the son of Lagus, continued the operation with the rest of the army split into three sections. The site presented such difficulties, and the work within it was so arduous, that their progress was limited to a stretch of no more than thirty feet by day, and rather less by night.

5   Their method was this. They went down into the ravine and drove piles into the riverbed where the flow was fastest, spacing them close enough to bear the weight of the infill and hold it together. Across these piles they placed wickerwork frames as a sort of bridge, tied them together, and then tipped earth down onto this framework, to build up a level surface for the army's access to the rock.

At first the barbarians took a dismissive view of this operation, 6 regarding it as completely hopeless. But as time went on the artillery began to find the range of the rock and the defenders above could do nothing to stop the Macedonians, who had erected screens to protect against missiles so the bridging work could continue in safety under them. Now alarmed at this developing situation Chorienes sent a herald to Alexander asking that Oxyartes should be sent up to him. This was done, and once there Oxyartes urged Chorienes to give himself 7 and the stronghold into the hands of Alexander. He argued that Alexander and his army could take anywhere they wanted by force, but if Chorienes were to go the way of trust and friendship, he himself could not speak too highly of the king's good faith and fair dealing, and he adduced his own treatment as a prime example to prove his point. Convinced by this, Chorienes came down to Alexander in per- 8 son, together with some of his kinsmen and associates. On his arrival Alexander gave him a courteous response and a pledge of friendship. He kept Chorienes with him and told him to send some of those who had accompanied his descent to return to the rock and order its surrender. The other refugees gathered there did surrender it, and 9 Alexander subsequently took five hundred of the foot guards with him to go up and see the rock for himself. So far from imposing any harsh penalty on Chorienes, Alexander put him in charge of this very same stronghold and allowed him to retain his position as regional overlord.

The winter had been hard on the army, and they suffered from a 10 heavy fall of snow during the siege: at the same time they were debilitated by a shortage of food. Chorienes offered to provision the army for two months, and made an immediate distribution to each mess of corn, wine, and salted meat from his stores on the rock. Even after this largesse he said he had not used up even a tenth of what they had laid in for the siege. This made Alexander respect him the more for what was a voluntary rather than an enforced surrender of the rock.

With this objective achieved, Alexander himself returned to Bactra, 22 but sent Craterus against Catanes* and Austanes, the only rebels left in Pareitacene: Craterus had with him six hundred of the Companion cavalry and four infantry brigades—his own, and those of Polyperchon, Attalus, and Alcetas.* There followed a fierce battle in which Craterus' 2 troops were victorious. Catanes died fighting in the field, and Austanes

was captured and brought before Alexander: the losses in their barbarian army were a hundred and twenty cavalry and about fifteen
hundred infantry. After this success Craterus and his force also
returned to Bactra, which is where Alexander then had to deal with
Callisthenes and the affair of the Pages.

3   Now that spring was over,* Alexander took his army out of Bactra
and advanced towards India, leaving Amyntas in Bactria with three
4 thousand five hundred cavalry and ten thousand infantry. He crossed
the Caucasus in ten days and came to the city of Alexandria [Begram]
which he had founded in Parapamisadae territory on his first campaign against the Bactrians. He dismissed from office the governor he
had originally put in charge of the city, deciding that his administra-
5 tion had been incompetent, and swelled the population of Alexandria
with more settlers drafted from the surrounding area and the members of his own army who were no longer fit for active service. As
administrator of the city itself he appointed Nicanor, one of the
Companions, and he installed Tyriespis* as satrap of the country of
the Parapamisadae and the adjoining land as far as the river Cophen
6 [Kabul]. After reaching Nicaea and sacrificing to Athena, Alexander
moved on towards the Cophen: he had sent a herald ahead of him to
Taxiles and the Indians on this side of the river Indus, asking them to
come to meet him at their individual convenience. Taxiles* and the
other princes did come as requested, bringing with them the gifts
which have the greatest prestige in their culture, and they promised
to give him the elephants in their possession, some twenty-five of
them.

7   Here Alexander divided his army, and sent Hephaestion and
Perdiccas* into the territory of Peucelaotis [Gandhara] towards the
river Indus. They took with them the brigades of Gorgias, Cleitus, and
Meleager, half of the Companion cavalry, and all the mercenary cavalry.
Their instructions were to take by force or negotiate the surrender of
all the towns on their route, and, once arrived at the Indus, to make
all necessary preparations for the crossing of the river. Taxiles and
8 the other princes were sent with them. When they reached the
Indus they set about the task Alexander had given them. But Astis,
the ruling prince of Peucelaotis, broke out in revolt, to his own ruin
and that of the city* where he and his followers had fled for refuge:
Hephaestion's troops took it after a thirty-day siege. Astis himself was
put to death, and Sangaeus was appointed governor of the city: he had

previously deserted Astis and gone over to Taxiles, which made Alexander confident of his loyalty.

Alexander took the foot guards, all the Companion cavalry not 23 allocated to Hephaestion, the brigades of the so-called 'Close Companions', the archers, the Agrianians, and the mounted javelin-men, and advanced towards the territory of the Aspasians, Guraeans, and Assacenians. After taking a rough mountainous path along the river 2 called Choes, and crossing the river with some difficulty, he ordered the bulk of the infantry to follow on after him at marching pace, while he himself pressed on at speed with all the cavalry and about eight hundred of the Macedonian foot mounted on horseback and carrying their infantry shields, as he was receiving reports that the barbarians inhabiting the area had gathered for refuge in the mountains of their country and the cities which had defensive fortifications. He made an 3 immediate assault on the first of these cities lying on his route, and in one quick attack routed the defenders drawn up in front of the city and shut them up inside. In this action he took an arrow wound in the shoulder through his breastplate (the wound did not give him much trouble, as the breastplate had prevented the arrow from passing right through the shoulder). Ptolemy the son of Lagus and Leonnatus were also wounded.

Alexander then made camp close to the city, where the wall seemed 4 most vulnerable to assault. There was in fact a double wall surrounding the city, and towards dawn on the next day the Macedonians easily broke through the first loosely built wall. The barbarians put up a brief stand at the second wall, but as soon as the scaling-ladders were in place and missiles began to inflict widespread damage on the first line of defenders, they abandoned any further resistance and came pouring out of the city gates, heading for the mountains. Some of 5 them were killed in the flight, and any caught alive were executed by the Macedonians in fury for their wounding of Alexander, but most escaped to the mountains, which were at no great distance from the city. Alexander razed the city, and moved on to another called Andaca, which agreed terms and surrendered into his hands. He then left Craterus to stay behind in the region with the other infantry commanders, to reduce any other cities which would not come over voluntarily, and to make arrangements in that area as best suited their present interests.

For his own operations Alexander took with him the foot guards, 24 the archers, the Agrianians, the brigades of Coenus and Attalus, the elite cavalry corps, some four units from the rest of the Companion cavalry, and half of the mounted archers. With this force he advanced to the river Euias, and from there to the Aspasian capital, where the prince had his seat, reaching the city on the second day of a long

2 march. On learning of Alexander's approach the barbarians fired the city and fled for the mountains. Alexander's troops pressed close in pursuit as far as the mountains, and there was massive slaughter of the refugees before they could get away into rough terrain.

3   The leader of the Indians in this region was spotted by Ptolemy the son of Lagus nearing one of the foothills with a group of his soldiers to escort him. Though his own company was much outnumbered Ptolemy still gave chase on horseback, and when the hill proved too steep for his horse to climb he left it there to be held by one of his

4 attendants and, just as he was, went after the Indian on foot. When the Indian saw Ptolemy closing on him, he and his soldiers turned to offer battle. The Indian aimed a thrust of his long spear at Ptolemy's chest through the breastplate, but the armour held good against the strike. Ptolemy then drove right through the Indian's thigh,* felled

5 him, and stripped the body. When the soldiers escorting him saw their leader lying there they abandoned their ground, but the men in the hills were outraged at the sight of the enemy carrying off the body of their prince, and came running down to join a fierce battle over the body close to the foothill. Alexander was already nearing the hill with those of his infantry who had dismounted: they now intervened and with some difficulty pushed the Indians back to the mountains and gained possession of the body.

6   Alexander crossed the mountains and came down to a city called Arigaeum [Nawagai], finding that it had been fired by the inhabitants and the population had fled. Here Craterus and his colleagues met

7 him with their army, after carrying out all the king's instructions.* As this city seemed well placed for a settlement, Alexander told Craterus to fortify it and settle the place with volunteers from the surrounding area and any members of the army now unfit for service. He himself advanced to the mountain where he was told that most of the barbarians in the region had taken refuge, and made camp at its foot.

8   It was at this point that Ptolemy the son of Lagus, sent out on a foraging expedition by Alexander, took a few of his men and went further ahead on his own initiative to spy out the land. He reported

to Alexander that he had seen the barbarian campfires, and they outnumbered the fires in Alexander's own camp. Alexander was not con- 9
vinced of the number, but he did recognize that he was faced with
some sort of concentration of the local barbarians. He left part of his
army camped where it was at the foot of the mountain, and took out
with him what seemed a sufficient force in view of the report. When
they were close enough to see the fires for themselves, he divided his
force into three parts. He put Leonnatus the Bodyguard in charge of 10
one, assigning him the units of Attalus and Balacrus; Ptolemy the son
of Lagus was given command of the second section, comprising one-
third of the royal foot guards, the brigades of Philip and Philotas,*
two regiments of archers, the Agrianians, and half of the cavalry; he
himself led the third section, and took it straight for what seemed the
greatest concentration of barbarians.

When the barbarians, from their commanding position on high 25
ground, saw the Macedonians approaching, confident in their own
numbers and contemptuous of the Macedonians' apparently small
force, they came down to the plain and a fierce battle ensued. Even
so, Alexander defeated this section of the barbarians without much
trouble. Ptolemy's troops could not deploy on level ground, as the 2
barbarians facing them were holding a hill with their companies
ranged in depth on a narrow front. Ptolemy advanced his troops to
what seemed the most vulnerable aspect of the hill, not completely
encircling it, but leaving an area open for escape, in case the barbarians chose to flee rather than fight. In fact there was a fierce battle 3
here also, compounded by the difficult terrain and the fact that these
Indians, in contrast to the other barbarians of the area, were by far the
best fighters of the local population. But these too were driven off the
hill by the Macedonians. Leonnatus and the third section of the army
were equally successful in defeating their opponents. Ptolemy says 4
that in total over forty thousand men were captured and over two
hundred and thirty thousand oxen:* and that Alexander, struck by
the exceptional good looks and size of these cattle, selected the finest
of them with the intention of sending them to Macedonia to work the
land.

From there Alexander marched towards the territory of the 5
Assacenians, as reports reached him that they had prepared for war
with some two thousand cavalry, over thirty thousand infantry, and
thirty elephants. Craterus had now finished the fortification of the

city he had been left behind to settle, and brought up to Alexander
the heavier-armed contingents of the army and the siege-train, in
6 case there was need for a siege. Alexander himself went on towards
the Assacenians, taking with him the Companion cavalry, the
mounted javelin-men, the brigades of Coenus and Polyperchon, the
thousand Agrianians, and the archers. His route lay through Guraean
7 country, and the crossing of the eponymous river Guraeus [Panjkora]
caused some difficulty—it was deep and fast-flowing, and the rounded
stones in its bed proved slippery to the tread. When the barbarians
became aware of Alexander's approach, they abandoned any brave
thoughts of a single concerted stand, and dispersed to their various
cities with the intention of fighting defensive campaigns for their
preservation, city by city.

26   Alexander marched first against Massaga,* the largest city in the
region. He had already come close up to the walls when the barbarians, confident in the seven thousand or so mercenaries they had
brought in from deeper India, suddenly charged out and made for
the Macedonians at the run when they saw them pitching camp.
2 Alexander realized that an immediate battle would be close to the
city, and he wanted to lure them out further from the walls, so that if
a rout ensued (and he was sure that it would) they would not have an
easy escape over a short distance to safety in their city. So as soon as
he saw the barbarians making their sally, he ordered the Macedonians
to turn about and withdraw towards a hill about three-quarters of a
3 mile away from his intended campsite. Emboldened by what they took
to be an instant Macedonian retreat, the enemy came on at them in a
disorderly rush. When the enemy arrows were just beginning to find
the range, at an agreed signal Alexander wheeled his phalanx and took
4 it back at the double against them. His mounted javelin-men, the
Agrianians, and the archers ran out ahead to engage the barbarians,
while he himself led on the phalanx in formation. The Indians were
stunned by this unexpected turn, and as soon as it came to hand-to-
hand fighting they gave way and fled for the city. About two hundred
of them were killed and the rest penned back inside their walls.
Alexander brought his phalanx up to the wall, and was then hit in the
ankle by a bow-shot* from the wall, but it was not a serious wound.
5 On the following day he brought up the siege-engines and easily battered down one section of the walls, but as the Macedonians attempted
to force their way in through this breach the Indians put up a stout

resistance, so that on this day Alexander had to recall his troops. The Macedonian attack was stronger on the next day, and a wooden tower was moved up against the walls, holding archers and catapults whose barrage of arrows and missiles kept the Indians a long way back, but even so they were unable to force an entry.

On the third day Alexander brought up the phalanx once more and 6 used a machine to lower a drawbridge across the breach in the wall: he then led the foot guards over it (they had been deployed in the same way in the capture of Tyre). The numbers crowding onto it in their enthusiasm overburdened the bridge, and it collapsed, taking the Macedonians with it. Seeing what was happening, the barbarians 7 on the walls gave a shout and began pelting them with stones, arrows, and anything else they happened to be holding or could lay their hands on at the moment, while others rushed out through the small gates in the curtain walls and struck directly at the Macedonians before they could recover from the fall. Alexander sent out Alcetas 27 with his brigade to recover the wounded and recall those still in combat to the camp. On the fourth day he had another drawbridge brought up to the wall on a different machine.

For as long as their local commander was alive the Indians contin- 2 ued to offer strong resistance. But when he was hit and killed by a catapult-bolt, and by then they had lost a number of their men in the sustained siege and most of them were wounded and out of action, they sent a herald to negotiate with Alexander. He was glad for the 3 opportunity to save the lives of brave men, and reached an agreement with the mercenary Indians on the condition that they should enrol as regular members of his army and join in his campaigns. They came out with their arms, and camped by themselves on a hill facing the Macedonian camp. In fact their intention was to make a dash for it at night and get away to their own homelands, as they had no wish to bear arms against fellow Indians. When Alexander heard of this, he 4 deployed his entire army in the night to ring the hill and cut down the Indians trapped inside:* he then took the city by storm, denuded now of its defenders, and captured the mother and daughter of Assacanus. In the whole siege the losses on Alexander's side amounted to some twenty-five men.

From there he sent Coenus to Bazira [Bir-kot], in the belief that 5 the inhabitants would surrender when they heard of the capture of Massaga. Attalus, Alcetas, and the cavalry commander Demetrius

were sent to another city, Ora* [Ude-gram], with instructions to
6 build a wall round it pending his own arrival. The people of Ora made
a sally against the troops with Alcetas, but the Macedonians had little
difficulty in routing them and sending them back inside their city wall.
Coenus had no success at Bazira. The people there were confident in
the strength of their site: it was very high and fully fortified all round,
and they gave no signs of submission.

7   On learning this Alexander started out for Bazira, but having heard
that some of the neighbouring barbarians, sent for that purpose by
Abisares,* were planning to make a covert entry into the city of Ora,
he marched first to Ora. He instructed Coenus to fortify a strong
position close enough to dominate Bazira, and to leave it with a sufficient garrison to deny the townspeople free use of their land: he
8 should then bring the rest of his force to join him. When the people
of Bazira saw Coenus leaving with most of his army, they disdainfully
thought that the remaining Macedonians would be no match for
them, and issued out into the plain. There followed a fierce battle in
which some five hundred of the barbarians were killed and more than
seventy captured alive. The rest fled back to the city, and were thereafter more closely debarred from their land by the garrison in the
9 fort. Alexander had no difficulty with the attack on Ora: he took the
city with one quick assault on the walls, and captured the elephants
left behind there.

28   When they heard of this the inhabitants of Bazira despaired of
their own situation, and round about midnight they abandoned their
city and fled to the Rock. The other barbarians of the area did the
same, all leaving their cities and fleeing for refuge on the rock in that
part of the country which is called Aornus* [Pir-Sar]. This rock is a
really massive feature of the landscape, and there is a tradition that
2 not even Heracles the son of Zeus could capture it. Whether Heracles
did in fact ever reach India—be it the Theban Heracles, the Tyrian,
or the Egyptian—I cannot confirm one way or the other. My own
view is that probably he did not,* but wherever something is difficult
men tend to exaggerate the difficulty by making up a story that even
Heracles would have found it impossible. So with this rock—I believe
3 that Heracles' name is invoked to add lustre to its reputation. The
circuit of the rock is said to be about twenty-two miles, and the height
of its plateau some six and a half thousand feet, with a rough man-
made track the only way up. At the top there is said to be a spring

with plenty of pure water positively gushing from it, and timber and enough good arable earth to occupy a thousand men in its cultivation.

As he heard all this Alexander was seized by a yen to add the cap- 4 ture of this mountain to his achievements, not least because of the legend told about Heracles. He turned Ora and Massaga into forts to garrison the area, and fortified Bazira as a city. The troops with 5 Hephaestion and Perdiccas had fortified another city for him, called Orobatis,* and left a garrison in it before proceeding on their way to the river Indus: once there, they set about following Alexander's instructions for the bridging of the Indus. And Alexander appointed 6 Nicanor, one of the Companions, as satrap of the whole region to the west of the river Indus.

He himself marched first towards the Indus, and secured the surrender by agreement of the city of Peucelaotis,* situated not far from the Indus. He installed a Macedonian garrison with Philip as its commander, and went on to take over some other small towns lying near the Indus. He had with him the local princes, Cophaeus and Assagetes. On arrival at the city of Embolima,* near the Rock of 7 Aornus, he left Craterus there with part of the army to gather as much food as possible into the city and all other necessities for a long stay, so the city could be the base for the Macedonians to wear down the occupiers of the rock with a lengthy blockade, if an immediate assault failed to capture it. He himself advanced towards the rock, 8 taking with him the Agrianians, Coenus' brigade, a select group of the fittest and also best-armed members of the phalanx, about two hundred of the Companion cavalry, and a hundred of the mounted archers. On that day he made camp in a suitable place of his choosing: on the next he moved a little closer to the rock and camped again.

At this point some of the local people came to surrender, and said 29 they would guide Alexander to the most vulnerable part of the rock, from which he could easily take the whole place. He sent Ptolemy the son of Lagus, the Bodyguard, to accompany them with the Agrianians, the other light troops, and a select unit of the foot guards: when Ptolemy had captured the position, he was to put a firm guard on it and signal its possession to Alexander. Following a rough and diffi- 2 cult route, Ptolemy managed to take the place without alerting the enemy, strengthened it with a surrounding stockade and ditch, and lit a beacon at a point on the mountain where Alexander would be able to see it. The fire was seen immediately, and on the next day Alexander advanced his army: but the barbarians fought back and he

3 could make no headway in the difficult terrain. When they were satisfied that Alexander could get nowhere on his line of attack, they turned and began their own attack on Ptolemy and his troops. A fierce struggle ensued between them and the Macedonians, the Indians making every effort to break down the stockade, and Ptolemy to keep his hold on the position. The barbarians had the worst of the exchanges of fire, and withdrew when night came on.

4 Alexander picked out one of the Indian deserters whom he had reason to trust and who knew the locality well, and sent him up to Ptolemy during the night with a letter. His written instructions were that when he made his own approach to the rock Ptolemy should move up the mountain against the Indians and not confine himself to the defence of his position: that way the Indians would come under

5 fire from two directions and find themselves compromised. At dawn Alexander left camp and led his army up the approach route which Ptolemy had used undetected: his thought was that if he could force his way up by this route and join Ptolemy's men, the rest of the task

6 should be easy. And so it happened. Until midday there was fierce battle between the Indians and the Macedonians, as they fought to gain the ascent and the Indians shot at them as they climbed up. But the Macedonians kept coming, group after group moving to the attack while their immediate predecessors rested, until after great effort and late in the afternoon they finally won control of the ascent and joined up with Ptolemy's force. Now united, the entire army moved up from there for another attempt on the rock itself, but the assault still proved physically impossible, and this was the end of operations for that day.

7 Shortly before dawn Alexander ordered all the soldiers to set about cutting a hundred stakes each. When these had been cut, he started the construction under his personal supervision of a huge ramp extending towards the rock from the summit of the hill on which they had camped: he reckoned that this ramp would bring his archers and missile-firing catapults within range of the defenders. All hands took part in the work of piling the ramp, and Alexander himself stood by to observe and commend hard-working progress and punish any instance of slackness.

30 On the first day the army built the ramp out to a length of about two hundred yards. On the next the slingers and the catapults could keep up fire on the Indians from the ramp so far constructed, which

deterred their sallies against the men working on it. For three successive days Alexander kept up the work of filling in the gap. On the
fourth day a few Macedonians forced their way through to capture a
small hill on a level with the rock. Without a moment's pause
Alexander drove forward the construction work to link the ramp to
the hill which this small group now held for him.

The Indians were stunned by the unimaginable daring of the 2
Macedonians who had forced through to the hill, and seeing the ramp
already joined to it they decided to put up no further resistance and
sent heralds to Alexander, offering to surrender the rock under formal treaty. Their plan was to spend the rest of the day in delaying
tactics to postpone ratification of the treaty, then scatter during the
night to their various home areas. When he heard of this, Alexander 3
granted them time for their withdrawal and agreed the removal of his
surrounding guard-posts. He waited until they had begun to withdraw, then took seven hundred of the bodyguards and foot guards
and climbed up to the part of the rock which was now deserted. He
himself was the first up, and the Macedonians followed, hauling one
another up by various routes. Then at a signal this force turned on 4
the retreating barbarians and killed many of them as they tried to
escape: in their panic to get away some threw themselves to their
death over the precipices. Alexander was now master of the rock
which had defeated Heracles. He made sacrifice on it and established
a garrison there, giving its command to Sisicottus, who had long ago
deserted from the Indians and joined Bessus at Bactra, then had taken
service in Alexander's army after his conquest of Bactria and shown
himself completely loyal.

Alexander now left the rock and struck into the country of the 5
Assacenians, where it was reported that Assacanus' brother had
holed up in the mountains, taking with him the elephants and a
good number of the local barbarians. When he arrived at a city called
Dyrta* he found it and the surrounding area devoid of inhabitants.
On the following day he sent out Nearchus and Antiochus, both
foot-guard battalion commanders, giving Nearchus the light-armed 6
Agrianians and Antiochus his own battalion and two more. They
were sent to reconnoitre the region and if possible capture some of
the barbarians to interrogate them about the local situation: Alexander
was particularly concerned to find out about the elephants.

He himself was now making for the river Indus, and the army had 7

to construct a road for the progress through what was otherwise impassable country. Here he captured a few of the barbarians, and learnt from them that the Indians of the region had fled to join Abisares, but had left their elephants where they were, grazing near the river
8 Indus. He ordered them to show him the way to the elephants. There are many elephant-hunters among the Indians, and Alexander was particular in keeping some of them with him: they now helped him to hunt these elephants. In the chase two of the beasts ran to their death over a precipice, but the rest were captured, submitted to mahouts,
9 and joined the army. He also found serviceable timber by the river, and had his army cut it down for shipbuilding. These ships then travelled down the river Indus to the bridge* which Hephaestion and Perdiccas had constructed on Alexander's orders some time ago.

BOOK FIVE

*IN this country which Alexander traversed between the rivers 1
Cophen and Indus there also lies the city of Nysa,* said to have been
founded by Dionysus after his conquest of the Indians—whoever
this Dionysus was, and whenever and from wherever he campaigned
against the Indians. I certainly have no means of deciding whether 2
the Theban Dionysus set out, either from Thebes or from Tmolus in
Lydia, and reached India at the head of an army, or how he managed
to pass through so many warlike peoples unknown to the Greeks of
the time without forcibly subduing any of them apart from the Indians. Except that one should not be a pedantic critic of the ancient
legends about the gods: what is incredible when judged by probability does not seem quite so far-fetched when one adds the divine
aspect to the story.

When Alexander came up to attack Nysa, the people sent out to 3
him the man of greatest authority among them, whose name was
Acuphis, accompanied on his embassy by thirty of the most distinguished citizens, to beg him to release their city into the god's charge.
It is said that the envoys came into Alexander's tent and found him 4
sitting there with the dust of the road still on him, in full armour with
the helmet on his head and spear in hand. Overawed at the sight they
fell to the ground and stayed silent for a long time. When Alexander
raised them up and told them to have no fear, Acuphis finally began
and spoke as follows:

'Your majesty, the people of Nysa beg you, out of respect for 5
Dionysus, to leave them free and independent.* When Dionysus was
on his way back to the Greek Sea [Aegean] after conquering the
Indian nation, he founded this city with those of his soldiers who had
become unfit for service: they were also his initiates. He wanted it to
be a memorial to posterity of his travels and his victory, just as you
yourself have founded Alexandria in the Caucasus and another
Alexandria in Egypt, and have left or will in time leave many other
foundations as proof that your achievements outnumber those of
Dionysus. Dionysus named the city Nysa, and the area Nysaea, after 6
his nurse Nyse. So also with the mountain near the city: he called this
Meros, as the legend goes that he grew to his birth in Zeus' thigh*

(*meros*). And from that time on Nysa has been a free city and we who live here have enjoyed independence and good government. And you can see further proof that Dionysus was our founder in the fact that ivy grows nowhere else in India except here.'

2   All this was congenial to Alexander's ears, and he wanted to believe the stories about Dionysus' travels. He also wanted Nysa to be a foundation of Dionysus, which would mean that he himself had already gone as far as Dionysus and would yet go beyond him: and he thought that the Macedonians would not be so reluctant to follow him on arduous campaigns still further on if they were spurred by the

2   ambition to surpass Dionysus' achievements.* So he granted the settlers of Nysa their freedom and independence. When he enquired about their institutions and learnt that their government was an aristocracy, he expressed his satisfaction, but at the same time demanded that they should send with him some three hundred of their horsemen, and select to go with him too the best hundred men of their governing elite, which happened to number three hundred also: Acuphis was to make the selection, and Alexander appointed him

3   governor of the Nysaea region. Acuphis is said to have smiled at this request, and when Alexander asked what had amused him, Acuphis replied: 'And how, your majesty, could a single city be deprived of a hundred good men and still remain well governed? No, if you care for the people of Nysa, take the three hundred horsemen, or more if you wish: but instead of the hundred best men you ask me to select, take twice that number of the commoners,* so that when you come back to Nysa you can find the city in the same good order you see now.'

4   This seemed a sensible response, and Alexander was persuaded by it. He ordered Acuphis to send him the horsemen, but dropped his demand for the select hundred and asked for no substitutes either: but Acuphis was required to send his own son and his grandson by his daughter.

5   Alexander was now taken with a yen to visit the place where the Nysaeans proudly claimed there was evidence of Dionysus. It is said that he went to Mount Meros with the Companion cavalry and the royal guard of infantry, and saw how the mountain was full of ivy and bay,* with all sorts of copses and shady thickets and every kind of

6   game there for the hunt. The Macedonians were delighted to see ivy after such a long time (as there was no other ivy in India, even in areas where there were vines), and hurried to make themselves wreaths of

it, which they put round their heads there and then, singing hymns to Dionysus and invoking the god by all his various names and titles. Alexander sacrificed there to Dionysus and joined his Companions in a celebratory feast. Some writers go on* to relate (if anyone wants to 7 believe this story) that once they were wreathed with ivy and had begun to invoke the god many Macedonians of some distinction in Alexander's circle became possessed by Dionysus, raised the cult cry of 'Euhoi', and fell into a Bacchic frenzy.

People can take these stories as they wish, and believe them or not. 3 For myself I do not wholly go along with Eratosthenes* of Cyrene, who says that everything set in a divine context by the Macedonians was a deliberately grandiose attribution to please Alexander. For 2 example he says that the Macedonians saw a cave in Parapamisadae country, and either hearing some local legend or making it up themselves spread the story that this was the cave where Prometheus was chained and the eagle came to feed on his innards, and that Heracles came by here to kill the eagle and release Prometheus from his chains. He also says that in their accounts the Macedonians transferred Mount 3 Caucasus from the Black Sea area to the far east, to Parapamisadae country towards India, calling Caucasus the mountain whose actual name is Parapamisus* [Hindu Kush], solely to glorify Alexander with the implication that he had in fact crossed the real Caucasus. And in 4 India itself the sight of cattle branded with the sign of a club* led them to deduce that Heracles had reached India. Eratosthenes is similarly sceptical about the travels of Dionysus. In my view the status of these stories must remain ambiguous.

When Alexander reached the river Indus* he found a bridge 5 already constructed across it by Hephaestion, and a collection of smaller boats as well as two thirty-oared vessels.* He also found that gifts had been sent there by Taxiles the Indian prince—about two hundred talents of silver, three thousand cattle and over ten thousand sheep for sacrifice, and some thirty elephants. In addition, seven 6 hundred Indian cavalry had arrived from Taxiles* to join his force, and Taxiles sent word that he was presenting Alexander with the city of Taxila, the greatest city between the rivers Indus and Hydaspes [Jhelum]. At the Indus Alexander made sacrifice to all his customary gods, and held athletic and equestrian competitions beside the river. The sacrificial omens were favourable for the crossing.

The river Indus is the greatest of all rivers in Asia and Europe 4

except for the Ganges, also an Indian river. Its source lies to the west
of Mount Parapamisus (or Caucasus), and it issues into the Great Sea
surrounding the southern part of India. The Indus has two mouths
and both of its outlets form shallows, like the five outlets of the
Danube: it creates a delta in India comparable to the Egyptian delta,
and this is called Patala in the Indian language. These are the most
salient undisputed features of the Indus, so let me record them here.

2 In fact the Hydaspes, the Acesines [Chenab], the Hydraotes [Ravi],
and the Hyphasis [Beas], which are all rivers of India, greatly surpass
all other Asian rivers in size, but are themselves smaller, and very
much smaller, than the Indus, just as the Indus is smaller than the
Ganges. Ctesias* (if indeed anyone regards him as a reliable witness)
says that at its narrowest the banks of the Indus are four and a half
miles apart, and eleven miles at its widest, with a breadth for most of
its course lying halfway between these figures.

3   So shortly before dawn Alexander and his army began crossing
this river Indus into the land of the Indians. *In this history I have
deliberately omitted any account of the customs and institutions of
the Indians, of any strange fauna their country produces, of the size
and nature of the fish or other monsters found in the Indus, Hydaspes,
Ganges, or the other Indian rivers, of the ants that mine their gold or
the griffins that guard it, or of all the other fabrications people have
made up as sensational stories rather than descriptions of reality, in
the certainty that no one was likely to disprove any far-fetched false-
4 hood peddled about India and the Indians. Yet in fact Alexander and
those with him on his campaign did disprove most of these stories
(except of course some which they invented themselves). They
proved that the Indians had no gold (at least that was true of the
various peoples—and they were many—encountered by Alexander
and his army); that their way of life was far from luxurious; that they
were physically tall, in fact the tallest in Asia, most of them measur-
ing seven feet or not much less, and darker-skinned than all men
except the Ethiopians; and that they were by far the finest fighters
5 among the inhabitants of Asia at that time. I have no means of making
a direct comparison between the Indians and the ancient Persians who
formed the army of Cyrus the son of Cambyses, when he set out to
wrest control of Asia from the Medes and by conquest or voluntary
submission extended his empire over other nations. But the Persians
too were poor at that time and lived in a rugged country, with a culture

very closely comparable to the Spartan discipline. As for the disaster suffered by the Persians in Scythia, again I have no precise means of deciding whether this came about because of difficult terrain or some error by Cyrus,* or whether the Persians were militarily outclassed by the Scythians of that region.

However, I intend to write a separate monograph about India, to 5 include the most reliable descriptions given by those who campaigned with Alexander, especially Nearchus,* who navigated the Indian coast of the Great Sea, as well as the accounts written by Megasthenes* and Eratosthenes, both of them men of repute: in this I shall record the customs and institutions of India, any strange fauna to be found there, and the actual voyage along the coast of the Outer Sea. For 2 present purposes I shall confine myself to what I judged relevant in the context of Alexander's life and work.

The boundary of Asia is Mount Taurus, which begins from Mycale, the mountain opposite Samos, cuts off Pamphylia and Cilicia, and stretches on from there to Armenia, and from Armenia to Media and past Parthyaea and Chorasmia. In Bactria it joins Mount Parapamisus, 3 which the Macedonians in Alexander's army called Caucasus,* allegedly to glorify Alexander with the implication that he had actually conquered his way over the real Caucasus. But it could well be that this mountain is in fact a continuation of the other Caucasus in Scythia, just as the Taurus is continuous with this Caucasus. For this reason I have called this mountain Caucasus on previous occasions and shall continue to use this name in future. This Caucasus extends all the way east 4 to the Great Sea round India.

So all the notable rivers of Asia rise in the Taurus and Caucasus mountains. Some flow to the north, and discharge either into Lake Maeotis [Sea of Azov] or into the sea called Hyrcanian [Caspian] (this too is a gulf of the Great Sea). Those that flow south are the Euphrates, Tigris, Indus, Hydaspes, Acesines, Hydraotes, Hyphasis, and all the rivers between these and the Ganges which either empty into the sea or, like the Euphrates, dissipate into shallow pools and vanish.

Considering the geography of Asia, if you think of it as divided 6 from west to east by the Taurus and Caucasus, you will see that this Taurus range separates the two main subdivisions of the continent, one facing south and south-west, and the other north and north-east. If the southern half of Asia is now divided into four, Eratosthenes and 2 Megasthenes make India the largest of these parts (and Megasthenes spent time with Sibyrtius the satrap of Arachosia, and often speaks of his visit to Sandracottus,* the king of the Indians). The smallest part, they say, is the region lying between the river Euphrates and our own Mediterranean Sea. The other two parts comprise the area between the Euphrates and the Indus, which even taken as a whole hardly merits comparison with the size of India.

3   India is bounded on its east side and down to the south by the Great Sea, and to the north by Mount Caucasus as far as its junction with the Taurus: to the west and west-north-west the river Indus forms its boundary all the way down to the Great Sea. Much of the country is low plain, which is inferred to be the result of alluvial
4 deposits by the rivers, as in other parts of the world plains near the sea have usually been created by the rivers of each particular region, and these regions have long taken their name from the river. For example we speak of a plain of the Hermus, a river which rises in Asia, in the mountain of Mother Dindymene,* and issues into the sea near the Aeolian city of Smyrna; again there is in Lydia the plain of the Caÿster, a river of that country, the Caïcus plain in Mysia, and in Caria
5 the Maeander plain which extends to the Ionian city of Miletus. Then there is Egypt. The historians Herodotus and Hecataeus (unless the book on Egypt attributed to him is by a different hand) both use the same term to describe Egypt as 'the gift of the river', and Herodotus has given patent proof of this, in that the country itself is in fact called after the river. That Aegyptus was the old name of the river which the Egyptians and the rest of the world now call the Nile is known on the sufficient authority of Homer, who says that Menelaus anchored
6 his ships at the mouth of the river Aegyptus.* If then in all these countries a single river—and not big rivers either—can create a large area of land in its course to the sea, when it brings down sediment and mud from the interior where it rises, there is no reason to doubt why it is that in India too the land is mostly low plain, and that this plain
7 was made by deposits from the rivers. Indeed if you put together the Hermus, the Caÿster, the Caïcus, the Maeander, and all the many rivers of Asia which flow into the Mediterranean Sea of ours, even that total does not bear comparison for volume of water with one of the Indian rivers, let alone the largest of them, the Ganges, with which the volume of the Nile in Egypt or the Danube flowing through
8 Europe cannot compare. In fact all of these rivers combined do not equal even the Indus, which is already a substantial river from its

very source and takes in fifteen tributaries, all larger than the Asian rivers and surrendering their names as they join the Indus in its course to discharge into the sea.

So much for the time being on the land of India. I shall keep what else I have to say on this subject for my Indian monograph.

Neither of my main sources, Aristobulus and Ptolemy, describes the 7 method used by Alexander to bridge the Indus. And I myself have no means of deciding with certainty whether the channel was bridged with boats (as the Hellespont by Xerxes, and the Bosporus and Danube by Darius), or whether a continuous solid structure was built across the river. I think it more likely to have been spanned by boats, as the depth of the water would not have allowed a bridge, nor could such an extraordinary feat of engineering have been completed in so short a time. Assuming that boats were used to span the channel, a further question I 2 cannot decide is whether an adequate bridge was formed by ships roped together and anchored in line across (which is how Herodotus says the Hellespont was bridged), or did they employ the method which has given the Romans their bridges over the Danube and the Celtic Rhine and was used whenever they were obliged to cross the Euphrates or Tigris. Yet since the Roman method with ships is the fastest bridge- 3 building technique I know, I shall describe it here for its own interest.

At a given signal the ships are released down stream, not head-on but stern-first, as if they were backing water. The current naturally carries them down, but they are slowed by an oared cutter until it brings them to a halt in their designated position. At this point cone-shaped wicker crates full of rough stones are lowered from the bows of each ship to hold it against the current. As soon as one ship 4 is made fast another is anchored alongside, prow facing upstream, at just the right distance to ensure the rigidity of the superstructure: hands on both ships then quickly lay beams across at right angles, with diagonal planks to clamp them together. This process goes on, ship after ship, for the number required to bridge the river. On either 5 side of the causeway ladders are laid horizontally and fixed down, to make transit safer for the horses and baggage-animals and also to stiffen the structure of the bridge. All is completed in short time and a flurry of activity, but discipline is maintained throughout, and the occasional burst of cheering from any ship or the bawling-out of slackers does not detract from the clear transmission of orders or the speed of the operation.

8   This then is the long-established method practised by the Romans. How Alexander bridged the Indus I cannot say, as even those who campaigned with him have not told us: but I think he must have employed a very similar technique. If he did in fact use some other means, so be it.

2   When he had crossed the river, Alexander sacrificed once more on the other side, as was his custom, then set out from the Indus and came to Taxila,* a large and prosperous city, the largest of the cities between the Indus and the Hydaspes. He was given a friendly welcome there by the ruler of the city, Taxiles,* and the Indian population of the area, and he made over to them as much of the neigh-

3   bouring territory as they wanted. There too he was visited by envoys from Abisares, the king of the highland Indians, together with Abisares' brother and a retinue of other notables, and also by another set of envoys bearing gifts from Doxares, one of the regional dynasts. At Taxila also, as elsewhere, Alexander made his customary sacrifices and held athletic and equestrian competitions. He appointed Philip the son of Machatas satrap of the Indians in this region, and left a garrison in Taxila together with the soldiers too sick for further service. He himself then led on towards the river Hydaspes.

4   The reason was that he had been receiving reports that Porus was on the far side of the Hydaspes, waiting there with his entire army to prevent him from crossing or to attack him as he made the attempt. On learning this Alexander sent Coenus the son of Polemocrates back to the river Indus, with orders to dismantle the boats gathered for the

5   crossing of the Indus and transport them to the Hydaspes. And so it was done: the boats were dismantled and transported, the shorter vessels split into two sections and the thirty-oared ships into three, and these sections were carried on ox-carts all the way to the bank of the Hydaspes. There they were put together again, and the whole flotilla now reappeared on the Hydaspes. Alexander himself advanced to the river with the force he had brought to Taxila, with the addition of five thousand Indians under Taxiles and the local princes.

9   Alexander pitched camp on the bank of the Hydaspes,* and Porus could be seen on the opposite bank with his entire army and his array of elephants. Porus stationed himself to guard the river at the point where he saw that Alexander had encamped, and posted detachments of guards, each with its appointed commanding officer, to all other stretches of the river where a crossing was easier: his plan was to close

off any opportunity for the Macedonians to cross. Seeing this, 2 Alexander thought the best counter was to confuse Porus by keeping his own troops on the move in various directions. So he split his army into several smaller units, some of which he himself led here and there up and down the country, ravaging enemy territory and also looking for places where the river might appear easier to cross: other units under various other commanders were likewise sent out constantly in different directions. He had corn brought in to the camp 3 from all over the country west of the Hydaspes, so it was clear to Porus that Alexander had decided to stay put on the riverside until the water-level fell in the winter and afforded him a range of possible crossing-places. With his boats plying up and down, leather rafts being stuffed with straw, the whole bank visibly crowded with troops, cavalry here, infantry there, Alexander kept Porus unsettled and prevented him from selecting a single vantage-point in which to concentrate his defensive capability. Besides, at that time of the year all the 4 Indian rivers were running swollen and muddy with a fast current. It was the season just after the summer solstice,* when there is continuous heavy rainfall over all of India and the melting of snow in the Caucasus, where most of the rivers have their source, greatly increases the volume of their flow. Then in winter the flow reduces, they shrink in size, turn clear, and, except for the Indus and Ganges and it may be one or two others, become fordable in places: the Hydaspes at any rate can certainly be forded.

So Alexander publicly declared that he would wait for this winter 10 season, if he were prevented from crossing for the time being: but he remained as alert as ever on the lookout for a chance to sneak across fast and unobserved. He realized that it was impossible to cross at the point where Porus himself had made his camp, because of the number of elephants there and the large, well-armed, and battle-ready army which would attack his troops as they tried to land. He thought that 2 the horses would refuse even to set foot on the far bank, with the terrifying sight and sound of the elephants coming straight at them, and even before that would not stay on the leather floats for the length of the crossing, but would be spooked by the sight of the elephants ahead and jump into the water. So he made plans to steal across, and 3 this is how he set about it. Night after night he took the bulk of his cavalry up and down the bank, shouting, raising war-cries, and generally making every sort of noise which suggested an army getting

ready to cross. Porus would replicate this movement, following the direction of the commotion with elephants and all, and Alexander got
4 him used to this constant tracking. When this had gone on for some time, and nothing happened except shouting and war-cries, Porus stopped responding in parallel to the cavalry excursions, but realized that these were false alarms and stayed put in his camp, though he had set sentries at several points along the bank. Having succeeded in lulling Porus into complacency about these night-time manoeuvres, Alexander now put the following stratagem into effect.

11   At a point where the Hydaspes described a sharp bend, the bank enclosed a projecting loop of land which was thickly wooded with a whole variety of trees: and opposite it there was an island in the river, also wooded and pathless, as it was uninhabited. When he learnt about this island opposite the loop, both places covered with trees and capable of concealing the launch of a crossing, Alexander decided
2 to take his army across at this point. The loop and the island were about seventeen miles from his main camp. Along the whole length of the bank he had posted groups of guards at intervals sufficiently short for them to maintain visual contact with one another and respond readily to orders coming from either direction. At night all along this line they made a great deal of noise and kept fires burning: this continued for many nights.
3   When Alexander had taken the decision to make the attempt, back at the camp he authorized overt preparations for a crossing. He had left Craterus in charge of the camp with his own cavalry unit, the cavalry from Arachosia and the Parapamisadae, the Macedonian phalanx brigades of Alcetas and Polyperchon, and the western Indian
4 princes with their five thousand men. His instructions to Craterus were that he should not begin to cross the river until Porus had decamped with his army to take on Alexander's force, or else he had learnt that the Macedonians were winning and Porus was in retreat. 'But if', Alexander continued, 'Porus takes part of his army against me and leaves part behind in the camp with elephants as well, you must still not make a move: if, though, he takes all his elephants with him against me, with some of the rest of his army left in the camp, then cross as fast as you can. It is only the elephants which make it impossible to land the horses—any other part of Porus' army will pose no problem.'
12   Such were his orders to Craterus. Between the island and the main

camp where Craterus was left in charge, Meleager, Attalus, and Gorgias* had been posted with the mercenary cavalry and infantry: their instructions too were to begin crossing in relays, section by section, as soon as they saw the Indians fully engaged in the battle.

For his own force Alexander selected the elite corps of the 2 Companion cavalry, the cavalry units of Hephaestion, Perdiccas, and Demetrius, the cavalry from Bactria, Sogdiana, and Scythia, and the Dahae mounted archers; from the phalanx the foot guards and the brigades of Cleitus and Coenus; and the archers and Agrianians. He took this force out of sight on a wide detour from the bank, to conceal his approach to the island and the loop, where he had decided to make the crossing. The leather casings for the floats had been 3 stockpiled there for some time, and the work of stuffing them with straw and stitching them tight had been taking place at night. On this particular night a violent rainstorm came on, which helped to smother the preparations for the crossing and the initial moves, with the thunder and the drumming of the rain serving to drown out the clatter of arms and the hubbub of command and response. Most of the boats, 4 including the thirty-oared ships, the triaconters, had been transported to this spot in dismantled sections, put together again out of sight, and hidden in the woods. Towards dawn the wind and the rain had quietened down. Part of the army now began the crossing, the cavalry on the leather rafts and as many infantry as the boats could accommodate: they kept close to the island, so that the scouts posted by Porus would not see them until they had skirted the island and already come near to the bank.

Alexander himself went on board a triaconter for the crossing, 13 together with the Bodyguards Ptolemy, Perdiccas, and Lysimachus, and one of the Companions, Seleucus* (who later became king), with half of the foot guards in his command. The rest of the foot guards were carried in other triaconters. As soon as this force had passed the island, there was no hiding the final approach to the bank. Porus' scouts saw them coming, and rode off to tell Porus as fast as each man's horse could carry him. Meanwhile a landing was made. Alexander 2 was the first ashore, and took off the foot guards from the other triaconters: with them he arranged the cavalry in immediate formation as more and more disembarked (he had given orders that the cavalry should be the first off the floats), and then took forward this combined force in full battle-order. What he had not realized was that, in the absence of local knowledge, he had landed not on the mainland but on another island, large enough to be mistaken for the mainland. It was separated from the far bank by a relatively narrow channel of

3 the river, but the violent rain which had lasted for most of the night had swollen the volume of water, so his cavalry could not find the fording-place, and there was the alarming prospect that he would have to repeat the first laborious exercise all over again in order to complete the crossing. In the end the ford was found, and Alexander led the way across, though it was hard going: at the deepest points the water came over the chests of the infantry and the horses had only

4 their heads above the surface. When this final stretch of the river had been crossed, Alexander brought round the elite corps of the cavalry and positioned it on his right wing, together with the best men selected from the other cavalry units, and placed the mounted archers in front of the whole line of cavalry. The infantry were drawn up behind the cavalry: first the king's household guards, commanded by Seleucus, then the royal corps of foot guards, and after them the rest of the foot guards in whatever order the various command units happened to come up at the time. At the wings of the phalanx on either side he placed the archers, the Agrianians, and the javelin-men.

14   With these dispositions made, Alexander ordered the infantry section, which numbered nearly six thousand, to maintain ranks and follow at marching pace, while he, assuming he had cavalry superiority with the five thousand or so in his force, took the cavalry ahead at speed and unsupported, though he did instruct Tauron, the commander of the archers, to bring his men along behind the cavalry at

2 their own best pace. His plan of engagement was that, if Porus' army met him with their full force, he would either secure a quick and easy victory with a cavalry charge, or at least fight them off until his infantry could join the action. If, though, his unexpected initiative panicked the Indians into flight, he would keep close after them as they ran: the greater carnage he could inflict on the retreating army, the less work would be left for him still to do.

3   Aristobulus says that Porus' son arrived with about sixty chariots before Alexander had made his further crossing from the smaller island, and that he could have prevented this crossing (which was difficult enough even without opposition) if the Indians had jumped down from their chariots and attacked the first wave of troops coming ashore. But in fact he drove past with his chariots, and so allowed

Alexander to cross in safety: Alexander then launched his mounted
archers against these Indians, and they were easily turned back, with
casualties sustained. Others say that there was a battle during the 4
landing between the Indians who had arrived with Porus' son and
Alexander and his cavalry. These claim that Porus' son had come
with a larger force, and that he wounded not only Alexander himself
but also Bucephalas, Alexander's favourite horse, who died at the
scene. But Ptolemy the son of Lagus gives a different account. He too 5
has Porus send out his son, but with more than just sixty chariots,
and I agree with him in this. It is not, after all, likely that Porus, on
hearing from his scouts that Alexander himself, or at least part of his
army, had crossed the Hydaspes, would have sent out his own son
with nothing more than sixty chariots. For reconnaissance purposes 6
that number of chariots was too many, and chariots are not suited for
a quick in-and-out mission: but if the aim was to prevent more of the
enemy from crossing and attack those already ashore, those chariots
would have had no hope of success. In fact Ptolemy says that when
Porus' son arrived he had with him two thousand cavalry and a hundred and twenty chariots, but was too late: by that time Alexander
had managed to complete his final crossing from the island.

Ptolemy agrees that Alexander first sent his mounted archers 15
against these arrivals, while he himself led out his cavalry in the belief
that Porus was approaching with his entire army, and that this cavalry
force with Porus' son was the spearhead sent forward in advance of
the rest of the army. But when he was given an accurate report of the 2
Indian numbers, he launched an immediate attack on them at the
head of his cavalry. They gave way when they saw that Alexander was
there in person and that what faced them was not a single line of cavalry but massed squadrons attacking in column. Some four hundred
of the Indian cavalry were killed, including Porus' son: the chariots
were captured horses and all, as the mud rendered them useless in the
actual engagement and weighed them down in the retreat.

When the cavalry who had survived and made their escape reported 3
to Porus that Alexander had succeeded in crossing the river with
what amounted to the strongest section of his army, and that his son
had died in the fighting, even so Porus was in two minds, as the troops
left with Craterus in the main camp opposite could be seen making a
start on their own crossing. In the end he chose to move against 4
Alexander and take his whole army into a decisive battle with the

strongest part of the Macedonian force and the king himself. Nevertheless he left a few of his elephants behind in the camp with a small contingent of troops, to frighten Craterus' cavalry away from the bank. He himself set out to confront Alexander, taking with him all his cavalry (some four thousand), all his three hundred chariots, two hundred of his elephants, and about thirty thousand serviceable

5 infantry. When he had found a place free of mud, a wide area of sandy soil giving a hard, flat surface for cavalry attacks and turns, he halted there and drew up his army in battle formation.

At the front he placed the elephants in a single long line, at intervals of at least a hundred feet,* so that this forward screen of elephants could cover the whole of his infantry phalanx and act as a deterrent to

6 Alexander's cavalry across the entire front. In any case he did not expect that any enemy units would attempt to force through the gaps between the elephants, either on horseback (as horses are frightened of elephants) or, still less, on foot: infantry units would be stopped in a frontal attack by his own hoplites, then trampled as the elephants

7 turned on them. After the elephants he ranged his infantry not quite on the same front, but in a second line slightly behind the beasts, close enough to have the various companies protruding a little way into the gaps. He had infantry also posted on the wings even beyond the line of elephants, and cavalry stationed on each flank of the infantry, with the chariots in front of the cavalry on either side.

16   This then was Porus' battle-order. When Alexander saw the Indians already taking up formation, he stopped any further advance by his cavalry, to allow the constant stream of infantry to catch up with him. They came to join him at the double, but even when he had the full complement of the phalanx gathered and added to his force, he did not immediately form them up and lead them into battle: they were exhausted and out of breath, and he was not going to commit them in that state to a fresh barbarian army. So he kept his cavalry circling while the infantry could rest long enough to restore their

2 fighting spirit. As he surveyed the Indian battle-line, he decided not to press an attack in the centre, where the elephants had been ranged ahead of the front line, with the phalanx drawn up in close order immediately behind and filling the gaps between them: he was cautious of this for the very reasons on which Porus had calculated in making this disposition of his forces. But since he had cavalry superiority Alexander took most of his cavalry with him and rode out to

make his attack on the enemy left wing. He sent Coenus,* with his 3
own and Demetrius' cavalry units, to the enemy right, with instructions to press close after them in their rear when the barbarians on
that wing saw the mass of cavalry attacking them on the left and rode
round in support. He had put the infantry phalanx under the command of Seleucus, Antigenes, and Tauron, with orders not to engage
until they saw that his cavalry attack had disrupted the enemy infantry line as well as their cavalry.

They were now within missile range, and Alexander sent his 4
mounted archers, about a thousand strong, against the Indians' left
wing, to create havoc among the troops stationed there with their
dense volleys of arrows and quick charges in and out. And he himself
took the Companion cavalry and rode at speed for the enemy left,
intent on attacking them in the flank while they were still in disarray
and before they could deploy their cavalry in line.

Meanwhile the Indians did indeed concentrate their cavalry from 17
all parts of the field to parallel Alexander's movement and extend
their line accordingly: and Coenus' squadrons, as ordered, began to
arrive in plain view at their rear. Their appearance forced the Indians
to form two fronts, with the larger and strongest part of their cavalry
facing Alexander, while the rest wheeled to confront Coenus and
his force. This of course caused immediate disruption to the Indian 2
battle-lines and their battle plans. Alexander saw his opportunity, and
at precisely the moment when the cavalry were executing this about-
turn he attacked those still facing him with such force that the Indians
did not even attempt to meet his cavalry charge, but were broken
and driven back on the elephants, as if to the protection of a home
city wall. At this point the mahouts began to turn their animals against 3
Alexander's cavalry, and the Macedonian phalanx responded with
their own attack on the elephants, spearing their riders and, with a
ring of men round them, inflicting multiple wounds on the animals
themselves. The consequent action was unlike anything they had
faced before. The beasts charged into the infantry lines and, wherever
they turned, began spreading carnage in the Macedonian phalanx
despite the density of its formation. Seeing the infantry in this trouble,
the Indian cavalry turned again and made a counter-attack on the
Macedonian cavalry: but once more they were penned back towards 4
the elephants, defeated by the far superior strength and experience of
Alexander's force. Alexander's cavalry was now amalgamated into a

single unit, a formation created naturally by the course of the battle rather than any specific order, and it made repeated charges into the Indian ranks, each time leaving a swathe of slaughter before the
5 Indians could break away. Crowded now into a narrow space, the elephants caused as much damage to their own side as to the enemy, turning round and round, barging, and trampling. The Indian cavalry, tightly corralled among the elephants, suffered massive carnage. Most of the mahouts had been shot down: wounded, exhausted, and with no one to control them, the elephants could no longer play their
6 specific role in the battle but, maddened by pain, they began attacking friends and enemies alike, crushing, trampling, and killing indiscriminately. The Macedonians, though, had plenty of room and could gauge their attacks on the animals, retreating whenever they charged, but keeping close behind them when they turned and firing javelins at them. Most of the damage done by the elephants was now
7 inflicted on the Indians attempting to rally among them. But as the animals tired and the strength went out of their charges, and all they could do now was trumpet and gradually retire like ships backing water, Alexander threw his cavalry in a cordon round the entire Indian force and gave the signal for his infantry to lock shields and advance the phalanx in the densest possible formation. In the ensuing action all but a few of the Indian cavalry were cut down, and with the Macedonians now pressing the attack on all sides of them there began the slaughter of their infantry also. When a gap opened up in Alexander's cavalry, the survivors all turned and ran.

18   At the same time Craterus and the other commanders of the army units Alexander had left on the far bank of the Hydaspes began to make their own crossing, once it became clear that Alexander was achieving a decisive victory. Coming fresh to take over the pursuit from Alexander's exhausted troops, they continued to slaughter the retreating Indians on no less massive a scale.

2   *The Indian losses were nearly twenty thousand infantry and about three thousand cavalry: and all their chariots were wrecked. Among the dead were two sons of Porus, the local Indian dynast Spitaces, and Porus' entire corps of army generals and officers commanding the elephants, the chariots, and the cavalry. All the elephants not
3 killed in the battle were captured. On Alexander's side about eighty at most were lost from the six thousand infantry involved in the main battle: cavalry losses were ten of the mounted archers (who were the

first to engage), about twenty of the Companion troop, and some two hundred of the other cavalry.

Porus had played a distinguished role in the battle, not only *4* as commander-in-chief but also as a fine soldier. Faced with the slaughter of his cavalry, his elephants either dead on the field or wandering in a pitiful state after the loss of their drivers, and most of his infantry killed, unlike the great King Darius he did not give way and start a general flight by his own example, but kept fighting on as long *5* as there was any Indian unit holding together sufficiently to offer resistance. It was only when he was wounded that he finally turned his elephant and began his own withdrawal. The wound was in his right shoulder, the only part of him exposed as he mingled in the battle: the rest of his body was protected from missiles by a corselet of remarkably strong and close-layered construction, as witnessed by those who saw it afterwards.

Alexander dearly wanted to save the life of a great man he had seen *6* fight a noble battle. So he first sent out Taxiles the Indian to reason with him. Taxiles rode up as close as he thought safe to the elephant carrying Porus, and asked him to halt the animal, as there was no escape, and listen to Alexander's proposals. Seeing an old enemy in *7* Taxiles, Porus turned and made for him with javelin in hand: and he could well have killed him if Taxiles had not been quick to spur his horse further away. Even after this Alexander did not harden against Porus, but sent out a succession of others, including finally an Indian called Meroes, who he had learnt was an old friend of Porus. Having heard what Meroes had to say, and overcome by thirst as well, Porus halted his elephant and dismounted: when he had drunk and revived, he told Meroes to escort him directly to Alexander.

Meroes did so. When Alexander heard that he was coming, he rode *19* out with a few of the Companions to meet Porus some way in front of the Macedonian line. He reined in his horse and gazed for a while at Porus, struck by the size of the man (he was over seven and a half feet tall), his handsome looks, and the way he seemed quite unbroken in spirit, more like one brave man meeting another after an honourable battle for his kingdom with another king. Alexander was the first to *2* speak. He asked Porus to say what he wished to be done with him. Porus is said to have replied: 'Treat me, Alexander, like a king.' Pleased with this answer, Alexander said, 'For myself, Porus, I shall do as you ask: tell me now what you expect for yourself.' Porus replied

3 that everything was contained in that one request. Yet more impressed
by this answer, Alexander granted Porus continued rule* over his
Indian kingdom and added to its original extent further territory
which more than doubled it. This was how he fulfilled his own com-
mitment to treat a brave man 'like a king', and Porus' response was
complete loyalty thereafter.

Such was the conclusion of Alexander's battle with Porus and the
Indians on the far side of the river Hydaspes. It took place in the
month Munychion of the year when Hegemon was archon at Athens
[April/May 326 BC].

4   Alexander founded a city on the site of the battle, and another city
where he launched his crossing of the Hydaspes. He called the one
Nicaea, after his victory (*nikē*) over the Indians, and the other
5 Bucephala,* in memory of his horse Bucephalas who died there. It
was no wound which caused his death, but rather exhaustion from
the heat and from old age—he was about thirty years old. Before then
he had kept company with Alexander in many a hardship and danger,
and only Alexander could mount him,* as he refused all other riders:
he was a big horse, with a thoroughbred spirit. The mark branded on
him was a bull's head (*boos kephalē*), from which his name Bucephalas
is said to derive: some, though, say that in an otherwise black body he
had a white star on his forehead which looked exactly like the head of
6 a bull. Once, in Uxian country, Alexander lost this horse,* and he had
a proclamation made throughout the land that he would kill every
inhabitant if they did not bring back his horse: this had immediate
effect, and the horse was returned. Such was Alexander's devotion to
his horse—and such the fear that Alexander inspired in the barbarians. Let this be my own tribute, for Alexander's sake, to the horse
Bucephalas.

20   After seeing to the payment of proper honours to those who fell in
the battle, Alexander made the customary sacrifices to the gods in
thanksgiving for the victory, and held athletic and equestrian competitions on the bank of the Hydaspes at the very point where he had
2 first crossed with his army. He left Craterus there with a section of
the army to build and fortify the cities he was founding, while he
himself moved on against the Indians bordering the area ruled by
Porus. The name of this tribe according to Aristobulus was
Glauganicae, but Ptolemy calls them Glausae: I have no wish to
3 decide between them. Alexander invaded their country with a force

consisting of half the Companion cavalry, select infantrymen from each of the brigades, all of the mounted archers, the Agrianians, and the foot archers. The agreed surrender of the entire population brought him some thirty-seven cities, the smallest of which had not 4 fewer than five thousand inhabitants, and many had more than ten thousand: the large number of villages also acquired were hardly less populous than the cities. Alexander added this country to Porus' domain, and effected a reconciliation between Porus and Taxiles: he then sent Taxiles back to his own home territory.

At this time there arrived envoys from Abisares,* offering 5 Alexander his personal surrender and that of the whole region in his control. Before the battle against Porus Abisares had been minded to join Porus in opposition to Alexander, but now he sent his own brother among the envoys to Alexander, bringing him a gift of money and forty elephants. Envoys came too from the autonomous Indian 6 peoples, and from another Indian prince also called Porus. Alexander ordered Abisares to come to him without delay, adding the threat that, if he failed to appear, he would see Alexander and his army coming to him, a sight he would not relish.

Meanwhile Phrataphernes* the satrap of Parthyaea and Hyrcania 7 reached Alexander bringing the Thracian troops which had been left behind in his command. And messengers also arrived from Sisicottus, satrap of the Assacenian region,* with news that the Assacenians had assassinated their regional overlord and revolted from Alexander. Alexander sent Philip and Tyriespis there with an army to deal with the situation and impose order on the region.

He himself advanced to the river Acesines [Chenab]. This is the 8 only one of the Indian rivers whose size is described by Ptolemy the son of Lagus. At the point where Alexander took his army across on the boats and leather rafts, Ptolemy says that the Acesines' current is fast and violent, seething and roaring over great sharp rocks in its path, and its width is about a mile and two-thirds. Those on the 9 rafts, he says, had an easy crossing, but several of the boats ran on the rocks and broke up, and quite a few on board were lost in the water. One can deduce, then, from this description that accounts of the size 10 of the river Indus are not far from the truth when they have estimated its mean width at about four and a half miles, contracting in the many stretches where it is narrowest (and therefore deepest) to a mile and two-thirds. And I would guess that with the Acesines too Alexander chose its widest part for his crossing, where the current would be slower.

21   *When he had crossed the river Alexander left Coenus and his brigade on the bank, with orders to supervise the crossing of the troops left behind, who were to transport the corn and other supplies from

2   the Indian territory already under his control. He sent Porus back to his own home country, instructing him to enlist a force of the best Indian fighters and bring it to him together with any elephants at his disposal. He himself was intending to take his fastest army units in pursuit of the other Porus, Porus 'the bad', who was reported to have

3   left his realm and taken flight. As long as there had been a state of hostility between Alexander and the first Porus, this Porus had been sending envoys to Alexander offering his own surrender and that of the area he ruled—an offer motivated more by hatred of the other Porus than friendly feeling for Alexander. But when he learnt that Porus had been set free and given control of his own territory and much more in addition, he turned fearful, not so much of Alexander as of this namesake of his, and fled his country, taking with him as many of his fighting men as he could persuade to join his flight.

4   In his pursuit of Porus Alexander reached the Hydraotes [Ravi], another of the rivers of India, which was as wide as the Acesines but not so fast-flowing. In all the territory he covered as far as the Hydraotes Alexander left behind guard-posts at the key points, to give protection across most of the country to the foraging parties

5   sent out by Craterus and Coenus. At the Hydraotes Alexander sent Hephaestion with a part of the army to annex the territory of the renegade Porus, giving him two infantry brigades, his own and Demetrius' cavalry units, and half of the archers: he was to hand over this territory to the other Porus, and also to win the surrender of any independent Indian tribes living along the banks of the Hydaspes

6   and put these too under Porus' control. He himself then crossed the river Hydraotes, with none of the difficulty experienced at the Acesines. As he advanced on the far side of the Hydraotes he met with voluntary surrender for the most part, but now some tribes offered armed resistance and were crushed by force, and others who attempted to escape were captured.

22   It was now reported to Alexander that prominent among the independent Indians intending to oppose him were the people called the Cathaeans, who were making their own preparations for battle,

should Alexander approach their territory, and were inciting all similarly independent tribes on their borders to join them in the campaign. The city in front of which they intended to make their stand, called Sangala,* was strongly fortified, and the Cathaeans were considered an exceptionally powerful and courageous fighting force: two other Indian tribes, the Oxydracae and the Mallians, had a similar reputation. In fact only shortly before now Porus and Abisares had mounted a campaign against them with their own forces together with support enlisted from many other independent Indian tribes, but had withdrawn when the expedition failed to achieve anything justifying its scale.

When he heard this report Alexander marched at speed against the Cathaeans. On the second day out from the Hydraotes he reached a city called Pimprama: the Indian tribe living here were called the Adraïstae. They agreed terms of submission to Alexander. On the day after this surrender he rested his army, then on the next day resumed his advance on Sangala, where the Cathaeans and the neighbouring tribes who had joined them were ranged for battle in front of the city on a not very steep hill: round the hill they had placed three rings of wagons, to form a triple rampart behind which they had made their camp. Observing the numbers of the barbarians and the physical nature of the site, Alexander made the dispositions for battle which he thought best suited the situation. As an immediate action there and then he sent out the mounted archers with orders to ride across the enemy front and shoot at long range, to prevent the Indians making any sallies before he had completed the arrangement of his forces, and to ensure they took some casualties while they were still inside their laager and the battle proper had not begun. With himself on the right wing Alexander posted the elite cavalry corps and Cleitus' cavalry unit, next to them the foot guards, and then the Agrianians; he stationed Perdiccas on the left wing with his own cavalry unit and the 'Close Companions' infantry brigades; and the archers, in two divisions, were placed on each wing. While he was making these dispositions he was joined by the infantry and cavalry of the rearguard. He divided this cavalry in two and sent them across to each wing, and used the newly arrived infantry to increase the density of the phalanx. He then took the cavalry posted on the right wing and led them against the wagons on the Indians' left, where there seemed an easier approach to the site and the wagons were not so closely packed.

23   The Indians did not come out from behind their wagons to meet
this cavalry attack, but climbed up on them and began shooting from
that height. Realizing now that this could not be a cavalry action,
Alexander jumped down from his horse and, on foot himself, led
2 forward the infantry phalanx. The Macedonians had no difficulty in
forcing the Indians back from the first line of wagons. The Indians
regrouped in front of the second line, and here they could offer more
effective opposition, as they were ranged closer together in a smaller
circle and the Macedonians no longer had an open space for their
attack—they had to drag the first wagons out of the way and then
charge through whatever gap they could find without any coordination. Even so, the Indians were driven back from this second line
3 also by the pressure of the phalanx. They made no further attempt to
resist at the third line, but retreated as fast as they could and shut
themselves in the city. For this day Alexander camped his infantry as
far round the city as the phalanx could cover. The extent of the wall
4 made complete encirclement impossible, but there was a lake close to
the section of wall he left unguarded, and he ringed this with the
cavalry: he had noticed that the lake was not deep, and guessed that
the shock of their earlier defeat would frighten the Indians into aban-
5 doning the city during the night. It turned out exactly as he had foreseen. Round about the second watch the bulk of them came pouring
out from behind the wall and ran straight into the cavalry outposts:
the first of them were cut down by the cavalry, and the rest, realizing
that the lake was guarded all round, turned back into the city.
6   Alexander now surrounded the city with a double stockade, except
where the lake formed a barrier, and here he put the circumference of
the lake under stricter guard. His intention was to bring up siege-
engines to batter a breach in the wall, but some of the people in the
city deserted to him and told him that the Indians were planning to
escape from the city that very night, on the lake side where there was
7 the gap in the stockade. Alexander posted Ptolemy the son of Lagus
to cover that area, assigning him three battalions of the foot guards,
all the Agrianians, and one unit of the archers. He pointed out to him
what he guessed was the most likely spot for the barbarians' break-
out, and continued: 'As soon as you see them breaking out here,
deploy your troops to stop them getting any further, and tell your
trumpeter to sound the alarm: and you, gentlemen,' (this to the other
officers) 'when the alarm is sounded form up your own units and follow

the trumpet-call to reach the disturbance. I shall not fail to attend the action myself.'

Such were Alexander's orders. Ptolemy collected as many as pos- 24 sible of the wagons abandoned by the Indians in their original defeat and placed them in staggered lines across the escape-route, to create an impression in the dark of multiple obstacles, and had his men bring the fencing-stakes which were cut but unused and pile them in heaps here and there between the lake and the city wall. His soldiers carried out this work in the night. It was now about the fourth watch, 2 and just as Alexander had been told, the barbarians opened the gates facing the lake and made for it at the run. But they did not get through without alerting the sentries posted on that side and their operational commander Ptolemy: his trumpeters immediately sounded the alarm, and Ptolemy brought up his troops ready armed and marshalled to meet the barbarians. The fugitives had to pick their way through the 3 wagons and the piles of stakes scattered in the intervening space, and when the trumpet sounded and Ptolemy's troops laid into them, cutting them down as soon as any got through between the wagons, they turned back and fled into the city. In this retreat some five hundred of them were killed.

Meanwhile Porus too had arrived, bringing with him the rest of 4 the elephants and about five thousand Indian troops, and Alexander's siege-engines had been assembled. They were now being moved up to the wall, but before any section was battered down the Macedonians began manually undermining the wall (as it was made of brick), then set up their ladders all round the circuit and took the city by storm. In the capture some seventeen thousand of the Indians were killed, 5 and over seventy thousand taken prisoner: there was also a haul of three hundred chariots and five hundred horses. The losses in Alexander's army amounted to slightly under one hundred over the whole siege, though the number of wounded was out of proportion to the dead—over twelve hundred, including several officers, most notably Lysimachus the Bodyguard.

After burying the dead with his customary honours, Alexander 6 sent his secretary Eumenes* to the two cities which had joined Sangala in revolt, assigning him some three hundred cavalry for this mission, which was to tell the occupants of those cities that Sangala had been captured and that they themselves would have nothing unpleasant to fear from Alexander if they stayed where they were and

gave him a friendly reception, as had been the experience of other
independent Indian peoples also who had voluntarily surrendered.

7 But they had taken fright at the reports they had already heard of
Alexander's storming of Sangala, and had abandoned the cities to
make their escape. When Alexander received the report of their flight,
he set out in hot pursuit. Most of the refugees got away in time, as
they had had a long start, but all those who were too sick to keep up
with the retreat were captured by Alexander's army and put to

8 death—a total of about five hundred. Alexander decided not to pursue the fugitives further, and returned to Sangala, where he razed the
city to the ground and gave its territory to those originally independent Indian peoples who had come over in voluntary submission. He
sent Porus and his accompanying force to install garrisons in the cities which had submitted, while he himself advanced with his army to
the river Hyphasis [Beas], intent on subduing the Indians yet further
to the east. In his mind there could be no end to the war as long as
there was any enemy left.

25   *Reports of the country beyond the Hyphasis* spoke of a fertile
land whose inhabitants were good farmers, brave in war, and in internal affairs well governed under an aristocracy which did not abuse its
power over the common people. It was also reported that these
Indians in the east had a far greater number of elephants than elsewhere in India, and that their elephants were distinguished for their

2 great size and courage. These reports spurred in Alexander a desire
to press on further. But the Macedonians' spirits were flagging by
now, as they saw their king taking on hardship after hardship and
danger after danger. They began to gather in groups* around the
camp, some simply complaining of their lot (these were the most
moderate of them), and others swearing they would go no further,
even with Alexander as their leader. When Alexander heard of this,
before the unrest and demoralization among the troops got worse, he
summoned his brigade commanders and addressed them as follows:

3   'Gentlemen—Macedonians and allies—I can see that you have
lost some of the conviction which so far has brought you with me in
dangerous enterprises. So I have gathered you together to persuade
or be persuaded: either I persuade you and lead on forward, or you
persuade me to turn back. If you have criticisms to make of the hard
campaigns we have endured up to now, or of my own leadership in
them, then there is no point in my speaking further.

'If, though, these labours have won us Ionia, the Hellespont, both 4
Phrygias, Cappadocia, Paphlagonia, Lydia, Caria, Lycia, Pamphylia,
Phoenicia, Egypt and the Greek part of Libya, some of Arabia, and
both Hollow and Mesopotamian Syria; if we have won control of 5
Babylon, the people of Susa, the Persians and Medes and all in their
empire, and then the countries they never ruled, beyond the Caspian
Gates, over the Caucasus, the Tanaïs, yet further than the Tanaïs,
Bactria, Hyrcania, the Hyrcanian Sea; if we have driven the Scythians
back to the desert; if, to crown all this, even the river Indus flows
through land that is now our own, if ours is the land of the Hydaspes,
the Acesines, the Hydraotes—why are you hesitant to add the
Hyphasis and the nations beyond the Hyphasis to this empire of ours,
this Macedonian empire? Are you afraid that there are barbarians out 6
there who will finally stop your advance? How so? These people
either offer their surrender—or if they run away we catch them—or
else they abandon their country and leave it empty for us: and then
we add it to the territory of our allies or those who have chosen to
come over to us.

'I myself think that for a man of spirit there is no limit to his labours 26
when those very labours are the price of achievement. But if anyone
longs to hear what limit there will be to this particular campaign,
I can tell him that we do not have far now to go to the river Ganges
and the Eastern Sea: and this, I assure you, will prove to be continuous with the Hyrcanian Sea [Caspian] as part of the Great Sea which
surrounds the entire world. And I shall then demonstrate to the 2
Macedonians and our allies that the Indian Gulf [Arabian Sea] links
with the Persian Gulf just as the Hyrcanian Sea links with the Indian
Gulf.* From the Persian Gulf we shall sail our fleet right round
Libya* to the Pillars of Heracles [Strait of Gibraltar]. Once we have
reached the Pillars all the interior of Libya becomes ours, just as we
are now winning the whole of Asia, and the bounds of our empire in
these continents become the self-same bounds which god himself has
set them.

'But if we turn back now we leave behind us many warlike tribes 3
between the Hyphasis and the Eastern Sea, many too from there
northwards to the Hyrcanian Sea, and the Scythian hordes not then
far away: so there is the fear that when we have gone back home the
areas we have conquered so far, but not secured, will be incited to
revolt by those whose conquest we shall leave unfinished. And then 4

our great labours will have brought us nothing, or we shall have to start all over again with more labour, more danger. So, gentlemen, Macedonians and allies, I ask you to persevere. Remember that labour and danger have their reward in glory: remember how sweet it is to live courageously and die with a legacy of immortal fame.

5   'Or have you forgotten our great ancestor? If Heracles had confined himself to Tiryns or Argos, or even the whole of the Peloponnese or Thebes, he would not have reached that height of glory which turned him from man into god, real or supposed. And even Dionysus, a more fastidious god compared to Heracles, was not without some labours to his name. But we have penetrated beyond Nysa, and we
6   have taken the Rock of Aornus which defeated Heracles. So make it your purpose to add the rest of Asia to what we have already won—most of it is done, and only a little remains. And what would we ourselves have achieved of any importance or distinction, if we had been content to sit tight in Macedonia and only expend what little effort was needed to protect our country by fending off the Thracians on our borders, or the Illyrians or Triballians, or even any Greeks unfriendly to us?

7   *'Now if I had led you through such labour and danger by simply giving you orders without sharing that labour and that danger myself, it would be understandable if your will to continue had flagged before mine—you would have done all the work and set up the rewards for others to enjoy. But as it is we share the labours, the dangers are common to us all, and the rewards are there in the open for all to claim.
8   All this land is yours, and you are its satraps. As for its treasure, the greater part is already coming to you, and when we have completed our conquest of Asia I swear that I shall not just satisfy you but surpass any man's hopes of the bounty to come. And then I shall send back those who want to return to home and country, or lead them back myself: and those who stay on I shall make the envy of the men who go.'

27   *After this and similar from Alexander, there was a long silence. No one dared there and then to disagree with their king, and no one either was willing to assent. In this vacuum Alexander repeatedly invited comments from anyone whose opinion differed from his own stated view. Even so the silence lasted long, and it was only after some time that Coenus the son of Polemocrates took the courage to speak in reply. This is what he said:
2   'By your own account, your majesty, you have no wish to exercise

command by diktat—you say that you will lead the Macedonians by persuasion, and if it is they who do the persuading you will not force your will on them. So in what I am about to say I shall not be speaking for those of us who are gathered here—given the preferment we enjoy, the rewards for our labours which most of us have already received, and our high standing compared to other ranks, there is no question of our absolute loyalty to you—but I shall speak for the army at large. And in so doing I shall not be espousing a populist 3 cause, but simply stating what I consider to be in your interest at the present time and the safest course for the future. I think my age entitles me not to hold back what I believe to be best—that and the status among my colleagues which I owe to you, and the unqualified determination I have shown so far in every labour and every danger.

'The very number and scale of the successes achieved under your 4 leadership by those who have been with you since we left our home together make me think that it is time now to put a limit to the labours we undergo and the dangers we face. You must be aware yourself how many Macedonians and Greeks came with you at the outset, and how many of us are now left. You sent the Thessalians straight home 5 from Bactra when you saw their loss of enthusiasm for further campaigning, and you were right to do so. As for the other Greeks, some have been settled in the cities you have founded, but they are not entirely happy to stay there. Others continue to share the labour and the danger of your campaigns, but they and the Macedonian army have lost some of their number in the battles, others have been wounded out of service and left behind in various parts of Asia, but 6 the largest category is those who have died of sickness. Few out of all those many are left, weakened now in physical condition, and yet more weary in spirit. Every one of them longs to see his parents, if they are still alive, longs to see his wife and children, and longs to see his own home country—and this longing for home is understandable when the bounty you confer for honourable service will send them back to enjoy the change from obscurity to prestige and from poverty to riches.

'You should not now lead on a reluctant army: you will not find 7 them as ready as they were to meet the dangers, when they have lost their own will for battle. But, if you agree, return with them to your own country, see your own mother, settle what needs to be settled in Greece, bring back all these mighty victories to adorn your father's house—and then, if that is your wish, start again and launch another expedition against these same Indian tribes in the east: or, if you want, an expedition to the Black Sea, or against Carthage and the rest of Libya beyond Carthage. That will be for you to determine at

8 the time. But it will be other Macedonians and other Greeks who follow you, young men in place of the old, fresh troops in place of the weary, men whose inexperience of war removes any immediate terrors and excites them with hopes for the future: and it is likely that they will be all the keener to go with you if they see their predecessors who joined you in hardship and danger coming back to their homes with poverty turned to wealth and what was once insignificance now

9 changed to celebrity. As fine a quality as any, your majesty, is moderation in the midst of success: and though with you as leader and an army such as ours at your command we have nothing to fear from any enemy, acts of god are another matter—they come unforeseen, and no human can guard against them.'

28   When Coenus had finished, it is said that the assembled company broke into applause at his speech, and several were even moved to tears, a yet stronger indication of their reluctance to prolong the dangers, and the joy with which they would welcome the retreat. Displeased at Coenus' plain speaking and the timidity of the other

2 officers, Alexander dismissed the meeting for the time being, but reconvened it in angry mood on the next day and told them that he himself was going on, but would not force any Macedonians to go with him if they did not wish to: he would have enough volunteers to follow their king, and those who wanted to go home were at liberty to do so—and to tell their friends that they had come back leaving their

3 king surrounded by enemies. After delivering that he is said to have retired to his tent and refused to admit even any of his Companions for the whole of that day and the two days thereafter: he was waiting to see if one of those sudden shifts of mood not uncommon in large bodies of troops would come over the Macedonians and their allies

4 and make them more amenable. When there was still a total lack of response in the camp, and it was clear that the men regretted Alexander's anger but had no intention of letting it change their minds, we are told by Ptolemy the son of Lagus that Alexander nevertheless made sacrifice to win sanction for the crossing of the river, but the offerings proved inauspicious.* It was only after this that he called together the oldest of his Companions and his particularly

close associates, and then, since everything now pointed to a withdrawal, announced to the army that he had decided to turn back.

The roar which greeted this was that of a huge motley crowd united **29** in a shout of joy. Most of them were in tears. Some came up to the royal tent and called down many blessings on Alexander for conceding to them his only defeat.

Alexander now divided the army into companies and ordered them to build twelve altars,* to the height of the tallest siege-towers but wider than a tower, as thank-offerings to the gods who had brought him victorious that far, and as memorials of his own labours. When **2** his altars were built, he made his customary sacrifices on them and held athletic and equestrian competitions. He added the land as far as the river Hyphasis to the territory ruled by Porus, and began his own return towards the Hydraotes. After crossing the Hydraotes he continued retracing his steps back to the Acesines. Here he found work **3** completed on the city which Hephaestion had been instructed to fortify. He populated it with volunteer settlers from the local tribes and those of his mercenaries no longer fit for active service, then turned to his own preparations for the voyage down to the Great Sea.

At this point he was visited by Arsaces, the dynast of the territory **4** next to Abisares,* together with Abisares' brother and his other relatives, bringing gifts of the highest prestige in India and the elephants from Abisares, some thirty of them: Abisares himself, they said, was unable to come because of illness. The envoys Alexander had sent to Abisares happened to arrive back at the same time, so it was easy to **5** confirm the facts as stated. With that confirmation Alexander granted Abisares the status of satrap over his own country, attaching Arsaces as a subordinate in Abisares' dominion, and fixing the tribute they would pay. He then made further sacrifice at the river Acesines, recrossed it, and came on to the Hydaspes, where he used the army to repair the monsoon damage to the cities of Nicaea and Bucephala, and made any other dispositions needed in the area.

BOOK SIX

1 WHEN Alexander had his flotilla built and ready on the banks of the Hydaspes*—large numbers of triaconters and sloops, large numbers of horse-ferries, and all the ancillary vessels needed for an army's transport by river—his plan was to sail down the Hydaspes to the Great Sea.

2 *He believed at first that he had found the origin of the Nile, as he had already seen crocodiles in the Indus (and in no other river apart from the Nile), had observed a type of bean native to Egypt growing along the banks of the Acesines, and had heard that the

3 Acesines flows into the Indus. So his idea was that the Nile rose somewhere in that part of India, flowed through a large tract of desert where it lost the name Indus, and then, when it reached inhabited land again, ultimately debouching into the Mediterranean Sea, the Ethiopians in those parts and the Egyptians called it the Nile (or, according to Homer, the Aegyptus, which gave its name to the coun-

4 try). Indeed it is reported that in a letter he was writing to Olympias about the land of India he included this belief of his that he had dis-covered the source of the Nile, reaching a momentous conclusion on

5 some very slender evidence: but on closer enquiry into the geography of the Indus he had learnt from the locals that the Hydaspes flows into the Acesines and the Acesines into the Indus, each surrendering its name at the confluence, and that the Indus then issues through two mouths into the Great Sea, and has no connection whatever with Egypt. He had then removed this passage about the Nile from the

6 letter to his mother.* So it was with the intention of sailing down the rivers to the Great Sea that he had ordered this fleet to be prepared. The ships' crews were made up from the Phoenicians, Cypriots, Carians, and Egyptians* accompanying the expedition.

2 *It was now that Coenus, one of Alexander's most faithful Companions, fell sick and died,* and Alexander gave him as magnifi-cent a funeral as the present circumstances allowed. He then sum-moned his Companions and all the Indian envoys who had come to visit him, and announced that Porus* was to be king of all the Indian land they had so far conquered—seven tribal territories in all, and more than two thousand cities among these tribes.

He turned now to the division of the army for the expedition. With 2 himself he took on board the ships all the foot guards, the archers, the Agrianians, and the elite cavalry corps. Craterus was to lead part of the infantry and cavalry along the right bank of the Hydaspes. And Hephaestion was to advance along the other bank in command of the largest and strongest part of the army, including the elephants, which now numbered some two hundred: this division had orders to proceed as fast as it could to the capital city of Sopeithes.* Philip, the 3 satrap of the region west of the Indus towards Bactria, was ordered to follow with his forces after an interval of three days. The cavalry from Nysa were sent back home. The admiral in command of the whole fleet was Nearchus, and the helmsman of Alexander's own ship was Onesicritus (one of the falsities in the history of Alexander written by Onesicritus is that he styles himself 'admiral', when in fact he was simply a helmsman).* According to Ptolemy the son of Lagus, 4 the main source I choose to follow, there were some eighty triaconters in the fleet, and the total number of vessels, including the horse-transports, corvettes, and all the other craft either in previous use on the rivers or constructed for this present purpose, came to little short of two thousand.

When Alexander had everything ready, the army began its embar- 3 kation just before dawn, and he made the customary sacrifices to the gods, and to the river Hydaspes, as specified by his seers. Embarking on his own ship, he poured a libation into the river from a golden bowl in the prow, and called on the Acesines as well as the Hydaspes, knowing now that it was the greatest of the other rivers joining the Hydaspes and that he was not far from the confluence: and he called too on the Indus, into which the Acesines and the Hydaspes jointly flow. With further libations to his ancestor Heracles, to Ammon,* 2 and to the other gods whom it was his custom to honour, he gave the order for the trumpet to signal departure, and at the signal the fleet immediately began to put out in disciplined order. Without coordination there would be collisions, so to avoid this specific instructions of the distance to be kept between them had been given to the freighters, the horse-transports, and the warships, and the faster ships were not allowed to get ahead out of formation. The noise of the simul- 3 taneous rowing by so many ships was like nothing else, what with the coxswains shouting the 'in . . . out' for every stroke and the oarsmen raising a cheer each time as they struck the churning water in unison.

The river banks, often higher than the ships, funnelled and ampli-
fied the noise, sending it reverberating from bank to bank, and here
and there wooded hollows on either side served as echo-chambers,
4 beating the sound back from their empty spaces. The horses visible
on the transports caused amazement to the barbarians watching the
spectacle, as horses had never been seen on ships before in India
(and the Indians had no traditional memory that Dionysus' expedition against them had also been ship-borne). So those who had
gathered when the fleet got under way followed it for some consider-
5 able distance, and wherever tribes now loyal to Alexander came within
earshot of the shouting of the rowers and the crash of oars they went
running along the bank and provided an escort, singing their native
songs. The Indians have a particular love of song and dance, ever since
Dionysus and his companions brought their revels to the country.

4   On the third day of this voyage Alexander put in at the place where
both Hephaestion and Craterus had orders to make camp, on opposite banks. He stayed there for two days, and then when Philip came
up with the rest of the army he sent him and the troops he had brought
with him to the river Acesines, with instructions to proceed down
along its bank, and Craterus' and Hephaestion's troops were sent on
2 again to follow the routes which Alexander prescribed for them. He
himself continued down the river Hydaspes, which at no point in the
voyage was less than two and a quarter miles wide. Every now and
then he put in to the banks to deal with the Indian tribes bordering the
Hydaspes: he made terms with those who surrendered, but he now
3 met some who took to resistance, and these he subdued by force. He
was, though, keen to make all speed to the territory of the Mallians
and the Oxydracae, on learning that these were the most numerous
and warlike tribes in this part of India, and receiving reports that they
had moved their women and children to safe keeping in their most
strongly fortified cities and were determined to do battle with him.
This made him hurry the voyage on, so he could come to grips with
these people before they had organized themselves and were still in a
flurry of incomplete preparation.

4   *On the fifth day from his second start he reached the confluence
of the Hydaspes and the Acesines. Where these two meet they form
one very narrow river, with a consequently fierce current swirling
into huge maelstroms, and the seething water gives out a roar and
5 crash which can be heard from far away. Alexander had warning of

this from the locals, and passed the warning to his men. Even so, when they neared the confluence the noise of the water was so dominant that the sailors stopped their rowing—this was nobody's order, but the coxswains calling the time had fallen silent in sheer amazement, and the rowers themselves were flummoxed by the din.

But when they were now close to the meeting of the waters the 5 ships' helmsmen ordered their crews to bend to their oars and row like fury through the narrows, to prevent the ships being caught in the whirlpools and capsized—with enough propulsion they could counteract the circular movement of the water. In fact, if any of the 2 broad-beamed boats were spun round by the current no harm was done except to the nerves of those on board, and the current itself eventually righted them and put them back on a straight course. The warships, though, did not come out of the maelstrom quite so unscathed. They did not ride so high over the seething rapids, and those with two tiers of oars could not keep the lower bank clear enough out of the water. So when the whirlpools swung them broad- 3 side on, those caught by the water had their oars shattered if they had not lifted them in time, and many ships were damaged: two collided and sank with the loss of many aboard. When the river finally broadened out the current was not so fierce and the eddies had less violent effect on the ships. So Alexander brought the expedition to anchor on 4 the right-hand bank, where there was shelter from the current and the ships could run in close: here there was a spit of land jutting conveniently into the river to enable the recovery of the wrecks and any survivors still on board. They were rescued and the damaged ships repaired. Alexander then ordered Nearchus to sail on down as far as the borders of the Mallian tribe, while he himself led a punitive raid through the territory of the barbarians who had not submitted, so preventing them from bringing aid to the Mallians. He then rejoined the fleet.

At this point Hephaestion, Craterus, and Philip joined him 5 once more with their troops. Alexander transported the elephants, Polyperchon's brigade, the mounted archers, and Philip's army to the other side of the Hydaspes and put them under Craterus' command. He sent Nearchus and the fleet on their way downstream, with orders to keep three days' march ahead of this army throughout their voyage. The rest of the land force he split into three parts. Hephaestion 6 was sent on five days ahead, so that any enemy attempting to escape

Alexander's own division by moving on at speed would run into Hephaestion's troops and be caught, and Ptolemy the son of Lagus was given a third section with orders to follow at an interval of three days, so that any turning back to escape Alexander would run into
7 these troops with Ptolemy. When they reached the junction of the Acesines and the Hydraotes, the leading division had instructions to wait until Alexander himself arrived, and Craterus and Ptolemy were ordered to meet him there with their troops.

6 He himself took the foot guards, the archers, the Agrianians, Peithon's brigade of the so-called 'Close Companions', all of the mounted archers, and half of the Companion cavalry, and led them through waterless country towards the territory of the Mallians, one
2 of the independent Indian tribes. On the first day he camped by a small source of water about eleven miles from the river Acesines. He fed and rested his army for a short while, then sent word for every-one to fill any container they had with water. Marching on through the rest of that day and the whole of the night he covered some forty-five miles before reaching at dawn one of the cities* in which large
3 numbers of the Mallians had gathered for refuge. Never thinking that Alexander would come to attack them through the desert, most of them were outside the city and unarmed: Alexander had clearly chosen this route for its very difficulty—the same reason which led his enemies to discount it as a possibility. So his onslaught took them by surprise, and he killed most of them without any resistance offered, unarmed as they were.* The rest were penned inside the city, and Alexander threw a cordon of cavalry round the wall to serve in place of a palisade, as the infantry phalanx had not yet come up with him.
4 As soon as the infantry arrived, he sent Perdiccas with his own and Cleitus' cavalry units and the Agrianians to another Mallian city where many Indians of the region had taken refuge, with orders to keep a close guard on the occupants of the city, but not to engage in any action until he himself arrived: here too they were to pre-vent anyone escaping to alert the other barbarians to the imminent approach of Alexander.
5 He then began his assault on the wall. The barbarians abandoned this outer wall, realizing that it was beyond them to defend it further when they had lost so many killed in the initial onslaught and others were incapacitated by wounds. Retreating to the citadel, they kept up resistance for some time from a commanding position which was

difficult to assault. But with the Macedonians pressing strongly on all sides, and Alexander himself conspicuously involved at various points of the action, the citadel was taken by storm and all those who had taken refuge there were killed. They numbered about two thousand.

Perdiccas meanwhile arrived at the city to which he had been sent 6 and found it empty. Learning that it was not long since the inhabitants had fled, he rode at full speed on the track of the fugitives, and his light infantry followed as fast as they could on foot. He overtook and massacred all of the fugitives who were not far enough ahead to make their escape into the marshes.

After seeing that his men had their dinner and resting them until 7 the first watch of the night, Alexander pressed on forwards. A long march through the night brought him at dawn to the river Hydraotes. There he learnt that most of the Mallians had already crossed, but he came on some of them still making the crossing and killed many of them in mid-stream. He kept straight on across the river by the same 2 ford they were using and went in close pursuit of those who had got away ahead of him. Many of these were killed, and some captured alive, but the majority escaped to take refuge in a strongly fortified position. As soon as his infantry came up with him, Alexander sent Peithon against these Mallians with his own brigade and two units of cavalry. They took the place* at one assault, and enslaved its entire 3 complement of fugitives who had not been killed in the attack. That accomplished, Peithon and his troops returned to camp.

Alexander had heard that some of the Mallians had taken collec- 4 tive refuge in one of the Brahman cities* as well, and he was already on the march against it. When he reached the city, he brought up his phalanx to surround the wall in close formation. Seeing that the wall was being undermined, and kept back from it by missile-fire, the occupants of this city too abandoned the outer defences and retreated in a body to continue resistance from the citadel. A group of Macedonians managed to press through with them into the citadel, but the defenders turned, consolidated their ranks, and drove them out again, killing some twenty-five as they attempted to withdraw. Alexander now gave orders for ladders to be set up on all sides of the 5 citadel and its wall to be undermined. The collapse of an undermined tower and the breach torn in that part of the curtain wall opened the citadel to assault, and Alexander was the first to mount the wall, standing conspicuously there in possession of it. This sight shamed 6 the rest of the Macedonians into climbing the wall* wherever they could. The citadel was now in their hands. Some of the Indians set fire to their houses, were trapped in them, and died there: but most of them were killed fighting. The dead numbered up to five thousand in all, and the courage of the Indians was such that few were taken alive.

8   Alexander stayed there one day and rested his army, then on the next day set out against the remaining Mallians. He found their towns abandoned, and learnt that the inhabitants had fled into the desert.

2 Here again he rested the army for one day, and on the following day sent Peithon and the cavalry officer Demetrius back to the river with the men under their command, giving them in addition as many com-

3 panies of light troops as they needed for their task. This was to proceed along the river bank looking for any fugitives hiding in the extensive woods which bordered the river, and to kill any they found who would not give themselves up. Peithon's and Demetrius' troops did in fact catch and kill a large number in the woods.

4   Alexander himself marched against the biggest of the Mallian cities, where there was reported to be a large concentration of fugitives from the other towns. But even this city had been deserted by the Indians when they learnt of Alexander's approach: they had crossed the Hydraotes* and taken up position in battle-order on the opposite bank, which was high above the river, to prevent Alexander

5 from using the ford. When he heard of this, he took all the cavalry he had with him and made for the Hydraotes at the point where the Mallians were reported to be massed, and ordered the infantry to follow. When he reached the river and saw the enemy lines on the far side, without any pause after the journey he plunged straight into the

6 ford, though it was still just him and the cavalry. The enemy watched him get halfway across, then made a hasty but disciplined retreat from the bank. Alexander went after them with just the cavalry, but as soon as the Indians realized that this mounted force had no infantry support they turned and began a vigorous counter-offensive. They numbered about fifty thousand, and Alexander, seeing the density of their ranks and still waiting for his own infantry, kept his cavalry circling and making quick charges in and out, but would not

7 engage the Indians at close quarters. Presently, though, the Agrianians and the archers arrived in support, together with the other companies of light troops he had picked to join his own force: and the phalanx of

heavy infantry could be seen not far behind. With all these threats converging on them the Indians turned and ran in headlong flight to the most strongly fortified city in the immediate area. Alexander fol- 8 lowed and killed a good number of them. Those who got away shut themselves in the city, and Alexander immediately threw his cavalry in a cordon round it: then when the infantry came up to join him he had them make camp for the rest of that day in a circle surrounding the city wall. There was little daylight left for an assault there and then, and besides his troops were exhausted, the infantry from their long march and the cavalry from the relentless pursuit, and for all of them the crossing of the river had been a particularly tiring trial.

On the following day Alexander divided the army in two for the 9 attack on the wall, leading one division himself with Perdiccas in command of the other. At this first stage the Indians did not resist the Macedonian onslaught, but abandoned the outer defences and congregated for refuge in the citadel. Alexander and his men now broke open a small gate and got inside the city long before the other troops under Perdiccas, who were slowed by their difficulty in negotiating 2 the wall, as most of them had not even brought ladders, in the belief that the city had already been taken when they saw the outer walls denuded of defenders. But when it became clear to Perdiccas' men that the citadel was still in enemy hands, and they could see large numbers marshalled for its defence, they made every effort to force their way in—undermining the wall, setting up scaling-ladders wherever they could. Alexander thought the Macedonians bringing up the 3 ladders were too slow* about it, so he seized a ladder from one of them, set it up against the wall himself, and, huddled under his shield, climbed up: Peucestas* came up after him bearing the sacred shield which Alexander had taken from the temple of Athena at Troy* and kept always with him, having it carried before him in his battles. He was followed up the same ladder by Leonnatus the Bodyguard,* and Abreas,* one of the soldiers on double pay, mounted by another ladder. The king was now up by the battlement at the top of the wall. 4 He had propped his shield against it, and by shoving some of the Indians back down inside the wall and killing others with his sword where he stood he had cleared that section of the wall. In extreme fear for their king's safety the foot guards rushed to jostle up the same ladder, and in the process broke it, so that those already on it fell to the ground, and the others had no means of ascent.

5   Standing there on the wall Alexander was the target of fire from all
       the surrounding towers within range (none of the Indians was pre-
       pared to approach him directly), and also from the men inside the
       citadel, who could shoot at short range from a pile of earth which
       happened to lie against the wall at that point. He could not conceal
       his identity—the magnificence of his armour and the exceptional
       show of courage betrayed him—and Alexander decided that to stay
       where he was without some dramatic move would put him in danger,
       but if he jumped down inside the citadel he could well cause panic
       in the enemy simply by that action: if not, and if he had to face the
       ultimate danger, he would die after putting up a heroic struggle fit for
       the wonder of future generations. This decision made, he jumped
6   down* from the wall into the citadel. There, with his back against the
       wall, he used his sword to deal with a number of Indians who con-
       fronted him and a rash direct attack by their commander: he killed
       them all. When others made to approach he stopped them one by one
       with the throw of a stone, and used his sword again on any who got
       too close. By now the barbarians were keeping their distance, but
       they formed a semicircle round him and began loosing at him all the
       missiles they had with them or could find on the spot.
10   At this point Peucestas, Abreas, the double-pay corporal, and after
       them Leonnatus (who were in fact the only men to get up on the wall
       before the ladders broke) also jumped down inside and began to fight
       in defence of their king. Abreas fell there, shot by an arrow in the
       face, and Alexander was hit too, the arrow passing right through his
       breastplate and into his chest above the nipple: Ptolemy says that
       the blood escaping from the wound was bubbling with the air from
2   his lung. As long as his blood ran warm, and although he was in a bad
       way, Alexander continued to defend himself: but when inevitably his
       breathing caused a massive haemorrhage he became dizzy and faint,
       and fell forward over his shield. Peucestas stood astride him as he lay
       there, protecting him with the sacred shield from Troy, and Leonnatus
       took his stand on the other side: these two were now the targets, while
       Alexander was slipping into unconsciousness from loss of blood.
3   The fact was that the rest of the Macedonians had particular diffi-
       culty in pressing the assault at this point. Those who had seen
       Alexander up on the wall under fire then jumping down into the cita-
       del were desperately afraid for their king's safety in this foolish risk.
       Their ladders were broken, but in the emergency they used any means

they could improvise to scale the wall: some hammered pegs into the clay of the wall and struggled to inch their way up by these hand-holds, and others tried standing on their companions' shoulders. The 4 first up on the wall threw himself down into the citadel, and all who followed mingled cries of grief with battle-shouts when they saw their king lying there. A fierce battle was quickly joined over his prone body, with one after another of the Macedonians defending him with their shields, until some of the troops outside cut through the bar holding the gate in the curtain wall and squeezed in a few at a time, while others put their shoulders to the gap and forced the gate all the way inside the wall, and so laid the citadel open on this side.

Now there was slaughter and rescue. The army set about kill- 11 ing the Indians—and they killed them all, no woman or child excepted*—while some carried out the king on his shield, in such a poor state that they could not yet tell if he would live. Some histor-ians have recorded that the incision to withdraw the arrow from the wound was made by Critodemus, a doctor of Asclepiad descent from Cos, but others say that it was Perdiccas* who, with no surgeon at hand in the crisis, and at Alexander's direct command, used his sword to cut round the wound and extract the arrow. There was a great rush 2 of blood as the arrow was pulled out, and Alexander fainted again, so the flow was stemmed by his loss of consciousness. Writers have con-cocted all sorts of other stories about this incident, and from the beginning tradition has taken these falsehoods at face value and kept them alive to our own day: and this transmission of false stories will continue unless I can put a stop to it with this history of mine.

In the first place, the universally accepted account is that Alexander 3 suffered this serious incident among the Oxydracae. This is not so. It occurred in the territory of the Mallians, an independent Indian tribe: the city was a Mallian city, and it was the Mallians who shot Alexander. They had indeed formed an offensive alliance with the Oxydracae, but Alexander was too quick on them with his march through the desert to allow any help to reach them from the Oxydracae, or vice versa. It is the same with the location of battles. The received tradi- 4 tion has Arbela as the site of the final battle with Darius, which saw Darius take to a prolonged flight ending only with his arrest by Bessus and his colleagues and his murder when Alexander was com-ing close—just as Issus is given as the location of the previous battle, and the Granicus of the first cavalry battle. Now it is true that there 5 was a cavalry battle at the Granicus, and the second battle with Darius took place at Issus, but Arbela is some considerable distance—estimates vary from fifty-five to sixty-five miles—from the actual place where Darius and Alexander fought their last battle. According to Ptolemy and Aristobulus this battle was fought at Gaugamela, by

6 the river Bumelus. Gaugamela was not a city, but only a large village, otherwise unknown and with an odd-sounding name: that is why I think the credit of the great battle was appropriated by the city of Arbela. Yet if we are to believe that Arbela was the site of an action fought so many miles away we might as well say that the naval battle at Salamis took place at the Corinthian Isthmus, and the battle of Artemisium in Euboea was fought off Aegina or Sunium.

7   Then again, there is the question of who came to his defence and shielded Alexander at the point of crisis. All agree that Peucestas was there, but there is divergence about the roles of Leonnatus and Abreas, the double-pay corporal. Then some say that Alexander was dazed and fell from a blow on his helmet by a club, and had got to his feet again when he was shot in the chest through his breastplate: but Ptolemy the son of Lagus speaks only of this one wound in the chest,

8 and no other blow. But I would say myself that the most significant error committed by Alexander historians is the statement by some that Ptolemy the son of Lagus joined Peucestas in climbing the ladder with Alexander and then protecting his fallen body, and that this is how Ptolemy acquired the title of 'Saviour'.* Yet Ptolemy himself has recorded that he took no part in this action and was not even there, as at the time he was commanding a force engaged in other battles against other barbarians. I trust that what I have set out here by way of digression will serve to make future historians more painstaking in their research when they write about actions and events of this importance.

12   While Alexander remained where he was under treatment for his wound, the first report to reach the base camp for the Mallian expedition was that he had died of the wound. As the rumour spread there was lamentation throughout the whole of the army, and then that first reaction gave way to desperate anxiety. Who would now lead them?

2 There was no clear choice among the many officers thought equally deserving both by Alexander himself and by the Macedonians at large. And how would they get safely back home, when they were surrounded by so many aggressive tribes, some still to submit and

likely to put up a strong fight for their freedom, and the others sure to revolt now that the fear of Alexander was removed? They thought they were now trapped between impassable rivers, and without Alexander they could see nothing but hopeless problems. When word *3* eventually came that Alexander was alive, they could hardly believe it and still had doubts of his ultimate survival: and when a letter arrived from him saying that he would shortly come to join them in the camp, most of them were so paranoid with fear that they doubted even this, and guessed that it was a forgery by his Bodyguards and generals.

In view of this situation, Alexander was concerned to prevent mat- *13* ters in the army getting out of hand. As soon as he was well enough he had himself carried to the banks of the river Hydraotes, and sailed downstream. The army was based at the junction of the Hydraotes and the Acesines, where Nearchus had the fleet and Hephaestion was in charge of the land forces. As the ship carrying the king came near to the camp, he ordered the removal of the awning over the stern, so that he would be plainly visible to all. Even so, the men were still *2* incredulous, thinking that what they saw on board was Alexander's dead body, until the very moment when the ship put in to the bank and Alexander raised his hand to the crowd. Then there was a great shout: men lifted their arms to the heaven or stretched them out towards Alexander, and many were forced to tears at this unexpected joy. As he was carried off the ship some of the foot guards brought him a stretcher, but he ordered his horse to be led up. When he was *3* seen once again mounted on his horse, the entire army broke into long applause which echoed from the banks and the surrounding woods. A little way short of his tent he dismounted, so that he could be seen walking too. His men crowded round him, touching his hands, his knees, his very clothing; some came up close just to see him and call out a blessing before they left; some festooned him with ribbons, or with the flowers then seasonal in India.

Nearchus tells us that Alexander was riled by the criticism of *4* some of his friends, who blamed him for going ahead of his troops and putting himself at personal risk: a soldier could do that, they said, but not a commander. I would guess that Alexander's resentment was because he recognized the truth of this charge and his own responsibility in incurring it. Yet the fact is that in battle he was a berserker, as addicted to glory as men are to any other overmastering passion, and he lacked the discipline to keep himself out of danger.

5 Nearchus says that one of the older soldiers, a Boeotian* whose name
he does not give, seeing that Alexander was resentful and sullen at his
friends' criticisms, came up to him and said in his country accent,
'A man will do what he has to do, Alexander,' then added a line of
verse to the effect that suffering is the debt which action must pay.
This delighted Alexander, and from that first approval the man
became a close friend.

14   Envoys now came to Alexander from the remaining Mallians,
offering the surrender of their people. A similar offer of surrender
was made by the Oxydracae, who sent their city and district governors in person, together with a hundred and fifty other dignitaries:
they had full authority to agree a settlement and brought with them
2 gifts of the greatest prestige among the Indians. They argued that
their failure to negotiate with him earlier was understandable, in that
like anyone else, but to a more than usual degree, they valued their
independence and wished to retain the freedom which they had preserved for all the time from Dionysus' arrival in India to that of
Alexander. However, since it was widely said that Alexander was also
of divine descent, if it were Alexander's pleasure they would accept a
satrap appointed at his discretion by Alexander, and pay such tribute
as Alexander determined: they were also willing to give as many hos-
3 tages as Alexander might require. He demanded a thousand of their
leading men, whom he would either keep as hostages, if he so wished,
or else conscript them to serve in his army until he had completed his
campaign against the rest of the Indians. They duly sent the men,
choosing a thousand of their greatest and best, and also an unsolicited
addition of five hundred chariots with their crews. Alexander now
appointed Philip as satrap* over the Oxydracae and the surviving
Mallians. He returned the hostages, but kept the chariots.
4   With these arrangements made, and the fleet expanded by a large
number of additional craft built during his convalescence after the
wound, Alexander put on board the ships seventeen hundred of the
Companion cavalry, the same number of light-armed troops as before,
and up to ten thousand infantry. He then sailed down the Hydraotes
for the short length before it joins the Acesines and yields its name to
the dominant river, continuing his voyage down what was now the
5 Acesines until he came to its confluence with the Indus. Four great
rivers, all of them navigable, are tributaries of the Indus, not always
retaining their original names. The Hydaspes flows into the Acesines,

losing to the Acesines its name as well as all its water; this enlarged Acesines then meets the Hydraotes and takes it in, still keeping the name Acesines; the next tributary it incorporates is the Hyphasis, and the Acesines continues under its own name until it flows into the Indus; after that confluence it finally surrenders its name to the Indus. From that point until it splits into the delta I can well believe that the Indus is up to eleven miles wide,* and perhaps even wider in the reaches where it is more like a lake than a river.

Alexander waited there at the junction of the Acesines and the 15 Indus until Perdiccas and his army came to rejoin him (on his way Perdiccas had subdued one of the independent tribes, the Abastanians). In this interval he received a consignment of new triaconters and freighters built for him in Xathrian country, and the Sogdians, another independent Indian tribe, came over to him. Envoys also arrived from the Ossadians (these too an independent race of Indians), offering their submission likewise. Alexander now fixed the boundary 2 of Philip's satrapy at the point where the Acesines joins the Indus, and left with him the entire Thracian contingent and as many men from the other units as seemed sufficient to garrison the country. He instructed Philip to found a city right at the junction of the two rivers, which he hoped would grow to fame as one of the great cities of the world: dockyards too were to be built there. At this time also 3 Alexander was visited by Oxyartes the Bactrian, the father of his wife Rhoxane. To add to his honours Alexander granted him the satrapy over the Parapamisadae, removing the previous occupant of that post, Tyriespis,* after reports of maladministration.

He now had Craterus ferried across to the left bank of the Indus 4 with most of the army and the elephants, as on that side of the river there appeared to be easier going for a heavily equipped army, and not all of the bordering tribes were friendly. Alexander himself sailed on down to the capital city of the Sogdians. There he built and fortified a new city, and constructed additional dockyards in which he had his damaged ships repaired. He appointed Peithon* as satrap of the region extending from the confluence of the Indus and Acesines down to the sea, including the entire coastline of India.

Sending Craterus and the army on again by land, Alexander sailed 5 downstream towards the kingdom of Musicanus, which was reported to be the richest in all India. Musicanus had not yet come to meet Alexander in person to offer his own and his country's submission,

nor was he sending any envoys to explore friendly relations: none of the usual gifts made to great kings had been sent, and he himself had
6 asked for nothing from Alexander. The voyage down the river was pressed at such a speed that Alexander was already on the border of his kingdom before Musicanus even heard that he was on his way against him. This shock had him hurrying to meet Alexander, conveying the gifts most highly valued by the Indians, bringing with him all the elephants in his possession, surrendering his people as well as himself, and acknowledging his failure to do as he should. This last was the surest way for anyone to win concessions from Alexander,
7 and so it proved in the approach taken by Musicanus. Alexander pardoned him, expressed his admiration for his city and his country, and granted him the continuation of his rule.* Craterus was ordered to fortify the city's acropolis, and Alexander stayed there while this was done and a garrison installed, as he could see the value of the place for keeping a watch and a hold over the surrounding tribes.

16   From here Alexander took the archers, the Agrianians, and the cavalry he had brought with him on the voyage and launched a punitive expedition against the local baron of this area, called Oxicanus,* who had neither appeared in person nor sent envoys to offer his own
2 submission and surrender his territory. The two largest cities under Oxicanus' control were taken by storm in an immediate assault, and Oxicanus himself was captured in the second of these. Alexander let his army have the plunder, but took the elephants for himself. The other cities in the same territory surrendered at Alexander's approach with no resistance offered—such was the abject despair to which all of the Indians had now been reduced by Alexander and the fortune which attended him.

3   Alexander now moved against Sambus, his own appointee as satrap of the highland Indians. Sambus was no friend of Musicanus, and was reported to have fled on learning that Musicanus had been par-
4 doned by Alexander and remained the ruler of his own country. As Alexander was coming close to the capital city* of Sambus' region, which was called Sindimana, the gates were opened to welcome his approach and the relatives of Sambus came out to meet him, bringing Sambus' elephants and an inventory of his personal treasure: Sambus' flight, they explained, was no sign of hostility to Alexander, but a
5 fearful response to the restoration of Musicanus. On this same expedition Alexander captured another city* which had rebelled, and

executed the Brahmans* responsible for the revolt: the Brahmans are the gurus of India, and I shall give an account of their supposed wisdom in my Indian monograph.

It was now that reports came in of a revolt by Musicanus. To deal 17 with the man himself Alexander dispatched a sufficient force under the satrap Peithon the son of Agenor, while he proceeded against the cities which owed allegiance to Musicanus: some he destroyed completely and sold the inhabitants into slavery; in others he fortified the citadel and installed a garrison. This done, he returned to the camp and the fleet. Here Musicanus was brought in under arrest by Peithon. 2 Alexander ordered him to be hanged in his own country, together with the Brahmans who had been the instigators of his revolt.

Here also Alexander was visited by the ruler of Patala, which, as I have mentioned before,* is the region of the delta formed by the river Indus, yet larger in extent than the Egyptian delta. He too offered the surrender of his entire territory and put himself and all he possessed at Alexander's disposal. Alexander sent him back to resume 3 rule in his country, with orders to make all preparations needed for the reception of the army. He then made his own dispositions. Craterus was ordered to take the route through Arachosia and Zarangiana to Carmania* with the brigades of Attalus, Meleager, and Antigenes, some of the archers, and all those of Companion or other rank now unfit for service and already destined for repatriation: Craterus was also given the elephants to take with him. Hephaestion 4 was put in command of all the remaining army units except those sailing down to the sea with Alexander, and Peithon was sent across the Indus with the mounted javelin-men and the Agrianians to operate on the bank opposite Hephaestion's line of march with the main army: his orders were to populate the cities which had already been fortified, deal with any rebellions among the Indians of that region, and then join up with Alexander at Patala.*

Alexander was on the third day of his voyage when news 5 reached him that the ruler of Patala had absconded, taking most of his people with him and leaving the country deserted. At this he set a more urgent speed down the river, and when he reached Patala he found the city empty of inhabitants and no men at work on the land. He dispatched his fastest troops in pursuit of the fugitives, and when 6 some of them were captured sent them on to give the others his message that they should not be afraid to come back—they were free

to live in their city and work their land as before. Most of them did
return.

18   *Meanwhile Alexander ordered Hephaestion to build a fortified
position in Patala, and sent men out into the adjoining desert country
to dig wells and make the area habitable. Some of the neighbouring
barbarians took this work party by surprise and in a sudden attack
killed a few of them, but their own losses were considerable and they
fled back into the desert. The original detachment was then able to
complete its task with the addition of further troops sent out by
Alexander to assist the work as soon as he heard of the barbarian
attack.

2   At Patala the water of the Indus divides into two great rivers, both of
which retain the Indus name from there to the sea. At this point of
divergence Alexander began the construction of harbour facilities and
dockyards, and when the work was well advanced he decided to sail
3 down the right-hand river to its outlet in the sea. He gave Leonnatus
about a thousand of the cavalry and eight thousand heavy and light
infantry and sent him out to march down the island of Patala* in parallel with the fleet, while he himself took the fastest of his ships—the
sloops, all the triaconters, and some of the corvettes—and began the
4 voyage down the western river. As all the Indians in the area had fled,
he had no local pilot, and navigation downstream proved that much
more difficult: and on the day after the fleet set out a storm* came on
with the wind blowing against the current and creating troughs in the
water which gave the hulls a thorough buffeting. As a result most of
his ships were damaged, and some of the triaconters were completely
broken up, though the crews managed to run them aground before
5 they actually fell apart in the water. So Alexander had new ships put
under construction, and sent a party of his lightest infantry to capture
some of the Indians on the far side of the bank: these then acted as his
pilots for the rest of the passage. When they came to the point where
the river spreads out wide, extending here to twenty-two miles at its
broadest, the wind was blowing in strong from the open sea and they
could hardly lift their oars in the heaving water: guided by their pilots,
they ran for shelter again into a side-channel.

19   They were anchored there when the tide ebbed and left their ships
high and dry. Tides are a regular phenomenon of the Great Sea, but
Alexander's men had never experienced them before: so they found
the ebb bewildering enough in itself, but their amazement was yet

greater when after some hours the tide came back in and re-floated the
hulls. When the tide caught them the ships which had settled on an 2
even keel in the mud were lifted intact and floated again without damage: but those which the ebb had left unbalanced on harder ground
were overwhelmed by the returning flood of water and either collided
with one another or scraped along the bottom until they broke up.
Alexander repaired the ships as best he could in the situation, and sent 3
some of his men downriver in two corvettes to reconnoitre the island
which the native pilots told him would provide anchorage on his way
to the sea: they said this island was called Cilluta. The men reported
that there were indeed places to anchor there, and the island itself was
large and had a supply of fresh water. So the rest of the fleet put in at
the island, while Alexander took his fastest ships and sailed on beyond
it, to take a look at the river mouth and check whether it offered a safe
passage out to the sea. They travelled about twenty miles down from 4
Cilluta and sighted another island,* this time in the open sea. For the
present they returned to the river island, and Alexander came to anchor
under its headland, where he sacrificed to those gods to whom he
always said that Ammon had instructed him to make sacrifice. On the
following day he sailed down to the other island out in the sea, put in
there too, and made sacrifice once more—but different sacrifices this
time, to different gods and in different rites, again claiming that these
had been enjoined by Ammon in his oracle. Then he took his own ship 5
further out from the Indus estuaries and deeper into the open sea, saying that he wanted to discover if there was any other land visible out
there not too far away, but I would guess that his main purpose was
simply the achievement of having sailed in the Great Sea beyond India.
Out at sea he slaughtered bulls in sacrifice to Poseidon and dropped
their bodies into the water, then made libation over the sacrifice from
a cup made of gold, and threw the cup and golden mixing-bowls with
it into the sea as thank-offerings, praying that Poseidon would grant
safe passage to the fleet he proposed to send under Nearchus to the
Persian Gulf and the mouths of the Euphrates and the Tigris.

    Returning to Patala, Alexander found the fortress built and Peithon 20
arrived with his army after accomplishing all the objects of his mission. Hephaestion was now charged with the arrangements for fortifying the harbour and constructing the dockyards, as Alexander
intended to leave behind another considerable fleet of ships at this
point near the city of Patala where the river Indus forked.

2 He now made a second voyage down to the Great Sea by the other branch of the Indus, to discover which of the outlets offered the easier passage to the sea (the two mouths of the Indus are about two hundred
3 miles apart).* On his way down he came to a great lake in the estuary, where the river spreads out to a vast extent, perhaps fed in this area by tributary waters, and looks just like a gulf in the sea: and in fact sea-fish could be seen in it, that far up, larger than those here in our Mediterranean. He put in and anchored by the side of the lake where his pilots directed him, and left Leonnatus there with the bulk of the
4 troops. He also left behind all of the corvettes, taking the triaconters and sloops with him to make the passage out beyond this mouth of the Indus and into the open sea once more, and thereby establishing that the Indus outlet on our side was the more easily navigable.* Alexander then anchored his ships by the shore and took a party of cavalry with him a distance of three days' march along the coast, reconnoitring the country along which the coasting voyage would be made and ordering wells to be dug to give the fleet a supply of water.
5 He then returned to his ships and sailed up again to Patala, sending a section of the army to carry on the same work along the coastline, with orders to return likewise to Patala. He went back downriver to the lake and constructed another harbour there and further dockyards, then left a garrison in the place, brought in enough grain to supply the army for four months, and made all other preparations for the voyage along the coast.*

21 At the time, though, it was not the season for sailing. This was the monsoon period, and unlike our own etesian winds which blow from the north the monsoons set in mainly from the south and blow inland
2 from the Great Sea. Alexander's information was that the navigable season in these parts was after the beginning of winter, from the setting of the Pleiades* until the winter solstice, a time when the heavily rain-soaked land naturally gives rise instead to light off-shore breezes well suited to a coastal voyage by oars or sail.
3 So while Nearchus, the appointed admiral of the fleet, waited for the right sailing season, Alexander set out from Patala* and advanced with his entire army as far as the river Arabius [Hab]. There he left Hephaestion in command of the rest of the army, while he himself turned westwards towards the sea, taking with him half of the foot guards and the archers, the brigades of the so-called 'Close Companions', the elite corps of the Companion cavalry together

with one squadron from each of the cavalry units, and all the mounted archers. He wanted to dig wells to ensure a plentiful supply of water for the fleet sailing along the coast, and also to make a surprise attack on the Oreitans, a long-independent Indian people in this area who had shown no welcome to Alexander and his army. Another 4 independent tribe living round the Arabius were the Arabitae: they realized they were no match for Alexander in battle, but were not prepared to submit either, so when they learnt of Alexander's approach they took flight into the desert. Alexander crossed the Arabius, which was a narrow river of little depth, traversed most of the desert in the night, and by dawn was close to the inhabited region. Here he ordered the infantry to follow in battle-order, while he went ahead into Oreitan territory with the cavalry, dividing it into squadrons to achieve maximum coverage of the plain. All who put up 5 resistance were cut down by the cavalry, and many were captured alive. Alexander made temporary camp by a small source of water, but continued his advance as soon as he was joined by Hephaestion's troops. On reaching the largest of the Oreitan villages, called Rhambacia* [Las Bela], he was sufficiently impressed by the site to think that a concentration of settlers there could make it a large and prosperous city. So Hephaestion was left there to see to it.

Alexander now moved on again to the border country between 22 Gedrosia and Oreitis, taking with him half of the foot guards and the Agrianians, the elite cavalry corps, and the mounted archers. He had been told that there was a narrow pass at the border, and that the Gedrosians and Oreitans had their joint forces camped in front of the pass to block his transit. They were indeed stationed there, but as 2 soon as they heard news of Alexander's imminent approach most of them deserted their posts and abandoned the pass, and the chiefs of the Oreitans came to surrender themselves and their people to Alexander. He told them to call a general meeting of their tribesmen and send them back to their homes with an assurance that they would come to no harm. Here too he imposed a satrap, appointing Apollophanes to that post, and in support he left Leonnatus the 3 Bodyguard in Ora with all the Agrianians, some of the archers and cavalry, and Greek mercenary troops as well, both infantry and cavalry. Leonnatus' instructions were to stay there until the fleet came by the coast in that region, and in the meantime to populate the new city and stabilize the situation in the country, to ensure the satrap had full compliance from the people. Hephaestion had now arrived with the troops left behind in Rhambacia, and Alexander set out for Gedrosia with the bulk of his army. The route was mainly through desert country.

4   In this desert Aristobulus says that there is a wealth of myrrh trees, larger than the usual species, and that the Phoenician traders following the army collected the gum of the myrrh and loaded it on their pack-animals for export: there was indeed plenty of it, given the size

5 of the tree trunks and the lack of any previous harvesting. He also says that a great deal of fragrant spikenard grows in the desert, this too gathered by the Phoenicians: it was there in such profusion that swathes of it were trampled by the army, and the plants crushed

6 underfoot spread a delightful fragrance over a wide area. Aristobulus speaks of other trees in the desert, one with a laurel-like leaf which grows in places flooded by the sea at high water. These trees are left on dry ground at ebb tide, but when the water comes back in they seem to be growing in the sea: some of them which grow in pools unaffected by the tides have their roots permanently submerged in

7 sea-water, and yet this does no harm to the tree. Some of the trees here, he says, are forty-five feet high: these tall trees were in flower at that season, with a blossom rather like the white violet, but much more fragrant. He speaks too of a long-stemmed thistle growing there, with spikes so strong that when they caught in a man's clothing as he rode past they would drag the rider from his horse before break-

8 ing from their stalk. It is said that hares running past would get these thorns entangled in their fur, and this was a way of catching hares like lime for birds or hooks for fish. The stalk was easily cut with a knife, and when cut this thistle exudes from its stalk an even greater quantity of more astringent juice* than figs in spring.

23   *From there Alexander marched on through Gedrosia. It was hard going, and supplies were short: in particular there was often no water for the army. They were forced to cover great distances at night and rather far inland, despite Alexander's anxiety to keep to the coastline, where he wanted to see what harbours existed and do all that he could on his land march to service the fleet, be it digging wells or arranging

2 here and there for a market or an anchorage. But the whole coastal strip of Gedrosia was nothing but desert, and he sent Thoas the son of Mandrodorus down to the sea with a few cavalrymen to find out if there were any places to anchor there, and any fresh water not too

far from the sea, or any other supplies. Thoas came back with the 3
report that he had found some fishermen on the beach living in
stifling huts put together out of shells and roofed with the backbones
of fish: these fishermen had to make do with the little water they
could find by laboriously digging in the shingle, and even this was not
always fresh.

When Alexander reached a part of Gedrosia where supplies were 4
more plentiful,* he loaded the food he had requisitioned on the
pack-animals, sealed it with his own seal, and ordered its transport to
the sea. But on the stage of the march which would bring a halt just
short of the sea the soldiers, including the men supposed to guard it,
helped themselves to the food without regard for the royal seal, and
distributed it to those of their colleagues in the greatest distress from
hunger. This was the measure of the overwhelming hardship they 5
faced: they deliberately chose to give greater weight to the manifest
and imminent likelihood of their death by starvation than to any subsequent retribution by their king, which was not such a certainty and
still in the future. In fact Alexander understood the dire need which
had driven them to act as they did, and pardoned them. He now made
forays scouring the area for what food he could collect to provision
the men in the fleet sailing along the coast, and put Cretheus, an
officer from Callatis, in charge of its delivery. He also ordered the 6
local inhabitants to grind and bring down from the upper country as
much flour as they could, together with dates and sheep for sale in a
market for the troops, and sent Telephus, one of the Companions, to
another place further on with a small supply of flour.

He himself marched on towards the Gedrosian royal capital, in the 24
area called Pura:* from his start in Oreitis to his arrival at Pura the
journey took sixty days in all. Most historians of Alexander say that
the hardships endured by the army on this march were beyond comparison with even the totality of all else they had suffered for him in
Asia. It was not that Alexander chose this route in ignorance of its 2
difficulty (only Nearchus maintains this), but because he had heard
that no one had yet succeeded in getting an army through here safely.
Semiramis had come this way on her forced retreat from India, but
the locals said that even she had only made it through with twenty
survivors of her army, and Cyrus the son of Cambyses likewise with
only seven. Cyrus had come to these parts on his way to invade India, 3
but he lost most of his army to the impossible conditions of this desert

route before he could get there. The consensus is that these stories inspired in Alexander a desire to outdo Cyrus and Semiramis,* and Nearchus says that he took this route both for that reason and also to keep close enough to the fleet to provide it with essential supplies.

4   However that may be, Nearchus relates that the scorching heat and the lack of water proved fatal to a large proportion of the army,* and took a particularly high toll of the baggage-animals. One factor was the depth of the sand and the temperature to which it was baked, but in most cases the animals finally died of thirst. They had to negotiate high dunes of deep loose sand, into which they sank as if they were
5   treading in mud or—a better analogy—a fresh drift of snow. While the horses and mules suffered from these climbs and descents, made worse by the uneven and shifting ground under their feet, the particular pressure on the men was the length of the marches: water was not available at intervals corresponding to a day's march, and it was this need more than anything else which came to dictate the distances
6   they had to travel. They marched at night, and when they covered enough ground throughout the night to bring them to a source of water at dawn, there was a limit to their suffering: but if the march had to be prolonged and they were caught still on the road as the day wore on, they would suffer terribly from the double oppression of burning heat and constant thirst.

25   Losses among the baggage-animals were extensive, and there was deliberate action by the army. Whenever they ran out of food the troops would gang together to kill most of their horses and mules and eat their flesh, saying that the animals had died of thirst or dropped from exhaustion. In the general distress no one was going to inquire
2   too closely, and they were all guilty of the same offence. Alexander was aware of what was going on, but saw that the way to treat the situation was by feigned ignorance rather than implied acceptance of an acknowledged practice. And it was not easy now to carry with them the troops who were sick or fell behind from exhaustion. There was a shortage of draught-animals, and the men themselves had been sabotaging the wagons, because they found it difficult to keep them moving through the deep sand, and in the earlier stages of the march this problem had precluded the shortest routes and compelled them
3   to go the way which was easiest for the wagon-teams. And so all along the route men were left behind—the sick, those suffering from exhaustion, heatstroke, or crippling thirst—and there was no

one to carry them or stay to look after them. The march was pressed on at all possible speed, and the concern for the general good necessarily involved the neglect of individual needs. With most of the marching at night, many simply fell asleep on the road. When they woke, those who still had the strength followed the tracks of the army in an attempt to catch up, but only a few survived: most were lost in the sand, like sailors lost overboard at sea.

The army suffered a further disaster of a different kind, as cruel as 4 any in its consequences for the men, the horses, and the baggage-animals. As in India, the monsoons bring heavy rain to Gedrosia, but it falls on the mountains rather than the plains, when the clouds driven by the winds hit the mountain peaks and release their moisture. The army had camped near a torrent bed which had a little 5 water in it (that, of course, being the reason for the choice of site), and about the second watch of the night this stream, fed by rains falling far beyond visible range, suddenly filled with such a spate of water that it drowned most of the womenfolk and children among the camp-followers, swept away the king's quarters with all the contents, and carried off all the remaining baggage-animals: the troops themselves only just survived, struggling to safety with nothing salvaged except their weapons, and not even all of those. Even the drinking of 6 water had its dangers. When the men happened to come on an abundant supply of water after hours of heat and thirst, their insatiable drinking often had lethal results. For that reason Alexander did not usually make camp close by the sources of water, but kept a distance of a good two miles, to prevent a fatal stampede into the water by both men and animals, and to stop the more impetuous from wading straight into the spring or stream and polluting the water for the rest of the army.

Now at this point I am determined not to leave unrecorded one of 26 Alexander's finest gestures: the occasion for it may have been here in Gedrosia, or somewhat earlier in Parapamisadae country, according to some other accounts. What happened was this. The army was marching through sand and had to keep on going until they reached water, even though it was now daytime and burning hot: the water was still some way ahead. Alexander himself was afflicted by thirst no less than anyone else, but for all the effort it cost him he persisted in leading his men on foot: the effect, as tends to happen in such examples of leadership, was that the rest of the troops were able to bear their own

hardship more cheerfully when they could see that the pain was
2 shared. A party of light troops had detached from the main army to go
in search of water, and they now found some—a pitiful dribble collected in a shallow torrent bed. They could only manage to gather a
small quantity, but they hurried back to Alexander with what they
thought a great prize, decanting the water into a helmet as they
3 approached and offering it to the king. He accepted the gift and
thanked them for their trouble: then, with the helmet in his hands and
everybody watching him, he poured its contents on the ground. The
effect of this gesture on the morale of the entire army was as if every
man had been refreshed by a draught of the water which Alexander
had poured away. For a combination of endurance and leadership
I find this action of Alexander's as admirable as anything he did.

4   The army now faced another problem in that part of the country.
The guides finally admitted that they had lost the way. The markers,
they said, had been obliterated by wind-blown sand, and there was
nothing else in the expanse of featureless dunes to indicate the
route—no trees which would elsewhere line a road, no solid outcrop
standing out in the sand: and they had not learnt how to navigate by
the stars at night or the sun by day, as sailors do using the Bears (the
Phoenicians go by the Little Bear, other seamen by the Great Bear).
5 In this quandary Alexander deduced that they needed a turn to the
left, and rode ahead in that direction with a small group of cavalry.
When their horses too began to tire from the heat, he left most of them
behind, rode on with only five others, and found the sea. By digging in
the shingle on the beach he came to pure, fresh water. So the whole
army followed, and for seven days they marched along the coast,* getting their water from the shore. Thereafter, when the guides could
now recognize the route, he turned course up into the interior.

27   When he reached the Gedrosian capital he rested his army there.
Deciding that the satrap Apollophanes had failed to carry out any of
his instructions, he removed him from his post* and appointed Thoas
to the satrapy of the region: then when Thoas died of sickness Sibyrtius
succeeded him in the satrapy. Alexander had recently appointed
Sibyrtius satrap of Carmania, but he now gave him the province of
both Arachosia and Gedrosia, and Carmania was taken over by
2 Tlepolemus the son of Pythophanes. Alexander was already on his
way towards Carmania when the news came that Philip, the satrap of
India,* had been murdered in a treacherous plot laid against him by

the mercenaries, and that Philip's Macedonian bodyguards had killed the assassins, some in the very act and others after subsequent capture. On receipt of this intelligence, Alexander sent letters to Eudamus and Taxiles in India telling them to take charge of what had been Philip's province until he sent out a new satrap to govern it.

When Alexander had now reached Carmania he was joined by 3 Craterus with his section of the army and the elephants: Craterus also brought Ordanes with him under arrest after he had revolted and attempted an insurrection. Here too there arrived Stasanor the satrap of Areia and Zarangiana, together with Pharismanes, the son of the satrap of Parthyaea and Hyrcania, Phrataphernes: and Alexander was joined also by the generals who had been left with Parmenion in command of the army in Media, Cleander, Sitalces, and Heracon, bringing with them the bulk of their troops. Several charges were 4 made against Cleander and Sitalces and their associates, brought both by the natives and by their own troops: they were accused of plundering temples, violating ancient tombs, and perpetrating other acts of gross injustice on the subject people. When this was reported to Alexander, he had both generals executed, as a stern warning to all others still in position as satraps or regional or district governors that any similar offences would bring the same penalty. And in fact the 5 most significant element in the control of the vast numbers of native peoples spread over a vast area who had come by conquest or submission under Alexander's rule was precisely this—that in Alexander's empire oppression of the ruled by the rulers was not tolerated. At the time Heracon was cleared of the charges: but soon afterwards some people from Susa had him convicted of plundering the temple at Susa, and he too paid the penalty.* Stasanor and Phrataphernes had 6 accurately foreseen the problems the army would face when they heard that Alexander was taking the route through Gedrosia, and the troops they sent brought Alexander a mass of baggage-animals and a good number of camels. The arrival of these troops was certainly a welcome help when help was needed, and so was the supply of camels and baggage-animals, which Alexander distributed throughout the army, to officers individually and to the squadrons, centuries, and companies in proportion to the total number.

*Some previous writers have recounted a story which I myself find 28 hard to believe. They say that Alexander had two carriages linked together, and drove through Carmania reclining on this contraption

with his friends to a serenade of pipes, while the army followed behind bedecked with garlands and generally making merry: all along the route supplies of food and other delights were there for the taking, laid on by the people of Carmania. All this is supposed to have been Alexander's
2 attempt to replicate the revels of Dionysus, as there was a story about Dionysus that after his conquest of India he led this sort of procession across most of Asia (hence his epithet 'Lord of the Triumph', and hence the term 'triumph' for the parades held in celebration of military victories). There is no mention of this in the accounts written by Ptolemy the son of Lagus or Aristobulus the son of Aristobulus, or in any other author who could be regarded as a reliable witness in such matters. I am content simply to record the story, with the caveat that I
3 do not believe it. Here though (and I am following Aristobulus now) are some historical facts: in Carmania Alexander made sacrifice in thank-offering for his victory in India and the army's survival of the march through Gedrosia, and organized festival games with competitions in the performing arts and athletics; and he enrolled Peucestas as an additional member of the Bodyguards. He had already decided to appoint Peucestas satrap of Persis, but before he took up that appointment Alexander wanted him to enjoy this accolade of ultimate trust for
4 his heroism in the Mallian campaign. Until then Alexander had had seven Bodyguards—Leonnatus the son of Anteas, Hephaestion the son of Amyntor, Lysimachus the son of Agathocles, Aristonus the son of Peisaeus (all these from Pella), Perdiccas the son of Orontes from Orestis, and Ptolemy the son of Lagus and Peithon the son of Crateuas* from Eordaea: now an eighth was added to their number, Peucestas the son of Alexander, who had shielded his king.
5   Meanwhile Nearchus had completed his voyage along the coast of Oreitis, Gedrosia, and the region of the Fish-Eaters,* and put in to the inhabited part of the Carmanian seaboard. From there he went inland with a few men to bring Alexander a report* of his voyage
6 in the ocean so far. Alexander sent him back to resume his coastal voyage all the way to Susiana and the mouths of the river Tigris. I intend to write a separate account, based on Nearchus' own, of the sea-journey from the Indus to the Persian Gulf, to complete this history of Alexander in Greek: but this is a project for the indefinite future, whenever I feel both the desire and the inspiration.
7   Alexander now ordered Hephaestion to take the bulk of the army, the baggage-train, and the elephants from Carmania into Persis,

telling him to go by the coastal route, as this was a journey in winter and the seaboard of Persis afforded relative warmth, as well as a plentiful supply of provisions.

He himself took the road to Pasargadae in Persis with the lightest 29 infantry units, the Companion cavalry, and a section of the archers, and sent Stasanor back to his own province. On reaching the border 2 of Persis he found that Phrasaortes was no longer satrap (he had in fact died of disease while Alexander was still in India), but Orxines had taken charge of the province without Alexander's sanction: he had simply decided that, in the absence of any other governor, he was the right man to do Alexander the service of keeping the Persians under control. One of those who came to meet Alexander at Pasargadae 3 was Atropates, the satrap of Media, bringing with him a Mede called Baryaxes, who was under arrest for assuming the upright tiara and calling himself King of the Persians and Medes. His associates in this revolutionary movement were brought in too, and Alexander had them all put to death.

Aristobulus tells of Alexander's distress at the desecration of the 4 tomb of Cyrus the son of Cambyses, when he found it broken into and plundered. The great man's tomb was in the royal park at Pasargadae, surrounded by a plantation of various trees and set in an irrigated lawn with a thick carpet of grass. The monument itself had a rectangular base 5 of squared stones, surmounted by a roofed chamber made of stone with an entrance door so small that even a short man would struggle to squeeze himself through. Inside the chamber there was placed a golden sarcophagus in which Cyrus' body had been buried, and next to it a couch with feet of beaten gold spread with purple blankets and a coverlet of Babylonian tapestry. On the couch there were laid out a sleeved jacket 6 and several tunics of Babylonian manufacture, and (Aristobulus adds) Median trousers, blue-dyed robes in deep purple and other hues, necklets, scimitars, and earrings of precious stones set in gold. There was a table set there, and the sarcophagus containing Cyrus' body stood between the table and the couch. Inside the precinct and close by the 7 approach to the tomb a small house had been built for the Magi who had guarded Cyrus' tomb ever since the time of his son Cambyses. This was an office passed down among the Magi from father to son: the king would give them a sheep each day, with a set allowance of wheat-meal and wine, and a horse every month to sacrifice to Cyrus. There was an inscription 8 on the tomb in the Persian language and script, with this meaning:

'Visitor, I am Cyrus son of Cambyses. I created the Persian Empire and was King of Asia. Do not therefore grudge me my monument.'

9   Alexander had made a particular point of visiting Cyrus' tomb each time he came to the Persian capital, and he now found it emptied of all but the sarcophagus and the couch. The thieves had even desecrated the body of Cyrus. They had removed the lid of the sarcophagus and thrown out the body, then attempted to hack or crush the rest of the sarcophagus into portable size and weight: this had failed,

10   and they had gone away leaving it where it was. Aristobulus says that he himself was instructed by Alexander to restore Cyrus' tomb to its original state: he was to put back into the sarcophagus what was still recoverable of the body and replace the lid, and repair the parts that had been damaged; to re-upholster the couch and dress it with exact replicas of every single article of its original ornament; and finally to block up the door with an infill of stone and an outer layer of plas

11   ter, stamped with the royal seal. Alexander arrested the Magi who guarded the tomb and had them tortured to force a disclosure of the culprits, but on the rack they said nothing to implicate either themselves or anyone else, and no other evidence was found of their complicity in the crime: and so Alexander let them go.

30   From Pasargadae Alexander went on to Persepolis, where on a previous occasion he had set fire to the royal palace, as I related earlier, making it clear that I could not condone his action:* and in fact on his return Alexander did not condone it either. Many allegations were now laid by the Persians against Orxines,* who had assumed control

2   of Persis on the death of Phrasaortes. It was proved that he had plundered temples and royal tombs, and illegally put to death numerous Persian citizens. He was hanged on Alexander's orders. As satrap of Persis Alexander appointed Peucestas, now one of his Bodyguards. He was confident of Peucestas' absolute loyalty, not least in view of his heroic action in the Mallian campaign, when at great personal risk he had helped to rescue Alexander, and in any case he thought him a suitable appointment given his adoption of the oriental way of life.

3   This was demonstrated as soon as he took over the satrapy. He was the only Macedonian to change to Median dress and learn the Persian language, and generally to assimilate himself to Persian norms. Alexander was all in favour of this, and the Persians were delighted that he preferred their own ways to the traditions of his native country.

BOOK SEVEN

WHEN he had come to Pasargadae and Persepolis Alexander was seized 1
by a yen to sail down the Euphrates and the Tigris to the Persian Gulf:
as with the Indus, he wanted to explore their outlets and experience
the sea into which they flowed. Some writers give a further account.* 2
They say that Alexander was planning to make a voyage round most
of Arabia, round Ethiopia and Libya and the Nomad country beyond
Mount Atlas, and so to Gadeira [Cadiz] and into our Mediterranean
Sea. With the conquest of Libya and Carthage he could rightly be
called king of all Asia, whereas the kings of the Persians and Medes 3
had ruled barely a fraction of Asia and had no justifiable claim to
the title of 'Great King' which they gave themselves. Some say that
thereafter he intended to sail into the Black Sea and Lake Maeotis*
[Sea of Azov] against the Scythians: others that his next destination
would have been Sicily and the Iapygian promontory of south Italy
[Capo S. Maria di Leuca], as he was beginning to feel some anxiety at
the fast-growing reputation of Rome.

I have no conclusive evidence for the sort of plans Alexander had 4
in mind, and I see no point in speculation. One thing, though, I agree
can be stated with confidence, and that is that no project of his would
be small-scale or unambitious: he would not have rested easy on any
of his conqueror's laurels, even if he had added Europe to Asia and
the British Isles to Europe, but would always be exploring further
into the unknown, and in the absence of any other rival would compete against himself. In this context I like the story told of some of the 5
Indian gurus, when Alexander came by the field where they held
their open-air classes. At the sight of Alexander and his army all they
did was to drum their feet on the ground where they stood. When
Alexander asked through interpreters what they meant by this action,
their answer was this: 'King Alexander, any individual human being 6
can occupy only as much of this earth as the patch under our feet
here. You are a human being like the rest of us,* except for the mon-
strous ambition which has you tramping over so much of the earth far
away from your home patch, making trouble for yourself and bringing trouble to others. And yet for all this you will soon be dead, and
occupying no more of the earth than will suffice for the burial of your
body.'

2   At the time Alexander declared himself pleased with this answer and those who gave it, though his actual practice was always quite incompatible with this professed approval. So too he is said to have admired Diogenes of Sinope* when he happened to come across him at the Isthmus. Diogenes was lying in the sun as Alexander passed with the foot guards and Companion infantry. Alexander stopped and asked him if there was anything he needed. Diogenes replied that he had only one request—that Alexander and his company should

2   move out of his sun. We can see, then, that Alexander was not completely out of sympathy with a higher philosophy, but the fact is that ambition for glory had an extraordinarily powerful hold over him. Another example is when he came to Taxila and saw there the Indian gurus who go naked:* he felt an immediate yen to have one of these people in his entourage, as he admired their powers of endurance. The senior guru, called Dandamis, said that he would not join Alexander, nor would he allow any of the others to do so (they were

3   all his disciples). His response, it is said, was that if Alexander was a son of Zeus, so was he; he did not need anything that Alexander could provide, as he was well content with his existing provision; and he could see that being with Alexander meant ranging far and wide over land and sea to no good purpose, with no limit set to this constant wandering. So he himself felt no desire for anything in Alexander's power to give, and no fear of exclusion from any benefit in his patron-

4   age. As long as he lived, the land of India, with the fruits it bore in season, was sufficient for his needs: and when he died, he would simply be released from the uncomfortable cohabitation of his body. Alexander recognized a free spirit, and did not even attempt to put pressure on him. But one of these gurus was seduced by the invitation to join Alexander. This was Calanus, who in the account given by Megasthenes was regarded by the gurus themselves as the most unstable among them, and reviled for rejecting the beatitude of their sect and going to serve a master other than god.

3   *I have recorded this because no history of Alexander can omit reference to Calanus. Though Calanus had never been ill before, his body began to fail him when he was in Persis. He did not want to adopt the regime of an invalid, and told Alexander that he was happy to make an end at this stage, before he faced a condition which would

2   oblige him to abandon his previous routine. Alexander put the counter-arguments at length, but when he saw that Calanus was not

to be dissuaded, but would take another exit if denied the way he had chosen, he finally gave orders for the building of a pyre in accordance with Calanus' own instructions, and put Ptolemy the son of Lagus, one of the Bodyguards, in charge of it. Some say that he also laid on a cortège of horses and men, some in full armour, others bringing every sort of incense to the pyre: in other accounts the offerings they brought were gold and silver cups, and royal clothing. A horse was *3* ready for Calanus, as he was too ill to walk, but he could not mount the horse either and made his approach carried on a litter, garlanded in the Indian tradition and chanting in the Indian language (the Indians say that these chants were hymns and praises to the gods). The horse on which he was to have ridden was one of the royal *4* Nesaean horses,* and before he went up on the pyre he gave it as a gift to Lysimachus,* who had been among those attending his seminars: and to others of his circle he distributed the cups and embroideries which Alexander had ordered to be placed on the pyre in his honour. Then finally he mounted the pyre and solemnly lay down on *5* it, with the whole army watching. Alexander found it distasteful that a friend's death was being made into a spectacle, but in fact the rest of the onlookers felt only admiration that Calanus kept his body absolutely still in the flames. When the pyre was lit by those assigned to *6* that duty, Nearchus says that in tribute to Calanus the trumpets sounded on Alexander's orders, the entire army gave voice to the shout they would raise when going into battle, and the elephants responded with their own piercing war-cry.

Good authorities have recorded this and similar stories about Calanus the Indian, which are not wholly without relevance to mankind in general, if anyone cares to learn how firm and invincible human resolution can be in the achievement of a chosen purpose.

On reaching Susa, Alexander now sent Atropates back to his satrapy, *4* and had Abulites together with his son Oxathres* arrested and executed for maladministration in Susiana. Now there had indeed been *2* widespread abuse by the governors of the territories Alexander had conquered—looting of temples and tombs, and crimes against the people subject to them—but the fact was that Alexander had been away a long time on his Indian expedition, and there seemed no likelihood that he could face all those tribes and all those elephants and come back safe: they thought he would meet his end somewhere beyond the Indus, Hydaspes, Acesines, and Hyphasis. And then *3* again his disastrous experience in Gedrosia encouraged these western satraps to dismiss any thought of his return. But it is also said that Alexander himself had by then become more inclined to jump to conclusions, convinced by any accusation as if it were tantamount to proof, and ready to inflict severe punishment on those found guilty of even minor misdemeanours, in the belief that the character of a petty offender was equally capable of more serious crimes.

4 *At Susa also Alexander celebrated arranged marriages for himself and his Companions. He himself married Darius' eldest daughter Barsine, and, according to Aristobulus, another wife as well, Parysatis, the youngest daughter of Ochus (he was already married to Rhoxane,*

5 the daughter of Oxyartes of Bactria). To Hephaestion he gave Drypetis, another of Darius' daughters and the sister of his own wife, as he wanted Hephaestion's children to be cousins of his own; to Craterus he gave Amastrine, the daughter of Darius' brother

6 Oxyatres; to Perdiccas the daughter of Atropates, satrap of Media; to Ptolemy the Bodyguard and Eumenes the Royal Secretary he gave two daughters of Artabazus, Artacama to Ptolemy and Artonis to Eumenes; to Nearchus the daughter of Barsine and Mentor; to Seleucus* the daughter of Spitamenes of Bactria; and similarly he gave as wives to his other Companions some eighty daughters of the most distinguished Persian and Median families. The marriages were

7 celebrated in the Persian style. A line of chairs had been set out for the bridegrooms, and after the toasts the brides came in and each took her seat beside her own groom: the men then took them by the hand and kissed them, following the lead set by their king, whose own marriage was part of the mass ceremony (this gesture was regarded as a prime example of Alexander's popular touch and sense of comrade-

8 ship). After this formal reception each man took his bride to his quarters, and Alexander provided every bride with a dowry. He also commissioned a register of all the other Macedonians who had married Asian wives: the total came to over ten thousand, and Alexander gave wedding gifts to them all.

5 He thought this also an appropriate occasion to pay off the debts incurred by members of the army, and invited them all to register the amount of their debt, with the promise that it would be paid. At first only a few registered their names, as there was a general fear that this was no more than a survey designed by Alexander to find out which of the soldiers were living beyond their salary or had extravagant

tastes. When Alexander was informed that most were not registering 2
themselves, but hoping to conceal any promissory notes they had
signed, he castigated the men for their lack of trust: a king's duty, he
told them, was to speak nothing but the truth to his subjects, and
likewise none of his subjects should suppose that what they heard
from the king was anything other than the truth. He had tables set up 3
in the camp piled with gold coins, and instructed the officials supervising the grants to pay the amount of their debt to anyone producing
a signed note, without any registration of names. This persuaded the
men that Alexander was speaking the truth, and they welcomed
the anonymity even more than the release from their debts. This largesse to the army is said to have been of the order of twenty thousand
talents.

He also made a variety of other gifts to individuals in recognition 4
of rank or conspicuous service in the face of the enemy. Golden
crowns were awarded to those who had displayed outstanding
bravery: first to Peucestas, who had protected Alexander with his
shield; then to Leonnatus* for the same service and for hazardous 5
operations in India and his success in Oreitis (with the force left
behind with him he had engaged the rebellious Oreitans and the
neighbouring tribes and defeated them in battle, and his general sta-
bilization of the country was regarded as a fine achievement); after 6
them the next honorand was Nearchus (he too had now arrived in
Susa), given the crown for his coasting voyage in the Great Sea from
India, and then Onesicritus, helmsman of the king's own ship. Crowns
were also conferred on Hephaestion and the other Bodyguards.

Here too he was joined by the satraps from his new-founded cities 6
and the rest of the territories he had conquered, bringing with them
about thirty thousand cadets, all of the same age and now old enough
for military service, who were kitted out in Macedonian battle-gear
and had been drilled in Macedonian techniques of warfare: Alexander
called them the Next Generation* (*Epigonoi*). It is said that their 2
arrival caused bad feeling among the Macedonians, as it seemed that
Alexander was looking for every means of reducing his dependence
on Macedonians. And there were other grievances. A sore point was
the sight of Alexander in Median dress, and most of the Macedonians
found it distasteful that the marriages had followed the Persian rite,
including even some of the bridegrooms involved, despite the great
honour of sharing it on a level with their king. They resented also the 3

fact that, with Alexander's evident approval, Peucestas the satrap of Persis was going native in his adoption of Persian dress and the Persian language. And they resented the dilution of the Companion cavalry regiments by the incorporation of cavalrymen from Bactria, Sogdiana, Arachosia, Zarangiana, Areia, and Parthyaea, and of the so-called Euacae cavalry from Persia, selected on the basis of rank,

4 good looks, or some other notable quality. As well as this there was also the creation of a fifth cavalry regiment, not entirely made up of barbarians, but the overall build-up of cavalry strength had certainly involved the enrolment of barbarians for that purpose. And then there were foreigners drafted into the elite corps—Cophes the son of Artabazus, Hydarnes and Artiboles the sons of Mazaeus, Sisines and Phradasmenes the sons of Phrataphernes, the satrap of Parthyaea and

5 Hyrcania, Itanes, the son of Oxyartes and brother of Alexander's wife Rhoxane, Aegobares and his brother Mithrobaeus: another foreigner was put in command, Hystaspes from Bactria, and they were all issued Macedonian lances in place of the thonged javelin used by the barbarians. All this was resented by the Macedonians, who thought that Alexander was now going completely native in outlook and showing no regard for the Macedonian way of life or the very Macedonians themselves.

7   Alexander ordered Hephaestion to take most of the infantry down to the Persian Gulf, while he himself went on board the fleet which had now sailed up into Susian territory. With him he embarked the foot guards, the royal guard of infantry, and a few of the Companion

2 cavalry, and set sail down the river Eulaeus to the sea. He left most of his ships, including those in need of repair, just short of the estuary, and took the faster vessels out into the sea and along the coast to the mouths of the Tigris. The rest of the fleet went back up the Eulaeus as far as the canal dug from the Tigris to the Eulaeus, and entered the Tigris by that route.

3   The two rivers Euphrates and Tigris enclose between them the land of Assyria—hence its local name of Mesopotamia ('the land between the rivers'). Of the two the Tigris is sunk much lower along its course, and so takes water from the many irrigation channels cut from the Euphrates, and a good number of tributary rivers as well: this added volume makes it a large river, not fordable at any point before it issues into the Persian Gulf, as none of its water is used up

4 on the land. The reason is that the surrounding land is higher than

the river, so the artificial channels and branch rivers flow into it rather than from it, and there is no possibility of its use for irrigation. The 5 Euphrates, on the other hand, runs in a higher bed and always flush with the land, so many side-channels have been cut from it: some are permanent canals maintained to bring their water to the inhabitants on either side of the river, and others are dug on demand to irrigate the land in times of drought (there is not much rain in this area). As a result the Euphrates finally dwindles to a swampy trickle and peters out.

So Alexander coasted along the stretch of the Persian Gulf which 6 lies between the Eulaeus and the Tigris, then sailed up the Tigris to the site where Hephaestion and his whole force had encamped. From there he sailed on to Opis, a city on the banks of the Tigris. In the 7 course of this voyage upstream he removed the weirs and returned the river to a uniform level. Not being a maritime nation, the Persians had constructed these weirs as a means of preventing any enemy with naval superiority from invading their country by bringing a fleet up-river from the sea, and the succession of artificial weirs did indeed make any such upward voyage difficult. Alexander dismissed these contrivances as symptomatic of military weakness, and said that he himself would have no use for this sort of defence: he went on to prove its futility by the ease with which he demolished all that Persian effort.

*On arrival at Opis Alexander called an assembly of the Macedonians 8 and announced that he was discharging from the army and sending home those no longer fit for active service by reason of age or disable-ment: to those who remained with him he promised a bonus which would make them the envy of their countrymen at home, and inspire more Macedonians to volunteer for this same life of tough adventure. Doubtless Alexander thought that this announcement would meet a 2 popular reception. But the Macedonians had by now formed the impression that they counted for nothing and were regarded by Alexander as quite superfluous to his military aims, so not surpris-ingly they took this speech of his as yet another ground for the resent-ment which had been building up throughout the whole of the campaign. There had already been many contributory sources of discontent—Alexander's adoption of Persian dress, the kitting out of the barbarian 'Next Generation' as young Macedonians, the intro-duction of foreign cavalry into the ranks of the Companions. So now 3 they were not prepared to take this latest in silence. They told Alexander that he might as well discharge the whole lot of them, and take his father with him on his next campaign—a sneering reference to Ammon. This infuriated Alexander. By that time he had become more quick to anger, and the oriental obsequiousness which now surrounded him had lost him his old easy relationship with the Macedonians. He jumped down from the platform with the officers who had shared it with him and ordered the arrest of the most conspicuous troublemakers, personally pointing out the men his guards should arrest. There were thirteen of these, and he ordered their removal for execution. The rest were stunned into silence, and Alexander mounted the platform again and spoke to them as follows:

9   *'What I shall say to you now, Macedonians, is not an attempt to counteract your desire for home—as far as I am concerned you can go wherever you wish. But if you do go I want you to understand on what terms you are leaving—what I have done for you, and how you
2   have treated me in response. I shall begin necessarily with my father Philip. When Philip took you in hand you were a collection of impoverished nomads, most of you dressed in skins and herding a few sheep and goats* on the mountains: you were fighting a losing battle to keep them out of the hands of the Illyrians and Triballians and the Thracians on your borders. Philip gave you cloaks to wear instead of skins, he brought you down from the mountains into the plains, he turned you into a fighting force ready to match your barbarian neighbours, with a security now based on trust in your own native courage rather than the strength of defensive positions: he made you citydwellers and gave you the benefits of law and a civilized way of life.
3 He brought under your control those same barbarians who used to raid you and take your people and property, so you were now their masters, not their slaves and subjects. He enlarged Macedonia by annexing most of Thrace, and took possession of the key positions on the seaboard, so opening the country to trade and removing any
4 threat to the exploitation of your mines.* For years you had been frightened to death by the Thessalians, but he gave you mastery over them; your access to Greece had been through a narrow and difficult corridor, but his crushing humiliation of the Phocians made it wide and easy; the Athenians and Thebans had always been watching for their chance to spring an attack on Macedonia, but Philip crushed them so low (and by now I myself was working with him in this

campaign) that instead of our paying tribute-money to the Athenians and taking prescription from the Thebans there was now a reversal of roles, and they were looking to us to give them protection.* Philip 5 moved on into the Peloponnese and effected a settlement there too. His appointment now as supreme commander of all Greece for the campaign against Persia was not just a personal triumph but an honour he had conferred on the whole Macedonian commonwealth.

'These services rendered you by my father are substantial enough 6 when considered in isolation, but they pale into insignificance in comparison with my own. From my father I inherited a few gold and silver cups, less than sixty talents in the treasury, and Philip's accumulated debts of some five hundred talents.* I borrowed another eight hundred talents and set forth from a country which could not even provide a decent subsistence for its own people. An immediate first act was to open up for you the channel of the Hellespont, despite Persia's naval supremacy at the time. My cavalry then defeated the 7 satraps of Darius* and I added to your empire the whole of Ionia, the whole of Aeolis, both Phrygias, and Lydia, and captured Miletus by siege. Other regions placed themselves voluntarily in my hands, and in every case I let you profit from them. The riches of Egypt and Cyrene, 8 which I won without a battle fought, come to you; Hollow Syria, Palestine, Mesopotamia are your possessions; Babylon, Bactra, Susa are yours; yours too the wealth of Lydia, the Persian treasure-houses, the riches of India, the freedom of the Outer Sea. Satraps, generals, battalion commanders—you are all of these. As for myself, what have 9 I left to show for these labours apart from this purple cloth and this diadem* on my head? I have made no personal gains: no one can point to any private hoard of mine separate from what you can see, which is all yours now or held in trust for you. And in any case I could have no motive for keeping back funds for my own benefit. I eat the same food as you, and sleep no more than you: though in fact I fancy my diet does not compare with the luxurious habits of some of you, and I know the nights I spend awake on your behalf, to ensure that you can have your sleep.

'All very well, you may say, but it was our labour and our suffering 10 which won you all this, and you just gave the orders without sharing these hardships. Well, is any one of you convinced that he has worked harder or suffered more for me than I have for him? Come on, then— if you have wounds, strip and show them, and I shall show mine in turn.

2 In my case I have been wounded in every part of my body except my back; every sort of weapon wielded or shot has left its mark on me; I have been cut by swords hand-to-hand, shot by arrows, struck by catapult bolts, taken innumerable blows from stones and clubs—all this in your interests, to win you fame and riches as I lead you victori-
3 ous over every land and sea, every river, mountain, and plain. I have shared your marriage-rites, and many of you will have children related to my own. What is more, I have paid off everyone's debts, without officious enquiry into how you came to incur them, when you earn so much in regular pay and acquire so much in kind from plunder after a siege. Most of you have gold crowns in recognition of your own bravery and my personal regard for you, and these will be
4 everlasting memorials. And if a man has given his life, he dies in glory and is buried with honour: a commemorative statue in bronze is commonly set up in his home town, and his parents are given the privilege of exemption from every state service and tax,* as under my command not one of you has died with the enemy at his back.

5   'And now I had intended to send home those of you no longer fit for active service and to make them the envy of their countrymen. But since you all want to go, go then—all of you! Go back to your homes and tell them there about your king Alexander. Tell them of
6 his victories over Persians, Medes, Bactrians, and Sacae; his subjection of Uxians, Arachosians, and Drangians; his conquest of Parthyaea, Chorasmia, and Hyrcania as far as the Caspian Sea; how he went over the Caucasus beyond the Caspian Gates, crossed the river Oxus and the Tanaïs, even the Indus which no one but Dionysus had ever crossed before, as well as the Hydaspes and Acesines and
7 Hydraotes, and would have crossed the Hyphasis too if you had not lost your nerve; how he burst out into the Great Sea by both mouths of the Indus, and came through the Gedrosian desert, where no one had taken an army before, acquiring Carmania and the land of the Oreitans along the way. Tell them this. And then tell them that, when his fleet had successfully completed its voyage along the whole coast from India to Persis and you were safe back in Susa, you deserted him and took yourselves off, leaving him to the mercy of the very barbarians he had defeated. A fine tale indeed, sure to raise you in men's esteem and meet with the gods' approval. Now go!'

11   That said, he jumped straight down from the platform and disappeared into the royal quarters, where he neglected all physical care of

himself and none of his Companions had sight of him: no sight on the following day either. On the third day he called inside the Persian elite and allocated the commands of the various army units between them: some he designated his 'kinsmen', and to these he gave the exclusive right to greet him with a kiss. The Macedonians were at 2 first stunned by Alexander's speech. They stood there in silence by the platform, rooted to the spot, and no one other than his supporting Companions and the bodyguards followed the king as he left. The rest had no idea what to do or say if they stayed, but were reluctant to leave. But then news reached them about the Persians and Medes, 3 about the commands being given to Persians, and barbarian troops being formed into army units with Macedonian titles—a Persian 'royal guard', Persian 'Companion infantry' and 'Close Companions' also, a Persian battalion of 'Silver Shields', and another 'King's squadron' added to the Companion cavalry. They could now contain themselves no longer. They ran in a mass to the royal quarters, threw down 4 their arms there in front of the doors to symbolize their supplication of the king, and stood there at the doors shouting and pleading to be let in. They offered to hand over the instigators of the recent trouble and the men who had started the barracking, and swore they would not leave the doors day or night until Alexander took some pity on them.

When this was reported to Alexander, he hurried out to meet them. 5 The sight of their abasement and the sound of so many voices raised in lamentation brought tears to his own eyes. He stepped forward as if to speak, but they kept up their litany. Then one of them, a man 6 called Callines, qualified both by age and by his rank as a squadron commander in the Companion cavalry, spoke out like this: 'Your majesty, what gives the Macedonians their grievance is that you have now made some of the Persians your kinsmen, so Persians are called "Alexander's kinsmen" and are permitted to kiss you, but no Macedonian has yet enjoyed this privilege.' To this Alexander made 7 an immediate response, saying, 'But I regard all of you as my kinsmen, and from now on that is what I shall call you.' With that said, Callines came up to Alexander and kissed him, followed by any others who wished to do the same. And so the whole gathering picked up their arms again and returned to the camp cheering and singing the paean of victory.

Thereafter Alexander made sacrifice to his customary gods, and 8 gave a public banquet, taking the chair himself with seats for all

arranged in order round him—first the Macedonians, then the
Persians in the next tiers, and after them the men of other national-
ities who were distinguished by rank or other claim to precedence.
The ceremony of libation was jointly conducted by the Greek seers
and the Persian Magi. Alexander and his circle drew their wine from
9 the same bowl and made the same libations, as Alexander prayed that
chief among their blessings should be a unity of purpose between
Macedonians and Persians and a partnership in empire.* The prevalent account is that there were nine thousand attending the banquet,
and that they all made the same prayer with their libation, following
it with a singing of the paean.

12   And now, with their own agreement this time, Alexander organized
the discharge of all the Macedonians who were no longer fit for
service by reason of age or any other circumstance: they numbered
about ten thousand. Alexander extended their regular pay beyond the
2 time already served to include the period of their journey home, and
gave each man a gratuity of one talent. He required them to leave
behind in his care any children they had by Asian wives, and not take
back to Macedonia a source of friction with the children and their
mothers they had left at home by bringing with them half-caste children of foreign wives. He promised that he would personally see to it
that these children were raised in the Macedonian way, especially in
their military training: and when they had reached adulthood he
would himself bring them back to Macedonia and return them to
3 their fathers. These were vague and unguaranteed assurances for
them to leave with, but Alexander did want to show them how much
he appreciated them and would miss them, and the clearest proof he
could give was to send Craterus with them to lead and protect them
on their journey—this was the man he trusted above all others, and
valued as highly as his own life. And so, with tears all round, including his, he bade them all farewell and sent them on their way.

4   Craterus' orders were to take the men home and once there to
assume charge of Macedonia,* Thrace, and Thessaly and the defence
of Greek freedom: and Antipater was sent orders to bring out fresh
drafts of adult Macedonians to replace the men being discharged
home. Alexander also sent Polyperchon* with Craterus as his second-
in-command, so that if anything happened to Craterus on the journey,
as he was known to be in poor health when given the commission,
there would still be a general to lead the men on their way back.

An unsubstantiated rumour was now gaining currency among 5 those who take royal secrecy as a challenge to exposure, and let guess-work and their own malice lead them to espouse the worst interpret-ation rather than the truth. This rumour had it that Alexander was falling under the influence of his mother's denigration of Antipater, and so wanted to remove him from Macedonia. It could well be that 6 Antipater's recall was not intended as a demotion, but as a means of preventing the quarrel between those two turning nasty on both sides, beyond any reconciliation that even Alexander could effect. The fact is that they were both endlessly writing letters to Alexander. Antipater would complain of Olympias' obduracy, her quick temper, and an interfering habit which did not sit at all well with her role as Alexander's mother: indeed Alexander is said to have remarked of his mother's reported doings that she was charging him a high rent for ten months' accommodation inside her. Olympias' complaint was 7 that Antipater's position and all the flummery that went with it had gone to his head: he was forgetting, she wrote, who had put him in that position in the first place, and assuming his own pre-eminence over all other Macedonians and the Greeks at large. It did seem that Alexander was increasingly swayed by these reports which tended to Antipater's discredit, as what they alleged was always a particular threat to a monarchy. And yet there is no record of any overt act or statement on Alexander's part which could have invited the conclu-sion that his affectionate regard for Antipater had in any way changed [. . .]*

[. . .] It is said that Hephaestion bowed to this argument and made 13 his peace with Eumenes, grudgingly offered but gladly accepted.

On his route from Opis to Ecbatana Alexander is said to have vis-ited the plain reserved for the pasture of the royal mares. This is called the Nesaean plain, and Herodotus tells us that 'Nesaean' is also the term for the horses. Apparently there were once about a hundred and fifty thousand of these mares, but by the time of Alexander's visit they numbered no more than fifty thousand, as rustlers had stolen most of them.

*While he was here they say that Atropates the satrap of Media 2 sent him a hundred women who he claimed were of the Amazon race. They were dressed and equipped like cavalrymen, except that they carried axes rather than spears and small targes instead of cavalry shields. Some say that their right breast was smaller, and they would

3 bare it in battle. The story goes that Alexander sent them away from the camp to avoid any problems of sexual molestation by the Macedonians or the barbarian troops, but told them to take his message to their queen that he intended to visit her and have a child by her. There is no mention of this story in the accounts written by Aristobulus or Ptolemy, or in any other writer qualified to judge the truth of such matters. In fact I doubt that the race of Amazons was still extant then, or even before Alexander's time, as otherwise Xenophon would have referred to them along with the Phasians and Colchians and the other barbarian races he mentions as encountered by the Greeks on their way back to Trapezus or the onward journey thereafter: they would certainly have met the Amazons too hereabouts, if any still remained. And yet I cannot believe that this race of women never existed at all, when so many authorities have celebrated them. There is, for example, the tradition that Heracles was sent against them and brought back to Greece a girdle taken from their queen Hippolyte, and that the Athenians under Theseus were the first to defeat these women in battle and repel their invasion of Europe. There is a picture painted by Micon of the Athenians' battle against the Amazons no less prominent than his picture of their battle with the Persians. And then Herodotus makes frequent reference to these women, and all the Athenians who delivered the funeral speech in honour of the war-dead included specific commemoration of this Athenian action against the Amazons. But if Atropates did present some female horse-riders to Alexander, I think he was exhibiting some other barbarian women who had been taught to ride and kitted out in what was supposed to be Amazon style.

14   At Ecbatana Alexander offered sacrifice, as he regularly did in celebration of a success, and put on festival games with competitions in athletics and the performing arts.* He also held drinking-bouts with his Companions. In the course of this Hephaestion fell ill. On the seventh day of his illness, it is said, the stadium was crowded for the day of the boys' sports when word came to Alexander that Hephaestion was in a serious condition: he hurried away to be at his side, but by the time Alexander reached him Hephaestion was dead.

2   At this point historians diverge in the accounts they give of Alexander's grieving. All relate that his grief was intense, but their accounts of how he expressed it in action vary with their own bias as supporters or detractors of Hephaestion, or indeed of Alexander

himself. The historians who report his excesses seem to me to fall *3*
into two camps: those who think that anything Alexander did or said
in the extremity of his grief for the man who was his dearest friend
can only redound to his credit, and those who take the opposite view,
that there was something shameful in behaviour below the dignity of
Alexander or any other king. Some say that Alexander spent most of
that day prostrate over the body of his friend and would not leave it
until he was dragged away by his Companions: others have him pros- *4*
trate on the body for that whole day and night. Some too report that
he had the doctor Glaucias hanged, either (in one version) for giving
the wrong medicine,* or (in the other) for not intervening when he
could see for himself that Hephaestion was drinking to excess.
Especially in the light of Alexander's emulation of Achilles, who had
been his role-model since boyhood, I think it quite likely that he did
indeed cut off his hair over the corpse. But I simply cannot believe *5*
the story told by some, that for a while Alexander himself took over
the reins of the hearse carrying Hephaestion's body: and, in yet
another account, his alleged order for the annihilation of the temple
of Asclepius at Ecbatana would have been a barbaric act quite out of
character for Alexander, and more in keeping with Xerxes' parox-
ysms of rage against the gods and his fantasy that he could 'punish'
the Hellespont, as the story goes, by throwing fetters into it. There is *6*
one recorded incident, though, which I do consider within the bounds
of possibility. This is the report that on his way to Babylon Alexander
was met by many embassies from Greece, including one from
Epidaurus. Alexander granted the Epidaurians' requests, and gave
them a votive offering to take back and dedicate to Asclepius, adding
as he did so, 'And yet Asclepius has not been kind to me: he failed to
save the friend I held as dear as my own life.' Most authorities agree *7*
that Alexander ordered the institution of a permanent hero-cult for
Hephaestion. Some say that he sent to the oracle of Ammon to ask if
the god would permit fully divine honours for Hephaestion, but
Ammon refused.

What is consistently reported in all the histories is that for two full *8*
days after Hephaestion's death Alexander took no food or attended to
any other physical need, but lay there on his bed consumed by grief,
sometimes expressed in open lamentation, sometimes kept silent
within him; that he ordered the construction of a funeral pyre in
Babylon* at a cost of ten thousand talents (some say even more); and *9*

that he had a period of national mourning proclaimed throughout the whole continent of Asia. There is agreement too that, to keep Alexander's favour, many of his Companions dedicated themselves and their arms to the dead Hephaestion: this was a ploy initiated by Eumenes (whose quarrel with Hephaestion we spoke of a little earlier), designed to prevent Alexander thinking that he took any satis-
10 faction in Hephaestion's death. In fact Alexander never appointed anyone else to take Hephaestion's place as overall commander of the Companion cavalry: he wanted Hephaestion's name to live on in the force, so 'Hephaestion's regiment' it continued to be called, and the standard carried at its head was that made to Hephaestion's own design. Alexander also planned funeral games with competitions in athletics and the performing arts more spectacular than any he had held before in the number of participating athletes and artists and the cost lavished in production. He presented a total of three thousand competitors: these same men, it is said, took part not long afterwards in the games at Alexander's own funeral.

15   Alexander was a long time in mourning, but eventually he began to pull himself out of it, and the efforts of his Companions to bring him round had more success. He now launched an expedition against the
2 Cossaeans, a warlike people next door to the Uxians. These Cossaeans are highlanders, living in mountain village strongholds, and their strategy on the approach of a hostile force was to retreat en masse, or each as best he could, to the summits of their mountains, so frustrating any army attempting to attack them. When the enemy had gone, they would return to the brigandage which was their livelihood.
3 Alexander wiped out the entire tribe,* even though he was campaigning in winter: but he never let bad weather or rough country stand in his way, and the same was true of Ptolemy the son of Lagus, who commanded one section of the army in the Cossaean campaign. It was characteristic of Alexander to find nothing impossible in any military operation once he had set his mind to it.

4   On his way back to Babylon he was met by embassies from the Libyans, congratulating him and presenting him with a crown as king of Asia, and envoys came for the same purpose from Italy, from the Bruttians, Lucanians, and Etruscans. It is said that the Carthaginians also sent envoys* at this time, that others came from Ethiopia and European Scythia, and that Celts and Iberians arrived to ask for Alexander's friendship. This was the first time that Greeks and

Macedonians had heard the names of these tribes or seen how they
were dressed and armed. Some, it is said, even appealed to Alexander *5*
for arbitration of their local disputes, and this was when Alexander
himself and those around him fully realized that he was indeed
master of every land and every sea. Two historians of Alexander,
Aristus and Asclepiades, speak of an embassy from the Romans* too.
They say that when he met their envoys he could see in these men a
discipline, a conscientiousness, and a freedom of spirit which,
together with their answers to his questions about their political
system, led him to predict something of the future power of Rome.
I record this as neither unquestionably true nor wholly incredible. *6*
I would simply observe that no Roman writer has ever made mention
of this embassy being sent to Alexander, nor have those whom I take
as my main authorities on the history of Alexander, Ptolemy the son
of Lagus and Aristobulus. And it would have been strange for the
Roman republic, at that time a model of freedom,* to send an embassy
to a foreign king, especially so far from home, when there was no
compelling fear or the hope of advantage, and of all people the
Romans had a fixed hatred of the whole tribe of kings, and even the
very name.

  After this Alexander sent Heracleides the son of Argaeus to **16**
Hyrcania with a party of shipwrights, with orders to cut timber from
the Hyrcanian mountains and build warships on the Greek model,
some decked and some undecked. This was because he was possessed *2*
by a yen to explore this Hyrcanian Sea as well (it is also called the
Caspian), and to find out what other sea it joins, whether that is the
Black Sea, or whether the Great Sea to the east of India circles round
to form a Hyrcanian Gulf, just as he had discovered that the Persian
Gulf (the so-called Red Sea) was exactly that—a gulf of the Great
Sea. No one had yet discovered where the Caspian Sea comes from, *3*
though there is quite a population of tribes round it and navigable
rivers flow into it: the Oxus [Amu-Darya], for example, the greatest
Asian river outside India, gives into this sea from Bactria; so does the
Jaxartes* [Syr-Darya] after its course through Scythia; and most
accounts have the Araxes [Arak] too flowing into it from Armenia.
These are the major rivers, but many others are either tributaries of *4*
these three or make their own way to an outlet in the Caspian. Some
of these rivers were found by Alexander's men when they campaigned
against the tribes in these parts, but there must be others on the far

side of the Gulf, in the Nomad Scythian country which is completely unexplored.

5 When Alexander had crossed the Tigris with his army on their way to Babylon he was met by the Chaldaean seers,* who took him aside from his Companions and implored him to halt his march to Babylon: they had an oracle, they said, from the god Bel warning that his entry

6 into Babylon at that time would be dangerous for him. The story is that Alexander answered them with a verse from the poet Euripides,* which goes like this: 'The best of prophets is the one whose guess comes good.' 'Well, your majesty,' they replied, 'at least do not aim for the west: you must not lead your army in from that direction. Go

7 round instead, and make your entry on the east side.' But Alexander encountered problems this way too, as the ground proved impassable: the truth was that divine power was leading him on to the point which once reached would seal his imminent death. And it may well be that it was actually better for him to die at the height of his fame and particularly when men would miss him most, before meeting any of the afflictions which are the lot of ordinary humanity. I imagine that is why Solon advised Croesus* to look to the end of a man's life, however long, and not to call any man happy until that end had come.

8 Though even Alexander had already suffered the great affliction of Hephaestion's death, and I believe he would have preferred to go first himself rather than live on in the shadow of that experience, just as I think Achilles too would have chosen to die before Patroclus rather than become the avenger of his death.

17 In fact Alexander had his suspicions of the Chaldaeans' motive in their attempt to prevent his march into Babylon at that time: he thought it not so much genuine prophecy as protection of their own interests. At the centre of the city of Babylon was the temple of Bel, which had been a huge edifice of unparalleled size, made of

2 baked brick cemented with bitumen. Along with the other sacred buildings in Babylon, Xerxes had totally destroyed this temple on his return from Greece. Alexander had proposed to rebuild it either, as some say, on the original foundations—and so he had ordered the Babylonians to clear the site of rubble—or, according to others, as

3 a new building yet larger than the old. In his absence since then the officials charged with the work had taken a relaxed approach to their responsibility, and he now intended to complete the project using his entire army. The Assyrian kings had given the god Bel

a large endowment of land and gold, which used to be applied to 4
the upkeep of the temple and meet the cost of sacrifices to the god,
but since then the Chaldaeans had enjoyed the god's revenue, as
there was nothing on which to spend the proceeds. This made
Alexander suspect that the reason they did not want him to enter
Babylon was to prevent the rapid completion of a new temple* which
would deprive them of the benefit of this income. Even so, Aristobulus 5
says that Alexander was prepared to accept their recommendation
of a change of direction for his entry into the city. So on the first
day he camped beside the Euphrates, and on the next day marched
north with the river on his right, intending to bypass the western
side of the city and then turn to the east. But in fact the nature of 6
the ground made this an impossible route for his army, as anyone
coming up on the west of the city and then turning east meets a
stretch of swamp with standing pools of water. So when Alexander
failed to comply with the god's direction this was both choice and
lack of choice.

In this context Aristobulus has also recorded the following story, 18
which concerns Apollodorus* of Amphipolis, one of Alexander's
Companions. He was the commanding officer of the force which
Alexander had left behind with Mazaeus, the satrap of Babylon, and
when he met Alexander on his return from India and witnessed the
harsh punishments Alexander was inflicting on a whole series of his
appointees to provincial satrapies, he wrote to his brother Peithagoras,
who was a seer practising divination from the innards of sacrificial
victims, and asked him to divine whether he himself was in danger.
Peithagoras wrote back asking who in particular posed the threat 2
which made him seek the help of divination, and Apollodorus replied
that it was the king himself and Hephaestion. So Peithagoras carried
out the sacrifices, using the first victim for a prediction concerning
Hephaestion. There was no sign of a lobe on the victim's liver, and
Peithagoras reported this in a sealed letter sent from Babylon to his
brother in Ecbatana, assuring him that he had nothing to fear from
Hephaestion, as he would soon be out of their way. Aristobulus says 3
that Apollodorus received this letter just one day before Hephaestion's
death. Peithagoras then sacrificed again with a view to Alexander,
and once more the victim's liver had no lobe. He wrote to Apollodorus
with the same prediction about Alexander, but Apollodorus did
not keep it to himself and told Alexander the contents of the letter,

thinking that it would confirm his loyalty to the king if he warned
him to take precautions against any potential source of immediate
4 danger. The story goes that Alexander thanked Apollodorus, and on
his arrival at Babylon asked Peithagoras what particular phenomenon
had caused him to write in those terms to his brother. He replied that
he had found the victim's liver lacking a lobe. Asked then what this
sign meant, he said, 'Something extremely grave'. So far from becoming angry at Peithagoras, Alexander actually held him in greater
5 regard for telling him the unvarnished truth. Aristobulus says that he
heard this at first hand from Peithagoras. He adds that Peithagoras
also made prophecies later for Perdiccas and Antigonus. In both cases
the sacrifices revealed this same ominous sign: Perdiccas was killed in
his campaign against Ptolemy, and Antigonus in the battle fought at
Ipsus* against Seleucus and Lysimachus.

6   And then there is also the story recorded of Calanus,* the Indian
guru, which goes like this. When Calanus was approaching the pyre
on which he would die, he gave a farewell embrace to his other friends,
but would not go up to Alexander and do the same, saying that he
would meet him in Babylon and embrace him there. At the time no
attention was paid to this remark, but later on, when Alexander died
in Babylon, it was recalled by those who had heard it and recognized
for what it was—a visionary prediction of Alexander's own death.

19   After entering Babylon Alexander was visited by several embassies
from the Greeks. Their particular purposes are not recorded, but I
imagine most of them came to offer him crowns and congratulate him
on his victories, especially those won in the Indian campaign, and to
express their pleasure at his safe return from India. We are told that
Alexander made them welcome, and paid them all due honours before
2 sending them back. He also entrusted into the envoys' care for transport back to Greece all the statues, religious art, and other dedications which Xerxes had removed from Greece to Babylon, Pasargadae,
Susa, or anywhere else in Asia. It is said that this is how the bronze
statues of Harmodius and Aristogeiton* and the seated figure of
Celcean Artemis were returned to Athens.

3   Aristobulus says that Alexander also found the navy waiting for
him at Babylon. Part of the complement was Nearchus' fleet,* which
had sailed up the Euphrates from the Persian Sea: the rest, consisting of two Phoenician quinqueremes, three quadriremes, twelve
triremes, and some thirty triaconters, had been brought up from

Phoenicia—transported in sections from Phoenicia to the city of Thapsacus on the Euphrates, then reassembled there and sailed down the river to Babylon. He says that Alexander had commissioned the 4 building of a new fleet in addition, for which he was felling the cypresses in Babylonia: these were the only trees in plentiful supply throughout Assyria, a country otherwise devoid of shipbuilding materials. To crew the ships and provide ancillary services large numbers of murex-divers* and others who made their living from the sea arrived from Phoenicia and the rest of the coast: and Alexander was dredging a harbour at Babylon big enough to afford anchorage for a thousand warships, and building dockyards to go with it. Miccalus of Clazomenae was sent to Phoenicia with a budget of five 5 hundred talents to hire or purchase men with experience of the sea.* The reason for this was that Alexander had it in mind to colonize the coast of the Persian Gulf and the outlying islands, thinking that this area had the potential to match the prosperity of Phoenicia. His naval 6 preparations were for use against the main body of the Arabs, ostensibly because they were the only barbarians in this region not to send him embassies or show respect for him in any other appropriate way: but the real motive, it seems to me, was Alexander's constant and insatiable appetite for further acquisition.*

According to the prevalent account Alexander had often heard that 20 the Arabs worshipped only two gods, Uranus and Dionysus—Uranus [Sky] because the god is in plain sight and encompasses all the stars and the sun, which is the prime and most conspicuous benefactor of all human life; and Dionysus for his famed expedition to India. This made Alexander think that he himself, with achievements no less spectacular than those of Dionysus, would qualify as the third god* in the Arab pantheon, if he did indeed conquer the Arabs too and then allow them, as he had the Indians, the maintenance of their own traditional institutions. A further attraction was the wealth of the 2 country. He had heard that there was cassia growing in the marshes, trees producing myrrh and frankincense, bushes yielding their crop of cinnamon,* and meadows full of wild spikenard. And then there was the pure size of Arabia. He received reports that its coastline was as extensive as that of India, that there were many islands lying offshore, and harbours all round the country offering suitable anchorage for his fleet and suitable sites for the establishment of cities with potential for a prosperous future.

3   These reports included intelligence of two islands out at sea opposite the mouth of the Euphrates. The first was not far from the outlets, just over thirteen miles from the shore and the river mouth. This
was the smaller of the two, and thickly wooded with a variety of trees.
It contained a sanctuary of Artemis, and the lives of the inhabitants
4 were centred on this sanctuary. The island supported wild goats and
deer, which were sacred to Artemis and given free range. Hunting
them was forbidden: the only lawful occasion for a hunt was if some-
5 one wished to sacrifice one of the animals to the goddess. According
to Aristobulus, Alexander decreed that this island should be called
Icarus after the Aegean island of that name, the place where (so the
usual story goes) Icarus the son of Daedalus fell to earth when the
wax attaching his wings melted. He had ignored his father's instructions to fly close to the earth, and had foolishly soared high, allowing
the sun to melt the wax and loosen the adhesion: he left his name both
6 to the island of Icarus and to the Icarian Sea. The distance from the
mouth of the Euphrates to the other island was said to be about a day
and night's sail for a ship with a following wind. This island was
called Tylus* [Bahrein]. It was of some size, for the most part low-
lying and free of tree-cover, and well suited to support cultivation
and every kind of seasonal produce.
7   This information reached Alexander from several sources. Some of
it came from Archias, who had been sent out in a triaconter to reconnoitre the coastal route for an expedition against the Arabs: he got as
far as the island of Tylus, but ventured no further. Then Androsthenes
was dispatched in another triaconter, and he sailed round part of the
Arabian peninsula. But the most extensive of the exploratory voyages
was that undertaken by the helmsman Hieron from Soli. He too was
8 given a triaconter by Alexander, with instructions to coast round the
entire Arabian peninsula and all the way up to Heroönpolis on the
Egyptian side of the Arabian Gulf [Red Sea]. He did not manage to
go the complete distance, but when he turned back he had sailed
round most of Arabia, and was able to report to Alexander that the
peninsula was of an amazing size, almost as large as India, with a
9 sharp tip extending far out into the Great Sea. Nearchus' men had
also caught close sight of this promontory before they turned north
into the Persian Gulf on their voyage from India, and they very nearly
crossed over to it. That had been the course chosen by the helmsman
Onesicritus, but Nearchus says that he personally countermanded

this decision,* as he had to complete the passage of the Persian Gulf and bring Alexander a report on the express objects of his voyage: he *10* had not been commissioned to sail out into the Great Sea, but to conduct a reconnaissance of the immediate coastal areas, gathering information about the local inhabitants and their way of life, potential harbours, water supplies, and the distribution of fertile and infertile land. And this, he says, is what ensured Alexander the safe return of this naval expedition: if they had sailed on past the desert parts of Arabia they would have come to grief. It is said that Hieron turned back for the same reason.

While his triremes were being built and the harbour at Babylon *21* excavated, Alexander sailed down the Euphrates from Babylon to the so-called 'river' Pallacotta. This lies about ninety miles from Babylon, and is in fact a canal branching from the Euphrates, not a river with its own independent source. Rising as it does in the Armenian moun- *2* tains, the Euphrates is not very full of water in the winter season, and flows within its banks. But from the first sign of spring, and culminating round about the summer solstice, it runs increasingly strong and overflows its banks to flood the surrounding Assyrian plain. This *3* is when the volume of water is hugely augmented by the melting of the snow-cover on the Armenian mountains, and the flooding occurs because the river is running high on a shallow bed. They prevent wider inundation by opening a sluice to divert the water along the Pallacotta canal into the marshes and lakes which begin from the canal and extend to the border with Arabia: thereafter it runs mostly into shoals, and eventually finds a multitude of tiny channels into the sea. When all the snow has melted, by about the setting of the Pleiades, *4* the Euphrates returns to a low level, but even so most of its water runs through the Pallacotta into the lakes. So if the Pallacotta were not now correspondingly dammed, to turn the flow back to its ori- ginal course through the river banks, the canal would have drained the Euphrates and left none of its water for the irrigation of the lower Assyrian plain. And so the satrap of Babylonia used to dam the sluices *5* which let the Euphrates run into the Pallacotta. These were easy enough to open, but to close them was a huge labour, as the soil in this area is mostly a soft, muddy clay which lets the river water through and makes it hard to stop this percolation. More than ten thousand Assyrians used to be employed in this task for two to three months.

6   Reports of this situation prompted Alexander to make some improvements in Assyria. At the point where the flow of the Euphrates was diverted into the Pallacotta he decided to block the outlet permanently. Then some three and a half miles further on he noticed that the earth was now stony, so that a cutting made from there to join the old Pallacotta canal through hard impermeable ground would prevent leakage and make it easy to redirect the flow whenever it was the

7   appropriate time. This, then, was what brought Alexander to the Pallacotta, and he sailed on down it to the lakes on the Arabian border. Here he found a promising site, and built and fortified a city which he settled with some of the Greek mercenaries, both volunteers and men no longer fit for active service by reason of age or disablement.

22   Thinking that he had proved the Chaldaeans' prophecy wrong, in that contrary to their predictions nothing untoward had happened to him in Babylon and he had left the city before anything could happen, with this confidence Alexander now sailed back up through the marshlands to the east of Babylon: on the voyage part of his fleet lost direction among the narrow channels for lack of a pilot, until Alexander himself sent them a guide to bring them back into the

2   main waterway. There is a story told about this voyage. Most of the tombs of the Assyrian kings had been built in the lakes and the marshlands. As Alexander was sailing through the marshes and, so the story goes, steering his trireme himself, a strong gust of wind caught the felt hat he was wearing with the royal diadem attached to it. The hat fell in the water, but the lighter diadem was carried away on the breeze and snagged on one of the reeds in a bed growing out of the

3   tomb of one of these ancient kings. This of itself was ominous enough of what was to come, and so was the fact that the sailor who swam out to recover the diadem from the reed did not bring it back in his hands, as he could not have kept it dry while swimming, but bound it round

4   his own head for the return swim. Most Alexander historians say that Alexander gave the man a talent in recognition of his prompt action, then had him beheaded in compliance with the interpretation of the seers, who advised that the head which had worn the royal diadem could not be allowed to live on. Aristobulus confirms the gift of a talent, but says that the man's punishment for wearing the diadem was

5   a flogging. In fact he relates that it was one of the Phoenician sailors who brought back his diadem to Alexander: but some say that it was Seleucus,* and that this portended both Alexander's death and

Seleucus' vast kingdom. I certainly take it as beyond doubt that Seleucus was the greatest king of all the successors to Alexander's empire: more than any other he had the mind of a king, and the extent of his rule was second only to that of Alexander himself.

On his return to Babylon Alexander found Peucestas arrived there 23 from Persis with an army* of some twenty thousand Persian troops: he had also brought a good number of Cossaeans and Tapurians, acting on information that these were the best fighting men of all the tribes bordering Persis. There too Alexander was joined by Philoxenus with an army from Caria, Menander with more troops from Lydia, and Menidas with the cavalry under his command. And at this time 2 also embassies came to visit him from Greece. The delegates wore ceremonial wreaths and offered Alexander golden crowns, to all appearances as if these were official pilgrimages to honour a god.* And as it turned out he was not far from his end.

Alexander thanked the Persian troops for their constant loyalty 3 under Peucestas' command, and congratulated Peucestas himself on his successful leadership. He then began integrating the Persians into the Macedonian brigades, in small units composed of a Macedonian sergeant, below him a double-pay Macedonian corporal and a ten-stater man, then twelve Persians and finally another Macedonian of 4 ten-stater rank (these ten-stater men, so called from their salary, were paid less than the double-pay corporals but more than the rank-and-file soldiers). So each unit comprised four Macedonians (the sergeant, and three on extra pay) and twelve Persians. The Macedonians carried the traditional arms of their country: the Persians were armed with bows or thonged javelins.

During this time Alexander kept his fleet in regular training, with 5 frequent races on the river between the triremes and such quad-riremes as he had, and team competitions for the rowers and helmsmen: there were crowns for the victors.

Now too there arrived back the envoys he had sent to Ammon to 6 enquire what category of posthumous honour was permissible for Hephaestion. They reported that Ammon declared it permissible to worship Hephaestion as a hero. Alexander was delighted with this oracular response, and immediately set about instituting a hero-cult. As part of this he sent a letter to Cleomenes, a reprobate official who was guilty of substantial abuses in Egypt. To the extent that this letter was an expression of his love for Hephaestion and desire to see

him remembered after death, I personally have no criticism: but there
7 is much else which I do criticize. The letter required the building of
hero-shrines to Hephaestion in Egyptian Alexandria, in the city itself
and on the island of Pharos next to the tower; they were to be of
unparalleled size and splendour, with no expense spared; Cleomenes
was to ensure that the shrines were named after Hephaestion, and
also that Hephaestion's name was written into all commercial con-
8 tracts. So far I cannot criticize anything more than a disproportionate
obsession with relatively trivial matters: but it is what follows that I
consider utterly deplorable. The letter continues: 'If I find the temples in Egypt and these shrines to Hephaestion in good order, I shall
ignore your previous offences and guarantee that any future offence,
of whatever nature, will not meet with any disagreeable consequence
at my hands.' There is no way that I can condone a mandate like that
from a great king to a man with authority over such a large and populous country, especially when the man was a known rogue.*

24   In fact Alexander's own end was now close upon him. Aristobulus
has this account of another sign portending what was to come.
Alexander was personally supervising the allocation into the existing
Macedonian brigades of the troops brought by Peucestas from Persis
and by Philoxenus and Menander from the coast. He felt thirsty and
walked away from the dais, leaving the royal throne unoccupied:
2 there were also couches with silver feet on either side of the throne,
where his attendant Companions had been sitting. They had accompanied Alexander when he left the dais, but the eunuchs were still in
position round the throne. Seeing the throne and couches empty, an
otherwise insignificant man (some say he was one of the prisoners
under open arrest) walked straight up through the cordon of eunuchs
3 and sat on the throne. Evidently some Persian taboo prevented them
from removing the man from the throne, and they tore their clothes
and beat their breasts and faces as if some great disaster had happened.* When this was reported to Alexander, he ordered the man
who had sat on the throne to be subjected to the rack, to discover if
his action had been part of a concerted plot. The man would only say
that the idea had come into his head and he acted on it. The seers took
this as confirmation that the incident boded no good for Alexander.
4   Not many days later, after making the usual sacrifices to the gods
for a successful outcome and adding some further offerings on the
advice of his seers, Alexander held a celebratory dinner with his

friends and drank far into the night. We are told that he had also distributed wine and animals for sacrifice to every company and platoon in the army. According to some reports, when he was ready to leave the drinking and retire to his bedroom, he was intercepted by Medius,* who at that time was the most influential of his Companions. Medius invited Alexander to come and join his own party, promising that he would enjoy it.

The Royal Journals* have this account. Alexander joined Medius' 25 party and continued drinking.* He then left the party, took a bath, and went to sleep. Later he dined again with Medius and again drank far into the night. When he left the drinking, he took a bath: after the bath he ate a little food and fell asleep on the spot, as he was already developing a fever. Next day he was carried out on a couch to per- 2 form the usual daily sacrifice, and after the imposition of the offerings he lay down in the men's quarters until dark. During this time he issued his officers their instructions for the land march and the naval expedition: the infantry commanders were to prepare for departure after three days, and the officers accompanying him by sea should be ready to sail a day later. From there he was carried on his couch to the 3 river and taken across by boat to the estate on the other side, where he bathed again and rested for the night. On the next day he bathed once more and made sacrifice as usual: he then went to lie down on the canopied bed and talked with Medius. After sending word to his officers to meet him early in the morning, he had a light dinner and 4 was carried back to the bed, where he spent the whole night in what was now a constant fever. On the next day he bathed first and then offered sacrifice: he then gave detailed instructions to Nearchus and the other officers about the naval expedition scheduled for departure in two days' time. On the next day he bathed again and made the requisite sacrifices, but thereafter there was no remission of his fever. Even so he summoned his officers and instructed them to make sure that all was ready for the sailing. In the evening he took a bath, and by now he was seriously ill. On the next day he was carried across to the 5 lodge by the swimming-pool and made the requisite sacrifices there: though in very poor shape he still summoned his most senior officers and gave further instructions for the naval expedition.* On the following day, though almost too weak for it now, he was carried out to the offertorium and made sacrifice, and despite all continued to brief his officers for the expedition. On the next day, his condition now 6 worsened, he still managed to make the requisite sacrifices, and sent word to the generals to wait for him in the palace courtyard and the battalion and company commanders outside the doors. By now in desperate condition, he was ferried back from the estate to the palace. When the officers came in he recognized them, but could no longer say anything: he had lost the power of speech. That night and the following day he was in an intense fever, and so again for the next night and day.

26   These are the records as written in the Royal Journals. The Journals go on to record that the troops were urgent to see him, either for a last sight of him while he was still alive, or because a rumour was going around that he was already dead, and I imagine some suspected that his death was being covered up by the Bodyguards: but for most their insistent demand to see Alexander was an expression of their grief and longing for the king they were to lose. They say that Alexander could no longer speak as the army filed past him, but he struggled to
2 raise his head and gave each man a sign of greeting with his eyes. The Royal Journals say that Peithon, Attalus, Demophon, and Peucestas, with Cleomenes, Menidas, and Seleucus too, slept the night in the temple* of Sarapis,* to solicit the god's answer to their question whether it would be meet and right for Alexander to be brought into the temple and given into the god's care as a suppliant. The divine response communicated to them was that he should not be brought
3 into the temple, but it was right for him to remain where he was. The Companions made this response public, and shortly afterwards Alexander died. This, then, was what was now 'right' for him.

In their histories neither Aristobulus nor Ptolemy has anything more to add.* Others, though, have recorded this further detail, that when his Companions asked him to whom he was leaving his kingdom, he replied, 'To the strongest':* and some have him adding that he foresaw some mighty 'funeral games' after his death.

27   I am aware that many other accounts have been written of Alexander's death. There is, for example, the story that Alexander died of a poison sent by Antipater.* In this story Antipater had the poison concocted by Aristotle, who was in growing fear of Alexander because of what had happened to Callisthenes, and had it delivered by his son Cassander (some have even written that he carried it
2 enclosed in a mule's hoof): it was administered by Cassander's younger brother Iollas, who was the king's butler and had been

offended in some way by Alexander not long before his death. Some also make Medius complicit in the affair, as he was Iollas' lover and it was he who had invited Alexander to the binge: they say that Alexander felt a sharp pain after drinking the cup, and left the party because of the pain. One writer has even brazenly asserted that when *3* he realized he was not going to live Alexander went out to throw himself into the river Euphrates, to disappear from human sight and leave posterity that much better reason to believe that he was indeed the son of a god, and had departed this earth to join the gods: but that his wife Rhoxane had seen him go out and stopped him, at which he groaned in frustration and accused her of evidently grudging him the everlasting fame of being truly born a god. I let these stories stand here simply to show that I am aware of their currency, and not to give them any credence.

*Alexander died in the hundred and fourteenth Olympiad, when *28* Hegesias was archon at Athens* [June 323 BC]. According to Aristobulus, he lived for thirty-two years and eight months into his thirty-third year, and he reigned as king for twelve years and those eight months. Physically he was very handsome, and possessed of exceptional endurance and energy; in character too he displayed to an exceptional degree the qualities of courage, ambition, enterprise against the odds, and scrupulous religious observance. In all that *2* gratifies the flesh he exercised complete control; but there was one gratification of the spirit for which he had an utterly insatiable appetite, and that was glory. He was remarkably skilful at intuiting the right tactic* when it was still far from self-evident, and remarkably successful at predicting the likely course of events once the initial evidence was to hand. In the management of an army—deployment in battle, supply of arms and equipment—his expertise was masterly: and he had an extraordinary natural gift for lifting the morale of his troops, inspiring them with confidence and banishing their fears in times of danger by the example of his own fearlessness. He was indeed *3* supremely bold when it came to direct and open action, but he was also supremely skilled at seizing the opportunity to steal a quick preemptive strike before the enemy had any warning of what was coming. He would keep to the letter any pact or agreement he made, and was never caught wrong-footed by others' false promises.* In money matters he was notably sparing in expenditure on his own pleasures, and notably generous in the interests of his fellows.

29   If Alexander did make some mistakes through impetuosity or anger, or if he did perhaps allow himself to be drawn too far into oriental pomp, I myself cannot regard these as serious faults, if one remembers in all fairness his youth, his unbroken sequence of success, and the harmful company of those flatterers who always do and always will surround a king without concern for his best interests. And yet of all kings in the past Alexander is the only one to my knowl-

2 edge who had the nobility to feel remorse for his mistakes. Most people conscious of making a mistake think they can conceal their error by defending it as an action with its own justification. They are wrong. In my view the only remedy for a mistake is to admit it and make your remorse clear. Then those adversely affected find the consequences easier to bear if the perpetrator admits that he acted wrongly, and he himself can salvage comfort from the hope that he will never do anything like that again, if he shows obvious dismay at his previous mistakes.

3   Again, I do not see it as a serious fault in Alexander that he attributed his birth to a god—which in any case could well have been nothing more than a political device to elevate his status in the minds of his subjects. In fact I would regard him as no less illustrious a king than Minos or Aeacus or Rhadamanthys:* the ancients attributed their birth to Zeus, and this carries no imputation of blasphemous intent. I put him on a par too with Theseus the son of Poseidon and

4 Ion the son of Apollo. So also with his adoption of Persian dress. I see this as a political device aimed at both constituencies—to show the barbarians that their king was not a wholly alien figure, and as a sign to the Macedonians that he was distancing himself from the national attitude of aggressive chauvinism. I imagine that it was for this reason too that he assimilated the Persian 'Golden Apple' troops into the Macedonian brigades and Persians of appropriate rank into the elite corps. As for his drinking sessions, as Aristobulus says they were not prolonged for the sake of the wine (Alexander was not in fact a heavy drinker), but as a social courtesy to his friends.

30   Anyone who vilifies Alexander should not just cite those actions which do deserve censure, but take an overall view of the entire course of Alexander's career. If he then still wants to criticize, he should first make some comparisons and reflect on them. Who is he, and what has he achieved, to assume the right to vilify a man of that stature who reached the height of human success and made himself unambiguously

king of two continents,* with his name spread throughout the whole world? By comparison the critic is an insignificant creature, toiling away at some insignificant work, and not even master of that.

I think it true that in Alexander's time there was no nation on 2 earth, no city, no individual unfamiliar with the name of Alexander. He was a man like no other man has ever been, and I cannot believe that he was born without some divine agency. In evidence of this there are the oracles reported at his death, the visions and dreams seen or experienced by many different people, and the more than human honour and remembrance in which men hold him to this day: even now, after such a passage of time, the people of Macedonia receive new oracles about the honours they should pay him.*

So, although I too have censured some of Alexander's actions in 3 my history, I make no apology for my admiration of the man himself. Where I criticize Alexander, I do so both to remain true to my own principles and also to provide an object-lesson of general use to the public. It was for that reason that I set out to write this history: and like Alexander I have had some help from god.*

THE INDICA

THE INDIGO

THE region which lies the other side of the river Indus to the 1
west, from there to the river Cophen [Kabul], is inhabited by the
Astacenians and the Assacenians.* These are Indian tribes, but they 2
do not have the physical stature of those who live within the boundary
of the Indus, and they lack both the courageous spirit and the dark
colour of most other Indians. They were subjected long ago to the As- 3
syrians, then to the Medes, and after the Medes to the Persians, paying
a set tribute in kind to Cyrus* the son of Cambyses. The Nysaeans, 4
on the other hand, are not of the Indian race. They originate from
the company which came to India with Dionysus, probably some
of the Greeks who had become unfit for active service in Dionysus'
wars against the Indians, and probably also some volunteers from the 5
local tribes established there by Dionysus in a joint settlement with
the Greeks. Dionysus called the country Nysaea,* and the city itself
Nysa, from the mountain of that name. This mountain, so close that 6
the city of Nysa is built on its foothills, is also called Meros ['thigh']
from the circumstances of Dionysus' birth.* Such at least is the story 7
told by the poets, and I am happy to leave interpretation to the scholars, Greek or foreign. Assacenian territory includes the large city of 8
Massaca, which is the regional centre of power, and another large city,
Peucelaïtis* [Gandhara], not far from the Indus. These, then, are the
inhabited areas to the west of the river Indus as far as the Cophen. My 2
definition, though, of India and the Indians properly so called is the
whole area and its inhabitants east of the Indus.

The northern boundary of India is the Taurus mountain range,
though that is not the name by which it is known in this country. In 2
fact, since the Taurus starts from the sea by Pamphylia, Lycia, and
Cilicia and extends all the way to the Eastern Ocean, cutting through
the whole of Asia, the range goes by different names in different 3
countries: it is variously called Parapamisus, Emodus, and Imaon,
and doubtless it has many other names too. The Macedonians on 4
campaign with Alexander called it Caucasus* (this being another
Caucasus, not the same as the Scythian range), so that the story
became current that Alexander had penetrated to the far side of
the Caucasus. On the west side the river Indus forms the boundary 5

of India all the way down to the Great Sea, into which it debouches
through two mouths. These mouths are not close together like the five
6 mouths of the Danube, but the Indus forms a delta like the Egyptian
delta at the mouths of the Nile, and no less extensive: in the local
7 language this Indian delta is called Patala. To the south* the land of
India is bounded by the Great Sea itself, and the same sea is also the
8 eastern boundary. The southern parts round Patala and the mouths
of the Indus were visited by Alexander and his Macedonians, and
have been seen by many Greek travellers. To the east Alexander did
9 not penetrate beyond the river Hyphasis [Beas], though a few writers
have given accounts of the country as far as the river Ganges, describing the mouths of the Ganges and the city of Palimbothra* [Patna],
the largest Indian city on the Ganges.

3   I shall take Eratosthenes* of Cyrene as the most authoritative
2 source, in view of his work on a complete map of the world. He says
that from Mount Taurus, where the Indus rises, and down the whole
course of the river to its mouths in the Great Sea, the length of that
3 side of India is fourteen hundred miles. The opposite side, taken
again from the Taurus range and down the whole eastern seaboard,
he reckons is rather longer than the west side, as a promontory runs
far out into the ocean for a distance of some three hundred miles:
so he would make this eastern side* of India seventeen hundred
4 miles long. That is his conclusion for the depth of India: as for its
length from west to east, he says he can give the distance to the
city of Palimbothra as officially measured in *schoinoi** along what is a
royal road, and this equates to eleven hundred miles, but beyond
5 Palimbothra there is a dearth of accurate information. Those who
base their accounts on hearsay give the further extent, including the
promontory running out into the sea, as about another eleven hundred miles, which would make the total length of India from west to
6 east about two thousand two hundred miles. Ctesias* of Cnidus states
that the land of India is equal in size to all the rest of Asia, which is
nonsense: nonsense too is Onesicritus' claim that it amounts to a third
of the entire world. Nearchus says that to cross the central plain of
7 India would be a journey of four months. Megasthenes* calls the
east–west dimension of India its width (all others speak of length),
and says that this width is seventeen hundred and fifty miles at its
8 narrowest extent. The north–south axis is then his length, and he
puts this at two thousand five hundred miles at its shortest.

*The Indian rivers are larger than any in the whole of Asia. The 9 greatest are the Ganges and the Indus (from which the country takes its name), both of these larger than the Nile in Egypt and the Scythian Danube, in fact larger than those two rivers combined. I would say 10 that the Acesines [Chenab] too is larger than the Danube and the Nile, at least when it has taken in the Hydaspes [Jhelum], Hydraotes [Ravi], and Hyphasis and reaches a width of over three miles at its confluence with the Indus. There may well be many other rivers larger than the Acesines flowing through India: but I cannot vouch 4 for the country beyond the Hyphasis, as that was the limit of Alexander's penetration. As for the two greatest rivers, the Ganges 2 and the Indus, Megasthenes wrote that the Ganges is far larger than the Indus, and all others who speak of the Ganges are in agreement. It is already (they say) a large river at its source, and it takes in as 3 tributaries the Caïnas, the Erannoboas [Son], and the Cossoanus, all these navigable rivers; then the Sonus, the Sittocatis, and the Solomatis, which are also navigable; then the Condochates, the 4 Sambus, the Magon, the Agoranis, and the Omalis. And it is joined by the Comminases (this is a large river), the Cacuthis, and the Andomatis, which flows into it from the territory of the Indian tribe called the Madyandini; thereafter by the Amystis at the city of 5 Catadupe, and the Oxymagis at the place called Pazalae; and the Erennesis flows into the Ganges in the territory of the Mathae, an Indian tribe. Megasthenes says that none of these rivers fails to match 6 the size of the Maeander in its navigable stretch. The Ganges at its 7 narrowest is about eleven miles wide, and it often forms great lakes such that the land on the other side is invisible, if it is low-lying country without an outcrop of hills.

The same goes for the Indus. The Hydraotes runs into the Acesines 8 in the territory of the Cambistholi: before then it has taken in the Hyphasis in Astrybae territory, and the Saranges and the Neudrus which flow into it from Cecaean and Attacenian land respectively. The Hydaspes also gives into the Acesines, in Sydracae territory, 9 bringing with it the Sinarus which joins in the land of the Arispae. The Acesines then has its confluence with the Indus in Mallian terri- 10 tory. Another large river, the Tutapus, also gives into the Acesines. All these rivers enlarge the Acesines, which keeps its own name unchallenged until it finally meets the Indus. The river Cophen, 11 bringing with it the Malamantus, the Soastus [Swat], and the Garoeas

12 [Panjkora], empties into the Indus in Peucalaïtis; further north, and close together, the Parennus and the Saparnus join the Indus; and the Soanus, flowing from the Abissarian highlands without any tributaries, also empties into it. Megasthenes reports that most of these rivers *13* are navigable. No cause, then, to doubt that the Danube and the Nile do not even begin to compare with the Indus and the Ganges in *14* volume of water. The Nile has no known tributary flowing into it, and in fact it loses water to the irrigation channels cut from it throughout *15* Egypt. The Danube is a small river at its source, and although it takes in many tributaries these are not as numerous as the Indian rivers which contribute to the Indus and the Ganges, and very few of them are navigable. From my own experience I know of the Enus [Inn] *16* and the Saus [Save] (the Enus joining the Danube at the border of Noricum and Raetia, and the Saus in Pannonia, in the area called Taurunus): if anyone knows of any other navigable tributaries of the Danube, I cannot imagine he knows of many.

5 Anyone who wishes to explain why there are so many large rivers in India is welcome to do so: my task, as always, is simply to record *2* what I have heard. Megasthenes does in fact give the names of many other rivers besides the Ganges and Indus which flow into the eastern or southern ocean, and concludes that the total number of Indian *3* rivers is fifty-eight, all of them navigable. But I do not think that even Megasthenes visited much of India, though he certainly saw more of it than the men who invaded with Alexander the son of Philip: he says, for example, that he spent some time with Sandrocottus, the *4* greatest king in India, yet greater than Porus. This same Megasthenes says that the Indians had never attacked, nor been attacked by, any *5* other people. Sesostris the Egyptian had subjugated most of Asia and taken an invading army as far as Europe, but then returned home; *6* Idanthyrsus the Scythian had set out from Scythia on a campaign which subjugated many of the nations in Asia and even brought him *7* a successful invasion of Egypt; Semiramis* the Assyrian queen did attempt an expedition against India, but died before she could give effect to her plans. It was only Alexander who did actually invade India.

8 *As for invasions before Alexander's, there is a strong tradition that Dionysus had also invaded India and subdued the population: *9* the similar tradition about Heracles is not so strong. Dionysus' expedition is amply evidenced by the city of Nysa, as well as the mountain called Meros and the ivy which grows on it, the practice adopted by the Indians of marching out for battle to the sound of drums and cymbals, and their clothing, which is dappled like that of Dionysian devotees. There is little to suggest a visit by Heracles. The story that *10* Heracles had tried and failed to take the Rock of Aornus which fell to Alexander's assault I would regard as a piece of Macedonian propaganda, comparable to their renaming of the Parapamisus [Hindu Kush] as the Caucasus, though this mountain has no relation to the real Caucasus: and when they came across a cave in Parapamisadae *11* country, they said this was the very cave in which Prometheus the Titan was hung in chains for his theft of fire. Again, when they saw *12* that an Indian tribe called the Sibae clothed themselves in skins, they claimed that the Sibae were the remnants of Heracles' invading army: moreover the Sibae carry cudgels and brand their cattle with the mark of a club,* so this too was taken as evidence of a tradition reflecting Heracles' own use of the club. If anyone is inclined to believe this, *13* the Heracles in question cannot have been the Theban Heracles, but either the Tyrian or the Egyptian Heracles, or perhaps some great king living up-country not far from the Indian border.

This digression can serve as a warning not to trust the accounts **6** some writers have given of the Indians on the far side of the Hyphasis: up to the Hyphasis those who were with Alexander on his campaign are not entirely untrustworthy. For example, Megasthenes has a story *2* about an Indian river called Silas, which flows from a spring of the same name through the land of the Silaeans, so named also from the river and the spring. He says that a peculiar phenomenon of this *3* water is its lack of resistance: nothing can swim in it or float on it, but everything sinks straight to the bottom. No other water, he says, is so insubstantial and gaseous.

Rain falls in India in the summer, especially on the mountains, *4* Parapamisus, Emodus, and Imaon, and the rivers rising there flow full and turbid. The plains of India also receive rain in summer, so *5* that large parts of them turn into lakes. Alexander's army had to escape this effect caused by the Acesines in midsummer, when the river overflowed onto the surrounding plain. This evidence suggests *6* a similar explanation for the flooding of the Nile: it is likely that summer rain on the mountains of Ethiopia swells the Nile until it overflows its banks onto the land of Egypt. Certainly the Nile flows turbid *7* at this time of year, as would not be the result of melting snow nor of

the contrary pressure exerted on it by the seasonal winds which blow
in summer: and in any case the climate is too hot for there to be snow-
8 cover on the Ethiopian mountains. But quite possibly they get rained
on like the Indian mountains, since in other respects too India and
Ethiopia are not dissimilar countries, and in the Indian rivers crocodiles are found as in the Ethiopian and Egyptian Nile, and in some of
them fish and other large river-creatures like those of the Nile, except
for the hippopotamus (though Onesicritus* says that hippopotamuses
9 are found too). There is no great difference either in the appearance
of the human inhabitants of India and Ethiopia. The southern Indians
are more like the Ethiopians in the black colour of their skin and hair,
though they are not as snub-nosed or woolly-haired as the Ethiopians:
the Indians more to the north have a greater physical resemblance to
the Egyptians.

7   *Megasthenes says that the total number of Indian tribes is a
hundred and eighteen. Now I agree with Megasthenes that there is a
large number of tribes in India, but I cannot see on what grounds he
could give a precise figure, since he visited hardly a fraction of the
whole country, and not all of these tribes are in communication with
2 one another. Originally, he says, the Indians were nomads, like those
non-farming Scythians who move about in their wagons from one
part of Scythia to another, without any permanent settlements or
3 centres of worship. In the same way the Indians at first had no settled
communities or edifices for worship of the gods, but simply clothed
themselves in the skins of the wild animals they killed, and ate the
bark of trees. These trees were called *tala** in the Indian language,
and what looked like balls of wool grew on them, similar to the growth
4 at the top of date-palms. They also fed on the animals they caught,
eating them raw—at least that was their practice before the arrival of
5 Dionysus in India. When he came and conquered the Indians, he
founded cities and established their code of law, brought the Indians
the gift of wine as he had to the Greeks, and gave them seed and
6 taught them to sow the land (either Triptolemus* had not driven this
way when Demeter sent him out to sow the entire earth, or this
Dionysus, whoever he was, had visited India before Triptolemus and
7 given the Indians the seeds of plants for cultivation). Dionysus was
the first to have them yoke oxen to the plough, and he turned most of
them from nomads to farmers, also equipping them with the arms of
8 war. Megasthenes says too that Dionysus taught them the worship

of gods, particularly of himself, with cymbals and drums; he instructed them in the satyric dance which the Greeks call the *kordax*; he intro- 9 duced the long hair and turban worn in the god's honour; and he taught them how to make perfumed lotions. So even much later the Indians still came out to their battles with Alexander to the accompaniment of cymbals and drums.

When Dionysus left India, with all these innovations in place, he 8 appointed Spatembas as king over the country, one of his Companions and the most faithful of them all to the Bacchic way. When Spatembas died his son Budyas succeeded to the throne. The father reigned over 2 India for fifty-two years, and the son for twenty. Budyas' son Cradeuas succeeded him as king, and for the most part thereafter the kingship 3 passed from generation to generation within that family, son succeeding father: if the family succession failed, kings of India were appointed on merit.

As for Heracles, commonly said to have visited India, the Indians 4 themselves hold that he was born from their earth. This Heracles is 5 particularly revered by the Suraseni, an Indian tribe whose territory includes two large cities, Methora and Cleisobora, and is traversed by the navigable river Iomanes. Megasthenes says that by the Indians' 6 own account this Heracles wore the same sort of outfit as the Theban Heracles. This Heracles too married many wives, and fathered a very large number of male children in India, but only one daughter. The 7 girl's name was Pandaea, and the country in which she was born and over which Heracles made her queen was called Pandaea after her: here her father endowed her with some five hundred elephants, four thousand cavalry, and a hundred and thirty thousand foot-soldiers. Some other Indians tell the following story of Heracles. After travel- 8 ling through every land and every sea and ridding the earth of all that troubled it, he discovered in the sea a new form of women's jewellery. Still to this day the merchants who bring us the produce of India are 9 keen to purchase and export this jewel, and the rich and prosperous among Greeks in the past and Romans today are yet keener to buy the sea margarita, as it is called in the Indian language. Anyway, Heracles 10 thought this would be a beautiful decoration to wear, and collected these pearls from every sea and brought them to India for the adornment of his daughter. Megasthenes says that the pearl-oysters are 11 caught with nets, and large numbers of them crowd together in the sea, like bees: and just like bees too the oysters have a king or queen.

12 Anyone who happens to catch the king then finds it easy to net the rest of the swarm of oysters: but if the king manages to escape, the others cannot now be caught either. The fishermen let the flesh
13 rot, and then use the shell as an ornament. Among the Indians too a pearl is worth three times its weight in refined gold, which is also mined in India.

9   In this country where Heracles' daughter was queen the girls are ready for marriage at age seven, and the men live for forty years at
2 most. The Indians have a story they tell about this. Heracles' daughter had been born to him late in life, and when he realized that his own end was near, in the absence of any potential husband for her of a distinction comparable to his, he slept with her himself when she was seven years old, so that he and she could leave a line of progeny
3 to rule India. So Heracles made her marriageable at that age, and ever since then the whole nation over which Pandaea was queen has
4 enjoyed this privilege as a legacy from Heracles. My own view is that if Heracles was capable of other feats just as extraordinary, he could have made himself live longer, to wait until she was mature before
5 sleeping with his daughter. But I suppose that if what is said about the early puberty of these girls is true, it is of a piece with the reported
6 lifespan of the menfolk, the oldest of them dying at forty. In a population where old age and consequent death come that much sooner, no
7 doubt the onset of maturity is proportionately earlier too. So the men there would be growing old at thirty, past their youth by twenty, and in their prime at around fifteen: on this scale the women could well be
8 ready for marriage at seven. By way of parallel, fruit ripens earlier in this country than elsewhere, as Megasthenes again has noted, and also decays earlier.

9   From Dionysus to Sandrocottus the Indians reckoned there were a hundred and fifty-three kings and a time of six thousand and forty-two years. During this time there were three periods when monarchy was replaced by a free political system: the first lasted for [. . .] years,* the second for a full three hundred years, and the third for a hundred
10 and twenty years. The Indians say that Dionysus was fifteen generations earlier than Heracles, and that no one else had made a military invasion of India, not even Cyrus the son of Cambyses, though he had campaigned against the Scythians* and was generally the most
11 expansionist of the Asian kings. But then Alexander had come and conquered every country he invaded by force of arms: he would have

gone on to conquer the entire world, if his army had been willing. For *12*
their part, none of the Indians ever launched a military expedition
outside their own country: that would have been contrary to their
moral principles.

It is also said that Indians do not put up monuments to their dead, 10
but consider that their virtues in life are sufficient memorials for the
departed, those and the songs which are sung at their funerals. As for *2*
the number of cities in India, it would be impossible to give an accurate figure, as there are so many of them. What can be said is that those
on rivers or by the sea are built of wood. If they were built of brick *3*
they would not last long because of the rain and the flooding of low
land when the rivers overflow their banks. Only the cities situated in *4*
elevated positions, on high and open ground, are built of brick and
clay. The greatest city in India is called Palimbothra [Patna], in *5*
Prasian territory at the confluence of the Erannoboas [Son] and the
Ganges. The Ganges is the largest of all rivers: the Erannoboas may
be the third river in India, but it is still larger than any river elsewhere, though it yields its name to the Ganges after the confluence.
Megasthenes says that at its greatest length the city of Palimbothra 6
extends for nine miles on either side, with a breadth of over one and
a half miles.* It is surrounded by a ditch two hundred yards wide and *7*
forty-five feet deep: the wall has five hundred and seventy towers and
sixty-four gates. Another notable feature of the country is that all *8*
Indians are free men, and no Indian is a slave. The Indians have this
in common with the Spartans, except that the Spartans have Helots
as their slaves to perform all servile functions. In India, though, there
are no slaves of any kind,* let alone any Indian slave.

*All Indians are divided broadly into seven castes. One caste con- 11
sists of the gurus: they form the smallest caste, but enjoy the highest
regard and honour. They are under no obligation to do any physical *2*
work or to contribute any material benefit to the community from
their activities. In fact nothing else is required of the gurus except to
preside over the public sacrifices made to the gods on behalf of the
whole Indian community. Any private sacrifice must be directed by *3*
one of the gurus, or it would not be acceptable to the gods. They are *4*
also the only Indians with the power of prophecy, and no one other
than a guru is allowed to prophesy. They prophesy only on questions *5*
concerning the seasons of the year, and whenever some public calamity strikes. It is not their business to prophesy on private matters to

individuals, either because trivial affairs lie outside the ambit of prophecy, or because it is beneath their dignity to bother with them.

6 The penalty for any guru who makes three errors in prophecy is simply enforced silence for the future, and no one will ever elicit any

7 speech from a man under this sentence of silence. These gurus live naked,* in the open air and sunshine during the winter, and in summer, when the sun is oppressive, in the meadows and marsh-lands under enormous trees* whose shade, according to Nearchus, extends for five hundred feet all round: such is their size that ten thousand

8 men could shelter under one tree. The gurus eat fruits in their season and also the bark of these trees, which is as sweet and nutritious as the dates produced by palm trees.

9 Second after the gurus come the farmers, and this is the most numerous of the Indian castes. They have no weapons and take no part in warfare, but work the land and pay a tax on their produce to

10 the kings or, as it may be, to the self-governing city states. If the Indians go to war with one another, they are forbidden to harm these workers on the land or to ravage the land itself—it is sacrilege to do so. So some can be at war and killing one another on this side or that, while others close by calmly continue with their ploughing, harvesting, pruning, or reaping.

11 The third caste of Indians are the herdsmen, the shepherds and cowherds. They do not live in the cities or villages, but are nomads making their living on the hills. They too pay taxes in kind from their flocks and herds, and hunt birds and wild animals out in the country.

12 The fourth caste is of artisans and shopkeepers. They are liable for public service, and they too pay a tax on the proceeds of their work, except those who manufacture weapons—these are actually paid a salary from the public purse. This caste includes the shipwrights and the sailors who man the river traffic.

2 The fifth caste consists of the soldiers, who are second only to the farmers in number, and more than any others enjoy a life of freedom and ease. Their only responsibility is the actual business of war.

3 Others make their weapons and provide their horses; others are there to serve them in the camps, grooming their horses, polishing their armour, riding the elephants, maintaining the chariots and driving

4 them. They themselves do fight as long as there is need for fighting, but in time of peace they simply enjoy themselves: and they are paid

a salary from the public purse which would easily support several others as well.

The sixth caste is made up of the Indians called 'inspectors'. They 5 supervise everything that goes on in the countryside and the cities, and make reports to the king (in those regions where there is a monarchy) or to the relevant authorities in the self-governing city states. It is strictly forbidden to give any false information to these inspectors, and no Indian has ever been charged with falsification.

The seventh caste consists of those who form an advisory council 6 on public affairs for the king or the authorities in the autonomous cities. This caste is small in number, but its members are distin- 7 guished more than any others for their intelligence and integrity. It is from this class that they select the men for public office—regional and local governors, treasury ministers, army generals, admirals of the fleet, paymasters, directors of agricultural works.

Marriage between castes is not allowed: so, for example, an artisan 8 cannot marry into the farmer caste or vice versa. It is also forbidden for anyone to combine two professions or to move from one caste to another—so a herdsman cannot become a farmer, or an artisan a herdsman. The only exception is that a guru can be drawn from any 9 of the castes, as there is nothing comfortable about the gurus' way of life—in fact it is the most rigorous of them all.

*For the most part the Indians hunt the same wild animals as the 13 Greeks, but their way of trapping elephants is unique, just as the animals themselves are unlike any other. They choose a level stretch 2 of ground open to the baking sun and dig a ditch round it in a circle wide enough to accommodate a large army at camp: the ditch is ten yards wide and eight yards deep. The spoil from the excavation is 3 heaped on either lip of the ditch to form a double wall. They then 4 make dug-out hides for themselves in the mound on the outer lip of the ditch, leaving small windows in them to let in light and give them a view of the animals as they approach and then charge into the enclosure. Now they put three or four of the tamest females inside the 5 enclosure, and leave just one entrance across the ditch, created by means of a bridge on which they heap a great deal of earth and vegetation to disguise it from the animals, who would otherwise suspect a trap. The hunters keep themselves out of sight, creeping into their 6 hides in the ditch, as wild elephants do not come near inhabited places in daylight (at night, though, they roam everywhere and feed

in herds, following the largest and most dominant male, as cows fol-
7 low bulls). When the elephants get near the enclosure and hear the
females calling and catch their scent, they run up to the surrounding
wall, work round the lip of the ditch until they find the bridge, then
8 jostle across it into the enclosure. When the hunters see that the wild
elephants have come inside, some of them quickly remove the bridge
and others run to the nearby villages to report elephants caught in the
9 enclosure. At this the villagers mount the best of their elephants for a
combination of courage and docility, and once up drive them to the
enclosure: once there they do not join battle immediately, but let the
10 wild elephants weaken from hunger and succumb to thirst. When
they think the elephants are in a sufficiently poor state, they replace
the bridge and ride into the enclosure. At first there is a fierce battle
between the tame bull elephants and those captured from the wild,
but in time the wild elephants are overcome, as you might expect
when they are so weakened by the combined effects of desperation
11 and hunger. The men then dismount and tie together the feet of the
now exhausted wild elephants, then order their tame animals to keep
punishing the wild ones with repeated buffets until they fall to the
ground in total distress. The men come up and slip nooses round the
12 elephants' necks, then mount on them where they lie. To prevent
them throwing their riders or doing any other mischief, they take a
sharp knife and make an incision all round the animals' necks and
pull the noose into the cut, so that this sore makes them keep their
13 head and neck still: any twist in an attempt to do mischief would have
the rope rubbing in the wound. So the animals keep quiet and, knowing that they are beaten, allow themselves to be roped to the tame
elephants and led away.

14 Any baby elephants and those not worth keeping because of some
2 defect are released back into the wild. The rest of the captured herd
are led off to the villages and first of all offered green bamboo shoots
3 and grass to eat. They are too depressed to have any appetite, so the
Indians form a circle round them and play and sing them to sleep
4 with drums, cymbals, and lullabies. For sensitive intelligence no
other animal can match the elephant. Elephants have been known to
pick up their mahouts who have been killed in battle and carry them
out for burial, to stand over them to protect their bodies on the
ground, and to risk their own lives in defence of the fallen. One elephant who killed his mahout in a fit of anger subsequently died of

remorse and despair. I myself have seen an elephant playing the 5
cymbals and other elephants dancing to his beat. The percussionist
had two cymbals fastened to his forelegs and another cymbal on
his trunk: he was rhythmically bashing his trunk on each of the leg 6
cymbals in turn, and the dancers were performing in a circle round
him, raising and bending their forelegs alternately in the same rhythm
as set by the cymbal-player. Elephants mate in the spring, like cattle 7
and horses, when the air-holes beside the temples of the females
open and breathe out. The period of gestation is sixteen months,
eighteen at most: like a mare, the she-elephant gives birth to a single
foal, which she suckles until its eighth year. The longest-lived ele- 8
phants live for two hundred years,* but many die of disease before
reaching that depth of old age. The Indians have various remedies for 9
elephants' ailments: for their eyes a lotion of cow's milk; for other
diseases a drink of red wine; and for wounds a poultice made out of
roasted pork.

The Indians regard the tiger as much stronger than an elephant. 15
Nearchus says that he had seen a tiger skin, but not a living tiger. The
Indians told him, he says, that a tiger is as big as the largest horse, and
for speed and strength superior to any other animal: when a tiger 2
meets an elephant it leaps onto the elephant's head and throttles it
easily. According to Nearchus, the creatures we see and call tigers are 3
in fact jackals, of a striped variety larger than the common jackal. As 4
for the ants, Nearchus says that he did not see any of the particular
sort which some writers have described as native to India, but he
did see many of their skins* brought into the Macedonian camp.
Megasthenes, though, reports that the story about gold-digging ants* 5
is true: these ants do dig up gold, not for the sake of the actual metal,
but it is in their nature to burrow in the earth to make their nests, just
as our smaller ants do, throwing up a little bit of earth in the process.
These Indian ants, though, are bigger than foxes, and so the amount 6
of earth they throw up is proportionate to their size: the earth is gold-
bearing, and this is where the Indians get their gold. However, 7
Megasthenes' report is just hearsay, and since I have no more accurate information than his to impart I am happy to leave the ant story
there.

Nearchus writes of parrots as if they were one of the wonders of 8
India, and describes the birds and their almost human voice. But 9
since I have seen many parrots myself and know that others are

familiar with the bird, I shall not go into detail as if parrots were some sort of oddity: nor shall I speak of the size of the apes in India, how fine-looking some of them are, or the methods used to hunt them, as all this too is common knowledge (except perhaps the handsomeness

10 of the apes). Nearchus also says that they hunt snakes which are multicoloured and fast-moving: he reports that the snake caught by Peithon the son of Antigenes was twenty-four feet long,* but that the Indians themselves say that the largest snakes are much bigger than

11 that. Greek doctors had never found an antidote to the bite of an Indian snake, but the Indians themselves could cure the victims of snakebite. Nearchus adds that Alexander had gathered all the most skilful Indian physicians and kept them with him, and had it announced in camp that anyone bitten by a snake should go straight

12 to the royal tent. These same physicians also took care of the other ailments and injuries. There are not many diseases endemic in India, as there is little variation between the seasons. Anyone taken seriously ill would inform the gurus, who were thought able to call on divine help to cure anything that could be cured.

16 According to Nearchus the Indians wear linen clothing, the linen coming from the trees* I have already mentioned. This Indian linen is brighter in colour than other linens, or else it may just seem brighter

2 by contrast with the people's dark skin. They wear a linen shirt down to mid-calf, another garment wrapped over their shoulders, and

3 another wound round their heads. Some wear ivory earrings, but this

4 is only common practice among the very wealthy. Nearchus says that the Indians dye their beards in various colours: some go for whiter

5 than white, others for dark blue, crimson, purple, or green. All Indians with any self-respect use parasols in the summer heat: and they wear elaborately fashioned sandals of white leather, with differently coloured soles built up high, to make them look taller.

6 The weaponry deployed by the Indians takes various forms. The foot-soldiers use a bow as tall as themselves, which they lower to the ground and brace with their left foot before drawing the string far back to shoot, as their arrows are nearly four and a half feet long.

7 Nothing can resist one of these arrows shot by an Indian archer: they penetrate through shields, breastplates, and any yet stronger form of

8 armour. On their left arms they carry rawhide shields which are nar-

9 rower than their bodies but not much shorter. Others have javelins rather than bows. All carry a broad cutlass not less than four and a half feet long. Whenever a battle becomes hand-to-hand (though the Indians are reluctant to come to this in their internal wars), they bring down this cutlass with both hands, to add force to the blow. Their *10* cavalry are armed with a pair of spears, more like javelins, and a small shield, smaller than the infantry shield. Their horses are not saddled and do not have bits of the Greek or Celtic type, but rather a band of *11* rawhide fitted round their muzzles with bronze or iron spurs, not very sharp, stitched into the underside (the rich have these spurs made of ivory). Inside their mouths the horses have an iron bar rather like a spit, to which the reins are attached. And so when the rider *12* pulls on the rein the spit controls the horse, as there is a direct connection from it to the spurs, and their pressure compels the horse to obey the rein.

Physically the Indians are lean, tall, and much more agile than *17* other men. For personal transport most Indians use camels, horses, or donkeys, and the wealthy use elephants. The elephant is regarded *2* by the Indians as the royal mount; second to it in prestige is a four-horse chariot, and camels come third; to ride on a single horse is thought lower-class. Their women are highly moral and not corrupt- *3* ible at any price, except that a woman will have sex with anyone who gives her an elephant: the Indians do not regard sex for an elephant as any disgrace, but rather a compliment to the women if their beauty is thought as valuable as an elephant. When they marry, no gifts are *4* given or received: when girls reach marriageable age their fathers bring them out and put them on public parade as prizes for the victors in wrestling, boxing, or running contests, or anyone excelling in any other manly quality. The Indians are mainly farmers with a cereal *5* diet, except for the highlanders, who eat game.

This must suffice for my description of the Indians, which includes *6* the most notable features recorded by Nearchus and Megasthenes, two recognized authorities. In any case it was not my main purpose in *7* this monograph to offer an Indian ethnography, but rather to give an account of the voyage of Alexander's fleet from India to Persia: so all so far must be regarded as a digression.

When Alexander had his fleet ready on the banks of the Hydaspes, *18* he manned his ships with crews picked from the Phoenicians, Cypriots, and Egyptians* who had joined the expedition into central Asia, selecting as oarsmen and ancillary crew those of them who had seafaring experience. There were also a good many islanders *2*

in the army with that sort of background, as well as Ionians and
3 Hellespontines. The list of those he appointed trierarchs* is as fol-
lows. The Macedonians were Hephaestion the son of Amyntor,
Leonnatus* the son of Eunus, Lysimachus* the son of Agathocles,
Asclepiodorus the son of Timander, Archon the son of Cleinias,
Demonicus the son of Athenaeus, Archias* the son of Anaxidotus,
Ophellas the son of Seilenus, Timanthes the son of Pantiades—all
4 these from Pella. From Amphipolis were Nearchus* the son of
Androtimus (who wrote an account of this voyage along the coast),
Laomedon* the son of Larichus, and Androsthenes* the son of
5 Callistratus; from Orestis, Craterus the son of Alexander and
Perdiccas the son of Orontes; from Eordaea, Ptolemy* the son of
Lagus and Aristonus* the son of Peisaeus; from Pydna, Metron the
6 son of Epicharmus and Nicarchides the son of Simus. Then there
was Attalus* the son of Andromenes from Tymphaea, Peucestas*
the son of Alexander from Mieza, Peithon* the son of Crateuas from
Alcomenae, Leonnatus* the son of Antipater from Aegae, Pantauchus
the son of Nicolaus from Alorus, and Mylleas the son of Zoïlus from
7 Beroea. All these were Macedonians. Of the Greeks, there were
Medius* the son of Oxythemis from Larissa, Eumenes* the son of
Hieronymus from Cardia, Critobulus* the son of Platon from Cos,
Thoas* the son of Mandrodorus and Maeander the son of
8 Mandrogenes from Magnesia, and Andron the son of Cabeleus from
Teos. The Cypriots were Nicocles the son of Pasicrates from Soli,
and Nithaphon the son of Pnytagoras* from Salamis. Alexander had
also appointed a Persian as trierarch, Bagoas the son of Pharnuches.*
9 The helmsman of Alexander's own ship was Onesicritus from
Astypalaea, and the secretary for the whole fleet was Evagoras the son
10 of Eucleon from Corinth. As admiral-in-chief he appointed Nearchus
the son of Androtimus, a Cretan by birth who lived in Amphipolis on
the Strymon [Struma].
11 When Alexander had made all these arrangements, he sacrificed to
all his ancestral gods and those prescribed by oracles,* to Poseidon,
Amphitrite, the Nereids, and Ocean himself, to the river Hydaspes,
where the expedition would start, to the Acesines, into which the
Hydaspes runs, and to the Indus, into which both these rivers run.
12 He then held festival games with competitions in the performing arts
and athletics, and distributed animals for sacrifice to every company
in the army.

When all was ready for the launch, Alexander ordered Craterus to 19
march down one side of the Hydaspes with a force of infantry and
cavalry, while Hephaestion* was already on his way down the other
side with another army yet larger than that assigned to Craterus: and
Hephaestion had with him the elephants, about two hundred in
number. Alexander himself took with him the so-called foot guards, 2
all of the archers, and that section of the cavalry called 'the
Companions'—a total of about eight thousand men.* The advance 3
contingents with Craterus and Hephaestion had orders to proceed to
a specified place where they were to await the fleet. Alexander sent 4
Philip, his appointee as satrap of this region, to the banks of the
Acesines with another large army, as by this time Alexander had at 5
his disposal a hundred and twenty thousand fighting men, made up
of the original force he had led into Asia from the coast, the reinforcements brought by the officers he had sent back on an enlistment drive,
and all sorts of barbarian tribes now with him, variously armed with
every type of weaponry. He himself set out with the fleet and sailed 6
down the Hydaspes to its confluence with the Acesines. The total 7
number of his ships was eight hundred,* including warships, freighters, and horse-transports, some of the vessels carrying provisions as
well as troops. In my earlier book written in Attic Greek* I have 8
already described the fleet's progress down the rivers, the tribes
Alexander conquered in the course of the voyage, the dangerous situation in which he put himself among the Mallians, the wound he
received there, and how Peucestas and Leonnatus* shielded him
where he fell. This present work is a description of the coastal voyage 9
on which Nearchus took the fleet through the Great Sea from the
mouths of the Indus to the Persian Gulf, also known as the Red Sea.

Nearchus' own account is as follows. Alexander had a yen* to sail 20
along the whole expanse of sea from India to the Gulf, but was wor- 2
ried about the length of the voyage and the risk of the expedition
coming to grief if they found stretches of the coastline were desert,
harbourless, or lacking in sufficient natural foodstuff: and that would
be a serious stain on his previous record of great achievements, obliterating all his success in the past. But in the end his constant desire
for some new extraordinary exploit triumphed over his doubts.
He could not decide, though, on a leader: whoever he chose would 3
have to be fully up to the proposed task and also capable of dispelling
fears among the ships' companies that this sort of voyage was an

4 ill-considered mission into obvious danger. Nearchus says that Alexander discussed with him the choice of an admiral to command the fleet. When he suggested various names, Alexander rejected them one after the other: this one was not prepared to run risks in the cause, that one was a coward, that one was homesick, and so on, all found

5 deficient in one way or another. Eventually Nearchus made his own offer. 'Your majesty,' he said, 'I will undertake the command of your fleet, and given god's help I will bring your ships and your men safely through to Persis—if, that is, anyone can navigate this sea and the

6 task is not beyond human skill.' Alexander professed reluctance to expose one of his own friends to that amount of hardship and danger,* but so far from discouraging him this made Nearchus all

7 the more insistent. Satisfied now with Nearchus' will for the task,

8 Alexander appointed him admiral-in-chief of the fleet. The troops and crews detailed for the voyage now took a happier view of it, thinking that of all people Alexander would never have sent Nearchus

9 into manifest danger, unless they were all likely to survive it. And then the pure splendour of the preparations, the trim of the ships, and the exceptional trouble taken by the trierarchs* to provide for rowers and crew—all this served to fortify men previously full of

10 doubt and to raise their hopes for the whole enterprise. And a strong contribution to army morale was the fact that Alexander himself had struck out into the ocean down both mouths of the Indus* and sacrificed victims to Poseidon and all the other gods of the sea, and given

11 magnificent gifts to the sea itself. Trusting in Alexander's established record of success against the odds, they thought there was nothing he could not dare and do.

21   They finally set out when the seasonal winds had died down. These winds set in for the whole of the summer season, blowing landwards from the sea and so making it impossible to sail. The launch took place in the year when Cephisodorus was archon at Athens, on the twentieth day of the month Boedromion,* by the Athenian reckoning: in the Macedonian and Asian calendar it was in the month of

2 Hyperberetaeus and the eleventh year of Alexander's reign. Before the departure Nearchus too sacrificed to Zeus the Saviour, and he too held athletic games. They moved out from the docks and on the first day came to anchor in the river Indus by a large canal, and stayed there for two days: the place was called Stura, about ten miles from

3 the docks. On the third day they set out again and sailed three miles

to another canal, which by now was salt, as the sea reached up to it, especially at high tide, and even on the ebb salt water stayed there, mixed with the river: the place was called Caumana. They sailed on 4 another two miles to Coreëstis and anchored there, still within the river. Starting out again from there they sailed only a little way before 5 they saw a great reef lying across this mouth of the Indus, mostly rocky and with waves crashing on its seaward side. But they found a 6 stretch where the reef was less solid and dug a channel through it half a mile wide, then took their ships through here when the flood tide came in from the sea. They then sailed out and round for fifteen 7 miles, and came to anchor at a sandy island called Crocala,* staying there for the next day. The inhabitants were an Indian tribe called the Arabies* (I mentioned them in my longer book, saying that they take 8 their name from the river Arabis [Hab], which runs through their country to its outlet in the sea and forms the boundary between their land and that of the Oreitans). From Crocala they sailed on with the 9 mountain they called Eirus on their right and a low-lying island on their left, which runs parallel to the coast and creates a narrow channel. They sailed through this and anchored in a fine natural harbour, 10 which for its size and amenity Nearchus decided to call 'Alexander's Harbour'. The harbour is formed by an island lying across its mouth 11 about three hundred and fifty yards from the shore and serving as a breakwater against the sea. The island is called Bibacta,* and the whole area Sangada. Here constant strong winds were blowing off the 12 sea, and Nearchus fortified their camp with a stone wall in case some of the natives might gang together and attempt to raid it. Their 13 enforced stay here lasted twenty-four days. Nearchus says that the men hunted for mussels, oysters, and the so-called razor-clams, of an enormous size compared to those in our own Mediterranean. They also had to drink brackish water.

As soon as the wind dropped they set out to sea, and after covering 22 about six miles anchored off a sandy beach fronted by a desert island called Domai, which acted as a breakwater and they could moor in its 2 lee. There was no water on the beach, but they found good water about two miles inland. On the next day they sailed till nightfall, 3 thirty miles to Saranga, and anchored off the beach: there was water just under a mile from the shore. The next leg took them to anchor at 4 a deserted place called Sacala. They then threaded between two rocks so close together that the oar-blades touched rock on either side, and

went on to anchor at Morontobara* [Karachi], a journey of some
5 thirty miles. Here there was a large circular harbour, deep and calm,
with a narrow entrance: in the local language this is called the
'Women's Harbour', as the first ruler of this region was a woman.
6 (After negotiating the rocks they met a large swell and strong cur-
rents, but it had seemed a risky business to sail out to sea round the
7 rocks.) For the next day they sailed with an island on their left shel-
tering them from the sea: it was so close to the shore that you would
have thought the intervening channel was an artificial canal. This
whole passage was about seven miles long. The shore was thick with
8 trees,* and the island too was a forest of every sort of tree. Towards
dawn they sailed clear of the island through a narrow rocky gap, as
the tide was still falling. After sailing another twelve miles they
dropped anchor at the mouth of the river Arabis [Hab]. There was
good capacious anchorage at the river mouth, but no drinking water,
9 as the outlets of the Arabis were polluted with sea-water. But a trek
of four miles inland brought them to a freshwater pond, where they
10 drew water and turned back. There was a hilly deserted island opposite the harbour, round which oysters and all sorts of fish could be
caught. The Arabis marks the limit of the land of the Arabies, the
most westerly of the Indians living in this area: from here on it was
Oreitan territory.

23   Leaving the mouth of the Arabis they coasted along the land of the
Oreitans and anchored at Pagala after sailing some twenty miles: it
was an area of rough shore, but still amenable to anchors. So the
crews rode it out on board ship, while some went ashore in search of
2 water and carried back a supply. On the next day they weighed anchor
at dawn and after covering about forty-three miles put in at evening
at Cabana, mooring off a deserted shore. There was rough surf here
3 too, so they anchored the ships well out to sea. It was on this leg of the
voyage that a fierce squall blew up from the sea and caught the fleet,
wrecking two warships and a corvette: the men were able to swim to
4 safety, as they were sailing quite close to the land. About midnight
they put out again and sailed as far as Cocala,* some twenty miles
from their starting-point. The ships were tossing at anchor, but
Nearchus disembarked the crews and made camp on land, as they
longed for a rest after all that discomfort at sea. The camp was fenced
as a precaution against barbarian attack.
5   It was here that Leonnatus, left in charge of the Oreitan situation

by Alexander, defeated the Oreitans* and the others who joined
their movement in a great battle, in which he killed six thousand of
them, including all their leaders. Of his own troops he lost fifteen
cavalry and a small number of infantry: Apollophanes, the satrap of
Gedrosia, was also killed. I have recorded this in my other history, 6
relating also how Leonnatus was rewarded for this achievement with
a golden crown conferred on him by Alexander in front of the whole
Macedonian army. On Alexander's orders corn had been stockpiled 7
here to provision the expedition, and they took on board ten days'
supply. Ships damaged during the voyage so far were repaired, and 8
any sailors who Nearchus thought were not pulling their weight were
transferred to infantry service under Leonnatus: he replenished the
ships' complements with soldiers from Leonnatus' army.

They set sail from here with a fresh breeze to speed them, and 24
covered about fifty miles before anchoring by a seasonal river called
Tomerus [Hingol]. There was a lagoon at the outlets of the river, 2
and in the shallows by the shore there were men living in stifling
huts. They were amazed to see ships sailing in, and formed themselves in a battle-line along the shore to repel a landing. They carried 3
thick spears about nine feet long, without iron tips, but the spear-
points had been hardened in fire to comparable effect. There were
about six hundred of them. When Nearchus saw them lined up and 4
ready to resist, he ordered his ships to ride at anchor within range,
so their own bow-shots could reach land: the natives' thick spears
looked effective for close fighting, but there was clearly no fear of
their use as missiles. He selected the most light of foot and lightly 5
armed of his men who were also strong swimmers, and briefed them
to dive in at a given signal and start swimming: as soon as any swim- 6
mer touched bottom and was able to stand in the water, he should
wait for a colleague to come up beside him, and no attack should be
made on the natives until they had a phalanx three rows deep; then
they were to raise the war-cry and charge them at the double. So the 7
men detailed for this operation dived off the ships into the sea simul-
taneously, swam fast, found footing in their proper places, then
formed themselves into a phalanx and charged at the enemy, shouting their battle-cry. The men on ship took up the cry and loosed a
barrage of bow and catapult fire on the natives. Panicked by the flash 8
of the weaponry and the speed of the charge, and with arrows and
other missiles raining down on them, half-naked as they were, the

natives offered no resistance at all, but turned and ran. Some were killed there as they fled and some were captured, but others made
9 their escape into the hills. The prisoners had thick hair on their heads and all over their bodies, and nails like animals' claws. They were said to use their nails like metal tools to slit open fish for consumption and to carve the softer woods: otherwise they used sharp stones for cutting, as they had no iron. As clothes they wore animal hides, or sometimes the thick skins of large fish.

25 The ships were beached here, and any damage repaired. On the sixth day they set out again, and after sailing about thirty miles they reached the furthermost point in Oreitan territory, a place called
2 Malana [Ras Malan]. The Oreitans who live up-country from the sea dress like Indians and are similarly equipped for war, but they speak
3 a different language and there are other differences of culture. The length of the voyage along the coast of the Arabies' territory was about a hundred miles from the original point of departure, and along
4 the Oreitan coast a hundred and sixty miles. Nearchus notes that when they were sailing along Indian land (from Malana on the population is no longer Indian) their shadows did not fall consistently.
5 When they were at sea on a broadly southerly course, they could see their shadows also falling to the south: but when the sun reached
6 midday, everything they saw was shadowless.* Another phenomenon was the stars. Those they were used to seeing high in the sky were now either completely invisible or shining low down on the horizon, and stars which had never set before were now seen setting and
7 immediately rising again. What Nearchus has described strikes me as quite plausible. In Syene in Egypt, when the sun is at its summer solstice, they show a well in which no shadow can be seen at midday:
8 and in Meroë at the same season everything is shadowless. So it seems likely that the same phenomenon obtains in India, given its southerly situation, and most particularly in the Indian Ocean, which faces yet further south. That must suffice on this subject.

26 Next to the Oreitans, in the interior, lived the Gedrosians. Alexander and his army had made their way through this country with great difficulty,* and suffered more hardship here than in all the rest of the campaign put together: I have described this in my larger
2 book. South of the Gedrosians the actual seaboard is inhabited by the so-called Fish-Eaters, and this was the coast along which the fleet sailed. On the first day they put out at about the second watch, and

came in to land at Bagisara, a voyage of sixty miles. There is good 3
anchorage there, and the village of Pasira lies six miles from the sea:
the local inhabitants are called Pasireans. On the next day they set out 4
earlier than usual and sailed round a high, precipitous cape jutting far
out to sea. They dug wells which yielded only a small amount of foul 5
water, and that day they rode at anchor, as there was heavy surf on
the shore. On the following day they put in at Colta after a voyage of 6
twenty miles. They left there at dawn and sailed sixty miles before
coming to anchor at Calima. There was a village near the beach, and
a few palms growing round it with unripe dates on them. About ten
miles from this beach there is an island called Carnine.* The villagers 7
here welcomed Nearchus with gifts of sheep and fish. He says that
the mutton had a fishy taste, like the meat of sea-birds, because there
is no grass in the place and the sheep too feed on fish. On the next day 8
they sailed about twenty miles and moored off a beach with a village
about three miles from the sea: the village was called Cysa, and the
beach Carbis. There they found some small boats suggesting a poor 9
fishing community, but there was no sign of the men, who had fled as
soon as they saw the ships coming in to anchor. There was no food in
the place, and most of their own supplies had been used up, but they
took some goats on board before they sailed away. After rounding a 10
high cape jutting some fifteen miles into the sea, they put into a calm
harbour, where there was water and a population of fishermen. The
harbour was called Mosarna.*

Nearchus tells that from this point on they were joined by a pilot, 27
a Gedrosian called Hydraces, who undertook to bring them as far as
Carmania: from there to the Persian Gulf the going was easier, and
there was better anchorage along that coast. They left Mosarna at 2
night and sailed seventy-five miles to a beach called Balomus. From
there another forty miles to the village of Barna, where there were
many date-palms and a plantation of myrtles and other flowering
shrubs, which the villagers wove into wreaths. There for the first
time they saw cultivated trees, and human beings living a not entirely
animal existence. From there they sailed on along the coast for twenty 3
miles and put in at Dendrobosa, where the ships had a rough ride at
anchor. Leaving there at midnight they came to the harbour of 4
Cophas after a voyage of about forty miles. There were fishermen 5
living here, with miserable little boats which they did not row in the
Greek way, with the oars in rowlocks, but like a river canoe, striking

into the water first on one side then on the other, like men digging the
6   earth. There was plenty of fresh water in the harbour. They set off
from here round about the first watch, and after covering some eighty
miles put in at Cyiza, where there was a deserted beach and heavy
surf: so the ships rode at anchor, and they had their supper on board.
7   *From there they sailed another fifty miles and reached a small town
8   built on a hill not far from the shore. Nearchus reckoned that the land
must be cultivated, and told Archias the son of Anaxidotus (a distinguished Macedonian from Pella, who was sailing with him) that they
9   had to take the place by surprise: he did not suppose that the inhabitants would voluntarily provision the army, and capture by force was
out of the question, as that would require a lengthy siege, and they
were already out of food. He deduced that there was arable farming
10 from the deep piles of straw they could see near the beach.* This
agreed, Nearchus ordered the rest of the fleet to make overt preparations as if for departure, supervised by Archias, while he was left
behind with a single ship and set off as if he just wanted to have a look
at the town.

28   As he approached the walls the inhabitants came out to welcome
him with gifts of tunny-fish baked in clay pots (these people were the
most westerly of the Fish-Eaters and the first they had seen cooking
2   their fish) and a few pastries and dates from the palms. Nearchus said
he was delighted to accept these gifts, but would like to see round
3   their town: and so they let him come in. Once inside the gates he told
two of his archers to secure the postern, while he himself with two
others and the interpreter climbed up on the wall on the seaward side
and gave the agreed signal to Archias* and his men (this had been
arranged in advance: Nearchus was to give a signal, Archias to see
4   what it meant and take action as instructed). When the Macedonians
saw the signal they quickly beached their ships, jumped out into the
sea, and came on at the double. Aghast at what was happening, the
5   natives ran to fetch their arms. The interpreter with Nearchus proclaimed that they must give the army corn if they wanted to save their
city. They said they had none, and tried to attack the men on the wall,
but the archers with Nearchus, shooting from above, were able to
6   keep them back. When they could see that their town was already
captured and in imminent danger of enslavement, the natives finally
begged Nearchus not to destroy the town but to take what corn they
7   had and go away. Nearchus ordered Archias to seize the gates and the

wall on either side, and sent some men with the natives to check they were coming clean about their stock of corn. They showed plenty of 8 meal ground from cooked fish, but only a little wheat and barley. In fact their bread was made from this fish-meal, and wheat loaves were for them a delicacy. Shown what there was, the fleet took on board 9 what corn was available and finally put back out to sea, coming to anchor by a headland which the local inhabitants held sacred to Helios, the sun-god. The headland was called Bageia.

They set out from there about midnight and sailed a hundred miles 29 to the harbour of Talmena, where there was good anchorage, and thereafter another forty miles to Canasis, a deserted town where they found a well dug and some wild date-palms growing. They cut out the hearts of the palms and ate them, as the army had run out of food. Hunger was now taking its toll on them, and they sailed on all day 2 and night, finally coming to anchor off a deserted beach. Morale was 3 so low that Nearchus was afraid that if the men disembarked they might desert ship, and so he deliberately kept the fleet anchored out at sea. Putting out again they covered about seventy-five miles before 4 anchoring at Canate, where there is a beach with shallow channels of fresh water. From there they sailed eighty miles to anchor at Taä. 5 There were some miserable small villages on the coast, but the inhabitants had fled. The men found a little corn there, and dates from the palms: they butchered the seven camels they caught and ate their meat. Setting out just before dawn they sailed thirty miles and 6 anchored at Dagaseira, where some nomad tribe was living. Putting 7 out from there they sailed non-stop all night and day, and after a voyage of a hundred and ten miles finally sailed past the Fish-Eater peoples, in whose land they had suffered badly from lack of basic supplies. They did not moor close to land, as there was a long stretch 8 of surf, but rode at anchor out to sea. The total length of the voyage along the coast of the Fish-Eaters was a little more than a thousand miles.*

As their name denotes, these Fish-Eaters live on fish. Few of them 9 actually go out fishing, as few have made boats for that purpose or learnt the techniques of catching fish in the sea, but for the most part they get their fish from the receding tide. For this they make nets, 10 usually some three hundred and fifty yards long, which they weave from the bark of the date-palm, twisting it into something like twine. When the sea recedes and exposes the shore, the areas of shore left 11

dry usually have no fish on them, but where there are hollows some
water remains with an enormous number of fish in it, mostly small,
but some larger fish too. They catch these by throwing their nets over

12 them. The tenderest fish they eat raw, straight out of the water. The
larger and tougher fish they dry in the sun, then grind the desiccated

13 flesh into flour and bake bread or cakes from it. Even their flocks are
fed on the dried fish, as the country has no green fields and does not

14 grow grass. There are plenty of places where they also catch crayfish,
oysters, and mussels, from which, with the salt found there in natural

15 deposits, they make a sort of sauce. Those who inhabit barren areas
without trees or cultivated crops have fish products as their sole diet,
but a few sow a little land with corn, and make some bread to accom-

16 pany the fish which is still their main food. The wealthiest among
them have houses made out of the bones salvaged from beached
whales and used like beams of wood, with doors constructed from
any flat bones they can find: but the poorer people, which is most of
them, have huts made from the backbones of ordinary fish.

30   Huge whales live in the outer ocean, and much larger fish than in

2 our own inland sea. Nearchus says that when they were sailing along
from Cyiza, at about dawn they were astonished to see water being

3 blown up from the sea with the force of a waterspout. They asked the
pilots what it was and what caused it: they replied that it was whales
spouting up the seawater as they swam. The sailors had been so star-

4 tled that the oars dropped from their hands, but Nearchus went up
and down to reassure and encourage them, and whenever he subsequently sailed past some whales he ordered the ships to turn in line
abreast as if to attack them, and had the men raise a shout with each
crash of the oars, increasing their stroke-rate and making a great deal

5 of noise. So the men took heart and made this concerted move at a
given signal. As they closed on the creatures they shouted at the top
of their voices, the trumpets sounded the signal, and the rowers kept

6 up the maximum possible din with their oars. So the whales, now in
view at the bows of the ships, took fright and dived down into the
depths, surfacing behind the ships a little later with more great spouts

7 over a wide area of sea. The sailors clapped at this unexpected deliverance and were full of praise for Nearchus' bold ingenuity.

8   Some of these whales beach themselves at various points along the
coast and are then stranded in the shallows when the tide goes out:
and others are driven ashore by fierce storms. They die and rot, the

flesh falling away to leave the bones the natives use for their houses. The large rib-bones serve as the main structural beams, and the 9 smaller bones as rafters: the jawbones are used as door-frames. That is the size of these creatures, many of them reaching a length of a hundred and fifty feet.

While they were sailing along the coast of the Fish-Eaters' country 31 they heard a story about an uninhabited island lying some ten miles off the mainland hereabouts. The locals said it was sacred to Helios 2 and called Nosala. No one would ever deliberately land on it, and anyone who did put in there in ignorance of the island's reputation immediately vanished. Nearchus says that one of his corvettes with 3 an Egyptian crew did vanish near this island, and the expedition's pilots were in no doubt that the disappearance of ship and crew must be because they had put in to the island in all ignorance. He sent a 4 triaconter round the island, with orders to sail in close without making a landing and to keep calling out to the men, calling by name on the helmsman and any other crew members whose names they knew. As there was no answer, Nearchus says that he himself then sailed to 5 the island and forced his reluctant crew to put in: he then went ashore and proved the story about the island a baseless myth. They heard of 6 another story in currency about this island, that one of the Nereids* lived there (her name was not told): she would have sex with anyone visiting the island, then turn him from man to fish and throw him into the sea. Helios lost patience with the Nereid and told her to leave 7 the island. She agreed to move elsewhere, and begged him to reverse the effect she had had. Helios consented, and out of pity for the men 8 she had turned into fish turned them back again into human beings: and these were the progenitors of the Fish-Eater race still extant in Alexander's time. Nearchus proves these stories false, but I wish he 9 had not made such a laboured disquisition of it. These things are easy enough to refute, and I consider it tedious to repeat all the old stories only to prove their falsity.

The interior above the Fish-Eaters is inhabited by the 32 Gedrosians—poor, sandy country in which Alexander's army and Alexander himself suffered all that hardship, as described in my earlier book. The fleet now passed Fish-Eater country and put in to the 2 Carmanian coast, though where they first stopped in Carmania there was a long line of rough surf extending out to sea, and they had to ride it out at anchor. From there on they no longer sailed due west, 3

but kept the ships' bows pointing more north-west,* and there
was a corresponding change in the country past which they sailed.
4 Carmania is better wooded and more fertile than the land of the Fish-
Eaters and the Oreitans, with more green fields and well watered.
5 They anchored at an inhabited place in Carmania called Badis, with
plantations of many sorts of cultivated trees (except the olive) and
6 good vines: the land also grew corn. Putting out from there they
sailed on for eighty miles and anchored off a deserted beach. They
could see a long promontory jutting far out into the ocean, which
7 seemed about a day's sail distant. Those with local knowledge said
that this extended promontory was part of Arabia, and was called
Maceta* [Ras Musandam]: it was from here, they said, that cinnamon
8 and other such spices were exported to Assyria. In my view, and that
of Nearchus, the bay formed between this beach where the fleet was
riding at anchor and the jutting promontory they had sighted opposite opens out into the interior, in what would seem to be the Red
9 Sea. When they saw this promontory Onesicritus proposed making
10 course for it, to avoid a wearisome row all round the bay. Nearchus
replied that it was foolish of Onesicritus to forget Alexander's pur-
11 pose in sending out this expedition. It was not through any doubt
of his ability to bring the whole army safely through on foot that
Alexander had commissioned this voyage, but from a desire to explore
the whole coastline along the route, the harbours and the islets, to sail
round every indenting bay, to gather information about all the coastal
settlements, and to find out what land was fertile and what was desert.
12 So they had no business to abort the enterprise when they had nearly
reached the end of their labours, especially as they no longer faced
any shortage of supplies for the voyage. Since that promontory ran to
the south, he feared they would find the land there desert, waterless,
13 and burning hot. These arguments prevailed, and I think it abun-
dantly clear that Nearchus saved the expedition* by this decision, as
it is generally reported that this promontory and the surrounding
country are completely desert and devoid of water.
33   *So in fact when they left this beach they sailed on hugging the
coast, and after a voyage of some seventy miles anchored at another
2 beach, called Neoptana. Setting off again before dawn they sailed
another ten miles and came to anchor by the river Anamis [Minab]
at a place called Harmozia.* Here at long last there was produce of
all kinds in abundance, except that there were no olives growing.

They disembarked and enjoyed a blessed relaxation after all that *3*
hardship, thinking back over what they had suffered at sea and along
the coast of the Fish-Eaters, and remembering desolate country, men
living like animals, and their own constant shortages. Some of them *4*
left the main camp and went up inland to scout for this or that. Here *5*
they sighted a man wearing a Greek cloak and otherwise dressed like
a Greek, who turned out to speak Greek also. The first to see him said
that they burst into tears at the apparent miracle of meeting a Greek
and hearing Greek spoken after all the miseries they had suffered.
They asked where he had come from and who he was. He said that he *6*
had wandered out from Alexander's camp, and the camp and
Alexander himself were not far away. Whooping and clapping they *7*
brought the man to Nearchus. He gave Nearchus a full report, and
said that the camp and the king were five days' journey away from the
sea. He undertook to introduce Nearchus to the district governor, *8*
and did so: in consultation with him Nearchus planned the journey
inland to meet the king. For the time being they returned to the ships, *9*
but at dawn Nearchus had the ships pulled up on shore, for repairs to
be made to any damaged in the course of the voyage, and also because
he intended to leave the bulk of his force stationed here. So he had a *10*
double stockade thrown round the dock, with an earth wall and a
deep ditch running from the river bank to the beach where his ships
had been dragged on shore.

While Nearchus was seeing to these arrangements the district *34*
governor, aware that Alexander was deeply worried about this expedition, thought that he would surely win a great reward from
Alexander if he were the first to bring him the news that the expeditionary force was safe and Nearchus would soon be coming into the
king's presence. So he rode off by the shortest route and announced *2*
to Alexander that Nearchus was there and coming up from the ships.
Though unconvinced of the truth of the report, Alexander naturally
expressed delight at the news. But as day succeeded day and the lapse *3*
of time from that first news confirmed Alexander's doubts of its credibility, as the search parties, sent out one after the other to find *4*
Nearchus and escort him in, either went a little way, found no one,
and returned empty-handed, or else went further on, missed Nearchus
and his group, and then themselves failed to return—in the end *5*
Alexander lost patience and had the man arrested for bringing him a
worthless report and raising empty hopes of joy which only served to

deepen his distress: and his look and mood revealed what a painful
6 blow this had been. In the meantime, however, some of those sent to
search for Nearchus, with horses and wagons to transport him and
his men, did actually come across Nearchus on the road, with Archias
and five or six others (that was the extent of his group making the
7 journey inland). At this meeting they did not recognize either
Nearchus or Archias, such was the great change in their appearance—long-haired, squalid, caked in brine, flesh shrivelled, pale
8 from lack of sleep and every other hardship. Nearchus and his company asked where they could find Alexander. The search party told
9 them where he was and began to drive on. Archias, though, worked it
out and said to Nearchus: 'My guess, Nearchus, is that these men
following the same road as us through desert country must have been
10 sent out specifically to find us. No surprise that they failed to recognize us—we are in such poor shape as to be unrecognizable. So let
us tell them who we are, and ask them why they are headed this way.'
11 Nearchus agreed that this was a sensible plan. So they asked where
the others were going, and they said that they were looking for
12 Nearchus and the men in his fleet. Nearchus said, 'Well, I am
Nearchus right here, and this is Archias. Take us to him, then, and
we will make our report on the expedition to Alexander.'

35   So the soldiers helped them onto the wagons and began driving
back. Some of the search party, eager to be first with the news, ran
ahead and told Alexander: 'Nearchus is here, and Archias with him.
Five others too. They are being brought to you right now.' They
could not, though, give any information in answer to his questions
2 about the fleet as a whole, and it was this that drove Alexander to
conclude that these few had been saved by some quirk of fortune, but
the whole of the rest of the expedition had been lost, so his emotion
was not so much joy at the survival of Nearchus and Archias as grief
3 at the loss of his entire force. Talk had gone no further than that when
Nearchus and Archias came in. It was some time before Alexander
could just about recognize them, and the sight of them with hair
uncut and squalid clothing served only to confirm his worst fears for
4 the whole naval expedition. He gave his right hand to Nearchus and
led him away from his Companions and guardsmen, then began to
5 weep, and wept long.* Eventually he recovered and said: 'Well, at
least we have you and Archias back safe among us, and that can give
me some consolation amid the total disaster. Tell me, how exactly did

the ships and the army in them come to grief?' Nearchus replied: 6
'Your majesty, your ships are safe and your army too. We have come
here to bring you the news of their safety.' At this Alexander wept yet 7
more, as the survival of the fleet had seemed beyond hope. He asked
where the ships were moored. 'They are here,' said Nearchus, 'pulled
up on shore at the mouth of the river Anamis and being repaired.'
Alexander then swore by the Greek Zeus and the Libyan Ammon 8
that this news had given him greater pleasure than his whole trium-
phant progress through Asia,* as his anguish at the loss of the fleet
threatened to outweigh all previous successes.

   *When the district governor, arrested by Alexander for a suppos- 36
edly false report, saw Nearchus there in person, he fell at his knees in
supplication and said: 'I am the one who brought Alexander the news 2
of your safe arrival—and now look what has happened to me.' So
Nearchus interceded for the man, and Alexander released him.
Alexander now set about making thank-offerings for the survival of 3
the expedition, sacrificing to Zeus the Saviour, Heracles, Apollo the
Protector, Poseidon, and all the other gods of the sea: and he held
festival games* with competitions in athletics and the performing
arts, and put on a parade. Nearchus was one of the leaders of the
parade, and the troops showered him with ribbons and flowers. At 4
the end of all this, Alexander said to him: 'Nearchus, I will not have
you exposed to danger and hardship any longer, so somebody else
will take command of the fleet from now on until he can bring it in to
Susa.' Nearchus replied: 'Your majesty, it is both my wish and my 5
duty to obey you in all things. But if it might be your wish to show
me some favour, please let it not be that. Allow me to command the
expedition through to the end, until I bring your ships safe to Susa.
I would not want you to have entrusted me with all the dangerous and 6
difficult work, only to relieve me of the final easy run and give this
imminent triumph to another man.' Alexander stopped him in 7
mid-flow to acknowledge the debt of gratitude he owed him, and in
that recognition sent him back to the fleet with a detachment of
troops to escort him—only a small force, as the route lay through
friendly territory.

   Even so, his journey down to the sea was not without problems. 8
The surrounding barbarians had gathered their forces and occupied
the dominant positions in Carmania, as their previous satrap had
been put to death on Alexander's orders, and the newly appointed

9 successor, Tlepolemus,* had not yet established firm control. So two or three times on the same day the troops with Nearchus had to fight off successive groups of barbarians who appeared out of nowhere, and there was no respite until with much difficulty they just managed to reach safety on the coast. Once there, Nearchus sacrificed to Zeus the Saviour and held athletic games.

37 *When Nearchus had completed the religious formalities they finally put out to sea. They coasted past a rocky, uninhabited island and after sailing thirty miles from their starting-point came to anchor

2 at another island, this one large and inhabited. The desert island was called Organa [Hormoz], and the one where they anchored Oaracta [Qeshm]: it was eighty miles long, with vines, date-palms, and corn-fields. The governor of the island, Mazenes, volunteered to act as

3 their pilot and sailed with them all the way to Susa. They said that the tomb of the first ruler of this region could be seen on this island. His name was Erythres,* and the sea was called Erythraean [Red Sea] after him. They put out from that part of the island and sailed on,

4 coasting about twenty miles along its length before anchoring again off the same island. From there they could see another island, about four miles distant from this large one, which was said to be sacred to

5 Poseidon and inviolate. Setting out towards dawn, they were caught in an ebb-tide so fierce that three of the ships grounded and were stuck fast on dry land, and the rest only just managed to drive through

6 the surf to the safety of deep water. The grounded ships were refloated by the next incoming tide, and on the following day joined the main

7 fleet where they had put in after a voyage of forty miles. This anchor-

8 age was at another island about thirty miles off the mainland. They sailed on from there just before dawn, passing a desert island called Pylora on their left, and anchored at [. . .], a destitute little township with nothing to offer except water and fish: the soil was poor, so these

9 people too were fish-eaters out of necessity. They took on water there and sailed another thirty miles to put in at Tarsias, which is a cape

10 running out into the sea. From there a voyage of thirty miles took them to Cataea [Kish], a low-lying uninhabited island said to be

11 sacred to Hermes and Aphrodite. Every year the local people dedicate sheep and goats to Hermes and Aphrodite and send them over to the island: they could be seen there living as wild animals now after so long without human tendance.

38 So far they were off Carmania: from here on it was Persian country.

The length of the voyage along the Carmanian coast was three hundred and seventy miles. (The Carmanians, being close neighbours of the Persians, have a similar way of life and there is no difference in their military arms and equipment.) Putting out from the sacred 2 island, and sailing now along the coast of Persis, they came to anchor after a voyage of forty miles at a place called Ilas, where a harbour is created by a small uninhabited island called Caïcandrus. At dawn 3 they sailed on to anchor at another island, this one inhabited, where Nearchus says there was pearl-fishing like that in the Indian Ocean: they sailed about four miles round the island's promontory to find their anchorage. Their next mooring was off a high mountain called 4 Ochus, in a fine harbour where some fishermen were living. From 5 there they sailed forty-five miles to anchor at Apostana, where many other boats were moored and there was a village six miles up from the sea. Setting out from there at night, they sailed into a gulf populated 6 with many villages—a voyage of forty miles. They came to anchor by some foothills covered with date-palms and every sort of fruit-tree which grows in Greece. They put out from here and sailed about 7 sixty miles along the coast to Gogana, an inhabited area, and anchored at the outlets of the seasonal river called Areon. This was not an easy manoeuvre, as the entrance at the river mouth was constricted by the shallows created on either side by the ebbing tide. Their next anchorage, after travelling some eighty miles, was at the mouth of another 8 river called Sitacus [Mand]. This was tricky too, and in fact the whole of this voyage along the coast of Persis was a succession of shallows, surf, and lagoons. At the Sitacus they found waiting for them a large 9 supply of corn stockpiled there on the king's orders to keep them provisioned. They hauled the ships on land, and stayed there for twenty-one days in all, repairing any ships which were damaged and carrying out maintenance on the rest.

Setting off again from there, they sailed seventy-five miles to reach 39 another inhabited area and the town of Hieratis. They anchored in a canal cut from the river to the sea which was called Heratemis. At 2 sunrise they sailed on to a seasonal river called Padargus. This whole area, called Mesambria [Bushēhr], forms a peninsula which was rich in orchards growing every sort of fruit-tree. From Mesambria they 3 set out to sail about twenty miles further along to Taoce, and came to anchor at the river Granis. There was a Persian royal palace near here, some twenty miles inland from the mouth of the river.

4 Nearchus says that on this leg of the voyage they saw a whale stranded on the shore, and some of his men sailed in to measure it. They
5 reported its length as seventy-five feet,* and said that its skin was scaly and up to eighteen inches thick, encrusted with oysters and other shellfish and a thick growth of seaweed. Nearchus adds that they noticed many dolphins near the whale, and these dolphins were
6 larger than those found in the Mediterranean. Sailing on again, they covered twenty miles before putting in to a good harbour by the sea-
7 sonal river Rhogonis. From there they sailed forty miles and camped by another seasonal river called Brizana. Anchorage was problematic here, as there were shallows, pounding surf, and reefs poking out
8 above sea-level. They waited for the flood tide before coming in to anchor, but when the water retreated again the ships were left high and dry. They were able to sail out when the flood tide duly
9 returned, and their next anchorage was at a river called Arosis,* which Nearchus says was the largest of all the rivers running into the ocean on this section of their voyage.

40 Thus far was Persian territory, but from here on it was Susiana (which is bordered inland by an independent people called the Uxians, described as brigands in my other book).* The length of the voyage along the coast of Persis was four hundred and forty miles.
2 The usual account divides Persis into three climate zones.* The coastal area adjoining the Red Sea is sandy and too hot for cultiva-
3 tion. The next zone to the north has a temperate climate. The country here is lush with water-meadows, extensively planted with vines
4 and all other fruits except the olive, and full of every sort of park and garden; rivers of clear water run through it, and there are lakes, so it is a good habitat for all sorts of water-birds, and good grazing too for horses and other draught animals; many areas are wooded, and there
5 is plenty of game. Further north still the country becomes wintry and snowy. In this context Nearchus tells of some envoys from the Black Sea who met Alexander, to his surprise, as he was travelling through Persis: they had come no great distance* at all, and they told Alexander
6 how short the journey was. I have mentioned the Uxians as bordering Susiana: then there are the Mardians (another brigand people)* on the border of Persis, and the Cossaeans* on the border of Media.
7 Alexander had pacified all of these tribes, catching them with inva-sions in winter, when they thought no one could get anywhere near
8 them. He followed this with the foundation of settled townships,* to

turn the people from nomads into farmers working the land, and to give them too much to lose from constant in-fighting.

So from now on the fleet was passing the coast of Susiana. Nearchus 9 says that he cannot report this part of the voyage in as much detail as before, other than the landfalls and the distances covered. This was 10 because the shoreline here was mostly shoals which extended far out to sea with consequent surf and gave no secure anchorage: so most of their travel was in the open sea.

They set out from the river mouth where they had camped at the 11 border of Persis, taking on board five days' supply of water, as the pilots warned that there was no water on the route. After travelling 41 fifty miles they came to anchor at the mouth of a lake called Cataderbis, which was full of fish: a small island lay at the mouth, called Margastana. They left here towards dawn and passed through a 2 stretch of shallows in single file. Poles driven in on either side marked the channel, just as in the narrow strait between the island of Leucas and Acarnania* there are clear markers to help navigators avoid grounding their ships in the shallows. The difference is that the 3 Leucas shallows are sandy-bottomed, so ships which run aground can be quickly righted, whereas here there is deep viscous mud on either side of the channel, and no means of rescuing a ship stuck there—bargepoles are of no use (they sink into the mud), and it is 4 impossible for the men to jump out and push the ship off into the navigable channel, as they would find themselves up to their chests in mud. They made this difficult transit, then, and sailed a total of sixty 5 miles before anchoring and turning their thoughts to supper on board, each ship catering for itself. They sailed on, now out in deep 6 water, through that night and the following day until late afternoon, covering ninety miles and coming to anchor at the mouth of the Euphrates, near a village in Babylonia called Diridotis (this is the 7 depot to which the spice-merchants bring frankincense from Gerrha and the other aromatics produced in Arabia). From the mouth of the 8 Euphrates to Babylon,* Nearchus says, is a voyage of about three hundred and thirty miles.

*Here they received information that Alexander was on his way to 42 Susa. So they travelled back the way they had come, in order to sail up the river Pasitigris [Karun] and meet Alexander. On this return 2 stretch they had the Susian coast on their left, and sailed round the lake into which the Tigris runs. The Tigris flows from Armenia past 3

the once large and prosperous city of Ninus [Nineveh], and gives the
area between it and the Euphrates the name of Mesopotamia ('the
4 land between the rivers'). The voyage up from the lake to the river
itself is sixty miles: at that point there is a Susian village called Aginis,
fifty miles from Susa. The distance along the Susian coast to the
5 mouth of the Pasitigris is two hundred miles. They then sailed up the
Pasitigris, passing now through populated and prosperous country.
They anchored some fifteen miles up-river to await the return of the
men Nearchus had sent out to establish the whereabouts of the king.
6 For his part Nearchus made sacrifices to the Saviour gods and put on
a festival of athletic games, and there was a holiday atmosphere
7 enjoyed by all members of the expedition. When news came of
Alexander's imminent approach, they sailed on again up-river and
anchored by the pontoon bridge* over which Alexander was going to
8 take his army on their way to Susa—and here the two forces met.
Alexander offered sacrifices in thanks for the preservation of his ships
and men, and games were held: wherever Nearchus appeared* among
9 the troops they showered him with flowers and ribbons. Here too
Nearchus and Leonnatus had golden crowns conferred on them by
Alexander, Nearchus for the safe return of the fleet, and Leonnatus
for his victory over the Oreitans and their neighbouring tribes.
10 This, then, is the story of how Alexander's fleet came safely through
from the start of its voyage at the mouths of the Indus.

43 *On the right of the Red Sea below Babylonia lies the bulk of
Arabia, a country which extends as far as the sea facing Phoenicia and
Palestinian Syria, and to the west borders Mediterranean Egypt.
2 A gulf running up beside Egypt from the Great Sea makes it clear
that, as far as continuity with the Great Sea is concerned, it would be
possible to sail round from Babylon into this gulf which leads to
3 Egypt. But in fact the heat and the desert conditions are such that
no one of any nationality has made this coastal circumnavigation,*
4 though there is some traffic across the open sea. The survivors of
Cambyses' army* who reached Susa from Egypt, and the troops sent
by Ptolemy the son of Lagus through Arabia to Seleucus* Nicator at
5 Babylon spent eight days in all crossing a narrow neck of land through
waterless desert, riding fast on camels with water for themselves carried on the camels: they travelled at night, as it was impossible to
6 stand the heat of the day out in the open. This illustrates why the
country beyond here, which as I have said forms a neck extending

between the Arabian Gulf [Red Sea] and the Red Sea [Persian Gulf],
is quite uninhabited, when its more northerly parts are nothing but
sand and desert. True, men have set out from the Egyptian side of the *7*
Arabian Gulf and sailed round most of Arabia in the quest to reach
the sea leading to Persis and Susa, but have had to turn back when
they got as far round the Arabian coast as their on-board supply of
water allowed. And although the men sent out by Alexander from *8*
Babylon* to sail as far as they could down the right-hand side of the
Red Sea to reconnoitre the lie of the land did investigate some islands
along their route, and doubtless put in here and there on the Arabian
mainland, no one has been able to round and double back along the *9*
far side of the promontory which Nearchus says they sighted running
out into the sea opposite Carmania. I am sure that if there had been *10*
the possibility of a navigable route along here, Alexander's restless
ambition would have found a way to prove its existence. Hannon* the *11*
Libyan set out from Carthage with Libya on his left and sailed out
beyond the Pillars of Heracles into the Outer Sea, continuing his
voyage then in an easterly direction for a total of thirty-five days:
but when he eventually turned south he met a number of crippling *12*
obstacles—lack of water, burning heat, streams of lava gushing into
the sea. The city of Cyrene lies in one of the more desert regions of *13*
Libya, but its site is green and soft, well-watered, full of woods and
meadows, and supports extensive cultivation and grazing—at least as
far as the silphium fields: the interior beyond the silphium belt is
sand and desert.

   This, then, can stand as the account I have written. Like its pre- *14*
decessor, it has its bearing on the history of Alexander the son of
Philip, Alexander of Macedon.

APPENDIX I

THE MACEDONIAN ARMY:
STRUCTURES AND TERMINOLOGY

HERE and in Appendix II, as in the translation and notes, capital letters are used to distinguish terms used by Arrian to designate specific titles or ranks from cases where he uses the same terms in a more general sense: thus, for example, we mark out the seven top-ranking Bodyguards from the humbler functional bodyguards. But some terms, for example 'companion', have more than two connotations, and it is not always clear which usage Arrian intends. Arrian may also sacrifice consistency to stylistic variation.

1. THE MACEDONIAN ARMY

The basic framework set out here starts with the situation that obtained when Alexander invaded Asia Minor in 334. But much changed over the next eleven years as the lines of communication lengthened, men were killed, or became unfit for front line service. The last sizeable force of reinforcements from Macedonia arrived in the winter of 329/8 (4.7.2 with Curtius 7.10.11–12). Thus Alexander became more dependent on troops recruited in Asia. Furthermore Alexander was a supreme innovator, willing to experiment and not inhibited by tradition when operational needs required ad hoc measures. Thus by 323 the command structure of the units with Alexander was quite different from what it had been in 334, and indeed presumably from the structure still preserved by the units which had been left in Macedon with Antipater.

As the evidence is generally partial and inconsistent the reconstructions offered here are tentative and open to debate.

A. Cavalry

(i) The Companion cavalry (Hetairoi)

Organized in seven squadrons (3.11.8), recruited territorially (1.2.5, 1.12.7, 2.9.3), each squadron (*ile*) with a complement of 225 men (if the seven squadrons, plus the squadron of elite cavalry, made up the initial force of 1800 Macedonian cavalry (Diodorus Siculus 17.17.4)). The order of precedence of the squadrons rotated day by day (1.14.6).

At the end of 331 Alexander incorporated the newly arrived reinforcements—some 500 Macedonian cavalrymen—into these units without regard for the region of Macedonia from which they had been recruited, and divided each squadron into two companies (*lochoi*: 3.16.11; the 'tetrarchy' of cavalry at 3.18.5 may represent an ad hoc formation of four such companies).

Philotas [4] was overall commander of the Companion cavalry, and after his death in late 330 the command was divided between Hephaestion and Cleitus [2] the Black, each with the title Captain of Horse (*hipparch*: 3.27.4; cf. 7.14.10). After the murder of Cleitus in 328 (4.8.1–9) no single grand commander of the cavalry is attested, and the cavalry was by now already divided into eight *hipparchies* (3.29.7, 4.4.7, 4.22.7 with 24.1, 5.11.3, 5.12.2, 5.16.3, 5.21.5, 5.22.6, 6.6.4 and 7.2).

The *hipparchy* was apparently made up of two squadrons (*ilai*: 6.21.3 and 6.27.6), each further divided into two companies (6.27.6, 7.24.4). Asian cavalrymen were gradually integrated into the Companions, perhaps from well before 324 (7.6.4 and 7.8.2), which, together with the reinforcements of late 331, would explain the increase in the total number of cavalrymen.

(ii) The Elite Corps

Referred to as the royal squadron (as at 1.18.3, 2.5.9, 3.1.4, 3.8.1, 3.11.8, 3.13.1, 3.18.5 and 3.19.8), and after 331 styled the *agema* (4.24.1, 5.12.2, 5.13.4, 5.22.6, 6.2.2, 6.21.3, 6.22.1, 7.6.4). Again the complement was initially 225 men. A second corps, made up of Persian cavalrymen, was established in 324 (7.11.3).

(iii) The advance guards

Or light cavalry (*prodromoi*), probably all Macedonians, in four or more squadrons (1.12.7, 1.14.6). Arrian seems to refer to them as *sarissa*-bearers (*sarissophoroi*) at 1.13.1, 1.14.1, 4.4.6; and at 3.12.3 Arrian mentions Aretes as the commander of the *prodromoi*, while Curtius (4.15.13) in the same context styles these men *sarissa*-bearers (meaning lancers, the cavalry *sarissa* being shorter than the infantry version). The *prodromoi* are styled Scouts by Heckel (*Quintus Curtius Rufus: The History of Alexander*, translated by J. Yardley, with an introduction and notes by W. Heckel (Harmondsworth: Penguin Books, revised edn. 2004)), but they seem to have functioned more generally in the role of light cavalry (1.14.1 and 6, 2.9.2, 3.7.7, 3.12.3, 3.18.2, 3.20.1–21.2). They are not mentioned after 329, and may have been absorbed into the Companion cavalry, and replaced by the mounted javelin-men (*hippakontistai*: 3.24.1, 4.25.6 and 26.4; cf. 4.4.7).

B. Infantry

(i) The Companion Infantry (Pezhetairoi)

In six brigades (1.14.2-3, 2.8.3-4, 3.11.9-10), which were recruited territorially (3.16.11). Each brigade (regularly styled a *taxis*, as at 1.8.1, but *phalanx* at 1.14.2–3, 5.20.3 and 21.5) was made up of 1,500 men, ranked in files, each file (*dekas*) with a notional strength of ten men. By 326 the number of brigades had risen to seven.

Men in three of the original six brigades are sometimes referred to as the Close Companions (as Heckel translates *asthetairoi*, thus rejecting the proposal of 'Townsmen Companions') (2.23.2, 4.22.7 with 23.1, 5.22.6, 6.6.1 and 21.3). One theory is that these three brigades were all recruited in Upper Macedonia; another is that the Close Companions were men from any of the regular brigades who had been 'decorated' for particular bravery in action, and who could be selected to take part in an operation in an ad hoc formation.

The brigade commanders are styled *strategoi* (generals: as at 1.28.3, 2.7.3) or *taxiarchs* (brigade commanders: 2.16.8, 3.9.6, 7.9.8).

The brigades were divided into companies (*lochoi*: as at 2.10.2, 3.9.6, 4.2.1, 6.27.6, or *pentacosiarchies* (units of 500 men): Curtius 5.2.3).

At the end of 331 the complement of each brigade was raised to 2,000, and the brigade was divided into two battalions (*chiliarchies*, units of 1,000 men). In a competition staged in Sittacene (Curtius 5.2.2–5, read with Arr. 3.16.11), Alexander selected officers to command these new divisions in an open process that allowed the candidates to compete for the favour of the ordinary troops. The battalion commanders (*chiliarchs*) ranked above the company commanders, but below the brigade commanders.

Major changes were made after Alexander's return to Susa in 324:

(a) Some 10,000 Macedonian veterans were discharged, and most of these would have been from the Companion Infantry (7.12.1);

(b) 30,000 young Persians, whose recruitment and training in the Macedonian manner had begun in 327, reached Alexander at Susa (7.6.1) and were set up as a separate force, referred to as the Next Generation (*Epigonoi*);

(c) Some 20,000 seasoned Persian troops were brought to Babylon in 323 to join Alexander's army (7.23.1). He then incorporated the infantrymen into the Companion Infantry, and in the same context he anticipated the eventual enrolment of the sons of mixed unions between Macedonians and Asian women (7.12.2 with Justin 12.4.2–8).

The complement of the smallest unit in the Companion Infantry, the file, was now increased from ten to sixteen men, each file made up of twelve Persian privates and four Macedonian non-commissioned officers (7.23.3–4; cf. 7.29.4). Thus the command structure of the brigade as a whole probably was:

brigade commander (*strategos* or *taxiarch*);

two battalion commanders (*chiliarchs*, as at 7.25.6);
four company commanders (*pentacosiarchs*, as at 7.25.6);
twenty centurions (each in charge of a century (*hekatostys*): 6.27.6,
  7.24.4);
about 120 file commanders (*decadarchs*): sergeants;

and in each file:

one double-pay NCO (*dimoirites*): corporal (cf. Abreas
  at 6.9.3);
two file officers (10-stater men): junior corporals;
twelve Asian 'privates'.

(ii) The foot guard

The *Hypaspists* (meaning literally 'shield-bearers', as at 1.1.11, 1.5.10,
1.6.6 and 9, 1.8.3–4, 1.14.2, 2.8.3, 3.17.2, 3.18.5, 3.21.8, 3.23.3, 4.30.3
and 5, 5.13.4); later called the Silver Shields (*argyraspids*), as anachronisti-
cally at 7.11.3. They constituted the elite infantry, and within this elite the
best men were enrolled in the royal guard (the *agema* of 1.1.11, 1.8.3–4,
2.8.3, 3.11.9, 5.2.5, 7.29.4; the royal bodyguards of 3.17.2; the royal *agema* of 5.13.4, or the Royal Shield-bearers of 4.24.10, and perhaps 3.13.6).
The picture is confusing because of the range of applications of the term
hypaspist.

The total strength seems to have been 3,000, which rose to 4,000 with
the arrival of reinforcements at the end of 331, when Alexander increased
the number of battalions (*chiliarchies*) from three to four, each of 1,000
men (cf. 3.29.7, 4.30.5–6, 5.23.7), and introduced a new level of command
by subdividing each battalion into two companies of 500, under *pentacosiarchs*.

At court they served as a (ceremonial?) bodyguard (4.8.8).

At Susa in 324, Alexander incorporated into the foot guard, but as a
separate battalion, 1,000 picked Persians (7.11.3, 7.29.4 with Diodorus
Siculus 17.110.1).

(iii) Light-armed troops

The *psiloi*: 1.7.9, 4.4.6.
Macedonians may have served as:

archers (*toxotai*: 1.2.4–5, 1.7.9, 3.12.2);
javelin-men (*akontistai*: 3.12.3, 3.13.5);
slingers (*sphendonetai*: 1.2.4);
mounted archers (*hippotoxotai*: 5.14.3);
mounted javelin-men (*hippakontistai*: 4.4.7).

But Alexander came to depend more on allied, mercenary and later Asian specialists in these roles (cf. 7.23.4).

(iv) Ancillary units

grooms (*hippokomoi*: 3.13.6);
shield-bearers (*hypaspistai*: 1.11.8, 4.24.3), or Royal Shield-bearers (if 3.13.6 is relevant).

C. Logistic and other support staff

Secretary (*grammateus*). Eumenes held this position under Philip and Alexander, and could also be used as a field commander (as at 5.24.6);
Administrative officer (*grammateus*), as at 3.5.3; and *Indica* 18.9 for a Greek as the administrative officer with the fleet on the Hydaspes;
Superintendents (*episkopoi*). Thus Aeschylus and Ephippus served as superintendents or overseers of the Greek mercenary units in Egypt (3.5.3); cf. 3.28.4;
Interpreter(s) (*hermeneus*). So Pharnuches, who could also be used as officer in charge of a special force (4.3.7).

D. Allied and mercenary units

(i) Balkan units, including:
Paeonian light cavalry (as at 1.14.1 and 6, 2.9.2, 3.8.1 and 12.3);
Agrianians (as at 1.6.6–7, 1.18.3, 2.9.2, 3.18.2, 4.25.6, 4.30.6; javelin-men: 1.14.1, 3.13.5);
Thracians (1.14.3, 4.7.2, 6.15.2; as cavalry: 1.14.3, 1.18.3, 3.5.1, 3.12.4 (Odrysians); as javelin-men: 1.28.4, 3.12.4–5).
(ii) Greek units supplied by the Corinthian League (see on 1.1.1, with some details in Diodorus Siculus 17.57.3 and Curtius 4.13.29), both infantry and cavalry (as at 1.29.4, 3.12.4, 4.3.7), and the Thessalian League (cavalry: 1.14.3, 1.24.3, 1.29.4, 2.9.1, 2.11.3, 3.11.10). Arrian sets their demobilization at Ecbatana in 330 BC, with provision for them to re-enlist, if they wished, and remain with his army as mercenaries (3.19.5; cf. 3.24.5).
(iii) Mercenary units. Greeks who had joined the Persian forces as mercenaries were given the chance of immunity if they switched to serving with Alexander (as at 1.19.6, 3.24.5).
Others were recruited in the Peloponnese or northern Greece or elsewhere (2.20.5, 3.5.1). They were assigned to separate infantry and cavalry units (cavalry: as at 3.12.2–5, 3.13.3, 4.3.7, 4.4.6, 4.22.7, 5.12.1; infantry: as at 1.18.1 and 5, 2.9.3–4, 2.18.1 and

5, 4.3.7; Cretan archers: 2.9.3). They were organized in companies (*lochoi*).

E. Weapons

(i) the *sarissa*: the trademark Macedonian pike, *c.*6 m long for infantry, and 4.5 m for cavalrymen. By contrast the Greek hoplite spear was *c.*2.5 m long;

(ii) the lance or thrusting-spear (*doru* or *xyston*): 1.6.1–4 (for its use in hilly terrain), 1.15.6–8, 1.16.1, 4.24.4;

(iii) the javelin (*lonchē*: 4.8.8, 4.9.2), or thonged javelin (*mesankulon*: 7.6.5, 7.23.4);

(iv) sword (*xiphos*: used by Alexander at Gordium: 2.3.7) or scimitar (*kopis*: 1.15.7);

(v) shields: depending on operational needs the Macedonians might carry the small bronze shield (the *peltē* at 7.13.2 of the Amazons, but of Alexander at Plutarch, *Alexander*, 16.7), *c.*575 mm in diameter, or the traditional large shield (*aspis*: 1.6.5, 6.9.3 with 10.2). The *aspis* differed from the shield normally carried by cavalrymen (4.23.2; cf. 3.21.7). There are references to body armour, for instance in 1.15.8, 4.24.4, and 6.10.1–11.7.

(vi) artillery and siege-gear: stones hurled from towers, as at 1.22.2 and 2.23.3, imply the use of torsion catapults; assault-bridges: 2.22.7, 4.26.6. Siege-engines: references include 1.19.2, 1.20.9, 1.21.5, 2.22.6 and *passim* to 2.27.5, 4.26.5, and 5.24.4. See too on 1.22.2.

2. THE NAVY

(i) Developments

Initially Alexander depended on warships (triremes) provided by the Greek allies. In 334 the fleet included some 160 triremes (1.11.6, 1.18.4), but it was sent back at the end of 334 (plan considered: 1.18.7–9; action taken 1.20.1). The creation of a fresh fleet began in the spring of 333 (2.2.3–5 and see 2.20.1 ff).

For crossing rivers Alexander improvised (as at 1.3.6, 3.29.4, 4.4.4, 5.12.3), or had boats built in sections that could be moved overland (5.8.4–5, 5.12.4, 7.19.3).

The Hydaspes fleet (326 BC): 2,000 ships; details at 6.2.4. The largest boats, triaconters, had thirty oarsmen as opposed to the 180 of a trireme.

In 324/3 Alexander planned two fleets: one of over 1,000 warships to sail down the Euphrates to the Persian Gulf (7.19.4), and another of 1,000 warships, larger than triremes, to operate in the Mediterranean (Diodorus Siculus 18.4.4). The numbers are incredible, and imply the availability of more than 360,000 oarsmen. Either Alexander had lost touch with reality, or these figures were made up after his death to ensure that the men scrapped the projects.

(ii) Ship types in Alexander's fleets

triremes: these and the few larger quadriremes and quinqueremes can be referred to as 'long ships' (*nēes makrai*: 6.5.2, 7.16.1, 7.19.4, *Indica* 19.7, 23.3);

penteconter: a fifty-oared ship (from Macedon: 2.20.2);

triaconters: thirty-oared ships (2.7.2, 2.21.6, 5.3.5, 5.8.5, 5.12.4, 5.13.1, 6.2.4, 6.15.1, 6.18.3–4, 6.20.4, *Indica* 31.4; some had two banks of oars: 6.5.2);

corvettes (*kerkouroi*: 6.2.4, 6.18.3, 6.19.3, 6.20.3, *Indica* 23.3, 31.3 (this one with an Egyptian crew));

sloops (*hemioliai*: 3.2.4, 6.1.1, 6.18.3, 6.20.4);

horse-transports (*hippagoga*: 6.2.4, 6.3.2, *Indica* 19.7);

freighters (*ploia skeuophora*: 6.3.2; *ploia strongula*: 1.11.6, 6.5.2 (referring to them as circular), 6.15.1, *Indica* 19.7).

(iii) The command structure

Admiral (*nauarchos*): 2.20.10, 3.5.5, 6.2.3. Nearchus served in this capacity from 326 (*Indica* 18.10), but the term could also be used of any captain of a trireme (as at 1.18.5);

Chief Helmsman (*kybernetes*: 6.2.3, 7.20.9; but again the term could be used of the helmsman of any warship);

Trireme commander (*trierarch*; but at *Indica* 18.3 and 8, and 20.9 the term is used as a courtesy title of captains of lesser ships in the Hydaspes fleet). See further on *Indica* 18.3–8.

APPENDIX II
THE MACEDONIAN AND PERSIAN COURTS AND IMPERIAL ADMINISTRATION

1. ALEXANDER'S COURT

(a) The Bodyguards (*Somatophylakes*, as at 2.12.2, 4.21.4; for example, Ptolemy [3], son of Seleucus: 1.22.4 and 24.1, 2.12.2, and Ptolemy [6], son of Lagus: 3.27.5). On the Persian model, the number of these officers was kept to seven, till Alexander made an exception with the appointment of Peucestas as the eighth in 325 (6.28.4).

(b) The Companions (*Hetairoi*, as at 1.6.5, 2.6.1, 2.27.6): an elite that rose in number to at least ninety by 324 (cf. 7.4.6), including some Greeks (like Demaratus: 1.15.6). They served in various military and administrative capacities.

(c) The Kinsmen (*syngeneis*): a lower rank of the elite, again on the Persian model, as at 7.11.1.

(d) Treasurer: Harpalus (3.6.4-6).

(e) Manager of the Royal Court (Peithon [2] at 4.16.6). His duties included supervising the training of the Pages.

(f) Favoured intellectuals (almost 'spin doctors'), including Callisthenes, as an embedded historian (4.9.10, 4.12.6), sophists and poets (4.9.9, 4.10.5).

(g) Assimilated Asian nobles (4.10.5).

(h) The Pages: young men from noble families, effectively serving as cadets (4.13.1-4, 4.16.6; at least one had the honour of assisting the king to mount his horse: 1.15.6).

(i) bodyguards (*hypaspists*, as at 4.8.8, 4.30.3).

2. THE EMPIRE AND ITS ADMINISTRATION

(a) In the Persian system a satrapy was an area controlled and taxed by the Persian king. The governor of a satrapy was the satrap, who might be a Persian viceroy, or a local dynast or grandee recognized by the king.

(b) Alexander took over the Persian satrapal system, starting with Hellespontine Phrygia and the appointment of a Macedonian as satrap (1.17.1-2). But where he appointed a Persian (as in Babylonia: 3.16.4) or local ruler (as in Caria: 1.23.7-8) or grandee (as in Media: 3.20.3) as satrap, he tended to appoint a Macedonian as satrapal general to keep an eye on the satrap (1.23.6, 3.5.5, 3.16.4 and 9, and perhaps 7.9.8), or a regional overseer with a similar function (3.22.1). Alexander might also appoint garrison commanders (as at 1.17.7–8, 3.5.3, 3.16.9), and a finance officer, charged with collecting tribute in the particular satrapy (as at 1.17.7), or with a wider mandate (3.5.4, 3.6.4).

(c) In both systems Arrian commonly refers to *hyparchs* as of lower rank. The term has a variety of connotations and has therefore not been translated by the same English word throughout. Arrian even uses it for stylistic variation to refer to a satrap (as with Mazaeus: 4.18.3 with 3.16.4; cf. 1.12.8, 1.16.3). The *hyparch* might be:

(i) an official with a designated rank in the administrative hierarchy.

(ii) a semi-independent regional overlord, baron or local leader (5.2.2), like the *nomarchs* in Egypt (3.5.2) and the Indus valley (6.14.1), or like Chorienes, left in control of his mountain fortress (4.21.9).

(iii) a 'war-lord', from the perspective of the authority being challenged.

3. DARIUS' COURT AND ARMY

(a) Senior Commander (*chiliarch*, representing the Persian term *hazaparati*): in the late Achaemenid period, there were two officers of this rank, one in command of the royal bodyguard of Melophoroi, and the other in command of the elite cavalry unit. They were subordinate to another top official. With regard to Nabarzanes, Arrian appears to refer to him as a cavalry commander at 3.21.1, and Alexander and the Successors seem to have taken over this institution; but some interpret 3.23.4 as meaning that under Darius III the *hazaparati* became the king's Grand Vizier.

(b) The Pomegranate-bearers (Herodotus 7.41) or Apple-bearers (*Melophoroi* in Arrian), whose spears were so adorned (3.11.5, 3.13.1, 3.16.1, 7.29.4). This royal bodyguard of 1,000 men was drawn from the elite infantry force of 10,000 Immortals (in Persian this meant that the number was kept constant at 10,000).

(c) *Proskynesis*: the established Persian form of respectful greeting to the king (2.12.6, 4.9.9, 4.10.5 ff.). Hostile sources wilfully took obeisance to be a defining element.

(d) Slave: term applied to all subjects of the Persian king. Slavery in the usual sense was also a feature of the Persian system.

APPENDIX III
FINANCE AND LINEAR MEASURES

1. MONETARY SYSTEMS

Drachm: silver coin worth 6 obols. The Athenian drachm weighed about 4.33 g. For an idea of its lowest value in your currency multiply the statutory or generally accepted minimum hourly wage rate by 8.

Stater: worth 2 drachms and weighed about 8.6 g.

Tertradrachm: a coin worth 4 drachms.

Talent: as a bar of silver it was worth 6,000 drachms, and in Athens weighed about 26 kg (1.26.3, 1.27.4, 2.11.10, 2.25.1, 3.16.7).

Daric: a Persian gold coin, continued by Alexander (4.18.7). Weight *c*.8.4 g, thus in effect a gold stater.

The gold: silver ratio varied above a base of 1 : 10.

2. LINEAR MEASURES

Finger's breadth (*daktylos*: 3.4.4), *c*.18.5 mm on the Athenian standard.

Cubit (*pechus*, 1.20.8, 4.21.4, 5.4.4, 5.19.1), *c*.44.4 cm on the Athenian standard.

Fathom (*orguia*), *c*.1.8 m, as at 2.18.3.

Plethron (5.15.5), *c*.29.6 m on the Athenian standard.

Stade: roughly 180 m, but the standard varied from city to city. In the *Indica* Arrian follows Nearchus, who may have used as a rule of thumb for sea distances *c*.50 stades (9 km or 5.6 miles) covered per hour sailed (cf. *Indica* 29.7–8; cf. Brunt, *Arrian* (Loeb edn.), Vol. I, App. XXV).

Parasang: the Persian measurement of distance, about 5.33 km (1.4.4).

Stathmos: a 'stage': in the Persian system this was taken as 5 parasangs, *c*.26.5 km or 16.5 miles (2.6.1, 3.29.7).

EXPLANATORY NOTES

THE numbers in the left-hand column refer to the chapter and section numbers in the margin of the text. In the notes 'Bosworth' refers to A. B. Bosworth, *A Historical Commentary on Arrian's History of Alexander*. Vol. 1: *Commentary on Books I–III* (Oxford: Oxford University Press, 1980); Vol. 2: *Commentary on Books IV–V* (Oxford: Oxford University Press, 1995). For other classical sources on Alexander (Plutarch, Diodorus Siculus, Quintus Curtius Rufus, etc.), see the Introduction, pp. xxx–xxxiii.

ANABASIS

PREFACE

1 *Where Ptolemy ... and Aristobulus agree ... unquestionably true*: as at 6.11.5 and 7.15.6 (cf. 5.7.1).

2 *as a king himself ... honour-bound to avoid untruth*: Arrian subscribes to the principle of *noblesse oblige*: kingship carried with it the burden of service to what was honourable (cf. 7.5.2).

   no compulsion or profit: the idea that, with Alexander dead, Ptolemy and Aristobulus would have been immune to any pressure to flatter or denigrate had some value in justifying Arrian's preference for their accounts over against that of Callisthenes, the 'embedded' historian, who wrote, and died, long before Alexander's death. But it avoids the issue that those who wrote their memoirs after his death clearly had their own diverse agenda in the power-struggle among the Successors.

3 *worth relating*: anecdotal material could be revelatory, as Plutarch noted with regard to remarks attributed to Alexander (*Alex.* 1.3; cf. Arr. 2.12.8).

BOOK ONE

1.1–3 Arrian starts in a rather affected way by giving the death of Philip and its aftermath as what other historians have recorded. By 1.6 he has switched to direct recording of Alexander's movements. In this way he defines the focus of this book: the circumstances of Philip's death and Alexander's accession are not relevant to his *Anabasis*. And from where he switches from summarizing generally accepted history to direct presentation of the facts we have what he claims to have verified from the best sources. The opening sentence recalls the opening line of Xenophon's *Cyropaedia*: 'History relates that Cyrus was the son of Cambyses ...' And Arrian, like Xenophon in his *Anabasis*, does not introduce himself at the outset, but leaves that to 1.12.4–5. Like Xenophon he plunges straight into the action.

1.1 *Philip died ... when Pythodelus was archon at Athens*: Philip II was murdered in the theatre at Aegae (Vergina) in about October 336, by one Pausanias, as Philip was presiding over the marriage of his daughter Cleopatra to Alexander I of Epirus, who was the brother of her mother, Olympias. Pausanias had personal reasons for murdering Philip, but it suited Olympias and Alexander to claim that there was a conspiracy behind the hit-man (cf. 1.25.1–2). Certainly Pausanias himself was killed as he ran away from the scene of the crime, thus before he could tell his story, and Alexander and his supporters acted immediately to secure his succession and eliminate possible rivals.

1.2 *called a meeting of the Peloponnesian Greeks*: this should be a reference to the Corinthian League, established by Philip II in 338/7 to reconfirm the Common Peace (see on 2.1.4) as the instrument for maintaining peace between the Greek states. The Peace was given a second arm when Philip used its structure to launch a military alliance against Persia with himself as its plenipotentiary general. The campaign was justified as retaliation for Xerxes' invasion of Greece in 480/79 and in particular for his desecration of Greek temples. Philip's alliance included city states and leagues from central and northern Greece and the islands. Arrian may have focused here on the Peloponnesian Greeks because Alexander had already forced the Thessalian League to recognize him as their leader, and likewise the states in the league centred on Delphi.

all . . . except the Spartans: it suited Alexander to leave the Spartans isolated among the Greek states, hence he made a point of celebrating Athens' heroic role in the war against Xerxes, while ignoring the Spartans' famous stand at Thermopylae (480 BC; implied at 1.16.7) and recalling Sparta's collaboration with the Persians in the last phase of the Peloponnesian War (431–404; reflected at 1.9.2).

1.4–6.11 **Campaigns into Thracian and Illyrian territory, 335 BC.** Alexander's route was probably eastwards past Amphipolis and then Xanthi to cut through the eastern end of the Rhodope range and then head north to Philippopolis [Plovdiv]. From there he would have headed north to cross the Haemus range via the Troyan Pass (2.1). Approaching Troyan he was in the territory of the Triballians, and fought a battle with them at the river Lyginus (2.1 and 4–7), perhaps a tributary of the Utus [Vit] near Pleven, otherwise the Osǔm.

1.5 *the. . . independent Thracians*: Philip II had clashed with them during his Thracian campaign of 342/1 in the Haemus mountains, but securing their full submission was unfinished business.

1.7 *phalanx*: the infantry line in battle formation. For all military matters refer to Appendix 1.

1.8 *hoplites*: heavy infantrymen.

2.1 *the Triballians*: living between the Haemus range and the Danube, they had tried to hold Philip to ransom when he was returning from his Scythian campaign in 339.

2.5 *Philotas* [4]: presumably the son of Parmenion, and the most senior cavalry officer. His main scene came with his trial for treason in 330, briefly covered by Arrian at 3.26.1–3.

3.1 *the river Danube*: a digression on the river and its peoples, perhaps in conscious imitation of Herodotus 4.48–50, but Arrian focuses more on the peoples than the rivers.

3.5 *yen*: he may have wanted to rival the crossing of the Danube by Darius in 512. Yen (*pothos*) is a leitmotif running through the Alexander legend: compare his urge to visit the palace where the Gordian knot was housed (2.3.1), to found the city of Alexandria (3.1.5), and to meet the Indian gymnosophists (7.2.2).

4.1 *to flatten the corn*: an indication of date: about June 335.

4.2 *Nicanor* [1]: brother of Philotas (2.5).

4.6–8 *envoys . . . from the Celts . . . a pretentious lot*: these Celts occupied territory between that of the Autariates (5.1) and the Adriatic. Strabo relates the same episode, though with less rationalization, and cites Ptolemy as his source (7.3.8.301–2): thus Arrian was surely following Ptolemy here. The Alexander story is dotted with anecdotes about people who, through ignorance, naivety, or sheer spirit, gave him frank answers to his questions and won his admiration, as, for example, the Indian gymnosophists (7.1.5–2.4).

5.1–6.11 **Alexander's campaigns against his northern, and western Illyrian neighbours.** His route was south via Sofia, Pataulia [Kjustendil], Stip, and Stobi [Sirkovo]. After the battle near Pellium Alexander headed east into the Eordaea canton of Macedonia (1.7.5).

5.1 *Cleitus* [1], *the son of Bardylis*: the brother of Philip II, Perdiccas I, was killed in a battle with the Illyrian king Bardylis in 359. On Bardylis' death *c*.358, Cleitus became king, but *c*.345 Philip campaigned against his people, the Dardanians, and he became a client king of the Macedonians. But their northern and western neighbours, the Autariates and Taulantians, remained independent.

5.4 *Cyna*: otherwise Cynnane, the daughter of Bardylis' daughter Audata-Eurydice, and thus half-Illyrian. She was available in 335, because after Philip's assassination Alexander liquidated her husband, Amyntas the son of Perdiccas III (Justin 12.6.14) for the threat he posed to the succession.

6.5 *Bodyguards and the Companions*: here probably referring to the elite group of seven Bodyguards and men of the next tier down in the hierarchy.

7.1–10.6 **The abortive revolt of Thebes and its aftermath.**

7.1 *garrison . . . Cadmea*: in 338 Thebes yielded to the call from Athens to participate in a campaign to block Philip's imperialist ambitions in Greece. The struggle ended swiftly with Philip's victory at the battle of Chaeronea in Boeotian territory, and in 337 Philip re-established the Common Peace, but now under the hegemony of the Macedonian king. Thebes was garrisoned by Macedonian troops, who occupied the acropolis, known as the Cadmea.

7.6 *Antipater* [1] . . . *another Alexander* [4] . . . *son of Aëropus*: Antipater had been a senior figure throughout Philip's reign, and played a major role in ensuring Alexander's accession. When Alexander was away campaigning he left Antipater in Macedonia as virtual regent. The Lyncestian, Alexander, son of Aëropus, was married to one of Antipater's daughters, which saved his life after Philip's murder, but he was destined to be charged with conspiracy (1.25).

7.11 *Boeotarchs*: elected officials of the Boeotian League, which was dominated by Thebes.

8.1 *Perdiccas*: Ptolemy had good reason to take a hostile line on Perdiccas, after the latter's bid, albeit unsuccessful, to wrest control of Egypt from him in 321/0.

9.2 *The Athenian debacle in Sicily*: in the Peloponnesian War (431–404), the Athenians opened up a second front against the Spartans and their allies in 415 by invading Sicily, but this ended in disaster at Syracuse in 413. Seven thousand men who escaped the final massacre or enslavement were thrown into the quarries of Achradina and kept prisoner for a further six months. In making the comparison Arrian echoes Thucydides 1.1.2 and 7.87.5.

9.3 *Aegospotami*: the battle of 405 marked Athens' final defeat in the Peloponnesian War.

9.4 *Leuctra* [371 BC] *and Mantinea* [362] . . . *Boeotian* . . . *attack on Sparta* [370/69]: key actions in the Theban bid for the hegemony of Greece, driven by Epaminondas.

9.5 *the capture of Plataea*: Athens had supported Plataea in its bid to remain independent of the Boeotian League, but in the spring of 431 the Thebans launched an abortive assault on the city, and Athens supported the Plataeans, but in 429, after the start of the Peloponnesian War, the Spartans began a long siege of Plataea, and took it in 427: the city was sacked and some 200 Plataeans, deemed anti-Spartan, were put to death (Thuc. 3.68; cf. 9.7).

Melos and Scione: the massacres at Scione (421) and Melos (416) (Thuc. 5.32.1 and 116.4) were in punishment for defections from the Athenian maritime empire.

9.7 *where the Greeks had stood . . . against the Persians*: after the Greek victory in the naval battle of Salamis (480), Xerxes returned to Persia and left Mardonius to continue the war, but his army was finally defeated in battle in August 479, near Plataea. The charge against the Thebans of 'betrayal of the Greeks in the Persian War' may have been a product of fourth-century campaigns against Thebes.

9.9 *consular representatives*: (*proxenoi*); rather like honorary consuls or lobbyists in the modern system, these were men who in their own city represented the interests of another state.

9.10 *Pindar*: Pindar (518–*c*.440) wrote, on commission, poems to celebrate the achievements, particularly in the various games, of the great and the good.

10.2 *the Great Mysteries*: September–October 335 BC. The week-long celebration began in the centre of Athens and culminated in the procession of the initiates from the city to the shrine of Demeter at Eleusis.

10.4 *Demosthenes and Lycurgus*: in the aftermath of Chaeronea (338) Demosthenes and Lycurgus engaged in chauvinist talk and promoted measures to strengthen Athens' defences and to train its young men for military action, but the programme was probably more about addressing social and economic problems than preparing for suicidal adventurism. Certainly for most of Alexander's reign Lycurgus did much to develop the city, increase its financial strength, and keep the hotheads in check. Demosthenes sounded the more belligerent in 338 and after, but his pragmatism showed through when Alexander struck at Thebes in 335: his promises of assistance came to nothing, and he may have dissuaded the Arcadians from intervening militarily.

10.4–6 *Charidemus*: he was from Euboea and had made his name as a mercenary captain, rewarded by the Athenians with citizenship in 358/7. In the chaotic situation after Chaeronea, the Athenian assembly voted Charidemus in as a general with special powers. In the same context Hypereides introduced a raft of radical proposals. But the council of elders, the Areopagus, took fright and removed Charidemus from office, replacing him with Phocion, who was more conservative and pragmatic.

10.6 *anger*: an important element in the Alexander myth. A link with the Homeric tale of the wrath of Achilles is suggested at 4.9.5–6, and at 1.11.8 Arrian alludes to Alexander's claim to descent from Achilles' son Neoptolemus.

11.1 *Archelaus* [reigned c.413–399] . . . *Aegae*: but in fact at Dium.

11.5 *Protesilaus*: Homer, *Iliad* 2.702.

12.2 *achievements . . . not published . . . as they deserved*: Callisthenes went into Asia as Alexander's official historian, but in 327 he took a principled stand against Alexander and so was put to death (Bk. 4.10–14), yet, ironically, his unfinished work was regarded by critics as an exercise in flattery, and not serious history.

Hieron, Gelon, Theron: these Sicilians—Hieron, the tyrant of Gela 485–478 and of Syracuse 478–466; Gelon, the tyrant of Gela 491–485 and of Syracuse 485–478; and Theron, tyrant of Agrigentum (in Greek, Acragas) 488–472—offered patronage to the leading poets of the day, like Pindar, Bacchylides, and Simonides, and were duly celebrated in verse.

12.3–5 In this 'second preface' Arrian makes the conventional point that his subject is one of exceptional historical importance in world history: cf. Herodotus 1, Preface, Thucydides 1.1.2, and even Josephus, *The Jewish War* 1.1. Then he signals the influence of Xenophon, but contrasts the latter's *Anabasis*, dominated by the retreat of the Ten Thousand losers, with the triumphal progression of Alexander through what had been the Achaemenid Empire. Immodestly he claims to feel worthy to undertake this greater task.

12.4 *another man's army*: an allusion to Xenophon, who served as a mercenary in the army of the Persian prince Cyrus in his attempt to seize the throne from his brother Artaxerxes.

12.5 *my country . . . my own land*: whether the *Anabasis* was written fairly early in Arrian's career or after his retirement from the imperial service, Arrian is here clearly stressing his Greek origins. Thus even if he wrote this after the crowning glories of the Roman consulship and the archonship in Athens, he may still be referring here to Bithynia and his home city of Nicomedia. Arrian lays claim to intellectual stature by his writings. The influence of Epictetus is suggested, for Epictetus, as we know from Arrian's summary of his teachings, emphasized that one had to exclude from any claim to wisdom accidents of birth, property, civic offices, etc.

12.9 *Memnon*: he married into the family of the Persian Artabazus (introduced at 3.21.4), but was still a Greek and could attract the suspicion or resentment of a Persian noble (12.10).

13–16 The battle of the Granicus.

13.1 *Granicus*: perhaps the modern Biga Çay, or its tributary, the Dimetoka.

13.2–7 Parmenion's exchange with Alexander. This is one of a series of episodes that serve to foreshadow the liquidation of Parmenion in 330, though this is not one framed to show him as disloyal or inept. See too 18.6–8 below and the note on 3.10.2.

15.8 *Cleitus* [2] *the son of Dropidas*: known as 'the Black', he commanded the Royal Squadron of the Companion cavalry (3.11.8), but in 328 he clashed with Alexander and was murdered (Bk. 4.8).

16.7 *except the Spartans*: see on 1.2 above.

17.9 *Amyntas* [2]: cf. 1.25.3.

17.11 *the statue of Philip*: the 'liberation' of Ephesus by Parmenion's expeditionary force in 335 and the promotion of ruler cult had not been universally welcome.

18.1–2 *Alcimachus*: although the declared purpose of the campaign in Asia Minor was the liberation of Greek cities from Persian control, it was only with the commission given to Alcimachus in Ephesus that Alexander set about the systematic removal of pro-Persian oligarchies. But he was no enthusiast for democracy per se (cf. 1.17.12).

18.6–8 Parmenion's advice rejected. As at 13.2–7 the exchange serves to illustrate the strength of Alexander's strategic thinking. His application of omens was another indicator of his leadership skills (18.9; cf. 11.2 and 25.6; 2.18.1).

19.6 *When he saw . . . served in his army*: while Alexander had good reason to take these mercenaries over into his own army, he had also learnt from the reaction to his enslavement of Greek prisoners taken captive at the Granicus (1.16.6). The Athenians made strong representations for the release of their people, first when he was in Gordium (1.29.5), but without success, and then in spring 331, when Alexander agreed to set the men free (3.6.2).

20.1 *no further need of a fleet*: this was to put a positive gloss on a decision rather forced on Alexander. Even though warships had a limited range between landings for water and supplies, a fleet gave the Persians a great strategic advantage. For Alexander the big fear was that the Phoenician fleet might be used to launch a counter-offensive in Greece, quite apart from maintaining pressure on the Greek islands of the Aegean. With the dismissal of the fleet, Alexander was unable, for example, to prevent the Phoenicians and their Greek allies from retaking Tenedos (2.2.2–3).

20.2–23.8 The siege of Halicarnassus.

20.2 *Halicarnassus*: there may once have been a Greek colony there, but it had developed as an essentially Carian city.

20.3 *Memnon*: see at 12.9 above.

20.4 *gates leading to Mylasa*: Alexander's camp was apparently at Yokuşbaşi, just north-east of the city, and the road from Mylasa crossed a saddle in the hills to enter the city from the east.

20.5 *Myndus*: the site, some 17 km west of Halicarnassus, had been occupied by Greek settlers from the Argolid in the late eighth century. The Persians supported successive Carian dynasties, giving them satrapal status, and Mausolus, the son of the founder of the Hecatomnid dynasty, had made Myndus his capital by about 360 BC.

20.8 *siege-towers*: this is picked up at 22.2.

20.10 *Neoptolemus* [1]: he may have deserted because he was a son of Arrhabaeus, executed in 335/4 because of his alleged involvement in the assassination of Philip (25.1 below). But Neoptolemus' brother Amyntas stayed and was one of Alexander's trusted commanders (1.12.7, 14.1 and 28.4). In the same way, while Alexander killed Arrhabaeus and his brother Heromenes, he kept their brother, the Lyncestian Alexander, in a high command for a lengthy period.

21.1 As at 8.1 Perdiccas is associated with some ill-discipline.

22.2 *large stones . . . from catapults*: Arrian is clearly referring to torsion catapults, firing stones 'over-arm', as opposed to 'belly-shooters', which were more like crossbows and used to fire bolts. The torsion catapult may have been invented *c*.340 (so D. Whitehead, *Aineias the Tactician* (Oxford, 1990), 195), but some argue that it was only introduced *c*.270 BC.

22.4 *the battalions of Adaeus and Timander*: according to Diodorus Siculus 17. 27.1–2 it was Macedonian veterans who came to the rescue, not least to shame the younger troops into fighting with greater determination.

22.7 *Adaeus . . . a battalion commander*: in this context the position held by Adaeus (as also Timander: 22.4), will have been the command of a battalion (chiliarchy) of the foot guards (the Macedonian elite infantry).

23.3 *Salmacis*: Salmacis was the promontory commanding the western point of exit from the main harbour, and the 'island' was the peninsula known as Zephyria, that marked the eastern point of the harbour mouth. These two elements were referred to jointly as the Citadel (Strabo 14.2.17.657). Zephyria became an island, quite probably as the result of deliberate action by Alexander to isolate the citadel (Diodorus Siculus 17.27.6).

23.5 *decided against besieging them*: the Persians held out for many months, till Orontobates was defeated in a minor battle, and Alexander only heard of this when he was at Soli in the latter part of 333 (2.5.7).

23.7 *Semiramis*: in legend the daughter of a Syrian goddess, who married the Assyrian king Ninus. The myth was built around the historical Assyrian queen Schammuramat (reigned 811–806 BC). Cf. on *Indica* 5.6–7.

Pixodarus: the brother of Ada and Hidrieus, and the father of Ada junior. Early in 336 he had proposed to Philip that his daughter, the younger Ada, should be married to Philip Arrhidaeus, Alexander's stepbrother. Alexander took it as a slight that he was not preferred, and his interference frustrated the plan (Plutarch, *Alexander* 10). Pixodarus then offered Ada in marriage to Orontobates (23.8).

25.1 *Alexander* [4] *the son of Aëropus*: he was of the royal house of Lyncestis, which Philip had incorporated into the Macedonian state. His two brothers, Arrhabaeus and Heromenes, had been executed as participants in the conspiracy to murder Philip, but Alexander survived, perhaps because he was the son-in-law of Antipater. Aëropus was a cousin of Eurydice, the mother of Philip II. Thus in 336 the sons of Aëropus may have appeared as a threat to Alexander's accession.

25.6–7 Arrian gives this in indirect speech, implying that the tale might be apocryphal.

25.10 *Alexander was arrested and kept under guard*: he was kept prisoner for three years, before being tried before the Macedonian troops and put to death, thus in 330. The case against him was obviously thin, and when he was finally brought to trial, of the key players in this drama, Parmenion was away from the main camp, Sisines had been murdered, and Amyntas was dead (2.13.2–3).

26.2 *not without divine intervention*: Arrian, Plutarch, and Strabo all indicate that Callisthenes and sensationalist writers made far more of the 'miracle' of the sea along the Pamphylian coast giving way to Alexander.

26.4 *The story they tell of themselves*: Arrian here adds contextual detail in Herodotean style.

BOOK TWO

1–2 The war in the Aegean.

1.1 *Memnon . . . Greece*: Memnon has been introduced at 1.12.9. He died in about August 333.

1.4 *the Peace of Antalcidas*: in 386 the Persian king Artaxerxes II (here erroneously styled 'the former King Darius'), acting as mediator in the power struggle between Greek alliances centred on Athens, Sparta, and Thebes, dictated an agreement that the Greeks would cease hostilities, and respect 'the Common Peace', based on the principle that the states, including the Aegean island states, would be autonomous, while accepting Persia's role as enforcer, and her control of the Greek cities of Asia Minor. It is referred to again at 2.2.2. Antalcidas was the Spartan naval commander who negotiated with Artaxerxes.

2.4 *Proteas*: apparently a nephew of Cleitus the Black (1.15.8). He had lost two brothers in the fighting at Miletus (Curtius Rufus 8.2.8).

3   Alexander and the Gordian knot.

3.6 *whoever could undo the knot . . . was destined to rule Asia*: Phrygian Gordium was seen as at the navel of Asia, in the sense of Asia Minor.

3.7 *Aristobulus says that he took out the pole-pin*: if Alexander had attacked the knot with a sword he might be seen as cheating, so Aristobulus has Alexander use brain rather than brawn to solve the conundrum. As elsewhere, Aristobulus adapts the story to present Alexander in more favourable light.

4.2 *the river Halys and much too beyond it*: even before Cyrus established the Persian Empire the Halys was recognized as the boundary between East and West. Crossing the Halys was thus a symbolic challenge to the Persian king (cf. Hdt. 1.103 and 72 ff.).

4.3 *the site where Cyrus had camped*: the camp of Cyrus II in 401 was perhaps at Podandus [Pozanti], *c.*20 km before the Cilician Gates [Gulek Bogaz] (Xen. *Anabasis* 1.2.21; cf. Arr. 1.12.2–3). Here as elsewhere the Gates denote a mountain pass.

4.6 *Arsames hurrying out of Tarsus . . . without doing any harm to the city*: in Curtius' account it was Parmenion who dashed ahead and saved Tarsus from destruction by fire. The variant points to Aristobulus as Arrian's source (cf. 4.7). Arsames was probably at that time the satrap of Cilicia.

4.7–11 Alexander falls sick and is warned of a plot to poison him. This may have been an attack or recurrence of malaria. Parmenion sent a report warning that the physician, Alexander's boyhood friend Philip, had been offered a bribe to poison him. This assassination plot does not figure in Alexander's list of grievances at 2.14.4, and the fuller version given by Curtius (3.5–6) reads like fiction, perhaps originating with someone concerned to portray Parmenion as a troublemaker.

4.7 *Aristobulus' account attributes it to exhaustion*: again Aristobulus alters the record to dismiss any suggestion that Alexander acted irresponsibly.

5.1 *the other Gates*: thus not the Gulek Bogaz of 4.2–3, but the coastal pass of Merkes Su, also known as the Pillar of Jonah, north of Iskenderun (cf. 6.1–2). Parmenion was expecting Darius to head towards Iskenderun, across the Amik plain and through the Belen Pass, and then presumably north towards Cilicia.

5.2 *Anchialus . . . founded by Sardanapalus*: a product of romantic revisionist history, reflecting the Cilician campaign of the Assyrian king Sennacherib in 696 BC.

5.5 *Soli . . . pro-Persian tendency*: perhaps some guilt by association, as Soli was a colony of Rhodes, and there were prominent Rhodians who had sided with Darius, including Memnon (1.12.9 and 2.1.1–2) and Lycomedes (2.1.5).

5.8 *Asclepius*: a sacrifice to the god of healing was appropriate after Alexander's brush with death at Tarsus (4.7–11).

5.9 *claimed descent from the Heracleidae of Argos*: Alexander named his son by Barsine Heracles, and at various points signalled his emulation of Heracles: for example at 4.28.1–2. Mallus was an oracular site, and the religious references in 5.8–9 provide some lead-in to the battle of Issus.

6.1–2 *Darius . . . at Sochi . . . about two days' march from the Assyrian Gates. . . . Alexander . . . on the second day passed through the Gates* [the Merkes Su Pass], *and camped by the city of Myriandrus*: there was some obfuscation of the facts because Alexander was the victim of some failure in intelligence: he was expecting Darius to descend to the coast via the Belen Pass, but after Alexander reached Myriandrus, he discovered that Darius had in fact headed north and had cut through the Gâvur Dağ via the Hasanbeyli Pass, and then headed west through the Toprakkale Pass, the Amanic Gates, and down to Issus (possibly Kinet Hüyük).

6.3 *Amyntas* [2]: a deserter (1.25.3), but still a Macedonian, gets the credit for giving wise advice, which Darius ignored (6.6), to his cost.

7.1 *Darius . . . advanced to the river Pinarus*: Darius, now in pursuit of Alexander, headed south from Issus, and reached the river Pinarus, perhaps the Deli Çay, if not the Payas.

7.3–9 Alexander's pre-battle speech. It is typical of the genre, in emphasizing that the battle cannot be avoided, but holds out every promise of victory. It is not unusual in offering no justification for the war in the first place. Arrian draws in a reference to Xenophon, *Anabasis* 3.3.6–20.

8.8 *was said to number some six hundred thousand fighting men*: Arrian's source for this incredible tally was probably Aristobulus, whom he used on Persian troop numbers for the battle of Gaugamela (3.8.3–6 with 11.3).

8.11 *took position at the centre of the whole line*: other sources moved Darius from the centre to the left of the Persian line to give him a more heroic role (see on 11.4 below). Arrian adds another reference to Xenophon, here *Anabasis* 1.8.22.

11.3 *riders in heavy armour*: before the next major battle, at Gaugamela, Darius acquired a new tactical force of Scythian cavalrymen whose horses were also armoured (3.13.4). By Arrian's day this latter combination was familiar to the Romans, and styled cataphract cavalry.

11.4 *Darius . . . one of the first to flee*: cf. 10.1: Alexander thought that Darius had lost all spirit for the fight, even before the battle began. But there was a counter-tradition that Darius was in the thick of the battle, and Alexander moved to engage him directly (so Polybius 12.22.2, citing Callisthenes, the 'embedded' historian), and Chares went further in claiming that Darius wounded Alexander in the right thigh with his sword. But Arrian's sources and Cleitarchus, the source followed by Diodorus Siculus and Quintus Curtius, clearly did not accept the attempt to present Darius as a more formidable opponent. The 'Alexander' mosaic from Pompeii may be another example of a bid to present Darius in heroic mould: here the charioteer has turned the chariot to flee, but Darius, towering in the centre of the scene, stays facing back and glaring at Alexander (fig. 20 in P. A. Cartledge, *Alexander the Great: The Hunt for a New Past* (London: Macmillan, 2004), and clearer in M. Wood, *In the Footsteps of Alexander the Great* (London: BBC, 1997), 58–9).

11.9 *his wife, who was also his sister*: cf. Plutarch, *Alexander* 30.3 and 10. But no source says that his wife, Stateira, was the daughter of his mother, Sisygambis, and Curtius labels Sisygambis Stateira's mother-in-law (4.10.19). Marriages between siblings or half-siblings seem to have happened in the late Achaemenid period in the royal family or the ruling class, but a more general practice of incestuous marriage was projected on Persians by hostile Graeco-Roman writers.

11.10 *Maemacterion*: this would be in about November 333 BC, which has a bearing on understanding the weather conditions at the time and the hours of daylight available.

12.1 *despite a sword-wound*: but not inflicted by Darius: see on 11.4.

12.5 *Leonnatus* [2]: one of the more than ninety Companions, and also of royal blood. After Alexander's death in 323 he was initially marked out to be regent, along with Perdiccas, for Alexander's unborn child.

control of Asia: Asia in the broader sense than in the Gordian oracle (3.6).

12.6 *Hephaestion*: introduced at 1.12.1. He was increasingly recognized as Alexander's homosexual partner (Bk. 7.14).

made obeisance to him: a reference to the Persian ritual of *proskynesis*, in its basic form amounting to no more than holding the thumb and forefinger to the lips, as if blowing a kiss, to show respect when coming into the presence of the king. Greeks and Romans chose to give it a religious significance, but ruler cult was not a feature of the Achaemenid kingship. Diodorus Siculus here gives that extended, erroneous sense, by stating that Sisygambis 'greeted him as a god' (17.37.4).

13.1 *Thapsacus*: the key crossing-point on the Euphrates for commercial and military traffic in the Persian and Greek periods. The location is disputed: some favour Jerablus, or Birecek (in the area of Zeugma), but Arrian and Xenophon point rather to Meskene, where the Euphrates turns to the east.

13.2 *Amyntas* [2]: cf. 1.17.9, 1.25.3, and 2.6.3.

13.4–8 The war in the Aegean and Alexander's campaign to seize control of the Phoenician cities that provided Darius with a navy.

13.4 *Agis*: the support given to the Spartan king led to the revolt against Macedonian rule, which began before the battle of Gaugamela (indicated by 3.24.4) in 331, and ended within a few months with Agis' defeat at Megalopolis.

13.7 *Hollow Syria*: strictly the area between the Lebanon and the Anti-Lebanon ranges. But as a label of an administrative territory its boundaries varied dramatically over the centuries. Menon's satrapy may have been northern Syria.

14 **The first diplomatic exchange.** Arrian mentions a second exchange when Alexander was at Tyre (25.1–3). The matching passages in Curtius are at 4.1.7–14 and 5.1–8, and he records another round, shortly before Gaugamela (4.11.1–22).

14.4 *Macedonia and the rest of Greece*: language (or rather dialect) and the monarchy had nurtured a long tradition of denial of the Greekness of Macedonia. Alexander thus identifies with the (flimsy) Greek justification for the war, alluding to the campaigns of Darius I and Xerxes (cf. 3.8.12), and then gives the purely Macedonian grievances relating to Artaxerxes Ochus' military activities in 340. Darius was surely not behind the assassination of Philip in 336 (1.1.1 above), but may have made such a boast. Significantly, Alexander now made an issue of the circumstances of Darius' accession. This enabled him to attack the man while leaving alone the institution of monarchy (cf. 3.30.1–5 and 4.7.3).

14.5 *Bagoas* [1]: by Arrian's day Bagoas had become identified in literature as the Persian name for a eunuch, with all its negative connotations.

15.2 *Iphicrates*: when the Macedonian king Alexander II was murdered in 368, Iphicrates senior, then commanding the Athenian fleet in the area, helped to remove the pretender, Pausanias, and 'saved the dynasty' for Philip II (Aeschines 2.29), the father of Alexander III.

16.1–24.6 **The siege of Tyre.**

16.1 *not the Argive Heracles*: thus not the Heracles from whom Alexander's family claimed descent, and so Alexander could not make his Heraclid ancestry an excuse for military action against the Tyrians. In 16.1–6 Arrian follows Herodotus and Hecataeus in trying to get beyond the myth; and in 16.6 he draws on his own knowledge of Ambracia and Amphilochia, which he would have acquired while studying at Nicopolis (see Introduction). The Tyrian 'Heracles' was the god Melqart.

16.2 *Oedipus the son of Laïus*: Laïus was the son of Labdacus, and Oedipus thus belonged to the fifth generation.

18.1 *an omen . . . a dream*: Curtius 4.2.3 has an oracular admonition, which would have made Alexander's demand more non-negotiable.

20.2 *penteconter*: a warship with fifty oars, thus smaller than a trireme, which had 180 oars.

20.5 *Cleander* [1]: cf. 1.24.2.

21.4 *walls . . . about a hundred and fifty feet high*: this figure (*c*.45 m) is surely an exaggeration. Alexander had mobile siege-towers drawn up against the walls (2.18.6; Curtius 4.2.23), and these were most likely the work of his specialist engineer Diades, who in his *Engineering Compendium* gave the specifications for a tower of 60 cubits (*c*.28 m). So it is surmised that at Tyre he deployed towers of his standard type, and thus that the walls were probably no higher than 60 cubits (so D. Whitehead and P. H. Blyth, *Athenaeus Mechanicus, On Machines* (Stuttgart, 2004), esp. 49 and 184).

23.2 *Coenus' brigade of the so-called 'Close Companions'*: this cannot mean that Coenus put onto one trireme a regular brigade of 1,500 men; and Alexander had with him the *agema* with a nominal strength of 500 men. Thus Coenus may have taken just a section of his brigade (see the guide at Appendix 1).

24.2 *Agenor*: in myth Agenor was the founder of Tyre (Curtius 4.4.15), and his son Cadmus sailed to Greece where he founded the city of Thebes (Aeschylus, *Seven against Thebes* 1; Herodotus 2.49), and introduced the Greeks to the art of writing.

24.5 *a delegation of Carthaginians*: their mission was simply to represent Carthage at the annual festival held in the mother-city in January to celebrate the awakening of Heracles. The vulgate sources Diodorus Siculus and Curtius Rufus (on whom see the Introduction on 'Arrian's Sources') say that the Carthaginians offered to take in Tyrian evacuees, and that when Alexander died he left behind plans for a campaign along the North African coast, one objective being the punitive conquest of Carthage.

24.6 *Hecatombaeon*: Tyre thus fell in July/August 332, in the seventh month of the siege.

25.1–3 **The second diplomatic exchange.** Darius had asked for a truce (14.1–3), and now offers incentives. Here too Parmenion is introduced as obstructively cautious.

25.4–27.7 **The siege of Gaza.** Curtius 4.6.7–31 offers more drama.

25.4 *a eunuch called Batis*: if a Persian eunuch, he would have been a garrison bureaucrat assigned to Gaza, so perhaps he was rather an Arab official recognized for his loyalty to the King.

27.3 *a ramp . . . two hundred and fifty feet high*: a doublet of the mound in 26.3, an indication that Arrian was marrying two accounts, and was blind to the improbability of the measurements.

27.7 *served . . . in his prosecution of the war*: Arrian stresses the strategic necessity of the capture of Gaza if Alexander was to advance into Egypt. Thus he tries to mitigate the atrocity—10,000 killed—and so too he omits the story that Alexander tied Batis to the back of his chariot and dragged him round the city till he was dead.

BOOK THREE

1.1–2.2 Alexander invades Egypt.

1.2 *Mazaces . . . welcomed him*: Mazaces had indirectly done Alexander a favour by blocking Amyntas' bid to pose as the liberator of Egypt (2.13.2–3).

1.4 *sacrifice to . . . Apis*: Alexander thus distanced himself from Artaxerxes Ochus, who, on his invasion of Egypt in 343 had killed the Apis bull, as had Cambyses in 518. But with this deference to Egyptian religion, Alexander combined a display of cultural imperialism with the celebration of the games (cf. 5.2).

2.1 *barley-meal . . . dribbled . . . along the line*: a Macedonian custom (Curtius 4.8.6), here rationalized.

2.3–7 Hegelochus' report, autumn 332, on the recovery of the Aegean islands. This picks up the story from Bk. 2.1–2.

2.6 *Chares* [1]: this is the Athenian mentioned at 1.10.4 and 12.1, and not the court official who wrote the *History of Alexander* mentioned in the Introduction.

2.7 *for whatever treatment the people might decide*: thus he put the onus on the cities to punish Persia's puppets (see further on 4.7.3 for the delegation of the responsibility to punish offenders; cf. 1.9.9).

3–4 The visit to the oracle of Ammon at Siwah.

3.1 *the shrine of Ammon*: the oracular shrine, as an element of the temple of Ammon, was at Aghurmi in the oasis of Siwah in the western desert, some 280 km west of Alexandria. Consultation of the oracle was, at least in its main form, by posing questions to the cult symbol (possibly an aniconic lump or meteorite, or a statuette of Ammon—Herodotus 2.42 and 4.181), and observing how the object swayed in response as it was being carried in procession. But Alexander was honoured with a private consultation (Callisthenes, Frag. 14).

3.2 *Perseus and Heracles*: Heracles was the great-grandson of Perseus, whose son, Perses, was the ancestor of the Persians (Herodotus 6.54). Alexander, as a Heraclid (2.5.9) invoked this myth to give himself an ancestral claim to the Persian Empire.

beginning to attribute part of his paternity to Ammon: as the new ruler of Egypt, Alexander might have been accorded—perhaps first at Siwah—the title held by each Pharaoh, Son of Ammon. Later he certainly claimed the sonship of Ammon (4.9.9; 7.8.3 with 27.3 and 29.3), but it seems unlikely that he did so even before his visit to Siwah.

3.3 *Paraetonium*: the Siwah oasis was some 300 km to the south of Paraetonium (mod. Mersa Matruh).

3.5 *Ptolemy says ... snakes ... led the way to the oracle*: the miracle of the guiding snakes was recorded only by Ptolemy, presumably as an element of his envisioned dynastic myth.

4.5 *put his questions to the god*: Curtius Rufus, dependent on the Alexandrian Cleitarchus, indicates that Alexander asked about his parentage (and was told that he was the son of Ammon), and whether he was destined to rule the world (an aspiration of each Achaemenid king), and whether all those involved in the murder of Philip had been eliminated (Curtius 4.7.25–8).

another route, direct to Memphis: had Alexander struck back through the Qattara Depression Ptolemy would not have been the only one to describe the feat. Ptolemy's version would backdate the foundation of Alexandria to before the journey to Siwah (January/February 331), even though in the Ptolemaic era 7 April was celebrated as the foundation anniversary.

5.2–7 **Arrangements for the administration of Egypt.** The limited use of locals assimilated into the system was not successful: Petisis declined to collaborate, and Cleomenes was later accused of appropriating powers and abusing his position (7.23.6–8).

5.5 *Peucestas* [1]: not to be confused with Peucestas [2] the son of Alexander from Mieza, introduced at 6.9.3.

5.6 *Leonnatus* [2]: cf. 2.12.5.

6.1 *the performing arts*: the contest included dithyrambic choruses and tragedies (Plutarch, *Alexander* 29.1).

6.3 *sent Amphoterus to support the Peloponnesians*: the resistance movement was against Macedonian rule in Greece. But Agis looked to Persia for financial and military support (2.13.4 and 6), so Alexander turned this against the Spartans by raising the spectre of the threat to Greece from Persia.

6.5 *they all went into exile*: in spring 336 Philip accused them of egging Alexander on in the Pixodarus affair (see at 1.23.7).

6.7 *Alexander* [1] *of Epirus*: the brother of Olympias, he had gone to Italy effectively as a mercenary leader to assist the men of Tarentum against their neighbours. He was killed in the winter of 331/0.

Harpalus: he was reinstated, but absconded a second time in 324 with treasure from the vaults in Babylon, and a record of scandalous behaviour (an episode probably covered by Arrian in the section of text missing after 7.12.7).

7 **From Thapsacus to Gaugamela.** Time references include July/August 331 for departure (7.1), the lunar eclipse datable to 20/1 September (7.6), and the date of the battle, 28 September, if not 1 October (Plutarch, *Alexander* 31.8 with *Camillus* 19.5). Alexander headed north from Thapsacus (perhaps Meskene: 2.13.1) and then east, as Darius could have anticipated. Darius had probably already left Babylon, heading north up the Tigris.

8–15 **The battle of Gaugamela.**

8.3–6 The composition of Darius' army: Aristobulus cited a captured Persian document for the battle-order (3.11.3–7), but Arrian chose to list the units with their commanding officers, as in Herodotus' catalogue of Xerxes' forces (Herodotus 7.61–88). The total Arrian gives at 8.6 is modest by comparison with Herodotus' 1,700,000 for Xerxes' army; but Curtius must be closer to historical reality with 200,000 infantry and 45,000 cavalry (4.12.6–13).

8.3 *Bessus*: given precedence perhaps as a leading commander on the Persian left (cf. 11.3), but he reappears later as the key character in the story of Darius' demise (chap. 21).

8.7 *Gaugamela*: Tell Gomel, north of Jebel Maqlub, *c*.108 km from Arbela [Erbil].

9.8 *duty . . . success*: in his commentary on this passage Bosworth notes that the vocabulary and rhetorical devices of this last sentence point to Thucydides as Arrian's model. The historical pep talk would have been less cerebral.

10.2 *won in open fight without trickery*: Arrian similarly advocates rational risk-taking over deviousness, in his *Tactics* 40.12 and *The Art of Hunting* 24.4. Other exchanges between Parmenion and Alexander are recorded at 1.13.2–7 and 18.6–9, 2.25.2–3 and 3.9.3–4, 18.11–12. They may go back to an unsympathetic treatment of Parmenion by Callisthenes. But Parmenion was an experienced commander, and Arrian here goes on to defend Alexander's decision (10.2–4).

12.4 *Sitalces . . . Agathon*: Sitalces, an Odrysian prince, and Agathon, a Macedonian, commanded Thracian infantry and cavalry respectively. Both men were used as agents in the murder of Parmenion in 330, and then executed in 325, albeit on charges of maladministration (3.26.3; 6.27.3–4 with Curtius 10.1.1–8).

15.1 *Parmenion . . . needed help*: Callisthenes' version of this episode represented the elderly commander as a torpid incompetent, petty-mindedly forcing Alexander to abandon the chase after Darius (Plutarch, *Alexander* 33.10).

15.7 *Pyanepsion*: an error for Boedromion [September] (Plutarch, *Alexander* 31.8, with Arrian 3.7.6), as could arise from faulty correlation of the Athenian, Macedonian, and Babylonian calendars.

16   **Babylon and Susa.**

16.4 *temples destroyed by Xerxes*: repeated at 7.17.2, but untrue as Herodotus saw the temple of Bel-Marduk, the Esagila, still intact (1.181.2 and 183.3).

Mazaeus satrap: he had a Babylonian wife, but Babylonians would not have been thrilled to be back under a Persian satrap.

16.5 *Chaldaeans*: Babylonian priests skilled in astronomy and revered for their power of prophecy (cf. 7.16.5–17.4).

16.6 *Philoxenus*: probably an error for Xenophilus, as at 16.9 Arrian certainly errs in naming the garrison commander appointed to Susa as Mazarus instead of Xenophilus (Curtius 6.2.16).

16.7 *reached Susa . . . in twenty days*: a distance of *c.*370 km. Alexander reached Susa, the administrative capital of the Persian Empire, *c.*14–25 December 331. Susa was unfortified and with a mixed population, hence the ready surrender.

Harmodius and Aristogeiton: heroized by the Athenians for assassinating the tyrant Hipparchus in 514, which led to the expulsion of the last of the Peisistratid dynasty and the establishment by 502 of Athens' proto-democracy. Xerxes seized the statues in 480/79, but Arrian's reference to the return of the statues at this point is premature (contrast 7.19.2; other sources date it long after Alexander's death).

16.9–10 **The despatch of Menes and the arrival of Amyntas.** Treasure sent 'for the Spartan war' should mean that Alexander had not yet heard if Agis had been defeated, or was allowing for follow-up operations. Thus Amyntas' arrival indicates that even with the threat from Agis, Macedon had the manpower resources to send reinforcements to Alexander. The reinforcements included six thousand Macedonian infantry and five hundred Macedonian cavalry (Diodorus Siculus 17.65.1; Curtius 5.1.40–2).

17.1–18.9 **War with the Uxians in the Zagros mountains.** Curtius 5.3–4 offers a fuller account. Alexander first secured a treaty with the lowland Uxians to the east of the Pasitigris [Karun] (17.1), in the area of Shushtar; then launched a campaign against the mountain Uxians (17.2–6).

18.1 *to Persepolis by the carriage road*: from Behbehan, and along the southern route via the Tang-i Muhammad Rizā pass.

18.2 *the Persian Gates*: this may be the pass known as the Darvāzeh-ye Fars, just north of Yasuj, *c.*80 km SE of Abadeh, *c.*55 km NE of Ardakan (the monographic study of H. Speck, 'Alexander at the Persian Gates', *American Journal of Ancient History*, NS 1: 1 (2002), exposes the flaws in earlier equations).

18.9 *Ptolemy*: some suggest that Ptolemy here claimed credit due to Philotas (18.6), or that a source with another agenda substituted Ptolemy for Polyperchon (Curtius 5.4.20).

18.10–12 **The occupation of Persepolis.** Alexander was in the area of Persepolis from January to early May 330. The occupation began with a massacre and looting, and ended with the destruction of the royal capital by fire. Arrian spares Alexander some bad press by the brevity of his treatment, and by omitting the tale of Ptolemy's mistress Thaïs' role in inciting the orgy of arson, but in the final, critical comment he shows that he was well aware of the basic facts.

18.10 *Pasargadae*: the royal city, *c.*45 km NE of Persepolis, founded by Cyrus the Great.

19.1 *rebellion might break out*: the four-month wait till Alexander could head north through the Zagros mountains tested his ability to keep his army motivated, and he had received reports back in 332 that Philotas was plotting against him (3.26.1).

19.2 *Caspian Gates . . . Ecbatana*: the Gates were possibly the Sar-i Darreh defile, east of Rhagae (20.2) and Tehran. Ecbatana in Media was the summer capital of the Persian kings.

19.5–6 **The discharge of allied units.** Other sources more credibly put this exercise later, in the Parthian capital, Hecatompylus [Shāhr-i Qūmis], and after Alexander had heard of the murder of Darius. His death could be taken as marking the end of the war initiated by the Corinthian League, and thus conscripts provided by league states could be discharged, but encouraged to stay on as mercenaries. The generous deal offered to Greek allied troops caused mutinous talk among the Macedonians, who would have been happy to 'take a package' and return home (Curtius 6.2.12–21; Diodorus Siculus 17.74.3). Arrian omits that episode.

20.1–22.6 **The pursuit of Darius and his murder.**

21.1 *Nabarzanes*: the title given him by Arrian, *chiliarch*, representing the Persian *hazaparati*, would mean that he was at least supreme commander of the Persian cavalry, if not the king's Grand Vizier (see Appendix II).

21.5 *Bessus . . . a relative of Darius*: kinship with Darius would explain why he took precedence over Nabarzanes. He was the satrap of Bactria (3.8.3), but the murder occurred further west in (Greater) Parthia/Parthyaea, whose satrap was Phrataphernes (23.4).

21.6 *a village*: perhaps Lasjerd.

22.1 *Darius' body . . . royal tombs*: ever the pragmatist, Alexander now dropped the line that Darius was a usurper, party to murder and not of royal blood (contrast 2.14.5).

22.6 *his daughter was married to Alexander*: Alexander married Stateira [2] at Susa in 324, though Arrian calls her Barsine (7.4.4).

23–5 **Campaigns in the Elburz mountains and into Areia.**

23.6 *Zadracarta*: perhaps the modern Sari, to the east of Amul and the territory of the Mardians (24.1).

23.7 *Artabazus*: he had been born into the Achaemenid royal house, and was appointed satrap of Hellespontine Phrygia, perhaps in 359. But he then joined the satraps who were in revolt against Artaxerxes III, and in 352 sought refuge in the court of Philip II, remaining there for many years. He was also the brother-in-law of Memnon (2.1.1–3) and Mentor, which would have added to his credibility as a mediator (23.9).

24.5 *peace and alliance*: cf. 3.23.8. The legalistic distinctions made in 24.4–5 mean that although Alexander had released the allied Greek troops at Hecatompylus, the Corinthian League remained in force, and its rules could be applied retrospectively.

25.1 *Zadracarta* [Sari]. . . *Susia*: he probably travelled via Shārūd to enter Areia at Susia [Tūs] near Mashhad. From there he could have headed north-east towards the Marv Oasis, but more likely turned south towards Herat, to enter Bactria via the valley of the Hari Rud. The trouble with Satibarzanes, however, took him further south to Farah.

25.5 *Artacoana*: often identified as Kalāt-i Nadirī, north of Mashhad, but more likely a settlement in the area of Herat.

25.6 *sixty-five miles in two days*: Arrian's account is much abbreviated. The picture may be that as Alexander made the final dash of *c.*104 km to Artacoana, Satibarzanes was already fleeing towards Bactria with a small cavalry force. The bulk of his infantry fled to a natural fortress (Curtius 6.6.23), and that may be where Alexander rejoined Craterus (25.8), and led the final assault on the Areian position.

25.8 *the Drangian royal capital*: Phrada, changed to Prophthasia, mod. Farah. Arrian oscillates between the forms Drangian and Zarangian.

26–7 **The judicial murders of Philotas and Parmenion.** Parmenion had been left in Ecbatana, and Philotas' brother had recently died (25.4). Arrian deals with this discreditable episode in the briefest possible way, and obscures it with more generous treatment of unrelated material (27.4–5). Even if there really was a conspiracy—perhaps intended to give the kingship to the Lyncestian Alexander—Philotas' crime emerges as misprision of treason, though a confession extracted under torture indicated worse. A mass meeting of Macedonians could not try Philotas in any proper sense, but could acclaim Alexander's clear verdict. On conspiracies real and imagined in Alexander's reign see especially E. Badian, 'Conspiracies', in A. B. Bosworth and E. Baynham, *Alexander the Great in Fact and Fiction* (Oxford: Oxford University Press, 2000), 50–95.

27.1 *Amyntas* [4]: introduced at 1.8.2. He had fallen foul of Olympias, who complained about him to Alexander, for she was given to accusatory letters. His seniority and good standing with a large section of the Macedonian infantry help to explain his acquittal.

27.4 *Hephaestion . . . and Cleitus* [2]: Hephaestion picked as Alexander's special friend (cf. 1.12.1; 2.12.6–7), and Cleitus as an older and highly experienced cavalry officer.

28–30 **The invasion of Afghanistan and the capture of Bessus.**

28.1 *march to Bactra*: via Qandahār and Ghazneh. The weather conditions point to the period January/February 329. The approach of envoys from the Makran, the area of the Gedrosians, and the north-western area of Pakistan was not to spare them from invasion later on. Arrian variously uses the form Bactra to refer to the satrapy of Bactria (as here) and its capital (Balkh), as at 29.1. The latter is also commonly styled Zariaspa (as at 4.1.5).

28.4 *Alexandria*: Alexandria by the Caucasus (Hindu Kush) was either close to Begram or at Opian north of Charikar and Kabul. It served as the capital of the Parapamisadae satrapy.

28.5 *Caucasus . . . Taurus . . . part of the Caucasus range*: at 5.5.1–4 Arrian corrects himself, noting that flatterers called the Parapamisus [Hindu Kush] the Caucasus to give Alexander the credit of crossing that range.

28.6 *silphium*: probably asafoetida, apparently used as a marinade (cf. Bosworth ad loc.).

28.9 *Nautaca*: probably Shakhrisyabz in Uzbekistan (cf. 4.18.1).

29.1 *Artabazus*: this appointment of a Persian as a satrap is worth noting, though Artabazus had a long association with the Macedonians, having found refuge in the court of Philip II for several years from 352 BC, and he was also the brother-in-law of the Rhodian brothers Memnon and Mentor.

29.2 *Oxus . . . discharging into the Great Sea*: in antiquity it was understood that the Oxus [Amu-Darya] flowed into the Caspian (not the Aral), and the Caspian was believed to be a gulf of the enveloping Great Sea (Oceanus).

30.5 *Aristobulus, though, says that it was the associates of Spitamenes and Dataphernes*: it may be that Ptolemy exaggerated his role in securing the arrest of Bessus (30.3), but equally possible that Aristobulus chose to transfer the demeaning brutality from Alexander to Spitamenes and Dataphernes. See further at 4.7.3.

30.8 *Herodotus . . . Tanaïs*: there was some confusion because of the mythis-torical equation of the Tanaïs [Don] and the Orxantes/Jaxartes [Syr-Darya]. Then there was some geographical confusion: the Jaxartes was believed to flow into the Caspian (not the Aral), and one theory was that the Caspian was the same as the Maeotis [the Azov]. Arrian cites Herodotus 4.57.

30.9 *Gadeira* [Cadiz] . . . *Libya*: the North African coast from the Straits of Gibraltar to Egypt could be styled Libya.

30.11 *Out of thirty thousand . . . eight thousand survived*: but Curtius says that only 20,000 were involved, and they promptly surrendered after Alexander was wounded (Curtius 7.6.2–6). Arrian's version means that Alexander's wound was decisively avenged.

BOOK FOUR

1.1 *Scythians known as the Abii*: if the Jaxartes [Syr-Darya] was the dividing line between these Scythians and the European Scythians, the Abii may have been nomads moving about the Kyzyl Kum, south of the Jaxartes and between Sogdiana and the Aral Sea.

'most civilized of all men': Homer, *Iliad* 13.6, a fine example of Utopian myth.

1.1–2 *European Scythians*: archaeological evidence suggests that their king, who died shortly after this first diplomatic exchange (4.15.1), was buried in the 'royal' burial mound at Chertomlyk (west of the Borysthenes [Dnieper]). The picture is complicated because Alexander historians con-fused the Jaxartes (Syr-Darya) with the Tanaïs (the Don) (so 4.3.6 with 3.30.8–9), and, unaware of the Aral Sea as a separate entity, equated the Caspian Sea with the Maeotis (the Sea of Azov).

1.3 *a city on the river Tanaïs*: this is referred to as Alexandria Eschate (the Furthermost) and is assumed to have been in the area of Khodzhent.

1.4 *Macedonian troops . . . in their cities*: the scale of the physical occupation of eastern Sogdiana provoked armed resistance. For many an immediate reason for deep anger was Alexander's appropriation of Sogdian horses (3.30.6).

1.5 *a pretext for revolt . . . Alexander had summoned . . . barons . . . for a joint conference*: a conference in Zariaspa/Bactra [Balkh], the satrapal capital, implies that the barons were Bactrians, whom the Sogdians were trying to frighten into joining the revolt.

2.1 *the seven cities*: in modern Kazak the area is called Jety-asar, the seven fortresses. The first mentioned, Gaza (mod. Nau), lies *c*.27 km ESE from Khodzhent.

2.2 *Cyropolis*: it was on the river Jaxartes (4.3.2), and the original local name may live on in the modern Kurkat.

2.4 *the second city*: perhaps the modern Ura-Tyube.

3.3 *Alexander . . . suffered a heavy blow to his head and neck*: Plutarch and Curtius say that Alexander was knocked unconscious, was almost blind for several days (perhaps the first attested case of transient cortical blindness), and his speech was affected. All this would have alarmed his followers, as the brain was regarded as 'the life substance'.

3.5 *Aristobulus says . . . Alexander . . . killed all*: Aristobulus is usually the apologist for Alexander, but here could excuse Alexander's murderous record in the killing fields of eastern Sogdiana. If Alexander was out of action for several days after the wound referred to in 3.3, then the injury was probably inflicted not at Cyropolis, but in the siege of the next city, that of the Memaceni (as Curtius 7.6.17 and 22 has it).

3.7 *In overall command . . . Pharnuches*: the idea of a Persian, even if he grew up in Lycia, being put in command over senior Macedonian army officers (cf. 4.6.1) as early as 329 BC is decidedly odd. Arrian explains that Alexander expected that Pharnuches would be able to negotiate agreements with the native population, and the troops were there more as a show of force than as an invasionary army. The failure of this operation means at least that Alexander underestimated the opposition.

4.1 *neighbouring barbarians who volunteered to be part of the settlement*: Arrian styles the process *synoecism*, but this term for relocation was often a euphemism for forced resettlement (*metoecism*), and Curtius 7.6.27 says that prisoners of war were assigned to the city. The Greek and Macedonian settlers needed a labour force.

4.3 *ridiculed . . . as Darius . . . had been*: his failed campaign of 509 BC against the Scythians living north of the Danube (Herodotus 4.83 ff.) is referred to again at 4.11.9.

Aristander refused . . . something else: but Curtius has Aristander yield to the intimidation (7.7.23–9).

4.5 *He put ashore the archers and slingers*: perhaps on something more substantial than leather floats stuffed with straw, as mentioned at 3.29.4, especially if he had artillery-pieces mounted on them (Curtius 7.9.1–4). But he did not have ships, thus perhaps floats rigged together and bridged with timber, of the type referred to in the Middle East as the *kelek*.

4.8 *some one hundred and fifty were captured*: but Curtius says that more were captured than were killed, and adds that some 1,800 horses were taken (7.9.16).

5.6 *withdrew towards the river Polytimetus* [Zeravshan]: if the battle was fought in the area of Ziadin, there would have been a stretch of the river to the east, behind them.

6.1-2 Aristobulus here, as elsewhere, seems to be careful to protect Alexander's reputation. The disaster occurred because the Scythians did not fight like gentlemen, but mounted an ambush. Secondly, Alexander was let down by his officers, who failed to accept the responsibility of directing the military operation when force, not diplomacy, was required. Aristobulus' version clearly differs from that attributable to Ptolemy (cf. note on 3.30.5), and from Curtius' version, which focuses on Menedemus' heroics (7.7.30–9).

6.2 *no more than forty cavalry and three hundred infantry left*: thus the casualty figures were respectively 820 and 1,200 (cf. 3.7).

6.4 *covered a hundred and seventy miles in three days*: a march rate of this order (*c*.270 km; *c*.90 km per day) with a mixed force seems quite incredible: in 1880 it took Lieutenant-General Frederick Roberts twenty days to rush with reinforcements from Kabul to Kandahar, a distance of *c*.305 miles. The feat attributed to Alexander by Arrian is suspiciously close to that heralded by Herodotus for the march of a smaller group of Spartans who sped to Attica in three days at the time of the battle of Marathon (Herodotus 6.120).

6.6 *the river does . . . disappear into the sand*: indeed the Zeravshan peters out near the village of Karakul. Arrian's source for this geographical digression was probably Aristobulus.

7.1 *Zariaspa . . . winter to be over*: thus Alexander spent the winter 329/8 in the Bactrian capital, Balkh.

  Stasanor . . . sent . . . to arrest Arsaces: cf. 3.25.7.

7.2 *Menes*: he had been sent with the convoy to the coast in late 331 (3.16.9).

  Menon and Asclepiodorus [1]: for their appointments see respectively 2.13.7 and 3.6.8. Curtius gives the total number of reinforcements to reach Alexander in Bactra as 19,400 infantry and 2,600 cavalry.

7.3 *charged him with treason to Darius*: the story is picked up from 3.30.4–5. It suited Alexander's purpose to show respect for Darius as the representative of the institution of monarchy: loyalty to the king was to be a non-negotiable. But the following episodes show that unquestioning loyalty did not come easily to the Macedonian officer class, whether veterans or cadets. The assembly, like that mentioned at 4.15, was clearly not deliberative, nor a judicial enquiry, but to witness, or acclaim, Alexander's decision. This was to be followed by a similar scene in Ecbatana with the local Medes and

Persians dragooned in to watch the killing of Bessus. Arrian criticizes the form of the punishment, but passes over the 'judicial' process.

7.4–14.4 The Great Digression (Bosworth). Arrian dilates on the damaging effect Alexander's victory over the Persians had on his own character. He draws in, out of their correct chronological context, Alexander's murder of Cleitus, Callisthenes' suicidal resistance to the imposition of Persian court ritual, and the conspiracy of the Pages.

7.4 *a descendant of Heracles*: cf. 3.3.1–2.

the Persian mitre: in ceremonial mode, the Persian king wore a tall cylindrical hat (cf. 3.25.3), and that may be what is referred to here as the mitre (Greek *cidaris*; Hebrew *keter*). There is no evidence that Alexander actually ever wore the *cidaris*, but he did take to wearing a Macedonian cap with a fillet, 'the diadem', tied round it (as mentioned at 7.22.2 with 29.4) in the Persian manner, and the 'diadem' became the symbol of monarchy in the Hellenistic period.

7.5 *to sail round the whole of Libya*: cf. 5.26.2. After Alexander's death a document was read out to the troops in Babylon, purporting to be the king's Last Plans. These included a campaign along the Mediterranean coast of North Africa, and then along the coast of Spain (Diodorus Siculus 18.4.4). This was embellished, whether by hero-worshippers or detractors, into a grand scheme to circumnavigate Africa. Arrian was sceptical about the more extravagant versions (7.1.2–4).

8.1 *somewhat later*: at Maracanda in the autumn of 328.

8.2 *the Dioscuri*: Alexander had Apelles paint a picture of him alongside Castor and Pollux (Polydeuces), and the goddess Victory. The myth of the Disocuri's shared parentage, with Zeus as their divine father and Tyndareus as the human father, and their absorption into the realm of the gods, suited Alexander's preoccupation with gaining recognition as of a rank with the gods.

drinking . . . on a more barbarian scale: Herodotus noted the Persians' fondness for wine, but generally Macedonians were regarded as the exemplars of binge-drinking.

8.6 *had saved Alexander's life . . . at the Granicus*: cf. 1.15.8.

8.9 *Aristobulus . . . holds Cleitus solely responsible for his fate*: again we have Aristobulus revising the historical tradition to exculpate Alexander.

9.4 *She had seen her sons die fighting for him*: two sons died in the assault on Miletus in 334, but there was at least one surviving son, Proteas.

9.5 *'sang of the wrath' of Dionysus*: a clear allusion to Homer, *Iliad* 1.1. There are other echoes of the *Iliad*, particularly in the story of Alexander's killing of Cleitus and the remorse that he then displayed. Such allusions were no doubt inspired by Alexander's claim to be descended from Achilles on his mother's side (cf. 1.12.1–2).

9.6 *admitted he had made an error*: this is picked up at 7.29.1.

9.7 *Anaxarchus the sophist*: as a follower of Democritus (born *c.*460), Anaxarchus would have believed that all matter is composed of atoms in freefall but with the propensity to swerve. This theory, as developed by the Epicureans, was opposed to determinism, and promoted the ethics of humanism and self-determination. But Arrian, as a Stoic, gives Anaxarchus the treatment he had heard Epictetus give the Epicureans, and continues the attack at 4.10.6. The idea here expressed, that the king was the law animate, was an element in the formulation of the ideals of monarchy in the Hellenistic period.

9.9 *formal obeisance*: this ritual (in Greek *proskynesis*) was practised in the Persian court as a mark of deference in greeting the king (as explained at 2.12.6). Alexander may well have come to believe by this time that he had a divine parentage, but it was certainly not Persian practice to consider their kings as having a divine nature. Greeks and Macedonians opposed to ruler cult chose to give *proskynesis*, especially with prostration, a religious significance.

Anaxarchus: he may have humoured Alexander's pretensions, but in other contexts he is reputed to have made fun of Alexander's ideas of his own divine nature, as when this self-proclaimed god called out for a bowl of soup when he was feeling ill.

Agis: he and Choerilus were the poets laureate of Alexander's court, universally lampooned for the execrable verse with which they constructed their eulogistic epics. By coupling Anaxarchus and Agis here Arrian underlines his contempt for the philosopher.

10.1 *Callisthenes*: Callisthenes of Olynthus had studied under Aristotle, to whom he was distantly related. Callisthenes had also written substantial works on contemporary history, and Alexander took him along as his 'embedded' historian. He duly delivered, but by 328 he was losing respect for Alexander. Unlike the court poets, he began to let his disenchantment show. Plutarch saw him as highly intelligent, but not very sensible (*Alexander* 54.1), as indeed did Arrian (4.12.7).

10.3 *Harmodius and Aristogeiton*: their killing of Hipparchus in 514 led to the expulsion of his brother Hippias in 510, and the final collapse of the tyranny of the Peisistratid family, and the transition to what was eventually called democracy. See on 3.16.7.

10.4 *Eurystheus*: Athenian victory over this mythical tyrant of Mycenae and Argos was probably concocted in the late fifth century.

10.7 *to award these divine honours to their own king*: in a Greek democratic state it would have been for the popular assembly to vote on the admission of any new cult into the city. Thus, for example, there was to be a debate in Athens in 324/3 on the proposal to accord Alexander divine honours. Indeed Callisthenes goes on to ask whether Alexander would want to force ruler cult on the Greeks, when the hallmark of the Greek *polis* was autonomy, literally the freedom to decide on their own laws. The surviving accounts of this debate in Bactria in 327 naturally reflect an issue of the early Roman Empire, whether the cult of the emperor was acceptable before an emperor's death and a formally recognized apotheosis.

11.7 *to add Asia to Greece*: the original aims were surely less ambitious: cf. 1.11.5 and 18.1–2. Alexander's reputed ambitions receive further expansion at 4.15.6.

11.9 *Cyrus . . . the first man to receive obeisance*: this is noted by Xenophon, *Cyropaedeia* 8.3.14.

Cyrus . . . Darius . . . Xerxes . . . Artaxerxes: Cyrus perished in battle against the Massagetae in 530; Darius crossed the Danube into Scythian territory in perhaps 513/12, but had to call off the invasion; Xerxes was defeated by the Athenian navy at Salamis, and the troops he left behind were then soundly defeated by the Athenians and Spartans at Plataea in 480/79 (though Alexander chose to play down the role of the Spartans: cf. 1.16.7); and Artaxerxes claimed a victory at Cynaxa in 401, despite the superiority of Cyrus' Greek mercenaries.

12.1 *caught the mood of the Macedonians*: there was a fault-line between the democratic culture and traditions of the Greek states, represented here by Callisthenes, and Macedonian monarchy, represented here by Anaxarchus' approval of royal diktat. Alexander would not have welcomed Callisthenes' encouragement of humanist rationalism over against submission to charismatic leadership, especially as the divide between the veterans and younger men in Alexander's army made Macedonian unity somewhat fragile.

12.2 *Leonnatus* [2]: introduced at 2.12.4–5, he had been promoted to the rank of Bodyguard in 332/1 (3.5.5). He was close enough to Alexander to be able to survive this mocking reaction to *proskynesis*. Curtius features Polyperchon in this episode and not Leonnatus.

12.3 *received a kiss*: like *proskynesis*, the kiss was an element of Persian court ritual. Alexander later revived the custom as a mark of recognition for Persian aristocrats whom he had admitted into his court (7.11.6).

12.7–14.4 The conspiracy of the Pages.

13.1 *sons of leading Macedonians*: these are the Royal Pages. The last group known to have joined Alexander before this event arrived with the reinforcements in late 331. By 327 they should have been about post-adolescent (cf. 16.6).

13.3 *life was not worth living without revenge taken on Alexander*: Hermolaus' sense of humiliation is intelligible, and his wish to take revenge echoes that of Pausanias, the assassin of Philip II. It is more difficult to see why these Pages, recruited in their early teens, should have conspired as a group against Alexander. The repeated references to homosexual ties (13.3 and 13.6) belong to a pattern of prurient comments in various sources and thus have limited value. The Pages may have been vengeful because of humiliations imposed on their fathers, and of course there is a common pattern for military coups to be initiated by junior, relatively obscure officers.

Arrian slips in a list of complaints as a brief summary of what Hermolaus said in his trial (14.2), but implies that it might not be historical. Thus he finishes up without any serious explanation of the conspiracy.

13.5 *Aristobulus has this account*: his revisionist account turns a night of binge drinking into a night spent by Alexander with drinkers at a seer's instruction. Aristobulus goes on to claim that under interrogation the Pages incriminated Callisthenes (14.1), though the stronger tradition indicates that there was no evidence against him: Alexander supposedly wrote in a letter that the Pages mentioned no other co-conspirator (Plutarch, *Alexander* 55.5). Aristobulus takes the fiction further by stating that Alexander did not have Callisthenes killed, but kept him in chains till he died of natural causes (14.3).

15.1 *For the second time an embassy . . . from the European Scythians*: their first approach is covered at 4.1.1–2. Arrian here appears to revert to the winter Alexander spent in Balkh, 329/8, since he only relates Alexander's return to the Oxus at 4.15.7. But Curtius 8.1.7–10, more credibly, sets the arrival of these Scythians in the summer of 328, when Alexander was in Maracanda.

15.4 *Chorasmians . . . Colchians and Amazons*: Arrian naively follows geographical fantasy and ethnographic myth, while Curtius puts the Chorasmians to the south of the Aral Sea.

15.5 *not the time to march to the Black Sea*: but the idea resurfaces at 7.1.3.

Artabazus . . . in charge of Bactria: 3.29.1.

15.6 *his immediate concern was India*: his goals, as set out at 4.11.7, are now expanded, and credible if Arrian means the area west of the Indus, as at 4.22.6, or the territory either side of the Indus. But there is debate whether he ever seriously intended to push on towards the Ganges (Bk. 5.25–6).

15.7 *Alexander . . . returned to . . . the Oxus*: this would be the spring of 328. Arrian omits two lengthy stages of marching and campaigning after Alexander left Balkh.

spring of oil: Alexander reported this in a letter to Antipater (Plutarch, *Alexander* 57.5–9).

16.1 *Polyperchon . . . Meleager*: the four were brigade commanders of the Companion Infantry.

16.3 *dispatched Coenus . . . into Scythia*: Coenus was sent on this mission ten days after the murder of Cleitus (Curtius 8.2.13), and before the winter of 328/7 (Curtius 8.2.19 with Arrian 4.18.2). Coenus invaded the territory of the Massagetae along the lower stretch of the Oxus, and, to the south, bordering on Bactria.

16.6 *Peithon [2] . . . and Aristonicus the musician*: it is implausible that the garrison force left behind in the satrapal capital, Zariaspa (Balkh), was answerable to no one more senior than a commissariat officer and a musician, even if Peithon's main function was the training of the Royal Pages. The episode reads rather like that of the ambush of the Macedonians on the Zeravshan, when the interpreter Pharnuches found himself out of his depth when required to give military leadership. Again an attempt to explain away a military failure exposes Alexander to the charge that he failed to provide the required command structure.

the Royal Pages: the conspiracy of the Pages (4.13) was still in the future, as it happened in Bactra in the following year, 327 (4.22.2).

17.3 *relieved Artabazus of the satrapy . . . on grounds of age*: after the outrageous raid by the Massagetae on Balkh perhaps Artabazus really did ask to be allowed 'to spend more time with his family'. Alexander initially designated Cleitus as the next satrap, but after his murder (4.8.8–9.1) Amyntas was appointed to the post.

17.4 *Gabae*: perhaps somewhere north of the Oxus, towards the western end of the Zeravshan.

17.5 *These Scythians . . . their families*: Arrian gives a similar stereotype of nomads in a different context at *Indica* 40.8.

17.7 *they decapitated Spitamenes and sent his head to Alexander*: but in Curtius' melodramatic version, Spitamenes' wife wished to be free of her bellicose, unstable husband, and tricked him into drinking himself comatose. She promptly decapitated him and delivered the head to Alexander as a peace offering. He was appreciative, but banished the woman from his camp lest she had a brutalizing effect on the sensitive Greeks (Curtius 8.3.1–15).

18.1–3 **A shake-up of the satrapal administration.**

18.1 *Nautaca*: cf. 3.28.9. Probably Shakhrisyabz in Uzbekistan. There Alexander spent the winter 328/7.

Stasanor: cf. 3.29.5 and 4.7.1. The scene presented here appears to be a doublet of that at 4.7.1. Stasanor now had added to his satrapy the formerly independent satrapy of Drangiana, whose capital was Farah.

18.2 *Phrataphernes*: Phrataphernes is introduced at 3.8.4. Alexander now made him satrap of Hyrcania as well as Parthia, thus restoring to him the position he had held under Darius. In addition he was given responsibility for the territory of the Tapurians and Mardians.

18.3 *to bring up the home army*: Alexander had last received Macedonian reinforcements in 331 (3.16.10). He now insisted that Antipater release troops from those available to him. There is no record of these officers completing their mission. As Sopolis was the father of Hermolaus, the central figure in the conspiracy of the Pages (4.13.2–4), he had good reason not to hasten back to Alexander's camp.

18.4–20.4 **The battle for the Rock of Sogdiana.** Arrian sets this episode and the following battle for the Rock of Chorienes (21) in the spring of 327, but Curtius, who calls the Sogdian Rock the Rock of Ariamazes, includes the earlier action in events of 328. Arrian relates the capture of Rhoxane at this rock, but others link it with the Rock of Chorienes, otherwise styled the Rock of Sisimithres. The last discrepancy can be resolved if Chorienes was the name which went with the chieftainship which Sisimithres held.

18.4 *the Rock of Sogdiana*: tentatively identified as a high point overlooking the gorge just north of Derbent, some 160 km south of Samarcand.

Oxyartes . . . had revolted from Alexander: this Bactrian, if not Sogdian, noble, introduced at 3.28.10, presumably joined the resistance movement referred to at 4.1.5.

18.7 *three hundred darics*: 300 gold darics or staters would be the equivalent of one talent of silver. Thus Alexander must mean that only the first twelve men up would receive the money prizes, ranging from twelve talents down to one.

19.5 *a virgin girl of marriageable age called Rhoxane*: Arrian records this story of love at first sight and Alexander's decision to marry her some time before her father, Oxyartes, learnt of her capture and went to surrender to Alexander (4.20.4). But vulgate sources set Alexander's first sight of Rhoxane at a banquet held by Oxyartes after his surrender to Alexander. In Arrian's sequence Alexander's falling for Rhoxane was entirely personal and honourable, and Arrian expands on this with a digression on his exemplary treatment of the female members of Darius' family after their capture at Issus (20.1–3). The reality no doubt was that Oxyartes was persuaded to give up Rhoxane as a victor's prize (Curtius 8.4.26 says that Alexander invoked the memory of his ancestor Achilles in his appropriation of Briseïs); and the marriage had a political function in building a link with the Bactrian nobility. Arrian's presentation seems designed to shed a positive light on an action that was resented by the Macedonians and called for some justification by Alexander (cf. Curtius 8.4.29–30 and 10.3.11).

Holt essays an understanding of this teenager's experience by reference to that of the young Afghan orphan given unwanted fame by the front-cover photograph of her in an issue of *National Geographic* (F. Holt, *Into the Land of Bones* (Berkeley: University of California Press, 2005), 86–91). But the trajectory of Rhoxane's life was very different: see further at 7.4.4.

19.6 *more praise than censure*: there were Macedonians in his army who did indeed resent Alexander's marriage to an Asian girl. Some 10,000 Macedonians acquired Asian partners (Arrian 7.4.8), but the issue was different over Rhoxane, because of the prospect of his producing an heir of mixed blood.

21 **The battle for the Rock of Chorienes** (or Rock of Sisimithres: note on 18.4–20.4).

21.1 *the Rock of Chorienes*: perhaps south of Faisabad, near Narak, overlooking the gorge where the Puli-Sang suspension bridge crosses (or crossed) the Wachsch.

22.1 *Catanes*: Curtius records that he was one of the conspirators who joined Sisimithres in arresting Bessus and handing him over to Alexander (Arrian 3.29.6–30.3).

22.2 *Alcetas*: he had taken over from his elder brother, Perdiccas, the command of the brigade from his own canton, Orestis, and Lyncestis.

22.3–30.9 From the Hindu Kush to Gandhara.

22.3 *spring was over*: the next temporal references at 5.9.4 and 19.3 indicate that Alexander left Balkh in the early summer of 327. He headed south over the Hindu Kush to Alexandria by the Caucasus (cf. 3.28.4).

22.5 *Tyriespis*: a Persian had the status of satrap, but the Macedonian, Nicanor, had the military clout. For Tyriespis' fate see 6.15.3.

22.6 *Taxiles*: persuaded by his son Omphis, he sought terms from Alexander, but died not long after the gift exchange. With Alexander's permission Omphis then took over the regnal name Taxiles in the spring of 326. His capital was in the area north-west of Rawalpindi (cf. 5.3.6).

22.7 *Hephaestion and Perdiccas*: after the murder of Cleitus, Perdiccas was given his command over half of the Companion Cavalry (cf. 3.27.4). Alexander needed a macho officer to balance the less bellicose Hephaestion.

22.8 *Peucelaotis . . . city*: the capital city of Peucelaotis (Gandhara) bore the same name, and may have been near Charsada. Arrian creates confusion by appearing to refer at 28.6 to another city called Peucelaotis closer to the Indus.

24.4 *Ptolemy . . . drove right through the Indian's thigh*: perhaps an intertextual reference to *Iliad* 16.307–11, Arrian's source, Ptolemy, casting himself in the role of Patroclus, Achilles' favourite.

24.6 *the king's instructions*: set out at 4.23.5. The main entry on Craterus is at 7.12.3–4.

24.10 *the brigades of Philip and Philotas*: probably light infantry, as suggested by 3.29.7.

25.4 *Ptolemy says . . . over forty thousand men were captured, and over two hundred and thirty thousand oxen*: Arrian here switches to indirect speech, not to claim Ptolemy as the guarantor of the historicity of the detail, but surely to mark his own scepticism about figures of biblical proportions.

26.1 *Massaga*: the capital of the Assacenians (cf. *Indica* 1.8) may have been just east of the Katgala Pass, to the west of the Wuch Khwar, and north-west of Chakdarra.

26.4 *hit in the ankle by a bow-shot*: Arrian downplays the seriousness of the wound and omits the anecdote that Dioxippus flattered Alexander by alluding to *Iliad* 5.339–40 on Aphrodite's wound, from which *ichor* flowed, the gods' equivalent of blood. Alexander snapped at Dioxippus that this was blood, and it hurt.

27.4 *cut down the Indians trapped inside*: other sources emphasize Alexander's violation of his agreement with the mercenaries, but Arrian, or his source (possibly Ptolemy), mitigates the treachery by making their bid to run away a violation of the condition that they should enrol in his army.

27.5 *Bazira . . . Ora*: Bazira was Bir-kot, across the Swat and upstream from Chakdarra, thus Ora is taken as a Ude-gram.

27.7 *Abisares*: his territory stretched from the Indus to beyond the Hydaspes (in the Hazara region of Pakistan), and lay to the north of Taxiles' kingdom. Abisares' support of the Gandharan resistance was no doubt a reaction to Taxiles' submission to Alexander (4.22.6).

28.1 *the Rock. The other barbarians . . . the rock . . . called Aornus*: if the text is sound, and means that the Bazirans fled to their mountain fortress, while others, less immediately threatened, fled to another stronghold, then the Baziran refuge was probably Mount Ilam (*c*.2,800 m), and the other the twin peaks of Una-sar (Aornus) and Pir-sar (2,670 m), closer to the Indus.

28.2 *Heracles . . . probably . . . did not*: Arrian returns to the issue at *Indica* 5.13. The 'Heracles' of Gandhara may represent the god Indra, who, in Indian myth, vanquished Vrita Aurnavābha (= Aornos?).

28.5 *Orobatis*: possibly Shahbazgarhi.

28.6 *secured the surrender . . . of Peucelaotis*: the position of this city, 'not far from the Indus', and its peaceful submission to Alexander, suggest that this is not the same as the Peucelaotis capital referred to at 22.7, but Arrian may have confused two accounts in his sources.

28.7 *Embolima*: close to Pir-sar, therefore perhaps Kabulgram rather than Ambela.

30.5 *Dyrta*: possibly Daggar, the capital of the modern Buner District.

30.9 *the bridge*: the crossing-point was probably north of Und/Udabhanda.

BOOK FIVE

1–2 On the track of Dionysus.

1.1–3.4 Digression on Alexander's fascination with Dionysus. Apart from expressions of uncertainty (1.2, 2.7, 3.1 and 4), Arrian distances himself a little from the myth by some use of indirect speech and archaic vocabulary.

1.1 *Nysa*: somewhere east of the river Kunar, but before Arigaeum [Nawagai] (4.24.6). Thus Arrian treats this episode out of its chronological context.

1.5 *to leave them free and independent*: cf. 1.17.4 and 3.27.5. Thus Acuphis speaks, not as a 'Brahman', but as a Greek, albeit an oligarch rather than a democrat.

1.6 *Meros . . . thigh*: as the largest bone in the body the thigh was particularly rich in marrow, which was of the same substance as ran up through the spine and filled the cranium as the brain. Marrow provided the life-force for the body, while the lungs (*phrenes*) were the organ of thought (R. B. Onians, *The Origins of European Thought* (Cambridge: Cambridge University Press, 1954) sets out the case). Hence the myth that Dionysus drew the seed of life from the thigh of Zeus; and there were parallels in Hindu myth.

2.1 *if . . . spurred by the ambition to surpass Dionysus' achievements*: this fore-shadows Alexander's use of the Dionysus myth as one way of motivating his men to advance beyond the Indus to the Ganges (5.26.5). They refused to accept the challenge.

2.3 *best men . . . commoners*: in Athenian-style democracy rights were proportional and hierarchic.

2.5 *full of ivy and bay*: as the legend developed, vines were added as appropriate for an area rich in associations with Dionysus.

2.7 *Some writers go on*: Alexander's role is thus limited to a perfectly respectable priestly celebration. Arrian was similarly protective of Alexander with regard to the Bacchic revels at Persepolis (3.18.11–12) and in Carmania (6.28.1–2).

3.1 *Eratosthenes*: the geographer, born in Cyrene, who *c*.245 took charge of the library in Alexandria. The main target of his attack on myth-makers was probably Cleitarchus.

3.3 *Caucasus . . . Parapamisus* [Hindu Kush]: Arrian here improves on what he took over from Aristobulus at 3.28.5.

3.4 *cattle branded with the sign of a club*: cf. *Indica* 5.12. Arrian does not repeat Eratosthenes' reasons for rejecting this story, and prefers to conclude this section by veiling a willingness to believe with an expression of agnosticism.

3.5 *reached the river Indus*: the crossing-point was probably upstream from Und (cf. 4.30.7–9), and Alexander arrived there before the end of February 326.

thirty-oared vessels: these triaconters were built in three sections, each perhaps of five metres, so that they could be moved overland where necessary (as at 5.8.5).

3.6 *Taxiles*: this was probably Omphis, who on the death of his father (perhaps the Taxiles of 4.22.6), was entitled to take the royal name Taxiles, but was now seeking Alexander's formal approval. His capital was in the area of Bhir Mound, *c*.35 km north-west of Rawalpindi.

4.2 *Ctesias*: he served as a doctor in the court of Artaxerxes II to 398/7, and wrote a 23-book *Persica* and a single-book *Indica*. A line of text must be missing: Arrian perhaps wrote that while Ctesias gave four and a half miles as its narrowest <and twenty-two at its broadest, others gave one and two-thirds,> and eleven miles respectively (as at 5.20.10).

4.3–6.8 Digression on India, serving to announce his plans for the *Indica*.

4.5 *disaster suffered by . . . Cyrus*: cf. 4.11.9 and Herodotus 1.208–14.

5.1 *Nearchus*: his long-time association with Alexander is recorded at 3.6.5, and his appointment as admiral of the fleet, initially for the voyage down the Indus, is recorded at 6.2.3.

Megasthenes: he probably wrote his *Indica* before about 310 (cf. Arrian, *Indica* 5.3).

5.3 *Mount Parapamisus . . . called Caucasus*: cf. 3.3 above and 3.28.5.

6.2 *Megasthenes spent time with Sibyrtius . . . visit to Sandracottus*: Sandracottus, or Chandragupta, seized control of the kingdom of Magadha, in Bihar, to the south of the Ganges, in 322 and established the Mauryan dynasty, with Pataliputra [Patna] as his capital. If Megasthenes visited Porus (as mentioned at *Indica* 5.1) on his way to Sandracottus, and while Sibyrtius was still satrap of Arachosia, that would have been in the period 322–317. After Porus' death in 318/7, Sandracottus extended his empire into his territory, and from 305 he controlled Gandhara. Megasthenes may have visited Sandracottus again, *c*.303.

6.4 *Hermus . . . Mother Dindymene*: the Great Mother goddess, Cybele, was associated with Mount Dindymus [the Murat Dağ] (cf. Herodotus 1.80.1).

6.5 *Menelaus anchored . . . at the mouth of the . . . Aegyptus*: Homer, *Odyssey* 4.581–2.

7.1–8.1 **The bridge over the Indus.** Arrian alludes to Herodotus 7.34–6 on Xerxes' bridge, but in this section he more obviously imitates Thucydides' prose style.

7.2 *bridges over the Danube . . . or Tigris*: as Bosworth observes in his commentary, Arrian probably wrote with the knowledge of Trajan's crossings of the Danube, first in AD 101, and then his achievement in 116 in being the first Roman to bridge the Tigris.

8.2–19.3 Into India and the battle of the Hydaspes [Jhelum].

8.2 *came to Taxila*: Alexander reached Taxila in early spring, 326.

the ruler of the city, Taxiles: Taxiles (3.6 above), like Abisares, was an independent local prince. Though he was honoured by Alexander, and allowed to keep the royal title, his kingdom became a satrapy, under Philip [5], the brother of Harpalus.

9.1 *pitched camp on the . . . Hydaspes*: this camp was about 27 km from the bend in the river where Alexander eventually crossed (11.2), hence the common view that the camp was at Haranpur and the crossing near Jalalpur. But it would have been difficult to reach Haranpur via the Nandana Pass with heavy wagons (8.5). Thus it is suggested that Alexander headed first for Jhelum, and crossed further north at Fort Mungla. But the issue is further complicated by the geographical evidence that the river has changed its course since antiquity.

9.4 *just after the summer solstice*: but the battle is dated before the solstice, to April/May 326 (19.3). By then the river-level had begun to rise, but it would only have reached its seasonal peak after the solstice.

12.1 *Meleager, Attalus, and Gorgias*: these were Macedonian brigade commanders reassigned for this operation to the command of mercenary units.

13.1 *Seleucus*: he had probably first been appointed to the command of the elite foot guards in 330. In the power-struggle after Alexander's death Seleucus had gained control of Babylon by 311, and he followed the lead of Antigonus and then Ptolemy in taking the royal title in 305. His rule extended to cover much of the old Persian Empire, but his dynasty was associated for the greater part with Syria.

15.5 *elephants . . . at intervals of . . . a hundred feet*: 200 elephants would thus have presented a front of 6 km, apart from the Indian units posted on the wings. That was to confront the Macedonian phalanx of 6,000 men, who, if deployed eight deep, would have occupied no more than 0.75 km. But Curtius, more credibly, mentions only eighty-five elephants, which if spaced every 13 metres (Polyaenus' figure) would have covered only 1 km.

16.3 *Coenus*: here in command of a cavalry unit, though he was an infantry commander (5.12.2).

18.2-3. Battle losses: the vulgate sources give lower Indian casualties: 12,000 killed, and 9,000 captured, and higher Macedonian losses: 700 infantry and 280 cavalry (Diodorus Siculus 17.89.1–3).

18.4–19.6 The surrender of Porus and the aftermath of the battle.

19.3 *granted Porus continued rule*: but now with the title satrap (Plutarch, *Alexander* 60.15).

19.4 *Nicaea . . . and . . . Bucephala*: on either side of the Hydaspes, the latter possibly near Fort Mangla, or Jalalpur (9.1 above).

19.5 *only Alexander could mount him*: the same was said of the horse of Julius Caesar.

19.6 *in Uxian country Alexander lost this horse*: this episode in the Zagros mountains should then have appeared at 3.17.3–5. Arrian may have omitted it because there were different traditions about where it took place, or he considered the manic threat of genocide in the Uxian context fatal to his nobler picture of that campaign.

20.5 *Abisares*: ruler in the area of Hazara running into Azad Kashmir (cf. 4.27.7).

20.7 *Phrataphernes*: cf. 4.18.2.

Sisicottus, satrap of the Assacenian region: but Sisicottus was a regional prince who had been left to guard Aornus, while answerable to the satrap of Swat, Nicanor (4.28.6 and 30.4). Thus the murder victim may have been Nicanor. Philip [5] was the satrap of India (5.8.3), and Tyriespis had been appointed satrap of Parapamisadae in 327 (4.22.5).

21.1–24.8 From the Acesines [Chenab] to the Hyphasis [Beas]. The space given to Alexander's clash with the Cathaeans and the capture of Sangala surely reflects Arrian's dependence on Ptolemy's proud record of his role in the action. Hence too Arrian's silence about Perdiccas' sweep in the area, known from Curtius' account.

22.2 *Sangala*: this city, some distance beyond the then course of the Hydraotes [Ravi] (22.3-4), may have been Amritsar.

24.6 *Eumenes*: he had served Philip in the same role as secretary, and was a prominent figure in Alexander's court. He became a very active player in the power-struggle after Alexander's death, and his role was the more controversial because he was a Greek. He is reputed to have compiled the *Ephemerides* ('Royal Journals'), which have not survived.

25.1–29.3 Mutiny at the Hyphasis. The term 'mutiny' may have anachronistic connotations, but Alexander's troops certainly demonstrated their unwillingness to advance deeper into India, and were horrified at the idea of pushing on to the Ganges and the 'Outer Ocean'. Conspiracy theorists have suggested that Coenus took advantage of this discontent to advance a plot against Alexander, or that Coenus was set up by Alexander to stage a protest that would provide him with an excuse for turning back. But war-weariness or even post-traumatic stress disorder, monsoon rains, and the perception of the futility of further advance may be sufficient explanation of the troops' refusal to indulge Alexander's fantasies any further.

25.1 *Reports of the country beyond the Hyphasis*: Phegeus, a Punjabi rajah, was said to be Alexander's main informant. According to one tradition Alexander received reports on the 'Prasii' (Sanskrit *pracya*, 'living in the east'), centred on Palimbothra [Patna] on the Ganges, and their king 'Aggrames', which may be a version of Anuruddha, the last of the Nanda dynasty. But Alexander was probably more concerned about what lay immediately beyond the Hyphasis.

25.2 *They began to gather in groups*: an echo of Xenophon, *Anabasis* 5.7.2. The troops were beginning to act like mercenaries, and, as H. W. Parke has noted, 'all mercenaries in an emergency [become] a democracy' (*Greek Mercenary Soldiers* (Oxford: Oxford University Press, 1933), 119).

26.2 *the Hyrcanian Sea links with the Indian Gulf*: Arrian's key source, Eratosthenes (cf. *Indica* 3.1–5.3) presented the Hyrcanian Sea [the Caspian] as the gulf in the Outer Ocean before the Persian Gulf, but that was long after Alexander's death. To the anachronism Arrian adds the novelty that the mouth of the Ganges formed a gulf, thus between the Caspian and the Persian Gulf (see Bosworth's commentary and his *From Arrian to Alexander* (Oxford: Oxford University Press, 1988), 129–30). The exotic geography was perhaps intended by Arrian to distance his work from the issues of his own day, after the failure of Trajan's expansionist policy.

we shall sail . . . right round Libya: Libya means Africa. The formulation in the Greek is rather less direct, as though Arrian was reluctant to credit Alexander with such an ambition, and indeed at 7.1.2–3 he registers his reservations. At 6.27.7 the focus is on Carthage and the North African coast.

26.7–8 Alexander's defence of his own record and reminder of his generosity to his troops foreshadows his speech to the mutineers at Opis: 7.10.1–4.

27 **Coenus' advice to Alexander.** Coenus, introduced at 1.6.9, was somewhat protected because this was an assembly of officers, and not a mass meeting (25.2; 27.2), but he was of the older generation (27.3) and there was tension between Alexander and the veterans of Philip's army (cf.

4.8.6). He had also been vulnerable as the brother-in-law of Philotas (Curtius 6.9.30). He died shortly after this episode (6.2.1).

28.4 *the offerings proved inauspicious*: a convenient excuse for calling off the advance into India. But Diodorus Siculus and Strabo add reference to the very demoralizing effect of the troops' exposure to seventy days of monsoon rains.

29.1 *twelve altars*: Arrian does not dwell on the details of the altars and bizarre associated structures, as described by Diodorus Siculus (17.95.1–2). It is likely that this set was created as a marker of Alexander's rivalry with Heracles and Dionysus.

29.4 *Arsaces . . . next to Abisares*: if Abisares, ruler of the Abissarians (*Indica* 4.12), held Hazara (cf. 4.27.7), then Arsaces' territory may have been in the Kashmir.

BOOK SIX

1.1 *flotilla . . . on the banks of the Hydaspes* [Jhelum]: picking up from 5.8.4–5.

1.2–5 **Digression on the Nile.** On the journey down the Hydaspes Arrian used mainly Ptolemy (2.4), but here he refers to Nearchus and Megasthenes (cf. *Indica* 17.6–7). Nearchus certainly mentioned the beans and the crocodiles (1.2), and quoted Homer on the name Aegyptus (1.3).

1.4–5 *the letter to his mother*: collections of letters of Alexander emerged early on as a genre of fictionalized history. But Arrian is here referring to a letter mentioned in a narrative source, presumably Nearchus, though that does not guarantee its historicity.

1.6 *The ships' crews . . . Egyptians*: the timber for this massive ship-building exercise (2.4) would have been floated in down the Jhelum, and the artisans had probably travelled with Alexander, but Alexander may have had to send for these experienced crewmen along with other reinforcements.

2.1–6.6 **The descent of the Hydaspes and Acesines.** Cf. *Indica* 18–19.7. From Aristobulus we learn that the operation began in early November 326 (Strabo 15.1.17). The monsoon was over, but the rivers were still very swollen (4.4–5). The next major stopping-point was Patala, reached in July 325.

2.1 *Coenus . . . died*: Arrian does not encourage suspicion: the book division and the digression distance this brief, positive death-notice from the confrontation with Alexander on the Hyphasis. His brother, Cleander [1], was executed later (6.27.3–4).

Porus: now paramount chief of all the territory between the Hydaspes and the Hyphasis.

2.2 *the capital city of Sopeithes*: Hephaestion was advancing along the eastern bank of the Hydaspes, but other sources put Sopeithes' kingdom beyond the Hydraotis [Ravi]. There were perhaps two kings of the same name.

2.3 *Onesicritus . . . in fact . . . a helmsman*: Onesicritus would indeed have been lower in rank than Nearchus, but he was the helmsman of Alexander's ship (*Indica* 18.9), and chief helmsman of the fleet. But someone was happy to put him down.

3.2 *Heracles . . . Ammon*: Arrian in *Indica* 18.11 mentions sacrifices to 'his ancestral gods', and also games.

4.4–5.4 **The ships caught in the rapids.** Curtius and Diodorus Siculus have similar purple passages, though Diodorus sets the episode at the confluence of the Indus and the Acesines, and has Alexander escaping death by jumping into the water, like Achilles doing battle with the bellowing river (Diodorus Siculus 17.97, with Homer, *Iliad* 21.233–41).

6.1–2 *waterless country . . . one of the cities*: perhaps the Sandarbar desert, leading to a settlement at Kot Kamalia.

6.3 *killed most of them . . . unarmed as they were*: see also 5 and 6. After the mutiny at the Hyphasis these massacres may have served the grim purpose of 'team-building'. This run of killings sets the scene for one of the bloodiest chapters in Alexander's campaigns.

7.1–11.8 **The battle for the chief city of the Mallians.**

7.2–3 *Peithon* [4] . . . *took the place*: the fortress may have been on the site of Tulamba Bhir, on the left bank of the Ravi, some 82 km north-east of Multan.

7.4 *one of the Brahman cities*: Arrian presents the status of the Brahmans more accurately at 16.5 below.

7.5–6 *Alexander . . . shamed the rest of the Macedonians into climbing the wall*: cf. 9.3. Disaffection did not stop with the resolution of the mutiny on the Hyphasis. There is mention of rumblings of discontent during the campaign down the Indus.

8.4 *they had crossed the Hydraotes* [Ravi]: Alexander had crossed the Ravi in pursuit of the Mallians (7.1), thus the Mallians now crossed in the opposite direction, heading west into the Rechna Doab (the area between the Ravi and the Chenab).

9.3 *Alexander thought the Macedonians . . . were too slow*: these Macedonians were under the command of Perdiccas, who in 321/0 invaded Egypt to attack Ptolemy. Thus Arrian may here reflect Ptolemy's hostile version of Perdiccas' role in this battle.

Peucestas [2]: Peucestas, from Mieza and of roughly the same age as Alexander, had served as a trireme commander on the Hydaspes (6.3.1 ff. with *Indica* 18.6). His defence of Alexander in this action won him an exceptional distinction (28.4).

sacred shield . . . from . . . Troy: cf. 1.11.7.

Leonnatus [2] *the Bodyguard*: introduced at 2.12.5. He had incurred Alexander's wrath by ridiculing *proskynesis* (4.12.2).

Abreas: a Macedonian NCO, on double pay, thus a corporal rather than a private.

9.5 *Alexander decided . . . he jumped down*: Arrian introduces a little soliloquy to check the pace and add to the suspense. Reckless, violent action, such as follows when Alexander leaps down, might be labelled berserking, as Arrian implies at 13.4.

11.1 *no woman or child excepted*: even though by now Macedonian officers and men had acquired Asian partners and children. The potentially mortal wounding of Alexander made it a matter of honour for his troops to exact revenge, and, as Arrian saw it, led writers before himself into shameless revamping of the core tradition.

Critodemus . . . Perdiccas: either the doctor performed the delicate task—Curtius calls him Critobulus, and describes him as moist-eyed and white as a sheet with fear and anxiety (9.5.25–6)—or the macho Perdiccas dug in with his sword. The divergence in the sources serves to introduce a digression on Arrian's authorial intent.

11.8 *Ptolemy . . . 'Saviour'*: the epithet Saviour (*Soter*) was a feature of ruler cult in the Hellenistic era. The king was honoured as being like the gods in his power to protect. Ptolemy only took the royal title in late 305 and was hailed Saviour God by Rhodes in 304 (Diodorus Siculus 20.100.3 plus epigraphic evidence).

12–17 From the country of the Mallians to Patala.

13.5 *a Boeotian*: Boeotians were stereotypically 'thick', but this one recites a line from a tragedy by Aeschylus.

14.3 *Philip [5] as satrap*: Philip already had responsibility for a vast area (5.8.3 and 6.2.3), and it was presently extended south to the junction of the Indus and Acesines [Chenab] (6.15.2).

14.5 *the Indus is up to eleven miles wide*: c.18 km. But Strabo 15.1.32 gives the maximum width as 9 km, reducing in places to 1.25 km according to more reasonable sources. Further on the rivers of the Punjab, *Indica* 3.10 and 4.8–10.

15.3 *Oxyartes . . . Tyriespis*: cf. 4.20.3 and 22.5 with 5.20.7.

15.4 *Peithon [4]*: featured above at 6.6.1, 7.2–3, and 8.2–3.

15.7 *granted him the continuation of his rule*: but effective power would be held by the garrison commander left in Musicanus' city. The city has generally been taken as in the area of Rorhi/Alor, near Sukkur.

16.1 *Oxicanus*: Curtius calls his people the Praesti (9.8.11), but that may be just a rendering of the Sanskrit term for people 'living in the east'.

16.4 *the capital city*: perhaps Sehwan, though P. H. L. Eggermont, *Alexander's Campaigns in Sind and Baluchistan* (Leuven: Leuven University Press, 1975), has argued for some site to the north of Shikarpur.

16.5 *another city*: Diodorus Siculus calls it Harmateleia (17.103.1) and links with it the Indian trick of smearing weapons with a poison. Thus Ptolemy fell sick, and his life was saved because Alexander found a herb with antidotal properties. This is but one of the amazing stories that Arrian judged unworthy of inclusion in his account of the Indian campaign.

the Brahmans: these were philosophers, or sophists, attached to the royal court as advisers, and thus to be distinguished from the gymnosophists, the naked ascetics, featured at 7.2.2. Arrian adds a programmatic reference to his *Indica* 11.

17.2 *Patala . . . as I have mentioned before*: at 5.4.1.

17.3 *Craterus was ordered to take the route . . . to Carmania*: Craterus was to take a substantial portion of the army, including some less mobile units, inland, via the Bolan Pass and Drangiana (here with the spelling Zarangian[a]), to Carmania, while Alexander would tackle the Gedrosian desert in Baluchistan, but even so with large numbers of camp-followers.

17.4 *join up . . . at Patala*: the site of the city of Patala is uncertain: possibly Bahmanabad, or Nisarpur.

18–20 The occupation of Patala and exploration of the delta. Much of this is probably from Nearchus (cf. 2.3), as is suggested by Alexander's deep concern for Nearchus at 19.5.

18.3 *to march down the island of Patala*: Arrian imagines the delta as an island, as did Onesicritus (Strabo 15.1.33).

18.4 *a storm*: the monsoon season had begun when Alexander reached the city of Patala, about July 325. There has even been the suggestion that the area was hit by a minor tsunami.

19.3–4 *Cilluta . . . and . . . another island*: Lambrick recognizes that the coastline was much further inland in antiquity, perhaps at an elevation of roughly 7 metres above the present sea-level, and he would identify the island in the open sea as what is now the hill Aban Shah, south-east of Pir Patho, which would put Cilluta somewhere closer to Mirpur Bathoro (H. T. Lambrick, *Sind: A General Introduction* (Hyderabad, 1964), 113).

20.2 *about two hundred miles apart*: the same exaggerated distance was given by Nearchus (cf. 19.5), while Aristobulus' estimate was more like 110 miles (180 km, Strabo 15.1.33). Again one must allow for the change in the coastline since antiquity.

20.4 *the Indus outlet on our side was the more easily navigable*: i.e. on the western arm. Alexander was now at the mouth of the eastern outlet, thus what follows was not direct preparation for the first phase of Nearchus' voyage, which was west from the western mouth, but either a sort of training exercise along a short stretch of the delta, or, if he turned left/east, it was in preparation for the development of a frontier outpost at the eastern end of the delta.

20.5 *dockyards . . . preparations for the voyage along the coast*: Arrian here adds to the confusion as the dockyards were developed on the eastern leg of the delta, while the planting of food stores for the navy would have been along the coast to the west of the western leg of the delta. The coastal stretch of the delta itself was said to be hardly manageable.

21.2 *from the setting of the Pleiades*: thus from the beginning of November 325. But Nearchus recorded that he actually set sail at the evening rising of the Pleiades, thus in September/October 325 (cf. *Indica* 21.1). The monsoon season is from July to September, but Nearchus was too quick off the mark, and had to wait for the winds to subside (*Indica* 21.13–22.1).

21.3 *Alexander set out from Patala*: Curtius 9.10.2 and 4 says that Leonnatus had been sent ahead along the overland route to dig wells, and that in Patala Alexander burnt all the ships which Nearchus could not use.

21.5 *Rhambacia*: Alexander had gone some distance beyond the Arabius [the Hab], so this settlement may have been Las Bela. From there he may have headed west towards Jau, via the Kumbh Pass, if that was the border between Oreitan territory and Gedrosia (22.1).

22.6–8 *trees . . . growing in the sea . . . long-stemmed thistle . . . astringent juice*: this refers to mangroves and perhaps cutch/catechu (cf. *Indica* 22.7 and Theophrastus, *Researches into Plants* 4.7.4).

23.1–26.3 The Gedrosian Disaster. See especially Bosworth, *Alexander and the East* (Cambridge: Cambridge University Press, 1996), chap. 6. After the mutiny at the Hyphasis, and Alexander's narrow escape from death at the city of the Mallians, this was the next major challenge to his leadership of his troops. Arrian was no doubt following mainly Ptolemy and Aristobulus, but also refers to the complementary account of the naval commander Nearchus (24.2 and 4), who had his own agenda and presented Alexander as a foil to his own persona in the story. Much of the drama in 24.4 to 26.3 is free composition (e.g. 25.3 and 24.5–6).

23.4 *where supplies were more plentiful*: taking the inland route through the eastern half of Gedrosia Alexander would have been able to seize crops harvested after the end of the monsoon season in September 325. He may have turned south towards the coast at Turbat, and from this point he was in serious trouble, as the western Makran was outside the monsoon belt, and would only have expected what little rain it gets in the period mid-December to mid-March.

24.1 *Pura*: perhaps Bampur.

24.3 *a desire to outdo Cyrus and Semiramis*: the emulation may have been real, but Arrian at *Indica* 5.4–7 follows Megasthenes in dismissing the Semiramis story as myth.

24.4 *fatal to a large proportion of the army*: Plutarch rather vaguely says that Alexander brought back no more than a quarter of 'the fighting men' who were with him in India (*Alexander* 66.4–5). But the numbers do not add up, and we may assume that losses in Gedrosia were disproportionately heavy among the camp-followers (25.5).

26.5 *seven days . . . along the coast*: probably from Pasni to Gwadar, a distance by the modern road of *c.*140 km.

27.1 *removed him from his post*: but Apollophanes had been left behind with Leonnatus to deal with the Oreitans (22.2–3), and was killed in action (*Indica* 23.5 with 7.5.5). Either Alexander had not yet heard of his death, or Arrian confused him with Astaspes, the satrap of Carmania (*Indica* 36.8). On Tlepolemus see 3.22.1.

27.2 *Philip* [5], *the satrap of India*: cf. 6.14.3. On Taxiles see 5.8.5 and 5.18.6–7.

27.4–5 *Cleander and Sitalces . . . executed, . . . Heracon . . . too paid the penalty*: but Cleander, Sitalces, and Heracon had been Alexander's agents in the killing of Parmenion (3.26.3 with Curtius 10.1.1), and needed to be silenced. Furthermore Cleander was the brother of Coenus, who spoke for the troops at the Hyphasis and died soon thereafter. Curtius adds that 600 of the troops brought in by Cleander and the other two were now executed as having been the agents of their crimes (Curtius 10.1.8). Arrian's presentation may seem rather naive.

28.1–2 **Dionysiac celebrations in Carmania.** Cf. Plutarch, *Alexander* 67. Nearchus preposterously made the offering of sacrifices and holding of games in Carmania Alexander's way of thanking the gods for the success of Nearchus' mission (*Indica* 36.1–7). Cleitarchus was probably the source for the seven-day extravaganza in Diodorus Siculus 17.106.1 and Curtius 9.10.24–8. This version served to illustrate how Alexander was corrupted by success, and was losing touch with reality. But by now it seems that Alexander was really trying to gain recognition as having a divine nature, and in this case seeking identification with Dionysus (cf. 5.1.1–2.7, 5.26.5; 6.14.2; 7.20.1).

28.4 *Peithon* [3] *the son of Crateuas*: (not to be confused with Peithon [4], introduced at 6.1). His career after Alexander's death was marked by intrigue and disloyalty to whichever leader of the day, and his presence in Babylon at Alexander's death (7.26.2) was turned into evidence of his involvement in the murder of Alexander (Pseudo-Callisthenes 3.31.8).

28.5 *the Fish-Eaters*: much more on these people at *Indica* 26.2 ff. Their territory may have stretched from Ras Malan to Ras el Kuh.

Nearchus . . . went inland . . . to bring Alexander a report: very early in 324. Nearchus landed at Harmozia, and eventually found Alexander's camp, perhaps in the area of Kahnu. Nearchus' expansive, problematic account of this march is summarized at *Indica* 33–6.

29.4–11 **Alexander's distress at the desecration of Cyrus' tomb.** As Aristobulus was commissioned to restore the tomb, he was probably Arrian's source here. The description of the tomb and its contents (29.5–6) suggests that the crime was the work of vandals out to loot. But the nature of the vandalism and the desecration of Cyrus' remains suggest that it was more iconoclastic, and Badian suggests that the Magi wanted to prevent Alexander using the tomb and its contents as the setting for a coronation ceremony (E. Badian, 'Alexander the Great Between Two Thrones', in A. Small (ed.), *Subject and Power: The Cult of the Ruling Power in Classical Antiquity* (Ann Arbor, Mich.: University of Michigan Press, 1996), 11–26).

29.7 *Magi*: originally members of a Median tribe, they were eventually drawn into the Persian royal court as priests, now of Ahura Mazda, with particular responsibility for the care of the dead.

30.1 *I could not condone his action*: cf. 3.8.12.

allegations . . . laid . . . against Orxines: Curtius' version stands the story on its head: Orxines welcomed Alexander with all due formality and generous gifts, but the eunuch Bagoas privately poisoned Alexander's mind and led him to believe that Orxines had plundered Cyrus' tomb, even though he was descended from Cyrus. The tomb, when opened, was taken as evidence of his guilt, and the innocent Orxines was executed (Curtius 10.1.22 ff.). This version is maximally hostile to Alexander, blinded by his love for a Persian eunuch, reckless in the administration of justice, and brutal. Not a story that Aristobulus would have repeated, even if it had borne any resemblance to the truth. (Incidentally, Mary Renault worked up Curtius' version: Orxines was indeed guilty of crimes including murder, and Bagoas was an unwilling agent in the exposure of Orxines, but was obliged to act because it was his father's dying wish that Bagoas punish Orxines for the betrayal of the father: *The Persian Boy* (London, 1972), 331–4.)

BOOK SEVEN

1-3 Encounters with Indian philosophers: ambition versus acceptance of the human condition.

1.2 *Some writers give a further account*: Alexander's untimely death in 323 generated a tidal wave of mixed emotions among the troops—overwhelming grief, remorse, and fear on being left leaderless in hostile territory. A reality check was needed and Perdiccas and other senior officers took the initiative by presenting to a massed meeting of the troops a document purporting to be Alexander's 'last plans'. This was sufficiently close to what they already knew to appear authentic, but so outrageously over-the-top for the war-weary troops to limit their idolatry to their memory of what he had achieved in his lifetime. A planned invasion of Arabia would explain the construction of a fleet on the Euphrates that was under way, and he may have threatened to attack Carthage, but hardly to circumnavigate Africa. The reference to his concern about the growing power of Rome seems purely anachronistic. Thus we should distinguish between Alexander's plans at the time of his death, the 'last plans' as unveiled by Perdiccas and as known to the first generation of Alexander historians, and later elaborations, as reflected here.

1.3 *into the Black Sea and Lake Maeotis [Azov] against the Scythians*: a similar ambition was attributed to Julius Caesar (Plutarch, *Caesar* 58).

1.6 *a human being like the rest of us*: some philosophers believed that all men are born equal, and others thought rather that, while God is the common father of all, He makes the best peculiarly his own (Plutarch, *Alexander* 27.11). The latter accommodated slavery, as did Zeno, the founder of Stoicism. The rival belief, here attributed to the Indian gurus, was hostile to the institution of slavery, and was akin to the thinking of Diogenes the Cynic (mentioned at 2.1) and Cleanthes, Zeno's successor (born *c.*331 BC).

2.1 *Diogenes of Sinope*: the anecdote about Diogenes (404–323 BC) appears in longer form in Plutarch, *Alexander* 14. He was also said to have opposed ritual prostration (cf. 4.12.2). Onesicritus supposedly studied under Diogenes.

2.2 *Indian gurus who go naked*: these would have been the Brahmans (cf. 6.7.4 and 16.5) whom Alexander met at Taxila in 326. They were philosophers loosely attached to the court, and are to be distinguished from the Indian ascetics (*Sramanas*), more accurately styled gymnosophists (from the Greek for 'naked philosophers'), who were more isolated from human settlements.

3.1 Calanus' suicide. Suicide by those seriously ill was condoned by Hindu law, but not suicide by fire, as Megasthenes attests (Strabo 15.1.68).

3.4 *Nesaean horses*: explained at 13.1.

Lysimachus: a Bodyguard, cf. 5.13.1, 24.5, and 6.28.4. After Alexander's death he married a daughter of Antipater, and took the royal title, probably in 305, with Thrace as his territory. For rhetoricians he was the exemplar of exceptional bravery, even credited with having survived being locked up by Alexander in a cage with a lion.

4.1 *Abulites . . . Oxathres*: the satraps of respectively Susiana (3.16.9) and Paraetacene (3.19.2). Badian ('Harpalus', *Journal of Hellenic Studies*, 81 (1961), 16) characterizes the purge of the satraps in 324 as a 'reign of terror'—perhaps an overstatement, but Arrian chose to be economical with facts, and to quote an explanation given for Alexander's paranoia.

4.4–5.6 The marriages at Susa, the settling of debts and awards for conspicuous bravery. With the king and the Companions the marriages projected a model for the integration of Persians into the Macedonian empire. At the level of the Macedonian troops this exercise addressed the realities of their situation: they had acquired sexual partners, had debts to settle, and wanted recognition for what they had achieved or suffered in the war.

4.4 *Barsine . . . Rhoxane*: Philip had taken numerous wives to secure control of Macedon's neighbours, but Macedonian chauvinists would have been alarmed that Alexander and his Companions were entering into a 'breeding programme' with Persian women. Indeed after Alexander's death Rhoxane, introduced at 4.19.5, murdered both Barsine (Stateira) and Drypetis, with the connivance of Perdiccas (Plutarch, *Alexander* 77.6).

4.6 *Seleucus*: Apame was the daughter of Spitamenes, the Sogdian hyparch (introduced at 3.28.10). By Seleucus she bore Antiochus I, and thus, ironically, she became the co-founder of the Hellenistic Seleucid dynasty. As Spitamenes had been murdered in 328/7 (4.17.7), this marriage may have given recognition to a partnership established even earlier than that.

5.4–5 *Peucestas . . . Leonnatus*: they had protected Alexander when he was struck down in the attack on the city of the Mallians (6.9.3–10.2).

6   The integration of Persians into the army dissolves any manufactured consent.

6.1 *thirty thousand . . . the Next Generation*: they had been conscripted in 327, effectively serving also as hostages. The full integration of Asian troops into the Macedonian Companion infantry came later, in 323, after the arrival of 20,000 more Persian recruits (7.23.1 and 4).

8–12 **The mutiny at Opis.** By now the Macedonians saw themselves as virtual mercenaries, and Alexander had to confront serious group solidarity (see the quotation from Parke's *Greek Mercenary Soldiers* cited at 5.25.2).

9–10 **Alexander's speech to the troops.** Alexander may indeed have adopted a very positive attitude towards Philip's record, but the version of recent Macedonian history in 9.2–4 seems implausible in context. Thus the speech is best taken as an exercise in rhetoric, attributed by some to Ptolemy. Bosworth (*From Arrian to Alexander*, 101–13) notes as indicators of Arrian's personal contribution to the base tradition the rhetorical embellishments, the intertextual references to Xenophon (e.g. 7.9.9 echoing Xenophon, *Anabasis* 7.6.36), 'self-borrowing' (especially in the echoes of his speech at the Hyphasis), and his adaptation of Megasthenes' account of Dionysus' mission to civilize the Indians (*Indica* 7) to describe Philip's campaign to convert a nation of rustic roughnecks into urbanized citizens (9.2).

9.2 *dressed in skins and herding . . . goats*: but much development had taken place long before Philip became king, and particularly in the reign of Archelaus (*c.*413–399).

9.3 *your mines*: Philip took the area north of Lake Prespa in 358 and so gained control of the mines of Damastion. Then to the east he captured Crenides in 357, renaming it Philippi. Thus he won control of the gold and silver mines in the area of Mount Pangaeum. The final phase of his campaign against the Odrysians in 341–340 added the Thracian mines to his resources.

9.4 *Philip crushed them . . . protection*: Philip finally brought Thessaly under his control in 344. In 346 he had secured the submission of Phocis and occupied the pass at Thermopylae, the key to the control of central and southern Greece. Greek resistance was finally broken at the battle of Chaeronea in 338 (see on 1.7.1).

9.6 *I inherited . . . sixty talents in the treasury . . . and . . . debts of some five hundred talents*: these details at least came from an external source, as Curtius gives the same figures. An Athenian rule of thumb of that era indicates that one talent would have covered the wages of six thousand hoplites for one day.

9.7 *defeated the satraps of Darius*: an allusion to the battle of the Granicus (334), and in 9.8 he alludes to the battles of Issus and Gaugamela.

9.9 *diadem*: this originated as a ribbon tied around the headpiece of the Persian king: see at 4.7.4, and cf. 7.22.2–5.

10.4 *commemorative statue . . . parents are given . . . exemption from . . . tax*: matching phraseology at 1.16.4–5.

11   **Reconciliation achieved and sealed with a banquet.**

11.9 *unity of purpose between Macedonians and Persians and a partnership in empire*: W. W. Tarn ('Alexander the Great and the Unity of Mankind', *Proceedings of the British Academy*, 19 (1933), 123–66) famously, but erroneously, took 'between Macedonians and Persians' to apply only to the prayer for partnership, and took the first element to be a pioneering affirmation of 'the unity of mankind'.

12.4 *Craterus' orders . . . to assume charge of Macedonia*: Antipater would quite reasonably have formed contingency plans in case of Alexander's death in Asia, and an element in that may have been the alleged secret negotiations with the Aetolians. A string of hostile letters from Olympias deepened Alexander's suspicions. Though Craterus' health problems might have delayed his departure from Cilicia, the fact that he was still there in June 323 suggests that he had no wish to clash with Antipater, whose position in Macedonia was so well established.

Polyperchon: one of the oldest of the veteran officers, and thus the right man to accompany Craterus. The two had regularly operated together during the Indian campaign. A few years after Alexander's death Polyperchon seized the regency, and claimed the respect of Macedonian nationalists, but his bizarre record in that period may explain why sources on Alexander's campaigns inserted or removed his name as suited their attitude to the man (notes on 3.18.9 and 4.12.2).

12.7 *in any way changed [. . .]*: the missing section at the end of 12.7 would have dealt with the flight of Harpalus with a large force of mercenaries and a large amount of bullion which he took from the treasury in Babylon. It must also have covered the quarrel between Hephaestion and Eumenes which is settled in 13.1.

13.2–6 **A meeting with a group of Amazons.** It was conventional to believe that some historical reality lay behind the Amazon myth, and it was built into Athenian 'national' epic (as in Lysias' *Funeral oration* of *c.*390 BC). But there was no agreement on where they lived. The vulgate sources say that Alexander met the Amazons in Hyrcania, at the south-east corner of the Caspian, which Cleitarchus thought was consistent with the tradition that they lived along the river Thermodon [Terme Çay], which actually flows into the Black Sea in northern Turkey. This chapter serves little except to show off Arrian's knowledge, and perhaps also to caution against ready acceptance of extravagances in the story of Alexander's reaction to the death of Hephaestion (next chapter).

14   **The death of Hephaestion.**

14.1 *games with competitions . . . in the performing arts*: such games could include tragedy and dithyrambic choruses (cf. 3.6.1), and even satyr plays, as in this case with the *Agen*, which mocked Harpalus (see on 3.6.7 and 7.12.7).

14.4 *Glaucias hanged . . . for giving the wrong medicine*: Mary Renault, in biographical mode (*The Nature of Alexander* (London: Pantheon Books, 1975), 208–10), analyses the record of Hephaestion's death and suggests that he may have been murdered, Glaucias acting in collusion with either Craterus (his hostility attested for example by Plutarch, *Alexander* 47.9–11), or more likely Eumenes (cf. 13.1 and 14.9).

14.8 *a funeral pyre in Babylon*: there is some confusion in the sources between the funeral pyre (cf. Diodorus Siculus 17.115), built in Ecbatana, and plans for a funerary monument (also called a 'pyre') to be built in Babylon (Diodorus Siculus 18.4.2). The latter was among the 'last plans' rejected by the army after Alexander's death.

15.3 *Alexander wiped out the entire tribe*: but some Cossaeans were captured and taken into Alexander's army (23.1). Arrian sandwiches a terse reference to the massacre between a justification for their elimination and a eulogy of Alexander's generalship in the most adverse conditions (the winter being that of 324/3). The snatch from Ptolemy's memoirs further serves his rhetorical purpose.

15.4 *Carthaginians . . . sent envoys*: Alexander had an encounter with Carthaginian envoys to Tyre in 332 (2.24.5).

15.5 *an embassy from the Romans*: Cleitarchus apparently mentioned a Roman mission to Alexander, but no context is given. Other first-generation Alexander historians could be excused for ignoring such an insignificant state in Italy. Much later in the Hellenistic period Aristus and Asclepiades could embroider this episode, whether historical or not, with a prediction by Alexander that Rome would become a major power, as indeed it was in their day.

15.6 *a model of freedom*: monarchy had been finally terminated in 509, but the conflict between the Patrician elite and the Plebeians dragged on, at least till the landmark legislation of 287 BC, and (Jupiter) Libertas (political freedom) was first honoured with a temple only in 238 BC. As it happened consuls were not appointed in Rome in 324, and supreme power was held by a Dictator. Arrian presents an idealized view of Roman politics and foreign policy in the late fourth century BC.

16.1–4 **Digression on the Caspian Sea.** Arrian summarizes Aristobulus' account, but indicates his own acceptance of Eratosthenes' conviction that the Caspian was a gulf of the Great Sea (cf. 3.29.2; 5.5.4 and 26.1). On the Araxes [Arak] he perpetuates the old uncertainty instead of giving established fact.

16.1 *Heracleides*: nothing more is heard of his commission, and this might have been one of the 'last plans' shelved after Alexander's death.

16.3 *so does the Jaxartes*: while the Oxus [Amu-Darya] probably did once flow into the Caspian (see on 3.30.7), the Jaxartes [Syr-Darya] did not, but into the Aral (as it was before its initial division into two in 1989, and the shrinkage of the Syr-Darya).

16.5 *Chaldaean seers*: cf. 3.16.5. Their bid to warn Alexander off entering Babylon may have been a form of resistance to Alexander (cf. on 6.29.4–11 on the Magi's desecration of Cyrus' tomb). But Arrian goes on in 17.1–4 to report a more mercenary motive imputed to the Chaldaeans.

16.6 *a verse from . . . Euripides*: Fragment 963 in Nauck's edition of fragments of the tragedies of Euripides.

16.7 *Solon advised Croesus*: Solon of Athens supposedly met Croesus, the king of Lydia, in Sardis in 553 BC, and Herodotus concluded his re-creation of their dialogue with the aphorism that no one should call a man happy until he is dead (Herodotus 1.32.7). Croesus in turn became the 'wise adviser' to Cyrus, persuading him to cross the 'Araxes' against the Massagetae (Herodotus 1.207), which Arrian may have had in mind with the mention of the Araxes in 16.3.

17.4 *to prevent the rapid completion of a new temple*: but Diodorus Siculus (17.112.2–3) says that the Chaldaeans urged Alexander to have the temple rebuilt as the way to avert danger, apart from not entering the city, and Nearchus, presumably Diodorus' source, communicated this message to Alexander. On the destruction of the temple and Alexander's instruction in 331 that it should be rebuilt cf. 3.16.4.

18.1 *Apollodorus*: he had been left behind to keep watch on Mazaeus (3.16.4). Arrian indicates that he took this story about Apollodorus and Peithagoras from Aristobulus (18.6), who smoothed over what Badian styled 'the reign of terror' (see on 7.4.1), here referred to as 'the harsh punishments', and extracted from Apollodorus' experience the positive element of Alexander's willingness to listen (18.4).

18.5 *Perdiccas was killed in his campaign against Ptolemy . . . Antigonus in the battle fought at Ipsus*: Perdiccas was killed when invading Egypt in 321/0 (see on 1.8.1 and 6.9.3). Antigonus, introduced as the satrap of Phrygia at 1.29.3, met his death at Ipsus, likewise in Phrygia, in 301. His grandson, Antigonus Gonatas, established the dynasty which ruled Macedon from 284 to 168 BC.

18.6 *Calanus*: cf. 7.2.4–3.6.

19.2 *statues of Harmodius and Aristogeiton*: see on 3.16.7 and 4.10.3.

19.3 *Nearchus' fleet*: cf. 6.28.6 and *Indica* 41.8.

19.4 *murex-divers*: the sea-snail (*murex*) was harvested for its purple dye.

19.5 *Miccalus . . . sent to Phoenicia. . . to hire or purchase men with experience of the sea*: Phoenicians, whether as hired hands or slave owners, saw the economic possibilities, and some Phoenician colonization in the Gulf area is mentioned, but would have been only after this activity.

19.6 *Alexander's . . . insatiable appetite for further acquisition*: presented as an authorial comment, but anticipated by Aristobulus. Cf. Megasthenes' judgement at *Indica* 9.11.

20.1 *Alexander . . . would qualify as the third god*: Arrian sets this common tradition between the formal reason for the campaign (19.6) and the economic and strategic considerations (20.2).

20.2 *cinnamon*: included in the list by Aristobulus, though it only grows in India, and the parallel reference in *Indica* 32.7 may mean that Arabs imported it from India for onwards trade.

20.3–6 *two islands . . . Icarus . . . Tylus*: although the coastline has changed considerably since antiquity, Icarus is generally taken to be Jazirat Failaka, *c*.15 km. ENE of Kuwait, and Tylus to be the island of Bahrein.

20.9 *countermanded this decision*: Nearchus rejects Onesicritus' proposal to head straight for the southern shore of the Persian Gulf. The story is told with more detail in *Indica* 32.9–13.

22.5 *Seleucus*: Seleucus, mentioned in Bk. 5.13 and 16, and 7.4.6, took the royal title in 306/5 and died in 281 BC. The diadem story is probably apocryphal, created to give an aura of entitlement to the kingship.

23.1 *Peucestas* [2] *arrived . . . with an army*: introduced at 6.9.3; satrap of Persia (6.28.3 and 30.2). On the consequential restructuring of the Companion Infantry see Appendix 1.

23.2 *as if . . . to honour a god*: after the death of Darius Alexander sought recognition as the equal of a god (*isotheos*), and that might be the sense in this context. But towards the end of his life he seems to have demanded recognition of his divine nature. Thus Demosthenes could tell the Athenian Assembly, 'Let him be the son of Zeus—and Poseidon too, if that is what he wants' (Hypereides, *Demosthenes* 31), and Hypereides in 322 referred to the imposition of ruler cult. Furthermore, if Hephaestion was to be worshipped as a hero (23.6), then Alexander could expect the higher rank.

23.6–8 *Cleomenes . . . a known rogue*: Arrian mentions at 3.5.4 the initial appointment of this Egyptian Greek to a governorship of an area of Egypt and to the position of receiver of revenue for the whole of Egypt. His bad reputation spread beyond what might be attributed to Ptolemy's hostility or Egyptians' resentment of his zeal as a revenue-collector.

24.2–3 *. . . as if some great disaster had happened*: in reality it was perhaps the enactment of a Mesopotamian ritual, carried out with Alexander's participation, whereby a 'substitute king' was made to fulfil the omen by being killed after taking the throne (as in Diodorus Siculus 17.116.2–4), and so protect Alexander.

24.4 *Medius*: a Thessalian, first mentioned as a trireme commander on the Hydaspes in 326 (*Indica* 18.7), but probably with Alexander from 334.

25–7 **Alexander's last days and death.**

25.1 *The Royal Journals*: not attested for any previous major event, and this record of Alexander's last days may have been created by his officers, who could expect to be the target of conspiracy theorists. It reads more like a court circular than a medical record. There are also divergences between Arrian's version and Plutarch's (*Alexander* 75–6), and since both claim to be quoting directly from the Royal Journals (*Ephemerides*), they must have worked from different recensions of the core text.

The texts are inadequate to establish the cause of death (before terminal pneumonia?), but the absence of any reference to any epidemic in Babylonia may tell against typhoid, malaria (unless it was a recurrence), or some water-borne disease.

continued drinking: excessive drinking is emphasized in numerous earlier episodes, but symptoms of acute pancreatitis or Boerhaave's Syndrome are not indicated (J. E. Atkinson, Elsie Truter, and E. Truter, 'Alexander's Last Days', *Acta Classica*, 52 (2009), 23–46).

25.5 *further instructions for the naval expedition*: thus the day originally set for mobilization passed without action, which would have played on his mind. Allowance should be made for the psychological factors: L. A. Tritle, 'Alexander and the Killing of Cleitus the Black', in W. Heckel and L. A. Tritle (eds.), *Crossroads of History: The Age of Alexander* (Claremont, Calif.: Regina Books, 2003), 127–46, esp. 140, finds evidence of post-traumatic stress disorder, with a suicidal streak, at least from 328.

26.2 *slept the night in the temple*: this was the ritual of 'incubation'—sleeping in a temple to await a vision or a dream with an omen (as in Diodorus Siculus 1.53.8).

Sarapis: 'Sarapis' might here be a substitute for Oserapis (a blend of Osiris and Apis), whose cult might have been taken to Babylon long before 323 BC.

26.3 *neither Aristobulus nor Ptolemy has anything more to add*: the interpretation of the Greek is much debated. We do not accept that it means that Aristobulus and Ptolemy ended their accounts with the death of Alexander. The following phrase 'others, though' does not relate to what followed Alexander's death and might have been missed by Ptolemy and Aristobulus; and it is improbable that Ptolemy, publishing *c*.310 if not earlier, passed up the opportunity to comment briefly on what happened in the immediate aftermath of Alexander's death. Thus we take Arrian to mean that Aristobulus and Ptolemy have nothing to add to the account of Alexander's death.

'To the strongest': perhaps an allusion to the myth of Strife throwing the apple of Discord in at the wedding of Thetis and Peleus, 'for the most beautiful'.

27.1 *died of a poison sent by Antipater*: the poisoning of Alexander is treated as a fact in the *Book on the Death of Alexander*, a product of the conflict between the Successors, and the *Alexander Romance*, which originated as a revisionist text in Ptolemaic Egypt. But much closer to the death, Olympias and the Athenian Hypereides treated Iollas as Antipater's agent in the murder plot. But obvious symptoms of poisoning are missing from accounts of Alexander's death.

28.1–30.1 **The obituary.** As is usual in the genre of biography, when the attitude of the readership is not presumed to be hostile, Arrian shows admiration for his subject, particularly here, where Alexander's faults are conceded and as far as possible excused, but the emphasis is more on his merits and achievements. Thus he does not load this obituary with the clichéd charges of the Stoic moralist, and at several points the final spin is at variance with the line taken in the narrative.

28.1 *died in the hundred and fourteenth Olympiad, when Hegesias was archon at*

Athens: Babylonian astronomical records indicate as the precise date 10/11 June 323 BC. The duration of his reign indicates that the accession was in about October 336 (cf. 1.1.1).

28.2 *skilful at intuiting the right tactic*: shown, for example, at 2.10.3 and 26.3; 4.2.5; and 5.23.5. Cf. Thucydides 1.138.3 on Themistocles, and Bosworth on Arrian 5.11.4.

28.3 *never caught wrong-footed by others' false promises*: well illustrated by his treatment of the Indian mercenaries trapped at Massaga (4.27.3–4, where note the counter-version of Plutarch, *Alexander* 59.6–7).

29.3 *Minos or Aeacus or Rhadamanthys*: Minos and Rhadamanthys were in myth the sons of Zeus and Europa, while Aeacus was the son of Zeus and Aegina, hence the name of his island kingdom. In Second Sophistic texts, as earlier, they were cited as exemplary wise judges.

30.1 *king of two continents*: but contrast the negative comments at 7.1.4–2.4, and 4.7.5, the latter leading into the tragedy of Cleitus' murder. Arrian offers no justification of Alexander's imperialism.

30.2 *new oracles about the honours they should pay him*: cults of Alexander continued, or were revived, particularly in Asia Minor in the Roman period, and this phenomenon, if seen as a form of assertion of a Greek identity, might be paralleled in the writings of the Second Sophistic Greeks, of whom Arrian was one.

30.3 *I have had some help from god*: it took a special person to produce the definitive history of one born not without some divine agency, just as Achilles needed a Homer (1.12.1–5; cf. Preface).

INDICA

1–17. Digression on the geography and peoples of India.

1–6. The country.

1.1 *Astacenians and the Assacenians*: at 4.22.8 Arrian mentions one Astis as the regional governor of the district of Peucelaotis (cf. note on 4.28.6). The Assacenians occupied the Swat valley and their territory stretched from the Panjkora to the Indus (cf. 4.23.1 and 25.5–7).

1.3 *paying . . . tribute . . . to Cyrus*: Gandhara as the territory centred on the Kabul valley had indeed fallen to Cyrus, thus before Darius I's accession in 518. But there is no evidence of previous Assyrian or Median conquests in the area.

1.5 *Dionysus called the country Nysaea*: cf. 5.1.1–2.7.

1.6 *Dionysus' birth*: Semele's unborn son was on her death sewn into Zeus' thigh, and at the due time was born the second time (cf. note on 5.1.6).

1.8 *Massaca . . . Peucelaïtis*: Massaca, or Massaga, was perhaps east of the Katgala Pass, and north-west of Chakdarra (cf. 4.26.1). The other city, close to the Indus, will be the 'Peucelaotis' of 4.22.8.

2.1–4 *the Taurus mountain range . . . the Caucasus*: cf. 3.28.4–5, where Aristobulus is cited, and 5.5.2–4, but here summarizing Eratosthenes (cf. 3.1), and repeating the point that the Parapamisus or Hindu Kush was styled the Caucasus by Alexander's followers for the greater glory of the conqueror (cf. 5.5.3).

2.7 *To the south*: the Greek here has a double-barrelled formulation as used by Herodotus 2.8, which if more than a literary ornamentation may mean 'to the south and south-west'.

2.9 *Palimbothra*: Sanskrit Pāṭaliputra [Patna], cf. 5.6.2 and chap. 10 below.

3.1 *Eratosthenes*: (*c*.275–194 BC), appointed director of the Library in Alexandria in about 245. His writings ranged from literary criticism and philosophy to mathematics and astronomy, but his special field was systematic geography. For detailed discussion of Eratosthenes' schematic map of the world and the geography of India see Bosworth, *Commentary*, ii. 236–46 on *Anabasis* 5.5.2–6.3.

3.3 *this eastern side*: from Bhutan down to Cape Comorin. Eratosthenes envisaged India as almost a trapezium, with the Indus marking the western boundary, running from north to south, almost parallel to its eastern seaboard.

3.4 *schoinoi*: an Egyptian measurement of length, roughly 10.5 km, and thus of more use than the Indian *yojana* (anywhere in the range from 6 to 15 km).

3.6 *Ctesias*: introduced at 5.4.2.

3.7 *Megasthenes*: see on 5.5.1 and 5.6.2.

3.9–5.2 **The river systems.** Von Hinüber, in G. Wirth and O. von Hinüber, *Arrian, Der Alexanderzug, Indische Geschichte* (Munich: Artemis, 1985), 1090–1100, summarizes the evidence for identifying these rivers. At 4.15–16 Arrian introduces an observation based on his own experience as a military officer in the Danubian provinces.

5.6–7 *Idanthyrsus . . . Semiramis*: a Scythian King Idanthyrsus was supposedly expansionist in the late seventh century BC, and Herodotus 4.120–8 deals with Darius' encounter with a later king of that name in about 508 BC. The Semiramis myth was built around the Assyrian queen Schammuramat (reigned 811–806 BC): cf. 6.24.2–3. Arrian was here following Megasthenes (quoted by Strabo 15.1.6).

5.8–13 **On Dionysus' and Heracles' supposed invasions of India.** Cf. *Anab.* 5.1.1–3.4, where Arrian suggests that Eratosthenes went too far in rejecting these myths, and in attributing so much to flatterers of Alexander. On Aornus see 4.28.1–4 and 5.26.5.

5.12 *brand their cattle with the mark of a club*: cf. 5.3.4. The practice is attested in the epic *Mahābhārata*, 3.240.5, and the club was an attribute of Krishna. On this and other links with Heracles speculation went back beyond Megasthenes to those with Alexander (cf. Strabo 15.1.8–9), though for 5.10–13 Arrian may have followed the critical line of Eratosthenes.

6.8 *Onesicritus*: the reference to the river animals is close to Strabo 15.1.13, and Arrian and Strabo probably both here cited Onesicritus second-hand from Eratosthenes.

7.1–9.12 The history of India, and Dionysus and Heracles. Arrian signals his scepticism by attributing all the detail to Megasthenes.

7.3 *tala*: there seems to be some confusion here between the sugar-palm (*Borassus flabellifer*) and the cotton shrub (*Gossypium herbaceum*), cf. 16.1.

7.6 *Triptolemus*: King Celeus of Eleusis gave hospitality to Demeter, and as a reward she taught his son Triptolemus the practice of agriculture, which he then spread throughout Greece. The myth found its way to India. Arrian seems to have developed a variant to credit Philip with civilizing the Macedonians (7.9.2; cf. *Indica* 40.8).

9.9 *the first lasted for [. . .] years*: for king-lists in pre-literate periods ancient writers generally allowed a generational gap in the range of 30 to 35 years, thus the missing number here may be about 280 years.

9.10 *Cyrus . . . campaigned against the Scythians*: cf. 4.11.9.

10–17 The Indians and their customs.

10.6 *Palimbothra extends . . . one and a half miles*: Megasthenes visited Palimbothra [Patna] (cf. 5.6.2) and here gives measurements that fit the archaeological evidence. The area would have been some 86 per cent greater than that enclosed by the Aurelian walls of the city of Rome (von Hinüber, *Arrian*, 1114).

10.8 *no slaves of any kind*: Sanskrit texts indicate that this is not true, and Onesicritus the Cynic lauded it as a peculiarity of the kingdom of Musicanus, a land which he chose to present as an almost utopian paradigm.

11–12 The Indian caste system. Arrian's version runs close to the summaries of Megasthenes' account in Strabo 15.1.39–49 and Diodorus Siculus 2.40–1, but with a reference to Nearchus in *Indica* 11.7. All give seven castes, though the Brahman system had four, styled *varnas*. The Brahmans came first, whose functions seem to have included those of Megasthenes' sixth and seventh castes, the inspectors and king's advisers. Second came the warriors, the *kshatriya* (Megasthenes' fifth caste), the third being the *vaishya* or commoners, including those involved in commerce, and the fourth the *shudra varna*, the farmers and manual workers.

11.7 *these gurus live naked*: cf. *Anabasis* 6.7.4; 7.1.5–2.4, and note on 6.16.5.

enormous trees: presumably banyans (*Ficus benghalensis*).

13–14 Indian elephants. On the method of hunting elephants Arrian is again close to Strabo's version of Megasthenes' account (15.1.42–3), but engages in literary elaboration: for example, whereas Strabo, following Megasthenes, gives the circumference of the area enclosed to trap wild elephants, Arrian imports the imprecise image of an area extensive enough for the encampment of a large army. There are echoes of Herodotus, and his phrase for a fierce battle (13.10) echoes a Homeric formula copied by Herodotus (cf. Bosworth, *From Arrian to Alexander*, 43–4). There is the element of bathos in the way Arrian tacks onto the picture of elephants acting heroically (14.4) a reference to his memory of elephants performing circus tricks.

14.8 *live for two hundred years*: in human society exceptional longevity is usually an indicator of illiteracy rather than a faultless lifestyle, and the same may apply to elephants, which when tied to written records rarely live beyond the age of seventy. But the period of gestation is now given as twenty-two months, rather than a maximum of eighteen as Arrian has it.

15.4 *Nearchus . . . did see many of their skins*: Arrian omits Nearchus' claim that they were like leopard skins (Strabo 15.1.44), and quotes Megasthenes only to dismiss the marvels as hearsay. After Herodotus' treatment of the subject (3.102–6), the ants could not be left out.

15.5 *gold-digging ants*: the 'ants' were perhaps a creation of folk etymology from some regional name or term for extraction.

15.10 *snake caught by Peithon* [1] *. . . twenty-four feet long*: this Peithon is not otherwise directly attested. The length given is not too much of an exaggeration for the Indian python, and Arrian chose to ignore reports attributed to Onesicritus of snakes kept by the Indian prince Abisares which were 120 feet and 210 feet long (cited by Strabo 15.1.28).

16.1 *linen coming from the trees*: as at 7.3, Arrian must be referring to cotton.

18.1–42.10 **Summary of Nearchus' record of his voyage from the Indus to the Euphrates.**

18.1 *Phoenicians, Cypriots, and Egyptians*: cf. 6.1.6, where he also mentions Carians. They were possibly recruited as mercenaries for the journey down the Indus in 326, but not all had experience of sailing on the open sea, and Arrian indicates that they were among the mercenaries who joined Alexander much earlier, and that this fleet was only put together after Alexander returned from the Hyphasis.

18.3–8 *The list of those he appointed trierarchs . . .*: the list is no doubt of historical value, but in literary terms it savours of the epic catalogue, such as the catalogue of ships in Homer, *Iliad* 2. As the fleet did not include triremes, the term trierarch is used in a rather inflated way to denote a ship's captain. In the Athenian system wealthy citizens were obliged to serve in this capacity as a civic duty, and the trierarch had to contribute to the cost of fitting out the warship which he commanded. But in Alexander's fleet not all trierarchs actually sailed.

18.3 *Leonnatus* [2]: though Leonnatus' father's name is variously given, this could be the officer introduced at 2.12.5, and made Bodyguard in 331 (3.5.5).

Lysimachus [2]: a Bodyguard (5.24.5, 6.28.4); cf. 7.3.4, 7.18.5.

Archias: he features as Nearchus' second-in-command in the episode at 27.8–28.9 below, and later on a mission to explore the Arabian coast (43.8 with 7.20.7).

18.4 *Nearchus*: see *passim* from *Anabasis* 6.28; his account of the campaign forms the basis of *Indica* 19.9–42.10.

Laomedon: his background is sketched at 3.6.5–6.

Androsthenes: he was originally from the island of Thasos. He wrote his own *Voyage along the Indian Coast*, which was used by the geographer Eratosthenes and cited by Strabo on the subject of shellfish (Strabo 16.3.2).

18.5 *Ptolemy*: the major source for Arrian's *Anabasis*.

Aristonus: a Bodyguard (6.28.4).

18.6 *Attalus* [3]: cf. 4.16.1 and 4.24.1.

Peucestas [2]: credited with saving Alexander's life at the city of the Mallians (6.9.3, 6.28.4).

Peithon [3]: a Bodyguard (6.28.4).

Leonnatus [1]: not to be confused with Leonnatus [2], son of 'Eunus', listed in 18.3.

18.7 *Medius*: a central figure in the story of Alexander's last days (7.24.4 and 27.2). He appears later as a fleet commander from 313 (Diodorus Siculus 19.69.3); and he too was a writer (if only attested on the subject of Armenia).

Eumenes: the secretary or commissariat officer introduced at 5.24.6. As P. A. Brunt notes in his Loeb edition (Cambridge, Mass., Harvard University Press), Vol. 2, p. 359), Eumenes was not 'naturalised' but yet was given the rank of Companion. He played a major role in the protracted power-struggle after Alexander's death.

Critobulus: possibly the physician who treated Alexander at the city of the Mallians (Curtius 9.5.25, though Arrian 6.11.1 calls him Critodemus).

Thoas: after the campaign down the Indus he left the fleet for the march into Gedrosia with Alexander (6.23.2 and 27.1).

18.8 *Nithaphon the son of Pnytagoras*: he had probably joined Alexander's camp sometime after his father's defection to the Macedonians in 332 (2.20.6 and 22.2).

Bagoas the son of Pharnuches: the father was probably the Lycian used for his language skills in the raid to apprehend Spitamenes (4.3.7 ff.).

18.11 *ancestral gods and those prescribed by oracles*: these included respectively Heracles and Ammon: cf. 6.3.2.

19.1 *Craterus . . . Hephaestion*: more details in 6.2.2. Hephaestion's first target was the capture of Sopeithes' capital.

19.2 *about eight thousand men*: cf. 6.2.2, adding Agrianians. This may mean about 2,000 of the Companion cavalry (cf. 6.14.4), the 3,000 men of the elite foot guard of the Companion Infantry, and about 3,000 archers and Agrianians.

19.7 *total number of his ships was eight hundred*: but at 6.2.4 Arrian cites Ptolemy as reporting a total of 2,000 boats, and of these only eighty were triaconters, warships but more like landing-craft when compared with the trireme (cf. 5.3.5). Thus if the text here is sound and Nearchus did not include the smallest boats in his count, the majority of the boats were still transport and support craft.

19.8 *my earlier book written in Attic Greek*: in switching from the *Anabasis* to the *Indica* Arrian took the odd decision to use the Ionic dialect for the latter (see Introduction, section on the *Indica*).

Peucestas and Leonnatus: cf. 6.11.8 with 7.5.5.

20.1 *Alexander had a yen*: this chapter opens and closes with two of the defining motifs of the Alexander legend: his urges and his extraordinary good fortune.

20.6 *professed reluctance to expose [Nearchus] to that amount of hardship and danger*: such feigned reluctance would have been labelled dissimulation if it had been applied to a Roman emperor, but in this context the intent is benign, serving to enhance the regard in which Alexander held Nearchus. The reality may have been that Alexander had real doubts about his friend's competence, and whereas in the Indus campaign Alexander had been personally in charge of the army moving with the fleet, Nearchus would now have responsibility for the troops as well as the crews.

20.9 *trierarchs*: explained above at 18.3–8.

20.10 *Alexander himself . . . down both mouths of the Indus*: cf. 6.18.3–20.5, with 19.4–5 for the sacrifices.

21.1 *when Cephisodorus was archon . . . on the twentieth day of the month Boedromion*: thus late September or early October 325, but the archon was Anticles, not Cephisodorus (the archon of 323/2). Nearchus left about a month after Alexander, but still was soon held up by the persistence of the adverse winds (21.13). The ship station from which they sailed (21.2) must have been some distance down the western branch of the Indus from Patala.

21.7 *Crocala*: possibly seaward of the island of Cilluta (6.19.3).

Arabies: the Arabitae of 6.21.4.

21.10–11 *'Alexander's Harbour' . . . Bibacta*: relating Nearchus' account to the topographical evidence, Lambrick, *Sind*, 117 suggests that this natural harbour was near Gujo, and that Bibacta was the hillock Tharri Gujo (p. 119). Central to Lambrick's reconstruction is the perception that the coastline in antiquity ran closer to due east of Karachi, and thus way to the north of the present coastline.

22.4 *Morontobara*: probably Karachi, in which case Sacala may have been at the estuary of the river Malir (Lambrick, *Sind*, 120).

22.7 *thick with trees*: related texts indicate mangroves.

23.4 *Cocala*: somewhere on the shore of Sonmiani Bay, and thus within relatively easy reach of Rhambacia [Las Bela] (6.21.5) on the river Purali.

23.5 *here ... Leonnatus* [2] *... defeated the Oreitans*: briefly mentioned at 7.5.5 (cf. 6.22.2–3). The following reference to the stockpile of corn left at the Purali for Nearchus does not mean that this was a synchronized amphibious advance. The monsoons and wind patterns ruled that out. Thus Nearchus' mission was not to establish food dumps for Alexander, but rather it was Alexander who left stores for Nearchus, where he could: next at the Sitacus (38.9).

25.5 *when the sun reached midday, everything ... was shadowless*: Nearchus probably did not witness this (or the setting of the stars) himself as he was way to the north of the Tropic of Cancer, and this was way after the summer solstice. In fact Arrian's wording allows the interpretation that Nearchus was reporting what he had learnt from traders who worked along the west coast of India, and there may also be the echo of Herodotus 4.41.4. It is quite credible that Nearchus included observations that might be of use to navigators.

26.1 *made their way through this* [Gedrosian] *country with great difficulty*: cf. 6.22–6. The conditions made it impossible for Alexander to move supplies down to the coast for Nearchus, as he did later (cf. 38.9); and there is no indication that Nearchus was supposed to land supplies along the coast for Alexander's convoy.

26.6 *Carnine*: some suggest that this was the island sacred to the Sun, later called Nosala (31.2).

26.10 *Mosarna*: perhaps Ras Pasni.

27.7–28.9 **Nearchus captures the last city of the Fish-Eaters by trickery.** The story serves to illustrate Nearchus' brilliance as a commander, able to interpret the evidence of the city's resources and the risks of a direct assault, to formulate a cunning plan, to lead the task force personally, and to motivate his troops to action.

27.9 *arable farming ... near the beach*: this may have been the shore of the Gwatar Bay.

28.3 *Archias*: listed at 18.3.

29.8 *a thousand miles*: the stages given by Arrian from Ras Malana (26.2) to Ras el Kuh (32.2–3) give a total of only 900, and the difference would be accounted for by the distances not given at 26.4 and 10, and 29.2.

31.6 *one of the Nereids*: she and her forty-nine or ninety-nine sisters were the daughters of the sea-god Nereus. In myth he was credited with great wisdom and the power of prophecy, and generally presented as in conflict with Heracles, but of more relevance to the Alexander myth is that Alexander's ancestor Achilles was the son of Thetis, a daughter of Nereus.

32.3 *kept the ships' bows pointing more north-west*: they must have entered Carmania in the area of Ras el Kuh, *c.*48 km west of Jask.

32.7 *promontory ... called Maceta*: Ras Musandam in Oman, but the headland seen from the Carmanian beach may have been Mount Hagim (3,000 m). Nearchus seems to have imagined that beyond Mount Hagim or Ras Musandam there was a channel leading through into the Red Sea (as opposed to the Persian Gulf).

32.13 *I think . . . that Nearchus saved the expedition*: cf. 7.20.10.

33.1–36.7 Nearchus' reunion with Alexander and renewed commission. A romantic story displaying Nearchus' literary panache and some liberty taken with the historical facts (as at 36.3).

33.2 *Anamis . . . Harmozia*: the river flowing past Harmozia would be the Minab. Nearchus would have arrived there in the period late December 325 to early spring 324. It took several days' march to get inland to where Nearchus met Alexander, which may therefore have been in the area of Gulašgerd-Kahnu. Diodorus Siculus is alone in setting the meeting-place at Salmous, on the coast (17.106.4).

35.4 *began to weep, and wept long*: on this and the following celebration (36) E. Badian, 'Nearchus the Cretan', *Yale Classical Studies*, 24 (1975), 169, comments that Nearchus presents himself as 'the only man whose fate could move the king to Homeric tears or Homeric celebration'.

35.8 *swore by . . . Zeus and . . . Ammon . . . through Asia*: in this climactic way Nearchus emphasizes that he was more than a close friend of Alexander, for he had pulled off a miraculous achievement in bringing the fleet through safely.

36.1–2 Nearchus' intervention saves the district governor. The story starts at 33.8 and finishes with this man, still under arrest, supplicating Alexander and giving Nearchus the credit for securing his release. A nice dramatic addition, but of dubious historical value.

36.3 *thank offerings . . . games*: at 6.28.3, following Aristobulus, Arrian sets these celebrations in Carmania, but before Nearchus' arrival (6.28.5), and not after. Nearchus presumably inverted the sequence to make the thanksgiving a tribute to his own survival and achievement. There is a complication in that Diodorus sets Nearchus' reunion with Alexander at Salmous (cf. 33.2) on the (Carmanian?) coast and not inland (17.106.4), with a second round of dramatic contests in progress as he appeared.

36.8 *previous satrap . . . put to death . . . successor, Tlepolemus*: the satrap, Astaspes, was axed early in 324 (Curtius 9.10.21 and 29), and was briefly succeeded by Thoas till Alexander appointed Tlepolemus (6.27.1).

37.1–4 Islands of the Strait of Hormuz and the Gulf of Oman. Nearchus sailed past a desert island, which he calls Organa, to reach Oaracta, an island about 80 miles (*c.*140 km) long. This latter must be Qeshm (in fact *c.*110 km long), in which case Organa would be Hormoz. The island seen to the south of Qeshm (37.4) would be Hengam. Arrian's account appears muddled, for Strabo's brief summary of Nearchus and Orthagoras (Strabo 16.3.5) indicates that the island where Erythres was buried, Ogyris (thus not Oaracta), was 2,000 stades (*c.*360 km) off the Carmanian Coast, and thus probably Masira. Nearchus did not get that far.

37.3 *Erythres*: the name means red, and Nearchus took this mythical character to be historical. The label the Red Sea was variously applied to the Indian Ocean, the Arabian Sea, the Persian Gulf, and the Red Sea as we know it.

39.4 *a whale . . . seventy-five feet*: but at 30.9 Arrian gives a whale's length as twenty-five fathoms (or twenty-three (*c.*41 m) according to Strabo 15.2.13). If the text is sound here, Arrian may have reduced the number to a more credible size.

39.9 *Arosis*: Strabo gives the form as Oroatis (15.3.1). Probably the Jarrahi with an estuary then near Bandar Mashur.

40.1 *Uxians, described as brigands in my other book*: not explicit in *Anabasis* 3.17, but they were able to extract subsidies or protection money from Persians wishing to travel between Susa and Persepolis (Strabo 15.3.4).

40.2–4 *three climate zones . . .*: the climatic zones of Persia are not particularly relevant to Nearchus' account, and Arrian may have taken this section from Eratosthenes (cf. Strabo 15.3.1).

40.5 *from the Black Sea . . . no great distance*: Eratosthenes was better informed (Strabo 2.1.26 and 15.3.1).

40.6 *Mardians (another brigand people)*: these are probably the 'Persian Mardi', as at 3.11.5 and 13.1, similarly characterized as bellicose and uncivilized by Curtius 5.6.17.

Cossaeans: mentioned in Arrian's reference to the second campaign which Alexander launched against the Uxian tribes, in the winter of 324/3 (7.15.1–3).

40.8 *foundation of settled townships*: Strabo likewise summarizes Nearchus, with anticipatory references to Hellenistic foundations, all this as justifying the imperialism.

41.2–3 *the narrow strait between . . . Leucas and Acarnania*: Arrian inserts a reference to his own observation when he was a student in Nicopolis, near Preveza.

41.8 *Babylon*: cf. 7.19.3.

42.1–9 The reunion with Alexander at Susa, at about the end of March 324. Noted at 7.5.6. This passage serves to reinforce the image of Nearchus' importance to Alexander as presented in 35.1–8.

42.7 *anchored by the pontoon bridge*: probably at Ahwaz, and thus not necessarily at the point mentioned at 3.17.1, which would have been further north.

42.8–9 *wherever Nearchus appeared . . .*: Nearchus shifts the focus onto himself by moving the general celebrations from Susa to the crossing-point on the Pasitigris, and by omitting the honour also paid to Onesicritus (contrast 7.5.6). Thus he also excluded the decoration of Peucestas and Hephaestion, but included Leonnatus as his fellow commander in the operations in Oreitis.

43 **Concluding observations.** This is a strange medley of facts and observations. As is suggested in the Introduction, Arrian's purpose may have been to draw the focus back on himself after what is presented as a digest of Nearchus' account.

43.3 *no one . . . has made this . . . circumnavigation*: this is an authorial comment, yet Arrian does not reflect the state of knowledge reflected in the roughly contemporaneous *Periplus of the Erythraean Sea*.

43.4 *survivors of Cambyses' army*: Cambyses lost a large number of men in Egypt when they tried to march back from the Libyan oases across the Qattara depression in or after 525 (Herodotus 3.26).

troops sent by Ptolemy . . . to Seleucus: this may refer to an action in 310/9 when Ptolemy gave support to Seleucus against Antigonus.

43.8 *men sent out . . . from Babylon*: at 7.20.7 Arrian identifies them as Archias, Androsthenes (cf. *Indica* 18.3 and 4), and the Cypriot Hieron.

43.11 *Hannon*: in the early fifth century BC Hannon, a Carthaginian, explored the west coast of Africa, possibly as far as Benin.

NOTES ON THE GREEK TEXT

For this translation I have used the text of the Teubner edition edited by A. G. Roos and revised by G. Wirth (Leipzig, 1967 (Vol. I), 1968 (Vol. II)). Noted below are the few places in which I have adopted a reading different from that in the Teubner text, and also the places where the manuscripts are evidently deficient and most editors (including the Teubner editors) have marked corruption or a lacuna: in the translation I have filled the lacunas with what seem the most likely supplements.

ANABASIS

1.1.6 The MSS ἐμπόρων ('merchants') is almost certainly corrupt: the sense required (*pace* Bosworth) is 'locals' or 'mountain people'.

1.7.2 Reading ἐλευθερίαν τε ⟨καὶ αὐτονομίαν⟩ προϊσχόμενοι (Abicht).

1.9.5 There is a small lacuna before τῶν ἐγκαταληφθέντων: Van Leeuwen's supplement ⟨καὶ ὀλίγων ὄντων⟩ gives the required sense.

1.12.1 There is a lacuna before the second οἱ δὲ: a μὲν clause has dropped out, beyond restitution.

1.12.6 Retaining, as a proper name, the MSS προσακτίῳ, which most editors emend to Πρακτίῳ, after Freinsheim.

1.14.2 Deleting, with the Teubner text, ἐπὶ δὲ ἡ Κρατεροῦ τοῦ Ἀλεξάνδρου as an interpolation.

1.15.6 Reading Ἄρετιν, with the MSS, not Ἀρέτην (Krüger).

1.17.2 Reading παραλαμβάνει for the second παραληψόμενον in the Teubner text (which seems simply a mistake by the editor).

1.17.11 Reading ἐπαγ⟨αγ⟩ομένους (Krüger), not ἐπαγομένους.

1.22.7 Reading Ἀδαῖος, χιλιάρχης οὗτος, καὶ... (Pflugk), not Ἀδαῖος ⟨ὁ⟩ χιλιάρχης, οὗτοι καὶ... (Schmieder).

1.24.4 Reading, with the MSS, εἰσβάλλων, not εἰσβαλὼν.

1.28.7 There is a lacuna before κοῦφοι γὰρ ὄντες: I translate the supplement suggested by Roos, ζῶντες δὲ ὀλίγοι ἐλήφθησαν.

2.8.9 Deleting καὶ τοὺς Μακεδόνας as a gloss (Schmieder).

2.16.7 Reading γενησόμενον (Lobeck), not γνωσόμενοι.

2.23.2 Reading ἀσθέταιροι (the MSS have ἀσθέτεροι), not πεζέταιροι, as substituted by the Teubner and most other editors. Also in 4.23.1, 5.22.6, 6.6.1, 6.21.3, 7.11.3.

2.24.6 After οὐχ ἄξιον μνήμης deleting τὸ ἐπίγραμμα as a gloss (Bosworth, after Polak).

3.2.1 Reading ἐπενόει (Krüger), not ἐποίει.

3.3.2 Reading with the MSS τῆς Ἡρακλέους...⟨sc. γενέσεως⟩, not τὴν Ἡρακλέους.....⟨sc. γένεσιν⟩ (Krüger).

3.5.5 The MSS give Λεοννάτον τὸν Ὀνάσου, and most editors mark Ὀνάσου as corrupt. Leonnatus is elsewhere (though not consistently) the son of Anteas.

3.6.6 Reading ἐς τὰ βαρβαρικά, γραμματέα ἐπὶ....(Sintenis), not ἐς τὰ βαρβαρικὰ γράμματα, ἐπὶ....

3.6.8 Reading Κλέανδρος (Sluys), not Κλέαρχος: cf. 3.12.2.

3.7.1 After ἱππέας μὲν ἔχων περὶ τρισχιλίους there is clearly a lacuna, in which the number of infantry was specified. I have translated Roos' suggested supplement ⟨πέζους δὲ ἴσους⟩.

3.7.7 Reading ἱππεῖς ἐστιν οἳ (Schmieder), not ἱππεῖς οὗτοι.

3.11.8 Deleting βασιλικῶν as a gloss (Roos).

3.13.3 Reading τοὺς περὶ Ἀρέτην τε ⟨καὶ⟩ τοὺς Παίονας (Bosworth).

3.20.4 Reading ἐπισιτισόμενος (Krüger), not ἐπισιτισάμενος.

3.24.5 Reading with the MSS Καρχηδονίων, not Καλχηδονίων (see Bosworth, *Commentary*, i. 353–4).

4.3.6 Reading with the MSS λόγου ἂν ἄξιον, not λόγου ὃν ἄξιον.

4.4.9 Reading ἐπὶ πᾶν τῶν Σκυθῶν (Pflugk), not ἐπὶ πάντων Σκυθῶν.

4.5.1 Reading with the MSS οὐκ ἀπὸ κοινοῦ, not οὐκ ἀπὸ ⟨τοῦ⟩ κοινοῦ.

4.5.3 The MSS reading ἐς τὰ βασίλεια τῆς Σογδιανῆς is probably corrupt. None of the emendations proposed is certain, but I translate the Teubner text ἐς τὰ βόρεια (Polak) τῆς Σογδιανῆς.

4.7.2 Reading Μενίδας (Hamilton), not Μελαμνίδας.

The MSS give Βῆσσός τε ὁ Συρίας σατράπης. The name Bessus is almost certainly corrupt, and there are other difficulties presented by this passage. There is no obvious solution of text or interpretation: the translation here given follows the suggestions made by Bosworth.

4.8.9 Deleting καὶ ταύτην (Castiglioni).

4.12.1 Retaining Μακεδόνας, which Roos deletes in the Teubner text.

4.24.1 The MSS have ἐπὶ τὸν ποταμὸν τὸν Εὔασ πόλεως προὐχώρει ἵνα.... The name of the river is probably Euias (Bosworth, comparing *Itinerarium Alexandri* 105), and there is evidently a lacuna of indeterminate length and content between Εὔασ and πόλεως (Roos).

4.28.4 Reading with the MSS τὰ Βάζιρα δὲ πόλιν, not τὰ Βάζιρα δὲ ⟨τὴν⟩ πόλιν (Roos, after Krüger).

4.29.4 Deleting τὸν Ἰνδόν (Polak).

5.2.6 Reading καὶ στεφανώσασθαι ὡς εἶχον (Vulcanius), not ὡς καὶ στεφανώσασθαι εἶχον.

5.3.6 Bosworth posits a lacuna in the sentence καὶ τὴν πόλιν Τάξιλα.... ἐνδίδωσιν, to provide a verb or clause introducing the indirect speech. The translation fills the lacuna conjecturally.

5.4.2 There is probably a lacuna between πλατύτατος and καὶ ἑκατόν. See Explanatory Note.

5.5.2 Bosworth posits a lacuna after ἐπὶ Μηδίαν. The translation assumes no more than ⟨καὶ⟩.

5.9.4 Reading ἡ μετὰ τροπὰς μάλιστα ⟨ἃς⟩ ἐν θέρει (Krüger), not ἢ μετὰ τροπὰς μάλιστα ⟨τὰς⟩ ἐν θέρει.

5.13.4 Reading with the MSS οἱ Ἀγριᾶνες καὶ οἱ ἀκοντισταί, where Roos deletes the καὶ.

5.18.2 There is probably a lacuna before ἐλήφθησαν δὲ καὶ, in which mention was made of the number of human captives (Krüger, accepted by Roos).

6.10.4 Reading ἐς τὸ ἔσω τοῦ τείχους (Krüger), not ἐς τὸ ἔσω τὸ τεῖχος.

6.17.4 Reading τῇ δὲ ἄλλῃ στρατιᾷ (Ellendt), not τὴν δὲ ἄλλην στρατιάν (MSS), which requires a lacuna before Ἡφαιστίων. The overall sense is not greatly affected.

6.25.5 Reading ὑπελείπετο (Castiglioni), not ἀπελείπετο.

6.26.2 Reading καὶ τούτου (Grundmann), not καὶ τοῦτο οὐ.

6.28.4 Reading, after Castiglioni, Πευκέσταν ⟨Ἀλεξάνδρου,⟩ τὸν Ἀλεξάνδρου ὑπερασπίσαντα.

6.29.6 Reading ἐν μέσῳ δὲ ⟨τῆς τραπέζης καὶ⟩ τῆς κλίνης (Polak).

6.29.9 Reading ὁπότε ἔλθοι ⟨ἐς⟩ Πέρσας (Pflugk and A. Miller), not ὁπότε ἕλοι Πέρσας.

7.3.6 Reading οὐκ ἀχρεῖα πάντη (Sintenis), not οὐκ ἀχρεῖα πάντα.

7.8.1 Reading ⟨τοῖς⟩ μένουσιν (Wüst), where Roos deletes μένουσιν and Krüger proposed ἀπιοῦσιν.

7.10.1 There is a lacuna after μᾶλλον. The simplest supplement, followed in the translation, is ⟨ἢ ταλαιπωρήσας ὑπὲρ ἐμοῦ μᾶλλον⟩ (after Polak).

7.12.7 A whole page of the original text is missing from the MSS. From other sources we know that the missing text recorded the absconding of Harpalus to Greece, and the march from Opis to Ecbatana. There must also have been an account of a quarrel between Hephaestion and Eumenes, the end of which is described in 7.13.1.

7.20.4 Reading ἐθέλοντα· ἐπὶ τῷδε γὰρ μόνον θηρᾶν οὐκ εἶναι ἀθέμιτον (Castiglioni), not ἐθέλοντα ἐπὶ τῷδε θηρᾶν μόνον· ἐπὶ τῷδε γὰρ οὐκ εἶναι ἀθέμιτον.

7.21.1 The MSS give the name of the canal as Pollacopas. A parallel passage in the historian Appian gives the name as Pallacotta, and we follow most recent editors in adopting that name here.

INDICA

1.5 Reading with the MSS ἀπὸ τοῦ ὄρεος τῆς Νύσης, not ἀπὸ τῆς τροφοῦ τῆς Νύσης (Roos).

4.8 Reading with the MSS Νεῦδρον, not Σύδρον (Marquart, Roos).

9.9 There is a lacuna after εἰς ἐλευθερίην. The translation gives the likely sense, but there is no means of conjecturing the number of years for which the first period of liberty lasted (except that it was almost certainly less than 300).

16.7 Reading οὔτε ⟨εἴ τι ἔ⟩τι καρτερ⟨ώτερ⟩ον ἐγένετο (Jacoby).

18.7 Reading Θόας Μανδροδώρου, as in *Anab.* 6.23.2, not Θόας Μηνοδώρου (MSS).

27.1 The MSS give μᾶλλόν τι †ὀνομαζόμενα†, which is almost certainly corrupt. No proposed emendation is convincing, but the translation gives the likely sense.

27.5 Reading with the MSS ὥσπερ ἐν ποταμῷ. Roos marks ποταμῷ as corrupt, but it seems to yield good sense.

37.8 The name of the 'destitute little township' is not recoverable from the corruption in the MSS.

40.5 There may be a lacuna after νιφετώδεα, providing a context for the otherwise weakly connected ὥστε....

INDEX

REFERENCES to the *Anabasis* are by Book and chapter (e.g. 1.17 refers to Book 1, chapter 17), and sometimes by Book, chapter, and section (e.g. 1.17.4 refers to Book 1, chapter 17, section 4): references to the *Indica* are by chapter number in italics, preceded by *Ind.* at the first occurrence (e.g. *Ind.21; Ind.21, 24, 37*). The chapters and sections are indicated in the text by marginal numbers in bold (chapters) and italics (sections).

Three-digit numerals in brackets (mainly from 336 to 323) are dates BC. Dates given in the form (e.g.) 326/5 denote the winter season, late 326 to early 325.

Numerals in square brackets after names of people (e.g. Amyntas [2]) are those used to distinguish homonyms listed in Waldemar Heckel's *Who's Who in the Age of Alexander the Great* (Oxford: Blackwell, 2006; New York and Oxford: Wiley–Blackwell, 2009): not all of the individuals listed in Heckel are mentioned in the *Anabasis* or the *Indica*, so homonyms listed in this index do not always have consecutive numbers in brackets. Numerals in round brackets after entry-headings (e.g. Achilles (1), Ora (2)) serve to distinguish places of the same name or people not listed in Heckel.

Where relevant, the entry for a place or country should be understood to include the inhabitants of that place or country.

The headings of the more important entries are given in bold capitals, and references of particular relevance or importance are printed in bold. The headings of a number of general topics are given in italics.

Abbreviations are A. for Alexander, and Mac. for Macedonian(s).

For the most part, this index does not include the names of fathers, unless they recur in another context.

Abastanians, independent Indian tribe 6.15

Abdera, city on coast of Thrace 1.11

Abii, Scythian people, perhaps N. of Samarcand 4.1

Abisares, Indian dynast, ruler of region to E. of upper Indus [Hazara], 'highland Indians' (5.8.3) 4.27, 4.30, 5.8, 5.20, 5.22, 5.29

Abissarians, Indian tribe in Hazara *Ind.4*

Abreas, Mac. corporal, killed defending A. in Mallian city (326/5) 6.9, 6.10, 6.11

Abulites, Persian confirmed by A. as satrap of Susiana (331): 3.8, 3.16, 3.19; executed for maladministration (324), 7.4

Abydos, city on Asian side of Hellespont 1.11

Acarnania, region of SW central Greece 2.4, 2.13, *Ind.41*

ACESINES [Chenab], Indian river 5.4, 5.5, 5.20, 5.21, 5.25, 5.29, 6.1, 6.3, 6.4–5, 6.6, 6.13, 6.14, 6.15, 7.4, 7.10, *Ind.3, 4, 6, 18, 19*

Achaean Harbour, on Asian side of Hellespont 1.11

Achilles (1), hero 1.12, 7.14, 7.16

Achilles (2), Athenian envoy to A. (331) 3.6

Acuphis, leading aristocrat in Nysa 5.1–2

Ada, daughter of Hecatomnos: appointed satrap of Caria by A. (334), 1.23; adopted A. as her son, 1.23.8

Adaeus, Mac. infantry commander: killed at Halicarnassus (334) 1.22

Admetus, Mac. infantry commander: killed at Tyre (332) 2.23, 2.24

Adraïstae, Indian tribe E. of Hydraotes 5.22

Aeacids, family claiming descent from Aeacus 2.27, 4.11

Aeacus, legendary king and judge, son of Zeus, grandfather of Achilles 7.29

Aegae, city in Macedonia 1.11, *Ind.18*

Aegean Sea 2.25, 5.1 ('Greek Sea'), 7.20
— war in the Aegean (333–2) 2.1–2, 2.13, 3.2
Aegina, island in the Saronic Gulf 6.11
Aegobares, Persian 7.6
Aegospotami, in Chersonese: Athenian defeat (405) 1.9
Aegyptus, old name of the Nile 5.6, 6.1
Aeolis, region of NW Asia Minor 1.18, 1.26, 3.22, 5.6, 7.9
Aëropus, father of Alexander [4], Heromenes, Arrhabaeus (qq.v.)
Aeschylus, superintendent of mercenaries in Egypt 3.5
Aetolia, region of W. central Greece 1.7, 1.10, 3.5, 3.16
Agamemnon 1.11
Agathon [1], son of Tyrimmas: commander of Thracian cavalry 1.14, 3.12
Agenor, father of Cadmus: his shrine in Tyre 2.24
Agesilaus, brother of Spartan king Agis 2.13
Aginis, village in Susiana Ind.42
Agis [1], king of Sparta 2.13
Agis [2], poet and flatterer in A.'s retinue 4.9
Agoranis, tributary of Ganges Ind.4
Agrianians, people in Paeonia 1.5, 2.7; their king Langarus 1.5
— light troops in A.'s army 1.1.11 and passim
Albanians, people bordering SW Caspian Sea 3.8, 3.11, 3.13
Alcetas, Mac. infantry commander 4.22, 4.27, 5.11
Alcias, commander of Elean troops joining A.'s army (333) 1.29
Alcimachus [1], son of Agathocles: sent to establish democracies in Aeolis and Ionia (334) 1.18
Alcmene, mother of (Argive) Heracles 2.16
Alcomenae, city in Macedonia Ind.18
Aleian Plain, in S. Cilicia 2.5
Alexander [1] of Epirus, brother of Olympias 3.6
ALEXANDER [2], the Great (356–323), son of Philip [1]: relative lack of literary celebration, 1.12; other historians of A., Preface, and see under

Arrian; Lysippus only sculptor allowed to portray A., 1.16
— ancestry, family, marriage: ancestry, 4.11; claimed descent from Aeacus, 4.11, Neoptolemus, 1.11, Heracles, 3.3, 4.7, 4.11, 5.26, 6.3, Heracleidae of Argos, 2.5, 4.10, 4.11, Perseus, 3.3; father Philip [1], 1.1, 1.16, 2.14, 3.6, 4.8, 4.11, 7.9, Ind.43; mother Olympias, 3.6, 4.10, 5.27, 6.1, 7.12; paternity attributed to Ammon, 3.3, 4.9, 6.14, 7.2, 7.8, 7.27, 7.29; sister Cyna, 1.5; nurse Lanice, 4.9; adopted as son by Ada (334), 1.23; married (327) Rhoxane (daughter of Oxyartes), 4.19, 4.20, 7.4, (324) Barsine/Stateira (daughter of Darius), 3.22, 7.4, (324) Parysatis (daughter of Ochus (1)), 7.4; offers of marriage, (332) a daughter of Darius, 2.25, (329/8) a Scythian princess, 4.15
— in Macedonia/Greece/Thrace (338–335): with Philip at battle of Chaeronea (338), 7.9; rift with Philip (337/6), 3.6; at Philip's death (336), 1.10, 1.25, 3.6; in Peloponnese, given leadership of Greek league against Persia (336), 1.1, 2.14; in Thrace (335), 1.1–6; march to Thebes (335), 1.7; at Thebes (335), 1.7–8; response to Athenian embassy (335), 1.10
— in Asia/Egypt/Libya (334–326): crossing to Asia (334), 1.11, 2.14; at Troy (334), 1.11–12; in Hellespontine Phrygia (334), 1.12–17 (battle of Granicus, 1.13–16); at Sardis (334), 1.17; at Ephesus (334), 1.17–18; at Miletus (334), 1.18–19; disbands navy (334), 1.20; in Caria (334), 1.20–4, 1.25; in Lycia and Pamphylia (334/3), 1.24, 1.26–7; in Pisidia (334/3), 1.27–8; in Phrygia (333), 1.29; at Gordium (333), 1.29 (the Gordian Knot, 2.3); in Galatia and Cappadocia (333), 2.4; in Cilicia (333), 2.4–12 (battle of Issus, 2.6–11); in Phoenicia (332), 2.13–25 (siege of Tyre, 2.18–24); in Palestinian Syria (332), 2.25–6; in Egypt and Libya (332/1), 3.1–5, 3.26 (foundation of Alexandria (1), 3.1–2; visit to oracle of Ammon, 3.3–4; organization of Egypt, 3.5); in

Phoenicia (331), 3.6; in Syria (331), 3.6–7; in Mesopotamia and Assyria (1) (331), 3.7–15 (**battle of Gaugamela, 3.8–15**); in Babylon and Susa (331), 3.16; in Uxian territory (330), 3.17–18; in Persis (330), 3.18; in Media and Parthyaea (330), 3.19–22; in the Elburz mountain area (330), 3.23–5; in Areia (330), 3.25; in Drangiana (330), 3.25–7; crossing of the Hindu Kush (329), 3.28; **in Bactria and Sogdiana (329–327)**, 3.29–4.22 (capture of Bessus (329), 3.29–30; first Sogdian revolt (329), 4.1–3; defeat of Scythians (329), 4.3–5; Polytimetus disaster (329), 4.5–6; second Sogdian revolt (328), 4.15–16; quarrel with and murder of Cleitus [2] (328), 4.8–9; Callisthenes and obeisance debate (328), 4.10–12; Pages' conspiracy (327), 4.13–14; capture of Rock of Sogdiana (327), 4.18–19; capture of Rock of Chorienes (327), 4.21); **from Bactria to the Indus (327–326)**, 4.22–5.2 (Swat campaign (327/6), 4.23–30; capture of Aornus (2) (326), 4.29–30)
— **in India (326–325)**: at the Hydaspes (326), 5.8–20 (**battle of Hydaspes, 5.14–19**); in the Punjab (326), 5.20–4 (Cathaean campaign, 5.22–4); mutiny at the Hyphasis, and turning back (326), 5.24–9; from the Hydaspes to the Indian Ocean (326–5), **6.1–20**, *Ind.18–19* (Mallian campaign (326/5), 6.6–11, *Ind.19*)
— **in Asia (325–323)**: (325–324) from Patala through Oreitis (6.21–2) and Gedrosia (6.22–7, 7.4, *Ind.26, 32*) to Carmania (6.27–8, *Ind.34–6*); in Persis and Susa (324), 6.29–7.6, *Ind.42* (mass marriage, 7.4); from Susa to Opis (324), 7.7; at Opis, and mutiny (324), 7.8–12; in Media (324), 7.13–14 (death of Hephaestion, 7.14); in Babylon (323), 7.19–27 (last illness and death, 7.25–6)
— **fleet sent from Indus to Persian Gulf (325–324)**: *see under* **NEARCHUS**; A.'s anxiety, *Ind.20, 34, 35*; reunion in Susa (324), 7.5, *Ind.42*
— **campaigns: 335**: against independent Thracians, 1.1, 1.3; against Triballians,

1.2–3; against Getae, 1.3–4; against Illyrians, 1.5–6; against Thebes, 1.7–8. **334: battle of Granicus**, 1.13–16, 1.29, 2.7, 2.11, 3.6, 3.22, 4.8, 6.11, 7.8; against Miletus, 1.18–19; against Halicarnassus, 1.20–3, 1.25, 2.5. **333: battle of Issus**, 2.6–11, 2.13, 6.11. **332**: against Tyre, 2.15–25; against Gaza (1), 2.25–6. **331: battle of Gaugamela**, 3.8–15, 6.11; against Uxians, 3.17; at Persian Gates, 3.18. **330**: in Elburz mountains, 3.23–5. **329**: against Sogdian cities, 4.2–3; against Scythians, 4.3–5; Sogdian revolts, 4.1–3 (329), 4.15–16 (328). **327/6**: in Swat, 4.23–30. **326: against Porus (1) at Hydaspes**, 5.14–19; against Cathaeans, 5.22–4. **326/5**: against Mallians, 6.6–11, 6.28, 6.30, *Ind.19*. **324/3**: against Cossaeans, 7.15, *Ind.40*
— **river-crossings**: Danube (334), 1.3–4; Eordaïcus (334), 1.6; Strymon (334), 1.11; Hebrus (334), 1.11; Black River (334), 1.11; Granicus (334), 1.14–15; Nile (331), 3.6; Euphrates (331), 3.7; Tigris (331), 3.7; Araxes (331/0), 3.18; Oxus (329), 3.29; Tanaïs (a) (329), 4.4; Choes (327/6), 4.23; Guraeus (327/6), 4.25; Indus (326), 5.4, 5.7, 5.8; Hydaspes (326), 5.11–13; Acesines (326), 5.20–21, 5.29; Hydraotes (326), 5.21, 5.29, 6.7, 6.8
— **sieges**: Miletus (334), 1.18–19, 7.9; Halicarnassus (334), 1.20–3; Tyre (332), 2.18–24, 4.26; Gaza (1) (332), 2.25–6; Massaga (327/6), 4.26–7; Sangala (326), 5.22–4; **rock assaults**: Rock of Sogdiana (327), 4.18–19; Rock of Chorienes (327), 4.21; Rock of Aornus (326), 4.29–30, *Ind.5*; **massacres**: Thebes (335), 1.8, 1.9; Greek mercenaries at Granicus (334), 1.16; Tyre (332), 2.24; Sogdiana (329), 3.30; Sogdian cities (329), 4.2, 4.3; Sogdiana (329), 4.6; Aspasians (327/6), 4.23, 4.24; Massaga (327/6), 4.27; Aornus (2) (326), 4.30; Hydaspes (326), 5.17–18; Sangala (326), 5.24; Mallians (326/5), 6.6, 6.11; Cossaeans (324/3), 7.15; **failures/disasters**: Myndus (334), 1.20; Polytimetus (329), 4.5–6; Hyphasis mutiny ('his only

defeat') (326), 5.29; Gedrosia (325), 6.23–6, 7.4

— (military): his armour, 1.11, 1.14, 6.9; the sacred shield, 1.11, 6.9, 6.10; his horse Bucephalas, 5.14, **5.19**; single combat, 1.15 (Granicus, 334), 6.9 (Mallians, 326/5); speed, 1.4, 1.7, 2.4, 2.10, 3.17, 3.18, 3.19, 3.20–1, 3.25, 4.6, 6.11, 6.15; guesses proved correct, 1.1, 1.27, 2.10, 3.18, 4.2, 5.23, 7.28; strategic thinking, 2.17, 3.10, 4.5, 6.15, 7.28; leadership, 1.14, 1.15, 1.28, 2.18, 2.23, 4.4, 6.7, **6.26**, 7.28; endurance, 6.26, 7.28; good fortune/success against the odds, 2.26, 3.28, 4.18, 4.21, 4.28, 6.6, 6.16, 6.24, 7.10, 7.15, 7.28, *Ind.20*; inspiring terror, 5.19, 6.12, 6.16; effect of personal appearance in battles/sieges, 1.8 (Thebes), 1.14 (Granicus), 1.21 (Halicarnassus), 1.27 (Aspendus), 2.4 (Cilician Gates), 2.22 (Tyre), 3.21, 5.15, 6.6

— (army management): reinforcements received, 1.29, 2.20, 3.5, 3.16, 4.7, 5.3 (Indian cavalry), 5.8 (Indians), 5.20 (Thracians), 5.24 (Indians), 7.23 (Persians, etc.), *Ind.19*; troops sent home, 3.19, 3.29, 5.27, 6.17, 7.8, 7.10, 7.12; convalescent centres, 2.7, 4.16, 5.8; veterans settled in Asia, 4.4, 4.22, 4.24, 5.27, 5.29, 7.21; army reorganization, 3.16, 3.19, 3.24, 3.27, 7.6, 7.8; integration of Asians, 7.6, 7.8, 7.11, 7.23, 7.24

— (political): desire to 'punish' Persia, 2.14, 3.18; to 'add Asia to Greece', 4.11; as *de facto* king of Asia, 2.14, 2.25, 3.18, 4.4, 4.7, 7.15; political interventions, 1.17 (Ephesus), 1.18 (Aeolis and Ionia), 2.5 (Soli (1)), 2.5 (Mallus), 3.5 (organization of Egypt, 331); conquered or surrendered regions allowed to retain their institutions or ruler, 1.17 (Sardis and Lydia), 3.5 (Egyptian nomarchs), 3.27 (Ariaspians), 5.2 (Nysa), 6.15, 6.16 (Musicanus), 6.17 (Patala), 7.20 (Arabia in prospect); tribute remitted, 1.18, 2.5; conquered territory given to local allies, 5.8, 5.19, 5.20, 5.21, 5.24, 5.25, 5.29, 6.2; purge of satraps (recalled/deposed/arrested/

punished), 3.29, 4.18, 6.27.1, 6.27.4–5 (generals), 6.30, 7.4, 7.18

— foundations: Alexandria in Egypt (332–1), 3.1–2, 5.1; Alexandria *in Caucaso* (330/29), 3.28, 4.22, 5.1; Alexandria Eschate (Sogdiana, 329), 4.1, 4.4; Arigaeum (327/6), 4.24, 4.25; Nicaea and Bucephala (326), 5.19, 5.20; at junction of Acesines and Indus (325), 6.15; in Sogdian (2) country (325), 6.15; Rhambacia (325), 6.21, 6.22; in S. Babylonia (323), 7.21; in Uxian, Mardian (1), Cossaean country, *Ind.40*

— (religious and ceremonial): 'scrupulous religious observance', 7.28.1; belief in divine signs and guidance, 1.17, 1.18, 1.20, 1.25, 1.26, 2.3, 2.7, 2.18, 2.26–7, 3.3, 3.3–4 (consultation of Ammon), 4.13, 7.18; sacrifice: 1.4, 1.11, 1.18, 2.5, 2.15, 2.24, 2.26, 3.1.4, 3.1.5 (for omens), 3.5, 3.6, 3.7 (for omens), 3.16.5 (Bel), 3.16.9, 3.25, 3.27, 3.28, 4.4.1, 4.4.3 (for omens), 4.8, 4.9, 4.15 (for omens), 4.22, 4.30, 5.2, 5.3 (for omens), 5.8, 5.20, 5.25 (for omens), 5.29, 6.3, 6.19, 6.28, 7.11, 7.14, 7.24, **7.25**, *Ind.18, 20, 36, 42*; games, festivals: 1.11 (Olympian games at Aegae, 335), 2.5, 2.24, 3.1, 3.5, 3.6, 3.16, 3.25, 4.4, 5.3, 5.8, 5.20, 5.29, 6.28, 7.14.1, **7.14.10** (for Hephaestion), *Ind.18, 36, 42*; parades: 1.18, 2.5, 2.6, 2.12, 2.24, 3.5, *Ind.36*; dedications: 1.11, 1.16, 1.17, 2.24, 5.29; pyre and hero-shrines for Hephaestion, 7.14, 7.23; funerals/burial for the dead: 1.16, 1.23, 2.12, 4.6, 5.20, 5.24, 6.2, 7.10, 7.14 (Hephaestion); cultivation of foreign gods: Tyrian Heracles, 2.24; Apis, 3.1; Isis, 3.1; Bel, 3.16, 7.17; Ammon (*q.v.*); claims to (semi-)divine status: 4.10–11, 6.14, 7.2, 7.20, 7.23, 7.27, **7.29**

— orientalizing: 'barbarian lifestyle', 4.8; prone to Persian luxury/pomp, 4.7, 7.29; adoption of Persian dress, 4.7, 4.9, 4.14, 7.6, 7.8, **7.29**; obeisance (*proskynesis*) issue, 4.9–12, 4.14; approval of Peucestas' [2] orientalizing (324), 6.30, 7.6; Persian elite designated 'Kinsmen', 7.11; banquet

promoting partnership with Persians (324), 7.11; mass inter-marriage, in Persian style (324), 7.4, 7.6; integration of Asians in Mac. army, 7.6, 7.8, 7.11, 7.23, 7.29; Macedonian resentment: 4.8, 4.11, 4.12, 4.14, 7.6, 7.8, 7.11
— plots against him: by Alexander [4], son of Aëropus (334/3), 1.25; supposed poison plot by Philip [9] (333), 2.4; plot by Philotas [4] (330), 3.26–7, cf. 4.10; Pages' conspiracy (327), 4.12–14, 4.22; alleged death by poisoning, 7.27; opposition: Cleitus [2] (328), 4.8; Callisthenes (328), 4.11–12; Hyphasis mutiny (326), 5.25–9; Opis mutiny (324), 7.8–12; murders: of Parmenion (330), 3.26, 4.14; of Cleitus [2] (328), 4.8, 4.14
— speeches: 2.7 (before Issus, 333); 2.12; 2.17 (Tyre, 332); 3.9 (before Gaugamela, 331); 5.25–6 (at the Hyphasis, 326); 7.9–10 (at Opis, 324); on his own achievements, 5.25, 7.9, 7.10
— wounds: 7.10; 2.12 (Issus, 333), 2.27 (Gaza (1), 332), 3.30 (Sogdiana, 329), 4.3 (Cyropolis, 329), 4.23.3, 4.23.5 (Swat, 327/6), 4.26 (Massaga, 327/6), 6.10, 6.11, Ind.19 (Mallians, 326/5); illness: 2.4, 2.6 (Tarsus, 333); 4.4 (N. of Tanaïs (a), 329); 7.25–6 (last illness, 323); rumours of his death: 1.7 (Thebes, 335), 6.12–13 (Mallian campaign, 326/5); 7.26; presages of his death: 7.16, 7.18, 7.22, 7.24; death (10 June 323): 7.26–8; games at his funeral, 7.14
— 'last plans': 4.7, 4.15, 5.26, 5.27, 7.1, 7.19; plans for Arabian expedition (323), 7.19–21, 7.25
— A. and Darius (1): capture (333) and considerate treatment of Darius' mother, wife, and children, 2.11, 2.12, 2.14, 2.25, 3.22; rejection of peace offers (332), 2.14, 2.25; pursuit: after Issus (333), 2.11, 2.17; after Gaugamela (331), 3.15; through Media and Parthyaea (330), 3.19–21; generous treatment after death (330), 3.22; marriage to Darius' daughter Barsine (1), 3.22, 7.4
— A. and Athens: 1.1, 1.7, 1.10, 1.16, 1.29, 2.15, 2.17, 3.6, 3.16, 3.18, 3.24,

7.19; and Sparta: 1.1, 1.7, 1.16, 2.15, 2.17, 3.6, 3.16, 3.24; and Achilles: 1.12, 7.14, 7.16; and Dionysus: 4.8, 4.9, 4.10, 5.1–2, 5.26, 6.28, 7.10, 7.20; and Heracles: 2.5, 2.18, 2.24, 3.3, 3.6, 4.7, 4.8, 4.10, 4.28, 4.30, 5.3, 5.26; and Antipater [1]: 7.12, 7.27; and Bessus: 3.30, 4.7; and Calanus (2): 7.2–3; and Callisthenes: 4.10–12, 4.22; and Cleitus [2]: 4.8–9, 4.14; and Hephaestion: 2.12 (his alter ego), 7.4; 7.14–15, 7.16 (grief at his death); 7.23 (hero-cult); and Nearchus: Ind.20, 35–36; and Parmenion: 1.13, 1.18, 2.25, 3.9, 3.10, 3.18, 3.26 (instructions for his murder); and Porus [1]: 5.18–19
— Character: ambition, 4.21, 5.24, 5.25, 5.26, 6.13, 6.24, 7.1, 7.2, 7.16, 7.19.6, 7.28, Ind.20, 43; anger, 2.16, 4.9, 4.13, 4.18, 5.28, 7.8, 7.29, Ind.34; care for his men, 1.16, 1.24, 2.12, 7.9, 7.12, Ind.15, and for the families of war-dead, 1.16, 7.10; common touch, 2.7, 2.10, 2.18, 6.13, 7.4, 7.8 (lost); consideration for women, 2.12 (Darius' mother and wife), 3.17 (Darius' mother), 4.19 (Rhoxane), 4.19–20 (Darius' wife); drinking, 4.8, 4.9, 4.13, 4.14, 7.14, 7.24–25, 7.29; susceptible to flattery, 4.8, 4.9, 5.3, 7.8, 7.29; generosity, 2.12, 3.19, 3.22 (to Darius after death), 5.18–19 (to Porus [1]), 5.27, 7.4–5, 7.12, 7.28; good faith, 4.21, 7.5, 7.28; indifferent to danger/reckless, 1.13, 2.27, 3.10, 6.9, 6.10, 6.13.4 ('berserker'), 7.29; intellectual interests, philosophy, 7.2–3, literature, 1.9 (reverence for Pindar), 7.16 (quotes Euripides); intolerant of abuse of power, 6.27, 6.30, 7.4; leniency/clemency, 1.17, 1.19, 1.23, 1.24, 1.25, 2.12, 2.15, 2.20, 2.24, 3.6, 3.23, 3.24, 6.23, Ind.36; loyalty to friends, 2.4, 2.12, 3.6, 3.26; paranoia, 4.8, 7.4, Ind.35; plain living, 7.9, 7.28; popularity, 1.24, 2.7, 6.13, 7.26; remorse, 2.15 (Thebes), 4.9 (Cleitus [2]), 6.30 (Persepolis), 7.29; respect for kings, 3.22, 3.23, 3.25, 3.30, 4.7 (Darius (1)); 5.18–19 (Porus [1]); 3.27, 6.29

(Cyrus (1)); **sexual restraint,**
4.19–20, 7.28; **sulking** (withdrawal in
anger or grief), 4.9, 5.28, 7.11, 7.14;
yens (Gk *pothos*), 1.3, 2.3, 3.1, 3.3,
4.28, 5.2, 7.1, 7.2, 7.16, *Ind.20*

Alexander [4], son of Aëropus, 1.7, 1.17;
Companion, A.'s general in Thrace,
commander of Thessalian cavalry, 1.25;
his plot against A. (334/3), 1.25

'Alexander's Harbour' *Ind.21*

Alexandria (1), in Egypt: foundation
(332–1), 3.1–2, 5.1; 7.23

Alexandria (2) *in Caucaso* [Begram]:
foundation (330/29), 3.28, 5.1; 4.22

Alexandria (3) Eschate, in Sogdiana
[Khodzhent]: foundation (329) 4.1, 4.4

Alinda, fortress in Caria 1.23

Alorus, city in Macedonia *Ind.18*

Amanic Gates, pass from Amanus
mountain range to plain of Issus 2.7

Amastrine, niece of Darius (1), married
by Craterus (324) 7.4

Amathus, city in Cyprus 2.22

Amazons 4.15, 7.13

Ambracia, city on coast of W. central
Greece 2.16

Amminapes, Parthyaean appointed satrap
of Parthyaea and Hyrcania (330) 3.22

AMMON, god 6.3, 6.19, *Ind.35*

— his shrine and oracle in Libya: visited
by A. (331), 3.3–4; 7.14, 7.23

— A.'s paternity attributed to
Ammon 3.3, 4.9, 6.14, 7.2, 7.8, 7.29

Amphilochia, region of W. central
Greece 2.16

Amphilochus, hero worshipped at Mallus
in Cilicia 2.5

Amphipolis, city in Thrace 1.1, 1.2, 1.11,
3.16, 7.18, *Ind.18*

Amphitrite, sea goddess *Ind.18*

Amphoterus, brother of Craterus, Mac.
officer, 1.25; in joint command of
Aegean fleet (333), 3.2; sent with fleet
to Peloponnese (331), 3.6

Amyntas [2], son of Antiochus, Mac.
defector, 1.17, 1.25, 2.6 (advises
Darius); killed in Egypt, 2.13

Amyntas [3], son of Arrhabaeus: Mac.
commander of light cavalry, 1.12; 1.14,
1.15 (at Granicus, 334); 1.20; overall
commander of left at Sagalassus
(334/3), 1.28

AMYNTAS [4], son of Andromenes
(mistakenly called son of Philip in
3.11.9), Mac. infantry commander: 1.8
(Thebes, 335), 1.14 (Granicus, 334),
1.17 (Sardis, 334), 1.20 (Halicarnassus,
334), 2.8 (Issus, 333); sent to levy
troops in Macedonia (332–331), 3.11,
3.16; 3.18, 3.23, 3.24, 3.25; charged
with complicity in Philotas' plot (330),
acquitted, 3.27; killed in battle (330),
3.27

Amyntas [5], officer of Mac. garrison in
Thebes, killed in the uprising
(335) 1.7

Amyntas [9], son of Nicolaus: appointed
satrap of Bactria (328) 4.17, 4.22

Amystis, tributary of Ganges *Ind.4*

Anamis [Minab], river in Carmania
Ind.33, 35

Anaxarchus, 'sophist' in A.'s retinue
4.9, 4.10–11

Anaxippus, Companion: Mac. officer in
Areia, murdered by Satibarzanes (330)
3.25

Anchialus, city in Cilicia 2.5

Ancyra, city in Galatia 2.4

Andaca, city in Aspasian territory 4.23

Andomatis, tributary of Ganges *Ind.4*

Androcles, king of Amathus in
Cyprus 2.22

Andromachus [1], son of Hieron:
Companion (4.6.1), Mac. commander
of mercenary cavalry, 3.12, 3.25, 4.3,
4.5, 4.6

Andromachus [3], Mac. naval
commander 2.20

Andron, trierarch (326) *Ind.18*

Andronicus [1], son of Agerrus, Mac.
officer 3.23, 3.24

Androsthenes, Mac. naval officer, 7.20;
trierarch (326), *Ind.18*

Antaeus, giant wrestled and killed by
Heracles 3.3

Antalcidas, Spartan statesman:
established peace of Antalcidas in
387/6, ceding Greek cities of Asia to
Persia 2.1, 2.2

Anthemus, district of Chalcidice 2.9

Antibelus, son of Mazaeus 3.21

Anticles, Page in conspiracy (327) 4.13

Antigenes [1a], Mac. infantry
commander 5.16, 6.17

Antigonus [1], son of Philip: commander of Greek allied infantry, then appointed satrap of Phrygia (333), 1.29; death (301), 7.18

Antilibanus, mountain range in Lebanon 2.20

Antiochus [1], commander of Mac. archers 2.9, 3.5

Antiochus [2], Mac. infantry commander 4.30

ANTIPATER [1] (399/8–319), son of Iolaus: A.'s regent in Macedonia and Greece, 1.7, 1.11, 2.2 (naval defence of Greece, 333), 3.5, 3.16; recalled (324), 7.12; relations with Olympias and A., 7.12; alleged poisoning of A., 7.27

Antipater [2], Page in conspiracy (327) 4.13

Aornus (1), city in Bactria 3.29

Aornus (2), Rock of [Pir-sar], mountain spur E. of Swat 4.28–30, 5.26, *Ind.5*

Aphrodite, goddess *Ind.37*

Apis, Egyptian god 3.1

Apollo, god 3.27, (4.11), 7.29, *Ind.36*

Apollodorus [1], Companion: given military command in Babylonia by A. (331) 3.16; 7.18

Apollonia, city in Chalcidice 1.12

Apollonides [1], Chian oligarch 3.2

Apollonius, appointed governor of Libya (331) 3.5

Apollophanes, appointed satrap of Oreitis/Gedrosia (325) 6.22, 6.27; *Ind.23* (killed, 325)

Apostana, harbour on coast of Persis *Ind.38*

ARABIA 2.20, 3.1, 3.5, 5.25, 7.1, 7.20, 7.21, *Ind.32, 43*

— A.'s preparations and motives for an Arabian expedition (323), 7.19–21, 7.25; exploratory voyages, 7.20, *Ind.43*

— Oman peninsula 7.20, *Ind.32, 43*

— spice trade *Ind.32, 41*

— Arab mercenaries 2.25, 2.27

Arabian Gulf [Red Sea] 7.20, *Ind.43*

Arabies, Arabis: *see* Arabitae, Arabius

Arabitae, Indian tribe in region of R. Arabius, 6.21; (Arabies) *Ind.21, 22, 25*

Arabius [Hab], Indian river W. of Indus, 6.21; (Arabis) *Ind.21, 22–23*

Arachosia, region W. of Indus, in Afghanistan 3.8, 3.11, 3.21, 3.28, 5.6, 5.11, 6.17, 6.27, 7.6, 7.10

Aradus, island off Phoenicia 2.13, 2.20

Araxes [Arak], river in Armenia 7.16

Arbela, city in Assyria (1) 3.8, 3.15, 3.16, 3.22, 6.11

Arbupales, Persian noble killed at Granicus 1.16

Arcadia, region of central Peloponnese 1.9, 1.10

Archelaus (1), king of Macedonia (413–399) 1.11

Archelaus [1], son of Androcles, Companion and Mac. commander 3.29

Archelaus [2], son of Theodorus, Mac. commander in Susiana (331) 3.16

Archias [1], son of Anaxidotus, Mac. naval officer, 7.20; trierarch (326), *Ind.18*; with Nearchus' fleet, *Ind.27–8, 34–5*

Archon, son of Cleinias, trierarch (326) *Ind.18*

Areia, region round Herat (Afghanistan), 3.8; A. in Areia (330), 3.25 (Satibarzanes' revolt, 3.25.5–7); Arsaces appointed satrap, 3.25.7; second Areian revolt (330), 3.28; 3.29, 4.6, 4.7, 4.18, 6.27, 7.6

Areius [Hari Rud], river in Areia 4.6

Areon, river in Persis *Ind.38*

Aretes, Mac. light cavalry commander at Gaugamela (331) 3.12, 3.13, 3.14

Aretis, groom in A.'s service 1.15

Argos/Argives, city in Peloponnese, 1.17, 2.5, 4.9, 5.26; Argive Heracles, 2.16, 4.10, 5.26

Ariaces, Persian commander at Gaugamela 3.8

Ariaspians, known as Euergetae, people in region S. of Drangiana (Seistan) 3.27, 4.6

Arigaeum [Nawagai], city in Aspasian territory 4.24, 4.25

Arimmas, dismissed as satrap of Syria (331) 3.6

Ariobarzanes [2], Persian commander, satrap of Persis: at Gaugamela (331), 3.8; at Persian Gates (331), 3.18

Ariobarzanes [3], son of Artabazus 3.23

Arisbe, city on Asian side of
Hellespont 1.12
Arispae, Indian tribe *Ind.4*
Aristander, seer from Telmissus 1.11,
1.25, 2.18, 2.26, 2.27, 3.2, 3.7, 3.15,
4.4, 4.15
ARISTOBULUS: charged with
restoration of Cyrus' tomb (324) 6.29
— as historian: Preface, 4.14, 5.7, 6.28,
7.13, 7.15, 7.26
— cited 2.3, 2.4, 2.12, 3.3, 3.4, 3.11,
3.26, 3.28, 3.30, 4.3, 4.6, 4.8, 4.13,
4.14, 5.7, 5.14, 5.20, 6.11, 6.22, 6.28,
6.29, 7.4, 7.15, 7.17, 7.18, 7.19, 7.20,
7.22, 7.24, 7.26, 7.28, 7.29
Aristogeiton *see* Harmodius
Aristomedes, Thessalian in Persian
service 2.13
Ariston [1], Mac. cavalry
commander 3.11
Ariston [3], commander of Paeonian light
cavalry 2.9, 3.12
Aristonicus [1], tyrant of Methymna 3.2
Aristonicus [4], musician in A.'s retinue:
fought and died at Zariaspa (328) 4.16
Aristonus: Bodyguard, 6.28; trierarch
(326), *Ind.18*
Aristophanes, Athenian archon 3.7, 3.15
Aristophon, Athenian archon 3.22
Aristotle, Greek philosopher, tutor of A.
4.10, 7.27
Aristus, historian of A. 7.15
Armenia, region of E. Anatolia, N. of
Mesopotamia 3.7, 3.8, 3.11, 3.16, 5.5,
7.16, 7.21, *Ind.42*
Arosis [Jarrahi?], river in Persis *Ind.39*
Arrhabaeus, son of Aëropus: father of
Amyntas [3], 1.12; party to the murder
of Philip [1], 1.25
ARRIAN: on himself, 1.12; on his own
work, Preface, 1.12, 6.11, 7.30, *Ind.5,
17, 18, 43*; advertisements for *Indica*,
5.4–5, 5.6, 6.16, 6.28; autopsy, 2.16,
3.16, 5.7, *Ind.4, 15, 41*
— sources and other historians: on
Ptolemy [6] and Aristobulus, **Preface**,
2.12, 4.14, 5.7, 5.14, 5.20, 6.2, 6.11,
6.28, 7.13, 7.15.6, 7.26.3; Aristus and
Aclepiades, 7.15; Ctesias, 5.4, *Ind.3*;
Eratosthenes, 5.3, 5.5, *Ind.3*;
Megasthenes, 5.5, *Ind.5, 6, 7, 17*;
Nearchus, 5.5, 6.28, *Ind.17, 31*;

Onesicritus, 6.2, *Ind.3*; Royal Journals,
7.25–6; other unnamed historians and
writers: Preface, 2.4, 4.14, 5.2, 5.4, 5.5,
5.14, 6.11 (their errors), 6.24, 6.26,
6.28, 7.1, 7.3, 7.14, 7.15, 7.22, 7.24,
7.26–7, *Ind.2, 3, 6*
— 'stories' about A.: **Preface**, 2.12, 3.2,
4.10–11, 4.12, 4.20, 5.2, 5.3, 6.28,
7.1–3, 7.13 (Amazons), 7.16, 7.18, 7.22,
7.27, *Ind.6*; professed agnosticism:
Preface, 2.3, 2.12, 3.3, 4.14, 4.28, 5.1,
5.3, 5.4, 5.7, 5.8, 5.20, 7.1, 7.14, 7.15,
7.27, *Ind.1, 4, 15*
— belief in divine influence, 2.6, 3.3,
7.16, 7.30; moralizing, 4.7, 4.8, 4.9, 7.3,
7.12, 7.23, 7.29, 7.30; on flattery of
kings, 2.6 (Darius), 4.8, 4.9, 7.29
(Alexander),
— assessments of A., 1.12, 2.12, 3.10, 4.7,
4.9, 4.19, 6.19, 7.1, 7.2, 7.28–30;
criticisms of A., 3.18, 4.7, 4.9, 4.12,
6.30, 7.23, 7.29–30; assessment of
Seleucus, 7.22; obituary of Darius, 3.22
— formal datings by Athenian archons:
1.1 (death of Philip), 2.11 (Issus), 2.24
(fall of Tyre), 3.7 (arrival at
Thapsacus), 3.15 (Gaugamela), 3.22
(death of Darius), 5.19 (defeat of
Porus), 7.28 (death of A.), *Ind.21* (start
of Nearchus' voyage)
see also geography
Arsaces [1], Persian: appointed satrap of
Areia (330), 3.25; arrested and deposed
(329), 3.29, 4.7
Arsaces [2], Indian dynast neighbouring
Abisares 5.29
Arsames [1], Persian: cavalry commander
at Granicus (334), 1.12; satrap of
Cilicia, fled from Tarsus at approach of
A. (333), 2.4; killed at Issus (333), 2.11
Arsames [2], son of Artabazus 3.23
Arses *see* Artaxerxes (3)
Arsimas, envoy from Darius to A.
(332) 2.14
Arsites, Persian: satrap of Hellespontine
Phrygia (334), 1.12, 1.17; suicide, 1.16
Artabazus, Persian loyal to Darius:
dissociated from Bessus' coup (330),
3.21; surrenders to A. (330), 3.23.7;
3.23.9, 3.28; appointed satrap of
Bactria (329), 3.29; 4.15, 4.16; relieved
of satrapy (328), 4.17

— daughters married to Ptolemy [6] and Eumenes, 7.4, 7.6

Artacama, daughter of Artabazus 7.4

Artacoana, capital city of Areia 3.25

Artaxerxes (1), Artaxerxes II, King of Persia 405/4–359/8 1.12, 1.16, 4.11

Artaxerxes (2), Artaxerxes III (Ochus), King of Persia 359/8–338 2.14, 3.19, 7.4

Artaxerxes (3), Artaxerxes IV (Arses), King of Persia 338–336 2.14

Artaxerxes (4), regal name assumed by Bessus (330) 3.25

Artemis, goddess: her temple at Ephesus, 1.17, 1.18; statue of Celcean Artemis returned to Athens, 7.19; her sanctuary on island in Persian Gulf, 7.20

Artemisium, promontory of Euboea: battle of (480) 6.11

Artiboles, son of Mazaeus 7.6

Artonis, daughter of Artabazus 7.4

Arybbas [2], Bodyguard: died in Egypt (332/1) 3.5

Asander [1], son of Philotas: appointed satrap of Lydia (334) 1.17; 2.5, 4.7

Ascania, lake in Phrygia 1.29

Asclepiades, historian of A. 7.15

Asclepiads, medical clan in Cos 6.11

Asclepiodorus [1], son of Eunicus: Mac. commander, 3.5; appointed satrap of Syria (331), 3.6, 4.7, 4.13

Asclepiodorus [2], son of Timander: trierarch (326), Ind.18

Asclepiodorus [3], son of Philon: appointed finance officer in Babylonia (331), 3.16

Asclepius, god of healing, 2.5, 7.14; his temple at Ecbatana, 7.14

ASIA: geographical divisions, 5.6; boundaries with Europe and Libya, 3.30; mountains, 3.28, 5.5; rivers, 3.29, 4.6, 5.4, 5.5, 5.6, 7.16

— legendary subjugations, Ind.5; sequence of empires, 2.6 (cf. Ind.1), 5.4; female rule accepted, 1.23; the expedition of the Ten Thousand (401), 1.12, 2.7, 4.11

— A.'s crossing from Europe to Asia (334), 1.11; Gordian Knot destining ruler of Asia, 2.3; A.'s purpose and ambition to rule over the whole of Asia, 2.7, 2.12, 2.14, 3.9, 4.11, 4.20, 5.26, 7.1;

A. as de facto king of Asia, 2.14, 2.25, 3.18, 4.4, 4.7, 7.15; national mourning for Hephaestion, 7.14

— Asians ('lazy and effeminate') contrasted with Europeans, 2.7; Asians integrated into Mac. army, 7.6, 7.8, 7.11, 7.23, 7.29

Aspasians, tribe in Swat region [Bajaur] 4.23, 4.24

Aspendus, city on coast of Pamphylia 1.26–27

Assacanus, Indian dynast, leader of the Assacenians 4.27, 4.30

Assacenians, Indian tribe in Swat region 4.23, 4.25–27, 4.30, 5.20 (revolt, 326), Ind.1, 4

Assagetes, Indian prince 4.28

Assyria (1), ancient kingdom in upper Tigris region, E. of Mesopotamia, 2.5.2–4, 2.6.7, 3.7, Ind.1, 5; Assyrian script and language, 2.5

Assyria (2), Mesopotamian Syria 2.5.1, 2.6.1, 2.6.3

Assyria (3), Mesopotamia 7.7, 7.17, 7.19, 7.21, 7.22, Ind.32

Assyrian Gates, coastal pass between Cilicia and Mesopotamian Syria 2.5, 2.6, 2.8

Astacenians, Indian tribe in Gandhara Ind.1

Astis, ruler of Peucelaotis (1) 4.22

Astrybae, Indian tribe Ind.4

Astypalaea, S. Aegean island Ind.18

Athena, goddess, 1.11, 4.22, 6.9; Trojan Athena, 1.11, 6.9; Athena of Magarsus, 2.5; Persian panoplies dedicated to Athena on Acropolis, 1.16

ATHENS/ATHENIANS: support of Heracleidae, 4.10; defeat of Amazons, 7.13; tyrannicides, 3.16, 4.10, 7.19; in Persian War, 3.18, 4.11; Sicilian disaster (413), 1.9; defeat at Aegospotami (405), 1.9; Spartan vote for destruction of Athens (404), 1.9; defeated by Philip [1] (338), 7.9; Athenians captured at Granicus (334), 1.29

— Great Mysteries, 1.10; worship of Dionysus, 2.16; state ship Paralus, 3.6; Acropolis, 1.16, 3.16; Long Walls, 1.9; altar of Eudanemoi, Cerameicus, Metroön, 3.16

— embassies to A.: honours offered (336),
1.1; after Theban revolt (335), 1.10;
requesting release of prisoners (333
and 331), 1.29, 3.6; embassies to
Darius (333 and 330), 2.15, 3.24
— A.'s suspicion of Athens, 1.1, 1.7, 1.10,
2.17; A.'s warmth towards Athens, 1.16
(Persian panoplies), 2.15, 3.6, 3.18,
3.16, 7.19
Atizyes, Persian satrap of Phrygia (334),
1.25, (1.29); cavalry commander at
Granicus, killed at Issus (333), 2.11
Atlas, mountain range [Great Atlas] in
NW Africa (Morocco) 7.1
Atropates, Persian: satrap of Media (331),
3.8; reappointed by A. (328/7),
4.18; 6.29, 7.4, 7.13
Attacenians, Indian tribe Ind.4
Attalus [2], Mac. commander of the
Agrianians 2.9, 3.12. 3.21
Attalus [3], son of Andromenes, Mac.
infantry commander: charged with
complicity in Philotas' plot (330), 3.27;
4.16, 4.22, 4.24, 4.27, 5.12, 6.17, 7.26;
trierarch (326), Ind.18
Attica 1.7
Austanes, rebel commander in
Pareitacene (327) 4.22
Autariates, Illyrian tribe N. of
Macedonia 1.5
Autophradates [1], Persian naval
commander in Aegean (333) 2.1–2,
2.13, 2.15, 2.20, 3.2
Autophradates [2], satrap of Tapuria:
surrendered to A. (330), 3.23;
appointed satrap of Mardians (2) also,
3.24; arrested (328/7), 4.18
Azemilcus, king of Tyre 2.15, 2.24

BABYLON 2.7, 2.17, 3.7, 3.16, 3.19,
5.25, 6.29, 7.9, 7.14, 7.15, 7.16, 7.17,
7.18, 7.19, 7.21, 7.22, 7.23, Ind.41, 43;
surrenders to A. (331), 3.16; temple of
Bel, 3.16, 3.17
— A. in Babylon: (331) 3.16, 7.17; (323)
7.19–27
Babylonia, region of S. Mesopotamia 3.8,
3.11, 4.18, 7.19, 7.21, Ind.41, 43
Bactra/Zariaspa [Balkh], capital city
of Bactria 3.19, 3.25, 3.28, 3.29,
3.30, 4.1, 4.7, 4.16, 4.22, 4.30,
5.27, 7.9

BACTRIA, region to NW of Hindu
Kush, 3.8, 3.11, 3.13, 3.16, 3.21, 3.23,
3.25, 3.28, 3.29, 4.1, 4.15, 4.16;
invaded by Spitamenes and Scythians
(328), 4.16–17; 4.17, 4.22, 4.30, 5.5,
5.12, 5.25, 6.2, 7.4, 7.6, 7.10, 7.16
— A. in Bactria: (329) 3.29; (329/8) 4.7,
4.15; (328) 4.10–12; (327) 4.13–14, 4.22
Badis, place on Carmanian coast Ind.32
Bageia, headland on Fish-Eater coast
Ind.28
Bagisara, place on Fish-Eater coast Ind.26
Bagistanes, Babylonian 3.21
Bagoas [1], eunuch at Persian court 2.14
Bagoas [2a], son of Pharnuches: trierarch
(326) Ind.18
Balacrus [1], son of Amyntas: replaced
Antigonus [1] as commander of Greek
allied infantry (333), 1.29; general in
Egypt (331), 3.5
Balacrus [2], son of Nicanor: Bodyguard,
appointed satrap of Cilicia (333) 2.12
Balacrus [3], Mac. commander of
javelin-men 3.12, 3.13, 4.4, 4.24
Balomus, beach on Fish-Eater coast
Ind.27
Bardylis, Illyrian king, father of Cleitus
[1] 1.5
Barna, village on Fish-Eater coast Ind.27
Barsaentes, satrap of Arachosia, 3.8, and
Drangiana, 3.21: in Darius' army at
Gaugamela (331), 3.8; arrested and
murdered Darius (330), 3.21, 3.25; put
to death by A., 3.25
Barsine (1), daughter of Darius (1), also
called Stateira: married by A. (324)
3.22, 7.4.4
Barsine (2), daughter of Artabazus 7.4.6
Baryaxes, Mede executed for attempted
revolution (324) 6.29
Batis, eunuch commanding Gaza (1) 2.25
Bazira [Bir-kot], city in Assacenian
territory 4.27–8
Bears (Little Bear and Great Bear),
constellations 6.26
Bel, god, 3.16, 7.16; temple at Babylon,
3.16, 7.17
Beroea, city in Macedonia 3.6, Ind.18
BESSUS, Persian commander related to
Darius (3.21.5): satrap of Bactria, in
Darius' army at Gaugamela (331), 3.8;
arrested Darius in coup and assumed

supreme command (330), 3.21, 4.8, 6.11; claiming to be king of Asia (330), 3.25; pursuit by A. (330–329), 3.28, 3.29–30 (arrest by Spitamenes); capture and sentence, 3.30; punishment (329/8), 4.7; 4.1, 4.7.1, 4.30

Bianor, Acarnanian in Persian service 2.13

Bibacta, island W. of Indus mouth *Ind.21*

Bisthanes, son of Ochus 3.19

Bithynia, region of Asia Minor bordering Propontis and Black Sea 1.29

Black River, river in Thrace 1.11

Black Sea [Gk *Euxeinos*] 1.3, 1.12, 1.29, 2.7, 3.30, 4.15, 5.3, 5.27, 7.1, 7.16, *Ind.40*

Bodyguards: (a) 'bodyguards', the royal guard of infantry: 3.17, 4.3, 4.30, 7.11.2(?). (b) 'Bodyguards', intimate group of 7 (later 8) high-ranking military commanders: 1.6, 1.22, 1.24, 2.12, 3.5, 3.6, 3.27, 4.8, 4.13, 4.15, 4.21, 4.24, 4.29, 5.13, 5.24, 6.9, 6.12, 6.22, 6.28, 6.30, 7.3, 7.4, 7.5, 7.26

Boedromion, month in Athenian calendar *Ind.21*

Boeotia, region NW of Attica, 1.7, 1.8, 1.9; Boeotarchs, federal officials, 1.7; cavalry in A.'s army, 2.7; Boeotian veteran comforting A., 6.13

Bosporus, strait between Black Sea and Propontis 5.7

Bottiaea, region of Macedonia 1.2

Brahmans, Indian caste 6.7, 6.16, 6.17

Brazanes, Persian appointed satrap of Parthyaea by Bessus 4.7

Brison, commander of Mac. archers 3.12

British Isles 7.1

Brizana, river in Persis *Ind.39*

Bruttians, people in toe of Italy 7.15

Bubaces [1], Persian killed at Issus (333) 2.11

Bucephala, city founded by A. on the Hydaspes (326) 5.19, 5.29

Bucephalas, A.'s horse 5.14, 5.19

Budyas, second king of India *Ind.8*

Bumelus, river in Assyria (1) 3.8, 6.11

Bupares, Persian commander at Gaugamela (331) 3.8

Busiris, murderous Egyptian king killed by Heracles 3.3

Byblus, city in Phoenicia 2.15, 2.20

Byzantium, city on Bosporus 1.3

Cabana, place on coast of Oreitis *Ind.23*

Cacuthis, tributary of Ganges *Ind.4*

Cadmea, citadel of Thebes 1.7, 1.8, 1.9

Cadmus, legendary founder of Thebes 2.16

Cadusians, people bordering SW Caspian Sea 3.8, 3.11, 3.19

Caïcandrus, island off coast of Persis *Ind.38*

Caïcus, river and plain in Mysia 5.6

Caïnas, tributary of Ganges *Ind.4*

Calanus (1), Mac. commander 3.5

Calanus (2), Indian guru in A.'s court 7.2–3, 7.18

Calas, Mac. officer: commander of Thessalian cavalry, 1.14 (Granicus, 334); appointed satrap of Hellespontine Phrygia (334), 1.17.1; 1.17.8, 1.25, 2.4

Calima, place on Fish-Eater coast *Ind.26*

Callatis, city on Thracian coast of Black Sea 6.23

Callines, Mac. cavalry officer 7.11

Callipolis, city in S. Caria 2.5

CALLISTHENES [1], 'official' historian in A.'s retinue: opposition to obeisance, 4.10–12; implicated in Pages' plot (327), 4.14, 4.22; 4.13, 7.27

Callistratidas, Spartan envoy to Darius (330) 3.24

Cambistholi, Indian tribe *Ind.4*

Cambyses (1), father of Cyrus (1) 3.27, 4.11, 5.4, 6.24, 6.29, *Ind.1*

Cambyses (2), son of Cyrus (1) 6.29.7, *Ind.43*

Canasis, deserted town on Fish-Eater coast *Ind.29*

Canate, place on Fish-Eater coast *Ind.29*

Canopus, city at W. mouth of Nile delta 3.1

Cappadocia, region of central Asia Minor 1.16, 2.4, 3.8, 3.11, 5.25

Caranus [2], Companion, Mac. commander 3.28, 4.3, 4.5, 4.6

Carbis, beach on Fish-Eater coast *Ind.26*

Cardaces, a corps of elite Persian infantry 2.8

Cardia, city in Chersonese *Ind.18*

CARIA, region of SW Asia Minor, 1.20, 1.23, 1.24, 3.22, 5.6, 5.25, 7.23; Carian troops in Persian service (333), 1.29; Carian crews in A.'s fleet (326), 6.1
— 'transplanted Carians', probably Carians deported to E. bank of Tigris 3.8, 3.11, 3.13
— A. in Caria (334) 1.20–4, 1.25
Carmania, region of S. Iran, W. of Makran 6.17, 6.27, 6.28, 7.10, *Ind.27, 32, 36, 38, 43*
— A. in Carmania (325/4) 6.27–8, *Ind.34–6*
Carnine, island off Fish-Eater coast *Ind.26*
Carthage, city in N. Africa (Tunisia) 2.24, 3.24, 5.27, 7.1, 7.15, *Ind.43*
Caspian Gates, pass through Elburz mountains from Media to Parthyaea 3.19, 3.20, 5.25, 7.10
Caspian Sea *see* Hyrcanian Sea
Cassander, son of Antipater [1] 7.27
Castor *see* Dioscuri
Cataderbis, lake on coast of Susiana *Ind.41*
Catadupe, city in India *Ind.4*
Cataea [Kish], island off Carmanian coast *Ind.37, 38*
Catanes, rebel commander in Pareitacene (327) 4.22
catapults 1.6, 1.22, 2.18, 2.21, 2.23, 4.2, 4.4, 4.21, 4.26, 4.27, 4.29–30, *Ind.24*
Cathaeans, Indian tribe E. of Hydraotes 5.22–4 (defeated by A., 326)
CAUCASUS, mountain range: (a) Scythian Caucasus (range between Black Sea and Caspian Sea), 5.3, 5.5, *Ind.2*; (b) Indian Caucasus (Hindu Kush), properly called Parapamisus (5.3.3), 3.28, 3.29, 3.30, 5.3, 5.4, 5.5, 5.6, 5.9, 5.25, 7.10, *Ind.2, 5*
— A.'s crossing of the Indian Caucasus: (329) 3.28, 3.30; (327) 4.22
— name transferred from (a) to (b) 5.3, 5.5, *Ind.2, 5*
Caumana, place on lower Indus *Ind.21*
Caunus, city on coast of Caria 2.5
Caÿster, river and plain in Lydia 5.6
Cecaeans, Indian tribe *Ind.4*
Celaenae, capital city of Phrygia 1.29
Celts 1.3, 1.4, 7.15, *Ind.16*
Cephisodorus, Athenian archon *Ind.21*

Cerameicus, district of Athens 3.16
Cercinitis, lake N. of Amphipolis 1.11
Chaeronea, in Boeotia, site of Philip's defeat of Athens and Thebes (338) 1.10, (7.9)
Chalcis, city in Euboea 2.2
Chaldaeans, Babylonian priests of Bel 3.16, 7.16, 7.17, 7.22
Chares [1], Athenian politician, 1.10, 1.12; in Persian service at Mytilene (332), 3.2
Charicles [1], son of Menander [1], revealed Pages' conspiracy (327) 4.13
Charidemus, Athenian politician, exiled on orders of A. (335) 1.10
Chios, E. Aegean island: captured by Memnon (333), 2.1; 2.13; recaptured by Hegelochus (332), 3.2
Choes [Alingar?], river in NE Afghanistan 4.23
Chorasmia, region S. of Aral Sea 4.15, 5.5, 7.10
Chorienes, dynast of Pareitacene, E. Sogdiana 4.21
— Rock of Chorienes, in Pareitacene: captured by A. (327) 4.21
Cilicia, region of S. central Asia Minor 2.4, 2.12, 3.7, 3.16, 3.22, 3.28, 5.5, *Ind.2*
— A. in Cilicia (333) 2.4–12
Cilician Gates, pass through Taurus range between Cappadocia and Cilicia 2.4
Cilluta, island in W. branch of Indus 6.19
Clazomenae, city in Ionia 7.19
Cleander [1], son of Polemocrates, Mac. commander 1.24, 2.20, 3.6, 3.12, 3.26 (instructed to execute Parmenion in Media, 330), 6.27 (accused of abuse of power and executed, 325/4)
Cleander [2], Mac. commander of archers, killed at Sagalassus (334/3) 1.28
Clearchus (1), Spartan officer with Cyrus (2), executed in 401 1.12, 4.11
Clearchus (2), Mac. commander of archers, killed at Halicarnassus (334) 1.22
Cleisobora, city in India *Ind.8*
Cleitus [1], son of Bardylis: king of Illyrian tribe, the Dardani, 1.5; revolt with Glaucias against A. put down (335), 1.5–6

CLEITUS [2], son of Dropidas, commander of Royal Squadron of cavalry: saves A. at Granicus (334) by killing Spithridates, 1.15, 4.8; at Gaugamela (331), 3.11; ill at Susa (330), 3.19; appointed one of two commanders of Companion cavalry (330), 3.27
— his quarrel with and murder by A. (328) 4.8–9, 4.14
Cleitus [3], Mac. infantry and cavalry commander 4.22, 5.12, 5.22, 6.6
Cleomenes [1]: appointed governor of Arabian sector of Egypt (331) 3.5; 7.23
Cleomenes [2], seer 7.26
Cnidus, E. Aegean peninsula *Ind.3*
Cocala, place on coast of Oreitis *Ind.23*
COENUS [1], son of Polemocrates, Mac. infantry commander: 1.6 (Pellium, 335); 1.14 (Granicus, 334); 1.24, 1.29 (sent home with newly-weds, and to levy troops, 334–3); 2.8 (Issus, 333); 2.23, 2.24 (Tyre, 332); 3.11, 3.15 (Gaugamela, 331: wounded); 3.18, 3.20, 3.21, 3.25, 4.16; 4.17–18 (victory over Spitamenes and Scythians, winter 328/7); 4.24, 4.25, 4.27, 4.28, 5.8, 5.12; 5.16, 5.17 (Hydaspes, 326); 5.21
— speech at Hyphasis (326) advocating a return, 5.27–8; death and funeral (326), 6.2
Coeranus [1], Mac. finance officer 3.6
Coeranus [2], commander of allied cavalry at Gaugamela (331) 3.12
Colchis, region on E. coast of Black Sea 4.15, 7.13
Colonae, city near Propontis 1.12
Colta, place on Fish-Eater coast *Ind.26*
Comminases, tributary of Ganges *Ind.4*
COMPANIONS (*see* Appendix I): (a) Companion cavalry, *passim*; reorganization (330), 3.27. (b) Companion Infantry (*pezhetairoi*), 1.28, 7.2, 7.11. (c) Close Companions (*asthetairoi*), 2.23, 4.23, 5.22, 6.6, 6.21, 7.11
— (d) elite officer cadre (*Hetairoi*), 1.6, 2.7, 2.23, 3.16, 4.1, 4.6, 4.8, 5.19, 5.28, 7.4, 7.11, 7.14, 7.15, 7.16, 7.24, 7.26, *Ind.35*; marriages at Susa (324), 7.4, 7.6, 7.10; forming advisory council, 1.25, 2.6, 2.16, 2.25, 3.9, 6.2

Condochates, tributary of Ganges *Ind.4*
consular representatives (Gk *proxenoi*) 1.9
Cophaeus, Indian prince 4.28
Cophas, harbour on Fish-Eater coast *Ind.27*
Cophen (1), son of Artabazus: member of Darius' court, 2.15; surrenders to A. (330), 3.23; drafted into A.'s Royal Guard (324), 7.6 (here called 'Cophes')
Cophen (2) [Kabul], river in NE Afghanistan 4.22, 5.1, *Ind.1, 4*
Coreëstis, place on lower Indus *Ind.21*
Corinth, 1.15, *Ind.18*; Corinthian Isthmus, 6.11, 7.2
Cos, SE Aegean island 2.5, 2.13, 3.2, 6.11, *Ind.18*
Cossaeans, tribe SW of Media, in N. Zagros mountains 7.15, 7.23, *Ind.40*
Cossoanus, tributary of Ganges *Ind.4*
Cradeuas, son of Budyas, third king of India *Ind.8*
CRATERUS, son of Alexander, brother of Amphoterus (1.25.9), Companion (7.4.5), Mac. infantry commander: at Granicus (334), 1.14; commanded left at Issus (333), 2.8, and at Gaugamela (331), 3.11; naval command at Tyre (332), 2.20; in Uxian campaign (331), 3.17; at Persian Gates (331), 3.18; 3.21, 3.23, 3.25; in Sogdiana (329–7), 4.2, 4.3 (wounded), 4.17, 4.18; in Pareitacene (327), 4.22; 4.23, 4.24, 4.25, 4.28; at the Hydaspes (326), 5.11–12, 5.15, 5.18, 5.20; 5.21, 6.2, 6.4, 6.5, 6.15, 6.17, 6.27, 7.4, *Ind.19*; trierarch (326), *Ind.18*; sent to escort veterans home and take charge in Macedonia (324), 7.12
Crete, 2.13, *Ind.18*; Cretan archers, 1.8, 2.7, 2.9, 3.5
Cretheus, Greek officer in A.'s army 6.23
Critobulus, trierarch (326) *Ind.18*
Critodemus, doctor 6.11
Crocala, island near mouth of Indus *Ind.21*
Croesus, 6th cent. BC King of Lydia 7.16
Ctesias, late 5th cent. BC author of an *Indica* 5.4, *Ind.3*
Curium, city in Cyprus 2.22
Cyclades, group of Aegean islands 2.2
Cydnus, river in Cilicia 2.4

Cyiza, beach on Fish-Eater coast *Ind.27, 30*

Cyme, city in Aeolis 1.26

Cyna, sister of A. 1.5

Cyprus/Cypriots, 2.13, 2.17, 2.21, *Ind.18.8*; Cypriot navy, 1.18, 2.13, 2.20 (defection to A., 332), 2.21–2, 2.24, 3.6; Cypriot crews in A.'s fleet (326), 6.1, *Ind.18.1*

Cyrene, city in Libya 3.28, 5.3, 7.9, *Ind.3, 43*

Cyropolis, city in Sogdiana 4.2, 4.3 (captured by A., 329)

Cyrus (1), Cyrus the Great, son of Cambyses (1), King of Persia *c*.557–530, 3.18, 3.27, 4.3, 4.11, *Ind.1*; defeated by Scythians (530), 3.27, 4.11, 5.4, *Ind.9*; attempt to invade India, 6.24, *Ind.9*; his tomb at Pasargadae, **6.29**

Cyrus (2), Persian, attempted coup with aid of Ten Thousand (401) 1.12, 2.4

Cysa, village on Fish-Eater coast *Ind.26*

Cythnos, Aegean island (Cyclades) 2.2

Daedalus, father of Icarus (1) 7.20

Dagaseira, place on Fish-Eater coast *Ind.29*

Dahae, Scythian tribe to E. of Caspian Sea, 3.11, 3.28; mounted archers in A.'s army, 5.12

Damascus, city in Syria 2.11, 2.15

Dandamis, Indian guru 7.2

Danube [Gk *Istros*], river 1.2, 1.3–4, 5.4, 5.6, 5.7, *Ind.2, 3, 4*

DARIUS (1), Darius III, King of Persia 336–330: his mother, wife, and family captured at Issus (333), 2.11, 2.12, 2.14, 2.25, 3.22, 4.20; his mother, 2.12, 3.17 (intercedes with A. for Uxians, 330); his wife, 2.11 (also his sister), 4.19–20; his daughter Barsine married by A. (324), 3.22, 7.4; his daughter Drypetis married by Hephaestion (324), 7.4; his children provided for by A., 3.22; his brother Oxyatres, 7.4

— alleged murder of Artaxerxes Arses (336), 2.14; receives exiled Athenian politician (335), 1.10; not present at **battle of Granicus (334)**, 1.12; attempts to exploit treason of Amyntas [2] (334/3), 1.25; gives command of

navy to Memnon (334), 1.20, 2.1, then to Pharnabazus (333), 2.1, 2.2; Memnon's death (333) a serious setback, 2.1; supposed plot to poison A. (333), 2.4; Greek envoys to Darius before Issus, 2.15; at Sochi, before Issus (333), 2.6; **at battle of Issus (333)**, 2.7, 2.8, 2.10, 2.11, 3.8; flees from Issus, 2.11, 2.13, 3.1, cf. 5.18.4; his goods sent to Damascus captured (333), 2.11, 2.15

— peace offers: **(a)** 2.14 (exchange of letters, early 332); **(b)** 2.25 (summer 332)

— attempt to defend Euphrates (331), 3.7; **at battle of Gaugamela (331)**, 3.8–15, 6.11; flees from Gaugamela, 3.14, 3.15, 3.16, 3.22, 6.11, cf. 5.18.4; his treasure captured at Arbela (331), 3.15

— pursued by A. after Issus, 2.11, 2.17, after Gaugamela, 3.15, through Media and Parthyaea (330), 3.19–21; his arrest and murder in coup led by Bessus (330), 3.21, 3.28, 3.30, 4.8, 6.11; body sent for burial to Persepolis, 3.22

— character: cowardice, 2.10, 2.11, 3.14, 3.22, 5.18; cruelty, 2.7; susceptible to flattery, 2.6, 3.8; uxorious, 4.20; recognition of A.'s decency, 4.20

— Arrian's obituary: **3.22**

Darius (2), son of Artaxerxes (1) 1.16

Darius (3), Darius II, King of Persia 424–404 2.1.4, 2.2.2 (in both places an error for Artaxerxes II)

Darius (4), Darius I, King of Persia (died 486), father of Xerxes 4.4, 4.11, 5.7

Dascylium, capital of Hellespontine Phrygia 1.17

Datames, Persian naval officer 2.2

Dataphernes, Persian involved in arrest of Bessus (329) 3.29–30

Delphi, oracle of Apollo at 4.11

Demades, Athenian politician 1.10

Demaratus [1], Companion 1.15

Demeter, goddess *Ind.7*

Demetrius [1], son of Althaemenes, Mac. cavalry commander 3.11, 4.27, 5.12, 5.16, 5.21, 6.8

Demetrius [2], Bodyguard: deposed on suspicion of complicity in Philotas' plot (330) 3.27

Demetrius [3], son of Pythonax, Companion 4.12

Demonicus, trierarch (326) *Ind.18*

Demophon [1], seer 7.26

Demosthenes, Athenian politician 1.10

Dendrobosa, place on Fish-Eater coast *Ind.27*

Dindymene, the goddess Cybele, to whom Mt Dindymus in Phrygia was sacred 5.6

Diogenes [1], 4th cent. BC Cynic philosopher 7.2

Diogenes [2], Mytilenaean oligarch installed by Persians as tyrant of Mytilene (333) 2.1

Dionysodorus, Theban envoy to Darius (332) 2.15

DIONYSUS, god, 2.16, 4.8, 4.9, 4.10, 5.1–2, 5.3, 5.26, 6.28, 7.20, *Ind.7–8, 9*; Theban and Athenian Dionysus, 2.16, 5.1; worshipped at Athens, 2.16, in Macedonia, 4.8, by Arabs, 7.20; founder of Nysa, 5.1–2, *Ind.1, 5*; Dionysus in India, 5.1–2, 5.3, 6.3, 6.14, 6.28, 7.10, 7.20, *Ind.1, 5, 7–8, 9*

— A.'s emulation of Dionysus 5.1, 5.2, 5.26, 6.28, 7.10, 7.20

Diophantus [2], Athenian envoy to A. (331) 3.6

Dioscuri (Castor and Polydeuces), gods 4.8

Diotimus, Athenian politician 1.10

Diridotis, village in Babylonia *Ind.41*

Dium, city in Macedonia 1.16

Doloaspis, Egyptian official 3.5

Domai, island W. of Indus mouth *Ind.22*

Doxares, Indian dynast 5.8

Drangiana (also Zarangiana), region W. of Arachosia, in Afghanistan 3.21, 3.25, 3.28, 4.18, 6.17, 6.27, 7.6, 7.10

— A. in Drangiana (330) 3.25–7

Drapsaca [Kunduz], city in Bactria 3.29

Dropides, Athenian envoy to Darius (330) 3.24

Drypetis, daughter of Darius (1): married by Hephaestion (324) 7.4

Dyrta, city in Assacenian territory 4.30

Earth (Ge), god 3.7

Ecbatana [Hamadan], city in Media, 3.19, 4.7, 7.13, 7.14, 7.18; temple of Asclepius, 7.14

—A. in Ecbatana 3.19 (330), 7.14 (324)

eclipse of moon (20 September 331) 3.7, 3.15

EGYPT: as Persian satrapy, 2.11, 2.17, 3.1; 2.13, 2.25–6, 3.1–5, 3.9, 3.22, 5.6, 5.25, 6.1, 7.9, 7.23, *Ind.2, 3, 4, 5, 6, 25, 43*; Egyptian Heracles, 2.16, *Ind.5*; Egyptians in A.'s fleet, 6.1, *Ind.18, 31*

— A. in Egypt (332/1), 3.1–5, 3.22, 3.26; organization of Egypt, 3.5

Eirus, mountain on coast W. of Indus *Ind.21*

Elaeus, city at SW extremity of Chersonese 1.11

Elephantine, city in S. Egypt 3.2

ELEPHANTS: in war, 3.8, 3.11, 3.15, 4.25, 5.9, 5.15, 5.16, 5.17, 5.18, 7.4, *Ind.8*; horses frightened by elephants, 5.10, 5.11, 5.15; acquired by A., 3.15, 4.22, 4.27, 4.30, 5.3, 5.18, 5.20, 5.21, 5.24, 5.29, 6.2, 6.15, 6.16, 6.17, 6.27, 6.28, 7.3, *Ind.19* ('about 200')

— intelligence, *Ind.14*; life-cycle and diseases, *Ind.14*; as status-symbols, *Ind.17*; elephants E. of Hyphasis, 5.25; elephant-hunting, 4.30, *Ind.13–14*

Eleusis, in Attica: Eleusinian Mysteries (1.10) 3.16

Eleutherae, town in Attica 1.7

Elimiotis, canton of Macedonia 1.7

Elis/Eleans, region of NW Peloponnese 1.10, 1.29

Embolima, city near Aornus (2) 4.28

Emodus, mountain range [Himalayas] *Ind.2, 6*

engineers 2.19, 2.21, 2.26

Enus [Inn], tributary of Danube *Ind.4*

Enylus, king of Byblus 2.20

Eordaea, canton of Macedonia 1.7, 6.28, *Ind.18*

Eordaïcus, river in Macedonia 1.5–6

Epaminondas, 4th cent. BC Theban general 1.9

Epardus, river in Mardian (1) territory 4.6

Ephesus, city in Ionia: A. in Ephesus (334), 1.17–18; temple of Artemis, 1.17, 1.18

Ephialtes, Athenian politician 1.10

Ephippus [1], superintendent of mercenaries in Egypt 3.5

Epidaurus, city on NE coast of Peloponnese 7.14

Epimenes, Page in conspiracy (327) 4.13

Epirus, region of NW central
Greece 2.16, 3.6

Epocillus, Mac. officer 3.19, 4.7, 4.18

Erannoboas [Son], tributary of Ganges
Ind.4, 10

Eratosthenes, geographer and polymath
(*c.* 275–194 BC), 5.3, 5.5, *Ind.3*; cited,
5.6, *Ind.3*

Erennesis, tributary of Ganges *Ind.4*

Erigon [Crna], river in Taulantian
territory 1.5

Erigyius, son of Larichus, brother of
Laomedon, Companion (3.28.2): exiled
by Philip [1] (336), 3.6; appointed
commander of allied cavalry (333), 3.6,
3.11 (at Gaugamela, 331); commander of
mercenary cavalry (330), 3.20; 3.23; kills
Satibarzanes in single combat (330), 3.28

Erytheia, mythical island in far west 2.16

Erythraean Sea, Persian Gulf (Red Sea
(a)) *Ind.37*

Erythres, legendary king in Persian Gulf
region *Ind.37*

Ethiopia 5.4, 6.1, 7.1, 7.15, *Ind.6*

Etruscans, people of NW Italy 7.15

Etymandrus [Helmand], river in
Ariaspian territory 4.6

Euboea, island off E. central Greece 2.2,
3.19, 6.11

Eudamus [2], Mac. commander 6.27

Eudanemoi, obscure: perhaps an
Athenian clan concerned with cult of
wind-gods 3.16

Euergetae ('Benefactors'), name given to
Ariaspians 3.27, 4.6

Eugnostus, Companion 3.5

Euias, river in Aspasian territory 4.24

Eulaeus, river in Susiana 7.7

Eumenes, A.'s Secretary, Companion
(7.4.6): 5.24, 7.4; trierarch (326),
Ind.18; quarrel with Hephaestion
(324), 7.13, 7.14

EUPHRATES, Asian river 2.13, 2.17,
2.25, 3.6, 3.7, 5.5, 5.6, 6.19, 7.1, 7.7,
7.17, 7.19, 7.20, 7.21, 7.27, *Ind.41, 42*

Euripides, dramatist 7.16

Euripus, channel between Euboea and
mainland 2.2

Europe, 1.3, 1.11, 2.7, 2.16, 4.7, 5.4, 5.6,
7.1, 7.13, *Ind.5*; boundaries between
Europe and Asia, Libya, 3.30

Eurybotas, Cretan: commander of the
archers, killed at Thebes (335) 1.8

Eurydice, royal name assumed by
Cleopatra [1] on marriage to Philip [1]
in 337 3.6

Eurylochus [2]: revealed Pages'
conspiracy (327) 4.13

Eurymedon, river in Pamphylia 1.27

Eurystheus, legendary king of Argolid,
taskmaster of Heracles 2.16, 4.10

Euthycles, Spartan envoy to Darius
(333) 2.15

Evagoras, Secretary of Hydaspes fleet
(326) *Ind.18*

FINANCE: A.'s inheritance from Philip,
7.9; navy disbanded for lack of funds
(334), 1.20; fines/taxes/tribute
imposed on conquered territories,
1.17.1, 1.17.7, 1.26, 2.5, 3.5, 3.17, 5.29;
Persian treasure captured, 2.11, 2.15
(Damascus, 332), 3.16 (Susa, 331),
3.18, 3.19 (Persepolis and Pasargadae,
330), 5.26, 7.9; A.'s travelling
exchequer, 3.6; regional finance officers
appointed, 1.17 (Lydia, 334), 3.5
(Egypt, 331), 3.6 (Phoenicia, W. Asia,
331), 3.16 (Babylonia, 331)

fire-ships 2.19 (Tyre, 332)

Fish-Eaters, tribe on Makran coast below
Gedrosia 6.23, 6.28, *Ind.26–9, 31,
32, 33*

Gabae, stronghold in Sogdiana 4.17

Gadeira [Cadiz], city in SW Spain 3.30,
7.1

Galatia, region of N. central Asia
Minor 2.4

Ganges, Indian river 5.4, 5.5, 5.6, 5.9,
5.26, *Ind.2, 3–4, 5, 10*

Garoeas [Panjkora] (Guraeus in 4.25.7),
tributary of Cophen [Kabul] 4.25,
Ind.4

Gates, passes: *see* Amanic Gates, Assyrian
Gates, Caspian Gates, Cilician Gates,
Persian Gates

GAUGAMELA, village in Assyria (1),
3.8, 6.11; battle of Gaugamela (331),
3.8–15, 3.22

Gaza (1), city in Palestinian Syria,
besieged and captured by A. (332),
2.25–7; fate of Gazaeans, 2.27; 3.1

Gaza (2), city in Sogdiana 4.2

GEDROSIA, desert region [Makran] of
SW Pakistan/SE Iran 3.28, 6.22,
6.23–7, 6.28, 7.4, 7.10, *Ind.23, 26, 27, 32*

— A. in Gedrosia (325) 6.22–7, *Ind.26, 32*

Gelon, tyrant of Gela in Sicily (*c.*
491–485), then of Syracuse (485–
478) 1.12

geography: boundaries of Europe/Asia/
Libya (Africa), 3.30; geographical
divisions of Asia, 5.6; alluvial plains,
5.6

— confusions/misapprehensions: Taurus
mountain range, 3.28, 5.5, *Ind.2*;
'Scythian' and Indian Caucasus, 3.28,
5.3, 5.5, *Ind.2, 5*; two Tanaïs rivers,
3.30; Hyrcanian/Caspian Sea, 7.16; *see
also* Great Sea

Geraestus, cape at S. tip of Euboea 2.1

Gerostratus, Phoenician, king of Aradus
district 2.13, 2.20

Gerrha, Arabian city on Persian Gulf
Ind.41

Geryones: Heracles tasked to carry off his
cattle 2.16

Getae, tribe N. of the Lower Danube, 1.3;
A's campaign against them (335), 1.3–4

Glaucias [1], king of Taulantians, joined
Cleitus [1] against A. (335) 1.5–6

Glaucias [2], Mac. cavalry
commander 3.11

Glaucias [3], doctor attending
Hephaestion 7.14

Glaucippus, Milesian 1.19

Glaucus, Aetolian mercenary commander
in Persian service 3.16

Glauganicae/Glausae, Indian tribe
bordering Porus' [1] domain 5.20

Gogana, area on coast of Persis *Ind.38*

Gordium, city in Hellespontine Phrygia,
1.29; A. in Gordium (333), 1.29, 2.3

Gordius, Phrygian, father of Midas, 2.3;
the Gordian Knot, 2.3

Gordyene, mountainous region N. of
Assyria (1) 3.7

Gorgias [1], Mac. commander 4.16, 4.22,
5.12

Gorgon (Medusa) 3.3

GRANICUS, river in Hellespontine
Phrygia ('little stream', 1.13.6): battle
at the Granicus (334) 1.13–16, 1.29,
2.7, 2.11, 3.6, 3.22, 4.8, 6.11, 7.9

Granis, river in Persis *Ind.39*

'Great King' of Persia, 1.9, 1.12, 1.24,
2.7, 3.17, 5.18, 7.1; trappings assumed
by Bessus (330), 3.25

GREAT SEA (also Outer Sea, 5.5, 7.9,
Ind.43), the Ocean surrounding the
entire world 5.26, 7.16

— (Atlantic), 2.16, *Ind.43*: (Caspian
Sea), 3.23, 3.29, 5.5, 5.26, 7.16:
(Indian Ocean/Arabian Sea), 5.4,
5.5, 5.6, 5.29, 6.1, 6.19, 6.20, 6.21, 7.5,
7.10, 7.20, *Ind.2, 3, 5, 43*; 'Indian
Ocean', *Ind. 25, 38*: (Indian Ocean/
Bay of Bengal), 5.5, 5.6, 7.16;
'Eastern Sea', 5.26; 'Indian Gulf',
5.26; 'Eastern Ocean', *Ind.2, 5*

— tides 6.19, *Ind.21, 29, 30, 37, 38, 39*

GREECE/GREEKS: Greek league
(Corinthian League) against
Persia: led by Philip [1], 1.1, 7.9, then
Alexander (from 336), 1.1, 2.14; 1.8,
1.9 (at Thebes, 335), 1.16, 2.1
(Mytilene), 2.2 (Tenedos), 2.14; A.'s
severity on Greeks not complying, 1.16
(Greek mercenaries at Granicus, 334),
1.29 (Athenian prisoners from
Granicus), 3.23 (Greek mercenaries
with Darius, 330), 3.24; A. as avenger
of Persian invasion of Greece, 2.14,
3.18, 4.11; Antipater left as regent in
charge of Macedonia and Greece (334),
1.11; Craterus sent out (324) to replace
him in 'defence of Greek freedom',
7.12; antagonism between Greeks and
Macedonians, 2.10

— allied troops with A., 1.8, 1.9 (at
Thebes, 335), 1.17, 2.5, 2.7, 2.13, 3.5,
3.6, 3.11, 3.12; sent home (330), 3.19;
some settled in Asia, 5.27

— Greek reaction to destruction of
Thebes (335), 1.9, 1.10; A.'s fear
of revolt/defection in Greece, 1.10,
1.18, 1.29, 2.17, 2.26, 3.6; Greek
embassies to A., 1.10, 1.29, 3.5, 3.6,
7.14, 7.19, 7.23; Greek envoys to
Darius before Issus (arrested, 332),
2.15; Greek artists in festivals held
by A., 3.1

— Greek Sea (Aegean) 5.1

see also mercenaries, Greek

guest-friends (Gk *xenoi*) 1.9 (of Philip
and A.)

Guraeans, tribe in Swat region 4.23, 4.25
Guraeus *see* Garoeas

Haemus, mountain in Thrace 1.1–2
HALICARNASSUS [Bodrum], city in
  Caria; siege and destruction by A.
  (334), 1.20–3, 2.5; 2.13, 3.22; Tripylon
  gate, 1.22; citadel Salmacis, 1.23
Halys [Kizilirmak], river in central Asia
  Minor 2.4
Hannon, early 5th cent. BC Carthaginian
  explorer *Ind.43*
Harmodius, with Aristogeiton assassinated
  the Athenian tyrant Hipparchus (514),
  4.10; statues, looted by Xerxes, sent
  back to Athens by A., 3.16, 7.19
Harmozia, place on Carmanian coast
  Ind.33
Harpalus, Mac. treasurer, with chequered
  career 3.6, 3.19
Hebrus [Maritza], river in Thrace 1.11
Hecataeus, late 6th cent. BC historian
  2.16, 5.6
Hecatombaeon, month in Athenian
  calendar 2.24, 3.7, 3.22
Hecatomnos, Carian dynast, father of
  Ada 1.23
Hegelochus, Mac. officer: light cavalry
  commander (334), 1.13; charged with
  reconstitution of Mac. fleet (333), 2.2;
  reports end of Aegean war to A. (331),
  3.2; cavalry commander at Gaugamela
  (331), 3.11
Hegemon, Athenian archon 5.19
Hegesias, Athenian archon 7.28
Hegesistratus, commander of Persian
  garrison at Miletus (334) 1.18
Heliopolis, city in Egypt N. of
  Memphis 3.1
Helios, sun-god *Ind.28, 31*
Hellanicus, Mac. officer 1.21
Hellespont, 1.11, 1.12, 1.13, 4.15, 5.7,
  5.25, 7.9, 7.14; Hellespontines in A.'s
  fleet, *Ind.18*
Hellespontine Phrygia *see* Phrygia,
  Hellespontine
Helots, servile population in Sparta
  Ind.10
HEPHAESTION (*c.*356–324), son of
  Amyntor, 6.28.4, Companion;
  Bodyguard, 6.28.4; trierarch (326),
  Ind.18; married to Drypetis (324), 7.4

— at tomb of Patroclus (334), 1.12;
  acknowledged as A.'s *alter ego* (333),
  2.12; wounded at Gaugamela (331),
  3.15; appointed as one of two
  commanders of Companion cavalry
  (330), 3.27, 7.14; quarrel with Eumenes
  (324), 7.13, 7.14; 4.12, 4.16, 4.22–3,
  4.28, 4.30, 5.3, 5.12, 5.21, 5.29, 6.2,
  6.4, 6.5, 6.13, 6.17, 6.18, 6.20, 6.21,
  6.22, 6.28, 7.5, 7.7, *Ind.19*
— death at Ecbatana (324), 7.14; foretold,
  7.18; A.'s grief, 7.14–15, 7.16;
  hero-cult, 7.14, 7.23; mourning
  proclaimed throughout Asia, 7.14;
  funeral games, 7.14; funeral
  monuments, 7.14, 7.23
Hera, goddess 2.16
Heracleidae, descendants of
  Heracles 2.5, 4.10
Heracleides [1], son of Antiochus, Mac.
  cavalry commander 1.2, 3.11
Heracleides [2], son of Argaeus: sent
  by A. to build ships in Hyrcania (323)
  7.16
Heracleides [3], Carthaginian envoy to
  Darius (330) 3.24
HERACLES: Argive, Tyrian, Egyptian
  Heracles, 2.16, 4.28, *Ind.5*; Tyrian
  Heracles, 2.16, 2.18 (A.'s dream at
  Tyre, 332), *Ind.5*; Egyptian Heracles,
  2.16, *Ind.5*; Indian Heracles, *Ind.8*;
  'Heracles' in India, 4.28, 5.3, *Ind.5*,
  8–9
— Argive/Theban Heracles, 2.16, 3.3,
  4.8, 4.28; deification, 4.11, 5.26;
  labours/exploits, 2.16 (cattle of
  Geryones), 3.3 (Antaeus, Busiris), 5.3
  (Prometheus' eagle), 7.13 (Hippolyte's
  girdle); said to have failed to take Rock
  of Aornus (2), 4.28, 4.30, *Ind.5*; Pillars
  of Heracles, 2.16, 5.26, *Ind.43*
— temples: at Thebes, 1.8; at Tyre, 2.16,
  2.24; at Tartessus, 2.16
— ancestor of A., 3.3, 4.7, 4.10, 4.11,
  5.26, 6.3; A.'s sacrifices to Heracles,
  1.4, 1.11, 2.15, 2.24, 3.6, 6.3, *Ind.36*;
  A.'s emulation of Heracles, 3.3, 4.28,
  4.30, 5.3, 5.26
Heracon, Mac. general in Media, accused
  of abuses and executed (325/4) 6.27
Heratemis, canal in Persis *Ind.39*
Hermes, god *Ind.37*

Hermolaus, son of Sopolis: Page, instigated Pages' conspiracy (327) 4.13–14

Hermotus, place near Propontis 1.12

Hermus [Gediz], river in Lydia 1.17, 5.6

Herodotus, 5th cent. BC historian 2.16, 3.30, 5.6, 5.7, 7.13

Heromenes, son of Aëropus: party to the murder of Philip [1] (336) 1.25

Heroönpolis, city in the Suez isthmus 3.5, 7.20

Heropythus, liberator of Ephesus 1.17

Hidrieus, Carian dynast, brother and husband of Ada 1.23

Hieratis, town on coast of Persis Ind.39

Hieron (1), tyrant of Syracuse (478–466) 1.12

Hieron (2), helmsman: sailed round most of Arabia (323) 7.20

Hippias, agent of Spartan king Agis 2.13

Hippolyte, queen of the Amazons 7.13

Hollow Syria see Syria

Homer, epic poet 1.12, 4.1, 5.6, 6.1

Hydarnes, son of Mazaeus 7.6

HYDASPES [Jhelum], Indian river, 5.3, 5.4, 5.5, 5.8; battle of Hydaspes (326), 5.8–19; 5.20, 5.21, 5.25, 5.29, 6.1, 6.2, 6.3, 6.4, 6.5, 6.14, 7.4, 7.10, Ind.3, 4, 18, 19

Hydraces, Gedrosian pilot Ind.27

HYDRAOTES [Ravi], Indian river 5.4, 5.5, 5.21, 5.25, 5.29, 6.5, 6.7, 6.8, 6.13, 6.14, 7.10, Ind.3, 4

Hyparna, fortress near border of Lycia 1.24

Hyperberetaeus, month in Mac. calendar Ind.21

Hypereides, Athenian politician 1.10

HYPHASIS [Beas], Indian river 5.4, 5.5, 5.24–5, 5.26, 5.29, 6.14, 7.4, 7.10, Ind.2, 3–4, 6

— mutiny at the Hyphasis (326) 5.25–9

Hyrcania, region bordering SE of Caspian Sea 3.8, 3.11, 3.19, 3.23, 5.20, 5.25, 6.27, 7.6, 7.10, 7.16

— A. in Hyrcania (330), 3.23, 3.24, 3.25; ship-building commissioned there (323), 7.16

Hyrcanian Sea [Caspian Sea] 3.23, 3.29, 3.30, 5.5, 5.25, 5.26, 7.10, 7.16

Hystaspes, Bactrian 7.6

Iacchus, god hymned in Eleusinian Mysteries 2.16

Iapygian promontory [Capo S. Maria di Leuca], at heel of Italy 7.1

Iassus, in Caria 1.19

Iazyges, Sarmatian tribe N. of the Lower Danube 1.3

Iberia, Spain 2.16, 7.15

Icarian Sea, gulf of Aegean N. of Icarus and Samos 7.20

Icarus (1), son of Daedalus 7.20

Icarus (2), E. Aegean island 7.20

Icarus (3), name given by A. to island in Persian Gulf [Failaka] 7.20

Ida, mountain range in Troad, NW Asia Minor 1.12

Idanthyrsus, Scythian king Ind.5

Ilas, harbour on coast of Persis Ind.38

Illyrians, tribes N. and W. of Macedonia, 1.1, 1.7, 1.10, 5.26, 7.9; A.'s campaign against them (335), 1.5–6; in A.'s army, 2.7

Imaon, mountain range [Himalayas] Ind.2, 6

INDIA: 4.15, 4.22, 5.3, 6.24 (Semiramis and Cyrus), 6.27; Arrian's definition of India, Ind.2; early history, Ind.7–8, 9; not invaded between Dionysus and A., Ind.5, 9; Indian language, 5.4, 7.3, Ind.2, 7, 8, 22; 'Indian Gulf' [Arabian Sea], 5.26; number of rivers, Ind.5; tribes, Ind.7, cities, Ind.10, kings, Ind.9; boundaries and dimensions, 5.6, Ind.2–3; physical geography, 5.6; climate: 5.9, 5.29, 6.21, 6.25 (monsoons); Ind.6, 10, 15, 21; flora: 5.1, 5.2, Ind.5 (ivy only in Nysa); 6.22 (myrrh, spikenard, mangroves); Ind.7, 16 (cotton); Ind.11 (enormous trees); fauna: gold-digging ants, 5.4, Ind.15; apes, Ind.15; crocodiles, 6.1, Ind.6; elephants, q.v.; hippopotamuses, Ind.6; jackals, Ind.15; parrots, Ind.15; pearl-oysters, Ind.8; snakes, Ind.15; tigers, Ind.15; phenomena: lack of shadows at midday, Ind.25; stars, Ind.25; products: gold, 5.4, Ind.8, 15; ivory, Ind.16; pearls, Ind.8, 38

— Dionysus in India, 5.1–2, 5.3, 6.3, 6.14, 6.28, 7.10, 7.20, Ind.1, 5, 7–8, 9; Heracles in India, 4.28, 5.3, Ind.5, 8–9

— A. in India (327/6–325), 4.23–6.22, 7.4, Ind.15; limit of A.'s penetration, Ind.2, 4, 5

Indian Ocean *Ind.25, 38*: *see* **GREAT SEA**
INDIAN RIVERS 3.29, 5.4, 5.6, 5.9, 5.20, 6.1, 6.3, **6.14**, 7.10, *Ind.3–5, 6, 10*
INDIANS, west of Indus: in Darius' army at Gaugamela (331), 3.8, 3.11, 3.13, 3.14, 3.15; 3.25; 4.22–30 (Swat campaign, 327/6, capture of Aornus (2), 326); 5.20, *Ind.1*; *see also* Arabitae, Oreitans
INDIANS, east of Indus: 'highland Indians', 5.8; allied to A., 5.3, 5.8, 5.11, 5.24, 6.3; hostile, 6.4, 6.5; autonomous/independent Indians, 5.20, 5.21, 5.22, 5.24 (*see also* Abastanians, Adraïstae, Cathaeans, Glauganicae, Mallians, Ossadians, Oxydracae, Sogdians (2)); Indians with Porus [1], **5.8–19**; bordering Porus [1], 5.20; E. of Hyphasis, 5.25, 5.27, *Ind.6*
— Indian losses in battle, 5.15, 5.18 (Hydaspes, 326); 5.24 (Sangala, 326); 6.6–7, 6.11 (Mallians, 326/5); 6.18
— physical appearance, 5.4, *Ind.1, 6, 17*; clothing, *Ind.5, 16*; diet, *Ind.17*; caste system, *Ind.11–12*; gurus (*see also* Brahmans), 6.16, 7.1–3, 7.18, *Ind.11, 12, 15*; doctors, *Ind.15*; social class, *Ind.16, 17*; puberty and life-expectancy, *Ind.9*; marriage, *Ind.9, 12, 17*; music, 6.3, *Ind.5, 7, 10, 14*
— political systems, 5.25, *Ind.9, 11, 12*; kings, *Ind.8, 9, 11, 12*; no slavery, *Ind.10*; warfare, 5.4, *Ind.5, 7, 11, 16*; courage, 5.4, 5.22, 5.25, 6.7, *Ind.1*; no aggression against others, *Ind.5, 9*; soldier caste, *Ind.12*; weaponry, *Ind.16*; cavalry horses, *Ind.16*; Indian mercenaries, 4.26, 4.27
INDUS, Indian river 3.25, 4.22, 4.28, 4.30, 5.1, 5.3, 5.4, 5.5, 5.6, 5.7, 5.8, 5.9, 5.20, 5.25, 6.1, 6.2, 6.3, 6.14, 6.15, 6.17, 6.28, 7.1, 7.4, 7.10, *Ind.1, 2, 3, 4–5, 18, 19, 20, 21, 42*
— Indus delta, 5.4. 6.14, 6.17, **6.18–20**, 7.10, *Ind.2*
interpreters 3.6, 4.3, 7.1, *Ind.28*
Iolaus, nephew and companion of Heracles: his precinct at Thebes 1.7
Iollas, son of Antipater [1], A.'s butler 7.27
Iomanes, Indian river *Ind.8*

Ion, eponymous ancestor of Ionians 7.29
Ionia, region of central W. Asia Minor, 1.12, 1.18, 3.22, 5.6, 5.25, 7.9; Ionians in A.'s fleet, *Ind.18*
Ionian Gulf 1.4
Iphicrates (1), Athenian envoy to Darius (333) 2.15
Iphicrates (2), father of Iphicrates (1), Athenian general 2.15
Ipsus, town in Phrygia 7.18
Isis, Egyptian god 3.1
ISSUS, in SE Cilicia, 2.7; battle of Issus (333), **2.6–11**, 3.6, 3.8, 3.22, 4.20, 6.11; effect of news of the battle, 2.13, 2.20, 3.1
Isthmus, Corinthian 6.11, 7.2
Italy 3.6, 7.1, 7.15
Itanes, son of Oxyartes 7.6

Jaxartes, another name for the river Tanaïs (a) [Syr-Darya], *q.v.* 7.16

Kore, mother of the Dionysus worshipped at Athens 2.16

Labdacus, father of Laïus, grandfather of Oedipus 2.16
Lade, island off Miletus 1.18, 1.19
Laïus, father of Oedipus 2.16
Lampsacus, city on Asian side of Hellespont 1.12
Lanice, sister of Cleitus [2], A.'s nurse 4.9
Laomedon, son of Larichus, brother of Erigyius: exiled by Philip [1] (336), 3.6; bilingual, appointed i/c Persian prisoners, 3.6; trierarch (326), *Ind.18*
Larissa, city in Thessaly *Ind.18*
Leonnatus [1], son of Antipater: trierarch (326) *Ind.18*
LEONNATUS [2], son of Anteas (son of Eunus in *Ind.18.3*): Companion, 2.12.5; appointed Bodyguard (332/1), 3.5, 6.28; 4.12, 4.21, 4.23 (wounded), 4.24, 4.25; trierarch (326), *Ind.18*; in Mallian campaign (326/5), 6.9, **6.10** (defends A.), 6.11, 7.5, *Ind.19*; in Oreitis (325), 6.22, 7.5, *Ind.23, 42*; 6.18, 6.20; crowned by A. (324), 7.5, *Ind.23, 42*
Lesbos, NE Aegean island 2.1, 2.13, 3.2
Leucas, W. Greek island *Ind.41*

Leuctra, in Boeotia: Spartan defeat there (371), 1.9
Leugaean squadron, a Mac. cavalry unit 2.9
LIBYA (= Africa), 3.3, 3.5, 3.30, 4.7, 5.25, 5.26, 5.27, 7.1, 7.15, Ind.35, 43; nomads, 3.30, 7.1; shrine of Ammon, 3.3, 3.4
— boundaries between Libya and Europe, Asia 3.30
Lucanians, people in toe of Italy 7.15
Lycia, region of S. Asia Minor 1.24, 2.2, 2.20, 3.6, 4.3, 5.25, Ind.2
— A. in Lycia (334/3) 1.24–5
Lycidas, Aetolian, mercenary commander 3.5
Lycomedes, Rhodian installed as commander of Mytilene garrison (333) 2.1
Lycurgus, Athenian politician 1.10
Lycus [Great Zab], river in Assyria (1) 3.15
Lydia, region of central W. Asia Minor 1.12, 1.17, 3.6, 3.22, 5.1, 5.6, 5.25, 7.9, 7.23
— A. in Lydia (334) 1.17
Lyginus, river in Thrace 1.2
Lysanias, Macedonian 1.2
Lysimachus [2], son of Agathocles: Bodyguard; trierarch (326), Ind.18; 5.13, 5.24 (wounded), 6.28, 7.3, 7.18
Lysippus, sculptor 1.16

MACEDONIA: development by Philip [1], 7.9; Mac. government, 4.11; traditional enemies, 5.26, 7.9; traditions, 4.7, 6.30, 7.6, 7.12; worship of Dionysus, 4.8, cf. 5.6–7; King's Pages, 4.12–14, 4.16, 4.22; consular representatives, 1.9; 'Macedonian empire', 5.25, 5.26, 7.9; Antipater regent of Macedonia and Greece, 1.11; Craterus sent to replace him (324), 7.12; Upper Macedonia (cavalry), 1.2; issue of half-caste children, 7.12; cult of A. in Macedonia, 7.30; Greek mercenaries imprisoned in Macedonia, 1.16, 1.29, 3.6
— recruitment in Macedonia 1.24, 1.29, 3.11, 3.16, 4.18, 7.8, 7.12, Ind.19
MACEDONIANS: reputation, 1.13, 2.10, 3.11; discipline/training, 1.6, 2.7,

3.9, 7.6, 7.12; contrasted with Persians, 2.7; xenophobia, 7.6, 7.29; A.'s banquet promoting partnership with Persians (324), 7.11; antagonism between Mac. and Greeks, 2.10; myth-making, 5.3, 5.4, 5.5, Ind.2, 5; first experience of tides, 6.19
— Mac. army at Gaugamela (331), 3.11–12; size of A.'s army in 326, Ind.19; Mac. army as court in capital trials, 3.26–7 (Philotas' plot), 4.14 (Pages' conspiracy); convalescent centres on campaign, 2.7, 4.16, 5.8; veterans sent home, 3.29, 6.17, 7.8, 7.10, 7.12; settled in Asia, 4.4, 4.22, 4.24, 5.27; Mac. married to Asian wives, 7.4, 7.10, 7.12; debts paid off by A. (324), 7.5, 7.10; newly-weds given compassionate leave (334), 1.24 (return, 1.29.4); exemptions for families of war-dead, 1.16, 7.10; statues of the dead, 1.16, 7.10; retirement bounties, 3.19, 5.27, 7.12; army pay and perks, 6.16, 7.5, 7.8, 7.9, 7.10, 7.12, 7.23; Companions, q.v.; 'Silver Shields', 7.11
— Mac. losses in battle, 1.2 (Triballians, 335); 1.8 (Thebes, 335); 1.15, 1.16 (Granicus, 334); 1.20, 1.22 (Halicarnassus, 334); 1.28 (Sagalassus, 334/3); 2.10 (Issus, 333); 2.24 (Tyre, 332); 3.13, 3.15 (Gaugamela, 331); 4.6 (Polytimetus, 329); 4.16 (Zariaspa, 328); 4.17 (Sogdiana, 328/7); 4.19 (Rock of Sogdiana, 327); 4.27 (Massaga, 327/6); 5.18 (Hydaspes, 326); 5.24 (Sangala, 326); Ind.23 (Oreitis, 325)
— anger at enemy, 2.24 (Tyre), 4.23 (Swat), 6.11 (Mallians); despair at potential loss of A. (326/5), 6.12–13; army hardships, 3.28, 4.21, 5.25, 5.27; (in Gedrosia) 6.23, 6.24–6, Ind.26, 32
— offended by A.'s behaviour/ orientalizing, 4.8, 4.11, 4.12, 4.14, 7.6, 7.8, 7.11; mutiny, at the Hyphasis (326), 5.25–9, at Opis (324), 7.8–12
Maceta [Ras Musandam], promontory of Oman Ind.32 (cf. 7.20.8–9)
Madyandini, Indian tribe Ind.4
Maeander (1), Greek from Magnesia: trierarch (326) Ind.18

Maeander (2), river and plain in Caria
1.19, 5.6 *Ind.4*

Maemacterion, month in Athenian
calendar 2.11

Maeotis, Lake [Sea of Azov] 3.30, 5.5,
7.1

Magarsus, city on coast of Cilicia 2.5

Magi, Persian priestly caste 6.29, 7.11

Magnesia, city in Ionia 1.18, *Ind.18*

Magon, tributary of Ganges *Ind.4*

Malamantus, tributary of Cophen *Ind.4*

Malana [Ras Malan], place on coast of
Oreitis *Ind.25*

Malea, cape at S. tip of Laconia 2.1

Mallians, Indian tribe in region of lower
Hydraotes, 5.22, 6.4, 6.5, *Ind.4*; A.'s
campaign against them (326/5),
6.6–11, 6.28, 6.30, *Ind.19*; surrender,
6.14

Mallus, city in Cilicia 2.5–6, 2.20

Mantinea, city in Arcadia: Spartan defeat
there (362) 1.9

Maracanda [Samarcand], capital city of
Sogdiana 3.30, 4.3, 4.5, 4.6, 4.16, 4.17

Marathus, city in Phoenicia 2.13–14, 2.15

Marcomanni, Celtic tribe N. of the
Upper Danube 1.3

Mardians (1), people on E. side of Persian
Gulf 3.11, 3.13, 4.6, *Ind.40*

Mardians (2), people to W. of Hyrcania,
bordering Caspian Sea: invaded by A.
and surrendered (330), 3.24; 4.18

Mareotis, lake at W. mouth of Nile 3.1

Margastana, island off coast of Susiana
Ind.41

Mariamme, city in Phoenicia 2.13

Maronea, city on coast of Thrace 1.11

Massaca *see* Massaga

Massaga, main city of the Assacenians
(Massaca in *Ind.1.8*) 4.26–7 (siege and
capture, 327/6) 4.28, *Ind.1*

Massagetae, Scythian tribe to NW of
Sogdiana, 4.17; invaded Bactria with
Spitamenes (328) 4.16–17, and
Sogdiana (328/7), 4.17

Mathae, Indian tribe *Ind.4*

Mauaces, commander of Sacae at
Gaugamela (331) 3.8

Mazaces, Persian satrap of Egypt
(332) 3.1, 3.22

Mazaeus, Persian commander: at
Euphrates (331), 3.7; at Gaugamela

(331), 3.8; appointed satrap of Babylon
by A. (331), 3.16, 4.18, 7.18; 3.21, 7.6

Mazarus, Companion: appointed garrison
commander at Susa (331) 3.16

Mazenes, governor of Oaracta *Ind.37*

MEDIA/MEDES, region SW of
Caspian Sea: 2.6, 2.7, 3.8, 3.11, 3.16,
3.25, 3.26, 4.7, 4.18, 5.4, 5.5, 6.27, 6.29,
7.4, 7.10, 7.13, *Ind.40*; empire, 2.6, 5.4,
5.25, 7.1, *Ind.1*; luxurious habits, 4.7;
practice of obeisance, 4.9, 4.11;
Median/Persian dress, 6.30, 7.6, 7.8;
high-born daughters married to
Companions (324), 7.4

— A. in Media: (330) 3.19–20; (324)
7.13–14

Mediterranean Sea 5.6, 6.1, 6.20, 7.1,
Ind.21, 30, 39

Medius, Companion: trierarch (326),
Ind.18; intimate of A. (323), 7.24–5,
7.27

Megareus, Chian oligarch 3.2

Megarid, region of Megara, W. of
Attica 3.6

MEGASTHENES, historian (*c.*350–290
BC), author of an *Indica*: as historian,
5.5, 5.6, *Ind.5, 6, 7, 17*; cited, 5.6, 7.2,
Ind.3, 4, 5, 6, 7, 8, 9, 10, 15

Meleager [1], son of Neoptolemus, Mac.
infantry commander 1.4, 1.14, 1.20,
1.24, 1.29, 2.8, 3.11.9, 3.18, 4.16, 4.17,
4.22, 5.12, 6.17

Meleager [2], Mac. cavalry
commander 3.11.8

Melos, Aegean island: destroyed by
Athenians (416) 1.9

MEMNON [1], Rhodian in Persian
service: at council of Zeleia (334), 1.12;
at Granicus (334), 1.15; 1.17;
appointed commander of Lower Asia
and whole Persian navy (334), 1.20,
2.1; at Halicarnassus (334), 1.20, 1.23;
in the Aegean (333), 2.1; death (333),
2.1

Memphis, city in Egypt below Nile delta
3.1, 3.4–5, 3.6

Menander [1], Companion, Mac. infantry
commander: appointed satrap of Lydia
(331) 3.6, 4.13, 7.23, 7.24

Menedemus, Companion (4.6.1), Mac.
commander 4.3, 4.6

Menelaus, brother of Agamemnon 5.6

Menes, Macedonian: appointed Bodyguard (333), 2.12; appointed governor of Syria, Phoenicia, and Cilicia (331), 3.16, 3.19, 4.7

Menidas, Mac. cavalry commander 3.12, 3.13, 3.15, 3.26, 4.7, 4.18, 7.23, 7.26

Meniscus, envoy from Darius to A. (332) 2.14

Menoetas, Mac. commander 3.5

Menoetius, helmsman of A.'s ship (334) 1.12

Menon [1], son of Cerdimmas: appointed satrap of Hollow Syria (333) 2.13, 4.7

Menon [2], appointed satrap of Arachosia (330) 3.28

Mentor, brother of Memnon, husband of Barsine (2) 2.2, 2.13, 7.4

MERCENARIES, Greek: (a) serving with Persians, (Granicus, 334) 1.12, 1.16, 1.29; (Ephesus, 334) 1.17; (Miletus, 334) 1.19; (Halicarnassus, 334) 1.20; 1.24, 1.26, 1.29, 2.7; (Issus, 333) 2.8, 2.10, 2.11, 2.13; 2.13.5, 3.7; (Gaugamela, 331) 3.11, 3.16; 3.21, 3.23, 3.24

— (b) serving with A., 1.18; (Miletus, 334) 1.18; 2.1–2, 2.5; (Issus, 333) 2.9; 2.20, 3.5, 3.6; (Gaugamela, 331) 3.9, 3.12, 3.13; 3.19, 3.20, 3.23, 3.25, 4.3, 4.4, 4.7, 4.16, 4.22, 5.12, 5.29, 6.22, 6.27, 7.21; settled in Asia, 4.4, 5.27, 5.29, 7.21

— Arab mercenaries, 2.25, 2.27; Indian mercenaries, 4.26, 4.27

Meroë, city in Ethiopia *Ind.25*

Meroes, Indian, friend of Porus [1] 5.18.7–19.1

Meros, mountain near Nysa 5.1, 5.2, *Ind.1, 5*

Mesambria [Bushēhr], peninsula on coast of Persis *Ind.39*

Mesopotamia, region between Euphrates and Tigris 3.7, 3.11, 7.7, 7.9, *Ind.42*

Methora, city in India *Ind.8*

Methymna, city in Lesbos 3.2

Metron [1], son of Epicharmus, trierarch (326) *Ind.18*

Miccalus, Greek sent to recruit seamen from Phoenicia (323) 7.19

Micon, 5th cent. BC Athenian painter 7.13

Midas, legendary king of Phrygia 2.3

Mieza, canton of Macedonia *Ind.18*

Miletus, city in Ionia 1.18–19 (captured by A., 334) 5.6, 7.9

Milyas, region to N. of Lycia 1.24

Minos, legendary king of Crete, son of Zeus 7.29

Mithraustes, Persian commander at Gaugamela (331) 3.8

Mithrenes, Persian: commander of Sardis garrison, surrendered Sardis to A. (334), 1.17, 3.16; appointed satrap of Armenia by A. (331), 3.16

Mithridates, son-in-law of Darius: killed by A. at Granicus (334) 1.15, 1.16

Mithrobaeus, Persian 7.6

Mithrobuzanes, Persian: satrap of Cappadocia, killed at Granicus (334) 1.16

Moerocles, Athenian politician 1.10

Monimus, Spartan envoy to Darius (330) 3.24

Moon (Selene), god 3.7

Morontobara [Karachi], place E. of R. Hab *Ind.22*

Mosarna [Ras Pasni?], harbour on Fish-Eater coast *Ind.26, 27*

Munichion, month in Athenian calendar 5.19

Muses 1.11

Musicanus, Indian dynast of region E. of lower Indus 6.15, 6.16, 6.17

Mycale, mainland promontory opposite Samos 1.18, 1.19, 5.5

Mycenae 2.16

Mylasa, in Caria 1.20, 1.21

Mylleas, trierarch (326) *Ind.18*

Myndus, city on coast of Caria 1.20, 2.5

Myriandrus, city just S. of Assyrian Gates 2.6

Mysia, region of NW Asia Minor 5.6

Mytilene, city in Lesbos 2.1, 3.2

Nabarzanes, Darius' Grand Vizier: in coup to arrest Darius (330), 3.21; surrenders to A. (330), 3.23

Naucratis, Greek city in Nile Delta 3.5

Nautaca [Shakhrisyabz], city in Sogdiana 3.28, 4.18

NAVY, Alexander's: crossing of Hellespont (334), 1.11, 7.9; at Miletus (334), 1.18, 1.19; inferiority to Persian navy, 1.18, 7.9; disbanded (334), 1.20;

reconstituted (333), 2.2; success in
Aegean (332), 3.2; augmented by
Phoenician and Cypriot defections
(332), 2.20; naval assault on Tyre (332),
2.20, 2.24; Tyrian counter-attack
crushed, 2.21–2; from Phoenicia to
Egypt (332/1), 3.1; in Egypt (331), 3.5;
ships sent to Peloponnese (331), 3.6
— Hydaspes/Indus fleet (326–5), 5.8,
5.9, 5.12–13, 6.1, 6.2, 6.14, 6.15,
6.18–20; size of Hydaspes fleet (326),
Ind.19; Nearchus' fleet (325–4), *see*
NEARCHUS; ships used from Susa to
Opis (324), *Ind.7*; fleet at Babylon
(323), 7.19; voyage down the Euphrates
(323), 7.21–2
— ships transported in sections, 5.8, 5.12,
7.19; ship-building: at the Indus (326),
4.30; for the Hydaspes fleet (326), 6.1,
6.2, 6.14; in Xathrian country (325),
6.15; in Hyrcania (323), 7.16; in
Babylonia (323), 7.19, 7.21
—naval preparations for Arabian
expedition (323) 7.19, 7.21, 7.23, 7.25
NAVY, Persian: at Miletus (334), 1.18,
1.19; 1.20.1; at Halicarnassus (334),
1.20.3; 1.24.3; Phoenician and Cypriot
contingents, 1.18, 2.13, 2.15, 2.17,
defect to A. (332) 2.20; Phoenician
crews, 2.2, 2.17
— in the Aegean (333–2) 2.1–2, 2.13,
2.17, 2.18, 3.2
NEARCHUS, son of Androtimus,
Cretan (*Ind.18*), Companion (7.4.6):
exiled by Philip [1] (336), 3.6;
appointed satrap of Lycia and
Pamphylia (334/3), 3.6; trierarch
(*Ind.18*) and admiral of Hydaspes/
Indus fleet (326–325), 6.2, 6.5,
6.13; 4.7, 4.30, 7.4, 7.19, 7.25
— as historian, 5.5, 6.28, *Ind.17, 31*;
cited, 6.13, 6.24, 7.3, 7.20, *Ind.3, 11,
15, 16, 20–42, 43*
— voyage from Indus to head of
Persian Gulf (325–324), 6.19, 6.20,
6.21, 6.28, 7.5, 7.10, 7.20, *Ind.17, 19,
20–42*; appointed admiral-in-chief
(326), *Ind.18, 20*; objectives of the
voyage, 7.20, *Ind.32*; size of fleet, 6.2,
Ind.19; support for the fleet, 6.21, 6.23,
6.24, *Ind.23, 38*; hostile encounters,
Ind.24 (coastal Oreitans), *27–8*

(Fish-Eaters), *36* (Carmania);
leadership, 7.20, *Ind.27–8, 29, 30, 31, 32*
— coastal route of voyage: Indus to
Arabis [Hab], *Ind.21–2, 25*; Oreitan
coast, *Ind.23–5*; Fish-Eater coast,
Ind.26–31, 33; Carmanian coast,
Ind.32–3, 37–8 (journey inland to
reunion with A., *33–6*); recommissioned
to continue voyage, *36*); coast of Persis,
Ind.38–40; coast of Susiana, *Ind.40–2*;
up Pasitigris to Susa, 7.5, *Ind.42*
— crowned by A. (324), 7.5, *Ind.42*;
mobbed by Macedonians, *Ind.36, 42*
Neiloxenus, Companion 3.28
Neoptana, beach on Carmanian coast
Ind.33
Neoptolemus [1], son of Arrhabaeus:
Mac. defector, killed at Halicarnassus
(334) 1.20
Neoptolemus [2], Companion, Mac.
infantry officer 2.27
Neoptolemus (3), son of Achilles 1.11
Nereids, sea goddesses 1.11, *Ind.18, 31*
Nesaean plain, in Media: the royal horses
pastured there 7.3, 7.13
Nestus, river in Thrace 1.1
Neudrus, tributary of Hydraotes *Ind.4*
'Next Generation' (Gk *Epigonoi*) 7.6, 7.8
Nicaea (1), city in Parapamasidae region
4.22
Nicaea (2), city founded by A. on the
Hydaspes (326) 5.19, 5.29
Nicanor [1], son of Parmenion, Mac.
infantry commander 1.4, 1.14, 2.8,
3.11, 3.21, 3.25 (death of disease, 330)
Nicanor [2], commander of Greek allied
fleet at Miletus (334) 1.18, 1.19
Nicanor [6], Companion: appointed
administrator of Alexandria *in Caucaso*
(327), 4.22; appointed satrap of whole
region W. of Indus (326), 4.28
Nicarchides [2], son of Simus: trierarch
(326) *Ind.18*
Nicetes, Athenian archon 2.24
Nicias, appointed finance officer for Lydia
(334) 1.17
Nicocles [1], Cypriot: trierarch (326)
Ind.18
Nicocrates, Athenian archon 2.11
Nile, river in Egypt, 3.1, 3.6, 3.30, 5.6,
6.1, *Ind.3, 4, 6*; old name Aegyptus,
5.6, 6.1; Nile delta, 5.4, 6.17, *Ind.2*

Ninus [Nineveh], city in Mesopotamia *Ind.42*

Niphates, Persian commander at Granicus (334) 1.12, 1.16 (killed)

Nithaphon, Cypriot, son of Pnytagoras: trierarch (326) *Ind.18*

nomads: Libyan, 3.30, 7.1; Scythian, 4.5, 4.17, 7.16, *Ind.7*; Indian, *Ind.7, 11*; Fish-Eaters, *Ind.29*; Uxians, Mardians (1), Cossaeans, *Ind.40*; Macedonians before Philip [1], 7.9

Noricum, Roman province S. of Danube *Ind.4*

Nosala, island off Fish-Eater coast, sacred to Helios *Ind.31*

Nysa, city E. of R. Kunar, in Aspasian territory 5.1–2, 5.26, 6.2, *Ind.1, 5*

Nysaea, region of Nysa 5.1, 5.2, *Ind.1*

Nyse, nurse of Dionysus 5.1

Oaracta [Qeshm], large island off Carmanian coast *Ind.37*

obeisance (Gk *proskynesis*) 2.12, 4.9–12, 4.14

Ocean, god *Ind.18* (*see also* **GREAT SEA**)

Ochus (1) *see* Artaxerxes (2)

Ochus (2), mountain on coast of Persis *Ind.38*

Odrysians, tribe in Thrace: cavalry in A.'s army 3.12

Oeagrus, father of Orpheus 1.11

Oedipus 2.16

Olympias, mother of A. 3.6, 4.10, 5.27, 6.1; relations with Antipater [1], 7.12

Olympic games, 2.15; Mac. Olympian games, 1.11

Olynthus, city in Chalcidice 4.10

Omalis, tributary of Ganges *Ind.4*

Omares, Persian commander killed at Granicus (334) 1.16

Ombrion, Cretan: appointed commander of Mac. archers (331) 3.5

OMENS, prophecies, signs 1.9, 1.11, 1.17, 1.18, 1.20, 1.25, 2.3.3–4 (Gordius), 2.3.8, 2.18, 2.26, 3.2, 3.3, 3.7 (eclipse), 4.15, 7.18, 7.22, 7.24

— validating omens sought by sacrifice 3.1, 3.7, 4.4, 4.15, 5.3, 5.28

Onchestus, city in Boeotia 1.7

ONESICRITUS: helmsman of A.'s ship (326), 6.2, 7.5, *Ind.18*; chief helmsman

of Nearchus' fleet (325–4), 7.20, *Ind.32*; crowned by A. (324), 7.5

— as historian, 6.2, *Ind.3*; cited, *Ind.6*

Onomas, Spartan envoy to Darius (330) 3.24

Opis, city on the Tigris, 7.7, 7.13; A. at Opis, and mutiny (324), 7.8–12

Ora (1) [Ude-gram], city in Assacenian territory 4.27, 4.28

Ora (2), capital city of Oreitis 6.22, 6.24

Ophellas [2], son of Seilenus: trierarch (326) *Ind.18*

oracles: Ammon, 3.3–4, 6.19, 7.14, 7.23; Bel, 7.16; Delphi, 4.11; Sarapis, 7.26; 2.3, 7.30, *Ind.18*

Orbelus, mountain in Thrace 1.1

Orchomenus, city in Boeotia 1.9

Ordanes, Persian arrested for revolt (325) 6.27

OREITIS/OREITANS, Indian people in region NW of Karachi, 6.21–2, 6.28, 7.5, 7.10, *Ind.21, 22, 23, 25, 26, 32, 42*; coastal Oreitans, *Ind.24* (cf. Fish-Eaters)

— A. in Oreitis (325) 6.21–2

Orestis, canton of Macedonia 6.28, *Ind.18*

Organa [Hormoz], desert island off Carmanian coast *Ind.37*

Orobatis, city in Gandhara region 4.28

Orontes, Persian commander at Gaugamela (331) 3.8

Orontobates: Persian satrap of Caria, 1.23; defending Halicarnassus (334), 1.23, (defeated) 2.5; at Gaugamela (331), 3.8

Orpheus 1.11

Orxantes, local name for river Tanaïs (a) [Syr-Darya] *q.v.* 3.30

Orxines, Persian commander: at Gaugamela (331), 3.8; assumed control of Persis, 6.29, accused and executed, 6.30 (324)

Ossadians, independent Indian tribe 6.15

Outer Sea *see* **GREAT SEA**

Oxathres, Persian commander: at Gaugamela (331), 3.8; appointed satrap of Paraetacene (330), 3.19; executed for abuse of power (324), 7.4

Oxicanus, Indian dynast in Sind region 6.16

Oxus [Amu-Darya], river of central Asia 3.28, **3.29**, **3.30**, 4.15, 7.10, **7.16**

OXYARTES, Bactrian/Sogdian noble, 3.28, 4.18, 4.21; father of Rhoxane, 4.19, 4.20, 6.15, 7.4, 7.6; appointed satrap of Parapamisadae (325), 6.15

Oxyatres, brother of Darius (1) 7.4

Oxydates, Persian: appointed satrap of Media (330), 3.20; deposed (328/7), 4.18

Oxydracae, Indian tribe E. of Hydraotes 5.22, 6.4, 6.11, 6.14

Oxymagis, tributary of Ganges *Ind.4*

Padargus, river in Persis *Ind.39*

Paeonia, region of Thrace, 1.5, 2.7; light cavalry in A.'s army, 1.14, 2.9, 3.8, 3.12, 3.13

Paetice, region of Thrace 1.11

Pagala, place on coast of Oreitis *Ind.23*

Pages, King's 4.12–14, 4.16, 4.22

Palestine/Palestinian Syria, 7.9, *Ind.43*; A. in Palestinian Syria (332), 2.25–6 (siege of Gaza)

Palimbothra [Patna], city in India *Ind.2, 3, 10*

Pallacotta, canal branching from Euphrates 7.21

Pamphylia, region of S. Asia Minor, 1.24, 3.28, 5.5, 5.25, *Ind.2*; A. in Pamphylia (334/3), 1.26–7

Pandaea, daughter of Indian Heracles, *Ind.8–9*; country named after her, *Ind.8*

Panegorus, Companion 1.12

Pangaeum, mountain in Thrace 1.11

Pannonia, Roman province S. and W. of Danube *Ind.4*

Pantaleon, Companion: garrison commander at Memphis 3.5

Pantauchus, trierarch (326) *Ind.18*

Pantordanus, Mac. cavalry commander 2.9

Paphlagonia, region of N. central Asia Minor 2.4, 5.25

Paraetacene/Paraetacae, region/people between Persis and Media 3.19

Paraetonium, city on Egyptian coast W. of Alexandria 3.3

Paralus, Athenian state ship 3.6

Parapamisadae, people of Hindu Kush region 4.22, 5.3, 5.11, 6.15, 6.26, *Ind.5*

Parapamisus [Hindu Kush], mountain range 5.3, 5.4, 5.5, *Ind.2, 5, 6; see also* Caucasus (b)

Paravaea, area of N. central Greece 1.7

Pareitacene/Pareitacae, region/people of E. Sogdiana 4.21, 4.22

Parennus, tributary of Indus *Ind.4*

PARMENION (*c.*400–330), Mac. general, father of Philotas [4] and Nicanor [1]: in charge of transport across Hellespont (334), 1.11; at the Granicus (334), 1.14; sent to take over Dascylium, 1.17, Magnesia and Tralles, 1.18; sent to Phrygia (334), 1.24; captures Sisines (334/3), 1.25; arrests Alexander [4] (334/3), 1.25; at Gordium (333), 1.29; at Cilician Gates (333), 2.4; warns A. of supposed poison plot (333), 2.4; sent to Assyrian Gates (333), 2.5; commander of left wing at Issus (333), 2.8; sent to capture Darius' goods at Damascus (333), 2.11, 2.15; commander of left wing at Gaugamela (331), 3.11, 3.14–15; 3.18, 3.19, 6.27
— execution of his son Philotas [4], and his own murder on A.'s orders (330) 3.26, 4.14
— advice to A. (usually rejected): 1.13 (before Granicus), 1.18 (Miletus), 2.25 (Tyre), 3.9, 3.10 (Gaugamela), 3.18 (Persepolis)
— Arrian's assessment 3.26

Parthyaea (Parthia), region to SE of Caspian Sea, 3.8, 3.11, 3.15, 3.19, 3.20, 3.22, 3.23, 3.25, 3.28, 4.7, 4.18, 5.5, 5.20, 6.27, 7.6, 7.10; A. in Parthyaea (330), 3.20–2

Parysatis, daughter of Ochus (1): married by A. (324) 7.4

Pasargadae, old capital of Persis, 3.18, 6.29, 7.1, 7.19; A. in Pasargadae (324), 6.29

Pasicrates [1], king of Curium in Cyprus 2.22

Pasira, village on Fish-Eater coast *Ind.26*

Pasitigris [Karun], river in Susiana 3.17, *Ind.42*

Patala, region and city of Indus delta 5.4, 6.17–18, 6.20, 6.21, *Ind.2*

Patara, city in Lycia 1.24

Patroclus 1.12 (his tomb), 7.16

Patron, Phocian mercenary commander in Persian service 3.16

Pausanias [1], Companion: appointed military commander at Sardis (334) 1.17

Pausippus, Spartan envoy to Darius (330) 3.24

Pazalae, place in India *Ind.4*

Peithagoras, seer, brother of Apollodorus [1] 7.18

Peithon [1], son of Antigenes *Ind.15*

Peithon [2], son of Sosicles 4.16 (at Zariaspa, 328)

Peithon [3], son of Crateuas: Bodyguard, 6.28, 7.26; trierarch (326), *Ind.18*

Peithon [4], son of Agenor, Mac. infantry commander 6.6, 6.7, 6.8, 6.15, 6.17, 6.20

Pelagon, Ephesian, son of Syrphax (*q.v.*) 1.17

Pelinna, city in Thessaly 1.7

Pella, capital city of Macedonia 1.5, 3.5, 6.28, *Ind.18, 27*

Pellium, city in Lyncestis, Macedonia (?), 1.5; fired by Cleitus [1] (335), 1.6

PELOPONNESE: 1.1, 1.7, 1.17, 2.13, 5.26, 7.9; recruitment in Peloponnese, 1.24, 1.29, 2.2, 2.20; Peloponnesian cavalry in A.'s army, 2.7, 2.8, 2.9; resistance movement (331), 3.6

Pelusium, city at E. mouth of Nile delta 3.1, 3.5

Peneius, river in Thessaly 4.6

Percote, city on Asian side of Hellespont 1.12

PERDICCAS [1], son of Orontes: Companion (7.4.5), Bodyguard (4.21.4, 6.28.4), trierarch (326) (*Ind.18.5*), Mac. infantry and cavalry commander; 1.6 (Pellium, 335), 1.8 (Thebes, 335, wounded), 1.14 (Granicus, 334), 1.20, 1.21 (Halicarnassus, 334), 2.8 (Issus, 333), 3.11 (Gaugamela, 331), 3.18, 4.16, 4.21, 4.22, 4.28, 4.30, 5.12, 5.13, 5.22, 6.6, 6.9 (Mallians, 326/5), 6.11, 6.15, 7.4; death (321), 7.18

Perge, city in Pamphylia 1.25–6, 1.27

Perinthus, city on European coast of Propontis 2.14

Peroedas, Mac. cavalry commander 2.9

PERSEPOLIS, royal capital of Persis, 3.18, 3.19, 7.1; royal palace fired by A. (330), 3.18, 6.30; Darius' body sent for burial in Persepolis (330), 3.22
— A. in Persepolis: (330) 3.18; (324) 6.30

Perseus, legendary hero 3.3

PERSIA/PERSIANS: in time of Cyrus (1), 5.4; Persian empire, 2.6, 5.4, 5.25, 6.29, 7.1, *Ind.1*; Persian language, 6.29, 6.30, 7.6; eunuchs, 7.24; Magi, 6.29, 7.11; 'Euacae' cavalry, 7.6; 'Golden Apple' guards, 3.11, 3.13, 3.16, 7.29; 'King's Kinsmen', elite cavalry squadron, 3.11, 3.16; practice of obeisance, 2.12, 4.9, 4.11, 4.12; luxurious habits, 4.7; contrasted with Macedonians, 2.7 ('soft living')
— A.'s invasion to 'punish' Persia, 2.14, 3.18; council of war at Zeleia (334), 1.12; Persian army at Issus (333), 2.8; Persian army at Gaugamela (331), 3.8, 3.11; Persian losses in battle, 1.16 (Granicus, 334), 2.5 (Halicarnassus, 333), 2.11 (Issus, 333), 3.14, 3.15 (Gaugamela, 331); Persian notables surrender to A. (330), 3.23, 3.25; pretenders to the Persian throne, 3.25 (Bessus, 330), 6.29 (Baryaxes, 324)
— Persians given or allowed to retain office by A., 2.4, 3.16, 3.18, 3.19, 3.20, 3.22, 3.23, 3.24, 3.25, 3.28, 4.18, 4.22; Persians at A.'s court, 4.10, 4.12, 7.8; Persian elite favoured by A. (324), 7.11; high-born daughters married to Companions (324), 7.4; A.'s banquet promoting partnership (324), 7.11; Persians enrolled in elite corps (324), 7.6, 7.8, 7.11, 7.29; Persians integrated into Mac. brigades (323), 7.23, 7.24, 7.29

Persian Gates, pass into Persis from Uxian territory 3.18

Persian Gulf, 5.26, 6.19, 6.28, 7.1, 7.7, 7.16, 7.19 ('Persian Sea'), 7.19, 7.20, *Ind.19–20, 27*; A.'s intended colonization, 7.19
see also Red Sea (a)

Persian War 1.9, 2.14, 3.18, 4.11, 6.11, 7.13

PERSIS, region to E. of Persian Gulf, 3.16, 3.17, 3.18, 6.28, 6.29–7.1, 7.3, 7.6, 7.10, 7.23, 7.24; *Ind.20, 38–40* (Nearchus' voyage); *Ind.40, 43*; climate, *Ind.40*
— A. in Persis: (330) 3.18; (324) 6.29–30, 7.3

Petenes, Persian commander at Granicus (334) 1.12, 1.16 (killed)

Petisis, Egyptian official 3.5
Peuce, island in the Danube 1.2, 1.3
Peucelaïtis *see* Peucelaotis (1)
Peucelaotis (1) [Gandhara], region and
   city in Cophen [Kabul] valley: 4.22;
   (Peucelaïtis) *Ind.1, 4*
Peucelaotis (2), city in Assacenian
   territory, near Indus 4.28
Peucestas [1], Mac. general in Egypt 3.5
PEUCESTAS [2], son of Alexander
   (*Ind.18.6*), Mac. commander: trierarch
   (326), *Ind.18*; heroism in the Mallian
   campaign (326/5), 6.9, 6.10, 6.11, 6.28,
   6.30, 7.5 (crowned by A., 324), *Ind.19*;
   appointed Bodyguard (325/4), 6.28,
   6.30; appointed satrap of Persis
   (325/4), 6.28, **6.30**, 7.23, 7.24;
   orientalizing, 6.30, 7.6; 7.26
Pharasmenes, king of Chorasmians 4.15
Pharismanes, son of Phrataphernes 6.27
Pharnabazus, son of Artabazus, nephew
   of Memnon: given Aegean command
   on death of Memnon (333) 2.1–2,
   2.13, 3.2
Pharnaces, Persian noble killed at
   Granicus (334) 1.16
Pharnuches, Lycian, father of Bagoas [2a]
   (*Ind.18.8*): A.'s interpreter in Bactria/
   Sogdiana, 4.3; given command against
   Spitamenes (329), 4.3, 4.5, 4.6
Pharos, island opposite harbour of
   Alexandria (1) 7.23
Pharsalus, city in Thessaly 3.11
Phaselis, city on coast of Lycia 1.24–5,
   1.26
Phasians, people of Phasis, city on E.
   coast of Black Sea 7.13
Pherae, city in Thessaly 2.13
Phesinus, Chian oligarch 3.2
PHILIP [1] (383/2–336), king of
   Macedon, 360/59–336; father of A.,
   1.1, 4.9, 4.11, 7.9; 1.5, 1.9, 1.10, 2.14,
   3.6, 4.8, 4.13, 7.9; his death (336), 1.1,
   1.10, 1.25, 2.14, 3.6
— marriage to Eurydice (Cleopatra [1])
   (337), 3.6; estrangement of A. and exile
   of A.'s associates (337–336), 3.6; leader
   of Greek league against Persia, 1.1, 7.9;
   Athenian honours, 1.1; statue at
   Ephesus, 1.17
Philip [2], son of Amyntas, Mac. infantry
   commander 1.14.2

Philip [3], son of Balacrus, Mac. infantry
   commander 1.4, 1.14.3
Philip [4], son of Menelaus, Mac. cavalry
   commander 1.14.3, 3.11, 3.25
Philip [5], son of Machatas, Mac. infantry
   commander: satrap of region E. of
   Indus (326), 5.8, and W. of Indus (326),
   6.2, and of Oxydracae and Mallians
   (326/5), 6.14; 4.24, 5.20, 6.4, 6.5, 6.15,
   6.27 (murdered, 325), *Ind.19*
Philip [9], doctor from Acarnania: treated
   A. at Tarsus (333) 2.4
Philip [13], Mac. officer, garrison
   commander of Peucelaotis (2) 4.28
Philippi, city in Thrace 1.1
Philotas [2], Mac. officer 1.2
Philotas [3] (Augaeus), Mac. officer 1.21
   (at Halicarnassus, 334)
PHILOTAS [4], son of Parmenion, Mac.
   cavalry commander: 1.2 (Triballian
   campaign, 335), 1.5 (at Pellium, 335),
   1.14 (Granicus, 334), 1.19 (Miletus,
   334), 2.5 (Cilicia, 333), 3.11
   (Gaugamela, 331); 3.18, 4.10
— accused of plot and executed (330)
   3.26–7, 4.14
Philotas [5], son of Carsis, Page in
   conspiracy (327) 4.13
Philotas [6], Mac. infantry
   commander 3.29, 4.24
Philoxenus [1], Mac. officer 3.6, 7.23,
   7.24
Philoxenus [2], sent by A. to accept
   surrender of Susa (331) 3.16
Phocis/Phocians, region N. of
   Boeotia 1.8, 3.16, 7.9
PHOENICIA, region on coast of Levant
   2.13, 2.16, 2.20, 2.21, 2.26, 3.1, 3.6,
   3.9, 3.16, 3.22, 5.25, 7.19, *Ind.43*
— Phoenician navy, 1.18, 2.13, 2.15,
   2.17, 2.20 (defection to A., 332),
   2.24, 3.6; Phoenician crews in
   Persian navy, 2.2, 2.17; in A.'s fleet,
   6.1, 7.19, 7.22, *Ind.18*; navigation,
   6.26; traders following A., 6.22;
   recruited for colonization of Persian
   Gulf (323), 7.19
— A. in Phoenicia: (332) 2.13–25; (331)
   3.6
Phradasmenes, son of Phrataphernes 7.6
Phrasaortes, Persian appointed satrap of
   Persis (330) 3.18, 6.29, 6.30

Phrataphernes, satrap of Parthyaea and Hyrcania 3.8, 3.23 (surrenders to A., 330), 3.28, 4.7, 4.18, 5.20, 6.27, 7.6

Phrygia, region of central Asia Minor, 1.16, 1.23, 1.24, 1.27, 1.29, 2.3 (story of Midas), 3.22, 5.25, 7.9; Mac. satrap appointed (333), 1.29, 2.4
— A. in Phrygia (333): 1.29

Phrygia, Hellespontine, region of NW Asia Minor 1.12, 1.17, 1.29, 3.22, 5.25, 7.9
— A. in Hellespontine Phrygia (333) 1.29, 2.3

Pieria, canton of Macedonia 1.11

Pillars of Heracles, rocks on either side of strait of Gibraltar 2.16, 5.26, Ind.43

Pimprama, city E. of Hydraotes 5.22

Pinara, city in Lycia 1.24

Pinarus, river in Cilicia, near Issus 2.7, 2.8, 2.10–11

Pindar, 5th cent. BC lyric poet: his house in Thebes spared 1.9

Pisidia, region of S. central Asia Minor, 1.24, 1.27–8; A. in Pisidia (334/3), 1.27–8

Pixodarus, brother of Ada, seized power in Caria from her 1.23

Plataea, town in Boeotia, 1.8, 1.9; destroyed in Peloponnesian War (427), 1.9

Pleiades, stars 6.21, 7.21

Pnytagoras, king of Salamis in Cyprus 2.20, 2.22, Ind.18

Polemon [1], son of Megacles, Companion: garrison commander at Pelusium 3.5.3

Polemon [2], son of Theramenes: admiral in Egypt (331) 3.5.5

Polemon [3], son of Andromenes: charged with complicity in Philotas' plot (330) 3.27

Polydamas, Companion: sent with instructions for murder of Parmenion (330) 3.26

Polydectes, legendary king of Seriphus 3.3

Polydeuces see Dioscuri

Polydorus, son of Cadmus 2.16

Polyeuctus, Athenian politician 1.10

Polyperchon, Mac. infantry commander 2.12, 3.11, 4.16, 4.22, 4.25, 5.11, 6.5, 7.12

Polytimetus [Zeravshan], river in Sogdiana, 4.5, 4.6; scene of Mac. defeat (329), 4.5–6

PORUS [1], Indian dynast of region E. of Hydaspes, NE Pakistan, 5.8–19, 5.20, 5.21, 5.22, 5.24, Ind.5; interview with A. after defeat (326), 5.19; his domain enlarged by A., 5.19, 5.20, 5.21, 5.29, 6.2; his son(s), 5.14–15, 5.18

Porus [2], 'the bad', Indian dynast of region E. of Acesines 5.20, 5.21

Poseidon, god: father of Theseus, 7.29; sacrifices to, 1.11, 6.19, Ind.18, 20, 36; island sacred to, Ind.37

Prasians, Indian tribe Ind.10

Priam, king of Troy 1.11

Priapus, city on Propontis 1.12

Proexes, Persian appointed satrap of Parapamisadae (330/29) 3.28

Prometheus 5.3, Ind.5

Propontis, Sea of Marmara 4.15

Prosactius, river running into Propontis 1.12

Proteas, Mac. naval commander 2.2, 2.20

Protesilaus, first Greek to land at Troy, killed on landing 1.11

Protomachus, Mac. commander of light cavalry at Issus (333) 2.9

Ptolemy [1], Bodyguard, killed at Halicarnassus (334) 1.22

Ptolemy [2], son of Philip, Mac. commander at Granicus (334) 1.14

Ptolemy [3], son of Seleucus, Bodyguard, Mac. infantry commander, 1.24, 1.29, 2.8; killed at Issus (333), 2.10, 2.12

Ptolemy [4], Mac. commander of Thracians 4.7

Ptolemy [5], Mac. officer in command of garrison of Caria (334) 1.23, 2.5

PTOLEMY [6], son of Lagus, Mac. commander: exiled by Philip [1] (336), 3.6; appointed Bodyguard (330), 3.6, 3.27, 6.28; trierarch (326), Ind.18; 2.11, 3.18, 3.29–30 (capture of Bessus, 329), 4.8, 4.13, 4.15, 4.16, 4.21, 4.23 (wounded, 327/6), 4.24–5, 4.29 (Aornus, 326), 5.13, 5.23–4 (Sangala, 326), 6.5, 6.11, 7.3, 7.4, 7.15, 7.18, Ind.43; title of 'Saviour' [Soter], 6.11
— as historian: Preface 4.14, 5.7, 6.2, 6.28, 7.15, 7.26

— cited 1.2, 1.8, 2.11, 2.12, 3.3, 3.4,
3.17, 3.26, 3.29, 4.3, 4.14, 4.25, 5.7,
5.14–15, 5.20, 5.28, 6.2, 6.10, 6.11,
6.28, 7.13, 7.15, 7.26
Pura [Bampur?], area of Gedrosia 6.24
Pyanepsion, month in Athenian
calendar 3.15
Pydna, city in Macedonia 3.5, *Ind.18*
Pylora, desert island off Carmanian coast
Ind.37
Pyramus, river in Cilicia 2.5
Pythodelus, Athenian archon 1.1

Quadi, Celtic tribe N. of Upper
Danube 1.3

Raetia, Roman Alpine province S. of
Danube *Ind.4*
RED SEA: (a) the Persian Gulf: 3.8,
3.11, 7.16, *Ind.19, 37, 40, 43*; (b) the
Arabian Gulf [mod. Red Sea]: 7.20,
Ind.32
Rhadamanthys, legendary king and judge,
son of Zeus 7.29
Rhagae, city in Media 3.20
Rhambacia [Las Bela], village in
Oreitis 6.21, 6.22
Rheomithres, Persian cavalry
commander 1.12, 2.11, 3.18
Rhine, river 5.7
Rhodes, SE Aegean island 2.1, 2.7, 2.20
Rhoesaces, Persian noble killed by A. at
Granicus (334) 1.15
Rhogonis, river in Persis *Ind.39*
RHOXANE, daughter of Oxyartes,
married by A. (327) 4.19, 4.20, 6.15,
7.4, 7.6, 7.27
rock assaults: see (Rock of) Aornus, (Rock
of) Chorienes, (Rock of) Sogdiana
ROME/ROMANS: administration of
Egypt, 3.5; river-bridging technique,
5.7–8; A.'s fear of growing reputation,
7.1; supposed embassy to A., 7.15;
import of pearls, *Ind.8*
Royal Journals 7.25–6

Sabictas, appointed satrap of Cappadocia
(333) 2.4
Sacae, Scythian tribe E. of Aral Sea 3.8,
3.11, 7.10
Sacala, place on coast E. of Karachi
Ind.22

Sacesinians, people to W. of Caspian
Sea 3.8, 3.11
Sagalassus, city in Pisidia 1.28
Salamis (1), island in Saronic Gulf: battle
of Salamis (480) 6.11
Salamis (2), city in Cyprus *Ind.18*
Salmacis, citadel of Halicarnassus 1.23
Sambus [1], Indian dynast adjacent to
Musicanus 6.16
Sambus (2), tributary of Ganges *Ind.4*
Samos, E. Aegean island 1.19, 5.5
Sandracottus, Indian king, 5.6;
Sandrocottus in *Ind.5, 9*
Sangada, area of coast to W. of Indus
mouth *Ind.21*
Sangaeus, appointed governor of
Peucelaotis (2) (327/6) 4.22
Sangala [Amritsar?], capital city of
Cathaeans: captured by A. (326)
5.22–4
Sangarius, river in Phrygia and
Bithynia 1.29
Saparnus, tributary of Indus *Ind.4*
Saranga, place on coast E. of Karachi
Ind.22
Saranges, tributary of Hydraotes *Ind.4*
Sarapis, god 7.26
Sardanapalus, legendary Assyrian
king 2.5
Sardis, capital of Lydia, 1.24; citadel,
1.17; A. in Sardis (334), 1.17, 3.16
Satibarzanes, Persian: satrap of Areia, 3.8;
arrests and murders Darius (330), 3.21;
submits to A., retains satrapy, 3.25;
leads Areian revolt, crushed by A.
(330), 3.25; leads second revolt, killed
by Erigyius (330), 3.28
Satraces, Scythian commander 4.4
Sauaces, Persian satrap of Egypt, killed at
Issus (333) 2.11
Sauromatae, Sarmatian tribe N. of Lower
Danube 1.3
Saus [Save], tributary of Danube *Ind.4*
Saviour gods *Ind.42*
Scione, city in Chalcidice, destroyed by
Athenians (421) 1.9
scythe-chariots 3.8, 3.11, 3.12, 3.13
SCYTHIANS: (a) European (NW of
Black Sea), 1.3, 3.30, 4.11, 7.15, *Ind.3*;
(b) Asian, E. of Caspian Sea (Dahae,
Massagetae, Sacae), 3.8, 3.19, 3.25,
4.1.1–3 [here and in 4.15.1 'European'

means N. of the Asian Tanaïs
  (Syr-Darya)], 4.3–6, 4.15, 4.16, 4.17,
  5.12, 5.25, 5.26, 7.1, 7.10, 7.16, *Ind.5*;
  defeat of Cyrus (1) (530), 3.27, 4.11,
  5.4, *Ind.9*; Scythian cavalry in Darius'
  army at Gaugamela (331), 3.11, 3.13;
  nomads, 4.5, 4.17, 7.16, *Ind.7*
Seleucus, Companion, Mac. infantry
  commander, 5.13, 5.16, 7.4, 7.18, 7.22,
  7.26; 'Nicator', *Ind.43*
Selge, city in Pisidia 1.28
Semele, daughter of Cadmus, mother of
  Dionysus 2.16
Semiramis, legendary queen of Assyria
  (1) in late 9th cent. BC 1.23, 6.24,
  Ind.5
Sesostris, legendary Egyptian king *Ind.5*
Sestos, city on Chersonese 1.11
Sibae, Indian tribe *Ind.5*
Sibyrtius, satrap of Carmania, then of
  Gedrosia and Arachosia 5.6, 6.27
Sicily, 7.1; Athenian disaster in Sicily
  (413), 1.9
Side, city in Pamphylia 1.26
Sidon, city in Phoenicia 2.15, 2.19–20,
  2.21, 2.24
siege mechanics: siege-engines, 1.19, 1.20,
  1.21–2, 2.21, 2.22–3, 2.24, 2.26, 2.27,
  4.2, 4.3, 4.26, 5.23, 5.24; siege-towers,
  1.20, 1.21, 1.22, 2.18, 4.26, 5.29;
  wickerwork shelters, 1.21; catapults,
  1.22, 2.18, 2.21, 2.23, 4.2; moles,
  ramps, 2.18 (Tyre), 2.26, 2.27, 4.21,
  4.29–30 (Aornus); bridging-ramps,
  2.22, 2.23, 4.26–7; undermining, 1.20,
  1.21, 2.27, 5.24, 6.7, 6.9; rock-
  climbing, 4.19
sieges: Miletus (334), 1.18–19, 7.9;
  Halicarnassus (334), 1.20–23; Tyre
  (332), 2.18–24, 4.26; Gaza (1) (332),
  2.25–6; Massaga (327/6), 4.26–7;
  Sangala (326), 5.22–4
Sigeum, city on Asian side of
  Hellespont 1.12
Sigon, city in Phoenicia 2.13
Sigrium, promontory at W. tip of
  Lesbos 2.1
Silaeans, Indian tribe *Ind.6*
Silas, miraculous Indian river *Ind.6*
'Silver Shields', elite Mac. infantry 7.11
Simmias [1], son of Andromenes, brother
  of Amyntas [4], Mac. infantry

commander, 3.11, 3.14; charged with
  complicity in Philotas' plot (330), 3.27
Sinarus, tributary of Hydaspes *Ind.4*
Sindimana, capital of region ruled by
  Sambus [1] 6.16
Sinope, city on S. shore of Black Sea
  (Paphlagonia) 3.24, 7.2
Siphnos, Aegean island (Cyclades) 2.2,
  2.13
Sisicottus, Indian dynast given command
  of Aornus (2) 4.30, 5.20
Sisines [1], Persian sent to encourage
  treason of Alexander [4] 1.25
Sisines [2], son of Phrataphernes 7.6
Sitacus [Mand], river in Persis *Ind.38*
Sitalces, commander of Thracian
  javelin-men, 1.28, 2.5, 2.9, 3.12, 3.26;
  accused and executed (325/4), 6.27
Sittacene, region NE of Babylonia 3.8,
  3.11
Sittocatis, tributary of Ganges *Ind.4*
Smyrna, city on coast of Aeolis 5.6
Soanus, tributary of Indus *Ind.4*
Soastus [Swat], tributary of Cophen
  [Kabul] *Ind.4*
Sochi, place in Amik plain,
  Mesopotamian Syria: Darius
  encamped there (333) 2.6
Socrates, Mac. cavalry commander 1.12,
  1.14, 1.15
SOGDIANA/SOGDIANS (1), region
  N. of Bactria, 3.8, 3.28, 3.30, 4.5, 5.12,
  7.6; first Sogdian revolt (329), 4.1–3;
  second Sogdian revolt (328), 4.15–16;
  Coenus in Sogdiana (328/7), 4.17
— A. in Sogdiana (329–327): (329)
  3.29–4.6; (328) 4.8–9, 4.16; (328–327)
  4.18–21
— Rock of Sogdiana, captured in spring
  327 4.18–19
Sogdians (2), independent Indian
  tribe 6.15
Soli (1), city in Cilicia 2.5, 2.6, 2.12, 2.20
Soli (2), city in Cyprus 7.20, *Ind.18*
Solomatis, tributary of Ganges *Ind.4*
Solon, 6th cent BC Athenian lawgiver and
  poet 7.16
Sonus, tributary of Ganges *Ind.4*
Sopeithes, Indian dynast E. of
  Hydaspes 6.2
Sopolis, Mac. cavalry commander 1.2,
  3.11, 4.13, 4.18

Sostratus, Page in conspiracy (327) 4.13

SPARTA, 1.9; in Persian War, 4.11; voted for destruction of Athens (404), 1.9; opposed to A.'s leadership of Greek league, 1.1, 1.16; hostility to A., 1.1, 1.7, 2.13, 2.14, 2.15, 3.6, 3.16; Spartan envoys to Darius, (333) 2.15, (330) 3.24; discipline, 5.4; Helots as slaves, *Ind.10*

Spatembas, first king of India *Ind.8*

Spitaces, Indian dynast 5.18

SPITAMENES, Bactrian/Sogdian warlord, 3.28; 3.29–30 (arrest of Bessus, 329); 4.1, 4.3; **4.5–6** (defeat of Mac. at Polytimetus, 329); 4.16; invasion of Bactria with Scythians (328), **4.16–17**; invasion of Sogdiana with Scythians, defeat and death (328/7), **4.17**; daughter married by Seleucus (324), 7.4

Spithridates, Persian: satrap of Lydia and Ionia, 1.12, 1.17; killed at Granicus (334), 1.15, 1.16

Stamenes, appointed satrap of Babylonia (328/7) 4.18

Stasanor, Companion: sent to arrest and replace Arsaces as satrap of Areia (329), 3.29, 4.7, 4.18; appointed satrap of Drangiana also (328/7), 4.18; 6.27, 6.29

Straton [1], Phoenician, son of Gerostratus, regent of Aradus district 2.13

Strymon [Struma], river in Thrace 1.11, *Ind.18*

Stura, place on lower Indus *Ind.21*

Stymphaea *see* Tymphaea

Sun, god 3.7; *see also* Helios

Sunium, S. promontory of Attica 6.11

Suraseni, Indian tribe *Ind.8*

SUSA, capital city of Susiana, and administrative capital of Persian empire 3.16, 3.17, 3.19, 3.20, 5.25, 6.27, 7.4, 7.6, 7.9, 7.10, 7.19, *Ind.36, 37, 42, 43*
— A. in Susa: (331) 3.16; (324) **7.4–6**, *Ind.42*

Susia, city in Areia 3.25

Susiana, region at N. end of Persian Gulf 3.8, 3.11, 3.17, 6.28, 7.4, 7.7, *Ind.40–2*

Sydracae, Indian tribe *Ind.4*

Syene, city in S. Egypt *Ind.25*

Syllium, city in Pamphylia 1.26

SYRIA, 3.1, 3.6, 3.16, 4.7, 4.13; (a) **Hollow Syria** (N. Syria), 2.13, 3.8, 3.9, 3.11, 5.25, 7.9; (b) **Mesopotamian Syria**, 3.8, 5.25; (c) **Palestinian Syria**, 2.25–6, 7.9, *Ind.43*: Syrian prophetess in A.'s entourage, 4.13

Syrmus, king of the Triballians 1.2, 1.4

Syrphax, pro-Persian oligarch at Ephesus 1.17

Taä, place on Fish-Eater coast *Ind.29*

Taenarum, promontory in Laconia 2.13

Talmena, harbour on Fish-Eater coast *Ind.29*

TANAIS, river(s): (a) **Asian** [Syr-Darya], 3.28, **3.30.7**, 4.1, 4.3, 4.4, 5.25, 7.10, 7.16; also called Orxantes (3.30.7) and Jaxartes (7.16.3); (b) **European** [Don], **3.30.8–9**

Taoce, place on coast of Persis *Ind.39*

Tapuria *see* Topeiria

Tarsias, cape on Carmanian coast *Ind.37*

Tarsus, capital city of Cilicia 2.4–5, 2.6

Tartessus, region of S. Spain 2.16

Taulantians, Illyrian tribe, N. and W. of Macedonia 1.5–6

Tauriscus, deserter 3.6

Tauron, Mac. commander of archers (326) 5.14, 5.16

Taurunus, area of Pannonia *Ind.4*

TAURUS, mountain range 2.4, 3.6, 3.28, 5.5, 5.6, *Ind.2, 3*

Taxila, city E. of Indus, NW of Rawalpindi 5.3, 5.8, 7.2

Taxiles, Indian dynast, ruler of Taxila 4.22, 5.3, 5.8, 5.18, 5.20, 6.27

Telephus, Companion 6.23

Telmissus (1), city in Lycia, renowned for prophetic families 1.11, 1.24, 2.3, 3.2

Telmissus (2), city in Pisidia 1.27–8

Tenedos, NE Aegean island 2.2, 3.2

Tempe, gorge in NE Thessaly 4.6

'Ten Thousand', Greek mercenaries supporting Cyrus (2) in Asia (401) 1.12, 2.4, 2.7, 4.11, 7.13

Teos, city in Ionia *Ind.18*

Thapsacus, city in Syria on Euphrates 2.13, 3.6, 3.7, 7.19

THEBES, city in Boeotia: occupied by Cadmus, 2.16; Theban Dionysus, 2.16,

5.1; medism in Persian War, 1.9; responsible for fate of Plataea (432–427), 1.9; voted for destruction of Athens (404), 1.9; defeated by Philip [1] (338), 7.9; *see also* Heracles
— revolt, and destruction by A. (335), 1.7–8, 1.9, 2.15; Greek reaction, 1.9, 1.10; Theban envoys to Darius (333), 2.15
— Ampheum, 1.8; Cadmea (citadel), 1.7, 1.8, 1.9; temple of Heracles, 1.8; precinct of Iolaus, 1.7
Thera, city in S. Caria 2.5
Thermopylae 1.7
Theron, tyrant of Acragas in Sicily (*c.*488–472 BC) 1.12
Thersippus, A.'s envoy to Darius (332) 2.14
Theseus, legendary king of Athens 7.13, 7.29
Thessaliscus, Theban envoy to Darius (333) 2.15
Thessaly, region of NE central Greece, 1.7, 4.6, 7.9, 7.12; Thessalian cavalry in A.'s army, 1.14, 1.24, 1.25, 1.29, 2.5, 2.7, 2.8, 2.9, 2.11, 3.11, 3.15, 3.18, 3.25; sent home, (330) 3.19, (329) 3.29, 5.27
Thoas, Mac. officer, 6.23, 6.27; trierarch (326), *Ind.18*
THRACE, 2.14, 5.26, 7.9, 7.12; Alexander [4] appointed general in Thrace (335?), 1.25; A.'s campaign in Thrace (335), 1.1–4; Bithynian Thracians, 1.29
— Thracians in A.'s army, 2.7, 4.7, 5.20, 6.15; cavalry, 1.14, 1.18, 2.7, 3.5, 3.19; infantry, 3.12; javelin-men, 1.28, 2.5, 2.9, 3.12; road-builders, 1.26
Thymondas, nephew of Mentor [1], Rhodian in Persian service 2.2, 2.13
Tigris, Asian river 3.7, 5.5, 5.7, 6.19, 6.28, 7.1, 7.7, 7.16, *Ind.42*
Timander, Mac. infantry commander 1.22
Timanthes, trierarch (326) *Ind.18*
Timolaus, officer of Mac. garrison in Thebes 1.7
Tiryns, city in the Argolid 5.26
Tlepolemus, Companion: superintendent of Parthyaea/Hyrcania (330), 3.22; appointed satrap of Carmania (325), 6.27, *Ind.36*
Tmolus, mountain in Lydia 5.1

Tomerus [Hingol], river in Oreitis *Ind.24*
Topeiria/Tapuria, region bordering S. of Caspian Sea 3.8, 3.11, 3.23, 3.24, 4.18, 7.23
Tralles, city in Ionia 1.18, 1.23
Trapezus, city on SE coast of Black Sea 7.13
Triballians, Thracian tribe, 1.1, 1.2–3, 1.4, 1.10, 5.26, 7.9; A.'s campaign against them (335), 1.2, 1.3
trierarchs Ind.18, 20
Triopium, city on Cnidian peninsula, E. Aegean 2.5
Tripolis [Tripoli], city in Phoenicia 2.13
Triptolemus, Eleusinian deity *Ind.7*
Trojan War 1.11
Troy, 1.11–12, 6.9, 6.10; A. in Troy (334), 1.11–12; temple of Trojan Athena, 1.11, 6.9; altar of Zeus of the Forecourt, 1.11
Tutapus, tributary of Acesines *Ind.4*
Tylus [Bahrein], island in Persian Gulf 7.20
Tymphaea (Stymphaea in 1.7.5), canton of Macedonia 1.7, *Ind.18*
Tyndareus, (human) father of Dioscuri 4.8
TYRE, city in Phoenicia, 2.15–19, 2.20–5, 2.27, 3.6; siege of Tyre (332), 2.18–24, 4.26; fate of Tyrians, 2.24; Tyrian navy, 2.18, 2.19, 2.20, 2.21–2
— two harbours, 2.20, 2.21–2, 2.23, 2.24; shrine of Agenor, 2.24; sanctuary of Heracles, 2.24
— Tyrian Heracles 2.16, 2.18, 3.6, *Ind.5*
Tyriespis, Persian, appointed satrap of Parapamisadae (327), 4.22, 5.20; deposed (325), 6.15

Uranus (Sky), god 7.20
Uxians, people in region between Susiana and Persis, 3.8, 3.11, 5.19, 7.10, 7.15, *Ind.40*; defeated by A. (331), 3.17, *Ind.40*

whales Ind.29–30, 39

Xanthus (1), river in Lycia 1.24
Xanthus (2), city in Lycia 1.24
Xathrians, Indian tribe in Punjab 6.15

Xenophon, historian and mercenary
    leader (*c*.428–*c*.354 BC) 1.12, 2.4, 2.7,
    2.8, 4.11, 7.13
Xerxes, Xerxes I, King of Persia 486–465,
    4.4, 4.11, 5.7, 7.14; destroyed temples
    in Babylon (482–481), 3.16, 7.17; art
    looted from Greece, 3.16, 7.19

Zadracarta, capital city of Hyrcania 3.23,
    3.25
Zarangiana *see* Drangiana
Zariaspa, alternative name for Bactra
    [Balkh] (*q.v.*) 4.1, 4.7, 4.16

Zeleia, city in Hellespontine
    Phrygia 1.12, 1.17
ZEUS, god: father of Dionysus, 2.16, 5.1;
    joint father of Heracles and of Perseus,
    3.3; joint father of Dioscuri, 4.8; father
    of Aeacus, Minos, Rhadamanthys, 7.29;
    4.9, 7.2, *Ind.35*
— Zeus of the Forecourt, 1.11; Zeus the
    King, 2.3, 3.5, 4.20; Olympian Zeus,
    1.11, 1.17; Zeus the Protector of
    Landings, 1.11; Zeus the Saviour, 1.4,
    Ind.21, 36

MAPS

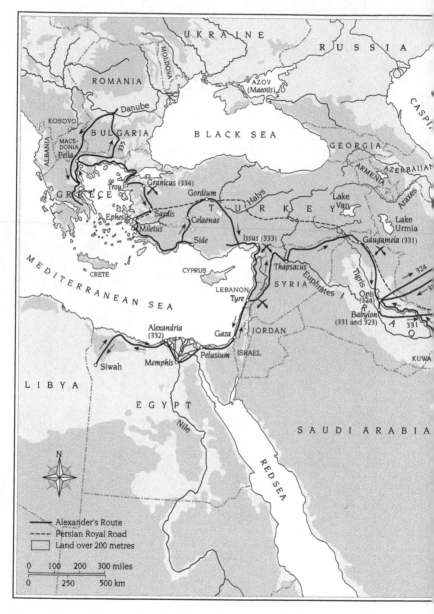

MAP 1 Alexander's campaigns in their modern geographical context

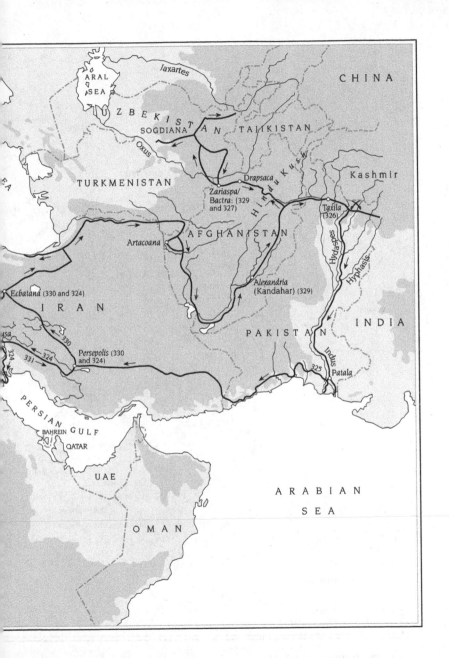

MAP 2 The Balkans and Asia Minor

A E

Triballians

even

Osûm

Troyan

T H R A C E

Philippopolis
(Plovdiv)

Xanthi

Byzantium

B L A C K

S E A

B I T H Y N I A

Nicomedia
(Izmit)

P R O P O N T I S

Priapus

Cyzicus

Sestos

Lampsacus

Arisbe

Zeleia

Abydos

Granicus

Dascylium

Hellespont

Troy

Gordium

H E L L E S P O N T I N E   P H R Y G I A

A E O L I S

P H R Y G I A

A E G E A N

Mytilene

Caicus

LESBOS

S E A

L Y D I A

Hermus

Sardis

CHIOS

I O N I A

Cayster

Ephesus

Magnesia

Maeander

Celaenae

Sagalassus

SAMOS

P I S I D I A

Miletus

C A R I A

'Telmissus' (2)
=Termessus

Selge

Myndus

Halicarnassus

P A M P H Y L I A

Perge

Aspendus

COS

L Y C I A

Phaselis

Telmissus

Xanthus

RHODES

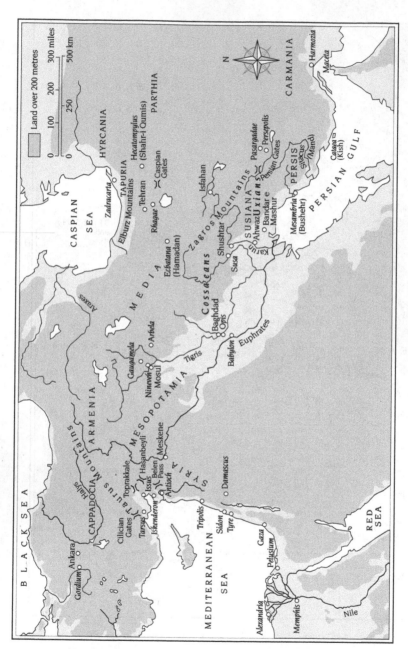

MAP 3 From Anatolia to Persia

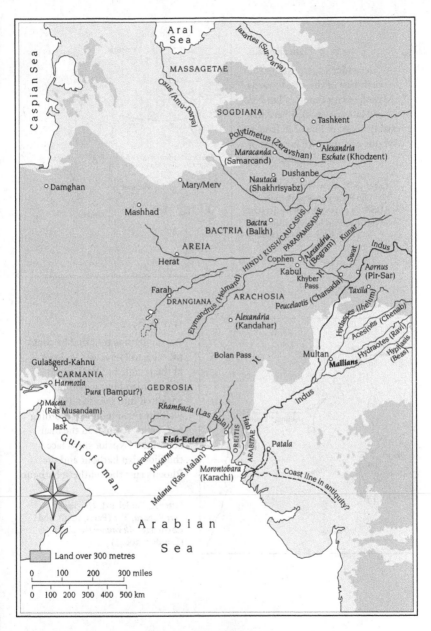

MAP 4 Bactria and India

MAP 5 Halicarnassus

Alexander's camp was to the north-east of the city, towards Mylasa (a city about 43 km NE of Halicarnassus). There was probably no outer line of defences. Myndus was about 16 km west of the Myndus Gate.

(after G. E. Bean and J. M. Cook, 'The Halicarnassus Peninsula', ABSA 50 (1955), and P. Pedersen, 'The fortifications of Halicarnassus', REA 96 (1994), 225)

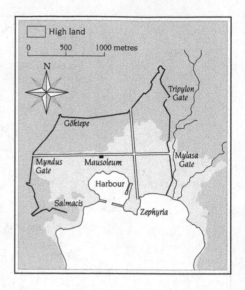

MAP 6 Tyre

Alexander was told that he could sacrifice to Heracles/Melqart at the temple in Old Tyre on the mainland but would not be admitted into the island city to visit the main temple (according to Curtius Rufus). In the final action the Cypriot ships faced the Sidonian harbour and the Phoenicians the southern harbour.

(after A. Poidebard, *Un grand port disparu*, Tyr (Paris, 1939), and Cartledge, *Alexander the Great* (London, 2004))

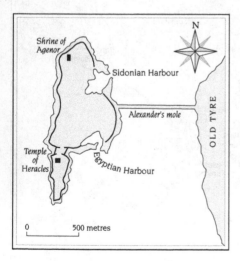

The Oxford World's Classics Website

www.worldsclassics.co.uk

- Browse the full range of Oxford World's Classics online

- Sign up for our monthly e-alert to receive information on new titles

- Read extracts from the Introductions

- Listen to our editors and translators talk about the world's greatest literature with our Oxford World's Classics audio guides

- Join the conversation, follow us on Twitter at OWC_Oxford

- Teachers and lecturers can order inspection copies quickly and simply via our website

www.worldsclassics.co.uk

American Literature

British and Irish Literature

Children's Literature

Classics and Ancient Literature

Colonial Literature

Eastern Literature

European Literature

Gothic Literature

History

Medieval Literature

Oxford English Drama

Poetry

Philosophy

Politics

Religion

The Oxford Shakespeare

A complete list of Oxford World's Classics, including Authors in Context, Oxford English Drama, and the Oxford Shakespeare, is available in the UK from the Marketing Services Department, Oxford University Press, Great Clarendon Street, Oxford OX2 6DP, or visit the website at www.oup.com/uk/worldsclassics.

In the USA, visit www.oup.com/us/owc for a complete title list.

Oxford World's Classics are available from all good bookshops. In case of difficulty, customers in the UK should contact Oxford University Press Bookshop, 116 High Street, Oxford OX1 4BR.

A SELECTION OF OXFORD WORLD'S CLASSICS

Classical Literary Criticism

The First Philosophers: The Presocratics and the Sophists

Greek Lyric Poetry

Myths from Mesopotamia

APOLLODORUS   **The Library of Greek Mythology**

APOLLONIUS OF RHODES   **Jason and the Golden Fleece**

APULEIUS   **The Golden Ass**

ARISTOPHANES   **Birds and Other Plays**

ARISTOTLE   **The Nicomachean Ethics**
Physics
Politics

BOETHIUS   **The Consolation of Philosophy**

CAESAR   **The Civil War**
The Gallic War

CATULLUS   **The Poems of Catullus**

CICERO   **Defence Speeches**
The Nature of the Gods
On Obligations
Political Speeches
The Republic and The Laws

EURIPIDES   **Bacchae and Other Plays**
Heracles and Other Plays
Medea and Other Plays
Orestes and Other Plays
The Trojan Women and Other Plays

HERODOTUS   **The Histories**

HOMER   **The Iliad**
The Odyssey

A SELECTION OF   **OXFORD WORLD'S CLASSICS**

HORACE	The Complete Odes and Epodes
JUVENAL	The Satires
LIVY	The Dawn of the Roman Empire
	Hannibal's War
	The Rise of Rome
MARCUS AURELIUS	The Meditations
OVID	The Love Poems
	Metamorphoses
PETRONIUS	The Satyricon
PLATO	Defence of Socrates, Euthyphro, and Crito
	Gorgias
	Meno and Other Dialogues
	Phaedo
	Republic
	Selected Myths
	Symposium
PLAUTUS	Four Comedies
PLUTARCH	Greek Lives
	Roman Lives
	Selected Essays and Dialogues
PROPERTIUS	The Poems
SOPHOCLES	Antigone, Oedipus the King, and Electra
STATIUS	Thebaid
SUETONIUS	Lives of the Caesars
TACITUS	Agricola and Germany
	The Histories
VIRGIL	The Aeneid
	The Eclogues and Georgics
XENOPHON	The Expedition of Cyrus

A SELECTION OF OXFORD WORLD'S CLASSICS

THOMAS AQUINAS   Selected Philosophical Writings

FRANCIS BACON   The Essays

WALTER BAGEHOT   The English Constitution

GEORGE BERKELEY   Principles of Human Knowledge and
                              Three Dialogues

EDMUND BURKE   A Philosophical Enquiry into the Origin of
                              Our Ideas of the Sublime and Beautiful
                            Reflections on the Revolution in France

CONFUCIUS   The Analects

DESCARTES   A Discourse on the Method

ÉMILE DURKHEIM   The Elementary Forms of Religious Life

FRIEDRICH ENGELS   The Condition of the Working Class in
                              England

JAMES GEORGE FRAZER   The Golden Bough

SIGMUND FREUD   The Interpretation of Dreams

THOMAS HOBBES   Human Nature and De Corpore Politico
                            Leviathan

DAVID HUME   Selected Essays

NICCOLÒ MACHIAVELLI   The Prince

THOMAS MALTHUS   An Essay on the Principle of Population

KARL MARX   Capital
                            The Communist Manifesto

J. S. MILL   On Liberty and Other Essays
                            Principles of Political Economy and
                              Chapters on Socialism

FRIEDRICH NIETZSCHE   Beyond Good and Evil
                            The Birth of Tragedy
                            On the Genealogy of Morals
                            Thus Spoke Zarathustra
                            Twilight of the Idols

A SELECTION OF   OXFORD WORLD'S CLASSICS

THOMAS PAINE   **Rights of Man, Common Sense, and Other
                       Political Writings**

JEAN-JACQUES ROUSSEAU **The Social Contract
                       Discourse on the Origin of Inequality**

ADAM SMITH   **An Inquiry into the Nature and Causes of
                       the Wealth of Nations**

MARY WOLLSTONECRAFT   **A Vindication of the Rights of Woman**

'He was a man like no other man has ever been'

So Arrian sums up the career of Alexander the Great of Macedon (356–323 BC), who in twelve years that changed the world led his army in conquest of a vast empire extending from the Danube to the rivers of the Punjab, from Egypt to Uzbekistan, and died in Babylon at the age of 32 with further ambitions unfulfilled.

Arrian (*c.* AD 86–161), a Greek man of letters who had experience of military command and of the highest political office in both Rome and Athens, set out to write the definitive account of Alexander's life and campaigns, published as the *Anabasis* and its later companion-piece the *Indica*. His work is now our prime and most detailed extant source for the history of Alexander, and it is a dramatic story, fast-moving like its main subject, and told with great narrative skill. Arrian admired Alexander and was fascinated by him, but was also alive to his faults: he presents a compelling account of an exceptional leader, brilliant, ruthless, passionate, and complex.

THIS EDITION INCLUDES

Introduction • **Bibliography** • **Chronology** • **Appendices**
Explanatory notes • **Textual notes** • **Maps** • **Index**

Translated by Martin Hammond
With an Introduction and Notes by John Atkinson

Cover illustration: detail of Alexander the Great, from a modern Greek coin.
© Marek Uliasz/Shutterstock.com.

OXFORD
UNIVERSITY PRESS

www.oup.com/worldsclassics

ISBN 0-19-958724-8

ALEXANDER THE GRT   90000

9 780199 587247